AN EXPLORER'S GUIDE

D0104109

Vermont

AN EXPLORER'S GUIDE

Vermont

Christina Tree & Alice Levitt

The Countryman Press ✳ Woodstock, Vermont

FOURTEENTH EDITION

DEDICATION

To Bill Davis, my companion on and off the road. —C. T.

To Drs. Bernard Raxlen and Amiram Katz for getting me back on the road, and James for traveling with me every step of the way. —A. L.

We welcome your comments and suggestions. Please contact Explorer's Guide Editor, The Countryman Press, P.O. Box 748, Woodstock, Vermont 05091, or email countrymanpress@wwnorton.com.

ISBN: 978-1-58157-281-0

Maps by Erin Greb Cartography, © The Countryman Press
Cover and interior design by Bodenweber Design
Text composition by PerfecType, Nashville, TN

Published by The Countryman Press, P.O. Box 748, Woodstock, Vermont 05091

Distributed by W. W. Norton & Company, Inc., 500 Fifth Avenue, New York, NY 10110

Printed in the United States of America

10 9 8 7 6 5 4 3 2 1

EXPLORE WITH US!

We have been fine-tuning *Vermont: An Explorer's Guide* for more than 30 years, a period in which lodging, dining, and shopping opportunities have more than quadrupled in the state. As we have expanded our guide, we have also been increasingly selective, making recommendations based on years of conscientious research and personal experience. What makes us unique is that we describe the state by locally defined regions, giving you Vermont's communities, not simply its most popular destinations. With this guide you'll feel confident to venture beyond the tourist towns, along roads less traveled, to places of special hospitality and charm.

WHAT'S WHERE

In the beginning of the book you'll find an alphabetical listing of special highlights, with important information and advice on everything from antiques to weather reports.

LODGING

Prices. Please don't hold us or the respective innkeepers responsible for the rates listed as of press time in 2015. Some changes are inevitable. We do not include the 9 percent Vermont state room and meals tax in rates unless stated. Many lodging establishments also add a gratuity to their listed rate, something we try to note but do not always catch. It's best to check ahead of time.

Smoking. State law bars smoking in all places of public accommodation in Vermont, including restaurants and bars.

RESTAURANTS

Note the distinction between *Dining Out* and *Eating Out*. By their nature, restaurants listed in the *Eating Out* group are generally inexpensive.

KEY TO SYMBOLS

- ✪ **Authors' favorites**. These are the places we think have the best to offer in each region, whether that means great food, outstanding rooms, beautiful scenery, or overall appeal.

- ♂ **Weddings**. The wedding-ring symbol appears beside establishments that frequently serve as venues for weddings and civil unions.

- ❀ **Special value**. The special-value symbol appears next to lodging and restaurants that combine high quality and moderate prices.

- 🐾 **Pets**. The dog-paw symbol appears next to lodgings that accept pets (usually with a reservation and deposit) as of press time.

- ✎ **Child-friendly**. The kids-alert symbol appears next to lodging, restaurants, activities, and shops of special appeal to youngsters.

- ♿ **Handicapped access**. The wheelchair symbol appears next to lodging, restaurants, and attractions that are partially or fully handicapped accessible.

- ((ᵠ)) **Wireless Internet**. Virtually all Vermont lodging places now offer Internet access. This symbols highlights cafés, restaurants, and public spaces with WiFi.

We would appreciate your comments and corrections about places you visit or know well in the state. Please email Chris: ctree@traveltree.net.

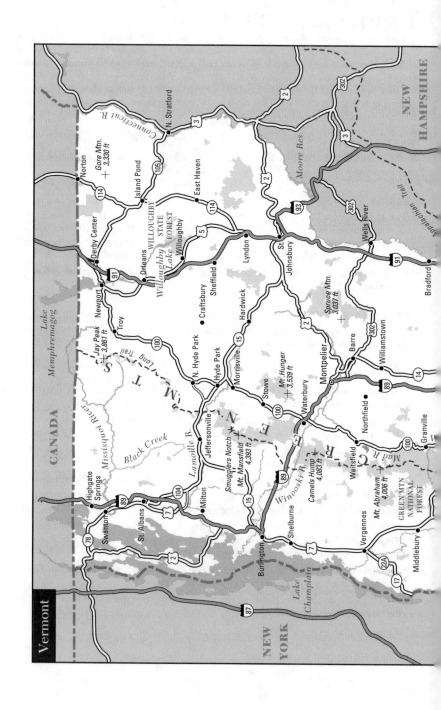

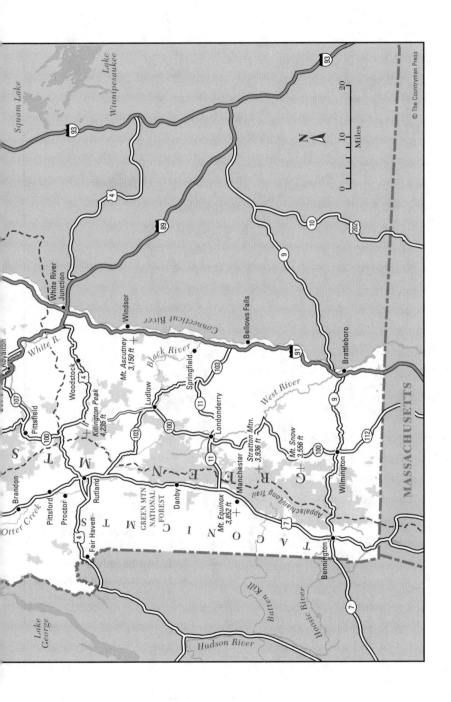

© The Countryman Press

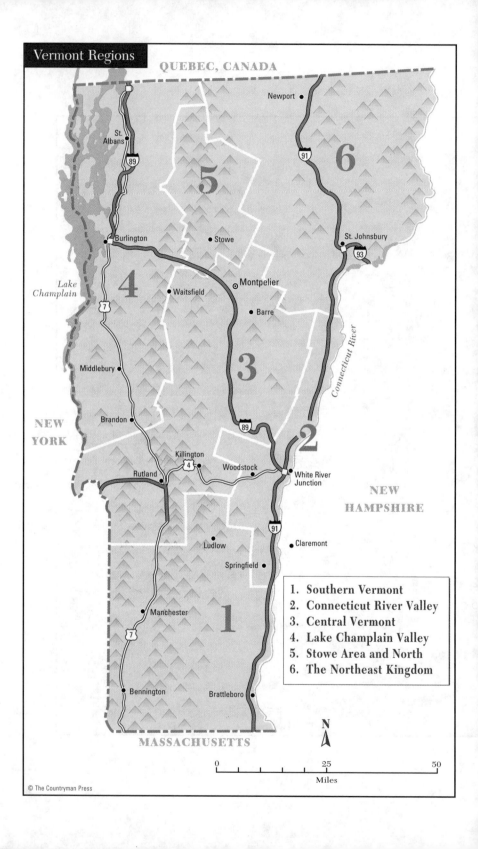

Vermont Regions

QUEBEC, CANADA

Newport

St. Albans

5

6

Burlington

Stowe

St. Johnsbury

Lake Champlain

4

Waitsfield

Montpelier

Barre

Middlebury

3

Connecticut River

Brandon

2

NEW YORK

Killington

Rutland

Woodstock

White River Junction

NEW HAMPSHIRE

Ludlow

Claremont

Springfield

1. Southern Vermont
2. Connecticut River Valley
3. Central Vermont
4. Lake Champlain Valley
5. Stowe Area and North
6. The Northeast Kingdom

Manchester

1

Bennington

Brattleboro

MASSACHUSETTS

N

0   25   50
Miles

© The Countryman Press

CONTENTS

MAPS

◼ INTRODUCTION

Welcome to the Green Mountain State and this 30th-anniversary edition of the most comprehensive guide to its distinctive landscape, character, things to do, and places to see and stay. No other portrait of Vermont gathers so much practical information between two covers—so much that even Vermonters find it useful.

We have divided the guide into generally accepted regions. Each section begins with a verbal snapshot of the area against a historical background, and includes descriptions of just about every legal form of recreation, from skiing and swimming to llama trekking and whitewater rafting.

We describe roughly half of Vermont's places to stay—B&Bs, farmstays, and family-owned (but not chain) motels. We are candid about what we like and don't like. We revisit with every new edition.

With this edition, we have to say, we are distressed by the ways in which online reservations for rooms and B&B in private homes are affecting Vermont's established B&Bs, which have invested big bucks in meeting safety and health codes. Of course vacation rentals can make sense if you are looking to accommodate a family or group for a week or more. If you're looking for a shorter stay, though, we have to put in a plug for hosts dedicated to hospitality and adept at tuning guests in to their surroundings.

We critique upscale restaurants (*Dining Out*) and everyday options (*Eating Out*), plus good delis, bakeries, country stores, and coffeehouses. Local entertainment, interesting shops, and special events round out coverage of virtually every city and town, and just about every village of interest to visitors.

We assume that our readers are not "tourists." We figure that anyone who buys a Vermont guidebook in this online era is interested in going beyond the obvious attractions and places to stay.

Vermont is not an in-your-face kind of place. Most of the things we like best about it are not obvious. Of course there are the ski resorts, country inns, and "attractions" like Ben & Jerry's, the Shelburne Museum, and the Rock of Ages. Vermont is found, however, along its vast network of unpaved roads and hiking paths, in crafts studios, visiting or staying at a farm, picnicking by a waterfall or covered bridge, eating at a community supper, and shopping at farmers markets.

Ironically, Vermont's fame as an autumn and winter destination has upstaged its original tourist season. Vermont's summer is soft, still, and deep, almost secretive. While traffic jams New England's coastal resorts, Vermont's roads and widely scattered lodgings remain blissfully quiet. Wooded paths and swimming holes are never far but rarely obvious.

A BARN AT THE INN AT MOUNTAIN VIEW FARM

Christina Tree

During the more-than-30-year life of this book Vermont's rural character has changed, but not essentially. Farming and processing locally grown and produced products is a flourishing industry that continues to evolve. Growing and eating locally sourced food and drink has become almost a religion in diners and delis as well as the most expensive restaurants and inns. Farms themselves are becoming dining venues.

True, today's shopping-center culture has made inroads here. Still, for every acre of open land paved for a parking lot, currently at least 10 acres are added to the holdings of the Vermont Land Trust, therefore shielded from development. The administrators of Act 250, the state's pioneering land-use program, also still exercise sensible controls over new commercial development, defeating sporadic efforts to dilute the

Vermont Department of Agriculture

act's provisions. Vermonters, prudently and in a spirit of thrift, have been loath to tear down the past. Abandoned farmhouses have been restored, and in a score of towns adaptive preservation techniques have been thoughtfully applied, frequently with the help of the Preservation Trust of Vermont, which works quietly—building by endangered building—to preserve the traditional look of the state.

Contrary to its image, Vermont's landscape varies substantially from north to south and even more from east to west. Rather than following the main tourist routes (east–west Rts. 9 and 4 and north–south Rt. 100), we suggest that (weather permitting) you drive the dramatic but well-paved "gap" roads (see Gaps, Gulfs, and Gorges in "What's Where") east or west across the state's relatively narrow width, bundling very different landscapes—mountain valleys and the broad sweep of farmland along Lake Champlain—into a few hours' drive.

While focusing on all the state's regions through the same lens (our format), we fervently hope that this book conveys the full spectrum of Vermont's beauty: the river roads of the Upper Valley, the high rolling farmland around Tunbridge and Chelsea, the glacially carved, haunting hills of the Northeast Kingdom, and the limestone farmsteads of Isle La Motte. Villages range from the elegant, gentrified resorts such as Stowe, Woodstock, and Manchester, to the equally proud but far less traveled villages of Craftsbury Common, Grafton, and Newfane, and the Victorian brick streetscapes of Brattleboro, Bellows Falls, and Burlington.

Vermont has never been a "rich" state. Except for machine tools, the industrial revolution passed it by; as one political scientist noted, Vermonters leaped from "cow chips to microchips." Nevertheless, at least a few 19th-century families made their fortunes from lumber, wool, marble, and railroads. The 14 years that it existed as a sovereign nation (between 1777 and 1791) stamped Vermont with a certain contrariness. Many examples of its free spirit animate its subsequent history, from the years when Ethan Allen's Rabelaisian Green Mountain Boys wrested independence from the grip of Hampshiremen, 'Yorkers, and "The Cruel Minestereal Tools of George ye 3d" to their quashing of British attempts to retake the Champlain Corridor. This autonomous spirit was later responsible for the abolitionist fervor that swept the state in the years before the Civil War and impelled Vermonters to enlist in record numbers when President Lincoln appealed for troops. Vermonters voted their consciences with much the same zeal when, in both world wars, the legislature declared war on Germany, in effect, before the United States did. More recently Vermont was the first state to legalize civil unions between same-sex couples. It boasts one of the nation's highest percentages of women in the legislature and a strict environmental policy, and is always prepared—if push comes to shove—to secede.

THE AUTHORS

A flatland author, born in Hawaii, raised in New York City, and living near Boston, Chris Tree claims to be a professional Vermont visitor. Her infatuation with the state began more than 40 years ago in college.

"The college was in Massachusetts, but one of my classmates was a native Vermonter whose father ran a general store and whose mother knows the name of every flower, bird, and mushroom. I jumped at her invitations to come 'home' or to 'camp' and have since spent far more time in Vermont than has my friend. As a travel writer for the *Boston Globe*, I spent more than 35 years writing newspaper stories about Vermont towns, inns, ski areas, and people. I interviewed John Kenneth Galbraith about Newfane, Pearl Buck about Danby. I rode the Vermont Bicentennial Train, froze a toe on one of the first inn-to-inn ski treks, camped on the Long Trail and in state parks, paddled a canoe down the Connecticut, slid over Lake Champlain on an iceboat as well as paddling it in a kayak, soared over the Mad River Valley in a glider, and hovered above the Upper Valley in a hot-air balloon. I have also tramped through the woods collecting sap, led a foliage tour, collided with a tractor, and broken down in a variety of places." Research for this edition represents the 14th time that Chris has combed regions around the Green Mountain State, traveling back roads to check out B&Bs, craftspeople, cheesemakers, and (yes!) swimming holes. It all seems to take longer than it once did, perhaps because there's more to talk about along the way. Vermont is as much about people as landscape, and both welcome old friends.

Alice Levitt has written about food for Vermont's alternative newsweekly, *Seven Days*, since 2007. A native of Greenwich, Connecticut, she has lived in Vermont since 1998, when a debilitating case of neurological Lyme disease (cured in 2003) spurred the then-teenager and her family to move north. At *Seven Days*, Alice reviews restaurants, reports on food news, blogs, and has helped to organize Vermont Restaurant Week since its inception. Alice also writes for *Seven Days*' other publications: dining guide *7 Nights*, bilingual airport magazine *BTV*, and college guide *What's Good*, as well as for the *Boston Globe*'s travel section. In 2014 she won the Daysie award for best print or online journalist in Vermont. She appears regularly on WCAX-TV's news magazine show *The :30* and WVMT's morning radio show *Charlie + Ernie + Lisa in the Morning!*

ACKNOWLEDGMENTS

Chris is deeply indebted to Peter Jennison, a sixth-generation Vermonter, who coauthored this book during its first eight editions, and many of the best words in it remain his. Peter was born on a dairy farm in Swanton, attended one-room schoolhouses, and graduated from Middlebury College. After 25 years in the publishing business in New York City, he became a "born-again" Vermonter, returning to his native heath in 1972 and founding The Countryman Press.

For help with research during this edition Chris owes special thanks to former coauthor Diane Foulds; many thanks too to Joan Gorman of Waitsfield, Beth Kennett of Rochester, Edie and Chuck Janisse of Bridgewater Corners, Jane Doerfer of Brookfield, Anne and Bill Mercier of Killington, Joan Seymour of Guilford, Jim and Mary O'Reilly of Lyndonville, Dennis and Carol Poutre of Irasburg, Ruth Sproull of Newport, Ray Wojckewych of Averill, Bonnie MacPherson of Okemo, and Greg Lucas of Montgomery.

Thanks, too, to those chamber of commerce directors who helped beyond the call of duty—especially to Susan Roy of the Mad River Valley, Beth Finlayson of Woodstock, Marji Graf of the Okemo Valley, Gloria Bruce of the Northeast Kingdom, and Lynn Barrett of Southern Vermont. Finally, a big thank-you to my husband, Bill Davis, proofreader and researcher during the endless inputting.

Both authors are grateful to Kermit Hummel and Lisa Sacks for launching this edition and to Fred Lee and Doug Yeager for shepherding it to fruition with the help of our ever-speedy and supportive copy editor, Laura Jorstad.

Christina Tree (ctree@traveltree.net)
vermontexplorersguide.com

WHAT'S WHERE IN VERMONT

AREA CODE The area code for all of Vermont is **802**.

AGRICULTURE AND AGRITOURISM Some 1.25 million acres of the state's total of 6 million acres are devoted to agriculture. The farmhouse and barn are still a symbol of Vermont, and a Vermont vacation should include a farm visit, whether to buy syrup, cheese, wool, or wine, maybe pick apples or berries, tour a dairy operation, or stay for a night or a week. Finding farms can be an excuse to explore unexpectedly beautiful backcountry.

Of course a "farm" isn't what it used to be. Fewer than 1,100 of Vermont's 6,400 farms are now dairy, compared with 10,000 dairy farms 40 years ago. Even so, the average size of dairy herds has increased: With just 15 percent as many dairy farms, the state produces more than twice as much milk as it did 45 years ago. Vermont remains New England's largest milk-producing state; gross sales of cheese, ice

Christina Tree

cream, dips, cream cheese, yogurt, milk, and milk powder total $1.2 billion per year.

Before cows, there were sheep. In the 1830s and '40s, meadowland was far more extensive, and was populated by millions of merino sheep. When the Civil War ended, so did the demand for wool blankets, and a significant number of sheep farms went under. Luckily railroads were expanding to every corner of the state by the 1870s, and railroad companies teamed up with state agriculture departments to promote farms to "summer boarders."

Now farmers are once again looking to visitors as well as new forms of agriculture to maintain their farms. Vermont farmers raise goats and llamas, beef cattle, miniature donkeys, Christmas trees, flowers, vegetables, fruit, trout, and more. Check the **Vermont Agency of Agriculture** website **vermontagriculture .com** for farmers markets. The **Vermont Farms Association** website, **vtfarms.org**, details farms that welcome visitors and overnight guests See also in this chapter *Apples, Cheese, Christmas Trees, Farmers Markets, Farmstays, Gardens, Maple Sugaring, Pick Your Own, Sheep and Wool*, and *Wine*.

AGRICULTURAL FAIRS The **Champlain Valley Exposition** (cvexpo.org) in Essex (lasting an entire week around Labor Day) is by far the state's largest agricultural fair. **Addison County Fair and Field Days** in early Aug. in New Haven, as well as the **Orleans County Fair** in Barton (orleanscountyfair.com, five days in mid-Aug.) and the **Caledonia County Fair** (vtfair.com), always the following weekend in nearby Lyndonville, all feature ox, pony, and horse pulling as well as a midway, live entertainment, and plenty to please all ages. The **Bondville Fair** (two days in late Aug.) claims to be Vermont's oldest continuous fair and is also the

genuine thing. The **Vermont State Fair**
(vermontstatefair.net) in Rutland lasts nine days
in early Sept. The **Tunbridge World's Fair**
(four days in mid-Sept.) is the oldest (it did miss
1918) and most colorful of them all (tunbridge-
fair.com).

AIR SERVICE Burlington International Air-
port (802-863-1889; burlingtonintlairport.com)
offers by far the most scheduled service in Vermont with flights to Atlanta, Chicago, Cleve-
land, Detroit, Newark, New York, Philadelphia,
and Washington, DC. Carriers include **Delta**,
United Airlines, **US Airways**, **JetBlue**, and
Porter, which offer some good deals. Curiously,
at this writing, the only commuter service to
Boston is from the **Southern Vermont
Regional Airport** (flyrutlandvt.com) in Rutland
and the **Lebanon Municipal Airport** (flyleb
.com) in New Hampshire, serving the Upper
Connecticut River Valley. For national service
to southern Vermont check **Bradley International Airport** in Windsor Locks, Connecticut
(bradleyairport.com), and **Albany Airport**
(albanyairport.com) in New York, convenient
for much of the western part of the state.
Manchester (New Hampshire) Airport (fly
manchester.com) is the largest airport in northern New England, with many domestic and
some international flights.

AIRPORTS Click on **airports.vermont.gov**
for details about Vermont's 16 airports, just 2
(see above) with scheduled flights, but all accessible to private and some to charter planes.
Request a copy of the *Vermont Airport Directory* from the Vermont Agency of Transportation (802-828-2587).

AMTRAK (800-USA-RAIL; amtrak.com).
Amtrak's **Vermonter** runs from Washington to
St. Albans with stops (at decent hours both
north- and southbound) in Brattleboro, Bellows
Falls, Claremont (New Hampshire), Windsor,
White River Junction, Randolph, Montpelier,
Waterbury, and Essex Junction (Burlington).
The **Adirondack** runs up the western shore of
Lake Champlain en route from Manhattan to
Montreal and stops at Port Kent, New York,
accessible to Burlington by ferry. The **Ethan
Allen Express** connects Rutland with New
York City via Albany—but it's a long haul. All
Vermont trains accept skis (but not bicycles) as
baggage.

ANTIQUARIAN BOOKSELLERS The Vermont Antiquarian Booksellers Association
(VABA) lists its members at **vermontisbook
country.com**.

Christina Tree

ANTIQUING The pamphlet *Antiquing in Vermont* lists more than 100 of the state's most
prestigious dealers, members of the **Vermont
Antiques Dealers' Association**, at **vermont
ada.com**. The association sponsors an **annual
antiques show** in July in Woodstock. Major
concentrations of dealers can be found in Bennington, Burlington, Dorset, Manchester, Middlebury, Woodstock, and along Rt. 30 in the
West River Valley. The **Weston Antiques
Show** (westonantiquesshow.org), usually the
first weekend in Oct., is the state's oldest and
still one of its best. Look for large group dealer-
ships in Quechee, Danby, East Arlington, Bellows Falls, and East Barre.

APPLES During fall harvest season the demand
is not only for bushel baskets already filled with
apples but also for an empty basket and the
chance to climb a ladder and pick the many
varieties grown in Vermont—primarily in the
Champlain Islands, the Champlain Valley
around Shoreham, and the Lower Connecticut
River Valley between Springfield and Brattleboro. Listings of orchards and apple festivals
can be found under descriptions of these areas
in this book and by requesting a map/guide to
farms from the Vermont Apple Marketing
Board (**vermontapples.org**). From the earliest
days of settlement through the mid-1800s, more
apples, it's said, were used for making hard
cider and brandy than for eating and cooking. In

Vermont Department of Agriculture

1810 some 125 distilleries were producing more than 173,000 gallons of apple brandy annually. Today wineries and cideries are once more making apple wines (see *Wine*).

ART GALLERIES Vermont's art collections (painting, sculpture, and decorative arts) are small, diverse, and widely scattered. The **Bennington Museum** is known for its works by Grandma Moses; there is also the **Robert Hull Fleming Museum** at the University of Vermont, Burlington, the **Middlebury College Museum of Art**; the **St. Johnsbury Athenaeum and Art Gallery**; the **Thomas Waterman Wood Art Gallery** in Montpelier; and the **Shelburne Museum** in Shelburne. While they lack permanent collections, the best changing exhibits in the state are usually found at the **Southern Vermont Arts Center** in Manchester, the **Brattleboro Museum & Art Center**, and the **Helen Day Art Center** in Stowe; also check out the nonprofit **Firehouse Center for the Visual Arts** in Burlington and the **Chaffee Center for the Visual Arts** in Rutland. Brattleboro, Woodstock, Brandon, and Bellows Falls offer the greatest number of private galleries. Burlington and Brattleboro hold open gallery tours the first Friday of every month.

AUCTIONS Most major upcoming auctions are announced in the Thursday edition of Vermont daily newspapers, with a listing of items that will be up for bid. Auctions may be scheduled at any time, however, during summer months. Check local chapters for details.

BALLOONING Year-round flights are offered by **Balloons of Vermont** (balloonsofvermont .com), based in Quechee, also the base for **Balloons Over New England** (balloons

overnewengland.com). **Brian Boland** at Post Mills Airport (802-333-9254) designs and makes his own balloons as well as offering ascents over the Upper Connecticut River Valley; he also showcases more than 100 balloons and many unlikely things that fly in his private museum. **Above Reality** (balloonvermont.com) operates year-round over northern Lake Champlain and the Champlain Valley. The **Annual Balloon Festival** in Quechee is held in June during Father's Day weekend, while the **Stoweflake Hot-Air Balloon Festival** (stoweflake.com) is a mid-July event with balloon launch and tethers.

BARNS Many barns along the highways and byways have distinctive touches, such as ornate Victorian cupolas, and still more are connected to farmhouses in the architectural style that served as shelter for the farmers' trips before dawn in deep snow. The few round barns that survive in Vermont were all built between 1899 and World War I. The concept of the round barn is thought to have originated with the Shakers in Hancock, Massachusetts, where the original stone barn, built in 1824, is now the centerpiece of a museum. The Vermont survivors include: the **Moore barn** in East Barnet; the **Hastings barn** in Waterford; the **Metcalf barn** (Robillard Flats) in Irasburg; the **Parker barn** in Grand Isle, converted into a housing center for the elderly; two barns in Coventry; the **Powers barn** in Lowell; the **Parker barn** in North Troy; one in Enosburg Falls; and **Southwick's** in East Calais. In Waitsfield the **Joslin round barn** is now a cultural center with a swimming pool in its bowels, attached to the **Inn at Round Barn Farm**; in Strafford the **Round Robin Farm**, a 350-acre working dairy farm with a 10-sided barn, takes guests. The **Welch Barn** on Rt. 12 in Morristown just north of Lake Elmore rises into view as you drive the beautiful stretch north from Montpelier.

Round-barn addicts should check at local general stores for exact location and to secure permission to photograph the structures. Among other Vermont barns open to the public are those at Shelburne Farms, including the vast, five-story, 416-foot-long Norman-style **Farm Barn**, the acre-large **Breeding Barn**, and the handsome **Coach Barn** in Shelburne. The round barn once in Passumpsic has been moved to the Shelburne Museum. Two lively, illustrated guides are *A Field Guide to New England Barns and Farm Buildings* by Thomas Visser and *Big House, Little House, Back House, Barn: The Connected Farm Buildings of New England* by Thomas Hubka (both from the University Press of New England).

Christina Tree

BED & BREAKFASTS The hundreds of B&Bs we have personally inspected are listed under their respective locations in this book. They range from working farms to historic mansions.

BICYCLE TOURING In Vermont the distance via back roads from swimming hole to antiques shop to the next inn is never far. John Freidin, author of *Backroad Bicycling in Vermont* (The Countryman Press), introduced the whole notion of guided bike tours for adults back in 1972. Woodstock-based **Discovery Bicycle Tours** (discoverybicycletours.com), formerly Bike Vermont, is the state's most respected inn-to-inn tour outfitter, providing a "sag wagon" (a support vehicle with spare parts and snacks), renting 27-gear hybrid bikes, specializing in small (under 20) groups and a wide variety of Vermont and foreign destinations. **POMG (Peace of Mind Guaranteed) Bike Tours of Vermont** (pomgbike.com). **Vermont Bicycle Touring** (vbt.com) specializes in "affordable" B&B-based biking tours throughout the state. In southern Vermont, **Diverse Directions** (vtcycling.com) offers self-guided tour packages that include baggage transfer, lodging, and routing, as does **Vermont Inn-to-Inn Walking** (vermontinntoinnwalking.com)—an association of innkeepers whose establishments are a comfortable bike ride (or hike) from one another. Participants are largely on their own, but rental equipment is available and baggage is transferred from inn to inn. **Craftsbury Outdoor Center** rents fat-tire bikes and serves as a popular base for cycling some 200 miles of surrounding farm roads.

Bicycle paths continue to grow and multiply in Vermont. Stowe's **"Rec" Path** is 5.3 miles with convenient rentals. The **Burlington Bike Path** follows the shore of Lake Champlain for 12 miles (rentals available). It connects six different parks, continuing across the Winooski River on a bike bridge and through Colchester to a (summer weekends only) bike ferry that links it with the Champlain Islands, arguably the most popular corner of Vermont for bicyclists. Check out the **Lake Champlain Bikeways** site (champlainbikeways.org) for an overview of 1,100 miles of routes on both shores of the lake and extending into Canada; also localmotion .org. The 26-mile **Missisquoi Rail Trail** follows an old railbed from St. Albans to Richford, and the 34-mile **D&H Recreation Trail** follows an abandoned railroad bed almost 20 miles from Castleton to West Rupert, with the remainder in New York State. Check individual chapters for long-distance races. Also see **trailfinder. info** for an overview of all Vermont rec trails.

Within each chapter we have described sources for local bike rentals. Also see *Mountain Biking*.

BIRDING While the hermit thrush, the state bird, is reclusive and not too easy to spot, Vermont offers ample opportunities for observing herons and ducks, as well as raptors like owls, hawks, falcons, ospreys, even bald eagles. It's home to more than 240 species of birds. Stop at the **Missisquoi National Wildlife Refuge** in Swanton even if you don't have time to walk the trails. The new visitors center is a must-see with exhibits showcasing local geology and the history of human habitation as well as bird and animal life. Other outstanding birding areas include the **Dead Creek Wildlife Refuge** in Addison, and the 4,970-acre **Victory Basin** east of St. Johnsbury. The 255-acre **Green Mountain Audubon Nature Center** in Huntington (vt.audubon.org/centers.html) is open year-round; inquire about guided walks and special programs. The neighboring **Birds of Vermont Museum** (birdsofvermont.org) in Huntington features life-like carvings of over 200 species, showing both male and female plumage, displayed in their natural habitats, all the work of master carver Bob Spear of Colchester. The **Vermont Institute of Natural Science (VINS)** maintains a nature center beside Quechee Gorge (vinsweb.org) open year-round, with owls, hawks, eagles, and other raptors in residence and a full program of naturalist walks and demonstrations.

BOAT EXCURSIONS If you don't own a yacht, there are still plenty of ways to get onto Vermont rivers and lakes. Possible cruises from Burlington include the *Spirit of Ethan Allen II*

Christina Tree

(soea.com), a 500-passenger excursion boat, and **Moonlight Lady** (vermontdiscoverycruises .com)—a three-deck converted swamp yacht with eight staterooms (private baths) offering overnight cruises on Lake Champlain. On Lake Memphremagog, Vermont's second largest lake, **Northern Star** (vermontlakecruises.com), a replica vintage canal cruiser, is now based in Newport, offering daily cruises out into international waters. Farther south the **M/V Carillon** (carilloncruises.com) sails between Fort Ticonderoga and the Vermont shore. For details, check under respective locations in this book. See also *Ferries*.

BOATING RULES For laws and regulations governing the use and registration of motorboats, see boatsafe.com/vt.

BOOKS In addition to the books we mention in specific fields or on particular subjects, here are some of the most useful current titles: *Vermont Atlas and Gazetteer* (DeLorme) and *Vermont Place Names: Footprints in History*, by Esther Swift (Vermont Historical Society). *Hands on the Land: A History of the Vermont Landscape*, by Jan Albers, published by the MIT Press for The Orton Family Foundation, is also essential reading for anyone truly interested in understanding why Vermont looks the way it does. Lovers of natural history should seek out *The Nature of Vermont*, by Charles Johnson (University Press of New England). Basic reference directories include the *Vermont Encyclopedia* (University Press of New England). Civil War buffs will be rewarded by Howard Coffin's *Full Duty: Vermonters in the Civil War*; *Nine Months to Gettysburg: Stannard's Vermonters and the Repulse of Pickett's Charge*; and *The Battered Stars: One State's Civil War Ordeal During Grant's Overland Campaign* (all published by

Christina Tree

The Countryman Press). For children, *Vermont: The State with the Storybook Past*, by Cora Cheney (New England Press), is the best.

Our favorite current Vermont fiction writer is Howard Frank Mosher of Irasburg, whose evocative novels include *On Kingdom Mountain*, *Disappearances*, *Northern Borders*, *Where the Rivers Flow North*, *A Stranger in the Kingdom* (the last two are also films), and *The Great Northern Express*. Joseph Citro is the author of several books about occult occurrences and folk legends in the state, including *Green Mountains, Dark Tales* (University Press of New England), and *Ghosts, Ghouls, and Unsolved Mysteries* (Houghton Mifflin). The Brattleboro-based mysteries of Archer Mayor, including *Open Season* and other titles in his Joe Gunther police-procedural series, are gaining momentum. And look for the charming little *Art of the State: Vermont* by Suzanne Mantell (Abrams). For a narrative guide to some off-the-beaten-path attractions, seek out *Off the Leash: Subversive Journeys Around Vermont* by Helen Husher (The Countryman Press). *Northeastern Wilds* (AMC Books), by Stephen Gorman, features stunning photography and includes informative text about Vermont's stretch of the northern forest.

Christina Tree

BREWERIES Civil War–era Vermont was New England's leading hops-producing state; in the United States only New York surpassed its output. In the late 19th century, however, temperance movements and other factors virtually eliminated its beer and wine industries. But Vermont brewing is back and growing with a vengeance. In fact there are more breweries here per capita than in any other state. Check out **vermontbrewers.com** for a list of the dozens of small breweries that seem to bloom across Vermont's hillsides on a weekly basis. Beer geeks traveled long distances to the **Alchemist Brewery** in Waterbury before it closed to guests, but after a move to Stowe soon, it will open to the public once again. Similar pilgramages to **Lawson's Finest Liquids**

in Waitsfield, and **Hill Farmstead Brewery** in Greensboro Bend continue. And the popular **Switchback Brewing Company** in Burlington, **Magic Hat Brewing Co.** in South Burlington, **Otter Creek Brewing** in Middlebury, **Long Trail Brewing** in West Bridgewater, **Rock Art Brewery** in Morrisville, and **Trout River Brewing Co.** in Lyndonville are all widely distributed and worth a visit, as is **Harpoon Brewery** (with a popular pub/restaurant) in Windsor.

BUS SERVICE "You can't get there from here" is no joke for would-be transit passengers to, from, and around Vermont. **Vermont Transit** has been absorbed by **Greyhound** (greyhound .com), which still maintains a Boston–Burlington run via White River Junction and Montpelier and New York City via Brattleboro and Bellows Falls to White River Junction. Regional bus services are taking up the slack. Bennington-based **Green Mountain Express** (greenmtncn.org) serves Bennington County including Manchester and Pownal with stops between. Rutland-based **Marble Valley Transit** (thebus.com) serves Manchester, Killington, Middlebury, Fair Haven, and points between. **Rural Community Transportation** (riderct.org) serves the Northeast Kingdom. See *Getting There* under each destination. New York City skiers should check **Adventure Northeast Bus Service** (adventurenortheast.com), offering daily service to Mount Snow, Stratton, and Killington from Thanksgiving weekend through April. Check with Okemo for similar services.

BYWAYS (vermont-byways.us). Most Vermont roads would qualify as byways anywhere else, but some are now officially recognized for their archaeological, cultural, historic, natural, recreational, or scenic qualities. You can download a map from the website. At latest count there were 10, several of which are among the most heavily trafficked roads in the state.

CAMPS, FOR CHILDREN For information about both day and residential Vermont summer camps for boys and girls, contact the **Vermont Camping Association** (vermont camps.org).

CAMPGROUNDS The *Vermont Campground Guide*, covering both private and public facilities, is published by the Vermont Campground Association and available online (**campvermont .com**), as well as at the welcome centers on Vermont interstates. Private campgrounds offer creature comforts such as snack bars, stores, playgrounds, electricity, cable TV, and WiFi.

For those same reasons, the state parks are quieter.

A map/guide to Vermont's 52 state parks is available from **Vermont State Parks** (802-241-3655; vtstateparks.com). The excellent website describes each park in detail with maps of the camping areas. Facilities include furnished cottages, unfurnished cabins, lean-tos, and tent and trailer sites. Fees vary with the class of the area. For reservations 14 days or less beforehand call the park directly (listed online); otherwise reserve online or by phone at 888-409-7579 weekdays 9–4. Trees separate most Vermont state park campsites from neighboring sites, and they are well maintained. Many offer organized programs such as hikes, campfire sings, films, and lectures. Most parks are relatively uncrowded, especially midweek; the most popular are Branbury, Stillwater, Groton Forest, Grand Isle, and Lake St. Catherine. This book describes state parks as they appear geographically.

Within the 400,000-acre **Green Mountain National Forest** seven designated camping areas are available on a first-come, first-served basis for a maximum 14-day period for $10 per night. These areas are **Hapgood Pond Recreational Area** near Peru, **Red Mill Brook Campground** near Woodford, **Grout Pond Recreational Area** (free) near Stratton, **Greendale Campground** north of Weston, **Silver Lake** (free) and **Moosalamoo** near Goshen, and **Chittenden Brook Campground** near Brandon. Camping is also permitted in the wilds without fee or prior permission unless otherwise posted, but before you pitch your tent, visit one of the district ranger offices; see *Green Mountain National Forest*. The **U.S. Army Corps of Engineers**, New England District, also maintains campsites close to flush toilets, showers, and swimming at the **Winhall Brook Camping Area** at Ball Mountain Lake in Jamaica and at **North Hartland Lake** near Quechee. For details, click on corpslakes.us. To reserve sites at any of these campgrounds, phone the National Recreation Reservation Service at 877-444-6777 or go to recreation.gov.

CANOEING AND KAYAKING Arlington-based **BattenKill Canoe** (battenkill.com), Vermont's oldest outfitter, offers day trips and inn-to-inn tours throughout the state; **Clearwater Sports** (clearwatersports.com) in Waitsfield offers guided tours, instruction, and special expeditions, as does **Umiak Outdoor Outfitters** (umiak.com) in Stowe. **Vermont Canoe Touring Center** (802-257-5008) in Brattleboro offers canoe rentals, shuttle service, and river camping on the Connecticut. **North Star**

Canoe Livery (kayak-canoe.com), based in Cornish, New Hampshire, offers rentals and shuttles for the scenic reach between White River Junction and the Cornish–Windsor bridge, one particularly rich in camping spots. **Wilderness Trails** in Quechee offers similar trips on the neighboring stretch of the river, on nearby ponds, and on the White River; so does **Great River Outfitters** in Windsor. For the upper reaches of the Connecticut check out **Hemlock Pete's Canoes & Kayaks** in North Haverhill, New Hampshire, and Passumpsic River Outfitters near St. Johnsbury. For canoeing and kayaking elsewhere in the Northeast Kingdom see Clyde River Recreation in West Charleston and Newport, and Montgomery Adventures near Jay Peak.

Check out the **Vermont Fish and Wildlife Department** website (vtfishandwildlife.com) for put-in places. **Recommended books:** Roioli Schweiker's third edition of *Canoe Camping Vermont and New Hampshire Rivers* (The Countryman Press) is a handy guide, and the *AMC River Guide: Vermont/New Hampshire* (AMC Books) is good for detailed information on canoeable rivers, as is *The Connecticut River Boating Guide, Source to the Sea* (Falcon Press) published in cooperation with the Connecticut River Watershed Council. The 740-mile **Northern Forest Canoe Trail** (northernforest canoetrail.org), which begins in Old Forge, New York, dips in and out of Vermont on its way to Fort Kent, Maine. The organization is headquartered in Waitsfield (802-496-2285).

CATAMOUNT TRAIL (catamounttrail.org). You may not want to ski the 300 miles from Massachusetts to Canada, but it's nice to know you can—along the longest cross-country ski trail in this country. Since 1984, when three young skiers bushwhacked their way the length of Vermont, the Catamount Trail has been evolving. The nonprofit Catamount Trail Association (CTA) now has over 1,800 paying members. Over the years countless permits and dozens of easements have secured use of private and public lands. Bridges have been built, trailhead parking created, and a 9th edition of *The Catamount Trail Guidebook* ($19.95) maps and describes each of the trail's 31 segments. The excellent website includes a "trip planning" section with suggested places to stay along the way. Members receive a regular newsletter and discounts at participating touring centers and retailers. Also see *Skiing, Cross-Country*.

CEMETERIES There's no better way to get close to Vermont's history than through its cemeteries. The Vermont Old Cemetery Association (voca58.org) provides a helpful starting point with its online listings of historical burial grounds, complete with maps and mentions of prominent people interred in some locations. International website FindAGrave.com is a good next step for research—many graves are listed with photographs, and some pages have detailed histories of the deceased. The **Old Bennington Cemetery** may be best known as Robert Frost's final resting place, but its denizens are a tightly packed group of Revolutionary War heroes and early Vermont governors. Near Putney, the **Westminster Old Cemetery** is uncommonly well preserved, making it an approachable ground zero for learning about the 1775 Westminster Massacre, viewed by some historians as the first battle of the Revolution. **Laurel Glen Cemetery** in Cuttingsville—down Rt. 103 in Rutland County—is home to Bowman Mausoleum. There, John Porter Bowman rests along with the two daughters and wife who each preceded him to the grave. On the memorial's steps, a sculpture of Bowman clutches the monument's key in one hand and a funeral wreath in the other. Inside, statues of the three female Bowmans reside eternally, along with the unsettling inscription, A COUCH OF DREAMLESS SLEEP. In New Haven, near Middlebury, **Evergreen Cemetery** is eternal host to Timothy Clark Smith, buried beneath a glass window and with a bell to alert passersby in case he was accidentally interred alive. Smith's neighbors, many buried almost 100 years before him in the 18th century, benefited from an exceptionally poetic stonecutter—the dark verse is present on nearly every stone. In Middlebury proper, **West Cemetery** is the location of Vermont's oldest burial. Museum founder Henry Sheldon committed the remains of 2-year-old

Alice Levitt

Amum-Her-Kepesh-Ef to Vermont soil after discovering the Egyptian mummy was too decayed to display. His stone marker lists his death date as 1883 BC. **Hope Cemetery** in Barre is deservedly Vermont's most famous (see the sidebar in "Barre/Montpelier Area") for its monuments carved for stonecutters by stonecutters. But **Green Mount Cemetery** in nearby Montpelier should not be overlooked. Positioned on a steep incline just past the city center, the memorials have a distinctly English feel to contrast with the lusty Italianate design at Hope. Victorian effigies of the deceased climb the hill alongside a gigantic boulder that marks the final resting place of William Stowell. Burlington has a **Green Mount Cemetery** of its own and it's tightly packed with members of the revolutionary Allen family. Ira Allen is certainly there, but there's some controversy around whether Ethan Allen's earthly form really lies under the soaring monument to him. Other Burlington luminaries repose at **Lakeview Cemetery**. The biggest name therein is that of Civil War general George Stannard, but the greatest attraction is the diversity of the lakeside park. There are specially consecrated Jewish and Muslim sections, as well as stones emblazoned with missives in Vietnamese and Chinese. It's a touch of the Queen City's modern profile, woven into Vermont's living (and deceased) history.

CHEESE Vermont's production of cheese rivals even its overactive mojo for beer. Similarly, there's more artisan cheese made per capita in this state than any other in the Union. It's not just quantity, either. The quality is legendary, leading to international garlands for cheeses made from sheep's, goat's, and cow's milk. Check out the following producers among the nearly 50 **Vermont Cheese Council** members currently listed on the downloadable **Vermont Cheese Trail map** (vtcheese.com).

A century ago most Vermont towns had a cheesemaker to which farmers brought the day's surplus milk. **Crowley Cheese** (crowley cheese-vermont.com), established in 1882 and billed as "the oldest continuously operated cheese factory in the U.S.," is the only survivor of this era, and welcomes visitors to its wooden factory just west of Ludlow on Rt. 103 in Healdville (open Mon.–Sat.). This distinctive cheese is creamier than cheddar and still made the traditional way. The public is invited to view a similarly old-fashioned cheesemaking process at **Plymouth Artisan Cheese** (802-672-3650; plymouthartisancheese.com), part of the Calvin Coolidge State Historic Site in Plymouth. **Cabot Creamery** (cabotcreamery.com) in

Grafton Cheese

Cabot is the state's largest, most famous producer. The cooperative has been farmer owned since 1919. Its visitors center is open daily, year-round, and offers plant tours (call ahead for cheesemaking days); its annexes in Waterbury Center south of Stowe and in Quechee sell a variety of the dairy products and cheeses that have made market inroads nationwide.

Award-winning **Vermont Shepherd Cheese** (802-387-4473; vtshepherdcheese .com), a rich, tangy sheep's-milk cheese from Westminster, opens its cave to visitors at certain times (call ahead). **Grafton Village Cheese Company** (800-472-3866; graftonvillagecheese .com) in Grafton had its beginnings around 1890 and was resurrected by the Windham Foundation in 1966; visitors view the cheesemaking from outside, through a picture window here and at the company's far larger new plant and retail store in Brattleboro, also showcasing 50 other artisan cheeses. **Taylor Farm** (802-824-5690; taylorfarmvermont.com) in Londonderry is reputed for its Gouda and open daily (try the smoked variety while you're there!), and **Woodcock Farm** (802-824-6538) in Weston has won top national honors for its Euro-style sheep cheese. In Randolph Center, minutes off I-89, Exit 4, at **Neighborly Farms** (802-728-4700; neighborlyfarms.com), you can walk down a hallway and view cows on one side and cheesemaking on the other (open Mon.– Fri.). **Vermont Creamery** (800-884-6287; vermontcreamery.com) in Websterville makes a wide variety of internationally beloved goat cheeses and will host guests with some notice. **Willow Moon Farm** (802-454-9916; willow moonfarm.com) produces cheese from tiny Nigerian dwarf goats. It's worth a trip off the beaten path to Plainfield to meet the animals and try some chèvre or feta. **Sugarbush Cheese & Maple Farm** (800-281-1757; sugar bushfarm.com), set high on a hill in Woodstock, smokes and packages several varieties of cheddar cheese and welcomes visitors—but beware the road in mud season.

At **Shelburne Farms** (802-985-8686; shelburnefarms.org) in Shelburne near Burlington, several varieties of prizewinning cheddar are made from the milk of a single herd of Brown Swiss cows. The farm store is open daily, year-round. In the northwest corner of the state, uncommon farmhouse cheeses are crafted at **Willow Hill Farm** (802-893-2963; sheep cheese.com) in Milton. In Highgate Center visitors are welcome at **Green Mountain Blue Cheese** (802-868-4193; boucherfamilyfarm .blogspot.com). The Northeast Kingdom also has more than its share of cheesemakers. **Bonnie View Farm** (802-755-6878; bonnieview .org) in Craftsbury makes a superb sheep's-milk cheese. **Jasper Hill Farm** in Greensboro is one of Vermont's most esteemed cheesemakers, but doesn't offer public tours. Grab some semi-soft Winnimere elsewhere, if you can. Check vtcheesefest.com for the July date of the Vermont Cheesemakers Festival, then purchase tickets as early as you can—the event always sells out.

CHILDREN, ESPECIALLY FOR Look for the ✿ symbol throughout this book; it designates child-friendly attractions as well as lodging and dining. Alpine slides delight children of all ages at **Bromley's** summer **Thrill Zone** (bromley .com). There are also alpine slides at **Stowe** (stowe.com) and at Pico, part of the **Killington/ Pico Adventure Center** (killington.com), which includes waterslides, a climbing wall, an in-line skate park, mountain biking, guided hikes, and more. Alpine lifts, which operate in summer, are also a way of hoisting small legs and feet to the top of some of Vermont's most spectacular summits. In Stowe, **Mount Mansfield**, Vermont's highest peak, and **Killington Peak**, second highest in the state, are accessible via gondola on weekdays. **Jay Peak's Pump House** boasts New England's biggest, most exciting water park, also weather-proofed with a sliding roof. Jay Peak also has an aerial tram the top of the mountain and an ice arena with rental skates and hockey equipment. At **Stratton Ski Resort** in southern Vermont, the gondola runs daily in foliage season.

The **Shelburne Museum** (shelburne museum.org) has many exhibits that please youngsters, as does the **Fairbanks Museum and Planetarium** (fairbanksmuseum.org), St. Johnsbury, which is filled with taxidermied animals, birds, and exhibits from near and far. The **Montshire Museum of Science** (montshire .org) in Norwich is a real standout, with hands-on exhibits explaining many basic scientific mysteries plus a 2-acre outdoor exhibit inviting plenty of water experiments (bring a towel) and

Manchester Chamber of Commerce

a beautiful riverside walk. **ECHO at the Leahy Center for Lake Champlain** (echo center.org) is a new science center and aquarium featuring 2,200 live fish, amphibians, and reptiles, with hands-on exhibits for kids 3–17. The **Billings Farm & Museum** (billingsfarm .org) and **Vermont Institute of Natural Science** (vinsweb.org), both in the Woodstock area, are child pleasers.

Over the past few years, as ski areas have come to compete for family business, resorts have developed special programs for children. **Smugglers' Notch** (smuggs.com) offers the largest, most extensive and reasonably priced full summer day camp and ski-geared programs for a wide range of ages. The **Tyler Place Family Resort** in Highgate Springs and the **Basin Harbor Club** in Vergennes are family-geared resorts with teens' and children's programs. The **Wildflower Inn** (wildflowerinn .com) and **Quimby Country** in the northeastern corner of the state offer summer half-day programs for children. Also check Farm Stays at vtfarms.org.

CHRISTMAS TREES Vermont's many Christmas tree farms generally open after Thanksgiving, inviting customers to come tag the tree they want, leaving it until the last moment to cut. Check the websites **vermontchristmastrees .org** and **vtfarms.org** for a list of the more imaginative marketers. For a do-it-yourself experience, contact the **Green Mountain National Forest Service** in Rochester (802-767-4261) and inquire about tagged trees you can cut for a nominal fee.

CIDERIES Records indicate that cider originally found its way to Vermont as frozen blocks transported by Samuel de Champlain. Production decreased during Prohibition, but the art of cider making has been forging a virile Vermont comeback. The nation's leading cider producer, **Woodchuck Cider** (802-385-3656; woodchuck .com), began the hard cider revival in 1991 in an old apple winery in Proctorsville. Its Middlebury Cider House now hosts guests Thurs.–Mon. **Citizen Cider** (802-448-3278; citizen cider.com) is a Burlington destination, known for its ever-expanding roster of bubbly beverages but also its tasting room, which serves handcrafted pub fare. **Champlain Orchards Cidery** (802-897-2777; champlainorchards .com) in Shoreham creates hard cider and ice cider in numerous varieties from fruit grown on-site. **Eden Ice Cider** (802-895-2838; eden icecider.com) in West Charleston trades in frozen apples made into sweet dessert wines. Visit their tasting room at the Northeast Kingdom Tasting Center in Newport. In Cambridge, **Boyden Valley Winery & Spirits** (802-644-8151; boydenvalley.com) produces Vermont ice ciders, as well as hard cider. Numerous small cideries are opening at a rate second only to breweries and are becoming organized through the Vermont Cider Makers Association. But for those looking to taste pressed Vermont apples without alcohol in the way, **Cold Hollow Cider Mill** (800-327-7537; coldhollow.com) in Waterbury can't be beat. **Shelburne Orchards** (985-2753; shelburneorchards.com) in Shelburne makes some fine juices that don't contain booze (including spicy Ginger Jack, which almost tastes like it does), but also its own imprint of apple brandy.

COLLEGES For information about all the state's colleges and universities, contact **Vermont State Colleges** (vsc.edu) and the **Consortium of Vermont Colleges** (vtcolleges.org).

COMMUNITY SUPPERS No website serves this elusive but ubiquitous Vermont institution.

Christina Tree

Check local papers and bulletin boards and try to catch at least one supper for a sense of local communities as well as regional food.

CONNECTICUT RIVER New England's longest river rises near the Canada–New Hampshire border and forms the boundary between that state and Vermont for some 255 miles. Not far below its source are a series of lakes: five in New Hampshire's North Country town of Pittsburg, and two—Moore and Comerford—near St. Johnsbury. The 145 miles between Barnet and Brattleboro are punctuated by four dams, each creating deeper pools that turn the river into a series of slow-moving, narrow lakes. But of the 275 miles the river runs from its source to the Massachusetts border, 134 miles are free flowing. The entire river is now the centerpiece of the 7.2-million-acre, four-state Silvio O. Conte National Fish and Wildlife Refuge. The **Connecticut River National Scenic Byway** includes 10 bistate "waypoint" information centers between Brattleboro and Colebrook, New Hampshire. Click onto **ctrivertravel.net** for a historical and cultural guide. Note that we include information about river towns in both states in our Connecticut River Valley chapters.

William Hays

COUNTRY STORES, also now referred to as "general stores," are a distinct species that is both endangered and evolving to fill the changing needs of the hundreds of villages for which they still serve as hubs. Most now offer hot food and a good deli. Some invite patrons to linger at tables or on couches. Within the book we've lovingly described the state's iconic general stores such as **Currier's** in Glover, **Willy's** in Greensboro, **Hastings** in West Danville, **Dan & Whit's** in Norwich, and **Mach's General Store** in Pawlet Village. We also note variations on the old model that offer eat-in options. Some of our favorite are **The Warren Store**, **Putney General Store**, **H. N. Williams General**

Store in Dorset, **Craftsbury General Store**, and **Newbury Village Store**. In recent years preservation and community groups have salvaged and revamped these community hubs; for examples see **Guilford**, **Shrewsbury**, **West Townshend**, and **Barnard**. For a complete list of independently owned markets and map, check out the **Vermont Alliance of Independent Country Stores** website (vaics.org). **The Vermont Country Stores** in Weston and Rockingham publish a thick catalog—a source of long underwear and garter belts and Healthy Feet Cream—and have become tourist destinations. **Farm-Way, Inc.**, in Bradford, is Vermont's L.L. Bean, billed as "complete outfitters for man and beast."

COVERED BRIDGES The state's 100 surviving covered bridges are marked on the official state map and on our maps and are described in the appropriate chapters of this book under *To See*. Bridge buffs should get a copy of *Covered Bridges of Vermont* by Ed Barna (The Countryman Press). The **Vermont Covered Bridge Museum** in Bennington features a theater production, dioramas, interactive exhibits, and a model railroad with covered railroad bridges (vermontcoveredbridgemuseum.org).

CRAFTS More than 1,500 Vermonters make their living from crafts. There are also more than 100 retail crafts venues in the state. During Vermont's **Open Studio Weekend** on Memorial Day weekend, and again the first weekend in Oct., hundreds of artisans welcome visitors in almost as many locations. Request a copy of the Vermont Crafts Studio Tour Map, available at

Vermont Crafts Council

information centers and on request from the **Vermont Crafts Council** (802-223-3380; vermontcrafts.com). It's worth having in the car any time of year, as many craftspeople welcome visitors informally. Within this book we have described studios, galleries, and shops as they appear geographically and have also included major crafts tours and fairs. The outstanding galleries are: **Frog Hollow Vermont State Craft Center** in Burlington (froghollow.org), **The Artisan's Hand** (artisanshand.com) in Montpelier, **Art on Main** (artonmain.net) in Bristol, **The Collective** (collective-theartof craft.com) in Woodstock, **Vermont Artisan Designs** (buyvermontart.com) in Brattleboro, and the **Brandon Artist's Guild** (brandon artistsguild.com). Craftspeople also sell at events ranging from farmers markets and church bazaars to juried shows and festivals. In late Nov. and early Dec. there are many open studios around the state. On the Thanksgiving weekend **Putney Craft Tour** (putneycrafts .com) and the **Walpole Artisan Open Studios Tour** (walpoleartisans.com) add up to a great way to explore back roads and take care of holiday shopping. Also see craftscenters vermont.gov.

CUSTOMS INFORMATION Vermont shares a 90.3-mile border with the Canadian province of Quebec. Since the September 11 terrorist attacks, all border crossings have become far stricter. Even in Derby Line (Vermont), where it's tempting to walk the few steps into Stanstead (Quebec) to a restaurant, repercussions can be serious. Travelers must present a passport, a passport card, a Trusted Traveler Card, or an Enhanced Driver's License and, if

Christina Tree

they are not American or Canadian, valid tourist visas. Pets are required to have a veterinarian's certificate showing a recent vaccination against rabies. At this writing it's possible to bring in Canadian cheese and all meats but lamb and goat—but check on your entry into Canada. For detailed information contact the U.S. Customs District Office in St. Albans (802-524-6527), in Montreal (514-636-3875), or in Toronto (416-676-2606). For U.S. customs information visit cbp.gov; for Canadian, cbsaasfc.ca.

DINERS Vermont will not disappoint old-fashioned diner buffs. Still, offerings tend to be on the simple side—don't expect the *Les Misérables*–length menus you might find outside New York City. Hearty meals at reasonable prices can be found in Burlington at **Henry's Diner** on Bank St., a Queen City staple since 1925. The South Burlington Worcester dining car known as the **Parkway Diner** serves the best hot turkey sandwiches in the state. Fare tends toward the modern at Middlebury's **The Diner**, where Korean beef-filled naan bread and jalapeño popper French toast might be the order of the day. The **Miss Lyndonville Diner** on Bond St., Lyndonville, is admired for its pies, even at breakfast. **Anthony's Restaurant** on Railroad St. in St. Johnsbury serves simple food that's grown locally.

Just off I-91 in Wells River, the **P&H Truck Stop** (open 24 hours but no longer full service at all hours) is a truckers' oasis that serves large, reasonably priced meals and up to 23 flavors of pie—but that doesn't mean to skip the doughnuts. The **Wayside Restaurant and Bakery** (Exit 7; follow signs for Rt. 302 and it's on your left) south of Montpelier has expanded gradually since its 1918 opening to become Vermont's ultimate family restaurant, replete with the salt pork and local perch that would have been popular the year it opened. **The Blue Benn Diner**, 102 Hunt St. in Bennington,

serves imaginative vegetarian as well as standard diner fare.

T. J. Buckley's in Brattleboro may look like a vintage Worcester diner, but inside oak paneling gleams and the upscale, dinner-only cuisine has long been recognized as some of the best in the state. Also in Brattleboro, the former Ed's Diner is now a venue for Mayan cuisine as the justly popular **Three Stones Restaurant**. West Brattleboro is home to the **Chelsea Royal Diner**, a great bet for families. In Chester, our pick is the friendly **Country Girl Diner**. Nearby, the 1920s **Miss Bellows Falls Diner** is on the National Register of Historic Places; equally historic (and tiny) **Dan's Diner** in Windsor has been lovingly restored with no kitsch lost. Check these establishments out in their respective chapters. Diner buffs should also find their way to **Martha's Diner**, a chrome classic in Coventry. (Also see *Highway Road Food*.)

DISTILLERIES At this writing there are 18 distilleries in Vermont, and they are multiplying quickly. See 802.spirits.com for a current list, which indicates those open for tours and tastings. Check out **American Crafted Spirits in Windsor** (silovodka.com), **Appalachian Gap Distillery** in Middlebury (appgap.com), **Boyden Valley Spirits** (boydenvalley.com) in Cambridge, **Caledonia Spirits** (caledoniaspirits.com) with a tasting room in Ferrisburgh, **Mad River Distillers** (madriverdistillers.com) in Warren, **Saxton's River Distillery** (sapling liqueur.com) with a tasting room in Brattleboro, **Smuggler's Notch Distillery** (smugglers notchdistillery.com) in Jeffersonville, **Vermont Distillers** (vermontdistillers.com) at the Hogback Overlook, Rt. 9 in West Marlboro, and **Vermont Spirits** (vermontspirits.com) with its tasting room on Rt. 4 in Quechee. Also see the **Northeast Kingdom Tasting Center** in Newport (nektastingcenter.com), showcasing local spirits such as Dunc's Mill rum from St. Johnsbury.

DOGSLEDDING Eden Dog Sledding (eden dogsledding.com) in Eden is sited in some of the snowiest backwoods of northern Vermont, a 75-acre property surrounded by protected wilderness with tours and lodging offered year-round. **Hardscrabble Mountain Dogsled Tours** in Sheffield is also well sited with its own woods trails but handy to Burke Mountain. **Montgomery Adventures** offers dogsledding near Jay Peak. **Great River Outfitters** in Windsor provides mushing by the Connecticut River, snow permitting, and shuttles patrons to snowier venues when necessary.

Vermont Crafts Council

EMERGENCIES Try **911** first. This simple SOS has finally reached most corners of Vermont. For state police phone 802-878-7111, for poison 800-222-1222, and for help with dental emergencies 800-640-5099.

EVENTS Almost every day of the year some special event is happening somewhere in Vermont. Usually it's something relatively small and friendly like a church supper, contra dance, community theatrical production, concert, or crafts fair. We have worked up our own *Special Events* for each region, and listings can also be found in various ways on the state's travel website, **vermontvacation.com**. Still, many of the best events are like fireflies, surfacing only on local bulletin boards and in the Thurs. editions of local papers. In northern and central Vermont check out the free and information-rich *Seven Days* and its funky weekly listing of local arts and entertainment, available in shops and grocery stores all over the region.

FACTORY OUTLETS Within the book we have mentioned only a small fraction of the factory outlets of which we are aware. Our bias has been to favor distinctly made-in-Vermont products. Among our favorites: **Johnson Woolen Mills** (quality wool clothing for all ages) in Johnson; **Bennington Potters** (dinnerware, housewares, and more) in Bennington and Burlington; and **Vermont Marble** in Proctor. **Charles Shackleton and Miranda Thomas** produce outstanding furniture and ceramics in an old mill in Bridgewater. **Copeland Furniture** in Bradford also has some seconds in its showroom. **Simon Pearce** in Quechee and Windsor sells seconds of his gorgeous glassware at affordable prices. **The Outlet Center** just off I-91, Exit 1, in Brattleboro harbors some genuine finds. Manchester merchants refuse to call the dozens of upscale stores clustered in their town "outlets," but the prices in designer name stores are lower than retail; this is in fact the state's prime destination shopping center.

FARMERS MARKETS One of Vermont's fastest-growing local industries, farmers markets can now be found in almost every Vermont community mid-June–early Oct. and monthly throughout winter in some areas. Count on finding fresh vegetables, fruit, honey, meat, eggs, flowers, crafts, wine, preserves, and much more at farm prices in commercial centers throughout the state. Look for listings within each chapter. Click on **nofavt.org** and **vermongagriculture .com** for current lists. Note **winter farmers markets**, now throughout the state.

FARMS OPEN TO THE PUBLIC For a list of farms open to the public for tours, to sell their products, or for farmstays, check on the Vermont Farms Association website, **vtfarms.org**.

FARMSTAYS A century ago hundreds of Vermont farms took in visitors for weeks at a time. "There is no crop more profitable than the crop from the city," an 1890s Vermont Board of Agriculture pamphlet proclaimed, a publication noted by Dona Brown in *Inventing New England* (Smithsonian, 1995). Articles advised farmers on how to decorate, what to serve, and generally how to please and what to expect from city guests—much as B&B literature does today. Our own family found a farmstay so enriching that we returned year after year. Within the book we have listed those farms that we have personally visited. For a fuller listing you can click on **vtfarms.org**.

Maple Crest Farm in Shrewsbury deserves special mention because it remains in the same family who have been taking in guests on this working farm since the 1860s. Beth Kennett at **Liberty Hill Farm** in Rochester has pioneered the resurgence in farmstays by successfully combining a working dairy farm with genuine hospitality and great food. **Allenholm Farm** in South Hero offers a B&B in the midst of a major apple orchard. In the Northeast Kingdom our favorite places to stay include **Emergo Farm Bed and Breakfast** in Danville, **Nancy and Jim Rodgers** in West Glover, **Cliff Haven Farm** in Newport Center, and **Mountain View Dairy** in Irasburg. In central Vermont we can recommend **Hollister Hill Farm** in Marshfield, **Round Robin Farm** in Sharon, and **Devil's Den Farm** in Chelsea. At the other extreme is lakeside **Shelburne Farms**, the most beautiful farm in the state—with its most elegant inn, the **Inn at Shelburne Farms**.

Vermont Farms! Association

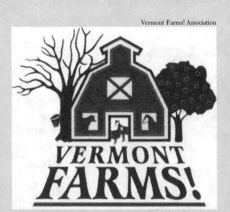

RM Eddy

Jacobson's *My Mother's Early Lovers* and *Nothing Like Dreaming* are absorbing narratives. By the same token, Tunbridge sheep farmer John O'Brien's film trilogy, *Vermont Is for Lovers*, *Man with a Plan*, and *Nosey Parker*, goes right to Vermont's still very real rural core. *Man with a Plan* launched its hero's real-life political campaign and, to the amazement of the country, retired Tunbridge dairy farmer Fred Tuttle not only defeated a wealthy carpetbagger for the Republican nomination but won a respectable percentage of the vote for a U.S. senatorial seat. O'Brien continues to make films. Samplings of Vermont-made films can be found on the **Vermont Film Commission**'s website (vermont film.com).

FERRIES A number of car-carrying ferries ply Lake Champlain between the Vermont and New York shores, offering splendid views of both the Green Mountains and the Adirondacks. The northernmost crosses to Plattsburgh, New York, from **Grand Isle**, on Rt. 314 (year-round; 12-minute passage). From **Burlington** they cross to Port Kent, New York (one hour); the **Essex Ferry** travels between Charlotte and Essex, New York (20 minutes). All three are operated by the **Lake Champlain Transportation Company**, descendant of the line founded in 1828 claiming to be "the oldest steamboat company on earth." Near the southern end of the lake, the car-carrying **Fort Ticonderoga Ferry** provides a seasonal, scenic shortcut (seven minutes) between Larrabees Point and Ticonderoga, New York. The Fort Ti Ferry has held a franchise from the New York and Vermont legislatures since circa 1800.

FIDDLING Vermont is the fiddling capital of the East. Fiddlers include concert violinists, rural carpenters, farmers, and heavy-equipment operators who come from throughout the East to gather in beautiful natural settings. The newsletter of the **Northeast Fiddlers Association** (nefiddlers.org) lists fiddling meets around the state, such as the **Cracker Barrel Bazaar & Fiddle Contest** in Newbury in July.

FILM A number of Hollywood hits have been filmed in Vermont, including *The Cider House Rules*, *Forrest Gump*, *The Spitfire Grill*, and *What Lies Beneath*. But Vermont filmmakers have produced independent hits of their own in recent years. Jay Craven's dramatizations of Howard Frank Mosher's novels—*Where the Rivers Flow North*, *A Stranger in the Kingdom*, and *Disappearances*—evoke life as it was in the Northeast Kingdom not so long ago. Nora

FISHING Almost every Vermont river and pond, certainly any body of water serious enough to call itself a lake, is stocked with fish and has one or more access areas. Brook trout are the most widely distributed game fish. Visitors ages 15 and over must have a 5-day, a 14-day, or a nonresident license good for a year, available at any town clerk's office, from the local fish and game warden, or from assorted commercial outlets. Because these sources may be closed or time consuming to track down on weekends, it's wise to obtain the license in advance from the **Vermont Fish and Wildlife Department** (802-241-3700; vtfishandwildlife .com). Request an application form and ask for a copy of *Vermont Guide to Hunting, Fishing and Trapping*, which details every species of fish and where to find it on a map of the state's rivers and streams, ponds, and lakes. Boat access, fish hatcheries, and canoe routes are also noted on the Fish Vermont Official Map & Guide. To prevent the spread of invasive aquatic species, felt-soled waders and boots are banned in Vermont.

The **Orvis Company**, which has been in the business of making fishing rods and selling them to city people for more than a century, has its flagship store in Manchester. Also in Manchester is the outstanding **American Museum of Fly-Fishing** (802-362-3300; amff.com.) Many inns, notably along Lake Champlain and in the Northeast Kingdom, offer tackle, boats, and advice on where to catch what.

Quimby Country (802-822-5533; quimby country.com), with a lodge and cabins on Forest and Great Averill Ponds, and **Seyon Ranch** (802-584-3829) on Noyes Pond in Groton State Forest, have all catered to serious fishermen since the 19th century. Landlocked salmon as well as rainbow, brown, brook, and lake trout are all cold-water species plentiful in the Northeast Kingdom's 37,575 acres of public ponds and 3,840 miles of rivers and streams. For guiding services check in those chapters. Warmwater species found elsewhere in the state include smallmouth bass, walleye, northern pike, and yellow perch.

Ice anglers can legally take every species of fish (trout only in a limited number of designated waters) and can actually hook smelt and some varieties of whitefish that are hard to come by during warmer months; the **Great Benson Fishing Derby** held annually in mid-Feb. on Lake Champlain draws thousands of contestants from throughout New England. The **Lake Champlain International Fishing Derby**, based in Burlington, is a big summer draw. Books to buy include the *Vermont Atlas and Gazetteer* (DeLorme), with details about fishing species and access; the *Atlas of Vermont Trout Ponds* and *Vermont Trout Streams*, both from Northern Cartographics Inc.; and *Fishing Vermont's Streams and Lakes* by Peter F. Cammann (The Countryman Press). Within this book we have listed shops, outfitters, and guides as they appear within each region. **Vermont Outdoor Guide Association** (voga.org) represents qualified guides throughout the state; check out their informative website.

FOLIAGE Vermont is credited with inventing foliage season, first aggressively promoted just after World War II in the initial issues of *Vermont Life*. The Vermont Department of Tourism and Marketing sends out weekly bulletins on color progress, which is always earlier than assumed by those of us who live south of Montpelier. Those in the know usually head for northern Vermont in late Sept. and the first week of Oct., a period that coincides with peak color in that area as well as with the **Northeast Kingdom Fall Foliage Festival**. By the following weekend central Vermont is usually ablaze, but visitors should be sure to have a bed reserved long before coming, because organized tours converge on the state. By the Columbus Day weekend your chances of finding a bed are dim. During peak color, we recommend visiting midweek and avoiding Vermont's most congested tourist routes; there is plenty of room on the back roads, especially those unsuited to buses. We strongly suggest exploring the high roads through Vermont's "gaps" (see *Gaps, Gulfs, and Gorges*) during this time of year.

GAPS, GULFS, AND GORGES Vermont's mountains were much higher before they were pummeled some 100,000 years ago by a mile-high sheet of ice. Glacial forces contoured the landscape we recognize today, notching the mountains with a number of handy "gaps" through which humans inevitably built roads. Gaps frequently offer superb views and access to ridge trails. This is true of the **Appalachian**, **Lincoln**, **Middlebury**, and **Brandon Gaps**, all crossing the Long Trail and linking Rt. 100 with the Champlain Valley; and of the **Roxbury Gap** east of the Mad River Valley. Note, however, that the state's highest and most scenic gap of all is called a notch (**Smugglers Notch** between Stowe and Jeffersonville), the New Hampshire name for mountain passes. Gaps at lower elevations are gulfs, scenic passes that make ideal picnic sites: Note **Granville Gulf** on Rt. 100, **Brookfield Gulf** on Rt. 12, **Proctorsville Gulf** on Rt. 103 between Proctorsville and Chester, and **Williamstown Gulf** on Rt. 14. The state's outstanding gorges include: 163-foot-deep **Quechee Gorge**, which can be viewed from Rt. 4 east of Woodstock; **Brockway Mills Gorge** in Rockingham (off Rt. 103); **Cavendish Gorge**, Springfield; **Clarendon Gorge**, Shrewsbury (traversed by the Long Trail via footbridge); **Brewster River Gorge**, south of Jeffersonville off Rt. 108; **Jay Branch Gorge** off Rt. 105; and (probably the most photographed of all) the **Brown River** churning through the gorge below the Old Red Mill in Jericho.

GARDENS Vermont's growing season is all the more intense for its brevity. Commercial herb and flower gardens are themselves the fastest-growing form of agriculture in the state, and many inns and B&Bs pride themselves on their gardens. **Historic Hildene** in Manchester also features formal gardens with thousands of peonies, and the **Shelburne Museum** holds an annual Lilac Festival in mid- to late May. Within this book we describe our favorite commercial gardens in *Selective Shopping*. For a listing of commercial nurseries log onto vermontagriculture.com/links. Within each chapter we list outstanding nurseries under *Farms*.

GOLF More than 60 Vermont golf courses are open to the public, and more than half of these have 18 holes, half a dozen of them justly famed throughout the country. A full program of lodging, meals, and lessons is available at Mount Snow, Killington, Okemo, Stratton Mountain, Sugarbush, and Stowe. The Woodstock Inn, Lake Morey Resort, and others also offer golf packages. The Manchester area boasts the greatest concentration of courses. Sixty-seven courses are identified on the Vermont Attractions Map; also see vermontvacation.com and vtga.org.

GREEN✿HOTEL
in the
Green Mountain State

GREEN HOTELS The Green Hotels in the Green Mountain State (vtgreenhotels.org) logo indicates lodging that has met environmental standards that include reducing waste, electricity, and more. A list of current members—which range from farms to Burlington hotels—can be found on the Vermont Chamber of Commerce website: visitvt.com.

THE GREEN MOUNTAINS Running 160 miles up the spine of this narrow state, the Green Mountains themselves range in width from 20 to 36 miles, with peaks rising to more than 4,000 feet. A part of the Appalachian Mountain chain, which extends from Alabama to Canada's Gaspé Peninsula, they were once far higher. The Long Trail runs the length of the range, and Rt. 100 shadows its eastern base. Also see *Hiking and Walking* and *Gaps, Gulfs, and Gorges*.

GREEN MOUNTAIN CLUB See *Hiking and Walking*.

GREEN MOUNTAIN NATIONAL FOREST The Green Mountain National Forest encompasses more than 400,000 acres spread across nearly two-thirds of Vermont's length, traversed by 900 miles of trails, including the **Appalachian Trail** and the **Long Trail**, which follows the ridgeline of the main range of the Green Mountains (see *Hiking and Walking*). The forest harbors six wilderness areas. Use of off-road recreational vehicles is regulated. Information—printed as well as verbal—about hiking, camping, skiing, berry picking, and bird-watching is available from the ranger stations in **Manchester Center** (802-362-2307), **Middlebury** (802-388-4362), and **Rochester** (802-767-4261). Request a free "mini map" from the **Green Mountain National Forest** (802-747-6700;

231 N. Main St., Rutland 05701). All four offices maintain visitors centers, open weekdays 8–4:30; Rochester is open 8–4 except Sun., weekdays only off-season.

HANDICAPPED ACCESS The wheelchair symbol & indicates lodging and dining places that are handicapped accessible.

HEALTH Almost every Vermont town has a health clinic or local physician. The two largest hospitals are in Burlington and just over the border from White River Junction, in Lebanon, New Hampshire. The **Dartmouth-Hitchcock Medical Center** (1 Medical Center Dr., Lebanon, NH; 603-650-5000; dhmc.org) oversees children's, cancer, spine, and cardiology centers, a medical school, and a level one trauma center. A branch of Dartmouth-Hitchcock is the 201-bed **Veterans Affairs Regional Medical and Office Center** (215 N. Main St., White River Junction; 866-687-8387; visn1.med.va.gov/wrj). **Fletcher Allen Health Care** in Burlington (111 Colchester Ave., Burlington 05401; 802-847-0000; fletcherallen.org)—also a level one trauma center—recently had a major expansion.

Other Vermont hospitals include (from south to north) **Brattleboro Memorial Hospital** in Brattleboro (802-257-0341; bmhvt.org); **Southwestern Vermont Health Care** in Bennington (802-442-6361; svhealthcare.org); **Grace Cottage Hospital** in Townshend (802-365-7357; gracecottage.org); **Springfield Hospital** in Springfield (802-885-2151; springfieldhospital.org); **Rutland Regional Medical Center** in Rutland (802-775-7111; rrmc.org); **Porter Medical Center** in Middlebury (802-388-4701; portermedical.org); **Mount Ascutney Hospital and Health Center** in Windsor (802-674-6711; mtascutneyhosp.hitchcock.org); **Gifford Medical Center** in Randolph (802-728-7000; giffordmed.org); **Central Vermont Medical Center** in Barre (802-371-4100; cvmc.hitchcock.org); **Copley Hospital** in Morrisville (802-888-4231; copleyhealthsystems.org); **Northwestern Medical Center** in St. Albans (802-524-5911; northwesternmedicalcenter.org); **Northeastern Vermont Regional Hospital** in St. Johnsbury (802-748-8141; nvrh.org); and **North Country Hospital** in Newport (802-334-7331; nchsi.org). For more general information, contact the **Vermont Association of Hospitals and Health Systems** in Montpelier at (802-223-3461; vahhs.org). As elsewhere in the country, when faced with a medical emergency, dial 911.

HIGH SEASON "High season" varies from Vermont community to community and even within a community such as Manchester (one side of town is nearer the ski resorts; the other is geared more to summer). While "foliage season" represents peak price as well as color everywhere, a ski condo can easily cost four times as much in Feb. as it does in July. Meanwhile, a country inn may charge half its July price in Feb.

HIGHWAY ROAD FOOD Cruising Vermont's interstates over the years, we have learned where to find good food less than a mile from exits. We strongly favor diners and local eateries over fast-food chains. All the following restaurants are described in their respective chapters. Along **I-91**, south to north: Just west of Exit 2 on Rt. 9 is the **Chelsea Royal Diner**. Off Exit 4 and just up Rt. 5 is the **Putney Diner**. **Isabell's Café** is just off Exit 14 in Thetford; in Fairlee the **Fairlee Diner** is just north of Exit 15. At Exit 16 there's the **Hungry Bear Pub & Grille**. The **Bliss Village Store** in the middle of Bradford town serves hot soups and deli sandwiches (try for the window seat), while for dinner there's **Colatina Exit** and the **Stone Mill Tavern**. Exit 17: **P&H Truck Stop**, Wells River (open 6 AM–10 PM.) Exit 23: Turn north onto Rt. 5 to find the **Miss Lyndonville Diner**. Along **I-89**: Exit 3: **Eaton's Sugar House** is right off the exit. Exit 7: Follow signs to Rt. 302, and the **Wayside Restaurant and Bakery** is on your left. Exit 9: **The Red Hen Café** is a bakery (great breads) and café just west of the exit on Rt. 2, Middlesex. Exit 10: Turn left, then left again, and you are in the middle of Waterbury and all its downtown restaurants. Exit 14W: Burlington is just down the hill, worth a detour. Exit 14E: Turn east onto Williston Rd. and head away from town to find **Al's French Frys**. Also see *Diners*.

HIGHWAY TRAVEL INFORMATION Dial 511 or click onto 511vt.com for road conditions and construction. From out of state, call 800-429-7623. See the *Information* sidebar for welcome and information centers along I-89, I-91, and I-93.

HIKING AND WALKING More than 700 miles of hiking trails web Vermont—which is 162 miles long as the crow flies but 255 miles long as the hiker trudges, following the Long Trail up and down the spine of the Green Mountains. But few hikers are out to set distance records on the Long Trail. The path from Massachusetts to the Canadian border, which was completed in 1930, has a way of slowing people down. It opens up eyes and lungs and drains compulsiveness. Even die-hard back-

packers tend to linger on rocky outcrops, looking down on farms and steeples. A total of 98 side trails (175 miles) meander off to wilderness ponds or abandoned villages; these trails are mostly maintained, along with the Long Trail, by the **Green Mountain Club** (802-244-7037; greenmountainclub.org), founded in 1910. The club also maintains about 66 shelters and 70 campsites, many of them staffed by caretakers during summer months. The mission of the GMC is to make the Vermont mountains play a larger part in the lives of the people by protecting and maintaining the Long Trail System and fostering, through education, the stewardship of Vermont's hiking trails and mountains. Check the website for current programs and for details about Wheeler Pond Camps rentals near Lake Willoughby. The club publishes the *Long Trail Guide*, which gives details on trails and shelters throughout the system, as well as the *Day Hiker's Guide to Vermont*. These and other guides are sold in the club's new visitors center (4711 Waterbury Rd., Waterbury Center 05677; open 9–5 daily, but closed on weekends in the off-season). The Appalachian Trail Conservancy (appalachiantrail.org) includes detailed information in its *Appalachian Trail Guide to Vermont and New Hampshire*, and a wide assortment of trails are nicely detailed in *50 Hikes in Vermont* (The Countryman Press).

Backpackers who are hesitant to set out on their own can take a wide variety of guided hikes and walks. Adventure Guides of Vermont (adventureguidesvt.com) and Vermont Outdoor Guide Association (voga.org) can put you in touch with guides and adventure-geared packages. For those who prefer to have their baggage transferred and to combine hiking with fine dining and lodging, **Country Inns Along the Trail** (inntoinn.com) has been offering

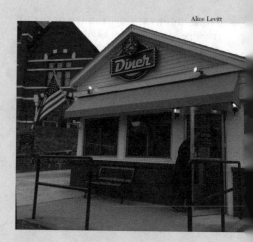

Alice Levitt

guided and self-guiding packages since 1975. Also see **Vermont Inn to Inn** (vermontinnto innwalking.com) for four-night, inn-to-inn walking tours (3–10 miles per day) with luggage transported.

Within this book we suggest hiking trails as they appear geographically. Also note the recent proliferation of trail systems: In the Northeast Kingdom check out **Kingdom Trails** (kingdom tails.org) in East Burke, the **NorthWoods Stewardship Center** near Island Pond, and the **Hazen's Notch Association Trails** (hazens notch.org). We should also note that both **Killington** and **Stowe** offer ridge hiking from the top of their lifts. (See also *Birding*, *State Parks*, *Mountain Biking*, and *Nature Preserves*.)

HISTORY Vermont is a small state, but it has had a dramatic life. In essence, the whole state is a living history museum, even though most towns were settled after the Revolution. Many often overlapped land grants issued by the royal governors of both New Hampshire and New York were not truly sorted out until 1791, when Congress admitted Vermont as the 14th state, after 14 years as an independent republic.

For an overview visit the outstanding exhibits collectively titled *Freedom and Unity* (the state motto) in the Vermont Historical Society Museum (vermonthistory.org), housed in a replica of the Pavilion Hotel that stands beside the Vermont State House in Montpelier. A pamphlet guide to *Vermont Historic Sites*, operated by the Division for Historic Preservation (historicvermont.org), is available at information centers throughout the state. See also *Historical Societies*.

The Abenaki presence in Vermont is far more pervasive than was acknowledged until recently. St. Anne's Shrine on Isle La Motte memorializes Samuel de Champlain's first landfall on the lake that bears his name; the site was an Indian village and by 1666 a mission as well as a French fort, which was abandoned in 1679 but remains an evocative place. Nearby in present-day Swanton, the Indian village of Missisquoi became a mission village, a way stop for Abenaki headed for Canada. Abenaki life is presented in an exhibit at the Abenaki Tribal Museum and Cultural Center. Native American settlements are also recorded at Otter Creek, and the 18th-century tavern at Chimney Point State Historic Site in Addison has a well-mounted display that explains the territory's Native American and French colonial heritage. In Newport the lakeside state office building displays the Memphremagog Historical Society's exhibit on northern Vermont's native people, from Paleolithic through current times, and

at the Fort at Number 4 in Charlestown, New Hampshire (see "The Lower Connecticut River Valley")—a community in which settlers and Indians lived side by side—the reconstructed fort exhibits Native American artifacts from the Connecticut River Valley.

Bennington, chartered by the avaricious Governor Benning Wentworth in 1749, the first chartered town west of the Connecticut River in the New Hampshire Grants, became the tinderbox for settlers' resistance to New York's rival claims, confirmed by King George in 1764. The desperate grantees found a champion in the protean Ethan Allen from Connecticut. This frontier rebel—land speculator, firebrand, and philosopher—recruited the boisterous Green Mountain Boys militiamen, who talked rum and rebellion at the Catamount Tavern in Old Bennington, pledged defiance of the 'Yorkers, and then fought the British. Ethan's rambunctious life is reflected in the Ethan Allen Homestead, the farm north of Burlington where he died in 1789.

In Westminster, on the bank of the Connecticut River, the 1775 "Massacre" was thought, incorrectly, to have been the first armed engagement of the Revolution. But the death of William French, shot by a 'Yorker sheriff, galvanized opposition to both New York and England, leading to a convention in Westminster in January 1777, where Vermonters declared their independence of everyone.

Formal independence was declared the following July, upriver in Windsor, where delegates gathered in Elijah West's tavern (now The Old Constitution House). They adopted a model constitution, the first to abolish slavery, before rushing off to attack the British, who had retaken Fort Ticonderoga. (While in Windsor, visit the American Precision Museum, a landmark showcasing early gun makers and the heyday of the machine tool industry.)

Since its discovery by Samuel de Champlain in 1609, Lake Champlain has been not only one of the nation's most historic waterways but also a strategic corridor in three wars. The French controlled the lake until 1759, when Lord Jeffery Amherst drove them out of Fort Carillon (now Ticonderoga) and then captured Montreal. In the American Revolution, the British used the lake as an invasion route to divide the colonies, but were thwarted when Ethan Allen's Green Mountain Boys captured Fort Ticonderoga in 1775.

Facing Ticonderoga across the lake's narrowest channel, the Mount Independence State Historic Site near Orwell dramatizes the struggle that ended with the decisive British defeat at Saratoga in 1777. The only battle of the

Revolution to have been fought on Vermont soil is commemorated at the Hubbardton Battlefield near Castleton, where a small force of Green Mountain Boys under Colonel Seth Warner stopped a far larger British contingent as Burgoyne's British troops marched south. The invaders were soon repulsed again in the Battle of Bennington—actually fought in New York—marked by the Bennington Battle Monument and by exhibits in the Bennington Museum.

The lake also figured in naval warfare when Benedict Arnold and a quickly assembled American flotilla engaged a heavier British squadron off Plattsburgh, New York, in the Battle of Valcour Island in October 1776. One of Arnold's small gunboats, the *Philadelphia*, sunk by the British, was salvaged in 1935 and reposes in the Smithsonian. An exact replica is moored at the Lake Champlain Maritime Museum at Basin Harbor near Vergennes. A number of ships and other artifacts of that battle have been found buried in the mud on the lake bottom in recent years. In 1814 the British again tried to use Lake Champlain as an invasion route. Thomas McDonough moved his headquarters from Burlington to Vergennes and a shipyard at the mouth of Otter Creek. His small fleet barely managed to defeat British ships at Plattsburgh Bay, a bloody engagement that helped end the War of 1812.

With Vermont in the vanguard of the antislavery movement of the 1840s, the Underground Railroad flourished, notably at Rokeby, the home of the Robinson family in Ferrisburgh, now a museum. Evidence of the state's extraordinary record in the Civil War and its greater-than-average number of per capita casualties may be seen in the memorials that dot most town and village greens. How Vermonters turned the tide of the battle at Cedar Creek is portrayed in Julian Scott's huge and newly restored painting that hangs in the State House in Montpelier. The anniversary of the October 1864 St. Albans Raid, the northernmost engagement of the Civil War, is observed annually.

There are few early 18th-century structures in the state, but the settlers who poured in after 1791 (the population nearly tripled, from 85,000 to 235,000 in 1820) quickly built sophisticated dwellings and churches. Dorset, Castleton, Chester (Old Stone Village), Middlebury, Brandon, Woodstock, and Norwich are architectural showcases of Federal-style houses. Several historic, outstandingly splendid mansions built by 19th-century moguls are open to the public: the Park-McCullough House, North Bennington; the Wilburton Inn and Hildene, Manchester; The Castle Inn, Proctorsville; Wilson Castle, West Rutland; the Marsh-Billings-Rockefeller

National Historical Park, Woodstock; and The Inn at Shelburne Farms (built by Lila Vanderbilt Webb and William Seward Webb), Shelburne.

Vermont's congressional delegations, especially in the 19th century, always had more influence in Washington than the state's size might suggest. For example, the Justin Morrill Homestead in Strafford, a spacious Gothic Revival house, reminds us of the distinguished career of the originator of the Land Grant Colleges Act, who served in Congress from 1855 to 1898.

The Vermont Historical Society maintains a research library in Barre with changing special exhibits. Arts, crafts, architecture, and transportation are featured in the Shelburne Museum in Shelburne. In Woodstock the Billings Farm & Museum re-creates a model 1890s stock farm and dairy, and the Marsh-Billings-Rockefeller National Historical Park traces the state's environmental history. Outstanding collections of the ways people lived and worked can be found in town historical societies, notably the Farrar Mansur House in Weston, the Sheldon Museum in Middlebury, and the Dana House in Woodstock. *Freedom and Unity: A History of Vermont*, published by the Vermont Historical Society, is a readable reference work that complements the society's permanent exhibit.

HISTORICAL SOCIETIES The attics of every town, historical societies are frequently worth seeking out, but because most are staffed by volunteers, they tend to be open just a few hours a week, usually in summer. Of Vermont's 251 towns, 200 have historical societies; we have tried to give accurate, current information on them within each chapter. The Vermont Historical Society publishes a free booklet, *Passport to Vermont History*, listing hours and contact phones, also available at vermonthistory.org. Outstanding local historical societies are found in Brownington, Newfane, Middlebury, and Woodstock.

HORSEBACK RIDING AND EQUESTRIAN SPORTS Horses are as much a part of the Vermont landscape as the famous black-and-white Holsteins. Resorts offering horseback riding include **Topnotch** in Stowe, the **Mountain Top in Chittenden**, and **Vermont Icelandic Horse Farm** (icelandichorses.com) in Waitsfield. The best options for trail rides are **Open Acre Ranch** in Fairlee, **Mountain View Ranch** in Danby, **Kimberly Farms Riding Stables in North Bennington**, and **D-N-D Stables** in East Burke. The Vermont Summer Horse Festival (vt-summerfestival.com), the largest of several hunter-jumper shows around the state, takes place in the Manchester area, mid-July–mid-Aug. The Vermont Quarter Horse Association (vtqha.com) hosts shows around the region in summer. The Green Mountain Horse Association in South Woodstock (802-457-1509; gmhainc.org) holds Dressage Days and other events open to spectators.

HUNTING *The Vermont Digest of Hunting, Fishing and Trapping Laws* and a useful State of Vermont Hunting Map are available from the Vermont Fish and Wildlife Department (802-241-3700; vtfishandwildlife.com). Of special interest to nonresidents: a reasonably priced, five-day small-game license. The ruffed grouse or "partridge" is the state's most abundant game bird, while woodcocks, or "timberdoodles," are found throughout the state. The wild turkey is considered "big game"—as hunters will understand when they try to bag them (in-season in Oct. and May). October is bow-and-arrow season for white-tailed deer, and Nov. is buck season. Hunting regulations for black bear and moose populations vary with the year.

ICE CREAM, CREEMEES, AND GELATO
Vermont's quality milk is used to produce some outstanding ice cream as well as cheese. The big name is, of course, **Ben & Jerry's**, proud producers of what *Time* once billed "the best ice cream in the world." Their plant on Rt. 100 in Waterbury (featuring factory tours, free samples, real cows, and a gift shop full of reproductions in every conceivable shape) is the state's most popular tourist attraction, but is now owned by Unilever. Look for **Wilcox Dairy** (try "sweet cream") in Manchester and throughout the state, at places like Cassie's Corner in Greensboro, just up from the beach. Soft-serve is known in Vermont as the "creemee" and is easy to find at any snack bar in the summer. We're especially fond of the **Dusty Miller** creemee sundae at **Maynard's Snack Bar** in Moretown: The vanilla creemee is topped with hot fudge and a thick pile of malt powder.

I. C. Scoops is worth seeking out in Stowe for uncommon homemade flavors; Depot Street Malt Shoppe around the corner is the place for sundaes and an old-fashioned experience. The 1950s soda fountain at Brandon's **The Inside Scoop** serves up everything ice cream inside a whimsical antiques shop. All in all it's hard to beat the World's Fair Sundae at the **Whippi Dip** in Fairlee: fried dough topped with vanilla ice cream, maple syrup, mixed nuts, and whipped cream.

As all artisan food production has grown, so has homemade ice cream, crafted from local ingredients. Scout's Honor at the **Sweet Spot**

in Waitsfield is ideally located next to the Mad River for an afternoon of lolling by the water with the most intense chocolate ice cream you've ever tasted. Eclectic lu°lu in Bristol is served at **Mary's Restaurant at the Inn at Baldwin Creek** as well as at its own store. In Burlington, the **Chubby Muffin** serves garden-fresh varieties such as strawberry-basil, harvested from the Intervale Center just down the road. Grabbing a scoop at **Artesano Mead** and ice cream is plenty of reason to find your way east from St. Johnsbury to Groton.

Birchgrove Baking in Montpelier serves exceptional ice cream in flavors such as Vietnamese coffee and passionfruit, as well as ice cream sandwiches in home-baked cookies. The state capital is also Vermont's top source for gelato. At **Simply Subs**, Angelo Caserta prepares his native frozen dessert in authentic Italian flavors. Downtown, **Chill Gelato** is more whimsical, with scoops that take their flavors from flowers, tea, and even speculoos cookies.

INNS It's probably safe to say that we have visited more Vermont inns, more frequently, than anyone else living today. We do not charge for inclusion in this book, and we attempt to give as accurate and detailed a picture as space permits. We quote 2014 rates—which are, of course, subject to change. Summer rates are generally lower than winter (except, of course, at lake resorts); weekly or ski-week rates run 10–20 percent less than the per-diem price quoted. Many inns insist on MAP (Modified American Plan—breakfast and dinner) in winter but not in summer. Some resorts have AP (American Plan—three meals), and we have shown EP (European Plan—no meals) where applicable. We have attempted to note when 15 percent service is added, but you should always ask if it has been included in a quoted rate and whether an additional local tax is added. Always add the 9 percent state tax on rooms and meals. It's prudent to check which, if any, credit cards are accepted. Many lodging places now insist on minimum two- or three-day stays during busy seasons. Within the text, special icons highlight lodging places that specialize in weddings ♂, those that offer exceptional value ✿, those that accept pets ☂, those that appeal to families ♂, and those that are handicapped accessible ⅃.

LAKES The state famed for green mountains and white villages also harbors more than 400 relatively blue lakes: big lakes like **Champlain** (110 miles long) and **Memphremagog** (boasting 88 miles of coastline, but most of it in Canada), and smaller lakes like **Morey**, **Dunmore**, **Willoughby**, **Bomoseen**, and **Seymour**. A

INFORMATION

The **Vermont Department of Tourism and Marketing** (800-VERMONT) offers vacation planning, information packets, seasonal highlights, and an excellent website (**vermontvacation.com**) with links to every aspect of exploring the state. A Vacation Planning packet can be requested through an online form on the website, or by calling the toll-free number above. The standard packet includes the *Official Vermont Road Map & Guide to Vermont Attractions* (a detailed road map with symbols locating attractions, covered bridges, golf courses, state parks and historic sites, ski areas, public boat and fishing access ramps, and more); request *The Vermont Vacation Guide*, a helpful and current magazine-format guide published by the Vermont Chamber of Commerce (vtchamber.com). You may also want to request the *Vermont Historic Sites Guide*, or the *Vermont Campground Guide*. All of these publications and more are available at Vermont's numerous welcome and information centers once you arrive in the state.

The **Vermont Information Center Division** maintains highway welcome and information centers with pay phones, WiFi, and bathroom facilities. At the Massachusetts border, northbound at **Guilford** on **I-91**, the state's largest and most complete **Welcome Center** (802-258-4503; facilities open 24 hours) showcases Vermont products. Other I-91 rest areas open daily are southbound at **Hartford**, **Bradford**, and **Lyndon**. Along I-89 your first stop should be the **Sharon Welcome Center** (802-281-5216), which is also the Vermont Vietnam Veterans Memorial, an architecturally striking building that tells its story well and also includes an octagonal greenhouse filled with exotic vegetation recycling Sharon's wastewater. Less elaborate rest areas are found southbound in **Randolph** at **Williston** and both north- and southbound in **Georgia**. There's also an inviting welcome center just over the state line from New Hampshire on **I-93** at **Waterford** (802-751-0472), as well as visitors centers at the New York–Canadian border on Rt. 2 in **Alburgh** (802-796-3980) and on the New York border on Rt. 4A in **Fair Haven** (802-265-4763). In **Montpelier**, the **Capital Region Visitors Center**, 134 State St. (802-828-5981), is the source of statewide information. The **Derby Line Welcome Center** (802-873-3311) on Rt. 91 southbound also welcomes visitors from Canada.

Waypoint Visitors Centers, along the Connecticut River Scenic Byway (**ctrivertravel.net**), serve communities on both sides of the river. Look for them in Brattleboro, Bellows Falls, Windsor, White River Junction, St. Johnsbury, and Wells River.

AAA Emergency Road Service: 800-222-4357. For **road conditions** dial 511 or click on 511vt.com. Also see *Highway Road Food* and *Weather Reports*.

First-time visitors may be puzzled by Vermont's **Travel Information System** of directional signs, which replace billboards (banned since 1968, another Vermont first). Stylized symbols for lodging, food, recreation, antiques and crafts, and other services are sited at intersections off major highways.

We have noted local chambers of commerce town by town in each chapter of this book under *Guidance*. In small towns inquiries are welcomed by the town clerk.

Christina Tree

century ago there were many more lakeside hotels; today just a handful of these classic summer resorts survive: **Quimby Country** in Averill, **Highland Lodge** in Greensboro, the **Tyler Place** in Highgate Springs, the **Basin Harbor Club** near Vergennes, and the **Lake Morey Resort** in Fairlee. Lakes are particularly plentiful and rentals reasonable in Vermont's Northeast Kingdom. There are also state parks with campsites on **Groton Lake**, **Emerald Lake**, **Island Pond**, **Maidstone Lake**, **Lake Bomoseen**, **Lake Carmi**, **Lake Elmore**, **Lake St. Catherine**, and **Silver Lake** (in Barnard). On Lake Champlain there are a number of state campgrounds, including those on **Grand Isle** (accessible by car) and **Burton Island** (accessible by public launch from St. Albans Bay). See *Campgrounds* for details about these, private campgrounds (we recommend Harvey's Lake Cabins and Campground), and those maintained by the Army Corps of Engineers on **Ball Mountain Lake** and **North Hartland Lake**. The **Green Mountain Club** (see *Hiking*) maintains two cabins for rental on Wheeler Pond near Lake Willoughby. There is public boat access to virtually every Vermont pond and lake of any size. Boat launches are listed on the state map.

LIBRARIES Along with general stores, libraries are central to Vermont communities. The 189 or so libraries in the state range from the one-room cottage at Joe's Pond in West Danville to opulent late-19th-century buildings gifted by wealthy native sons. Notable examples are the **Aldrich Public Library** in Barre, the **Kellogg Hubbard Library** in Montpelier, the **Norman Williams Public Library** in Woodstock, and the **St. Johnsbury Athenaeum and Art Gallery**. Some of our favorites are, however, found in very small places. The **Lincoln Library**, destroyed by flood a decade ago, has been replaced with a new building with porch rockers, also the signature of the new **Craftsbury Public Library** with its handsome interior (visitors are requested to remove their shoes). In Peacham the library marks the center of the village and is also an art center. The **Grafton Public Library** is an elegant vintage-1822 house but remarkably homey. The **Tunbridge Pubic Library** is also in a renovated historic brick house, as is **Alice M. Ward Memorial Library** (with historical exhibits upstairs) on the green in Canaan. The **Pope Memorial Library** on the common in Danville is said to have ghosts, and the small **Fairlee Public Library** has an excellent collection. For research, the **Vermont Historical Society Library** in Barre is a treasure trove of

Vermontiana and genealogical resources; likewise the **Wilbur Collection** of the Bailey-Howe Library at the University of Vermont and the **Russell Collection** in Arlington. Three of the Vermont state colleges—Castleton, Johnson, and Lyndon—have collections of Vermontiana in the Vermont Rooms of their libraries. In East Craftsbury there's also the **John Woodruff Memorial Library**, a former general store open just seasonally two days a week but well stocked, especially with children's titles.

LLAMAS AND LLAMA TREKKING We list these within our chapters. Treks are offered by **Applecheek Farm** in Hyde Park and **Northern Vermont Llama Co.** in Waterville; **Agape Hill Farm** in Hardwick offers a kid-geared farm tour that includes guiding a llama around an obstacle course.

MAGAZINES *Vermont Life* (vtlife.com), the colorful quarterly published by the Agency of Commerce and Community Development, chronicles Vermont's people and places, featuring distinguished photographers. *Seven Days* (sevendaysvt.com) is Vermont's alternative weekly newspaper, available for free throughout the state. Besides news, arts and food coverage, its calendar of events, both online and in print, is the most comprehensive around. (Full disclosure: Coauthor Alice Levitt is the senior food writer at *Seven Days*.) *SO Vermont Arts & Living* (vermontartsliving.com) is a lively quarterly magazine that covers galleries, museums, and arts happenings throughout southern Vermont. *Vermont Magazine* (vermontmagazine .com) is a statewide bimonthly that deals in the state's townscapes, products, and personalities.

Christina Tree

MAPLE SUGARING (vermontmaple.org).Vermont sugarhouses welcome visitors on **Maple Open House Weekend** in mid-March. Vermont produces some 400,000 gallons of maple syrup each year, over a third of the national supply and more than any other state. Approximately 2,000 maple growers tap an average of 1,000 trees each. About a quart of syrup is made per tap; it takes 30 to 40 gallons of sap to make each gallon of syrup. The process of tapping trees and boiling sap is stubbornly known as sugaring, rather than syruping, because the end product for early settlers was sugar. Syrup was first made in the early 19th century, but production flagged when imported cane sugar became more accessible. The Civil War revived the maple sugar industry: Union supporters were urged to consume sugar made by free men and to plant more and more maples.

We urge visitors to buy syrup direct from the producer, any time of year (finding the farm is half the fun), but also to seriously consider making a special trip to a sugarhouse during sugaring season in March and April. It's then (not in autumn) that sugar maples really perform, and it's a show that can't be seen through a windshield. Sugaring season begins quietly in February as thousands of Vermonters wade, snowshoe, and snowmobile into their woods and begin "tapping," a ritual that has changed since plastic tubing replaced buckets. But the timing is the same. Traditionally, sugaring itself begins on Town Meeting Day (the first Tuesday in March). But sap runs only on those days when temperatures rise to 40 and 50 degrees during the day and drop into the 20s at night. When the sap does run, it must be boiled down quickly. What you want to see is the boiling process: sap churning madly through the large, flat evaporating pan, darkening as you watch. You are enveloped in fragrant steam, listening to the rush of the sap, sampling the end result on snow or in tiny paper cups. Sugaring is Vermont's rite of spring. Don't miss a sugar-on-snow party: plates of snow dribbled with viscous hot syrup, accompanied by doughnuts and dill pickles. Vermont maple syrup is 100 percent pure, no additives. The **Vermont Maple Festival**, held in late April in St. Albans, is a three-day event that includes tours through the local sugarbush (vtmaplefestival.org). **Maple Grove** in St. Johnsbury bills itself as "the world's oldest and largest maple candy factory." Videos on maple are also shown in the **New England Maple Museum** in Pittsford. Within this book we list maple producers in the areas in which they are most heavily concentrated. There are many more than are found on any formal lists. Ask locally.

MAPS The *Official Vermont Road Map & Guide to Vermont Attractions* (see *Information*) is free and extremely helpful for general motoring but will not suffice for finding your way around the webs of dirt roads that connect some of the most beautiful corners of the state. Among our favorite areas where you will need more detail: the high farming country between Albany, Craftsbury, and West Glover; similar country between Chelsea and Williamstown; south from Plainfield to Orange; and between Plymouth and Healdville. We strongly suggest securing a copy of the *Vermont Atlas and Gazetteer* (DeLorme) if you want to do any serious back-road exploring. Among the best regional maps for anyone planning to do much hiking or biking are those published by Map Adventures (mapadventures.com). Also see *Hiking and Walking*.

MARBLE The Vermont Marble Trail (vermontmarbletrailweb.pdf), described in a glossy booklet (phone 800-VERMONT), focuses on the visual evidence of Vermont's once all-important marble industry. One trail leads from Bennington via Dorset and Danby to Rutland, where the nearby **Vermont Marble Museum** in Proctor is a must-see. Here the history and extent of the industry in Vermont are dramatized in exhibits and in a film that depicts, among other things, the ongoing underground quarrying in Danby. The **Dorset Historical Society** also has impressive exhibits and a diorama pinpointing all the onetime quarries in that area, some now popular swimming holes. Additional trails includes the marble works at the center of **Middlebury**, as well as the **Fisk Quarry** preserve and ancient reefs on Isle La Motte, with a film at the Goodsell Ridge Preserve that describes the evolution of limestone.

MONEY Each inn has its own policy about credit cards and checks. Personal checks are frequently more acceptable to craftspeople and small lodging places than credit cards.

MORGAN HORSES The Vermont state animal is a distinctive breed of saddle horse popular throughout America. The first "Morgan" was born in the late 1790s to singing teacher Justin Morgan of Randolph. Colonel Joseph Battell began breeding Morgans on his Weybridge farm in the 1870s and is credited with saving the breed (America's first developed breed of horse) from extinction. The farm is now a breeding and training center operated by the **University of Vermont** (uvm.edu/morgan), open to the public. For more about Morgan horse sites and events, visit vtmorganhorse.com.

MOUNTAIN BIKING In recent years Vermont mountain biking options have dramatically broadened as the potential for the state's hundreds of miles of dirt and Class 4 roads as well as cross-county trail systems has been recognized. The nonprofit **Kingdom Trails Association** (kingdomtrails.org) in East Burke maintains a more-than-100-mile mix of trails across woods and meadows that have been rated among the top networks in the country and attract many fans from Canada. In the **Mad River Valley** trails begin with lift service at Sugarbush Adventure Center and link with a 60-mile network maintained by the Mad River Riders. In Windsor **Sport Trails at Ascutney** is an evolving network of trails. In the Burlington area the **Catamount Family Center** (catamountoutdoor.com) and **Sleepy Hollow Inn, Ski, and Bike Center** (skisleepyhollow .com) in Huntington both offer extensive cross-country trail networks and bike rentals. **Blueberry Hill Inn** (blueberryhillinn.com) is set high in Goshen with easy access to trails in the Moosalamoo region of the Green Mountain National Forest and to Silver Lake. **Trapp Family Lodge** rents bikes for use on its extensive cross-country trails.

Several ski areas offer lift-assisted mountain biking. The **Mount Snow Mountain Bike School** (mountsnow.com) offers 45 miles of trails, some served by lifts Memorial Day to Columbus Day. **Stratton Mountain** (stratton .com) offers more than 100 miles of trail, primarily in its Sun Bowl; lifts accessing trails off the summit run during foliage season. The 45 miles of trails at **Mountain Bike Park at Killington** (killington.com) are accessed by lift from Rt. 4 July–Columbus Day weekend (weather permitting). **Jay Peak Resort** (jay peakresort.com) also permits mountain biking on ski trails, accessible via its tramway. The **Craftsbury Outdoor Center** (craftsbury.com), also in the Northeast Kingdom, offers fat-tire rentals for exploring over 200 miles of dirt roads through glorious farm country, as well as 20 km of singletrack snowshoeing trails on its own 400 acres. In East Barre, **Millstone Hill Touring and Recreation Center** (millstonehill.com) offers 70 miles of singletrack trail in 350 acres of wooded terrain, spotted with abandoned granite quarries. In Putney the **West Hill Shop** (westhillshop.com) publishes its own map to an extensive network of singletrack trails and forgotten roads.

The nominally priced Topographic Maps & Guides produced by **Map Adventures** (map adventures.com) are useful map/guides outlining rides in various parts of Vermont: the Burlington and Stowe areas, the White River Valley, the Upper Valley, and southern Vermont, among others. Also check out the **Vermont Mountain Bike Association** (vmba.org).

MOUNTAINTOPS While Vermont can boast only seven peaks above 4,000 feet, there are 80 mountains that rise more than 3,000 feet and any number of spectacular views, several of them accessible in summer and foliage season to those who prefer riding to walking up mountains. **Mount Mansfield**, which at 4,393 feet is the state's highest summit, can be reached via the Toll Road and a gondola. The mid-19th-century road brings you to the small Summit Station at 4,062 feet, from which the 0.5-mile Tundra Trail brings you to the actual summit. The Mount Mansfield gondola, an eight-passenger, enclosed lift, hoists you from the main base area up to the Cliff House Restaurant, from which a trail also heads up to the Chin. The big news about **Killington Peak**, Vermont's second highest at 4,241 feet, is **Peak Lodge**, a state-of-the-art glass-walled summit lodge, open year-round, accessible via a 1.2-mile gondola ride. The gondola carries mountain bikes, and there are trails for both hiking and biking back down. **Jay Peak**, a 3,861-foot summit towering like a lone sentinel near the Canadian border, is accessible via a 60-passenger tram, and a "four-state view" from the top of **Stratton Mountain** is accessible via the ski resort's six-passenger gondola, Starship XII (daily in fall). Honestly we don't recommend the Auto Road to the 3,267-foot **Burke Mountain** in East Burke—too rough on the gears coming down. We love the Toll "Parkway" to the parking area below the 3,144-foot summit of **Mount Ascutney** in Ascutney State Park. It has been nicely upgraded, and there is a turnout for picnicking with a view up the Connecticut River, as well as a summit fire tower with a view that sweeps from New Hampshire's White Mountains to Mount Monadnock on the east and up the spine of the Green Mountains to the west. From Sunderland, southwest of Manchester in southern Vermont, Skyline Drive snakes up **Mount Equinox** to a new observatory maintained by the Carthusian monks. There are also chairlift rides to the tops of **Bromley** (you don't have to take the alpine slide down) and **Mount Snow**.

MUD SEASON The period from snowmelt (around the middle of March) through early May (it varies each year) is known throughout the state as mud season for reasons that few visitors want to explore too deeply. Dirt roads can turn quickly into boggy quagmires.

MUSEUMS Within this book, we have listed museums in their geographic areas. They vary from the immense **Shelburne Museum**—with its 39 buildings, many housing priceless collections of art and Americana, plus assorted exhibits such as a completely restored lake steamer and a lighthouse—to the **American Precision Museum** in Windsor, an 1846 brick mill that once produced rifles. They include a number of outstanding historical museums (our favorites are the **Bennington Museum** in Bennington, the **Sheldon Museum** in Middlebury, the **Old Stone House Museum** in Brownington, and the **Dana House** in Woodstock) and some collections that go beyond the purely historical: The **Bennington Museum** is famed for its collection of Grandma Moses paintings as well as early American glass and relics from the Revolution, and the **Fairbanks Museum and Planetarium** in St. Johnsbury has vaulted wooden halls filled with taxidermied birds and animals. The **Billings Farm & Museum** in Woodstock shows off its blue-ribbon dairy and has a fascinating, beautifully mounted display of 19th-century farm life and tools.

MUSIC The Green Mountains are filled with the sounds of music each summer, beginning with the **Discover Jazz Festival** (discoverjazz .com), more than 100 concerts held over a week around Burlington in early June. In Putney a late-June–July series of three evening chamber music concerts each week is presented in the **Yellow Barn Festival** (yellowbarn.org). In July and Aug. options include the internationally famous **Marlboro Music Festival** (marlboro music.org) at Marlboro College, presenting chamber music on weekends. The **Killington Music Festival** (killingtonmusicfestival.org) is a series of Sunday concerts at Rams Head Lodge from late June to early Aug., and the **Manchester Music Festival** (mmfvt.org) brings leading performers to various venues around Manchester. Also well worth noting: the **Central Vermont Chamber Music Festival** (centralvt chambermusicfest.org) at the Chandler Music Hall in Randolph in mid- to late Aug., the **Summer Music School** in Adamant (adamant.org /summer.htm), and concerts at the Town House in Hardwick by the **Craftsbury Chamber Players** (craftsburychamberplayers.org).

Other concert series are performed at the **Southern Vermont Arts Center** (Thurs. and Sun.; svac.org), Castleton State College (csc.vsc .edu), the **Dibden Center for the Arts**, Johnson State College (jsc.edu), and Middlebury College's **Mahaney Center for the Arts** (middlebury.edu). The **Vermont Symphony**

Christina Tree

Orchestra (vso.org), the oldest of the state symphonies, figures in a number of the series noted above and also performs at a variety of locations, ranging from Brattleboro's Living Memorial Park and the State House lawn to Wilson Castle, throughout summer. In Weston the **Kinhaven Music School** (kinhaven.org) offers free concerts on summer weekends, and in Brattleboro the **Brattleboro Music Center** (bmcvt.org) brings in world-renowned classical groups for its year-round Chamber Music Series. See also *Fiddling*.

NATIONAL PUBLIC RADIO See Vermont Public Radio (VPR).

NATURE PRESERVES The **Vermont Land Trust** (vlt.org), founded in 1977, is dedicated to preserving Vermont's traditional landscape of farms as well as forest (it has helped protect more than 700 operating farms), and many local land trusts have acquired numerous parcels of land throughout the state. Many of the most visitor-friendly preserves are owned by **The Nature Conservancy** (nature.org), a national nonprofit that has preserved close to 7 million acres throughout the United States since its founding in 1951. Its Vermont branch is at 27 State St., Montpelier 05602.

OPERA HOUSES Northern New England opera houses are a turn-of-the-20th-century phenomenon: theaters built as cultural centers for the surrounding area, stages on which lecturers, musicians, and vaudeville acts as well as opera singers performed. Many of these buildings have long since disappeared, but those that survive are worth noting. The **Hyde Park Opera House**, built in 1910, has been restored by the Lamoille County Players, who stage four annual shows, including both plays and musicals. The **Barre Opera House**, built in 1899, is an elegant, acoustically outstanding, second-floor theater, home of the Barre Players; productions are staged here year-round. In Derby Line, in the second-floor **Opera House** (a neoclassical structure that also houses the Haskell Free Library), the audience sits in Vermont watching a stage that is in Canada. Tom Thumb and Houdini performed at Rutland's 1914 **Paramount Theater**, which has been restored and now offers a full repertory from cabaret to jazz, comedy, and musicals. The theater company **Northern Stage** has taken up residence at White River Junction's **Briggs Opera House**, offering year-round performances and courses for children and young adults in summer months. The **Chandler Center for the Arts** in Randolph and the opera houses in **Vergennes** and **Enosburg Falls** have been restored for cultural events. Each of these is described under *Entertainment* within its respective chapter.

PETS We note lodging places that accommodate pets with the symbol 🐾. For a small additional fee, many B&Bs and inns now accommodate dogs as well as their owners. Among the most elegant to do so are **Topnotch** in Stowe, the **Basin Harbor Club** in Vergennes, the **Woodstock Inn and Resort** in Woodstock, and the **Mountain Top Inn and Resort** in Chittenden. **Layla's Riverside Lodge** in West Dover (at Mount Snow) caters to guests with dogs, supplying dog-sitters and off-leash areas as well as equipping each room with dog bowls, beds, and biscuits.

PICK YOUR OWN Strawberry season is mid- to late June. Cherries, plums, raspberries, and blueberries can be picked in July and Aug. Apples ripen by mid-Sept. and can be picked through foliage season. For specifics on where, see *Apples* and *Farms Open to the Public*.

QUILTS A revival of interest in this craft is especially strong in Vermont, where quilting supply and made-to-order stores salt the state. The **Vermont Quilt Festival** (vqf.org) is held for three days in late June in Essex Junction, including exhibits of antique quilts, classes and lectures, vendors, and appraisals. **Shelburne Museum** has an outstanding quilt collection, and the **Billings Farm & Museum** holds an annual show.

RAILROAD EXCURSIONS Trains Around Vermont (rails-vt.com) runs a number of excursion trains around the state. Check the website for current info.

RESTAURANTS Culinary standards are rising every day, along with the commitment to using local ingredients. You can lunch simply and inexpensively nearly everywhere and dine superbly in a score of places. Further boosting culinary standards is the **Vermont Fresh Network**; see the entry below. Fixed-price menus (prix fixe) have been so noted. We were tempted to try to list our favorites here, but the roster would be too long. Restaurants that appeal to us appear in the text in their respective areas. Note that we divide restaurants in each chapter into *Dining Out* (serious dining experiences) and *Eating Out* (everyday places). See also *Highway Road Food*.

ROCKHOUNDING The most obvious sites are the **Rock of Ages Quarry and Visitor Center** in Barre and the **Vermont Marble Museum** in Proctor, both with interactive exhibits. Vermont fossils, minerals, and rocks (including dinosaur footprints) may be viewed at the **Perkins Museum of Geology** at the University of Vermont, Burlington (uvm.edu/perkins/visitor .htm), and the **Fairbanks Museum** in St. Johnsbury. The 480-million-year-old coral reef at Fisk Quarry on Isle La Motte is another mustsee. And an annual **Rock Swap and Mineral Show** is held in early Aug., sponsored by the Burlington Gem and Mineral Club (burlington gemandmineralclub.org). Gold, incidentally, can be panned in a number of rivers, notably Broad Brook in Plymouth; the Rock River in Newfane and Dover; the Williams River in Ludlow; the Ottauquechee River in Bridgewater; the White River in Stockbridge and Rochester; the Mad River in Warren, Waitsfield, and Moretown; the Little River in Stowe and Waterbury; and the Missisquoi in Lowell and Troy.

SHEEP AND WOOL Specialty sheep and alpaca farms are numerous in Vermont. A number of farmers specialize in processing wool and fiber. Check vermontsheep.org. The annual **Vermont Sheep and Wool Festival**, featuring sheep shearing, spinning, weaving, and plenty of critters, is held the last weekend in Sept. at the Tunbridge Fairgrounds.

SHIPWRECKS Well-preserved 19th-century shipwrecks are open to the public (licensed divers) at any of nine underwater historical preserves in Lake Champlain near Burlington. Check with the **Lake Champlain Maritime Museum** (lcmm.org) in Vergennes, which is charting underwater remains. Nondivers can explore the lake's shipwrecks at the museum's Nautical Archaeology Center, which has interactive exhibits, a touch-screen "Virtual Diver," and archaeologists on site.

SKIING, CROSS-COUNTRY The **Vermont Ski Areas Association** (skivermont.com) lists some 20 cross-country centers on its website and profiles them in its useful free *Ski Vermont Alpine and Nordic Directory* and *Ski Vermont Magazine*. Centers are also listed in the *Vermont Winter Guide*, published by the Vermont Chamber of Commerce and available free by phoning 800-VERMONT. Within this book we have described each commercial touring center as it appears geographically. It's important to check conditions before you jump in the car. Vermont's most dependable snow can be found on high-elevation trails in **Stowe**, at **Craftsbury Outdoor Center** in Craftsbury Common, **Hazen's Notch** in Montgomery Center, **Bolton Valley Resort** between Burlington and Stowe, **Burke Mountain Cross-Country** in East Burke, and **Blueberry Hill** in Goshen. **Mountain Top Inn** in Chittenden and **Grafton Ponds** in Grafton offer some snowmaking. All the cross-country ski centers mentioned above are located on the 300-mile **Catamount Trail**, a marked ski trail that runs the length of the state (see *Catamount Trail*). **Prospect Mountain Nordic Ski Center** (prospectmountain.com), a former alpine area in the southwestern corner of the state, also tends to have reliable conditions because of its site in the state's highest town. **Mad River Glen** and **Bolton Valley** are two alpine resorts that specialize in telemarking. Also see *State Parks* and *Green Mountain National Forest*.

SKIING, DOWNHILL Since the 1930s, when America's commercial skiing began with a

SkiVermont.pdf

Model T Ford engine pulling skiers up a hill in Woodstock, skiing has been a Vermont specialty. Twenty ski areas are members of the **Vermont Ski Areas Association** and accessible with daily updated snow conditions and weather on the website **skivermont.com**. Request a free *Ski Vermont Alpine and Nordic Directory* and a *Ski Vermont Magazine* and/or phone 800-VERMONT for a glossy *Vermont Winter Guide*. Daily lift tickets are, of course, not the cheapest way to ski. A season's pass aside, there are always deeply discounted multiday lift and lodging packages, and there are frequently discounts for ordering ahead online.

The areas vary widely in size and character. **Killington/Pico** is the largest ski resort in the East. **Mount Snow**, Vermont's second largest area, is the most convenient to New York City; **Stratton** is a close second (there's daily shuttle service to all three areas from Manhattan). **Stowe** remains the Ski Capital of the East when it comes to the quantity and quality of inns, restaurants, and shops. **Sugarbush**, with a lower profile and almost equal options on and off the slopes, is preferred by many New England skiers, especially given the local option of skiing **Mad River Glen**, a famously old-fashioned ski area with minimal snowmaking, a single chair, and a ban (the only one in the East) against snowboarders. **Okemo** is known for its outstanding snow grooming and facilities and **Jay Peak** for its natural snow, off-piste and glade skiing, and facilities that include a spectacular water park, ice arena, and recently expanded slope-side bed base; Jay's owners have recently acquired **Burke** (now **Q Burke**), and a major new midmountain condo-style lodge is due for completion in 2015. We describe these and smaller areas as they appear geographically.

Burke Mountain Ski Resort

SLEIGH RIDES Sleigh rides are listed under *To Do* as they appear geographically in the book.

SNOWBOARDING This international sport was first popularized by Burton Snowboards (born in Manchester, long since moved to Burlington). Snowboarding lessons, rentals, and special terrain parks are offered at every major Vermont ski area except Mad River Glen.

SNOWMOBILING Vermont's roughly 6,000 miles of well-marked, groomed trails are laced in a system maintained by the **Vermont Association of Snow Travelers** (vast.com). VAST's corridor trails are up to 8 feet wide and are maintained by 140 local snowmobile clubs; for detailed maps and suggestions for routes, activities, and guided tours, check the website. Due to insurance laws, snowmobile rentals and tours are relatively few. The Northeast Kingdom in general and Island Pond in particular are best geared to snowmobiling, with storage facilities and a wide choice of lodging handy to trails. The **Northeast Kingdom Chamber of Commerce** (nekchamber.com) publishes a snowmobiling map/guide to the area. Within the book we list snowmobile rentals and tours as they appear geographically.

Okemo

SNOWSHOEING Snowshoeing is experiencing a rebirth in Vermont, thanks to the new lightweight equipment. Virtually all ski-touring centers now offer snowshoe rentals, and many inns stock a few pairs for guests.

SOARING Sugarbush Soaring, in the Mad River Valley, is known as one of the prime spots in the East for riding thermal and ridge waves. The Sugarbush Airport is a well-established place to take glider lessons or rides or simply to watch the planes come and go. The **Fall Wave Soaring Encampment** held in early Oct. (weather permitting) draws glider pilots from throughout the country. Glider and airplane rides are also available at the **Stowe-Morrisville Airport** (802-888-7845) and from the **Post Mills Soaring Club** at the Post Mills Airport (802-333-9992), where soaring lessons are also a specialty, along with simply seeing the Connecticut Valley from the air.

SPAS Vermont is home to the lion's share of New England's resort spas. In Stowe, **Topnotch Resort and Spa** (topnotchresort.com) and **Stoweflake Mountain Resort & Spa** (stoweflake.com) are among the region's biggest and best, but the spa at **Stowe Mountain Lodge** (stowe.com) is in its own class. The revamped **Equinox Resort** (equinoxresort.com) in Manchester Center offers a magnificent full-service spa. The **Castle Hill Spa** (castlehillspa.com) in Cavendish, near Okemo, is small but lovely, and **The Woodstock Inn** maintains the luxurious Serenity Spa. Many independent day spas are open through the state—we describe them under *To Do* in almost every chapter.

SPIRITUAL CENTERS/RETREATS Karmê Chöling Shambhala Meditation Center (karmecholing.org) is a long-established retreat in Barnet with many special programs. **Yoga Vermont** in Burlington (yogavermont.com) draws Ashtanga yoga practitioners from throughout the country. The **Green Mountain Dharma Center and Maple Forest Monastery** (greenmountaincenter.org) in Hartland is the scene of a major retreat (families welcome) in July and throughout winter, and the **Weston Priory** (westonpriory.org) in Weston is a longtime Benedictine monastery known for its music, offering unstructured retreats.

STATE PARKS Vermont's more than 50 exceptionally well-groomed state parks include camping and/or day-use facilities, and are so diverse an assortment of properties that no one characterization applies. Within this book we attempt to describe each as it appears geographically. Vermont state parks are also detailed in an exceptional website (vtstateparks.com) and are part of the **Department of Forests, Parks and Recreation** (vtfpr.org), which manages more than 157,000 acres of state land, offering opportunities for hunting, fishing, cross-country skiing, mountain biking, snowmobiling, and primitive as well as supervised camping. Also see *Campgrounds*.

SUMMER SELF-IMPROVEMENT PRO- GRAMS Whether it's improving your game of tennis or golf, learning to take pictures or to weave, cook, identify mushrooms, fish, or bike, or simply to lose weight, there is a summer program for you somewhere in Vermont. See *Tennis*, *Golf*, *Canoeing and Kayaking*, and *Fishing* for lodging and lesson packages. Intensive language programs are offered at **Middlebury College** (among the offerings are Arabic and Japanese, as well as more standard ones; middlebury.edu), and a writers' conference is held at its Bread Loaf summer campus. Senior citizens can take advantage of some outstanding courses offered at bargain prices (which include lodging) as part of the **Road Scholar** program (formerly Elderhostel; roadscholar.org). The state's oldest, most respected crafts program is offered by the **Fletcher Farm School for the Arts and Crafts** (fletcherfarm.org) in Ludlow: off-loom weaving, wooden-spoon carving, quilting, pottery, bookbinding, gourd or birch-bark vessel design, virtually every craft imaginable, including meals and lodging (minimum age 18, except for Young Artists programs). The nonprofit **Shelburne Art Center** (shelburneart center.org) offers similar courses though on a smaller scale, and the **Vermont Studio Center** in Johnson (vermontstudiocenter.org) has a national reputation. Working visual artists and writers come to renew their creative wellsprings or to explore completely new directions during intensive sessions that feature guidance and criticism by some of the country's premier artists. **Craftsbury Outdoor Center** in Craftsbury (craftsbury.com) has summer programs for all ages in running, bicycling, and sculling; also inquire about Road Scholar programs.

SWIMMING On the *Official Vermont Road Map & Guide to Vermont Attractions*, you can pick out the day-use areas that offer swimming, most with changing facilities, maintained by the Vermont State Department of Forests, Parks and Recreation (**vtstateparks.com**). Similar facilities are provided by the Green Mountain National Forest at **Hapgood Pond** in Peru,

and the U.S. Army Corps of Engineers has tidied corners of its dam projects for public use in Townshend and North Springfield. There are also public beaches on roughly one-third of Vermont's 400 lakes and ponds (but note that swimming is prohibited at designated "Fishing Access Areas") and plenty on Lake Champlain (in Burlington, Charlotte, Colchester, Georgia, and Swanton). Add to these all the town recreation areas and myriad pools available to visitors—and you still haven't gone swimming Vermont-style until you've sampled a Vermont swimming hole. These range from deep spots in the state's ubiquitous streams to 100-foot-deep quarries (**Dorset Quarry** near Manchester and **Chapman Quarry** in West Rutland are famous) and freezing pools between waterfalls. We have included some of our favorite swimming holes under *Swimming* in each section but could not bring ourselves to share them all. Look for cars along the road on a hot day and ask in local general stores. You won't be disappointed.

TAXES Vermont's lodging and meals tax has recently become more complicated and cumbersome. Until recently it was simply 9 percent statewide, but in 2008 many communities adopted an optional 1 percent meals and alcoholic beverage tax and/or a local option rooms tax. In Burlington the total tax is 11 percent rooms and meals and 12 percent alcohol. In Rutland the total tax is 10 percent rooms and meals. It can all add up. Our recent tab for three people lodging and two meals was $300 + $27 (9 percent tax) plus a bottle of wine ($30) + 10 percent alcohol tax = $360. This didn't include service, which is frequently added as 15–18 percent of the total.

TENNIS Vermont claims as many tennis courts per capita as any other state in the Union.

Christina Tree

These include town recreation facilities and sports centers as well as private facilities. For a listing of both public and private facilities see **ustavermont.com**. Summer tennis programs, combining lessons, lodging, and meals, are offered at **Bolton Valley**, **Killington**, the **Village at Smugglers' Notch**, **Stratton**, **Topnotch Resort** in Stowe, and both the **Bridges Family Resort and Tennis Club and Sugarbush Resort in Warren**. Check *Tennis* in each area.

THEATER Vermont's two long-established summer theaters are both in the Manchester area: the **Dorset Playhouse** and the **Weston Playhouse**. Other summer theater can be found in Stowe (**Stowe Theatre Guild** and the **Lamoille County Players** in Hyde Park each put on four shows a year), in Castleton, in Saxtons River, in Waitsfield (the **Valley Players**), and **Northern Stage** at the Briggs Opera House in White River Junction. There's also the **Lost Nation Theater** in Montpelier, and in Brattleboro the **New England Youth Theatre** and the **Vermont Theatre Company**. The **Flynn Theater** in Burlington and the **Paramount Theater** in Rutland are the scene of year-round film as well as live entertainment, including Vermont's largest community troupe, **Lyric Theatre**.

TRAINS See *Amtrak* and *Railroad Excursions*.

VACATION RENTALS There are plenty to choose from; Google "vacation rentals" plus "Vermont."

VERMONT FRESH NETWORK (802-434-2000; vermontfresh.net). Vermont's better restaurants share more than an interest in fine cuisine. Among discerning Vermonters, it's taken for granted that spots worth visiting display a distinctive green sign flaunting their affiliation with an exclusive club: Vermont Fresh Network, a nonprofit that partners chefs with local farmers. The idea came to Pam Knights in 1994, while she was public relations director at the New England Culinary Institute. Such a network, she felt, would not only provide restaurateurs with the freshest ingredients—from venison to just-picked berries—but also keep local producers in business, which in turn would help preserve Vermont's rural landscape. Today most of Vermont's finest dining establishments are members, and the little green sign has come to be regarded as a prestigious badge of culinary savvy. Now the real achievement is a Gold Barn Honor, bestowed only to the restaurants whose use of local foods is among the association's top 20 percent.

VERMONT PUBLIC RADIO Stations for those addicted to National Public Radio can be found throughout the state on the FM dial (click onto vpr.net). Recently VPR Classical has been added to the VPR World Channel, a collaboration with St. Michael's College. For this news channel in the Burlington area, tune in to WVPS (107.9); in the Windsor area WVPR (89.5); in the Rutland area WRVT (88.7); in St. Johnsbury WVPA (88.5); in Manchester 106.9; in Brattleboro 88.9; in Bennington WBTN (94.3); in Middlebury 99.5; in Montpelier 94.1; and in Rupert 101.1.

WATERFALLS Those most accessible and worth seeing include (north to south): the falls at **Brewster River Gorge**, Rt. 108 in Jeffersonville and, farther south off Rt. 108 (the Mountain Road) in Stowe. At **Bingham Falls** (an unmarked pull-off on the north side of the road), a trail leads downhill to the falls and gorge, recently conserved and deeded to the state. In Stowe also look for **Moss Glen Falls**, a 125-foot drop off Rt. 100. (About 3 miles north of the village, turn right onto Randolph Rd., then right again onto Moss Glen Falls Rd.; park at the area on your left just before a 90-degree turn across from a narrow bridge and look for the well-worn trail.) Beware **Big Falls** in Troy (directions are in our Jay Peak chapter): The top of this series of drops and cascades is a dramatic but rather scary spot; they represent the largest undammed waterfall on any major Vermont river (the Missisquoi). Also in northern Vermont: the **Great Falls of the Clyde River** in Charleston; **Duck Brook Cascades** in Bolton; **Little Otter Creek Falls** in Ferrisburgh; the seven falls on the **Huntington River** in Hanksville; **Shelburne Falls** in Shelburne; and **Cady's Falls** in Morrisville.

On the east–west roads linking the Champlain Valley with Rt. 100 (see *Gaps, Gulfs, and Gorges*), several falls are worth noting. On Rt. 17 look for the parking area, picnic table, and a short trail leading to the 45-foot **Bartlett Falls** in Bristol Memorial Park. On Rt. 125 check out **Middlebury Gorge** in East Middlebury; off Dugway Rd. note the scenic **Huntington Gorge** in Huntington (responsible for at least 20 drowning deaths); and in Hancock you'll find the 35-foot **Texas Falls**. North on Rt. 100 from Hancock also look for 45-foot **Moss Glen Falls** in Granville Gulf; here a boardwalk leads back to the falls, passing **Little Moss Glen Falls**. In the Upper Valley of the Connecticut River look for **Cow Meadows Ledges** in Newbury, the falls on the **Waits River** by Rt. 5 in the village of Bradford, and **Glen Falls**, a 75-foot drop in Fairlee almost opposite the fishing access on Lake Morey Rd.

In southern Vermont look for **Buttermilk Falls** (a popular swimming hole) in Ludlow; **Old City Falls** in Strafford off Old City Falls Rd.; the **East Putney Falls** and **Pot Holes**; and, our favorite of all, 125-foot **Hamilton Falls** in Jamaica, cascading down a schist wall with pools (responsible for more than one death over the years). Ask locally for directions to 160-foot **Lye Brook Falls** in Manchester. Most of these sites can be located on the invaluable *Vermont Atlas and Gazetteer* (DeLorme); also check

Dean Goss's fact-filled northeastwaterfalls.com and the colorful newenglandwaterfalls.com.

WEATHER REPORTS For serious weather travel information in Vermont, check with the Vermont Agency of Transportation's weather line: Dial 511 or 800-ICY-ROAD, or go to 511vt.com. Listen to "An Eye on the Sky" on Vermont Public Radio (see *Vermont Public Radio* for stations; fairbanksmuseum.org). The show, produced by the Fairbanks Museum and Planetarium, reports entertainingly as well as informatively on life's most constant variable. The site **vermontvacation.com** also carries current weather information.

TOURISM IN VERMONT

Contrary to common belief, tourism (for lack of a better word to describe the phenomenon of visitors "from away") is an integral part of Vermont's history, one that has affected its landscape— not just since the 1950s but for 150 years.

Before the Civil War, southerners patronized mineral spas in every part of the Green Mountain State, from Brattleboro to Brunswick Springs. You can still see glimpses of these antique establishments in such off-the-beaten-track places as Clarendon Springs. After the war, Vermont's burgeoning railroads teamed up with the state's Board of Agriculture to promote farm vacations. Railroad guides also promoted Newport, with its elegant four-story Lake Memphremagog House ("one of the largest and finest hotels in New England"), and Lake Willoughby ("one of the most remarkable places in the continent"). Carriage roads were built to the top of Jay Peak, Mount Mansfield, and Mount Equinox, and of course there was a summit hotel atop Mount Mansfield (the highest peak in the state) as well as a the Green Mountain Inn in Stowe Village.

In the 1850s the Equinox House was recognized as one of New England's leading hotels. By 1862 the *Manchester Journal* could report that the previous summer, "Every house in the village was as full as a 'Third Avenue car,' almost entirely New Yorkers." Woodstock was equally well known in the right Manhattan circles by the 1890s.

All 19th- and early-20th-century visitors arrived by train (the exception being those who crossed Lake Champlain by ferry), and Vermont was slower than many other states to provide roads suitable to touring. The flood of 1927 washed out a number of major highways and bridges. In 1936 a proposal for building a federally funded, 260-mile Green Mountain Parkway the length of the state—passing just below the crests of Pico, Killington, and several other peaks—was roundly defeated in a public referendum.

After World War II, however, Vermont launched what may be the world's first and most successful campaign to turn off-season into peak season.

"If you can pick and choose, there is no better time for a motor trip through Vermont than in autumn," Abner W. Coleman wrote in the first issue of *Vermont Life*, a state publication. The autumn 1946 article continued: "To the color photographer, Vermont during the autumn months offers delights indescribable. Should film become more plentiful this year, hundreds of camera enthusiasts will be roaming around these hills, knocking themselves out in a happy frenzy of artistic endeavor. For the autumn woods run the entire spectrum's course, from the blazing reds of the maple through the pale yellows of beech and birch to the violet of far-off mountain walls." The story was illustrated with the first of many vividly hued photos for which *Vermont Life* remains famous.

While Vermonters can't claim to have invented skiing, the state does boast America's oldest ski resorts. In the 1930s skiers began riding rope tows up slopes in Woodstock, at Pico, and on

WEB PAGES In this edition we list hundreds of websites within each region. Among the most helpful statewide sites are the following: **vermontvacation.com** is maintained by the Vermont Department of Tourism and Marketing. The Vermont Outdoor Guide Association, **voga.org**, maintains the best overall site for activities of every kind in the state; **vtstate parks.com** includes locator maps and special programs related to state parks. This guide is a search engine in its own right, listing Vermont websites with phone numbers throughout the book.

WEDDINGS Destination weddings have become big business in Vermont, so big and so ubiquitous that we use the wedding-ring symbol ⚭ to designate establishments that specialize in them. Same-sex marriages are now officially recognized in Vermont, helping to give rise to this booming industry. Contact **vermontwedding book.com** to request a free copy of the promotional *Vermont Wedding Resource Guide*. *Vermont Bride Magazine* and *Vermont Vows* also provide resources.

WHITEWATER During whitewater season beginning in mid-April, experienced canoeists and kayakers take advantage of stretches on the **White**, the **Lamoille**, and the **West Rivers**, among others. Whitewater rafting is also available on the **West River** during dam releases.

Mount Mansfield; after World War II, Stowe became "Ski Capital of the East." Patrons at Mad River Glen built the country's first slope-side lodging, and in the early '60s nearby Sugarbush opened with the East's first bottom-of-the-lifts village. In ensuing decades more than a dozen Vermont ski areas have evolved into year-round resorts, several (Stowe, Sugarbush, and Killington) spawning full-fledged communities. Stowe and Warren were towns before they were resorts.

Vermont's ski communities mirror (in reverse) the story of its mill towns. Whereas mills were positioned on waterfalls—and no longer need the water to generate power—ski resorts have grown around mountains chosen for their good terrain and "dependable" snowfall. Only in recent years has it become apparent that access to enough water—to make snow—is crucial.

The question of whether skiing or any other manifestation of "tourism" (again that inadequate term) contributes to the preservation or destruction of the Vermont character and landscape can be argued interminably. But the fact is that it has been here for 150 years. Today Vermont inns and B&Bs outnumber farms, and Vermont visitors outnumber cows.

Today's visitor is more likely than not to be welcomed by ex-visitors: More than 40 percent of the state's population of 626,431 has come "from away," a post–World War II phenomenon that has profoundly affected the cultural and political landscapes.

Much has been made of the proverbial "Vermont mystique," that indefinable quality of life and character. It is, we are happy to report, alive and well, especially along the back roads and in villages and hamlets where "neighboring" still reigns. While the portrait of the legendary Vermont Yankee—frugal, wary, taciturn, sardonic—has faded somewhat in today's homogenized culture, independent-minded Vermonters (many of them ex-"tourists") take care of one another, tolerate eccentricities, and regard the world with a healthy skepticism.

TROPICAL STORM IRENE

Tropical Storm Irene, which ripped through southern Vermont on August 28, 2011, was the state's most devastating natural disaster since "The Great Flood" of 1927. Six people died, some 1,400 households were displaced, and damage to roads, bridges, and property was estimated at more than $1 billion. The storm deposited massive amounts of water along its path, turning normally placid rivers and streams into raging torrents with water levels nearly 20 feet above normal, approaching those of 1927. Dozens of towns were inundated and often cut off for days; thousands of people were without power for weeks, with repair crews unable to reach them because of fallen trees and road damage. The base lodge at Killington collapsed. Two iconic wooden covered bridges were destroyed and more than a dozen badly damaged. More than 500 miles of road and 200 bridges in all required repair, almost isolating some communities.

It's the kind of situation that could have resulted in massive chaos—but this is Vermont. From all around the state volunteers rushed to stricken areas to help their neighbors. The Vermont National Guard was mobilized, and seven other states also sent units to assist. The building housing the state's emergency planning agency was severely damaged, but authorities moved quickly and decisively. State government was put on an emergency footing, eliminating red tape so that work on necessary projects could begin immediately.

The bulk of Vermont's visitors come during the fall foliage and winter ski seasons—which did not leave much time to clear and repair essential roads and bridges. Yet within a month of the storm 84 of the 118 sections of state roads that had been closed were reopened, along with 28 of the 34 closed state bridges.

We delayed the 2012 edition of this guide to revisit all areas affected by the storm. What we saw was impressive enough, but what we saw in 2014 was downright amazing. Several of the communities most devastated by the storm had rebuilt such that we dubbed them "Comeback Towns." Check out **Brattleboro** (a fire in the iconic Brooks House Block was followed by flooding along Flat St.), **Wilmington** (downtown has been rebuilt and then some), **Woodstock** (two covered bridges were damaged along with many riverside properties—but take a look now), **Rochester** ("We're still farming" says Beth Kennett of Liberty Hill Farm, a triumph when you understand the odds), and **Killington** (significant improvements). Along Bridge Street in **Waitsfield** most businesses are back, and new ones have opened. **Waterbury** has bounced back as a foodie and craft beer destination. Of course it's what most of us don't notice—new bridges, improved roads and infrastructure throughout the state—that is the real story here.

Vermont Standard

Christina Tree

Vermont Crafts Council

WINE Vermont has traditionally made apple and other fruit wines, but grape has become the fruit of choice. Grape vineyards and wines are proliferating so quickly that it's best to check **vermontgrapeandwinecouncil.com** to keep abreast. Download a map/guide to more than 20 vineyards and orchards, along with a passport to present at tasting rooms. The pioneers are two wineries in the northern reaches of the state: **Boyden Valley Winery** in Cambridge, and **Snow Farm Vineyard and Winery** in South Hero. Other newcomers include **Honora Winery and Vineyard** in West Halifax and Jacksonville (south-central Vermont), with hundreds of acres of vineyards and a Napa Valley–style tasting center, and **Lincoln Peak Vineyard** in New Haven. Among producers who offer tours and tastings are **Shelburne Vineyard**, open daily for tastings, and **Neshobe River Winery** with tastings in a vintage post-and-beam barn in Brandon. **North River Winery** (northriverwinery.com), Vermont's first vintner, produces fruit wine; the associated **Ottauquechee Valley Winery** (802-295-9463) is in Quechee. **Flag Hill Farm** (flaghillfarm .com) in Vershire produces hard apple cider (the traditional state drink), **Grand View Winery** (grandviewwinery.com) in East Calais near Montpelier offers tastings of a variety of fruit wines (also maintains a tasting room in Waterbury), and **Putney Mountain Winery** makes cider and apple wine and brandy.

WOODWORKERS *Vermont Woodshop & Forest Tours* is a glossy pamphlet guide available from the Vermont Department of Tourism and Marketing (800-VERMONT) and vermont forestheritage.org. It details and locates dozens of woodworking concerns, ranging from furniture makers to sculptors, throughout the state.

Southern Vermont

BRATTLEBORO, PUTNEY,
AND THE WEST RIVER VALLEY

THE MOUNT SNOW VALLEY

BENNINGTON AND
THE SOUTHSHIRE

MANCHESTER AND THE MOUNTAINS
Including Arlington, Dorset, Danby,
Peru, Londonderry, and Pawlet

OKEMO VALLEY REGION
Including Ludlow, Chester, Cavendish,
Mount Holly, Andover, Plymouth,
and Weston

Windham Foundation

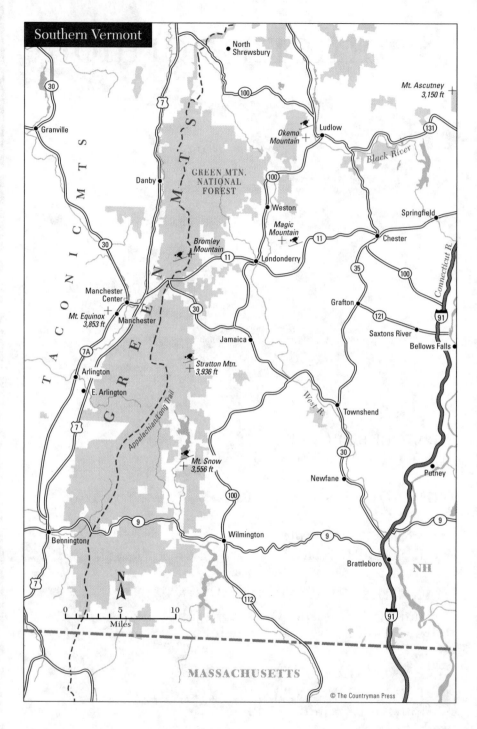

Southern Vermont

North Shrewsbury
Mt. Ascutney 3,150 ft
30
100
131
Granville
Ludlow
Okemo Mountain
Black River
GREEN MTN. NATIONAL FOREST
Danby
7
100
Weston
Springfield
Magic Mountain
Chester
Bromley Mountain
11
11
Londonderry
35
100
Manchester Center
30
Grafton
121
Mt. Equinox 3,853 ft
Manchester
Saxtons River
Jamaica
91
7A
Bellows Falls
Arlington
Stratton Mtn. 3,936 ft
E. Arlington
West R.
Townshend
Appalachian/Long Trail
G R E E N   M T S
T A C O N I C   M T S
Mt. Snow 3,556 ft
30
7
Newfane
Putney
100
9
Bennington
Wilmington
9
9
Brattleboro
NH
N
7
112
0   5   10
Miles
91

MASSACHUSETTS

© The Countryman Press

BRATTLEBORO, PUTNEY, AND THE WEST RIVER VALLEY

V ermont's southeastern corner is a major gateway, and many visitors—a number of them now residents—get no farther. It's said that Vermont is a state of mind; in Brattleboro, the area's commercial and cultural hub, you quickly understand why. The world's only Brattleboro is home to a vibrant artistic and activist community with the contagious energy of a community many times its size.

Repeatedly this community has shown amazing resiliency, most recently bouncing back from a fire that destroyed the splendidly built 1870s, 80-room hotel at its heart. Totally renovated, retaining its mansard roof, atrium, and tower, Brooks House how houses branches of two state colleges as well as residents, shops, and restaurants.

Another Main Street icon, the 1930s art deco Latchis Theater and Hotel, has been lovingly restored, the former rail station (where Amtrak still stops) is now an art museum, the downtown supermarket is an expansive state-of-the-art co-op with café, and several Main Street buildings are honeycombed with artists' studios. Along with Elliot and High Streets, it's a rich mix of traditional stores and galleries, restaurants and cafés, owner-operated bookstores, and boutiques.

Brattleboro has long drawn earnest and energetic young people. World Learning, now an international institution, began more than 50 years ago just north of town on a campus that is now its SIT Graduate Institute, granting degrees in such subjects as sustainable development and social justice. Similar degrees can also be earned downtown at Marlboro College's graduate center. Add to this mix the Brattleboro Music Center and the New England Center for Circus Arts, housed in the Cotton Mill, a building also known for its annual December Open Studios tour.

Year-round, the first Friday of every month is Gallery Walk, showcasing local art and music in some 50 venues. These in turn represent a small fraction of studios and galleries salted through the surrounding hills and valleys, most open by appointment and during annual open studio tours.

Putney, a dozen miles up the Connecticut River (next exit on I-91), is closely linked to Brattleboro in spirit. This rural village has been a center of progressive thinking since the 1840s when it spawned a group that practiced Bible Communism. It's home to the nationally recognized Putney School and Landmark College, also to the Yellow Barn Music School and Festival, The Sandglass Theater, and Next Stage (live performances and films).

Northwest of Brattleboro, Route 30 shadows the West River, threading the white-clapboard villages of Newfane, Townshend, and Jamaica—strung like pearls along a couple of dozen miles with back roads branching off to widely scattered inns and B&Bs, antiques dealers, galleries and shops, swimming holes and hiking trails to unexpected vistas.

Despite its accessibility, this is far from the most touristed corner of Vermont. The confluence of the Connecticut and West Rivers at Brattleboro is itself a beautiful, placid place to paddle. Beyond, roads web the area, connecting villages in sometimes extraordinarily beautiful ways.

GUIDANCE Brattleboro Area Chamber of Commerce (802-254-4565; 877-254-4565; brattleboro chamber.org), 180 Main St., Brattleboro 05301, is good for walk-in information (open year-round, Mon.–Fri. 9–5). It maintains a seasonal information booth just north of Main St. on Rt. 5.

(ᵠ) **The River Garden** (157 Main St.) is a welcoming weather-proofed downtown public space hung with changing local art and overlooking the river, year-round home base for Strolling of the Heifers (strollingoftheheifers .com). It offers local info, public restrooms, and WiFi, and serves as a venue for frequent free brown-bag lunch programs.

The Southeast Vermont Welcome Center, I-91 in Guilford (open daily 7 AM–1 AM), is Vermont's most elaborate visitors center, with displays on all parts of the state, featuring local attractions and events. **Restrooms** are open 24 hours.

Newspapers: The ***Brattleboro Reformer*** (802-254-2311; reformer.com) publishes a special Thursday calendar that's the best source of current arts and entertainment. Also check out ***The Commons*** (commonsnews.org).

GETTING THERE *By bus:* **Greyhound Bus Lines** (802-254-9727; greyhoundbus.com) stops south of town on Rt. 5.

By train: **Amtrak** (800-USA-RAIL; amtrak .com) trains from Washington, DC, and New York City stop twice daily at Brattleboro's vintage railroad station, now a museum.

William Hays
BRATTLEBORO MOON, A LINOCUT PRINT

By air: **Bradley International Airport** (bradleyairport.com) in Connecticut and **Manchester Airport** (flymanchester.com) in New Hampshire offer connections with all parts of the county; both are 1½ hours.

GETTING AROUND Brattleboro Taxi (802-254-6446) will meet trains, buses, and planes.

Connecticut River Transit (802-885-5162; 888-869-6287; crtransit.org) offers shuttle service among Brattleboro, Putney, Westminster, and Bellows Falls.

Parking: Main St. has metered parking; side streets are possible. A large parking area (Harmony Place) in the rear of the Brooks House is close to shops on High, Elliot, and Main Sts. Brattleboro's **Transportation Center** offers multilevel parking with access from Elliot or Flat Sts. Another large lot runs between High and Grove Sts.

WHEN TO GO Brattleboro itself is appealing in almost any weather. Summer brings riverside eating and strolling, twice-weekly farmers markets, hiking, paddling, and **Marlboro Music**. Off-season the shops and cafés seem even more inviting. The June **Strolling of the Heifers** up Main St. is a big draw. Foliage brings day-trippers, and it's wise to avoid Rt. 9. Luckily, there are many options (see *Scenic Drives*). Canny shoppers know about December open studios in Brattleboro's Cotton Mill. In summer and winter alike, gracious West River Valley inns and B&Bs beckon.

MEDICAL EMERGENCY Call **911**. **Brattleboro Memorial Hospital ER** (802-257-8222), 17 Belmont Ave., Brattleboro. **Grace Cottage Hospital** (802-365-7357), Rt. 35, Townshend.

✳ Towns and Villages

Brattleboro (population 12,400). This largely 1870s brick and cast-iron town is the commercial hub for rural corners of three states. Brattleboro is also a state of mind. The present mix of native Vermonters and flatlanders was seeded in the 1970s by former members of the communes that flourished in this area. Artists, musicians, and social activists continue to be drawn by local educational institutions (see the chapter introduction). The town's old landmark stores like Sam's Outdoor Outfitters and Brown & Roberts Hardware continue to thrive, but art galleries, crafts stores, and dozens of independently owned, one-of-a-kind enterprises are the rule, not the exception.

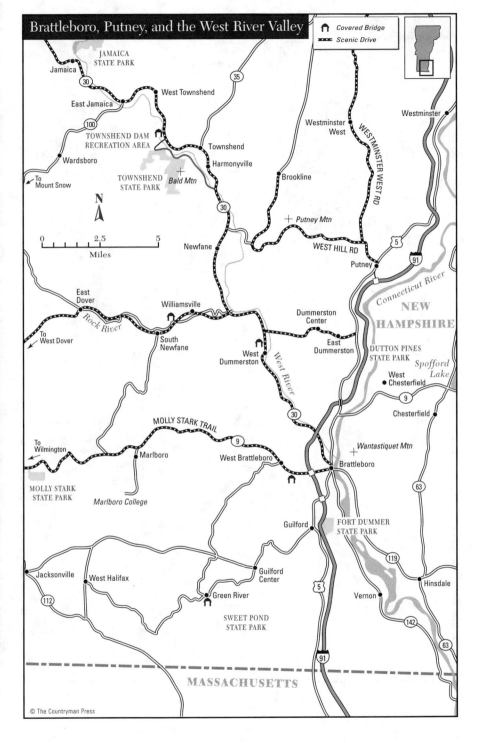

Brattleboro, Putney, and the West River Valley

Covered Bridge
Scenic Drive

JAMAICA STATE PARK

Jamaica

30

West Townshend

35

East Jamaica

100

TOWNSHEND DAM RECREATION AREA

Wardsboro

Townshend

Harmonyville

Westminster West

Westminster

WESTMINSTER WEST RD

To Mount Snow

TOWNSHEND STATE PARK

Bald Mtn

Brookline

N

0   2.5   5

Miles

Newfane

30

Putney Mtn

WEST HILL RD

Putney

5

91

East Dover

Williamsville

Dummerston Center

Connecticut River

NEW HAMPSHIRE

To West Dover

Rock River

South Newfane

East Dummerston

DUTTON PINES STATE PARK

West Chesterfield

Spofford Lake

West Dummerston

West River

9

MOLLY STARK TRAIL

9

Chesterfield

To Wilmington

Marlboro

West Brattleboro

30

Wantastiquet Mtn

Brattleboro

63

MOLLY STARK STATE PARK

Marlboro College

Guilford

FORT DUMMER STATE PARK

119

Jacksonville

West Halifax

Guilford Center

5

Hinsdale

112

Green River

Vernon

142

SWEET POND STATE PARK

63

91

MASSACHUSETTS

SOUTHERN VERMONT

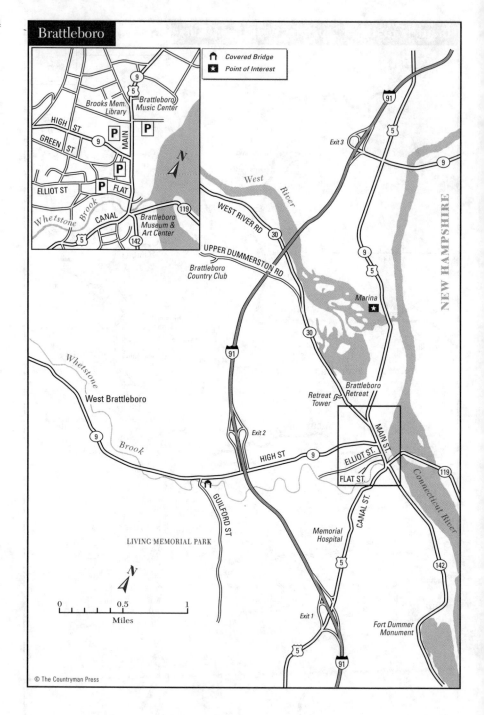

Brattleboro

Covered Bridge
Point of Interest

Brooks Mem. Library
Brattleboro Music Center

HIGH ST
GREEN ST
MAIN
ELLIOT ST
FLAT
Whetstone Brook
CANAL
Brattleboro Museum & Art Center

West River
WEST RIVER RD
UPPER DUMMERSTON RD
Brattleboro Country Club

Exit 3

NEW HAMPSHIRE

Marina

Whetstone
West Brattleboro

Brook

Brattleboro Retreat
Retreat Tower

Exit 2

HIGH ST
ELLIOT ST.
MAIN ST.
FLAT ST.

Connecticut River

GUILFORD ST

LIVING MEMORIAL PARK

Memorial Hospital

CANAL ST.

Fort Dummer Monument

Exit 1

0   0.5   1
Miles

© The Countryman Press

William Hays

CONGREGATIONAL CHURCH ON MAIN
STREET: *ILLUMINATION*, LINOCUT PRINT

During its long history, this town has shed many skins. The site of Fort Dummer, built in 1724 just south of town, has been obliterated by the Vernon Dam. Gone, too, is the early-19th-century resort town; no trace remains of the handsome, Federal-style commercial buildings or two elaborate hotels that attracted trainloads of customers who came to take the water cure developed by Dr. Robert Wesselhoeft. The gingerbread wooden casino in Island Park and the fine brick town hall, with its gilded opera house, are also gone. However, the slate-sided sheds in which hundreds of thousands of Estey organs were made are slowly being restored—one houses the new Estey Organ Museum.

In the center of town Brooks House, built splendidly in 1871 as an 80-room hotel, is currently under restoration after a devastating fire. Blocks down, the 1930s art deco Latchis Hotel and Theater remains both a hotel and a theater.

Brattleboro is full of pleasant surprises. The former railroad station is now the outstanding **Brattleboro Museum and Art Center**. The Connecticut River is accessible by rental canoe and kayak and can be viewed from a hidden downtown park and several restaurants. Whetstone Brook, once the power turning the town's mills, is increasingly visible. Twice-weekly seasonal farmers markets are among the liveliest in New England; a winter version is housed in the **River Garden**, a weather-proofed mid–Main Street space with public restrooms. Frequents concerts, dance and circus performances, and a film festival are presented without hoopla.

Putney (population 2,616; iputney.com). This town's riverside fields have been heavily farmed since the mid-18th century, and its hillsides produce one-tenth of all the state's apples. Putney is an unusually fertile place for progressive thinking, too. In the 1840s a group here practiced Bible Communism, the sharing of all property, work, and wives. John Humphrey Noyes, the group's leader, was charged with adultery in 1847 and fled with his flock to Oneida, New York, where they founded the famous silverplate company. Known today for experimental education rather than religion, Putney is the home of the **Putney School**, a coed, college preparatory school founded in 1935, with a regimen that entails helping with chores, including raising animals. **Landmark College** is a fully accredited college specifically for dyslexic students and those with other learning disabilities. In July the **Yellow Barn Music School and Festival** is housed in a barn behind the library; concerts are staged there and at other local venues throughout the month. The **Sandglass Theater** (serious puppetry) and **Next Stage** (live performances and films) are also based in Putney Village, which offers interesting shopping, augmented by exceptional artisans. During the three days following Thanksgiving some two dozen local studios are open for the **Putney Artisans Craft Tour** (putneycrafts.com). Putney's scenic roads are also well known to serious bicyclists, and **Putney Mountain** (see *Hiking*) is beloved by both hikers and mountain bikers.

Putney's native sons include the late George Aiken, who served as governor before going on to Washington as a senator in 1941, a post he held until his retirement in 1975. Frank Wilson, a genuine Yankee trader who was one of the first merchants to enter Red China, built **Basketville**, "The World's Largest Basket Store," in the village. The **Putney Historical Society** (802-387-5862; putneyhistory .org) is housed in the town hall, open when it's open. The **Putney General Store** at the heart of the village burned twice in recent years but is now fully restored, complete with an elevator accessing a second-floor pharmacy.

Guilford (population 2,121; guildfordvt.org). Back-roaded by I-91 (which has no exit between Brattleboro and Bernardston, Massachusetts), this old agricultural town rewards with quiet rural scenery anyone who drives or pedals its roads. Check out **Sweet Pond State Park**, a former 125-acre estate (the pond has been drained). Labor Day weekend is big here, the time for the old-fashioned **Guilford**

Fair and for the annual two-day, free concerts sponsored for more than 40 years by **Friends of Music at Guilford** (802-254-3600; fomag .org) in and around the **Organ Barn**. The **Guilford Historical Society**, 236 School Rd., is open Memorial Day–Columbus Day, Tues. and Sat. 10–2 and by appointment (802-257-0147). It maintains exhibits in the 1822 town hall, in the 1837 meetinghouse, and in the 1797 one-room brick schoolhouse. Guilford was the largest town in Vermont in 1817, the year the **Guilford Country Store** opened. Recently reopened after a lengthy community-funded restoration, it offers a welcoming café.

Christina Tree

PENNY CANDY SHOPPING AT THE NEWFANE COUNTRY STORE

Along Route 30 in the West River Valley
Newfane (population 1,700; newfane connection.org). A columned courthouse, matching Congregational church, and town hall—all grouped on a handsome green—are framed by dignified, white-clapboard houses and a four-columned inn. When Windham County's court sessions began meeting in Newfane in 1787, the village was about the same size it is now but it was 2 miles up on Newfane Hill. Beams were unpegged and homes moved to the more protected valley by ox-drawn sleighs in the winter of 1824. Check out the exceptional **Historical Society of Windham County** (see *To See*). Newfane is also home to a big Sunday flea market and to antiques shops.

Brookline (population 467; brooklinevt.com). Half as wide as it is long, Brookline is sequestered in a narrow valley bounded by steep hills and the West River. (Turn off Rt. 30 at the Newfane Flea Market.) Its population is four times what it was 50 years ago but a small fraction of what it was in the 1820s and '30s, when it supported three stores, three schools, two hotels, and a doctor. Its surviving landmark is a round schoolhouse, designed by John Wilson, a schoolteacher who never mentioned his previous career as Thunderbolt, an infamous Scottish highwayman. He gave the schoolhouse six large windows, the better to allow him to see whoever approached from any side. Wilson later added "Dr." to his name and practiced medicine in Newfane, then in Brattleboro, where he married, fathering a son before his wife divorced him "because of certain facts she learned." When he died in 1847, scars on Wilson's ankles and neck suggested chains and a rope. Today several of Thunderbolt's pistols are preserved in local museums.

JAMAICA TOWN HALL, AS SEEN FROM THE DINING ROOM OF THE THREE MOUNTAIN INN

Christina Tree

Townshend (population 1,190; townshend vermont.org). The village green is a splendid 2 acres, complete with Victorian-style gazebo. The classic white 1790 Congregational church is flanked by clapboard houses and a former brick tavern, and there's a columned and tower-topped stucco hall belonging to Leland and Gray Union High School (founded as a Baptist seminary in 1834). On the first Saturday in August the common fills with booths and games to benefit Grace Cottage Hospital, a complex that has grown out of the back of a rambling old village home and now includes assisted living buildings. Rt. 30 continues through West Townshend with its recently restored country store, by Vermont's largest single-span covered bridge, and past a public swim beach. The town includes 15 cemeteries and several good places to stay and to eat.

Jamaica (population 900; jamaicavt.com). The small village includes a white Congregational church (1808), another 19th-century church that's now the red-clapboard town hall, a standout country store, an exceptional art gallery, and two welcoming lodging places. Jamaica is the kind of town you can drive through in two minutes, or stay a week. Scott and Helen Nearing came in 1932 and chronicled their stay in *Living the Good Life: Being a Plain Practical Account of a Twenty-Year Project in a Self-Subsistent Homestead in Vermont*. It remains a back-to-the-earth bible. As nearby Stratton ski area began to expand, the Nearings moved on to Maine, but vestiges of the community they spawned survive. Stop by the Elaine Beckwith Gallery and leaf through *Almost Utopia*, picturing and describing "The Residents and Radicals of Pikes Falls, Vermont 1950." The actual Pikes Falls remains a popular swimming hole. **Jamaica State Park** also offers swimming, camping, and extensive hiking trails. While the village of Jamaica is small, the town is large, with many hidden corners worth exploring. These include glorious Hamilton Falls, Bald Mountain Dam, and the chapel of Our Lady of Ephesus, a replica of the house in Turkey said to be the last residence of the Virgin Mary. There is a spectacular view and amazing story there (ourladyofephesushouseofprayer.org). The Jamaica Historical Foundation (jamaicahf.info) housed in the village's former bank is open building mid-May–mid-Oct., Thurs. 1–3 and Sat. 10–1, or by special appointment. Exhibits of early Jamaica history, including Civil War and Native American memorabilia.

✳ To See

MUSEUMS

♿ **Brattleboro Museum & Art Center** (802-257-0124; brattleboromuseum.org), 10 Vernon St. (corner of Canal and Rt. 119), Brattleboro. Open Sun.–Thurs. 11–5, Fri. 11–7, Sat. 10–5. $8 adults, $6 seniors, $4 students. The town's 1915 rail station makes a handsome home for increasingly compelling changing exhibits with an emphasis on contemporary art. Check the website for the current exhibit and a lively calendar of receptions, readings, music, lectures, and more.

Brattleboro Historical Society and History Center (802-258-4957). The Society **History Room** at 230 Main St., third floor, open Thurs. 1–4, Sat. 10–noon is all about genealogical research. **The History Center**, 196 Main St., open Thurs., Fri. 2–4 (until 8 during Gallery Walks), Sat. 10–noon, exhibits a model of Fort Dummer, historical prints, and artifacts along with multimedia presentations and changing exhibits.

Brooks Memorial Library (802-254-5290), 224 Main St., Brattleboro (open daily except Sun.), mounts changing exhibits of regional art and has a fine collection of 19th-century paintings and sculpture, including works by Larkin G. Mead, the Brattleboro boy who first won recognition by sculpting an 8-foot-high angel from snow one night at the junction of Rts. 30 and 5.

Historical Society of Windham County (802-365-4148), Rt. 30, south of the common (open Memorial Day–Columbus Day, Wed., Sat., Sun. noon–5). It looks like a brick post office, but exhibits fill both the main floor and the second-floor gallery. In addition to changing shows, there are permanent displays on the West River Railroad, which operated between Brattleboro and South Londonderry (1880s–1927) and is remembered as "36 miles of trouble" (the Newfane RR Station is being renovated as a museum to tell the tale); Porter Thayer's photographs of local turn-of-the-20th-century scenes; and the saga of John Wilson (see Brookline under *Towns and Villages*).

COVERED BRIDGES In Brattleboro the reconstructed **Creamery Bridge** forms the entrance to Living Memorial Park on Rt. 9. North on Rt. 30 in West Dummerston, a Town lattice bridge across the West River is the longest still-used covered bridge in the state (for the best view, jump into the cool waters on either side; this is

BRATTLEBORO MUSEUM & ART CENTER
Christina Tree

a popular swimming hole on a hot summer day). The **Green River** in Guilford also boasts a recently rebuilt covered bridge connecting the village to Bernardston, Massachusetts. The **Scott Bridge**, Vermont's longest single-span bridge, stands by Rt. 30 in West Townshend just below the Townshend Dam, but it's closed to traffic. The region's oldest covered bridge spans the **Rock River** between Williamsville and South Newfane.

FOR FAMILIES ✎ **Retreat Petting Farm** (802-257-2240; theretreatfarm.com), 350 Linden St., and the neighboring **Grafton Village Cheese Company** (802-246-2221), both at the beginning of Rt. 30 as you head north from Brattleboro. The farm is open Memorial Day–Columbus Day weekends, Wed.–Sat. 10–4, Sun. noon–4, also holiday Mondays. $5 ages 2–11, $6 ages 12 and over. This was the Brattleboro Retreat's working dairy farm. It's now owned by the Grafton-based Windham Foundation, which has replaced the cows with a major cheesemaking facility and shop. There are still plenty of farm animals in residence: llamas, pigs, emus, lambs, sheep, goats, oxen, donkeys, horses, chickens, kittens, shaggy Highland cattle, and more. Next door the new cheese shop includes a window in which to watch cheese being made and a big retail store full of Vermont specialty foods and gifts. Also note the adjoining **Retreat Trails**, a 9-mile network with an entrance at the farm.

Estey Organ Museum (802-246-8366; estey organmuseum.org), 108 Birge St. (rear), Brattleboro (turn off Canal St. at the Sunoco station). Open June–Columbus Day, Sat., Sun. 2–4. Visits are also available by special arrangement; call 802-246-8366. Admission $5. For many years Brattleboro's largest employer, the Estey Organ Co. produced thousands of organs each year between 1846 and its demise in 1960. This evolving museum, founded in 2002, is housed in a former engine house, a large, airy, well-lit space in which exhibits trace the history of organs in general and of Estey organs in particular. There are examples of reed organs from the 1860s and the ornately carved parlor organs found in countless Victorian homes. There are also the pipe organs Estey made for small churches throughout the county, and finally there are electronic organs, highly innovative when they first appeared. Inquire about frequent special events.

Tasha Tudor Museum (802-258-6664; tashatudormusem.org), 974 Western Ave., West Brattleboro. Open days vary with the season; hours are 10–4. $6 per adult, $4 children and seniors. Tasha Tudor (1915–2008) wrote and illustrated children's stories depicting America's idyllic rural past. The museum's changing exhibits depict her life, and there are frequent programs. This is not her home—that's in Marlboro, privately owned by her family and open for limited tours (tashatudorandfamily.com). Inquire about Tasha Tudor teas.

Also see the **Southern Vermont Natural History Museum** at Hogback Mountain (west of Brattleboro) in "The Mount Snow Valley" and the **Nature Museum** of Grafton in "The Lower Connecticut River Valley."

SCENIC DRIVES The hilly, heavily wooded country between the West and Connecticut River Valleys is webbed with roads, most of them dirt. Our favorites include:

West Dummerston to West Dover. Beautiful in a car or on a bike, the 13 miles between Rt. 30 and Rt. 100 form a shortcut from Newfane to Mount Snow. Turn west off Rt. 30, 2 miles north of the covered bridge. Follow the Rock River (in summer, clumps of cars suggest swimming holes) west from West Dummerston and Williamsville, on through the picturesque village of South Newfane; detour 0.5 mile into the old hill village of Dover, very different from West Dover down on busy Rt. 100.

Route 30 from Brattleboro to Jamaica (you can loop back on Rt. 100) shadows the West River, passing two covered bridges and threading the photogenic villages of Newfane and Townshend, as well as passing Townshend Dam (good for swimming). Plenty of reasons to stop along the way to shop for crafts and antiques.

East Dummerston to West Dummerston. A handy shortcut from Rt. 5 to Rt. 30 (or vice versa), just 2 miles up one side of a hill to picturesque Dummerston Center and 2 miles down the other. This was long known in our family as the Gnome Road because of the way it winds through the woods to Vermont's longest (refitted) traffic-bearing covered bridge. It's generally known as the East/West Rd.

Putney Mountain Road to Brookline. (Closed in winter.) From Rt. 5 in the middle of Putney, turn left onto Westminster West Rd. and left again about a mile up the hill onto West Hill Rd. Not far above the Putney School, look for a dirt road on your right. It forks immediately; bear right to Putney Mountain. Trees thicken and sunlight dapples through in a way that it never seems to do on paved roads. Chipmunks scurry ahead on the hard-packed dirt. The few drivers you pass will wave. The road curves up and up—and up—cresting after 2.1 miles. Note the unmarked parking area on your right (see Putney Mountain under *Hiking*). The road then snakes down the other side into Brookline.

Brattleboro to Guilford Center to Halifax and back. This can be a 46-mile loop to Wilmington and back; ask locally for shortcuts back up to Rt. 9. Take Rt. 5 south from Brattleboro to the Guilford Country Store, then right into Guilford Center. Continue for 0.5 mile and bear right on Stage Rd. to Green River with its covered bridge, church, and recently restored crib dam. Bear right at the church (before the bridge) and then left at the Y; follow Green River Rd. (along the river) and then Hatch School Rd. into Jacksonville. To complete the loop, see *Scenic Drives* in "The Mount Snow Valley."

The **Molly Stark Scenic Byway**—Rt. 9 between Brattleboro and Bennington—is dedicated to the wife of General John Stark, hero of the Battle of Bennington. The 20-mile stretch west from Brattleboro bypasses the village of **Marlboro**, climbing high over **Hogback Mountain** with its **Southern Vermont Natural History Museum** before winding down into Wilmington. For details about Marlboro and Hogback, see *Scenic Drives* in the Mount Snow chapter. Note that this route is heavily trafficked during foliage season.

✳ To Do

BICYCLING Some 200 miles of dirt and abandoned roads, along with miles of off-road trails, add up to a well-established mecca for cyclists. Download maps from the Windham Regional Commission: windhamregional.org/bikemap. Amtrak no longer permits bikes, but the train from NYC still stops in Brattleboro, where you can rent a hybrid at the **Brattleboro Bicycle Shop** (802-254-8644; 800-BRAT-BIKE; bratbike.com), 178 Main St., and pick up plenty of advice about where to use it.

Road biking is popular in this area thanks to many interlinking back roads and river roads.

In Putney the **West Hill Shop** (802-387-5718; westhillshop.com), open daily, just off I-91, Exit 4, offers mountain and road bike rentals. It's also still home to the **Putney Bicycle Club**, which organizes races and (hard-core) tours. The **Ranney-Crawford House** in Putney and **Jamaica House** in Jamaica (see *Lodging*) are geared to cyclists.

BOATING Vermont Canoe Touring Center (802-257-5008), 451 Putney Rd., Brattleboro. Located on the West River at the cove at Veterans Memorial Bridge, Rt. 5, just north of the junction with Rt. 30. Open daily Memorial Day weekend–Labor Day weekend, 9–dusk; also spring and fall weekends, weather permitting. John Knickerbocker rents canoes and kayaks. The 32 miles from Bellows Falls to the Vernon Dam is slow-moving water, as is the 6-mile stretch from below the dam to the Massachusetts border.

Whitewater on the West River. Once a year, on the last weekend in September, the Army Corps of Engineers releases water from the **Ball Mountain Dam** (802-874-4881) in Jamaica, creating whitewater rafters as well as kayakers and canoeists to take advantage of the flow.

FISHING In the **Connecticut River** you can catch bass, trout, pike, pickerel, and yellow perch. There is an access on Old Ferry Rd., 2 miles north of Brattleboro on Rt. 5; another is from River Rd. on the New Hampshire shore in Westmoreland (Rt. 9 east, then north on Rt. 63). The **West River** is a source of trout and smallmouth bass; access is from any number of places along Rt. 30. In Vernon there is a boat access on **Lily Pond**; in Guilford on **Weatherhead Hollow Pond** (see the *DeLorme Vermont Atlas and Gazetteer*).

GOLF Brattleboro Country Club (802-257-7380; brattleborogolf.com), 348 Upper Dummerston Rd., Brattleboro, offers 18 holes along the contours of rolling hilltops and includes a full driving range, practice areas, and instructional range. Also see **Mount Snow** and **Stratton** ski resorts under *Downhill Skiing*; both offer golf schools and 27 holes.

HIKING ❀ The Retreat Trails (theretreatfarm.com). In Brattleboro 9 miles of well-kept, mostly wooded trails web the 457-acre retreat farm, now owned by the Windham Foundation. The trails were built in the 19th century by patients and staff of the Retreat, a pioneering mental hospital first opened in 1836. The Retreat Petting Farm (see *To See*) is the obvious access point, but there are many others. Popular paths lead to a 19th-century observation tower (now closed but still good views), a former ice pond, and the Harris Hill Ski Jump.

Putney Mountain between Putney and Brookline, off Putney Mountain Rd. (see *Scenic Drives*), is one of the most rewarding 1-mile round-trip hikes anywhere. A sign nailed to a tree in the unmarked parking area assures you that this is indeed Putney Mountain. Follow the trail that heads gently uphill through birches and maples, then continues through firs and vegetation that changes remarkably quickly to the stunted growth usually found only at higher elevations. Suddenly you emerge on the mountain's broad crown, circled by a deep-down satisfying panorama. The view to the east is of Mount Monadnock, rising in lonely magnificence above the roll of southern New Hampshire, but more spectacular is the spread of Green Mountain peaks to the west. You can pick out the ski trails on Haystack, Mount Snow, and Stratton.

The West River Trail follows the abandoned railbed of the West River Railroad (1879–1927), known in its time as "36 miles of trouble." Access to its first stretch is off Rt. 5 north of town; take the second left turn after crossing the bridge. Other sections are found from Jamaica State Park to Ball Mountain Dam (3.5 miles) and from East Jamaica to Townshend Dam (3 miles). Jamaica State Park (see *Green Space*) offers a choice of three interesting trails. The most intriguing and theoretically the shortest is to Hamilton Falls, a 125-foot cascade through a series of wondrous potholes. It's an obvious mile (30-minute) hike up, but the return can be confusing. Beware of straying onto Turkey Mountain Rd.

Wantastiquet Mountain, overlooking Brattleboro from across the Connecticut River in New Hampshire, is a good 1½-hour hike. From Main St. take Rt. 119 across the Connecticut and immediately after the second bridge turn left; the parking area is on your right.

Black Mountain Natural Area, maintained by **The Nature Conservancy of Vermont** (802-229-4425). Cross the covered bridge on Rt. 30 in West Dummerston and turn south on Quarry Rd. for 1.4 miles. The road changes to Rice Farm Rd.; go another 0.5 mile to a pull-off on your right. The marked trail begins across the road and rises abruptly 1,280 feet to a ridge, traversing it before dropping back down, passing a beaver dam on the way back to the river. The loop is best done clockwise. Beautiful in laurel season.

SWIMMING ✤ **Living Memorial Park**, west of downtown Brattleboro on Rt. 9, offers an Olympic-sized public pool (mid-June–Labor Day). In the West River Valley at the **Townshend Lake Recreation Area** (802-874-4881) off Rt. 30 in West Townshend, you drive across the top of the massive dam, completed in 1961 as a major flood-prevention measure for the southern Connecticut River Valley. Swimming is in the reservoir behind the dam, with a manmade beach and gradual drop-off, good for children. Changing facilities provided; small fee. The **West River** itself offers a few swimming holes, notably under the West Dummerston covered bridge on Rt. 30 and at Salmon Hole in Jamaica State Park. **Hamilton Falls**, accessible from the park, and **Pikes Falls**, also in Jamaica (ask directions locally), are favorite swimming holes, but not advised for children. Just off Rt. 30, a mile or so up (on South Newfane Rd.), the **Rock River** swirls through a series of shallow swimming spots; look for cars. Also handy to Brattleboro, **Wares Grove** is across the Connecticut River in Chesterfield, New Hampshire (9 miles east on Rt. 9, the next left after the junction with Rt. 63). This pleasant beach on Spofford Lake is good for children; you'll find a snack bar and makeshift changing facilities.

✳ Winter Sports

CROSS-COUNTRY SKIING Brattleboro Outing Club Ski Hut (802-254-4081; brattleboroouting club.org), 348 Upper Dummerston Rd., Brattleboro. Warming hut open weekends, trails daily in-season. Trails through woods and a golf course, 33 km machine tracked, plus rentals, lessons, and moonlight ski tours. **West Hill Shop** (802-387-5718), just off I-91, Exit 4, in Putney rents cross-country skis and snowshoes. **Jamaica State Park** in Jamaica (see *Green Space*) offers marked trails.

See also **Grafton Ponds Recreation Center** in "The Lower Connecticut River Valley."

ICE SKATING Living Memorial Park Skating Rink (802-254-5808), Rt. 9 west, Brattleboro. Open late Oct.–mid-Mar. with skate rentals. A seasonal weather-proofed rink. Call for public skate times.

DOWNHILL SKIING The big ski areas are a short drive west into the Green Mountains, either to **Mount Snow** (Rt. 9 from Brattleboro and then up Rt. 100 to West Dover—see "The Mount Snow Valley") or up Rt. 30 to **Stratton** (see "Manchester and the Mountains").

SNOWMOBILING See **Mount Snow** (in "The Mount Snow Valley") and **Stratton** (in "Manchester and the Mountains") ski resorts for tours and rentals. The VAST (Vermont Area Snow Travelers; vtvast.org) trail system can be accessed in West Brattleboro.

✳ Green Space

Fort Dummer State Park (802-254-2610), Guilford. Located 2 miles south of Brattleboro (follow S. Main St. to the end). Surrounded by a 217-acre forest, overlooking the site of its namesake fort, built in 1724 to protect settlements along the Connecticut River. It was flooded by the Vernon Dam in

RUDYARD KIPLING AND NAULAKHA

Rudyard Kipling first visited Brattleboro in the winter of 1892 and determined to build himself a house high on a hill in Dummerston (just north of the Brattleboro line), on property purchased from his wife's brother. The young couple then headed for Samoa to see Robert Louis Stevenson but got no farther than Yokohama; at that point their bank failed, taking virtually all their money. Returning to Vermont, they rented a cottage while building Naulakha; the name is a Hindi word meaning "great jewel." The shingled house is 90 feet long but only 22 feet wide, designed to resemble a ship riding the hillside like a wave. Its many windows face east, across the valley to the New Hampshire hills with a glimpse of the summit of Mount Monadnock.

Just 26 years old, Kipling was already one of the world's best-known writers, and the four following years here were among the happiest in his life. Here he wrote the *Jungle Books*. Here the local doctor, James Conland, a former fisherman, inspired him to write *Captains Courageous* and also delivered his two daughters. Kipling's guests included Sir Arthur Conan Doyle, who brought with him a pair of Nordic skis, said to be the first in Vermont. Unfortunately, in 1896 a highly publicized falling-out with his dissolute brother-in-law drove the family back to England. They took relatively few belongings from Naulakha, and neither did the property's two subsequent owners, who used it as a summer home.

The house has been restored and is maintained by The Landmark Trust USA, which has preserved every detail of the home as Rudyard and Carrie Kipling knew it. Though the house is not available for functions and rarely for tours, it can be rented for a week ($350–450 per day, three-night minimum). There are four bedrooms (three baths). Some 60 percent of the present furnishings are original, including a third-floor pool table. A game of tennis, anyone, on the Kipling court? Or how about curling up with the *Jungle Books* on a sofa by the fire, only a few feet from where they were written? Or steeping in Kipling's own deep tub? The **Carriage House** has also been restored to Kipling's design ($275 per night). For details about renting Naulakha, contact The Landmark Trust USA (802-254-6868; landmarktrustusa.org), 707 Kipling Rd., Dummerston 05301. *Rudyard Kipling in Vermont: Birthplace of the Jungle Books* by Stuart Murray (Images from the Past) offers an excellent description of Kipling's relation to and portrayal of the area.

Landmark Trust USA has restored two more historic buildings at neighboring 571-acre Scott Farm (scottfarmvermont.com). **The Sugarhouse**, a classic century-old sugarhouse, has been fitted with radiant floor heating and a gas log stove, a bedroom (sleeping two), and a fully equipped kitchen with a dishwasher and linens ($135–170 per night, pets permitted, two-night minimum). The eight-room **Dutton Farmhouse** is an 1837 Greek Revival white-clapboard homestead set near the highest point of the farm with 30-mile views over the Connecticut River Valley to Mount Monadnock. There are four bedrooms—two doubles and two with twins—two and a half baths, a full kitchen, a living room with gas log fireplace, a dining room, and a fully equipped kitchen ($300–350 per night, three-night minimum). Both properties offer access to hiking trails on the farm and to the tennis courts at Naulakha. Landmark Trust has also restored the **Amos Brown House**, a brick Cape-style home built circa 1802 on 30 aces of meadow and forest in Whitingham. With three bedrooms and two baths, it sleeps six ($250–300 per night, three-night minimum, dogs welcome).

1908. There are 50 tent/trailer sites and 10 lean-tos, hot showers, and a dump station but no hookups, also hiking trails and a playing field.

🐾 ✍ **Living Memorial Park** (802-254-5808), just west of Brattleboro on Rt. 9. This 56-acre park includes a swimming pool (mid-June–Labor Day), an enclosed ice-skating rink, two tennis courts, wooded walking trails (dogs are welcome, but pick up), a playground, ball fields, picnic shelter, and a ski hill serviced by a T-bar.

Dutton Pines State Park, Rt. 5, 5 miles north of Brattleboro, is a picnic area with a shelter.

Townshend State Park (802-365-7500), Townshend, marked from Rt. 30 south of Townshend. Open early May–Columbus Day. Up a back road, an attractive, classic '30s Civilian Conservation Corps (CCC) stone-and-wood complex with a picnic pavilion, set in an 856-acre state forest. The camping area (30 tent/trailer campsites, four lean-tos) is near the start of the 2.7-mile (steep) climb to the summit of Bald Mountain; trail maps are available at the park office.

Christina Tree
A SWIMMING HOLE IN JAMAICA STATE PARK

✍ **Jamaica State Park** (802-874-4600), Jamaica. This 758-acre wooded area offers riverside camping, swimming in a great swimming hole, a picnic area, and an organized program of guided hikes. An old railroad bed along the river serves as a 3-mile trail to the Ball Mountain Dam, and an offshoot mile-long trail leads to Hamilton Falls. A weekend in spring and again in fall is set aside for whitewater canoe races. There are 41 tent/trailer sites and 18 lean-tos. A large picnic shelter is handy to the swimming hole; a playground includes swings, a teeter-totter, and slides.

Ball Mountain Lake (802-874-4881), Jamaica. This 85-acre lake, created and maintained by the U.S. Army Corps of Engineers, is a dramatic sight among the wooded, steep mountains, conveniently viewed from the access road off Rt. 30. Over 100 campsites are available on Winhall Brook at the other end of the reservoir, open mid-May–Columbus Day; it's accessible off Rt. 100 in South Londonderry. A controlled release from this flood dam provides outstanding canoeing on the West River below Jamaica each spring and fall (see *Boating*).

See also *Hiking* and *Swimming*.

✳ Lodging

COUNTRY INNS & A DOWNTOWN HOTEL

🎭 **Latchis Hotel** (802-254-6300; latchis.com), 50 Main St., Brattleboro 05301. This downtown, art-deco-style hotel first opened in 1938 and has recently been resurrected after a thorough restoration by a local group dedicated to turning the hotel's grand theater into a performance center. Push open the door into the small but spiffy lobby, with its highly polished terrazzo marble floors. Take the elevator up to one of the 30 air-conditioned rooms; request one with views down Main Street and across to Wantastiquet Mountain. Rooms are comfortably furnished in art deco style, some individually themed, all with private bath, phone, fridge, and coffeemaker. The hotel is solidly enough built to muffle the sound of traffic below. For more about the theater, see *Entertainment*. $99–190; $165–225 for the suite includes continental

breakfast. More during foliage. Inquire about a variety of packages.

♂ **Windham Hill Inn** (802-874-4080; 800-944-4080), West Townshend 05359. High above the West River Valley, this 1825 brick farmhouse is a luxurious retreat. Several of the 21 guest rooms have soaking tub, private deck, Jacuzzi, and fireplace or gas stove. All have private bath and phone, and are furnished with antiques and interesting art. Eight are in the White Barn Annex, some with a large deck looking down the valley. Common space in the inn itself includes a living room and an airy sunporch with wicker armchairs. Two sitting rooms are country elegant with wood-burning fireplace, Oriental carpets, and wing chairs, and the dining room also has a fireplace, a formal dining table, and tables for two (see *Dining Out*). A nicely landscaped pool overlooks the mountains and tennis court. The 160-acre property also includes an extensive network of hiking paths, groomed as snowshoe trails in winter. Inquire about weddings, for up to 50 guests, both inside (there's a small conference center in the barn) and outside. $255–545 per couple B&B. Check the website for packages.

♂ ✿ 🏃 **Four Columns Inn** (802-365-7713), Newfane. Reopening under new ownership in May 2015.

♂ ✿ **Three Mountain Inn** (802-874-4140; 800-532-9399; threemountaininn.com), Rt. 30, P.O. Box 180, Jamaica 05343. Ed and Jennifer Dorta-Duque welcome you to their 1790s inn in the middle of a classic Vermont village. There are seven upstairs rooms and seven in neighboring Robinson House, all nicely decorated, several with whirlpool tub, gas or wood fireplace or stove. Sage Cottage in the garden has skylights and a stained-glass window. Common space includes the old tavern room with its large hearth and a cozy corner bar. There are two small but elegant dining rooms (see *Dining Out*) and a private gallery/dining room. Jamaica State Park and its trails are a short walk away. From $119 off-season for a small room in the inn to $360 high-season for the ground-floor two-room Jamaica Suite opening onto the patio; $325–360 for Sage Cottage; a three-course breakfast is included. Less for solo travelers.

♂ ✿ **Chesterfield Inn** (603-256-3211; 800-365-5515;), P.O. Box 155, Chesterfield, NH 03443. On Rt. 9, 2 miles east of Brattleboro. The original house served as a tavern from 1798 to 1811 but the present facility is contemporary, with a large attractive dining room, spacious parlor, and 13 guest rooms and two suites divided between the main house and the Guest House. All rooms have sitting area, phone, controlled heat and air-conditioning, optional TV, and wet bar, and some have a working fireplace or Jacuzzi. Innkeepers Phil and Judy Hueber have created a popular dining room and a comfortable, romantic getaway spot that's well positioned for exploring southern Vermont as well as New Hampshire's Monadnock region. $149–269 includes a full breakfast. Inquire about pet packages.

BED & BREAKFASTS

In Brattleboro 05301

✪ ♂ **1868 Crosby House** (802-257-7145; crosbyhouse.com), 175 Western Ave. An Italianate-Victorian mansion built by a local mill owner, this is a gem. Marble or slate mantels in the three second-floor guest rooms frame gas fireplaces; TVs are hidden in crafted cupboards

above. Bathrooms are luxurious, featuring either a double shower or a whirlpool bath. Two efficiency suites add a shared porch, garden views, and cooking facilities. Innkeeper Lynn Kuralt charges $160–195 per room (inquire about longer stays in the suites). The house is nicely positioned within walking distance of downtown but backing on an expansive landscaped garden with a gazebo and lily pond, adjacent to conservation land with extensive walking trails.

🏃 **Forty Putney Road** (802-254-6268; 800-941-2413; fortyputneyroad.com), 192 Putney Rd. Just north of the town common and within walking distance of downtown shops and restaurants, this house with steeply pitched, gabled roof, reminiscent of a French château, was built in 1930 for the director of the nearby Brattleboro Retreat. There are five guest rooms, each with phone, TV, and private bath, one with a whirlpool bath and fireplace, one a suite with a gas fireplace and garden views. Common space includes a sunny living room and a bar. We would request one of the rear rooms overlooking the gardens, away from Rt. 5 (Putney Rd.), but front rooms are air-conditioned so noise is muted. Common space is plentiful and attractive, and landscaped grounds border the West River. $156–299 includes a two-course full breakfast, snacks, and beverages.

The One Cat (802-579-1905; theonecat vermont.com), 34 Clark St. There's nothing fancy but plenty of comfort and warmth to this new B&B a short walk from downtown shops. Pat and her Brit hubbie, Conrad, at present have one big, bright guest room (named Brighton for the place they met) and two cats. The

WINDHAM HILL INN, WEST TOWNSHEND
Christina Tree

bath is private but down the hall. Rates include a full English breakfast, served in the library, which doubles as a private bath. $125–165 also includes tax.

In Putney 05346

🐾 ♂ **Hickory Ridge House** (802-387-5709; 800-380-9218; hickoryridgehouse.com), 53 Hickory Ridge Rd. south. An 1808 brick mansion, complete with Palladian window, set on 12 acres with walking/cross-country ski trails. Gillian and Dennis Petit offer six softly, authentically colored guest rooms in the inn. Pets and children are welcome in the neighboring cottage, available either as two rooms or together. Inn rooms come with and without gas fireplace, but all have private bath, phone, and TV/VCR. The original Federal-era bedrooms are large and there's an upstairs sitting room. The cottage consists of a room and a separate suite with its own living room and kitchen; it can also be rented as a whole ($395–525). A swimming hole lies within walking distance, and cross-country touring trails are out the back door. $175–245 per couple includes a full breakfast.

♂ **Ranney-Crawford House** (802-387-4150; 800-731-5502; ranney-crawford.com), 1097 Westminster West Rd. Another handsome brick Federal (1810) homestead on a quiet country road, surrounded by fields. Innkeeper Arnie Glim is an enthusiastic bicyclist who knows all the local possibilities for both touring and

HICKORY RIDGE HOUSE IN PUTNEY

Christina Tree

mountain biking. Four attractive guest rooms—two spacious front rooms with hearth, along with two smaller back rooms, all with private bath—are $170–200, including a three-course breakfast served in the formal dining room.

In Guilford 05301

✪ ♂ **Green River Bridge House** (802-257-5771; 800-528-1861; greenriverbridgehouse .com), 2435 Stage Rd., Green River. Technically just 7 miles south of Brattleboro, this 1830s house is one of the most remote-feeling and peaceful places to stay in Vermont. It's tucked into the slope just above the Green River and a covered bridge that connects Vermont's southeasternmost village with Bernardston, Massachusetts. There's a waterfall (you can sit in) just above the bridge and landscaped grounds below the house along the river. Longtime host Joan Seymour has totally renovated the house, filling it with whimsical touches, like a former confessional repurposed as the reception window and specially designed ceilings to display her collection of crystal chandeliers. Amenities range from Jacuzzis to hair dryers; there's a guest pantry. There are three guest rooms with private bath. It's lovely to hear the river from your bed and to walk or run along the dirt road. Gardens and lawn stretch back along the river, with a "meditation garden," a venue for weddings. $175–235 per couple includes a full breakfast, organic by prearrangement. Inquire about spa services.

In the West River Valley (listed geographically along Route 30)

✪ **Gillian's Guest House** (802-365-7215; gilliansguesthouse.com), 505 Rt. 30, Newfane 05345. Gillian and Jack Winner are longtime innkeepers who have "retired" to this comfortable old house in which they continue to host guests. The three rooms share two baths; two have a double bed, and the third offers a single with a trundle as well. Guests have their own entrance and sitting room. $95 double, $55 single includes a full breakfast; more in foliage season. Jack is a long-established antiques dealer (see *Selective Shopping*), and the Winners are a font of information about the area.

✪ **Fieldstone Lodge** (802-365-0265; 866-771-3585; fieldstonelodgevt.com), 51 West St., Newfane 05345. Hidden away off across Smith Brook from Newfane's West Street, this is a handsome, 1930s Adirondack-style shingle lodge with a massive fieldstone hearth in its amazing, art-hung, open-timbered common room. Veteran innkeepers Bob and Gary have raised the profile of this sleeper, spiffing up the three appealing guest rooms ($150–175) and their

Christina Tree

GREEN RIVER BRIDGE HOUSE

baths and the two cottages. Squirrel Cottage with two bedrooms (sleeping four to six), an inviting common room with woodstove, and full kitchen, is a real beauty ($300 per night). Walk to the village and jump from the grounds into a popular swimming hole in the brook.

☙ **West River Inn** (802-365-7745; westriver lodge.com), 117 Hill Rd., Brookline 05435. With its big red barn and white, black-shuttered farmhouse, this is a classic country B&B, just enough off the beaten track to feel like the find it is. The Kaisers bring new energy to this comfortable old place, keeping the antiques but adding a king bed in one of the eight rooms (the rest are queens and twins) and replacing the ubiquitous horse pictures left from years as a horse farm. There are now six resident dogs. $80–110 per couple, more in foliage—some shared baths, some private. Rates include a full breakfast.

✪ ✿ **Boardman House** (802-365-4086; 888-366-7182), village green, Townshend 05353. We like the friendly feel of this 1840s Greek Revival house tucked into a quiet (away from Rt. 30 traffic) corner of one of Vermont's standout commons. Sarah Messenger and Paul Webber offer four attractive guest rooms (one can be a suite) with private bath. There's also a two-bedroom suite, a parlor, and an old-fashioned kitchen. Breakfast usually includes fresh fruit compote and oven-warm muffins with a creative main dish. $80 for rooms, $120 for a suite sleeping four. The couple volunteer in Tanzania each summer and sell Tanzanian jewelry, art, and fabric.

✿ **Ranney Brook Farm** (802-874-4589; ranneybrookfarm.com), P.O. Box 1108, West Townshend 05359. Set back from Rt. 30 in wooded grounds, this comfortable old red farmhouse is just up the road from boating and swimming at Townshend Dam. It's an informal, relaxing place with a piano in the den, a "great room" in the rear (a former 1790s barn), and a cheerful dining room in which a full breakfast is served family-style. Residents include a dog, two cats, and a parrot. The four rooms are upstairs; two have private bath. Diana Wichland is innkeeper. $70–80 (no surcharge for foliage season).

Olde Farmhouse B&B (802-365-4704; olde farmhouse.net), 1169 Grafton Rd. (Rt. 35), Townshend 05353. A vintage-1790 roadside farmhouse on 15 acres with wide pumpkin floors, three guest rooms with queen beds and handmade quilts, private baths. There's a fireplace in the living room and birds to watch at the feeders. A full breakfast is included in $95 per room.

✪ ♂ ✿ **Jamaica House Bed and Breakfast** (802-874-4620; jamaica-house.com), 3849 Rt. 30, Jamaica 05343. Built in 1814 as the village hotel, this handsome clapboard building has been thoroughly renovated by Valerie and David Heisler. There are three large, cheerful, antiques-furnished second-floor guest rooms with bath, one with an adjoining second room that works for families. The pleasant living room offers a TV, books, games, and DVDs; there's a fridge for guest use. $145–175 per room, $195–225 for the suite, includes continental breakfast served at small tables either in the original tavern, on the front porch, or in the outside garden. Appropriate for weddings up to 40 people. The Heislers are warm hosts and knowledgeable about the area's back-road bike routes as well as more obvious attractions.

Stone Boat Farm Bed and Breakfast (802-297-9929; stoneboatfarm.com), 7240 Rt. 30, Jamaica 05343. This roadside B&B is particularly popular in winter, probably the reason its four units are named for the four nearby ski areas (Mount Snow, Stratton, Magic, and Bromley). The building dates in part to the early 19th century and for a while was a sawmill used to build "stoneboats"—sleds used for hauling rocks. Joseph and Jeffrey have transformed this longtime motel into something more, especially in summer when their extensive flower gardens are in bloom and walking trails lead down through the property to the river. In winter cross-country skis and snowshoes are available. $135–150 per night.

♂ **Cold Moon Farm** (802-988-0775; cold moonfarm.com), 251 Pratt Bridge Rd., Jamaica 05343. This is not your typical Vermont farm or B&B. High on a wooded back road a few miles from Stratton, it's Irene and Ed Glazer's contemporary-style dream home, one with guest rooms (private baths) and plenty of space to relax. Brooklyn born and bred, the Glazers are now enthusiastic farmers who delight in introducing guests to their goats, chickens, and veggie garden. Irene is also a professional bread maker. Amenities include a pool table and hot tub; breakfast features freshly laid eggs. $200–300 per night.

OTHER LODGING 🐾 🐈 🐕 **Colonial Motel & Spa** (802-257-7733; 800-239-0032; colonial motelspa.com), 0.5 mile south of the I-91, Exit 3 roundabout at Putney Rd., Brattleboro 05301. A 70-room (with phones) motel, family owned and geared, with a 75-foot heated lap pool in a glass greenhouse. There's an indoor Jacuzzi and outdoor hot tub and pool. $69–189. Restaurant on premises.

CAMPGROUNDS See *Green Space* for information on camping in Fort Dummer State Park.

✳ Where to Eat

DINING OUT

In Brattleboro

✪ **T. J. Buckley's** (802-257-4922;), 132 Elliot St. Open Wed.–Sun. 6–9. Reservations suggested. From the outside this small (eight tables) but classic red-and-black 1920s Worcester diner looks unpromising, even battered. Inside, fresh flowers and mismatched settings (gathered from yard sales) brighten the tables, walls are oak paneled, and chef-owner Michael Fuller prepares the night's fish, fowl, and beef (vegetarian is also possible) in the open kitchen behind the counter. Fuller buys all produce locally, and what's offered depends on what's available: The menu might include roasted local rabbit or bluefin tuna with roasted lobster stock accompanied by a risotto with ginger-pheasant stock. The $40 entrée includes salad; appetizer and dessert are extra.

🐾 **Peter Havens** (802-257-3333), 32 Elliot St. Open from 6 PM Tues.–Sat. Just 10 tables in this nifty restaurant decorated with splashy artwork, and with an inspired menu to match. The ownership—but not the quality—has recently changed. The menu might include wild Maine mussels steamed in white wine and honey-brined pork chop, grilled and finished with a rosemary-apricot gastrique. Daily specials always include fresh seafood. Entrées $28–32, including salad.

duo (802-254-4141; duorestaurants.com), 136 Main St. Open (except Tues.) for dinner from 5, brunch Sat., Sun. Duo seems equal to its star spot at the heart of downtown in newly renovated Brooks House. Not exactly a chain, it's the second of two; the other has been a 10-year hit in Denver, cited among the country's best farm-to-table restaurants. Here the locally sourced menu might include fennel lamb meatballs with braised greens, ratatouille, and pistachio picada ($22), or braised rabbit with kale, corn, and cherry tomatoes ($18).

✪ 🐾 **Three Stones Restaurant** (802-246-1035; 3stonesrestaurant.com), 105 Canal St. Reservations (by phone only) recommended. Open Wed.–Sat. 5–9. Who knew that a former diner styling itself a "Mexican Mayan Cocina" would be so crowded on a winter Wednesday night? Luckily there was room at the bar (beer and wine)! The attractive interior space and menu are limited. No guacamole or Tex-Mex, rather this is simple, fresh, and authentic fare from the Yucatán. The name is from the three stones on which Mayan Indians still place their outdoor cooking griddle with a fire underneath. A choice of tortillas, tamales, and empanadas come with rice, beans, greens, and fresh-made salsa. The specialty is pumpkin seed "onzicil," topped with sautéed zucchini and smothered in a tomato pumpkin seed salsa ($13). For dessert try the Boca Negra, a chocolate delicacy with a hint of chili pepper. Beer and wine are served. Chef and co-owner Mucuy Bolles comes by her culinary enthusiasm and skill from her Mayan mother. Entrées $12–15.

In Putney

The Gleanery (802-387-3052; thegleanery .com), 133 Main St. Open for dinner Wed.–Sat. A middle-of-village organic farm-source menu that might include braised veal with nutmeg-roasted cauliflower, onion-raisin couscous, and grilled fennel ($27); or grilled pea and oyster mushroom risotto, chèvre, roasted winter squash, and broccoli rabe ($26). Also open for lunch 11:30-2 daily, see *Eating Out*.

Along Route 30

♂ ♿ **Four Columns Inn** (802-365-7713), Newfane. Reopening under new ownership in May 2015.

Windham Hill Inn (802-874-4080; 800-944-4080; windhamhill.com), West Townshend. The attractive, candlelit dining room, overlooking a pond, is open to the public for dinner (6–8:30) by reservation. On a summer night you might begin with inn-smoked duck breast with garden rhubarb, then dine on braised short rib, parsnip puree, roasted beets, and wilted greens; entrées are $27–35. A tasting menu with paired wines is $88. Wines are extra.

Three Mountain Inn (802-874-4140), Rt. 30, Jamaica Village. Open by reservation. Candlelit

THE MARINA RESTAURANT IN BRATTLEBORO

dinner is served in front of the fireplaces in the two small dining rooms of this 18th-century village house. It's a $55 prix fixe menu with an amuse bouche; starters that might include Vermont cheddar and ale sole or a grilled wild boar chop; a mixed salad; and a choice of five entrées, maybe crab-stuffed locally raised chicken breast, pan-seared ahi tuna, or a roasted root vegetable risotto with Vermont Alpine cheese.

🍴 **Asta L'Auberge du Village** (802-874-8000), 3894 Main St. (Rt. 30), Jamaica. Open by reservation for dinner; usually open weekends. Chef-owner Michel de Preux hails from the Swiss canton of Valais and has a sure touch with everything he prepares, from chicken Provençal, roast half duckling à l'orange (finished with Grand Marnier and green peppercorn sauce), and choucroute garnie to a choice of Wiener schnitzels and gnocchis. Entrées come with a choice of authentic rosti or spaetzle as well as freshly baked bread. The ambience is warm. $25–38 includes salad and sides. Wine and beer.

EATING OUT

In Brattleboro

✪ 🍴 ♪ **The Marina Restaurant** (802-257-7563; vermontmarina.com), Rt. 5 just north of the West River bridge. Open year-round, daily 11:30–10; Sunday brunch 10–1, dinner till 9. Sited at the confluence of the West and Connecticut Rivers, this place is bigger and better than ever, totally rebuilt with windows to maximize the view as well as seasonal patio and dockside tables. The reasonably priced menu includes plenty of seafood and vegetarian choices at both lunch and dinner, but also burgers. Full liquor license. A great place to enjoy a margarita while watching the sunset. Many lunch salads as well as a standout Middle East

plate for summer lunches, also pizzas, pastas, fried clams, and sandwiches. Dinner favorites include New York strip steak and broiled sea scallops. Sunday brunch buffet. Full bar, 12 draft beers, good wine list.

✪ 🍴 **Amy's Bakery Arts Café** (802-251-1071), 113 Main St. A great lunch spot. There are river views from tables in the back of this attractive storefront café, and the food is as good as can be: hot sandwiches such as Vermont croque monsieur, fresh salads including Niçoise and Cobb, daily soups, and sandwiches such as chicken salad du jour and hummus and avocado on fresh-baked bread. Worth the line.

(((•))) **Whetstone Station Restaurant & Brewery** (802-490-2354; whetstonestation.com), 36 Bridge St. Open daily for lunch and dinner. A large, welcoming fish-and-chips kind of menu and pub atmosphere with a fireplace, a long bar facing out on the river, a rooftop "Biergarten" in summer, and 17 beers on tap featuring local brews.

✪ **Flat Street Pub** (802-257-1911), 6 Flat St. Open from 4 PM. Where the locals go to get away from the tourists at Whetstone Station. Casual, friendly atmosphere with 18 to 20 beers on tap, blackboard specials like Guinness stew, and the best burgers in town.

✪ ♪ (((•))) **Superfresh! Organic Café** (802-579-1751; superfreshcafe.com), 30 Main St. Open Mon.–Wed. 9–3; Thurs., Fri. 9 AM–10 PM; Sat. 10–10; Sun. 10–9. A vegetarian's delight with many gluten-free options, from breakfast hash browns served over a bed of greens, topped with pumpkin seeds and seasonal produce, to

WHETSTONE STATION RESTAURANT & BREWERY

pizzas with a "raw" grain-free/nut-free crust made from zucchini, soaked pumpkin, and more. We had a great salad here in the colorful dining area overlooking the Whetstone Brook. Children's menu.

♣ ♪ **Top of the Hill Grill** (802-258-9178), 632 Putney Rd. Open mid-Apr.–Oct., 11–9. You have to be looking for this unusual BBQ place. It comes up fast just north of the bridge as you head north on Rt. 5 out of town. You order, get a card, take in the view of the river and "Retreat Meadows," and sit at a picnic table or in the screened deckhouse (muffling traffic noise, including restrooms) until your card is called (could be the Queen of Hearts). Indiana-born Jonathan Julian hickory-smokes his brisket and pork ribs, and apple-smokes his turkey. He also makes corn bread and coleslaw from scratch. You can get a tempeh burger, Cajun dishes, a salad, or a hot dog, too. Sides include red beans and rice, garden greens, and garlic-rosemary potatoes.

♪ **Fireworks** (802-254-2073; fireworks restaurant.net), 73 Main St. Open for dinner nightly, bar open late. Handy to the Latchis Theater for a great pizza after a movie or before a live performance. Pastas, burgers, and delicacies like miso-roasted salmon are also available. Children's menu.

Milagros Mexican Kitchen (802-251-8226), 97 Main St. The latest venture by Fireworks owner Chef Blau, a bright, casual, and very popular restaurant with a wide choice of well-spiced tacos, tortillas, and burritos with unusual combinations. Place your order and bus your table.

Shin La Restaurant (802-257-5226), 57–61 Main St. Open 11–9, closed Sun. Yi Soon Kim is the dynamo behind Vermont's only devoted Korean restaurant, really a standout that has evolved over its years at this storefront. It's known for homemade soups, dumplings, and kimchi among other Korean fare. Want Japanese instead? There's a sushi bar, too.

Back Side Cafe (802-257-5056), Harmony parking lot. Open weekdays for breakfast and lunch until 3; first Fridays for dinner; Sunday brunch. A great place for breakfast if you like an omelet with lots of fresh garlic or homemade salsa. Lunch features homemade soups, salads, deli sandwiches, and bagels; dinner runs from burgers to roast chicken, with a full bar featuring Vermont beers. Brunch both Sat. and Sun.

((ψ)) **Tulip** (802-490-2061), 12 Harmony Place. Open weekdays 7–5, weekends 9–5. A pleasant, laid-back lunch spot with well-spaced tables. Order from the menu or a blackboard listing specials and wait—not long—to be called. On a

summer day the sliced avocado salad with snow peas, feta, and greens hit the spot.

Brattleboro Food Co-op (802-257-0236), 2 Main St., Brookside Plaza. Open Mon.–Sat. 8–9, Sun. 9–9. An outstanding natural food market and deli, newly rebuilt, worth checking out for its stellar choice of Vermont cheeses—but while you're there, take advantage of the Café and Juice Bar featuring creative smoothies, first-rate sandwiches, and salads.

Thai Bamboo (802-251-1010; thaibamboovt .com), 7 High St. Open daily for lunch (11:30–3) and dinner (5–10). Sign of the times! This is genuine Thai. Try deep-fried fish cakes served with cucumber sauce topped with crushed peanuts, followed by a wide choice of hot curries or stir-fried duck with black mushrooms and veggies. Wine and beer are served.

EATING OUT BEYOND BRATTLEBORO

In and around Putney

JD McCliment's Pub (802-387-4499; jd mcclimentspub.com), 26 Bellows Falls Rd. (Rt. 5, just north of the village). Open Tues.–Sat. 5–midnight. Cozy in cool weather with pure pub atmosphere, a piano and fireplace, and an upstairs with booths. In summer there's a large deck, a great spot with umbrella-shaded tables. There's a house root beer as well as a choice of brews on tap, classic pub grub, flatbread pizza, summer dinner salads, and veggie options.

The Gleanery (802-387-3052; thegleanery .com), 133 Main St. Hours vary with the season. The trendy newcomer to town, good kimchi with black rice, flatbread with sausage, corn puree, basil, Swiss cheese, greens, and caramelized onions. Also see the dinner write-up under *Dining Out*.

❂ ♣ ♪ **Putney Diner** (802-387-5433), Main St. Open 6 AM–3 PM daily. Another pleasant option in the middle of Putney Village. Good for corned beef hash or kielbasa and eggs, gravy and hand-cut fries, grilled liver and onions, and juicy big burgers. Children's menu.

♪ **Curtis' Barbeque** (802-387-5474). Summer through fall, Wed.–Sun. 10–dusk. Follow your nose to the blue school bus parked behind the Mobil station on Rt. 5 in Putney, just off I-91, Exit 4. Curtis Tuff and his family cook up pork ribs and chicken, seasoned with his secret barbecue sauce; also foil-wrapped potatoes, grilled corn, and beans flavored with Vermont maple syrup. There are picnic tables and a weatherproofed pavilion.

Putney Food Co-op (802-387-5866), Rt. 5 just south of the village. Open for lunch at 11. This is a great, quick lunch stop at a supermarket-

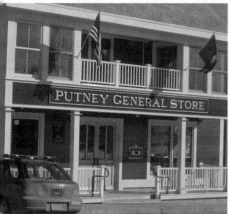
Christina Tree

THE NEW PUTNEY GENERAL STORE IS BACK IN BUSINESS WITH AN ELEVATOR

sized cooperative with a pleasant café area: daily soups, salads, and deli.

Putney Village Pizza (802-387-2203), 84 Main St. These are Turkish-style pies, handmade by Erhan Oge and Tugce Okumus with all the toppings; also Turkish plates like ezme, grilled eggplant, lentil soup, shish kebab wrap, and kofte wrap (grilled Turkish meatballs with grilled tomatoes and chopped red onion wrapped in pita bread). Subs, salads, and pastas; beer and wine available.

(☂) **Putney General Store** (802-387-4692; putneygeneralstore.com), 4 Kimball Hill Rd. Open 7 AM–9 PM. Looking much as it always has, this red-clapboard landmark was actually rebuilt from scratch after it burned to the ground in 2009. It had been rehabbed after a fire the previous year. It remains the village center, more than ever given the serious deli and blackboard menu, Mocha Joe coffees, and plenty of seating. Upstairs (there's an elevator!) owner Jim Heal presides over a full-service pharmacy.

Along Route 9 west

⚘ **Chelsea Royal Diner** (802-254-8399; chelsearoyaldiner.com), 487 Marlboro Rd. (Rt. 9), West Brattleboro. Open 6 AM–9 PM. A genuine '30s diner that's been moved a few miles west of its original site (it's a mile west of I-91, Exit 2). Plenty of parking and diner decor. Serving breakfast all day as part of a big menu that includes pizza, burgers, platters, daily blue plate specials, and great ice cream.

Vermont Country Deli (802-257-9254), 436 Western Ave. Open 7–7. A great to-go deli, full stock of Vermont specialty foods.

◆ (☂) **Guilford Country Store** (802-490-2233; guilfordcountrystore.com), 475 Coolidge Hwy., Guilford. Open 7–7, Sat. 7:30–6, Sun. 8–5. There's a saga to this attractive oasis at the center of one of Vermont's southernmost towns—which was briefly, in 1817, the year the store originally opened, the most populated in Vermont. Check out the store's framed history back in the sunny café section. Chef-owner Marc Tessitore tells us that the windows were boarded and hidden with grocery shelves until this historic landmark was totally but oh so carefully renovated and reopened in 2013. That took four painful years as the community raised the funding. Now it's once more the hub of this rural community, good for all three meals—breakfast off the grill and then exceptional deli offerings, as locally sourced as possible, until closing. Plenty of WiFi users in between.

Along Route 30

◆ **Newfane Creamery Café** (802-365-4442), 550 Rt. 30, south of Newfane Village. Open except Mon. 7–7, later Fri., Sat. for thin-crust pizzas. Nothing here is what you expect: It's all far more imaginative and tasty. The printed menu lists specialty panini, sandwiches, and prepared foods such as the "tortilla critter" we feasted on: layers of tortillas, onions, peppers, corn, black beans, cheese, and salsa. Yum! Everything comes with mixed greens. Beer and wine.

Rick's Tavern (802-365-4310), 386 Rt. 30 south of Newfane Village. Open except Tues. for lunch and dinner, live jazz Thurs., and

GUILFORD COUNTRY STORE

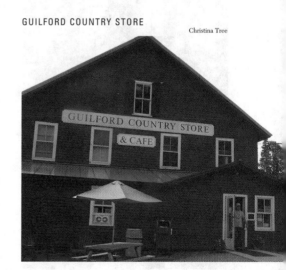
Christina Tree

acoustic music Sat. night. The bar was built around 1890 in Bismarck, North Dakota, but the draft beers are Vermont microbrews. Daily blackboard specials, pizza, homemade desserts.

Williamsville Eatery (802-365-9600; williamsvilleeatery.com), 26 Dover Rd., Williamsville. Currently open for dinner Fri. and Sat. 5–10:30, but expanded hours are promised. This vintage-1828 village store is once more open, serving craft beers and small vineyard wines, locally sourced food. It's an open kitchen and open feel, just far enough off the main drag.

West Townshend Country Store & Café (802-874-4800; westtownshend.org), 6573 Rt. 30, West Townshend. Open daily 7–7. Built originally in 1848, this store stood at the center of an otherwise vanished village and still retained a post office, but nothing else, in 2012 when a local community group began renovating it. To help finance the renovations they built a clay oven beside it for Friday-night pizza parties; the local farmers market set up beside it on Fridays as well, 4–7. A thrift store, opened upstairs, also helped finance the project. Check out the café, hung with local art, good for locally sourced breakfast through lunch and on, all day. Frequent music.

♥ ⌘ **The Townshend Dam Diner** (802-874-4107), Rt. 30, 2 miles north of the Townshend Dam. Open daily except Tues. 5 AM–8 PM. Breakfast all day. There's a big U-shaped

MOCHA MORNING, A LINOCUT PRINT
William Hays

counter and plenty of table seating, the greenery is genuine, and the waitresses are friendly. Specialties include homemade French toast, home fries, muffins and biscuits, the "best dam chili," soups, and bison burgers (from the nearby East Hill Bison Farm). Dinner staples include roast turkey, spaghetti, and garlic bread; daily specials. Peanut butter and jelly comes with chips and pickle.

D&K's Jamaica Grocery (802-874-4151; dks jamaicavermont.com), 3816 Rt. 30, Jamaica. Open daily 7 AM–8 PM. Dale and Karen Ameden's friendly, genuine old-fashioned country store is the heart of Jamaica Village, source of sandwiches and salads for picnics in Jamaica State Park, also soups and hot food, pastries (including breakfast sandwiches), and wines. In 2008 "D&K" bought back this store that they had sold in 1990 but missed almost immediately.

BREWS ✪ ⸘ **Mocha Joe's Coffee House and Coffees Roasters** (802-257-7794), 82 Main St., Brattleboro. Open daily weekdays from 7 AM, 7:30 on weekends, until 8 PM weekdays, 9:30 Fri. and Sat. There's a funky, friendly feel to this basement-level landmark that's a must-stop in town. The coffee that's been roasted here for more than 20 years is now sold throughout the country, but this original Mocha Joe's remains its own place. The free-trade, certified-organic coffee itself—from espressos to pumpkin spice lattes—is the best. Worth a wait in line. Chai, hot chocolate, and more also served, along with pastries, light food. Check out the Mocha Joe's espresso bar at the Putney General Store.

Hermit Thrush Brewery (802-892-0258; hermitthrushbrewery.com), 28 High St., Brattleboro. Belgian-inspired ales brewed using green technology and aged in oak casks. Tours and tastings.

McNeill's Brewery (802-254-2553), 90 Elliot St., Brattleboro. Open at 4 PM Mon.–Thurs., 2–2 Fri., and 1 PM–2 AM Sat., Sun. This brewery was once the town firehouse/offices/police station/jail. Ray McNeill was working on a graduate degree in music when he decided to focus instead on his second passion. Dark and pubby, hung with art; mixed reviews but not for the quality of the brews. A dozen are usually on tap.

Also see **Flat Street Pub** under *Eating Out*.

WINE & SPIRITS Putney Mountain Winery (802-387-5925; putneywine.com). Winery and tasting room inside Basketville, 8 Bellows Falls Rd. (Rt. 5), 11–5 daily. Music professor and composer Charles Dodge has established a

Christina Tree

SAXTONS RIVER DISTILLERY, BRATTLEBORO

reputation for the quality of his sparkling fruit wines.

Saxtons River Distillery (802-246-1128; saplingliqueur.com), 485 West River Rd. (Rt. 30), Brattleboro. Open for tastings 9–5 Mon.–Fri., 10–5 Sat., Sun. Christian Stromberg's family fled Lithuania in 1906, bringing with them the family tradition of crafting fine liqueurs, including maple bourbon and rye. Stromberg's Sapling maple syrup liqueur garnered a gold medal at the 2011 World Spirits Competition. His newest venture is a coffee liqueur.

CHEESE 🧀 **Grafton Village Cheese** (802-254-2201; graftonvillagecheese.com), 400 Linden St., Brattleboro. Open Mon.–Sat. 10–6, Sun. 10–5. This large facility for the Grafton-based cheese company is beside the Retreat Farm (see *For Families*) at the beginning of Rt. 30. It's a must-stop. While the store features its own handcrafted cheeses, more than 80 varieties are available, along with Vermont microbrews, fresh bread, and Vermont specialty foods and gifts. Cheesemaking can be viewed and samples are offered.

✳ Entertainment

The Latchis Theater (802-254-6300; latchis .com), 50 Main St., Brattleboro, shows first-run and art films, also the Metropolitan Opera in HD plus concerts and live performances. For film buffs, this 900-seat art deco movie house with three screens is itself a destination. Apollo still drives his chariot through the firmament on the ceiling; walls are graced with Doric columns, and the lobby floor bears the zodiac signs in multicolored terrazzo. Along with the Latchis Hotel in which it's housed, the theater is owned by the Brattleboro Arts Initiative; there's also an art gallery.

🎭 **New England Youth Theatre** (802-246-6398; neyt.org), 100 Flat St., Brattleboro. Fabulous year-round productions of children's and all-time classics in a beautiful new theater. New England Youth Theatre is a state-of-the-art acting school for children ages 6–18; its performance space seats 125. Theater, music, dance, and circus performances occur frequently at this and other venues in the Brattleboro area. Not just the actors but the set builders, costumers, stage managers, and technicians in the light and sound booth are youths. Check the website for current productions.

Hooker-Dunham Theater (802-254-9276; hookerdunham.org), 139 Main St., Brattleboro. Check out what's going on at this middle-of-town venue: theater, music, classic films, and lectures.

Whittemore Theater and other performance venues at Marlboro College (802-257-4333; marlboro.edu), in Marlboro Village (10 miles west of Brattleboro) are the setting for frequent presentations.

The New England Center for Circus Arts (802-254-9780; necenterforcircusarts.org), 74 Cotton Mill Hill, #300, Brattleboro. A full program of circus arts is offered year-round in the Cotton Mill; check the website for performances.

Brattleboro Music Center (802-257-4523; bmcvt.org), 38 Walnut St., Brattleboro. Housed in a former convent, this burgeoning music school sponsors a wide variety of local musical events and festivals as well as a fall-through-spring Chamber Music Series.

Vermont Jazz Center (802-254-9088; vtjazz .org), 72 Cotton Mill Hill, Studio 222, S. Main St., Brattleboro, stages frequent musical, vocal, and jazz happenings.

Friends of Music at Guilford (802-254-3600; fomag.org), 39 Church Dr., Guilford. A series of concerts throughout the year at various locations. Note the free Labor Day weekend concerts under *Special Events*.

Actors Theatre Playhouse (877-233-7905; actorsplay.org), corner of Brook and Main Sts., West Chesterfield, NH. Ten minutes from Brattleboro, seasonal performances, reasonably priced. With a diverse variety of plays and exceptional performances by local actors, this is not your run-of-the-mill community theater.

In Putney

Sandglass Theater (802-387-4051; sandglass theater.org), Kimball Hill. A resident theater company performs original work combining live theater with puppetry performances. When not

Marlboro Music, Persons Auditorium, Marlboro College (marlboromusic.org), 10 miles west of Brattleboro off Rt. 9. This internationally famous series of chamber music concerts has been performed Fri.–Sun., mid-July–mid-Aug., since 1951. The festival is a seven-week gathering of 70 or so world-class musicians who come to work together. It is held on this rural campus because Rudolf Serkin, one of its founders, owned a nearby farm. Pablo Casals came every year from 1960 to 1973. Some concerts are sold out in advance, but you can frequently find good seats before the performance (chairs are metal, and regulars bring cushions). There are (almost) always bargain-priced seats in the tent just outside the auditorium's sliding glass doors (tickets are $15–37.50, with last-minute, unsold seats $5).

on tour they perform in a 60-seat renovated barn theater in Putney Village.

Yellow Barn Music Festival (802-387-6637; yellowbarn.org), 63 Main St. Begun in 1969, this is a center for chamber music study and performance presenting a series of chamber music concerts in July and early Aug. Most are staged in a 150-seat, air-conditioned barn just north of the Putney Co-op in Putney Village. Artists include both well-known professionals and students chosen each summer from leading conservatories.

Next Stage Arts Project (nextstagearts.org), 15 Kimball Hill. A former 1841 Congregational church owned by the Putney Historical Society is now the home of the 160-seat **Next Stage Theater**, a year-round performing arts center with a full schedule of classical and folk/rock music as well as as well as film (**Next Stage Cinema**).

✴ Selective Shopping

ANTIQUES Twice Upon a Time (802-254-2261; twicetime.com), 63 Main St., Brattleboro. Open Mon.–Wed. 10–6, Thurs.–Sat. 10–7, Sun. 11–6. "I always wanted a consignment shop that would be able to display anything that anyone wanted to give me," says Randi Crouse, proprietor of this shop that now fills the entire three-level space created in 1906 for the E. J. Fenton Department Store. In the '50s it was chopped into smaller storefronts, but the two-story-high Corinthian columns, bubble glass, and wooden gallery are back, a setting for clothing, antique furniture, and furnishings. The markdown schedule is patterned on that of the late Filene's Basement. More than 100 dealers and thousands of consigners.

Jack Winner Antiques (802-365-7215; winnerantiques.com), Rt. 30, Newfane. Open Thurs.–Mon. 10–5. Specializing for over 30 years in 18th- and 19th-century formal and country furniture, equestrian antiques, Spode china, brass, and hunting prints.

Townshend Auction Gallery (802-365-4388), Rt. 30, Townshend. Over 30 years Kit Martin and Art Monette have established a solid reputation for their frequent auctions, usually Sat. mornings. Previews Fri.

Newfane Flea Market, Rt. 30 north of Newfane Village. Sundays, May–Oct.; assorted junk and treasure.

ART AND CRAFTS GALLERIES *Note:* The first Friday of each month is **Gallery Walk** (gallerywalk.org) in Brattleboro: open house with refreshments and music at dozens of downtown businesses that hang works by local artists and at studios as well as at formal galleries, usually 5:30–8:30.

✪ **Vermont Artisan Designs** (802-257-7044; buyvermontart.com), 106 Main St., Brattleboro. Open daily. Gallery 2 on the second floor displays Vermont's best artists. Special exhibits change with every Gallery Walk (first Fri.), when there are opening receptions with live music. The store's main floor is an outstanding contemporary crafts gallery displaying the well-chosen work of hundreds of artisans. There's also a kitchen store. This was the town's department store when Greg Worden acquired a portion of the space circa 20 years ago to establish the town's first quality gallery.

✪ **Gallery in the Woods** (802-257-4777; galleryinthewoods.com), 145 Main St., Brattleboro. For decades Dante and Suzanne Corsano's gallery has been a standout, featuring folk art, finely crafted furniture, and known painters and artists in a variety of media from throughout the world. Changing exhibits.

Mitchell-Giddings Fine Arts (802-251-8290; mitchellgiddingsfinearts.com), 183 Main St., Brattleboro. Open Wed.–Sun. 11–5. Hidden downstairs below A Candle in the Night, this is a serious contemporary gallery.

✪ **Fulcrum Arts** (802-257-2787; fulcrumarts.com), 485 West River Road (Rt. 30), Brattleboro. Open Mon.–Sat. 10–6. This is a major new gallery in a big blue metal building (formerly a candy-making factory). It combines work and gallery space for two well-established artists, Randi Solin and Natalie Blake, who had neighboring studios in the Cotton Mill and subsequently searched for seven years for a larger, more visible venue. The handsome gallery showcases Solin's colorful glass and Blake's striking tile mosaics as well as work of juried artists in varied media. Glass is blown in the adjoining open hot shop and clay is shaped in an equally open studio at the opposite end of the building. Inquire about workshops.

Artist's Loft Gallery (phone/fax 802-257-5181; theartistsloft.com), 103 Main St., Brattleboro. Realistic landscapes as well as portraits and other worth-checking oils by William Hays.

Vermont Center for Photography (802-251-6051; vcphoto.org), 49 Flat St., Brattleboro. Squirreled back in a corner beside the Transportation Center. Open Fri. 2–7, Sat.–Sun. noon–5. Quality changing exhibits. Worth checking.

In Putney

Note: See putneycrafts.com for an overview of a sampling of resident craftspeople. **The Putney Craft Tour** (putneycrafts.com), held for more than 30 years for three days after Thanksgiving, showcases the work of more than two dozen craftspeople within a dozen miles of Putney.

Brandywine Glassworks (802-387-4032; robertburchglass.com), Fort Hill Rd. (off Rt. 5 north). Visitors are welcome, but call first. Robert Burch, a pioneer in art glass, hand-blows his signature cobalt perfume bottles and vases, veiled with delicate silver bubbles, and amber and ruby swirling paperweights in a 200-year-old barn beside his home. He supplies some 200 shops and galleries across the country and is also a respected teacher of his craft, drawing students regularly from Boston. Seconds are available.

Green Mountain Spinnery (802-387-4528; 800-321-9665; spinnery.com), just off I-91, Exit 4. Open daily. Founded as a cooperative more than 30 years ago and now worker owned, this is a real spinning mill in which undyed, unbleached fibers—alpaca, mohair, wool, and organic cotton—are carded, spun, skeined, and labeled. You can buy the resulting yarn in various plies in natural and dyed colors. Many original patterns are shown in the catalog. The store also carries buttons and knitting supplies. Inquire about guided mill tours.

Dena's Weavings (802-387-2656; vermont weaver.com), 4 Signal Pine Rd. (corner of Westminster West Rd.). Open by chance or appointment. Built as Putney's high school in 1909, this building now houses the Vermont Weaving School (vermontweavingschool.com) with ongoing classes and workshops. Looms and weaving supplies also sold along with woven scarves, shawls, and hats by founder Dena Gartenstein Moses.

West River Valley, along Route 30
Note: See **Fulcrum Arts**—described with Brattleboro galleries because it's technically in Bratt. We recommend beginning here and continuing up Rt. 30.

((ɯ)) **Pots** (802-465-9768; zpots.com), 21 Grassy Brook Rd., Brookline. Open daily 10–6 but call ahead. Noelle and Eric are a husband-and-wife team whose work is internationally known; Eric shapes the pottery and Noelle adds her poetry. Not far off Rt. 30.

Robert DuGrenier Glass Art Gallery (802-365-4400; dugrenier.com), 1096 Rt. 30, Townshend. Open weekdays and most Saturdays 10–5. Robert DuGrenier's work can be seen in custom installations throughout the United States and Europe. The gallery features DuGrenier's glass handblown on site, including colorful glasses and decanters and small seashells; inquire about weekly glassblowing demonstrations.

○ **Elaine Beckwith Gallery** (802-874-7234; beckwithgallery.com), 3923 Rt. 30, Jamaica Village. Open daily (except Tues.) 10–5:30. This is a long-established, destination gallery with a strong contemporary collection, representing some 30 artists in a variety of styles and media, painting, sculpture, and hand-pulled prints.

GREEN MOUNTAIN SPINNERY, PUTNEY
Christina Tree

Superb artist-printmaker Joel Beckwith is also featured. A must for art lovers.

Note: Also check **rockriverartists.com** (802-348-7865 or 802-348-7440) for information about a collective of artists who welcome visitors by appointment any time of year and host an open studio tour in mid-July. The Rock River flows into the West River in Newfane, and most studios are not far off Rt. 30.

Along Route 9, west of Brattleboro

Applewoods Studio & Gallery (802-254-2908), 2802 Rt. 9, Marlboro. Open in summer 10–5 or when the sign is up; also by appointment. This long-established gallery showcases one-of-a-kind vases, bowls, furniture, and much more that's been created from hardwood burls.

Also see **brattleboro-west-arts.com** for artists on back roads off Rt. 9 who host an annual late-September open studio tour.

BOOKSTORES Everyone's Books (802-254-8160; everyonesbks.com), 25 Elliot St., Brattleboro. This is an earnest and interesting alternative bookstore, specializing in women's books; also a great selection of children's and multicultural titles.

Brattleboro Books (802-257-0777), 34 Elliot St., Brattleboro. Open 10–6 daily except Sun. An extensive selection of used and out-of-print books; over 60,000 titles fill a storefront and a basement. Browsing strongly encouraged.

Mystery on Main Street (802-258-2211; mysteryonmain.com), 119 Main St., Brattleboro. Open daily 10–6 except Wed. The Brattleboro area is home to Archer Mayor, Vermont's most

THE ELAINE BECKWITH GALLERY IN JAMAICA
Christina Tree

Christina Tree
EVERYONE'S BOOKS, BRATTLEBORO

famous detective novelist, a fitting home to its first mystery bookstore. Many special events.

Old & New England Books (802-365-7074), 47 West St., Newfane. Open late May–Oct., Fri.–Mon. noon–5; also by appointment. Delightful browsing with an interesting stock of books old and new, cards, and posters.

SPECIAL SHOPS

In Brattleboro

Sam's Outdoor Outfitters (802-254-2933; samsoutfitters.com), 74 Main St. Open daily, varying hours. The business that Sam Borofsky started in 1934 now fills two floors of two buildings with a full stock of hunting, camping, and sports equipment. The big thing is the service—skilled help in selecting the right fishing rod, tennis racket, or gun. There are also name-brand sports clothes and standard army and navy gear. Fishing and hunting licenses, free popcorn.

Delectable Mountain (802-257-4456), 125 Main St. Fine-fabric lovers make pilgrimages to Jan Norris's store, widely known for its selection of fine silks, all-natural imported laces, velvets, cottons, and upholstery jacquards. It also offers a wide selection of unusual buttons.

Borter's Jewelry Studio (802-254-3452; bortersjewelry.com), 103 Main St. Tues.–Fri. noon–5:30, Sat. noon–4, and by appointment. Gemstones; silver and gold jewelry handcrafted into stunning settings on the premises.

Altiplano (802-257-1562), 42 Elliot St. Open daily. The shop features contemporary clothing and other crafted products, some with the store's own widely distributed label, designed in-house but made in Guatemala.

Penelope Wurr (802-387-3915; penelopewurr .com), 167 Main St. Open Thurs.–Sun. noon–5. Known for her own distinctive glass, Wurr now maintains a shop filled with furnishings, crafted items, gifts, and cards, a great place to browse, next door to the Front Porch Café.

Brattleboro Food Co-op (802-257-0236), 2 Main St., Brookside Plaza. Open Mon.–Sat. 8–9, Sun. 9–9; deli and fresh-baked products. Recently rebuilt, better than ever. The cheese counter showcases Vermont cheeses; local produce, grains, wines, and a café.

A Candle in the Night (802-257-0471), 181 Main St. Donna and Larry Simons have built up a vast knowledge as well as inventory of Oriental and other handcrafted rugs over the decades.

Beadniks (802-257-5114), 115 Main St. Beads, baubles, and whimsical wonders.

Turn It Up (802-251-6015; turnitup.com), 2 Elliot St. Open Mon.–Thurs. 10–9, Fri.–Sat. 10–10, Sun. 11–7. Discounted new, rare, and overstock compact discs, records, and more. In-store listening available. Will order for you at no extra charge.

Renaissance Fine Jewelry (802-251-0600), 151 Main St. A handsome shop in a former bank showcasing quality designer and estate jewelry.

The Outlet Center (802-254-4594), 580 Canal St., Exit 1 off I-91. Open daily 9:30–8 except Sun. 10–6. This former factory building that once produced handbags is now an old-fashioned factory outlet center with varied stores worth checking, including Carter's Children's wear and locally based Northeast Mountain Footwear.

In Putney
Basketville (802-387-5509; basketville.com), Rt. 5. Open daily 9–6. Founded by Frank Wilson, an enterprising Yankee trader in the real sense, this is a family-run business. The vast store features woodenware, wicker furniture (filling the entire upstairs), wooden toys, and exquisite artificial flowers as well as traditional baskets and myriad other things, large and small. *Note:* Check out the Columbus Day weekend Basketville Seconds Sale. This is also the venue for Putney Mountain Winery tastings.

FARMS TO VISIT One of the state's concentrations of farms and orchards is here in the Lower Connecticut River Valley, some offering "pick your own," others welcoming visitors to their farm stands, sugaring houses, or barns. Call before coming.

Note: Also see vtfarms.org for details and directions for many of the following.

Robb Family Farm (802-258-9087; robb familyfarm.com), 827 Ames Hill Rd., Brattleboro. This farm has been in the same family since 1907, and visitors are welcomed. The shop here sells the family's maple syrup and maple candies, gift baskets and farm-raised beef.

Olallie Daylily Gardens (802-348-6614; day lilygarden.com), 129 Augur Hole Rd., South Newfane. Open late May–Labor Day. Grass paths crisscross the bed of blooms. Pink irises in mid-June; daylilies June–Sept. Garden shop and potted plant nursery. Inquire about the Daylily Festival.

🌷 **Dutton Berry Farm Stand** (802-365-4168), farm stands at 407 Rt. 30, Newfane, and 308 Rt. 9, West Brattleboro (also Rt. 11, Manchester). Open daily, 9–7 year-round. This is a local institution, showcasing fruit and produce from Paul and Wendy Dutton's orchards and farms in Windham, Dummerston, Newfane, and West Brattleboro. The "stands" (year-round shops) feature their own apples, pears, plums, veggies, maple syrup, and nursery plants; greenhouses produce winter greens, flowers, Christmas trees, PYO, and more.

Hickin's Mountain Mowings Farm (802-254-2146), 1999 Black Mountain Rd., Dummerston. Retail shop open by appointment. "Tickle your pickle palate," Randy Hickin advises. Pickles are his pride. Maple pickles have to be tried to be believed. Jams, jellies, syrup, and (seasonal) fruitcake are also specialties. Marked off the East/West Rd. between Putney and Rt. 30 (see *Scenic Drives*).

Dwight Miller & Son Orchards (802-254-9158), 581 Miller Rd., East Dummerston. Open late Aug.–Sept. One of Vermont's oldest family farms. A retail stand with the farm's own organic fruit and vegetables, preserves, pickles, and syrup; seasonal pick-your-own apples and varied fruit in-season.

🐄 **The Scott Farm** (802-254-6868; scottfarm vermont.com), 707 Kipling Rd., Dummerston. Turn off Rt. 5 at the sign and follow it up beyond the hardtop to this historic 571-acre farm, now owned by The Landmark Trust USA (see the Rudyard Kipling sidebar for lodging on the property). The extensive orchard here produces 90 varieties of apples as well as peaches, plums, pears, cherries, grapes, quince, nectarines, and a variety of berries. The farm stand also carries the farm's heirloom apple cider. Inquire about workshops on how to make everything from peach tarts to hard cider. This is also a popular wedding venue.

Walker Farm (802-254-2051; walkerfarm.com), Rt. 5, Dummerston. A 200-year-old farm and garden center (open mid-Apr.–Thanksgiving, 10–6), specializing in hard-to-find annuals and perennials and garden books by local authors. Jack and Karen Mannix have made this a destination for serious gardeners. Choose from 30 kinds of heirloom peppers and 50 kinds of tomatoes as well as a peerless selection of flowers (30 varieties of pansies and 1,200 other annuals and perennials started from seed, plus 700 other plants nurtured in 17 greenhouses) and a full line of produce June–Thanksgiving, featuring the Mannixes' own organic vegetables and local fruit. Display gardens.

Walker Farm's Elysian Hills Tree Farm (802-257-0233; elysianhillsfarm.com), 209 Knapp Rd., Dummerston. New ownership but Bill and Mary Lou Schmidt still maintain this 100-acre Christmas tree farm. Retail sales of wreaths and ready-cut Christmas trees begin the Saturday after Thanksgiving and end at 4 PM Dec. 24. Inquire about "Tag Days" in the fall.

Green Mountain Orchards (802-387-5851; greenmtorchards.com), 130 West Hill Rd., Putney. Open daily in-season. Pick-your-own apples and blueberries; cider available in-season. Christmas trees, local crafts, and produce also

sold, gift shop, horse-drawn wagon rides on fall weekends, wedding sites.

Harlow's Sugar House (802-387-5852; harlowssugarhouse.com), Rt. 5 north of Putney Village. Open Mar.–late Dec., Harlow's is one of the most visitor-oriented operations. The Sugar House lets you watch maple production in-season, and there's a film and maple museum; the big store sells their own syrup and honey and offers pick-your-own apples, blueberries, and strawberries. The produce stand features a wide variety of apples in-season.

✳ Special Events

Note: **Gallery Walk** (gallerywalk.org) in Brattleboro is the first Friday of every month.

February: **Brattleboro Winter Carnival**, a full week of celebrations, climaxed by the Washington's Birthday cross-country ski race. The annual **Harris Hill Jumping Competition** (harrishillskijump.org) may or may not coincide with the carnival.

May–October: **Brattleboro Farmers Markets**. Saturday is the big day just west of town by the Creamery Bridge. A live band and crafts, as well as produce vendors, are usually on hand.

Strolling of the Heifers (strollingoftheheifers.com). Local educational consultant Orly Munzing had recently witnessed the Running of the Bulls in Pamplona when she conceived the idea of a slower, friendlier version—a parade of heifers and calves led by their owners up Brattleboro's Main Street—as a way of honoring and supporting local farmers. That first parade in 2002 has since expanded into a full weekend (the first in June) of farm-geared events with the Saturday-morning parade leading watchers to a Slow Living Expo on the common—with plenty of live entertainment and events ranging from cooking demonstrations to goat races. Sunday begins with a Farmers Breakfast and features **Tour de Heifer** cycling tours (not races) geared to all abilities, kids included, along with farm tours. Strolling of the Heifers is now nonprofit, based at the River Garden, downtown Brattleboro's weatherproofed public space (see *Guidance*) to which it brings art, volunteers, and a program of weekday brown-bag presentations and performances. Only in Brattleboro?

STROLLING OF THE HEIFERS IS THE FIRST SATURDAY IN JUNE

Jason Henske

Christina Tree

PHOTOGRAPHER CHRIS TRIEBERT IS AMONG
PARTICIPANTS IN THE ROCK RIVER ARTISTS
OPEN STUDIO TOUR.

On Wednesday it's downtown off Main St. at
the Brattleboro Co-op. (The winter farmers
market is held Sat. in the River Garden, Main
St.).

May: **May Day dancing**, Eliot St., Brattleboro.
Memorial Day weekend **open studios**.

✪ *First Saturday of June:* **Strolling of the
Heifers** (strollingoftheheifers.com). See the
sidebar.

Late June: **Annual Strawberry Supper**,
Grange Hall, Dummerston Center.

July–August: **Marlboro Music** in Marlboro.

July 4: A big parade winds through Brattleboro
at 10 AM; games, exhibits, refreshments in Living Memorial Park; fireworks at 9 PM.

Mid-July: **Rock River Artists Open Studio
Tour** (rockriverartists.com)—open studios
sponsored by artists in Williamsville and South
Newfane. **Southern Vermont Dance Festival**, a weekend of performances and classes in
and around Brattleboro.

August: **Free concert** on the Newfane common every Wed. ✪ **Grace Cottage Hospital
Fair Day**—held the first Sat., with exhibits,
booths, games, rides on the green in
Townshend.

September: Labor Day weekend in Guilford is
observed both with the old-style **Guilford Fair**
and with the annual two-day music festival in
Guilford's Organ Barn (802-257-1961). Concerts are free. **Heritage Festival Benefit** in
Newfane, sponsored by the Newfane Congregational Church. **Puppets in the Green Mountains**—every other year, performances by
puppet theaters from near and far in varied ven-

ues, mostly in Brattleboro and Putney
(puppetsinthegreenmountains.com).

Late September: **Annual Tour de Grace**—a
21-mile expert ride from Stratton Mountain
to Grace Cottage Hospital, Townshend. **Townshend Dam Release** at Ball Mountain Dam.
Brattleboro–West Arts Studio Tour
(brattleboro-west-arts.com).

October: The **Newfane Heritage Festival**
(newfaneheritagefestival.org), Columbus Day
weekend—crafts, dancing, raffle, sponsored by
the Newfane Congregational Church.

Mid-October: The **Apple Pie Festival** in Dummerston features hundreds of Dummerston's
famous apple pies, also crafts, at the Dummerston Center Congregational Church and
Grange. The annual **Pumpkin Festival** on the
Townshend common features biggest-pumpkin
and best-pumpkin-pie contests, plenty of vendors, food. **Brattleboro Literary Festival**
(brattleboroliteraryfestival.org) with nationally
known authors.

Late October: **Brattleboro Film Festival**
(brattleborofilmfestival.org), a 10-day extravaganza based at the Latchis Theater.

Thanksgiving weekend: **Putney Craft Tour**
(putneycrafts.com).

Early December: **Christmas Bazaar** on the
common, Newfane. **Community Messiah
Sing** at Centre Congregational Church in Brattleboro. **Cotton Mill Open Studio & Holiday
Sale** (thecottonmill.org) featuring some 50 resident artists, also in Brattleboro.

December 31: **Last Night Celebrations**, Brattleboro. Fun family day and night with fireworks
at the Retreat Meadows about 9 PM.

HOSPITAL FAIR DAY IS THE BIG DAY ON
TOWNSHEND GREEN.

Christina Tree

THE MOUNT SNOW VALLEY

Long before this steep-sided valley drew skiers, summer visitors arrived via the Hoosac Tunnel and Wilmington Railroad, staying in hotels at Sadawga Springs in Whitingham and on Lake Raponda in Wilmington. In the 1890s a number of these urbanites transformed local farms into summer homes. The shingle-style Child's Tavern (now the Crafts Inn, a time-share resort—craftsinn.com), designed by no less an architect than Stanford White, opened in the center of the village of Wilmington in 1902 and soon became part of the "Ideal Tour" through New England, widely promoted for "pleasure driving," promising auto travelers "A First Class Hotel at the End of Each Day's Run."

In the 1920s and '30s cars became affordable (between 1908 and 1927, 15 million Ford Model T's were produced) and ordinary folks began motor touring (ergo "tourists"). In 1938 the 48 miles of Rt. 9 between Brattleboro and Bennington was formally pronounced a scenic driving route, the Molly Stark Trail. It's now an official Vermont Scenic Byway, still named for the wife of the New Hampshire general who traveled this route in August 1777 on his way to defeating the British at the Battle of Bennington.

The compact village of Wilmington sits at the junction of Rts. 9 and 100 north. Site of one of the state's first rural traffic lights, it's midway between Brattleboro (20 miles) and Bennington (21 miles). West Dover, another picturesque village clustered around its church and tavern, is 6 miles north of Wilmington. The intervening stretch of Rt. 100 is now lined with restaurants, lodges, and shops, reflecting the vagaries of the ski industry since 1954, the year Reuben Snow's farm was transformed by ski lifts, trails, and lodges, varying in style from Tyrolean to 1950s futuristic.

Mount Snow is one of Vermont's best family-geared ski resorts, with a loyal following among skiers of all levels. It also deserves credit as one of the pioneering resorts in snowboarding; local Olympian Kelly Clark won the gold in the half-pipe in 2002, the first woman gold medalist in snowboarding in the Winter Olympics. Mount Snow's Carinthia Park (once an independently owned ski area) is now a 100-acre freestylers' domain with eight terrain parks. This is one big mountain with plenty of skiing challenge on its 80 trails and 100 acres of hand-cleared "tree terrain." Wilmington's Devin Logan earned a silver medal at the 2014 Olympics for slope-side skiing.

MOUNT SNOW

Mount Snow

Over the years the ski resort has spawned a large number of condos, many available for rental. More traditional lodging places are scattered along back roads, an unusual number offering dinner as well as breakfast, perhaps because Mount Snow is the most convenient major ski mountain to New York City.

Beyond this narrow corridor, mountains rise on all sides. The village of Dover is a knot of white-clapboard buildings on the crest of a hill. Rt. 100 is heavily forested north to the village of Wardsboro, south to the delightfully

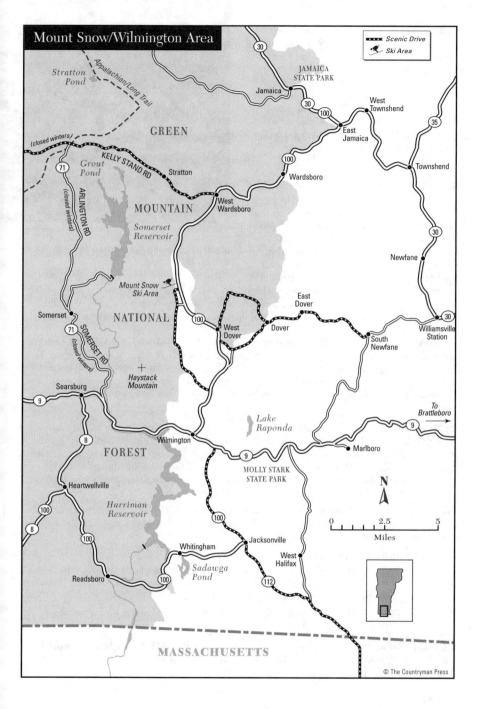

Mount Snow/Wilmington Area

Scenic Drive
Ski Area

Stratton
Pond

Appalachian/Long Trail

JAMAICA
STATE PARK

Jamaica

30

West
Townshend

(closed winters)

GREEN

30

100

East
Jamaica

35

71

Grout
Pond

KELLY STAND RD

Stratton

100

Wardsboro

Townshend

ARLINGTON RD

(closed winters)

MOUNTAIN

West
Wardsboro

Somerset
Reservoir

30

Newfane

Mount Snow
Ski Area

East
Dover

Somerset

NATIONAL

100

West
Dover

Dover

30

Williamsville
Station

71

SOMERSET RD

(closed winters)

South
Newfane

+
Haystack
Mountain

Searsburg

9

Lake
Raponda

To
Brattleboro

9

8

Wilmington

9

Marlboro

FOREST

MOLLY STARK
STATE PARK

N

Heartwellville

0   2.5   5

100

Harriman
Reservoir

100

Miles

8

100

Whitingham

Jacksonville

West
Halifax

Readsboro

100

Sadawga
Pond

112

MASSACHUSETTS

© The Countryman Press

back-roaded towns of Jacksonville and Whitingham, and east to the college town of Marlboro, site of the world-class Marlboro Music Festival in July and August.

The surrounding hills were once lumbered extensively. Two former logging villages actually lie at the bottom of the sizable Harriman and Somerset Reservoirs, which have transformed the Deerfield Valley into one of the most watery parts of Vermont, good for fishing, boating, and swimming as well as hiking and biking.

One of the Vermont regions impacted by 2011's Hurricane Irene, the Mount Snow Valley pulled together as one community, and in the aftermath of the flooding restored and renovated buildings in downtown Wilmington, which probably hasn't looked this good in a century. In summer lodging prices are "off-season." The newly completed 14-mile Valley (recreational) Trail, linking West Dover with Wilmington,

Christina Tree

DOWNTOWN WILMINGTON HAS MADE A DRAMATIC COMEBACK FROM TROPICAL STORM IRENE.

invites walkers and cyclists. Another recent addition, the Zoar Adventure Center, encourages paddling the valley's magnificent lakes and touring their surrounding backcountry on two wheels. At the end of the day you can expect lodging and dining just as "first class" as it was for your 1902 counterparts.

GUIDANCE Mount Snow Valley Chamber of Commerce (802-464-8092; 877-887-6884; visit vermont.com) maintains a major Vermont Information Center on 21 W. Main St. in Wilmington (Rt. 9 west, seven doors from the junction of Rts. 9 and 100). Open seven days a week. Pick up the useful visitors guide. Also check the detailed visitor-geared website **wilmingtoninthemountains.com**, maintained by the Wilmington Downtown Association. It's especially good for events and community news.

GETTING THERE The obvious route to Mount Snow from points south and east is I-91 to Brattleboro, then Rt. 9 to Wilmington. There are also **two scenic shortcuts**: (1) Rt. 30 north from Brattleboro 11.1 miles to the marked turnoff for Dover; follow the road through the covered bridge in South Newfane past Dover to West Dover; (2) turn off I-91 onto Rt. 2 in Greenfield, Massachusetts; follow Rt. 2 for 3.6 miles to Colrain Rd. and proceed 17.3 miles to Jacksonville, where you pick up Rt. 100 into Wilmington (under *Scenic Drives* see this route detailed in reverse).

From New York City: **Adventure Northeast Bus Service** (917-861-1800; adventurenortheast.com) goes in both directions daily during ski season, typically Thanksgiving weekend–Apr. Call/check the website for reservations and timing details.

GETTING AROUND The MOO-ver (802-464-8487; moover.com) is a free community bus service operated by the Deerfield Valley Transit Association (DVTA). It connects points of interest in the valley along Rts. 9 and 100 year-round and offers a Mount Snow shuttle in winter. Look for its Holstein cow logo and check the website for specific routes.

Valley Cab (802-348-7827; valleycabvermont.com). Located in West Dover, at the base of Mount Snow, Valley Cab offers both local and long-distance transportation.

MEDICAL EMERGENCY Emergency service is available by calling **911**. **Brattleboro Memorial Hospital** (802-257-0341; bmhvt.org) in Brattleboro and **Southwestern Vermont Medical Center** (802-447-1536; svhealthcare.org) in Bennington.

To Do

BIKING Mountain Biking at Mount Snow (802-464-6640; mountsnow.com) offers mountain biking clinics, tours, rentals, and maps to its 35 miles of trails, with the Canyon Express lift servicing a portion daily July–mid-Oct., then weekends until Columbus Day weekend. Lift-serviced trails are designed for experienced mountain bikers; the lower loops are geared to novices. Inquire about lodging/biking packages. Check in at Mount Snow Sports.

First Trax Sports Shop (802-464-3464; firsttraxsportsshop.com), 5 Mountain Park Plaza, West Dover. Mountain and road bikes to rent as well as the area's repair center.

BOATING ✪ Both Lake Whitingham (Harriman Reservoir) and Somerset Reservoir are spectacular boating lakes. Smaller bodies of water such as Grout Pond, Lake Raponda, and Sadawga are also excellent for canoeing and kayaking.

Zoar Adventure Center (800-532-7483; zoaradventurecenter.com), 36 Main St., Wilmington on the western edge of the village with access to the Valley Trail and via the river to Lake Whitingham (Harriman Reservoir). This long-established outfitter opened a Wilmington facility in 2014, offering kayaks and stand-up paddle-boat rentals as well as bikes, guided kayaking on the two local reservoirs and Lake Raponda, and guided cycling tours of the back roads around the periphery of the lakes. Since 1989 ZAC has offered whitewater rafting on the Deerfield River, timed for regular dam releases south of the state line in Massachusetts. For details about rafting, zipline canopy tours, rock climbing, and much more at its Charlemont base, see zaroutdoor.com.

CHAIRLIFT (800-464-4040; mountsnow.com). After exploring from the ground, you might as well get a bird's-eye view from up above. The Bluebird Express Lift operates from the main base lodge to the summit on weekends in summer and daily through peak foliage season. You can ride back down or position yourself for mountain biking and hiking.

FISHING The **Deerfield River** is known for rainbow and brook trout (the season runs from the second Saturday in April through October). The remote Harriman Bypass Reach, a 4.5-mile stretch of the river between the dam in Whitingham and Readsboro, is a good bet. **Somerset Reservoir**, 6.5 miles west of Wilmington then 10 miles north on Somerset Rd., offers bass, trout, and pike. There is a boat launch at the foot of the 9-mile-long lake. Smaller **Sadawga Pond** in Whitingham and **Lake Raponda** in Wilmington are also good for bass, trout, perch, salmon, pickerel, northern pike, and smelt. **Harriman Reservoir (Lake Whitingham)** is stocked with trout, bass, perch, and salmon; a boat launch is located off Fairview Ave.

Adams Farm (see *Farms*) offers an Orvis fly-fishing school and guide service.

Fishing licenses are available in Wilmington at C&S Beverage (802-464-8062), in Whitingham at the Whitingham General Store, and online at **vtfishandwildlife.com**.

FOR FAMILIES **Southern Vermont Natural History Museum** (802-464-0058; vermontmuseum .org), 7599 Rt. 9. Open daily. Admission $5 adults, $3 seniors, $2 ages 5–12. Sited at the most dramatic pullout along Rt. 9, formerly the summit of Hogback Mountain ski area, the view here can stretch for 100 miles. Bigger than it looks from outside, the museum began with the extensive collection of taxidermist Luman R. Nelson, which includes more than 500 stuffed New England birds and mammals in 80 dioramas. It has expanded to include live birds of prey, also fish and reptiles. The museum continues to evolve with local and environmentally focused exhibits. More than 600 acres of adjacent preservation land offer extensive hiking.

✍ **Mount Snow Day Camps** (802-464-3333; mountsnow.com), Mount Snow. Mini Camp (ages 6 weeks–12 months), Kids Camp (ages 5–8), and Sports Camp (ages 9–12) run during summer, Mon.– Fri. 9–4. Activities include swimming, chairlift rides, arts and crafts, nature hikes, field trips, and more.

✍ **North Star Bowl & Mini Golf** (802-464-5148), Rt. 100, Wilmington, open daily for indoor mini golf and candlepin bowling; also videos and pool tables, with ice cream and pizza parlor.

Also see **Adams Farm** and **Zoar Adventure Center**.

GOLF **Mount Snow Golf Club** (802-464-4254; mountsnow.com), Country Club Rd., West Dover. Billing itself as "The Original Golf School," this program has been evolving since 1978. Weekend and two- to five-day midweek golf school packages are offered May–Sept.; the 18-hole, Cornish-designed championship golf course is also open on a daily basis.

Sitzmark Golf & Tennis Club (802-464-3384), 54 East Dover Rd., Wilmington; 18 holes, club and cart rentals. No tee times.

HIKING Along with the trails in **Molly Stark State Park** and **Grout Pond Recreation Area** (see *Green Space*), there are a number of overgrown roads leading to ghost towns. The **Long Trail** passes through the former logging town of Glastenbury (261 residents in 1880), and a former colonial highway in **Woodford State Park** (see the Bennington chapter) leads to a burying ground and

18th-century homesites. Somerset is another ghost town. The **Hogback Mountain Overlook** on Rt. 9 is the starting point for a hike up the old ski area access road to the Mount Olga fire tower. Inquire at the Mount Snow Valley Chamber of Commerce about accessing the 12-mile trail along the undeveloped shore of **Lake Whitingham**, a lake trail around **Lake Raponda**, and the **Lisle Hill/White's Road Trail** just north of Wilmington off Rt. 100. To venture out for the 5-mile round-trip hike up **Haystack Mountain**, head west on Rt. 9 from Wilmington about 1.1 miles and turn north onto Haystack Rd. Follow into Chimney Hill; at the Binney Brook Rd. end stop sign, turn right onto Upper Dam Rd. Bear left at the next intersection and look for a trailhead marker on your right. Limited roadside parking. Well-marked trails can be found in the **Crosstown Area** at Mount Snow, which is the resort's trail system for hiking and mountain biking (see *Biking*).

Note: As with all hiking in Vermont, make sure to sign in at trailheads.

HORSEBACK RIDING *♘* **Flames Stables** (802-464-8329), Rt. 100 south, Wilmington. Western saddle trail rides, half-hour horse-drawn wagon rides, pony rides for young children.

♘ **Brookside Stables** (802-464-0267; brooksidestables.com), Rt. 100 north of Wilmington. Lessons, camps, boarding.

SCENIC DRIVES East along the Molly Stark Scenic Byway (mollystarkbyway.org). Five miles east of Wilmington on Rt. 9 you come to **Hogback Mountain**. Formerly a ski area, this is now a major overlook, said to offer a 100-mile view (weather dependent) facing south. This is also the site of the **Southern Vermont Natural History Museum** (see *For Families*). Continue along the Molly Stark Trail east some 5 miles to the turnoff to **Marlboro Village**, home of Marlboro College. From mid-July until mid-August its campus is the venue for the **Marlboro Music Festival** (marlboromusic .org). Continue into Brattleboro and return via the Dover Hill Rd. or follow the road past the college to the T, turn right, and you are soon in Jacksonville. See the following tours.

Jacksonville and Whitingham. From Wilmington follow Rt. 100 south 6 miles, past **Flames Stable** (see *Horseback Riding*) and the turnoff for Ward's Cove, to the village of Jacksonville. Near the junction of Rts. 100 and 112 stop by **Stone Soldier Pottery** (see *Selective Shopping*). Just down Rt. 112 is the **Honora Winery** (see *Wineries*). Follow Rt. 100 another 1.5 miles south and turn left onto Town Hill Rd. (marked for the **Brigham Young Monument**) into Whitingham. At the top of Town Hill a monument commemorates the Mormon prophet who led his people into Utah and is hailed as the founder of Salt Lake City. He was born on a hill farm here, the son of a poor basket maker. The view takes in surrounding hills; there are picnic benches, grills, a playground, and a parking area. Continue down the hill to **Brown's General Store** and turn right onto Stimpson Hill. Look on the right-hand side of the road near the top of this hill for a small marker that proclaims this to be the homestead site of Brigham Young: BORN ON THIS SPOT 1801 . . . A MAN OF MUCH COURAGE AND SUPERB EQUIPMENT. (Young fathered 56 children by 17 of his 52 wives.) Before leaving the village, note the 25-acre "floating island" in the middle of Sadawga Pond. Whitingham was once a busy resort, thanks to a mineral spring and its accessibility via the Hoosac Tunnel and Wilmington Railroad. The old railroad bed is now a **12-mile walking trail** along this remote shore of Lake Whitingham. (Continue 1 mile south on Rt. 100 beyond the store, and take a right onto Dam Rd.; park and walk across the dam. Note the "Glory Hole," a large concrete overflow funnel that empties into the Deerfield River.) If you are still feeling adventurous, continue on to **Readsboro**, a truly remote town with an inn and arts scene. See the Bennington chapter for details. From there it's 11 more miles through high country back to Rt. 9.

Dover Hill Road, accessible from Rt. 100 via either Dorr Fitch Rd. in the village of West Dover or East Dover Rd. farther south (just below Sitzmark). The road climbs steeply past the tiny village center of Dover. Here you could detour onto Cooper Hill Rd. for a few miles to take in the panorama of mountains. On an ordinary day, you can pick out Mount Monadnock in New Hampshire beyond Keene. You can either loop back down to Rt. 100 via Valley View Rd., or continue down the other side of the hill through East Dover to the general store, covered bridge, and picturesque village center in South Newfane, following Augur Hole Rd. back to Rt. 9—or, if you're out for a real ride, continuing to Rt. 30, then south to Brattleboro and back to Wilmington on Rt. 9.

Handle Road runs south from Mount Snow, paralleling Rt. 100, turning into Cold Brook Rd. when it crosses the Wilmington line. The old farmhouses along this high, wooded road were bought up by city people to form a summer colony in the late 1880s. It's still a beautiful road, retaining some of the old houses and views.

Arlington–Kelley Stand Road heads west from West Wardsboro through the tiny village of Stratton. At 6.3 miles the Grout Pond turnoff is clearly marked and leads 1.3 miles to the pond. Hiking trails loop around the pond, through the woods, and continue to **Somerset Reservoir**. Beyond this turnoff is the monument to Daniel Webster, who spoke here to 1,600 people at an 1840 Whig rally. The hiking trail to Stratton Pond that begins just west of the monument is the most heavily hiked section of the Long Trail. It's possible (your vehicle and conditions permitting) to return to Rt. 9 through the Green Mountain Forest via the Arlington–Somerset Rd. (closed in winter). Roughly halfway down you pass the turnoff for Somerset Reservoir.

Also see the West Dummerston (Rt. 30) road through South Newfane to West Dover under *Getting There*.

SWIMMING ♂ There are several beaches on 11-mile-long Harriman Reservoir, also known as Lake Whitingham. **Mountain Mills Beach** is 1 mile from Wilmington Village, posted from Castle Hill Rd. **Ward's Cove Beach** is on Rt. 100 south of Wilmington—turn right at Flames Stables and follow signs. Inquire locally about less publicized places.

Sitzmark Lodge (802-464-3384), north of Wilmington on Rt. 100, has a pool that's open to patrons who use the golf course or lunch here; call ahead for hours and rates. Snacks and a bar are available poolside.

TENNIS Municipal courts at **Baker Field** off School St. in Wilmington are open to the public; also courts at Sitzmark (see above).

✳ Winter Sports

CROSS-COUNTRY SKIING Timber Creek Cross Country Ski Area (802-464-0999; timbercreek xc.com), West Dover. Just across Rt. 100 from the entrance to Mount Snow, a high-elevation, 14 km wooded system of mostly easy and intermediate trails that hold their snow cover, access to backwoods trails, and an additional 6 km of snowshoe trails. Ski and snowshoe rentals, instruction available. Full- and half-day trail fees and special packages.

The Hermitage (802-464-3511; hermitageinn.com), 25 Handle Rd., West Dover, offers some 45 km of cross-country trails including high elevation and ridgeline, also separate trails for snowshoeing. Rentals available.

✪ **Prospect Mountain Nordic Ski Center** (802-442-2575; prospectmountain.com), Rt. 9, Woodford. This former downhill ski area features more than 30 km of groomed trails with access to backcountry trails; special trails for snowshoeing; and a comfortable base lodge with a fireplace, home-cooked food, and baked goods. Rentals. Because of its elevation, Prospect Mountain often has snow when other areas are bare. Inquire about moonlight dinners and ski tours.

DOWNHILL SKIING AND SNOWBOARD-ING ✪ ♂ **Mount Snow** (information 802-464-3333; snow report 802-464-2151; reservations 800-245-SNOW; mountsnow.com), West Dover. Peak Resorts, the mountain's current owner, has invested heavily in snowmaking and new chairlift technology, which has enhanced this 590-acre area, one of the largest mountain resorts in the Northeast. The snowmaking system is anchored by over 250 high-output fan guns, the most of any resort in North America. New for 2014–15 are 645 state-of-the-art, low-energy snow guns, which means the resort can make high-quality snow while using very little power. The sprawling **Grand Summit Resort Hotel** offers 197 rooms plus shops and services. Farther down by a small lake is the more modest and recently renovated **Snow Lake Lodge**, popular with college students and young families for its inexpensive, basic rooms. But the vast majority of the area's 2,100 "on-mountain" beds

MOUNT SNOW

Rachel Carter

Mount Snow

MOUNT SNOW BUBBLE LIFT

are rentals and multi-bedroom condos spread out around the foot of the mountain. As for skiing, there are four distinct areas: the Main Face, the expert North Face, the intermediate Sunbrook, and Carinthia, which is home to eight different terrain parks and a half-pipe. Mount Snow's vertical drop is 1,700 feet. Base area facilities include three lodges, rental/repair shops, retail, and restaurants, plus the Ski and Snowboard School at the Discovery Center, a dedicated instruction area with a learning slope and special lifts where beginners can go at their own pace. See the chapter introduction for the resort's history.

Lifts: 20 chairlifts—1 high-speed 6-passenger bubble lift, 3 high-speed and 1 fixed quad, 6 triples, 4 doubles. There is also 1 surface lift and 4 Magic Carpets.

Ski/snowboard trails: 83, including 14% "easier," 73% "more difficult," 13% "advanced," and 1 "double black diamonds." There are numerous hand-cleared tree skiing areas on all four mountain faces.

Snowmaking: 80% of the mountain.

Facilities: 3 base lodges, a summit lodge, the Snow Barn (nightclub with entertainment, dancing), and nature spa at the Grand Summit Resort Hotel.

Ski and Snowboard School: Over 400 instructors and dozens of clinics.

For children: Ski and Snowboard School: Burton Riglet Program (3- to 6-year-olds), Cub Camp (3-year-olds), Snow Camp (4- to 6-year-olds), and Mountain Camp and Mountain Riders (7- to 14-year-olds).

FOOD TASTING AT MOUNT SNOW

Rachel Carter

Rates: See mountsnow.com for lift ticket prices, which vary with the day ($55 weekend adult in Jan. if purchased online). The website also has a full schedule of events.

SLEIGH RIDES ♦ Sleigh rides are offered at **Adams Farm** (802-464-3762; adamsfamilyfarm .com), Wilmington, with a refreshment stop at a cabin in the woods. They are also offered at **Flames Stables** (802-464-8329) on Rt. 100 south of Wilmington, and at **The Hermitage** (hermitageinn.com) in West Dover.

SNOWMOBILING Snowmobile Vermont at Mount Snow (802-464-2108; mountsnow snowmobiletours.com), 39 Mount Snow Rd., West Dover, offers two-hour backcountry tours in the Green Mountain National Forest daily during ski season; two-passenger machines can take up to 350 pounds. $154 single, $199 double, $99 with guide.

Sitzmark (802-464-3384), 54 East Dover Rd., Wilmington, registers and garages sleds for use on the VAST trails.

✳ Green Space

❦ **Molly Stark State Park** (802-464-5460; vtstateparks.com), Rt. 9 east of Wilmington Village. This 158-acre preserve features a hiking trail through the forest to the Mount Olga fire tower, at 2,415 feet, from which there is a panoramic view. The 34 campsites include 11 lean-tos. Open Memorial Day to Columbus Day; pets permitted in this park.

Grout Pond Recreation Area (802-362-2307), west of West Wardsboro, off the Arlington (aka Kelley Stand) Rd. A 1,600-acre piece of the Green Mountain National Forest designated for hiking, picnicking, fishing, boating, and camping. In summer a ranger resides at the Grout Pond Cabin, and campsites are available on a first-come, first-served basis (6 vehicle sites, 11 walk-in campsites, and 4 sites accessible by canoe). Twelve miles of trails, which circle the pond and connect with Somerset Reservoir, are open in winter for skiing (they are not groomed). At the north end of the pond there are five picnic sites.

Lake Raponda. This hidden treasure, a town-owned 200-acre pond, is accessed by Stowe Hill Rd. from Rt. 100, and via Lake Raponda Rd. from Rt. 9 west of Molly Stark State Park. Good for fishing and paddle boats.

✳ Lodging

This area offers a choice of mountainside inns, condominiums, and ski lodges. The **Mount Snow Valley Chamber of Commerce** keeps track of vacancies and refers callers; it also maintains a website with direct links to lodging places, and you can reserve online (877-887-6884; visitvermont.com).

Mount Snow Central Reservations (802-464-8501; 800-451-4211; mountsnow.com). A reservation service that includes area lodges, inns, and condos that are slope-side or at the base of the mountain; from studios to three-bedroom units with full kitchens and access to pools, saunas, and fitness rooms.

RESORTS ♂ ✿ **The Hermitage Inn and Club** (802-464-3511; 877-464-3511; hermitage inn.com), 25 Handle Rd., West Dover 05356. Originally built in the 1840s as a farmhouse and for some years the summer home of an editor of the Social Register, The Hermitage Inn (15 rooms) has been an inn since the 1960s. In 2007 it was acquired by Jim Barnes as the core of a still-evolving 1,400-acre resort/private club that includes former **Haystack Mountain** and its 18-hole golf course, extensive cross-country ski trails, and several more inns, including the elegant White House of Wilmington (11 guest rooms), a former paper baron's estate on the eastern edge of Wilmington, and 10-room **Vermont House**, a newly rehabbed 1850s stagecoach inn at the center of Wilmington Village. Inn guests as well as Hermitage Club members have access to Haystack's lifts and trails, and the public is welcome at the golf course and cross-country trails. At The Hermitage Inn itself, environmental innovations include a solar-powered photovoltaic system for their electrical needs. Amenities include a massage-centered spa, a game room, a fitness room, and numerous outdoor facilities and activities; hot tub, stocked trout pond, ice skating and tubing, horse-drawn sleigh rides, and multiple networks of trails groomed for cross-country skiing, snowshoeing, and snowmobiling (machines are available for guests), as well as hiking. The dining room is open to the public by reservation for all three meals (see *Dining Out*). Rates vary seasonally; $229.95–615.58.

SNOWMOBILING AT THE HERMITAGE
Rachel Carter

The Grand Summit Resort Hotel at Mount Snow (802-464-8501; 800-498-0479; mountsnow.com), 89 Grand Summit Way, West Dover 05356. At the base of the ski lifts, this 198-room, ski-in, ski-out condo hotel and conference center is a 1998 version of an Austrian chalet. It features one- to three-bedroom suites (many with kitchen) as well as the usual hotel rooms. Amenities include a heated outdoor pool and hot tubs, an arcade, a spa and fitness center, and, of course, ski lifts. In summer there are golf and mountain biking programs. **Harriman's Restaurant** (see *Eating Out*) is open for breakfast and dinner; the **Grand Country Deli & Convenience Store** offers take-out. Rates vary seasonally as well as for midweek and weekend stays: Rooms range from a basic two-person studio to a two-bedroom deluxe suite. The ritziest option is the three-bedroom, three-bath penthouse on the top floor, sleeping 12 ($337 in low season, $1,237 in high). The standard rooms and one-bedroom suites (consisting of a bedroom, bath, living room, and galley kitchen) run $100–520, including continental breakfast in winter.

INNS

In Wilmington/West Dover

The Inn at Sawmill Farm (802-464-8131; 800-493-1133; 800-493-8131; theinnatsawmillfarm.com), on Crosstown Rd. just off Rt. 100, West Dover 05356. Each of the 21 guest rooms in several buildings (including 3 cottages) is different, most with king-sized bed, some with jetted tubs, each individually decorated with an eye to comfort and detail. With the exception of those in the main house, all have TV and most have wood-burning fireplace; several cottages overlook the trout-stocked ponds. There's a resident blue heron and lawns that slope to the edge of a pine forest. You'll also find a tennis court, a heated pool, a workout room, and wide floorboards that creak underfoot. A Vermont country breakfast is included in rates of $175–375, depending on room/cottage selection. Pets allowed in some rooms for a fee. Italian cuisine is served in Nonna's Restaurant (see *Dining Out*).

The White House of Wilmington (802-464-2135; 800-541-2135; whitehouseinn.com), 178 Rt. 9 east, Wilmington 05363. Built in 1915 on a knoll overlooking Rt. 9 as a summer residence for Martin Brown, founder of Brown Paper Company, the interior of this gorgeous Colonial Revival mansion lives up to its elegant facade. Common rooms are huge, light, and atmospheric, but also stay warm in winter—with the help of 14 yawning hearths. At the front is an inviting sunken bar overlooking the

Rachel Carter

THE HERMITAGE

valley. Otherwise the decor is Old World, including genuine French wallpaper. There are hand-carved mahogany mantelpieces and marble-topped antiques in a total of 16 rooms, 9 with fireplace, some with two-person whirlpool tub, terrace, or balcony. There's a small indoor pool on the lower level and a sauna and steambath. The spa offers a good range of spa services and treatments. The inn is now owned by The Hermitage Club, and guests have access to skiing at Haystack Mountain. Rates range $125–350 and include breakfast, based on double occupancy. Also see *Dining Out*.

Deerhill Inn (802-464-3100; deerhillinn.com), 14 Valley Rd., West Dover 05356. Ariane Burgess and Scott Kocher maintain this delightful farmhouse with an additional wing providing luxurious accommodations, all with private bath, some with jetted tubs and fireplaces. Several rooms are suites. One comfortable sitting room adjoins a quaint bar and two spacious dining rooms, walled with the work of local artists; upstairs is another lounge for guests, plus a library nook. In summer, flowers abound inside and out and around the patio of the swimming pool. Dinner and spa treatments can be arranged. Small dogs are allowed for a fee. Children over 12 welcome. Rates include a sumptuous breakfast; $210–355 for suites, $135–295 for rooms.

Nutmeg Inn (802-464-3907; 855-8-NUTMEG; nutmeginn.com), 153 Rt. 9 west, Wilmington 05363. A delightful 1777 roadside farmhouse on Rt. 9 west recently purchased by Paul and Shelly Lockyear. Situated on the western edge of Wilmington, it offers 14 guest rooms, 6 with fireplace. There are four suites, all with hourglass-shaped two-person whirlpool and wood-burning fireplace. All rooms have central air-conditioning and private bath. There is a cozy antiques-filled living room, library, and BYOB bar, plus three intimate dining rooms for a breakfast buffet and prix fixe dinner for guests only (arrange in advance). Summer and winter $99–249, fall $119–225 includes breakfast, less weekdays than weekends.

Wilmington Inn & Tavern (802-464-3768; 800-845-7548; thewilmingtoninn.com), 41 W. Main St., Wilmington 05363. A big, gracious 1894 house on the edge of the village within walking distance of shops and restaurants. The nine nicely furnished guest rooms include two suites with fireplace. The tavern is furnished with an assortment of old oak tables and antique tools. There are several comfortable common areas. Rates are $119–229 and include country breakfast with a choice of menu items such as frittatas. Children are welcome if arrangements are made in advance.

West Dover Inn (802-464-5207; westdoverinn .com), 108 Rt. 100, West Dover 05356. Built in 1846 as the village inn and now on the National Register of Historic Places, Phil and Kathy Gilpin's handsome inn includes modern amenities and country-style appointments in each of its 11 guest rooms, some fireplace suites with jetted tubs. All rooms have double or queen beds, private bath, and cable TV. Guests enjoy a homey common room with a fireplace, as well as the 1846 Tavern & Restaurant (see *Dining Out*). $209–309 in winter, less off-season; rates include breakfast. Some minimum stays required during holidays. Children welcome (pets not).

♂ ❀ 🐾 ♪ **Layla's Riverside Lodge** (802-464-7400; laylasriversidelodge.com), 145 Rt. 100, West Dover 05456. Located on a paved portion of the Valley Trail, this is a great place to stay if you are traveling with Fido. Grounds include an in-ground pool, a gazebo, flower gardens, quiet sitting areas along the Deerfield River, outdoor dining, and a dog kennel. The two-story inn has 17 guest rooms, 10 of which are luxury suites featuring king and queen beds and full-sized baths with spa tubs. Each of the rooms is individually furnished; some have fireplace and balcony. Dinner is served in The Hunt Club (see *Dining Out*). Room rates range $159–379 include breakfast. Pet stays are additional.

BED & BREAKFASTS ❂ ♂ ♪ **Cooper Hill Inn** (802-348-6333; 800-783-3229; cooperhill inn.com), 117 Cooper Hill Rd., East Dorset 05341. High on a hilltop on a quiet country road with one of the most spectacular mountain

panoramas in New England, this spacious white farmhouse has 10 bright, tastefully decorated guest rooms, all with private bath. At the heart of the house, dating from 1797, is a gracious living room with a fireplace and piano. Lee and Charles Wheeler have reserved one wing of the house for families, creating kid-friendly suites, and the other for romantic getaways, featuring rooms with fireplace, king beds, Jacuzzi, and balcony. There's a large dining room, game room, deck, and covered porch as well as spacious grounds, with fields for softball, tag, and long walks. Lee has also created formal flower gardens and a landscaped hollow for weddings. The house can hold 24 and is frequently rented in its entirety. You can watch the sun rise on one side of the house and see it set on the other. The Wheelers lived 12 years in Singapore, which explains the Asian antiques throughout. $169–240 per room, depending on the season, includes breakfast.

🍷 ♪ ♿ **Shearer Hill Farm** (802-464-3253; 800-437-3104; shearerhillfarm.com), 297 Shearer Hill Rd., Wilmington 05363. Off Rt. 9, 2 miles southeast of Wilmington: Turn right onto Shearer Hill Rd., bearing left at the fork to Bill and Patti Pusey's restored 200-year-old farmhouse, where they raise cows, make maple syrup, and grow raspberries. Six guest rooms are offered in either the main farmhouse or the carriage house, each with private bath; one can become a two-room suite with additional living area. The pleasant large living room in the farmhouse has a VCR library. $125 double, $90 single with full breakfast.

❂ **Brass Bed B&B** (802-464-5523; brassbedbb .com), 30 Not-A-Road, Wilmington 05363.

BRASS BED B&B

Brass Bed B&B

Laraine and Skip Morrow offer two third-floor rooms with views of forest and mountains beyond. A shared bathroom and living space with a balcony overlooking a solarium make this an ideal accommodation for two couples traveling together. Otherwise only one room is rented at a time, keeping the bath and sitting room—which has a small fridge, microwave, and toaster as well as a TV—private. Breakfast is brought up. Shade gardens, trails, and sculptures cover the grounds. Snowshoes are available for use in winter. Both hosts are talented artists and musicians: Skip operates **The Art of Humor Gallery** (see *Art Galleries & Crafts Studios*) and Skip and Laraine perform at local venues. Rates (with breakfast) are $150; $250 for the suite. Children over 12 welcome.

🌢 �//images☼ **Whetstone Inn** (802-254-2500; whetstoneinn.com), 550 South Rd., Marlboro 05344. Handy to the Marlboro College and to the Marlboro Music Festival, this is a 1786 tavern with a Palladian window, part of the cluster of white-clapboard buildings—including the church and post office—that form the village core. Innkeeper Jean Boardman has been welcoming guests more than 35 years, and there's a worn but casually comfortable feel to the place. Most guests have been here before and have their own favorite rooms, of which there are 11, 7 with private bath and 2 with kitchen. Singles with private bath run $55–80; doubles, $90–110. Breakfast, served daily, is $10 extra. Prix fixe dinner can be arranged. There's swimming in a spring-fed pond.

MOTELS ☼ 🌢 ☼ **Viking Motel** (802-464-5608; 800-722-4427; vikingmotel.net), Rt. 9, Wilmington 05463. This family-owned motel is the best value in Wilmington. Eleven nicely decorated units have two doubles each, four rooms have a queen-sized bed, and all have cable TV, a small fridge, AC, direct-dial phones, and more ($75–95); the Viking Suite has two bedrooms and cooking facilities. Pets accepted.

🌢 ✐ **Austrian Haus Lodge** (802-464-3911; 800-487-3910; austrianhaus.com), 6 Abroad Rd., West Dover 05356. Three miles from the mountain off Rt. 100. Thirty double-occupancy rooms with a few variations. Geared mostly to families with amenities including indoor heated pool, sauna, game room, BYOB gathering lounge with fireplace, and common space for kids. High-season rates of $89–160 include continental breakfast From $59 in summer. Inquire about discounted ski-and-stay packages.

CONDOS/RENTALS Mountain Resort Rentals (802-464-1445; 888-336-1445; mountain resortrentals.com). Rentals ranging from the humble to the sublime for short- or long-term stays. Open daily, year-round.

Mount Snow Vermont Rentals (800-451-6876; mountsnowvermontrentals.com) offers one- to four-bedroom condos to rent for short- or long-term stays.

Chimney Hill (802-464-2181; chimneyhill .com) provides vacation rentals within their resort community.

☼ **The Amos Brown House** (802-254-6868; landmarktrustusa.org). The oldest house in the back-road town of Whitingham has been meticulously restored by the nonprofit Landmark Trust USA. The brick Cape-style farmhouse, built around 1802 with connected barn and sheds, is set in 30 acres of meadow on a quiet dirt road. With three bedrooms and two baths, it sleeps six ($250–300 per night, 3-night minimum, dogs welcome).

CAMPGROUNDS See Molly Stark State Park and Grout Pond Recreation Area in *Green Space*.

✳ Where to Eat

DINING OUT Nonna's Restaurant at the Inn at Sawmill Farm (802-464-8131; theinnat sawmillfarm.com), Crosstown Rd., just off Rt. 100, West Dover. Open for dinner Thurs.–Mon. Nonna's meatballs are a must-have, followed by a solid assortment of finely executed meat, fish, and pasta dishes. Entrées $17–35. Daily specials.

The Hermitage Inn (802-464-3511; hermitage inn.com), 25 Handle Rd., West Dover. Open daily for breakfast, lunch, and dinner. Reservations essential. The casually elegant, many-windowed inn dining rooms are attractive, hung with distinctive artwork. Entrées $12–32.

Two Tannery Road (802-464-2707; two tannery.com), 2 Tannery Rd., Rt. 100, West Dover. Open for dinner Tues.–Sun. The building itself is said to date in part from the late 1700s, when it stood in Marlboro, Massachusetts, and has moved several times within this valley, serving for a while as a summer home for Theodore Roosevelt's son. The bar began service in the original Waldorf-Astoria (present site of the Empire State Building). The food is highly rated, flavorful, and creative. Entrées $25–37. Nightly specials, reservations encouraged.

☼ ᕦ **The Roadhouse** (802-464-5017), Rt. 100 and Old Ark Rd., halfway up the mountain, Wilmington. Dinner nightly and Sunday brunch. The name and exterior disguise the elegant atmosphere, distinguished food, and inviting bar—which is good, because this place is a hidden gem. Crab-stuffed trout ($24) is a staple, along with traditional dishes such as the Roadhouse burger ($13) or filet mignon ($29). Light bite menus for $12.95. The homemade bread served with entrées is mouthwatering.

Layla's Riverside Lodge (802-464-7400), 145 Rt. 100, West Dover. Dinner Wed.–Sun., lunch Fri.–Sun.; best to check ahead. The boast is that 80 percent of what's served is locally produced. A favorite among the locals. Entrées might include chicken potpie, organic beef, and crispy duck confit.

The White House of Wilmington (802-464-2135; 800-541-2135; whitehouseinn.com), 178 Rt. 9 east, Wilmington. Open for dinner Thurs.–Sun. The wood-paneled dining room in this hilltop mansion (see *Inns*) is warmed by a hearth. This is fine dining, with locally sourced ambience and menu; $26 for miso salmon, $30 for steak. Lighter, reasonably priced fare is available in the Black Dog Tavern around a sunken mahogany bar overlooking the valley.

♪ & **Harriman's Restaurant** (802-464-1100; mountsnow.com), located in the Grand Summit Hotel at Mount Snow Resort. Serving breakfast and dinner daily. Casual fine-dining atmosphere with a culinary focus on local meats and produce, homemade desserts, and an extensive wine and martini list. Try the venison osso buco or the five-spice lamb shank (in-season). Pub fare also served. Entrées $14–30.

EATING OUT ✪ ❀ *♪* **Dot's Restaurant** (802-464-7284; dotsofvermont.com), 5 W. Main St., Wilmington. Open 5:30 AM–8 PM, until 9 Fri. and Sat. The real center of Wilmington, a beloved icon by the Deerfield River that was

DOT'S RESTAURANT, DEVASTATED BY IRENE, ONCE MORE MARKS THE CENTER OF WILMINGTON.

Christina Tree

severely damaged by Hurricane Irene but back and better than ever, called a "National Treasure" by *Gourmet* magazine. Still the long Formica counter, also seating in the side room, overlooking the river. Breakfast (5:30–3), great omelets, waffles, and corned beef hash. Then there's housemade soups and blue plate specials; dinner from 4 PM offers plenty of choices. Try the Vermont maple berry chicken. Pies are a must. Beer and wine served.

✪ *♪* & (ᵥ) **Dots of Dover** (802-464-6476; dotsofdovervt.com), 2 Mountain Park Plaza, Rt. 100, West Dover. Dot's offspring. Open daily for breakfast and lunch, also dinner on winter weekends. Berry-berry pancakes at breakfast (served until 1) and flame-grilled burgers at lunch are big sellers, but there are plenty of choices. Soups are from scratch; grilled meatloaf, salads, and much more. This is a great place for kids, who have a special menu.

✪ *♪* **Jezebel's Eatery** (802-464-7774), 26 W. Main St., Wilmington Village. Open breakfast, lunch, and dinner, serving farm-fresh comfort food. Lunch specials include panini, soups, and salads, with fresh-baked desserts a specialty; also inquire about occasional dinner seatings, which are well worth it. Full bar, craft beers.

♪ **Valley View Saloon** (802-464-9422; valleyviewsaloon.com), Mount Snow Market Place, 131 Rt. 100, West Dover. Open daily for lunch and dinner, Sunday brunch 10–2. Big-screen games but also room to get away from the screens, a wide range of pub food, kids' menu.

❀ **Maple Leaf Tavern** (802-464-9900), 3 N. Main St., Wilmington. Open daily, offering a wide choice of crafted microbrews and a large, reasonably priced all-day pub menu with the likes of ribs, pesto chicken, beer-battered fish, and specials. Open late.

🐾 *♪* & (ᵥ) **Wahoos Eatery** (802-464-0110; wahooseatery.com), 2 White's Rd., Wilmington. Open daily for lunch and dinner May–Sept. Local entrepreneur Adam Grinold started Wahoos in 2000 and has grown this colorful roadside fast-food stop into a successful franchise. The *food* is fresh and made to order; the *fast* comes from using social media applications to order ahead. Burgers, wraps, and ice cream as well as daily specials.

♪ **Anchor Seafood House & Grille** (802-464-2112; anchorseafood.com), 8 S. Main St., Wilmington. Daily lunch and dinner, Sunday brunch. An intimate, upscale spot with a marble and oak bar. Daily specials like Parmesan-baked tilapia, fresh Maine lobsters, and horseradish-encrusted salmon. Lunch $8–15, dinner $17–25. Children's menu.

Jerry's at Old Red Mill (877-733-6455; oldredmill.com), Rt. 100 north on the edge of Wilmington. Dinner served on the covered and heated deck Memorial Day–Columbus Day. Jerry Osler has owned this converted 1828 sawmill for almost 40 years. The large, rustic restaurant and tavern features fascinating antique fixtures dating to the mill's early days and offers plenty of atmosphere. We especially recommend the riverside deck in summer; traditional New England local and comfort-food menu. Accommodations also available.

TC's Family Restaurant (802-464-5900; tcsrestaurant.com), 178 Rt. 100, West Dover (2 miles south of Mount Snow). Open for dinner nightly, lunch on seasonal weekends. Owned by Olympic gold medalist Kelly Clark's family, this is a casual. affordable place with nightly specials. Outdoor riverside dining in summer.

The Sitzmark Pub & Grill (802-0464-3784), 54 East Dover Road, Wilmington. This is a great place for lunch with or without kids in warm weather. The food is incidental though okay—but there's a lot going on here: golf (see *Golf*), a pool, volleyball, and lawn games. Beers on tap and an après-ski scene in winter (also see *Snowmobiling*). This is a longtime village establishment, doing a lot of useful this and that to get by.

In Wardsboro (13 miles up Route 100 from West Dover)
Bittersweet Memories Bakery Café (802-896-1130), 11 Fortune Rd. (just off Rt. 100). Open daily 6–3 for breakfast and lunch. The village of Wardsboro is a dozen miles north up Rt. 100 from the Mount Snow access road so it's

THE SILO

Rachel Carter

good to know about this attractive café if you are on your way there. It features breakfast sandwiches, assorted pancakes and omelets, the usual lunch choices, plus veggie options and pies by Cindy.

APRÈS-SKI The Silo (802-464-2553; thesilo mountsnow.com), **Dover Bar & Grill** (802-464-2689), and **Last Chair Bar & Grill** (802-464-1133; lastchairvt.com) are all happening après-ski venues within a mile of Mount Snow. Of course, the best après-ski action is right at the at Mount Snow lodges, accessed with ski boots still on (mountsnow.com).

✴ Entertainment

Note: Be sure to check out the **Marlboro Music Festival** (marlboromusic.org) under *Entertainment* in the Brattleboro chapter.

Memorial Hall Center for the Arts (802-464-8411; memhall.org), lodged in the McKim, Mead & White–designed theater next door to the historic Crafts Inn, Wilmington. This nonprofit center hosts community theater productions as well as films, a range of live musical performances, and community events.

✴ Selective Shopping

ANTIQUES Wilmington Antique & Flea Market (802-464-3345), junction of Rts. 9 and 100. Open May–Oct., Sat. and Sun. Bills itself as southern Vermont's largest outdoor flea market.

Chapman's Antique Barn (802-464-8344; chapmansantiques.com), 38 New England Power Rd., Wilmington. Open Fri.–Sun. 10–4, Memorial Day–Columbus Day. Large barn filled with antiques, vintage collectibles, and handmade crafts.

ART GALLERIES & CRAFTS STUDIOS
✪ **Quaigh Design Centre** (802-464-2780), Main St., Wilmington. Open daily in summer and fall, weekends much of the rest of the year. This is a long-established showcase for top Vermont crafts, pottery, and artwork; imported Scottish woolens and British handiwork are also specialties. Lilias MacBean Hart, the owner, has produced a Vermont tartan. There are also many woodcuts by Vermont artists Mary Azarian and landscapes by Ann Coleman.

✪ **The Art of Humor Gallery** (802-464-5523; skipmorrow.com), Not-A-Road, Wilmington. Open daily 10–5, but a call ahead is appreciated. Humorous illustrator, greeting card designer, book and calendar artist, and entertainer Skip Morrow operates a beautiful two-story gallery showcasing his work and collections, like the

Christina Tree

QUAIGH DESIGN CENTER IS ONE OF THE
OLDEST ART/CRAFTS GALLERIES IN VERMONT.

famous *The Official I Hate Cats Book* and its
subsequent editions. Just five minutes from
Wilmington Village. Skip and his wife, Laraine,
also perform music on weekends and operate
the **Brass Bed B&B** (see *Lodging*).

The Vermont Bowl Company (802-464-5296;
vermontbowl.com), 111 W. Main St., Rt. 9,
Wilmington. Adjacent to the John McLeod Ltd.
Store and factory. A Scottish engineer, McLeod
fell in love with the state and decided to settle
here and make a living from woodturning.
Hardwood bowls, clocks, mirrors, cutting
boards, and furniture on the western edge of
the village; open daily.

Gallery Wright (802-464-9922; gallerywright
.com), 103 W. Main St., Wilmington. Open
Thurs.–Mon. 11–6. The area's finest selection of
fine art, including landscapes, figures, and still
lifes in oil, pastels, and prints.

Stone Soldier Pottery (802-368-7077; stone
soldierpottery.net), Jacksonville Village. Connie
Burnell is the second generation of her family to
handcraft functional stoneware pottery in this
classic pottery shed/showroom. Connie's work
differs somewhat from that of her father, the
late Robert Burnell, who created the iconic
stone soldier that still resides in the shop—
which is large, displaying dinnerware, mugs,
vases, bakeware, and more, most pieces are
hand decorated and all hand glazed, some
deeply colored. Visitors welcome, call ahead.

Applewoods (802-254-2908; holzapfelwood
working.com), 8 miles east of Wilmington on
Rt. 9, in Marlboro. Open in summer Thurs.–
Mon. 10–4, or by appointment. David and
Michelle Holzapfel create amazing tables,

benches, and vessels from burls and other wood
forms.

BOOKSTORES ✪ **Bartleby's Books and
Music** (802-464-5425; myvermontbookstore
.com), 17 W. Main St, Wilmington. Open daily.
An exceptional two-story independent bookstore
featuring a well-chosen wide assortment of
titles, featuring Vermont and local-interest
books, cookbooks, and children's books. Owners
Lisa Sullivan and Phil Taylor were in the store
that Sunday morning in 2011 when the floodwa-
ters from Hurricane Irene came surging in. Lisa
now downplays the effort it took to build back
and talks about the sense of community that
ensued. The store itself is a community gathering place with self-serve coffee, frequent
authors' events, and monthly openings for the
changing art upstairs. Greeting cards, CDs, art
supplies, stationery, games, and music are also
carried.

Austin's Antiquarian Books (802-464-8438;
austinsbooks.com), 123 W. Main St. on Rt. 9,
0.5 mile west of downtown Wilmington. Open
daily. Maps, prints, and 15,000 used, rare, and
out-of-print books, many with leather bindings.
Inquire about local and regional book fairs.

FARMS ✿ **Adams Farm** (802-464-3762;
adamsfamilyfarm.com), 15 Higley Hill Rd., off
Rt. 100, Wilmington. A sixth-generation visitor-
friendly farm with livestock, a farm store, a petting farm, sleigh and wagon rides. Inquire about
special events. Also about certified Orvis fly-
fishing programs, paintball courses, and
farmstays.

♂ ✿ **Boyd Family Farm** (802-464-5618;
boydfamilyfarm.com), 125 East Dover Rd.,
Wilmington. A fifth-generation working hillside

SKIP MORROW'S GALLERY

Rachel Carter

farm, with pick-your-own flowers, raspberries, and blueberries June–Sept., then pumpkins, gourds, mums, kale, and cabbage. Always beautiful homemade wreaths; wedding venue.

Wheeler Farm (802-464-5225), 36 Woffenden Rd. (Rt. 100) north of Wilmington Village. A third-generation working farm with Jersey and Dutch belted cows, part of the cooperative that produces Cabot cheese. Maple syrup is produced and sold, along with maple cream and sugar. Call ahead and also inquire about fishing on the property.

SPECIALTY SHOPS 1836 Country Store Village (802-464-5102; 1836countrystore.com), W. Main St., Wilmington, has an eclectic stock of decorative brasses, pierced-tin lanterns, toys and games, Vermont specialty foods, and the usual souvenirs. Note the amazing old floors.

Norton House (802-464-7213; norquilt.com), adjacent to the 1836 Country Store at 30 W. Main St., Wilmington, was pulled here by oxen in the 1830s and dates from 1760, making it Wilmington's oldest structure. A quilter's paradise with over 3,000 fabrics and every quilting accessory. Note the yawning brick hearth and the historical objects upstairs in the windowed closet.

Pickwell's Barn (802-464-3198; pickwellsbarn .com), 22 W. Main St., Wilmington, has pottery, clocks, prints, colorful glassware, Vermont wines, and specialty foods.

WINERY & SPIRITS ♂ ♿ **Honora Winery & Vineyards** (802-368-2226; honorawinery .com), 202 Rt. 112, Jacksonville. Open daily. Honora has combined with North River Winery and specializes in cold-weather varietals of both red and white wines. More traditional wines are also crafted with growers specifically in the Paso Robles region. The tasting room and store are open Wed.–Sun., 11–5. See *Scenic Drives* for directions. A few miles down the road are the vineyards, which can be toured (best to call) and are also a site for weddings. Ten thousand vines are planted on 11 acres, a truly lovely sight. In 2014 Jville Craft Brewery (jvillebrewery.com) was added to the Jacksonville (former North River Winery) venue. Inquire about winemaking and other programs, events.

Vermont Distillers (802-464-2003; vermont distillers.com), tastings at the Hogback

Mountain Gift Shop, 5494 Rt. 9. Open daily. Locally made raspberry and maple cream liqueur.

✳ Special Events

Late February: **Harriman Ice Fishing Derby** on Lake Whitingham (doververmont.com).

First weekend in April: **Mount Snow Winter Brewer's Festival** (mountsnow.com), first weekend. In late April, **Club Mud** celebration with music, mud, and fun at The Hermitage (hermitageinn.com).

May: **Tough Mudder**—a hard-core 12-mile obstacle course challenge (toughmudder.com).

♪ Memorial Day: **The Great Duck Race**— over 1,500 rubber ducks are released at noon at Wilmington's bridge. BBQ, games, prizes, duck quacking contest (visitvermont.com).

July 4 weekend: A very big celebration in these parts with fireworks, parades, et cetera (visit vermont.com). The most famous parade is in the tiny village of Wardsboro, 12 miles north on Rt. 100 from Mount Snow.

July: Second installment of **Tough Mudder** challenge (toughmudder.com).

Late July–mid-August: **Marlboro Music Festival** (802-254-2394; marlboromusic.org).

Memorial Day weekend: **Fiddlehead Festival** (vermontfiddleheadfestival.com), Dover.

♪ Early August: **Deerfield Valley Blueberry Festival**, a happening throughout the valley with messy and excellent pie-eating contests among many things (vermontblueberry.com).

Labor Day weekend: Second installment of **Mount Snow Brewer's Festival** (mountsnow .com).

September: **Taste of the Deerfield Valley** under the tent at Mount Snow showcasing some of the area's hidden gems in dining (celebrate thevalley.com). **Vermont Wine and Harvest Festival**, last weekend, has grown to be a spectacular showcase of wines and harvest tastings over a full weekend of events (thevermont festival.com).

October: **Octoberfest and Craft Fair** with brews and crafts at the mountain; the chairlift is running for great views (mountsnow.com).

BENNINGTON AND
THE SOUTHSHIRE

Bennington is the name both of Vermont's southwesternmost town, and of its southwestern-most county. It's the only county divided into North and South "shires," each with a venerable court-house, one in Manchester and one in the town of Bennington. The name honors Benning Wentworth, the avaricious governor of the New Hampshire Grants. The town, settled in 1749, was the first he designated west of the Connecticut River. In 1770 Bennington became a hotbed of sedition when the "Bennington Mob"—better known as the Green Mountain Boys—formed at Fay's Catamount Tavern, choosing Seth Warner and Ethan Allen as their leaders and vowing to expel the "Yorkers" who claimed the territory and, eventually, the British.

The August 16, 1777, Battle of Bennington—more precisely, the Battle for Bennington—deflected General Burgoyne's occupation of the area, thanks to New Hampshire general John Stark's hastily mobilized militiamen. They beat the tar out of Colonel Baum's overdressed Hessians on high ground near the Walloomsac River, across the New York border. The story is memorialized in the Bennington Battle Monument, a 306-foot high obelisk that towers over Old Bennington and the surrounding countryside. The tale is dramatized through paintings and memorabilia in the nearby Bennington Museum and finds a human form in the exceptionally preserved memorials of soldiers at the Old Bennington Cemetery.

Major old north–south and east–west highways (Historic Rt. 7A and Rt. 9) cross at downtown Bennington's "Four Corners." However, limited-access highways (Rts. 7 and 279) now circumvent the town. Along with outlying commercial strips and loop roads, these have back-roaded the community's three distinctive centers—Old Bennington, North Bennington, and downtown. All are worth finding.

A MEMBER OF THE CATAMOUNT PROWL, BENNINGTON

Alice Levitt

North Bennington is a gem of a former mill village with mansions hidden down leafy side roads. The most ornate of these, the Park-McCullough House, is open to visitors; another estate forms the core of Bennington College campus. The town also offers a choice of B&Bs, fine and casual dining, three of the county's five covered bridges, several waterfalls, extensive walking paths, and Lake Paran.

GUIDANCE The **Bennington Area Chamber of Commerce** (802-447-3311; 800-229-0252; bennington.com), 100 Veterans Memorial Dr., maintains a cheerfully staffed, well-stocked information center, open year-round Mon.–Fri. 9–5; also on weekends mid-May–mid-Oct.

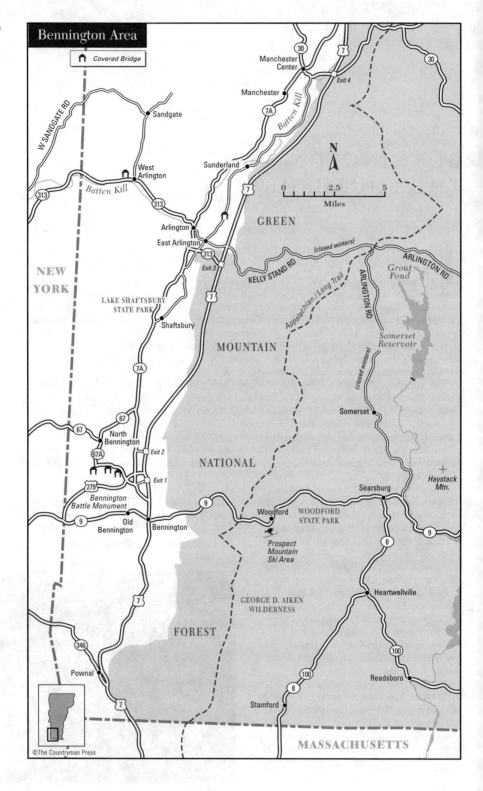

Bennington Area

Covered Bridge

©The Countryman Press

Christina Tree

THE JUNCTION OF RTS. 7 AND 9 IN DOWNTOWN BENNINGTON

Their free Bennington guide and their fold-out map/guides are both excellent.

Downtown Welcome Center (802-442-5758; betterbennington.com), 215 South St. Open year-round Mon.–Sat. 9–5. A 19th-century stone building, originally a smithy, then a police station, now an information center.

Also check the **Shires of Vermont** regional tourism website: shiresofvermont.com.

GETTING THERE *By car:* From New York City/New Jersey: Take I-87 to Exit 23, then I-787 to Exit 9E; continue to Rt. 7 east to Bennington.

From Boston: Rt. 90 to I-91 to Brattleboro and Rt. 9 (the Molly Stark Scenic Byway).

GETTING AROUND Going north can be confusing; watch the signs carefully to choose between the limited-access Rt. 7 to Manchester and the more interesting but slower Historic Rt. 7A to Shaftsbury and Arlington.

MEDICAL EMERGENCY Call **911**. **Southwestern Vermont Medical Center** (802-442-6361; svhealthcare.org), 100 Hospital Dr., Bennington.

❋ Must See

🐚 **Old Bennington and the Bennington Battle Monument** (802-447-0550; historicvermont.org), Old Bennington. Open late-Apr.–late-Oct., daily 9:30–5:30, $5 adults, $1 children. Parking area at its base, just off Rt. 9 west. There's an elevator to the observation floor, with a three-state view. The focal point in Old Bennington, this 306-foot, blue limestone shaft was dedicated in 1891 and remains the tallest manmade structure in Vermont. It commemorates the battle in which General John Stark defeated invading British and Hessian forces at Walloomsac Heights, 5 miles to the northwest, on August 16, 1777. Given the busy traffic pattern, it's wise to keep your car parked at the monument and stroll down Monument Ave., by the fine early houses and the Old Academy to the imposing **Old First Church** with its triple-decker belfry and Palladian windows, built in 1806. A slew of Revolutionary War heroes and villains, five Vermont governors, and Robert Frost repose in its exceptionally well-preserved, hilly burial ground. The home once known as the Walloomsac Inn is now private.

THE BENNINGTON BATTLE MONUMENT

Christina Tree

✪ ⛦ **Bennington Museum** (802-447-1571; benningtonmuseum.org), 75 Main St., Rt. 9, Bennington. Open daily except Wed. and holidays, 10–5. The centerpiece of this museum is the Grandma Moses Gallery, which features the world's largest collection of the naive work of the artist formerly known as Anna Mary Robertson. Down the hall, the one-room schoolhouse that she attended as a child now houses some of her personal possessions and a hands-on look at school, clothing, and toys from that era. A look at the artifacts from the Battle of Bennington,

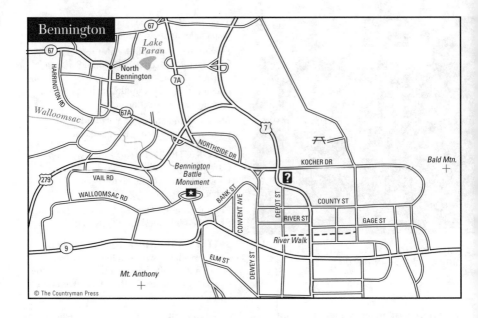

including one of the oldest American Revolutionary flags in existence, is extremely helpful before visiting Old Bennington. The rest of the eclectic collection includes medical tools, hair jewelry, modern art, and a gallery and study center devoted to historic Bennington Pottery, notably an extraordinary 10-foot ceramic piece created for the 1853 Crystal Palace Exhibition in London. Give yourself a few hours to absorb it all. $10 adults, $9 students/seniors, under 18 free.

✳ To Do

CANOEING BattenKill Canoe Ltd. (802-362-2800; 800-421-5268; battenkill.com), River Rd., off Rt. 7A, Arlington, is the center for day trips—with van service—canoe camping, instruction, rentals, and equipment. Customized inn-to-inn tours with hiking as well as paddling.

CULTURAL ATTRACTIONS Bennington Center for the Arts and the **Vermont Covered Bridge Museum** (802-442-7158; thebennington.org), 44 Gypsy Lane, Bennington. Open Mon., Wed.–Sat., 10–5. Adults $9, seniors/students $8, children under 12 free. These are two adjoining but very different museums. The Bennington Center has several fine art galleries, including Native American arts and fine art bird carvings, changing exhibits, wind sculptures, and an ongoing performance schedule. The second museum presents Vermont's covered bridges and their lore, delivered through videos, dioramas, and interactive exhibits, part of the Bennington Center for the Arts.

NORTH BENNINGTON'S MILE-AROUND WOODS PATH

⌀ **The Dollhouse and Toy Museum of Vermont** (802-447-2496; dollhouseandtoymuseum ofvermont.com), 212 Union St., Bennington. Open Sat.–Sun. 1–4 or by appointment. Admission is $4 for adults, $2 for children. The house in which this permanent collection of dollhouses resides looks like a dollhouse itself. Dollhouses and dolls of many styles as well as trains, trucks, and other educational toys. Open every day Christmas and New Year's weeks.

GOLF ✔ **Mount Anthony Country Club** (802-447-2617; mtanthonycc.com), 180 Country Club Dr. (just below the Battle Monument): 18-hole golf course with pro shop and clinics open Apr.–Nov. The Grille restaurant is open year-round. See *Dining Out*.

HIKING/WALKING The Appalachian Trail crosses Rt. 9 several miles east of Bennington. There's a parking area and an easy hike south to Harmon Hill for a 360-degree view. Allow three or four hours round-trip.

✔ **Mile-Around Woods** (northbennington.org), Park St., North Bennington. West of the Park-McCullough House, look for the break in the stone wall and the marked entrance to this foot and bridle path across lovely woods and meadows, part of the original estate.

HISTORICAL ATTRACTIONS ✔ **The Park-McCullough House** (802-442-5441; parkmccullough .org), 1 Park St., North Bennington just off Main St. Open for tours Fri. 10–4, Mar.–Dec., and by appointment. A 35-room Victorian mansion built in 1865 by Trenor W. Park. Born poor, Park was a self-educated lawyer who married the daughter of a former governor at age 23. In 1852 he took his young family to California, where he made a fortune in the gold rush. Back in Vermont, he bought his

ANNA MARY ROBERTSON "GRANDMA" MOSES

Anna Mary Robertson Moses lived in a county fair world. When she entered her first, "I won a prize for my fruit and jam, but no pictures," she recalled. She brought her preserves along with her to gallery shows in New York City, too.

Moses began painting in Bennington in 1932, when she moved to the city to care for her daughter Anna who was suffering from tuberculosis. Painting replaced pictures embroidered with wool when Moses' arthritis prevented her from stitching. Holding a paintbrush was gentler on her joints.

Her naive depictions of her childhood in Greenwich, New York, attracted no notice, and once her daughter healed, Moses returned to her farm in Hoosick Falls, New York. It was there that wealthy art collector Louis J. Caldor first spied Moses' work in the window of a drugstore. What attracted him isn't clear. Perhaps it was the sparkles?

More likely, it was a vogue for outsider art, and Moses' candy-colored representations of what she called "old-timey" scenes certainly fit the bill. At first her Yankee pragmatism prevented her from leaving the farm to appear at exhibitions. Once won over, she made the big-city scene complete with baked goods and jam to share with her fans.

The Bennington Museum hosts the world's largest public collection of Moses' paintings. They are almost completely lacking in perspective or depth. Faces are pink blobs that resemble smiley faces. And yes, winter scenes are speckled with glitter, much to the chagrin of Moses' handlers.

A pair of paintings on display at the museum depicts the town of Bennington. They don't bear much of a resemblance to the Bennington of today. But they don't look much like the Bennington of Moses' time, either. One was painted from life, another from a photograph a decade later. But Moses admitted that she had little regard for accuracy.

Instead, her childish paintings capture a feeling. *A Country Wedding* is a more accurate time capsule of a sunny late-19th-century wedding day than any photograph. *Sugaring Off* conjures every sense of boiling maple sap around an outdoor fire and enjoying a taste of sugar on snow.

At the Bennington Museum, the sensory experience of Moses' life isn't limited to her canvases. The schoolhouse she attended until becoming a "hired girl" at age 12 has been transported to Bennington and installed down a short hallway from the gallery devoted to Moses' work. There her early years, including items she owned and contemporary clothing and dolls, come to three-dimensional life.

Moses was born nearly a year before Abraham Lincoln took office. She died at 101, having enjoyed TV appearances, an Oscar-nominated biographical documentary, and a *Life* magazine cover devoted to her 100th birthday. Perhaps she was less a "genuine American primitive" than one of America's first ironic celebrities.

father-in-law's farm and built this three-story, mansard-roofed mansion with a grand staircase and hall, stained-glass skylight, and richly paneled woodwork. Park's son-in-law, John G. McCullough, became governor of Vermont in 1902 and raised his family in the capacious home. It has been open to the public since 1965 and is on the National Register of Historic Places, functioning as a community arts center. The house is filled with artwork, furniture, artifacts, clothing, and toys, more than 100,000 items belonging to the Hall-Park-McCullough family. There's an appealing children's playhouse replica of the mansion; also a gift shop. The **Carriage Barn** houses a collection of carriages and doubles as an events and reception site. Inquire about concerts, lectures, and other special events.

Robert Frost Stone House Museum (802-447-6200; frostfriends.org), 121 Rt. 7A, S. Shaftsbury. Open May–Oct., days vary seasonally. $6 adults, $5 seniors, $3 ages 18 and under; 6 and under free. The poet lived and worked for a time in the 1920s in this stone-house-turned-museum; it was here that he wrote "Stopping by Woods on a Snowy Evening." From the windows you can still see the apple trees, stone walls, and country lanes that inspired him. Biographical exhibits and a few of his personal belongings are on display.

🌢 **The Shaftsbury Historical Society** (802-375-2776; vermonthistory.org), Rt. 7A, Shaftsbury. Open May–Oct., weekends 2–4. This gradually developing cluster of historic buildings includes two schools and an 1846 Baptist meetinghouse. Free.

HORSEBACK RIDING Kimberly Farms Riding Stables (802-442-5454; kimberlyfarms.org), 1214 Cross Hill Rd., North Bennington, offers trail rides, lessons, and an overnight horse camp on its 60-acre farm.

✍ **Lively's Livery** (802-447-7612; 802-379-1299; livelyslivery.com), 193 Crossover Rd., Bennington. Horse-drawn carriage service, wagon rides, trail rides, sleigh rides, bridge tours.

SCENIC DRIVES Bennington County's five covered bridges. The **Silk Road Bridge** (1840), the **Paper Mill Village Bridge** (1840s), and the **Henry Bridge** (rebuilt 1989) are all within a couple of miles just off Rt. 67A, south of the village of North Bennington. Continue north on Rt. 67A as it turns into Main St., then left on Rt. 67 to Rt. 7A and follow it north, past the Robert Frost House and Lake Shaftsbury State Park to the village of Arlington. Note the historic marker in front of the home of writer Dorothy Canfield Fisher. Turn left onto Rt. 313 and follow the Battenkill for 4.4 miles through woods and farmland to West Arlington to find the frequently photographed tableau of the classic green-shuttered church with a spiky steeple, a farmhouse (painter Norman Rockwell's home from 1939 until 1953), and the red **West Arlington Bridge** (1872). Return to Arlington Village and, at the sign for East Arlington, turn north on the East Arlington Rd., following it 1.9 miles to the **Chiselville Bridge**, built high above Roaring Branch Brook in 1879. Continue along this road until it veers to join Rt. 7A in Sunderland, near the toll road to the top of Mount Equinox.

Readsboro. This road less taken is our favorite way to Bennington from Massachusetts. Follow Rt. 2 west from Greenfield, Massachusetts, for 3.6 miles to Colrain Rd. Continue for 17.3 scenic miles through Colrain, Massachusetts, to Jacksonville, Vermont. Here Rt. 100 splits, the more traveled road heading north to Rt. 9 (see below) at Wilmington, the other branch meandering west through Whitingham and on 14 miles to Readsboro—arguably the most remote town in southern Vermont and one that's recently become a center for artists and craftspeople. It was its proximity to the Hoosac Tunnel and its status as a roundhouse for the Wilmington Railroad that spawned this late-19th-century mill village (population 809), which was later known for its large chair factory. The **Readsboro Inn** (802-423-5048; readsboroinn.com) marks the center of town with its lounge and cheerful, reasonably priced dining room and lodging. Readsboro Glassworks (see *Selective Shopping*) is another draw. Several more studios are open periodically, and a crafts festival is held every September (readsboroarts.org). The **Readsboro Historical Society** (802-423-5630; 7009 Main St.) is open by appointment. It's 11 more miles northwest through high backcountry to Rt. 9 at Searsburg, 14 miles east of Bennington.

Molly Stark Byway. For a map and details about the 48 miles of Rt. 9 between Bennington and Brattleboro, see the introduction to "Southern Vermont" and *Scenic Byways* in the Mount Snow chapter. Also see mollystarkbyway.org.

SWIMMING Lake Paran (802-688-6270; northbennington.org), Rt. 67, North Bennington. This hidden gem, a town recreation area centered on a small lake with facilities for swimming, also has good fishing. Daily rates.

Also see Lake Shaftsbury State Park and Woodbury State Park under *Green Space*.

Bennington Tennis Center (802-447-7557; benningtontenniscenter.com), 200 Lovers Lane, Bennington. An indoor tennis club complete with lessons.

✳ Winter Sports

CROSS COUNTRY SKIING ✔ **Prospect Mountain Nordic Ski Center** (802-442-2575; prospect mountain.com), 204 Prospect Access Rd., Woodford (you may need to set your GPS for Bennington). Open daily 9–5, as long as there's snow. Little Woodford has the highest elevation of any town in the state. The base at this cross-country skiing area is 2,250 feet, increasing the odds for consistent snow. Frequently it's snowing here when it's raining (literally) down the road. Phone or check the website for conditions. A former downhill family ski area, the focus is now on 30 km of cross-country trails groomed for skating and classic skiing plus extensive backcountry connecting with the Green Mountain National Forest trails. The base lodge has a big stone hearth, a woodstove, and a modest restaurant. Moonlight dinners and ski tours during full moons.

Also see **Woodford State Park** under *Green Space.*

✳ Green Space

✔ **Lake Shaftsbury State Park** (802-375-9978; vtstateparks.com), 262 Lake Shaftsbury Rd., Shaftsbury. Open Memorial Day weekend–Labor Day weekend. A private resort until 1974, this 84-acre area surrounding Lake Shaftsbury offers swimming, picnicking, rental kayaks, rowboats and pedal boats, a concession stand, a lakefront cottage rental sleeping six, and 15 lean-tos clustered for group camping. The Healing Spring Nature Trail circles the lake.

✔ **Woodford State Park** (802-447-7169; vtstateparks.com) 142 State Park Rd., Bennington. This 400-acre heavily wooded area includes 103 camping sites, 20 with lean-tos; swimming in Adams Reservoir from a small beach; a children's playground; picnic spots; and canoe, kayak, and rowboat rentals. Several hiking trails—including the 2.7-mile trail around the lake—are excellent for cross-country skiing in winter.

✳ Lodging

INNS AND BED & BREAKFASTS

In Bennington 05201

♂ ❧ **The Four Chimneys Inn** (802-447-3500; fourchimneys.com), 21 West Rd. (Rt. 9) in Old Bennington. This stately, 1910 Colonial Revival home, once the estate of businessman Phillip Jennings, offers 11 luxurious rooms, all spacious with private bath, TV, and phone, most with fireplace and Jacuzzi, and two with glassed-in porch. Firewood provided. The grounds are beautifully landscaped, but the inn is not suited to pets or children under age 12. $129–299 per room, including country breakfast. (See also *Dining Out.*)

South Shire Inn (802-447-3839; southshire .com), 124 Elm St. This attractive turn-of-the-20th-century mansion features 10-foot ceilings with plaster moldings, a library with a massive mahogany fireplace, an Italianate formal dining room, and comfortable bedrooms furnished with antiques. Three of the nine guest rooms have a fireplace, and all have a private bath; two can be joined as a suite. Carriage House rooms have whirlpool tub, fireplace, and TV. Tea is served many afternoons. $169–239 with breakfast. Unable to accommodate pets or children. Senior discounts offered.

In North Bennington 05257

✪ **The Eddington House** (802-442-1511; 800-941-1857; eddingtonhouseinn.com), 21 Main St. This sunny, elegantly comfortable vintage-1857 manse is in the middle of a picturesque village, within walking distance of a waterfall and handy to walking paths and swimming. Patti and Steve Eddington offer three tastefully furnished, unfussy rooms with private bath and boast "the best beds anywhere." A full breakfast and afternoon tea are included in $109–179. Patti is a font of local information, which she delights in sharing along with her homemade truffles. Children over 12 welcome.

♂ ❧ **The Henry House** (802-447-7612; the henryhouseinn.com), 1338 Murphy Rd. Steps away from the Henry Covered Bridge lie these beautiful guest rooms, four with private bath, and common rooms in a home built in 1769 (it's on the National Register of Historic Places). Among the guest rooms, the Ballroom, with its vaulted 14-foot ceiling, four-poster canopy bed, and a sitting area with working fireplace, is the most notable ($155). The others are also distinctive. $100–140, including breakfast. Children over 12 are welcome. With its gracious rooms and expansive grounds, this is a great venue for weddings.

♂ **Taraden** (802-447-3434; taraden.com), 183 Park St. The Tudor-style manor, part of a former 500-acre estate, still retains 19 acres, its barn (for small weddings and events), and a guest cottage. Bob and Nan Lowary offer three suites: The two-room Night Pasture upstairs sleeps four and has a fridge, microwave, and TV; the West Wing suite sleeps three (fridge and TV); and the Cottage sleeps two with French doors opening onto a deck (fridge and microwave). $165–185 per couple, $35 per extra person, includes a full breakfast. Children over 12 welcome.

MOTELS

In Bennington 05201

♦ **Paradise Motor Inn** (802-442-8351; 800-575-5784; theparadisemotorinn.com), 141 W. Main St., close to the Bennington Museum, with 77 air-conditioned rooms, a pool, and a tennis court, set in 8 landscaped acres on a knoll above Rt. 9. From $70 for a standard room (two king beds) off-season to $240 for a suite with living room and kitchen in foliage season.

♦ ♥ **Knotty Pine Motel** (802-442-5487; knottypinemotel.com), 130 Northside Dr. (Rt. 7A). The locals use this family-owned motel to put up their guests, not a bad sign. There's a pool and an adjacent diner. Pets are welcome as long as they are not left alone. The clean, no-frills rooms range $65–99. Continental breakfast included.

♦ ♥ **Harwood Hill Motel** (802-442-6278; 877-442-6200; harwoodhillmotel.com), 864 Harwood Hill Rd. Perched on a hilltop north of Bennington, this motel "with the million dollar view" offers eight deluxe rooms, three cottages, and three economy units, all with air-conditioning, refrigerator, and cable TV. The deluxe rooms have microwave and phone, $73–95; pets (with restrictions) $8 per night.

CAMPING See Vermont State Parks (vtstateparks.com) under *Green Space*. Also see private campgrounds listed at bennington.com.

✱ Where to Eat

DINING OUT Pangaea Restaurant & Lounge (802-442-7171; Lounge 802-442-4466; vermontfinedining.com), 1 Prospect St., North Bennington. Dinner is served in the restaurant Tues.–Sat. 5–9. The Lounge is open nightly, 5–10. This chef-owned eatery in the center of tiny North Bennington is southern Vermont's culinary star. William Scully aims to draw the best from every continent, and it shows in his menu. His wine cellar has won *Wine Spectator* awards, and beers include imports from India

and the Czech Republic. Most menu items can be made as starters or entrées to formulate your own tasting menu. Perhaps a scallop and black trumpet mushroom tart will whet your palate? In summer, seating extends to an outdoor terrace overlooking the river. Entrées $30–39.

The Four Chimneys Inn (802-447-3500; four chimneys.com), 21 West Rd. (Rt. 9), Old Bennington. Only open for dinner Aug.–Oct., so plan ahead (closed Tues. and Thurs.). The setting is a casually elegant dining room and an enclosed porch where many celebrities have dined for decades. Dinner could begin with Brie en croute for two ($12) and continue with sea bass en papillote flavored with lemongrass and red curry ($36). Full bar, reservations essential.

♂ ♿ **The Grille at Mount Anthony Club** (802-442-2617; mtanthonycc.com), 180 Country Club Dr., Bennington. Open year-round for lunch and dinner. With a winter hearth and seasonal terrace, it's a great place to stop after visiting the nearby Bennington Monument. For lunch try a wrap, panini, or burger. Dinner choices range from sliders to rack of lamb. Entrées $18–27.

✪ ♦ **Allegro Ristorante** (802-442-0990; allegroristorante.com), 520 Main St., Bennington. Despite being prepared with ingredients from small, local farms, the creative Italian fare here is perhaps the best value in the area. Appetizers, which top out at $10, are enough to satisfy a smaller appetite. Pastas and entrées range from $12 to $20. If you're lucky enough to be there when the menu includes rabbit-and-ricotta meatballs over potato gnocchi with cherry tomatoes, don't miss pairing it with an Italian wine or beer.

EATING OUT

In Bennington

♦ **Blue Benn Diner** (802-442-5140), 314 North St. (Rt. 7). Open daily for breakfast and lunch. This 1940s diner combines "road fare" with a few surprises, including tabouleh and falafel. A 10-minute wait for a seat is not uncommon.

✪ ♦ ♂ **Lil' Britain** (802-442-2447), 116 North St. Open Tues.–Sat for lunch and dinner. The red English phone booth in the corner says it all: This is southern Vermont's only authentic chip shop. Order your fish-and-chips with mushy peas and a side of curry for dipping, then take home a sausage roll or steak-and-kidney pie. There are Brit groceries, too.

♦ ♂ ♿ **Madison Brewing Company** (802-442-7397; madisonbrewingco.com), 428 Main St.

Rachel Carter

STREET FOOD IN BENNINGTON

Open for lunch and dinner daily. A long-standing local family, the Madisons, began brewing as a hobby before opening this brewpub. It has become a destination stop for beer lovers. Outdoor seating in warm weather and a huge pub menu are the other attractions, including bison meatloaf.

In North Bennington

🍴 **Kevin's Sports Pub & Restaurant** (802-442-0122; kevinssportspubandrestaurant.com), 27 Main St. Open daily for lunch, dinner, and late night. Live entertainment on weekends, and the game is always on. The community gathering spot, frequently packed for dinner—but you can always find space at the bar.

((ᵧ)) **Powers Market** (802-442-6821; powers market.com), 9 Main St. (Rt. 67A). Open daily 7–6. Sited on the village's triangular square, this columned establishment was built in 1833 as a company store for the local paper mill. There's still an old-fashioned soda fountain, with flavors including cherry cola, root beer, and pomegranate, with or without ice cream. House specialty sandwiches are available on gluten-free bread upon request.

🍴 ((ᵧ)) **Marigold Kitchen** (802-445-4545; marigoldkitchen.info), 25 Main St. Open Tues.–Sun for dinner, lunch on Fri.–Sat. Pleasant atmosphere, organic and artisan freshly made pizzas and salads. Sit down or take out.

BAKERIES 🍴 **Bakkerij Krijnen** (802-442-1001), 1001 Main St., Bennington. Open daily. Hidden in a residential neighborhood, it's easy to miss this Dutch scratch bakery, but don't. You'll be a happier person for having tucked into marzipan-filled Flemish pastries and naturally leavened bread stamped with the shape of Vermont. Comforting soups are served at lunchtime.

🍴 **Crazy Russian Girls Neighborhood Bakery** (802-442-4688), 443 Main St., Bennington. Open until 5 PM Mon.–Sat. Every Friday is Peasant Lunch Day, when diners can binge on homemade pierogi, sauerkraut, and borscht. Russian bread and pastries are always available, but the bulk of the offerings are all-American cookies, cakes, and simple lunches.

✳ Entertainment

Oldcastle Theatre Company (802-447-0564; oldcastletheatre.org), 331 Main St., Bennington. This professional theater company performs a mix of warhorses and new works alike, as well as both musicals and straight plays. Check the website for lodging and restaurant deals available with theater tickets.

Bennington College (802-442-5401; bennington.edu), 1 College Dr., Bennington. This beautiful campus hosts many events open to the public; check the website for a calendar.

Vermont Arts Exchange (802-442-5549; vtartxchange.org), 29 Sage Street Mill, North Bennington. Basement Music Series concerts, art classes, art shows, yoga, performances, special events, facility rental.

Also see **The Bennington Center for the Arts** under *Cultural Attractions*.

✳ Selective Shopping

ART GALLERIES & CRAFTS STUDIOS

Hawkins House (802-447-0488; hawkinshouse .net), 262 North St. (Rt. 7), Bennington, is a crafts market complex filled with the work of 400 diverse artisans. Open daily.

Bennington Arts Guild (802-442-7838; benningtonartsguild.com), 103 South St., Bennington. Open Thurs.–Mon. Showcasing the work of more than two dozen local artists, photographers, and craftspeople; changing exhibits.

Fiddlehead at Four Corners (802-447-1000; getartbehappy.com), 338 Main St., Bennington. Open 7 days a week. This downtown gallery is itself a work of art—housed within the marble walls of a historic bank complete with high ceilings and brass chandeliers. Former teacher Joel Lentzner and his wife, Nina, produce one-of-a-kind hand-painted furniture. The fine art and contemporary crafts include Dr. Seuss art, glass, sculpture, jewelry, and ceramics.

Mount Nebo Gallery (800-328-6326; will moses.com), 60 Grandma Moses Rd., Eagle Bridge, New York. Open daily. Off Rt. 67, less than a dozen miles west of North Bennington, the original white frame farmhouse that was home for Grandma Moses now belongs to her

Bennington Potters Yard
(802-447-7531; bennington
potters.com), 324 County St.,
Bennington. Open year-round,
Mon.–Sat. 9:30–6, Sun. 10–5.
Bennington was known for its
stoneware pottery in the early
and mid-1800s, and ornate
samples can be viewed in the
Bennington Museum. But the
brand lives on. In 1964 Bennington Potters expanded into
its present home, once a business supply outlet for coal, firewood, ice, and lumber. Over
the years the company has
grown while retaining its quality, design, and a dozen full-
time potters. This flagship
factory store also stocks specialty foods, housewares, and
gifts.

BENNINGTON POTTERS

Christina Tree

great-grandson, artist Will Moses. Is his work a
rip-off of his ancestor's? Sure, but if it's your
thing, this is the place for numbered and signed
prints, cards, and other products.

Visit vermontcrafts.com for all area artisans and
note that Memorial Day weekend is **Open Studio Weekend** in Vermont.

BOOKSTORES Bennington Bookshop (802-
442-5059), 467 Main St., Bennington. Open
daily 9–5:30, Fri. until 9, Sun. noon–4.
Extended hours in summer. A full-service,

BENNINGTON POTTERY GALLERY AND STUDY
CENTER

Alice Levitt

independent bookstore specializing in Vermont
books, adult and children's titles, and greeting
cards.

Now and Then Books (802-442-5566; now
andthenbooksvt.com), 439 Main St., 2nd floor,
Bennington. Open Wed.–Mon. The oldest
used- and collectible-book shop in the area,
with an emphasis on fiction, cookbooks, and
Vermont. With more than 55,000, this is one of
New England's largest antiquarian collections.

BREWERIES Northshire Brewery (802-681-
0201; northshirebrewery.com), 108 County St.,
Bennington. Tours and tastings Saturday or by
appointment; microbrews include Equinox Pil-
sner, Battenkill Ale, Chocolate Stout, and Summer Lager.

Madison Brewing Company (madison
brewingco.com) in downtown Bennington. See
Eating Out.

**FARMS ✐ The Apple Barn & Country Bake
Shop** (802-447-7780; 888-8-APPLES; theapple
barn.com), 604 Rt. 7 south, Bennington. Open
daily May–Oct. Up to 30 varieties of apples to
pick, six types of strawberries, and blueberries;
also plenty of produce, candy, cheese, pies, and
food specialties in the farm store complete with
bakery and coffee shop.

Shaftsbury Alpacas (802-447-3992; shaftsbury
alpacas.com), 12 S. Stateline Rd., Shaftsbury.
Sandy and Johan Harder invite you to spend

Alice Levitt

MORRIS AND BETTY AT THE VILLAGE
CHOCOLATE SHOPPE, BENNINGTON

a day as an alpaca farmer—or just to shop in
the Alpaca Shack for throws, slippers, outer-
wear, and more. Open weekends 11–4, weekdays after 2.

Clear Brook Farm (802-442-4273; clearbrook
farm.com), 983 Myers Rd., Shaftsbury. Open
10–6 mid-May–mid-Oct. Bedding plants, produce, farm store on a growing organic farm.

Wing and a Prayer Farm (802-233-6031;
wingandaprayerfarm.com), 47 Hidden Valley
Rd., Shaftsbury. Visits by appointment. Meet
the alpacas, sheep, and goats whose hair is made
into wool at this small farm. Occasional
workshops.

**FARMERS MARKET Walloomsac Farmers
Market**, behind Bennington Station at River-
walk Park. Info at vermontagriculture.com.

SPECIALTY SHOPS ⚭ **Hemmings Old-
Fashioned Filling Station** (802-442-3101;
hemmings.com), 216 Main St., Bennington.
Open daily 7–7. A full-service classic Sunoco
filling station and convenience store—and the
home of the world's largest collector car marketplace. Vintage vehicle displays include a 1937
Hudson and a 1910 Buick; there's also a quasi-
museum selling auto-related memorabilia.
Check the website for frequent cruise-ins and
events.

Mahican Moccasin Factory (802-823-5294;
mahicanmoccasins.com), 2970 Rt. 7 in Pownal,
6 miles south of Bennington on the right.
Charles Gray crafts handmade footwear from
deerskin, elk, cow, and buffalo hide to order.
Call ahead for hours, open most of the year.

Camelot Village (shopsatcamelotvillage.com),
located in a string of renovated 18th-century
barns just west of the Old First Church on
Rt. 9 in Bennington. Open 9:30–5:30 daily.
The **Antique Center** (802-447-0039) displays
antiques and collectibles from more than
140 dealers, and the **Artisan Center**

(802-447-0228) represents the work of more
than 100 artisans and craftspeople. **Bennington
Vintage Sewing** (802-688-9919) offers antique
and vintage fashions from the 1860s to the
1970s. The **Furniture Barn & Gallery**
(877-BEDDING) sells new, used, vintage, and
antique furniture.

The Village Chocolate Shoppe (802-447-
3789; villagepeddlervt.com), 471 Main St., Bennington. Open daily; closed Sun. Jan.–May.
Meet Morris and Betty, a mated pair of 100-
pound chocolate moose. You can't eat them, but
their "moose stuff" is for sale, as are gelati, and
olive-oil-infused chocolate bars.

✳ Special Events

May 1: **Annual Bennington Road Race**
(bkvr.org)—the local marathon, at the Park-
McCullough House, North Bennington.

Memorial Day weekend: **Bennington Mayfest**
(betterbennington.com)—a 10–5 street festival
downtown with artisans, local food vendors, and
entertainment.

⚭ *July 4:* **Annual 4th of July Celebration**
(bennington.com) with evening fireworks,
Willow Park.

⚭ *June or July:* **Pownal Valley Fair** (802-823-
5683)—exhibits, antique tractor pull, bingo,
music, fireworks, petting zoo, and more.

A GAS STATION/VINTAGE CAR MUSEUM IS
HOME TO HEMMINGS MOTOR NEWS.

Christina Tree

Mid-August: **Bennington Battle Day Week of Celebrations** (bennington.com), with the annual fire department's Sunday parade. Battle reenactments, special museum events, family activities.

❧ *Labor Day weekend:* **Southern Vermont Garlic & Herb Festival** (lovegarlic.com), Camelot Village. Sample garlic jelly and ice cream, pickled and roasted garlic, garlic golf, also crafts and music.

Mid-September: **Annual Bennington Car Show & Swap Meet** at Willow Park, Bennington (bennington.com). Car show, swap meet, crafts festival, car corral, tractor pull, food, and entertainment. **Annual Bennington Quilt Fest** (benningtonquiltfest.com)—an exhibit of statewide quilts, plus lectures and demonstrations at the middle school.

Weekend before Halloween: **Fallapalooza! Fall Festival** (betterbennington.com) held in downtown Bennington with food, vendors, entertainment, Walloomsac farmers market, and activities.

Late November–mid-December: **Festival of the Trees**, Bennington Museum. Silent auction, food, and tour of decorated trees and wreaths throughout the museum's galleries (bennington museum.org).

MANCHESTER AND
THE MOUNTAINS
INCLUDING ARLINGTON, DORSET, DANBY, PERU, LONDONDERRY, AND PAWLET

Manchester has been a summer resort since the Civil War. The nearby Green Mountains have drawn skiers since 1939 when Bromley opened, augmented in the 1960s by Stratton and Magic and by several dependably snowy cross-country centers.

Manchester itself is an up-and-down town consisting of two villages that once varied in status with their altitude. Hilltop Manchester Village is a gathering of mansions along marble sidewalks around the Congregational church, the gold-domed Bennington County Courthouse, and the white-columned, tower-topped Equinox Resort. Mrs. Abraham Lincoln and her sons spent two seasons here, booking a third for the entire family for the summer of 1865; the president, unfortunately, never made it.

Other presidents—Taft, Grant, Theodore Roosevelt, and Benjamin Harrison—came to stay at the Equinox, but it was Lincoln's family who adopted the village. Robert Todd Lincoln, president of the Pullman Palace Car Company, selected Manchester Village as his summer home, building Hildene, the lavish mansion that's now such an interesting place to visit. Other opulent "summer cottages" are sequestered off River Road and nearby country lanes. Several are now B&Bs.

In the 19th century the opulence of Manchester Village contrasted sharply with the poverty of neighboring "Factory Point" down the hill, home to sawmills, marble works, and a tannery. The era is memorialized in Sarah Cleghorn's 1917 quatrain:

> The golf links lie so near the mill
> That almost every day
> The laboring child can look out
> And see the men at play.

Today Manchester Center (alias Factory Point) is the bustling, attractive center of town, a walk-able mix of factory outlets and specialty stores. While the villages retain separate zip codes and zoning, the lines between have been blurred by the lineup of shops and restaurants along Rt. 7A. Some 30 top brand outlets fill old homes and house-sized compounds, blending nicely with shopping landmarks like the Orvis Retail Store, which has been supplying the needs of fishermen and other sporting folk since 1856.

Luckily the 1930s Work Progress Administration plan to carve ski trails on Mount Equinox never panned out, and Manchester Village retains its serene, white-clapboard good looks, at least for the time being. A stray peak from the Taconic range, Mount Equinox thrusts up 3,800 feet from behind its namesake hotel. Much of it now owned by the Carthusian monks, it's accessible by hiking trail and by a toll road from Rt. 7A in Sunderland, south of town.

The Battenkill, beloved by fishermen and canoeists, runs south from Manchester through Sunder-land and Arlington, one of Vermont's oldest towns with more than its share of covered bridges, antiques stores, and genuine beauty.

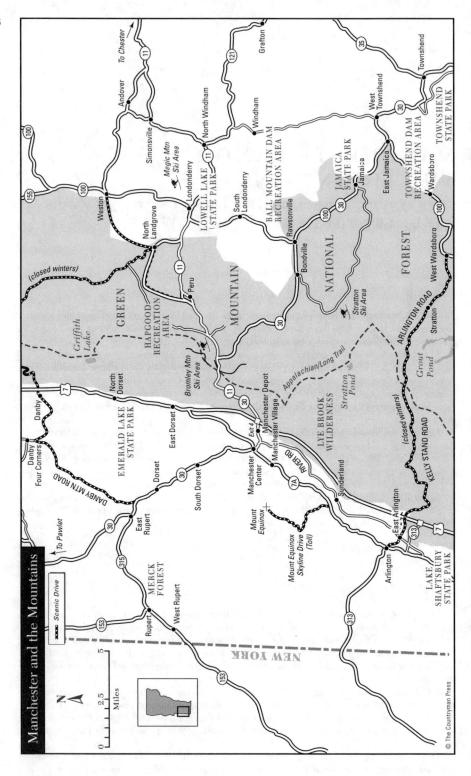

Manchester and the Mountains

- - - Scenic Drive

N

Miles
0   2.5   5

© The Countryman Press

NEW YORK

To the east the Green Mountains rise even within Manchester town limits to 3,100 feet, rolling off into heavily forested uplands punctuated along Rt. 11 by picturesque villages like Peru, Landgrove, and Londonderry. In winter there's skiing at Bromley and Magic Mountains and the area's largest ski resort, Stratton Mountain at 3,900 feet.

Manchester Center is sited at the confluence of major roads north and south, east and west. From Manchester, Rt. 30 leads to the elegant village of Dorset, known for its year-round playhouse and destination dining. It then veers northeast through the lovely, long-farmed Mettawee River Valley to the intriguing village of Pawlet and beyond. Heading directly north, Rt. 7 follows the Otter Creek from North Dorset to Danby through a steep-sided, heavily wooded, and lonely valley, a hiking haven.

Manchester itself remains a cultural as well as shopping center, home to the Southern Vermont Arts Center and the Manchester Music Festival, as well as to the monthlong Vermont Summer Festival Horse Show.

GUIDANCE Manchester and the Mountains Regional Chamber of Commerce (802-362-6313; 800-362-4144; visitmanchestervt.com), 39 Bonnet St., Manchester Center. Open Mon.–Fri. 9–5, Sat. 10–4, Sun. 11–3. The chamber's splendid air-conditioned building is just off Main St., behind Northshire Books. It offers restrooms and well as live advice and walls of printed info. Also check the Shires of Vermont regional tourism website: shiresofvermont.com.

GETTING THERE *By car:* From Bennington, US 7 to Manchester is a limited-access highway that's speedy but dull, except for viewing Mount Equinox. You get a more interesting taste of the area, especially around Arlington, by clinging to Historic Rt. 7A, now the Shires of Vermont Scenic Byway. From the southeast, the obvious access is I-91 to Brattleboro, then Rt. 30 north.

From New York City, take I-87 to Exit 23, then I-787 to Exit 9E to Rt. 7 east to Bennington; continue on Rt. 279 to Rt. 7 north to Exit 4, or follow Historic Rt. 7A from Bennington.

MEDICAL EMERGENCY Emergency service is available by calling **911. Northshire Medical Center** (802-362-4440), Main St., Manchester Center. **Mountain Valley Medical Clinic** (802-824-6901; ourclinic.org), Rt. 11, Londonderry. **Carlos Otis Clinic** (802-297-2300; carlosotisclinic.org), at Stratton Mountain.

✳ Villages

In addition to Manchester, the area's picturesque places include Arlington, 7 miles south along Rt. 7A; Dorset, 8 miles to the northwest; Pawlet, another 7 miles to the north on Rt. 30; and Danby, 8 miles north of Dorset and 10 miles east of Pawlet.

Arlington (population 2,400; arlingtonvt.org). Although never formally the capital of Vermont, this was the de facto seat of government during most of the Revolutionary period. Fearing British attacks in the north, Vermont's first governor, Thomas Chittenden, moved south from Williston, liberated a Tory property in Arlington (the area known as Tory Hollow), and conducted affairs of state from there, making it one of Vermont's most historic villages.

Dorothy Canfield Fisher, early American author and longtime Book-of-the-Month Club judge, made her home here. Another famous resident was artist Norman Rockwell, who lived in West Arlington from 1939 to 1953 and incorporated local scenes into his paintings of small-town Americana. One of his models was Dr. George A. Russell, the country doctor immortalized in the Rockwell print that hangs in thousands of doctors' offices. Russell amassed an important collection of Vermontiana (including S. C. Fisher materials, works by Norman Rockwell, and many photographs dating from 1860–90),

NORMAN ROCKWELL LIVED HERE IN WEST ARLINGTON, WITHIN SIGHT OF THE CHURCH AND COVERED BRIDGE.

Christina Tree

now on view in the Martha Canfield Memorial Free Library (802-375-6153; marthacanfield library.org), 528 East Arlington Rd. Turn east off Rt. 7A to find antiques shops and the way along the Battenkill to the Chiselville Covered Bridge.

Dorset (dorsetvt.com). This pristine village of a little more than 2,000 souls is visible evidence that it takes money to prevent the future. A fashionable summer refuge for years, few signs of commerce mar its green lawns and marble sidewalks. Today's tranquility, making it a haven for artists, writers, and the affluent, contrasts sharply with the hotheaded days of its youth. In 1776 the Green Mountain Boys gathered in Cephas Kent's tavern and issued their first declaration of independence from the New Hampshire Grants, signed by Thomas Chittenden, Ira Allen, Matthew Lyon, Seth Warner, and other Founding Fathers of Vermont. Today the Dorset Inn (see *Lodging*), said to be the state's old-

Alice Levitt

A PLAQUE IN DORSET MARKING THE SITE OF NH INDEPENDENCE

est continuously operating hostelry, is the village's focal point, along with the Dorset Playhouse (see *Entertainment*), one of New England's most venerable summer theaters, and the private Dorset Field Club, an 18-hole golf course billed as the state's oldest. The first marble to be quarried in North America came from Dorset, and one quarry—now a popular swimming hole—supplied the marble for New York City's Public Library. The newly expanded Bley House Museum (802-867-0331; dorset-vthistory.org) at the junction of Main St. and Rt. 30 offers displays about the history of local marble quarrying.

Pawlet (pawletvermont.com). Not far north of Dorset, this hamlet on Rt. 30 is an unexpected delight, with a mix of architectural styles in buildings that cling to the rather steep slopes leading up from Flower Brook, over which Johnny Mach's General Store extends. Gib Mach harnessed the rushing brook to a turbine that generated his electricity and built a glass-topped counter at the end of a store aisle through which you can still peer down at the water surging through the narrow gorge below. The clutch of shops and restaurants are worth investigating—it won't take long to give the town a thorough exploration.

✳ Must See

♿ **Southern Vermont Arts Center** (802-362-1405; svac.org), 930 SVAC Dr. off West Rd., 1 mile north of the Equinox, Manchester Center. Open all year, Tues.–Sat. 10–5, Sun. noon–5. $6 nonmembers, $3 students; free for members and children under 13. The Elizabeth de C. Wilson Museum is a work of art in itself with its soaring, light-filled galleries that house some first-class touring shows of paintings, sculpture, prints, and photography. Concerts, including the summer Manchester Music Festival series, ballet performances, and lectures, are held in the adjacent, 430-seat Arkell Pavilion; there are special events throughout the year. Lunch and dinner are served in the café in summer and fall, and there are also pre-performance dinners. Trails run through the woods, among them a botany trail featuring rock formations, wildflowers, and birches; sculptures are salted through the property.

The American Museum of Fly Fishing (802-362-3300; amff.com), next to the Orvis Company's flagship store on Rt. 7A, Manchester Village. Open Tues.–Sun.10–4; $5 adults, $3 ages 5–14, $10 for a family. Closed Sun. off-season. Manchester native Charles Orvis perfected the ventilated reel, accelerating the drying of fishing line on a fishing reel. He opened his first store in 1856. The museum displays the beautiful flies of Mary Orvis Marbury as well as hundreds of rods and reels made by famous rod builders and owned by such luminaries as Daniel Webster, Bing Crosby, Ernest Hemingway, and Presidents Hoover and Eisenhower. Permanent collections and rotating artist exhibitions. Museum store; inquire about select special events.

Hildene, the Lincoln Home (802-362-1788; hildene.org), Rt. 7A, Manchester Village. Open year-round, seven days a week, 9:30–4:30. $18 adults, $5 ages 6–14. Members and children under 6, free. Limited handicapped accessibility. Built as the summer home of Robert Lincoln and his wife Mary Harlan Lincoln, the estate comprises 412 acres of land with views of both the Green Mountains and the Taconic range. Bring a picnic lunch and plan to stay at least half the day.

Visits begin at the Carriage Barn, an extensive welcome center with a museum store and a film about the Lincoln family and the Hildene experience, as well as the

Historic Hildene

ONE OF LINCOLN'S STOVEPIPE HATS IS ON DISPLAY AT THE HILDENE LIBRARY.

restoration of the Pullman car, Sunbeam. You learn that Robert, the eldest and only child of President Abraham and Mary Todd Lincoln to survive to adulthood, first came to the village in 1864 as a young man with his mother for a stay at the Equinox House; his father was assassinated before the family could return, as they had intended, in the summer of 1865. Forty years later, following a successful career as a lawyer and statesman and while he was president of the Pullman Company, Robert returned to Manchester to build the place he called his ancestral home, Hildene, a name chosen for its meaning: "hill and valley with stream." Robert died here in 1926, and members of the family, three generations of Lincolns, lived at Hildene until 1975, some 70 years. From the welcome center, transportation is provided to the various venues on the property, with the first stop at Hildene's meticulously restored 1903 wooden Pullman palace car, Sunbeam. Built during Robert's tenure as president of the company, it evokes its era through varied voices, those of Pullman Company executives, of wealthy passengers who would have chartered it, and of black Pullman porters who would have worked on it. The fourth voice is that of the visitor interacting with other visitors and staff in civil civic discourse about the difficult questions the exhibit stimulates.

Next stop is Hildene Farm with the solar-powered Rowland Agricultural Center, set in an expansive meadow. There's a timber-frame barn designed to house Hildene's goat herd and for viewing the cheesemaking process, from milking of the goats to the processing of artisanal cheese.

The mansion itself is a standout among Vermont's historic houses. The 24-room Georgian Revival manor is furnished almost entirely with the family's belongings. Guides provide an introduction and then play a short piece for guests on Mr. and Mrs. Lincoln's 1,000-pipe Aeolian organ, originally playable both manually and with one of 240 player rolls of music. The house contains many treasures, including one of three of President Lincoln's stovepipe hats still in existence. There are also special exhibits.

Immediately behind the house are the restored formal gardens, featuring the family's original peonies in June and later perennials, beautiful well into October. Be sure to walk to Mr. Lincoln's observatory on promontory next to the house. Picnic tables outside the welcome center command a pleasant view of the less formal cutting, kitchen, and butterfly gardens. Totaling 12-plus miles, walking trails are also used for cross-country skiing and snowshoeing in the winter; rentals available.

The newest addition here is the 100-acre lower portion of the property, known as the Dene, once more used for agriculture as it was during the Lincoln years. It includes a year-round greenhouse, pollinator sanctuary, and protected bobolink habitat. Guests can access this area anytime throughout the year on foot, spring through fall by tram or daily guided wagon rides. The wagon also stops at the 600-foot floating boardwalk through the wetlands and at Dene Farm to visit the animals.

✳ To Do

BICYCLING In Manchester, mountain bike, hybrid bike, and touring bike rentals and touring information are available from **Battenkill Sports Cycle Shop** (802-362-2734; battenkill sports.com), open daily 9:30–5:30, less in winter, at 1240 Depot St., in the Stone House at the junction of Rts. 7 and 11/30.

Stratton Mountain (802-297-4321; stratton .com) at Stratton Mountain rents mountain and road bikes for adults and kids through First Run Ski Shop. Bike trails continue to be developed at and around the mountain.

Equipe Sport and Mountain Riders (802-297-2847; equipesport.com), junction of Rts. 30 and 100 in Rawsonville; also in the Village Square at Stratton Mountain (802-297-3460); sales, rentals, and bike maps.

Christina Tree

THE SOUTHERN VERMONT ARTS CENTER FEATURES VERMONT'S LARGEST SCULPTURE PARK.

BOATING The Battenkill makes for satisfying canoeing in spring; the Manchester-to-Arlington section is relatively flat water, but it gets difficult a mile above Arlington.

BattenKill Canoe Ltd. (802-362-2800; battenkill.com), 6328 Rt. 7A in Arlington. An outfitter offering inn-to-inn canoe trips throughout the state but specializing in this area with combination hiking-and-paddling tours. Canoe rentals and shuttle service on the Battenkill are also offered.

Stratton Mountain (802-297-4321; stratton.com), at First Run Ski Shop. Canoe and kayak tours, rentals, and sales.

Equipe Sport (800-282-6665; equipsport.com), at the junction of Rts. 30 and 11 in Rawsonville, also offers kayak rentals.

❦ **Emerald Lake State Park** (802-362-1655; vtstateparks.com) rents canoes, kayaks, rowboats, and pedal boats.

BUSHWHACKING Land Rover Driving School at the Equinox Resort (802-362-0687; equinox resort.com), Manchester Village, at the Equinox. Off-roading driving instruction on an 80-acre course, as well as on back-roads trails for more experienced drivers. Expert instructors offer techniques over all terrain, depending on the driver's skill level. Extra passengers are welcome; drivers must have a valid license.

Backroad Discovery Tours (802-362-4997; backroaddiscovery.com). Special touring vehicles for six to eight guests traverse the back roads and byways of southern Vermont, stopping along the way to give you a taste of local history and the best places to watch sunsets and view fall foliage. Tours offered spring, summer, fall, and winter; also special history tours.

FISHING AT EMERALD LAKE
Rachel Carter

FISHING Fly-fishing has been serious business on the Battenkill since the mid-19th century. The Orvis Company began manufacturing bamboo rods in Manchester Village near the spot where they are still produced. Fishing licenses at vtfishandwildlife.com.

The Battenkill is generally recognized as Vermont's best wild trout stream; access is available at a number of places off Rt. 7A. Brown trout can also be found in Gale Meadows Pond, accessible via gravel road from Rt. 30 at Bondville. Emerald Lake in North Dorset is stocked with pike, bass, and perch; rental boats are available at the state park facility.

Orvis Fishing Schools (802-531-6213; orvis.com), the name in fly-fishing instruction as well as equipment; one- and two-day courses are offered Apr.–Oct. Classes conducted across from the Orvis flagship store in fully stocked casting ponds and on the Battenkill.

The Battenkill Angler (802-379-1444; battenkillangler.com). Tom Goodman offers tours blending the art and science of the craft of fly-fishing.

GOLF The Golf Club at the Equinox (802-362-7870; playequinox.com), 108 Union St., Manchester Village, was established in the 1920s for guests of the Equinox House, expanded and redesigned in 1991 by Rees Jones to 18 holes. The Dormy Grill (see *Eating Out*) offers pleasant dining with a beautiful view of the course.

Stratton Mountain Golf Course (800-STRATTON; stratton.com) is a 27-hole championship course with full clubhouse including the Green Apron restaurant (open seasonally for lunch and for farm-to-table dinners), pro shop, and practice facility. Each of the three nine-hole courses is perfectly positioned as a forest, then lake, then mountain course. **The Stratton Golf School** offers weekend and midweek sessions, including professional instruction, and a special 22-acre training site.

HIKING From the Green Mountain National Forest District Office (802-362-2307), request hiking maps for Lye Brook Wilderness, a 14,600-acre preserve south of Manchester with a 2.3-mile trail to the Lye Brook Waterfalls and the Long Trail. This Massachusetts-to-Quebec path doubles as the Appalachian Trail throughout the area; portions of the trail make good day hikes, either north over Bromley Mountain or south over Spruce Peak from Rt. 11/30. Another popular route is the Stratton Pond Trail, which starts at Kelley Stand Rd. and stretches to Stratton Pond; there is one shelter in the immediate area, and swimming is permitted. Griffith Lake, accessible from Peru and Danby, is a less crowded swimming and camping site on the trail. For details, consult the Green Mountain Club's *Long Trail Guide.*

🐾 **Merck Forest & Farmland Center** (802-394-7836; merckforest.org), 3270 Rt. 315, Rupert (west of Dorset). A beautiful find near the New York border. Open year-round, free admission, with unexpected bird-watching opportunities.

Mount Equinox. Details about the rewarding, 6-mile Burr and Burton Trail from Manchester Village to the summit are available in *Day Hiker's Guide to Vermont* (Green Mountain Club). At 3,825 feet, this is the highest mountain in the state that is not traversed by the Long Trail.

See also *Green Space.*

HORSEBACK RIDING, ETC. 🐎 **Karl Pfister Farm** (802-824-4663; karlpfistersleigh.com), off Rt. 11, Landgrove. Wagon treks through the fields and woods, and special-event carriage rides.

🐎 **Taylor Farm** (802-824-5960; taylorfarm
vermont.com), Rt. 11, Londonderry, offers carriage rides in summer and fall as well as tours of the farm. In winter box-style sleighs are pulled by Belgian draft horses courtesy of cheesemakers Jon and Kate Wright, on Rt. 11 in Londonderry. (The benefit here is that you can buy some of their wonderful cheese at the same time.)

🐎 **Horses for Hire** (802-297-1468; horses
forhire.net), Rt. 30, Bondville. Deb Hodis offers one- and two-hour and half-day trail rides, sleigh rides, and riding lessons for individuals and groups, even in winter, weather permitting.

🐎 **Mountain View Ranch** (802-293-5837; mountainviewranch.biz), 502 Easy St., Danby. Horse and pony rides; carriage rides for special occasions and village tours. Inquire about sunset and picnic rides. Winter brings sleigh rides in a wagon made for the snow with hot chocolate and s'mores.

AT THE STRATTON MOUNTAIN GOLF COURSE
Stratton Mountain Resort

Bromley Mountain Resort

THE BROMLEY ALPINE SLIDE

⚘ **Chipman Stables** (802-293-5242; chipman stables.com), Danby Four Corners. Year-round horse and pony rides, family-friendly hayrides in fall, and kids' camp by the day or week, Western-style. Sleigh rides in conjunction with The Equinox during winter holidays.

MOUNTAIN RIDES *⚘* **Bromley Mountain** (802-824-5522; bromley.com), Rt. 11, Peru (6 miles east of Manchester). This 3,284-foot-high mountain offers excellent views of Stratton and Equinox Mountains. It's traversed by the Long Trail and also accessible by hiking the ski trails from the midpoint exit on the chairlift. This lift, serving the alpine slide, is open Memorial Day–mid-Oct., weather permitting; days and hours very, check ahead. The Bromley Alpine Slide, the longest in this country, is a great ride with fabulous views whatever your age. The Big Splash waterslide (biggest in Vermont) and the Giant Swing are huge draws for the teen set. You'll also find miniature golf, a 24-foot climbing wall, space bikes, a parabounce, the "trampoline things," and an extreme zipline—the Sun Mountain Flyer, five stories high, half a mile long, with speeds up to 50 mph on four tracks. Lunch, snacks, and drinks are available at the base lodge.

⚘ **Stratton Mountain** (800-STRATTON; stratton.com) offers a four-state view from its summit, accessible by gondola from the ski resort (Rt. 30, Bondville). The gondolas run summer and fall; check the website for days and hours.

SCENIC DRIVES *⚘* **Mount Equinox** (802-362-1115; equinoxmountain.com). The summit of Mount Equinox is 3,848 feet high. A toll road (open May–Oct., 9–4:30; $15 per car and driver; $5 per passenger; $12 per motorcycle) climbs more than 5 miles from Rt. 7A in Arlington. This can be a spectacular ride on a clear day, even more dramatic if the mountain is in the clouds and the road keeps disappearing in front of you. Be sure to drive back down in low gear and total sobriety. Much of the mountain is owned by the Carthusian monks who occupy a monastery high on its slopes and maintain the viewing center at the summit. It offers a glimpse of austere Carthusian life as well as restrooms and one of the most panoramic views in southern Vermont.

Green Mountain National Forest Road Number 10, Danby to Landgrove. Closed in winter. A long (14 miles) and isolated byway, the road (beginning in Danby) climbs through the White Rocks Recreation Area, crossing a number of tempting hiking paths as well as the Long Trail. There are some fine views as you continue along. You might want to picnic somewhere in the middle of the forest, as we did by a beaver pond. The road follows Tabor Brook down into Landgrove, itself a tiny, picturesque village.

East Rupert to Danby. Danby Mountain Rd. is the logical shortcut from Dorset to Danby, and it's quite beautiful, winding up and over a saddle between Woodlawn Mountain and Dorset Peak. Well-surfaced dirt, with long views in places. If you're coming from East Rupert, be sure to turn right at Danby Four Corners and follow Mill Brook into Danby.

Kelley Stand Road. From Rt. 7A, follow East Arlington Rd. past Candle Mill Village and continue until you cross a one-lane bridge. Turn right onto Kelley Stand Rd., which is a great foliage-viewing trip all the way to Stratton. Closed in winter.

SWIMMING *⚘* **Dorset Quarry**, Rt. 30 between Manchester and Dorset (turn at the historic marker), is a deep, satisfying pool but lacks easy access, making it unsafe for small children. Though the land is private property, the owners allow access by members of the public who treat it respectfully.

Christina Tree

THE DORSET QUARRY IS A POPULAR SWIMMING HOLE.

✔ **Hapgood Pond** (802-362-2307) in the Green Mountain National Forest, Rt. 11, 6 miles east of Peru, with its sand and calm, shallow drop-off, is favored by families with young children, a real oasis in the woods. There are also campsites here with picnic tables and fire rings.

✔ **Emerald Lake State Park** (802-362-1655; vtstateparks.com), Rt. 7, North Dorset, offers clear lake swimming.

See also *Green Space*.

TENNIS ✔ **Cliff Drysdale Tennis School at Stratton Mountain** (802-297-4236; 800-STRATTON; stratton.com). Tennis legend Cliff Drysdale offers tennis weekends in summer; his well-reputed tennis school directs adults in a series of camps, programs, and instructions as well as junior camps and programs.

Equinox Hotel Tennis (802-362-4700; equinoxresort.com), Rt. 7A, Manchester Village. Three Plexicushion all-weather courts are open to the public for a $15 hourly fee; $65 for private lessons. Inquire about clinics and round robins.

✳ Winter Sports

✔ **CROSS-COUNTRY SKIING AND SNOWSHOEING Viking Nordic Centre** (802-824-3933; vikingnordic.com), 615 Little Pond Rd., Londonderry. Trail fee. The Viking trail system includes 35 km of groomed trails, 3 km lighted for night skiing (arranged ahead for groups), and dedicated snowshoe trails. You'll also find instruction, rentals, a retail shop, on-snow kid-sitters (by reservation), and a café serving drinks, light breakfasts, and lunches. The Viking Nordic House, a home with a library, hearth, and four bedrooms that sleeps 10, is available for rental by the weekend or week.

✔ **Wild Wings Ski & Yoga** (802-824-6393; wildwingsski.com), North Rd., Peru. A family-oriented touring and yoga center located within the Green Mountain National Forest, 2.5 miles north of Peru. Trails are narrow, geared to beginning and intermediate skiers. This area tends to get a heavier snowfall than other local touring centers; the 28 km of groomed one-way trails are at elevations between 1,650 and 2,040 feet. Instruction and rentals; no skate skiing or dogs.

Stratton Mountain Nordic Center (802-297-4567; stratton.com), Stratton Mountain. Based at the Sun Bowl, a 13 km series of groomed loops plus adjoining backcountry trails. Guided backcountry and snowshoe tours are offered. Hot lunch and snacks available at the Sun Bowl Base Lodge.

Hildene (802-362-1788; hildene.org), Rt. 7A, Manchester Village. The historic Lincoln home, property, and working farm offers cross-country skiing trails and rentals. Trail fee.

DOWNHILL SKIING AND SNOWBOARDING ✔ **Bromley** (802-824-5522; bromley.com), 3984 Rt. 11 in Peru, 6 miles east of Manchester. In winter there's a reservations service for condominiums. Founded in 1936 by Fred Pabst of the Milwaukee brewing family, this is among the oldest ski areas in the country. The only southern-facing ski mountain in Vermont, it was also one of the first to develop snowmaking, a slope-side nursery, chairlifts, and condominiums.

HAPGOOD POND IS A QUIET SPOT FOR A GOOD SWIM.

Christina Tree

Pabst set up a rope tow in what is now the parking lot. Later he invented the J-bar, which allowed skiers to be pulled up the mountain rather than having to clutch a rope. Fred sold the area to Stig Albertsson in 1971, but remained president until his death in 1977. Albertsson brought the first alpine slide to North America, helping Bromley develop into more than just a winter destination. Today the resort is owned by Boston-based Joe O'Donnell, who made extensive renovations, adding a snowboarding park, a high-speed quad chairlift that gets skiers from base to summit in six minutes, and a new lodge. The Halo Terrain Park is wired for sound and has its own T-bar, tabletops, glades, gaps, spines, quarter-pipes, and dedicated groomer. There are three more terrain parks: Exhibition Park for intermediates, focusing on rails and boxes; the Unforgiven Boardercross Park, featuring tons of higher-

Rachel Carter

BROMLEY MOUNTAIN RESORT

speed terrain with whoops, gaps, and banked turns; and the Bonanza Park, a progression for beginner boarders. This is a popular family mountain, with many trails suited to beginners and intermediates, but there are a number of challenging runs on the mountain's east side, particularly Stargazer, Blue Ribbon, Avalanche, Havoc, and Pabst Peril.

The Bromley Summer Adventure is one of the largest summer amusement parks in the state. It includes the Giant Swing—which looms as tall as a four-story building—an 18-hole mini golf course, a 0.7-mile triple-track alpine slide, a 24-foot climbing wall, and a variety of spinning, splashing rides. For the youngest set there's KidZone Fun Park, with a 24-foot inflated slide, Bounce House, and bumper boats. Adults can settle in with a snack at the Sun Café and enjoy the view.

Lifts: 9: 1 high-speed detachable quad, 1 fixed-grip quad, 4 doubles, 1 T-bar, 1 Mighty Mites, and 1 covered Magic Carpet.

Trails: 46 trails—evenly divided among intermediate, beginner, and expert.

Vertical drop: 1,334 feet.

SKIING AT BROMLEY

Bromley Mountain Resort

Snowmaking: 85% of terrain from base to summit.

Facilities: The base lodge offers two cafeterias as well as a more formal tavern upstairs. Skiers unload right at the base lodge; the driver then parks in an area across Rt. 11 and rides back on a shuttle bus. Valet parking is another option.

Ski school: Ski and snowboard school are of particular pride and have been recognized nationally. New kids program, Kidsrule for ages 4–14, one stop for lessons and rentals. Brand-new indoor facility dedicated to kids for lesson registration, rentals, and lunch. A Star Carpet lift has been added to the beginner learning area. There is also a new warming cabin for bathroom/hot chocolate breaks in the learning area. Parents are finding it a great place to watch their kids in a lesson.

Lift tickets: $71 adults, $61 teens, $45 juniors on weekends; tickets for 2 days and half days are available; check the website for ways to save.

✆ **Stratton** (800-STRATTON; ski report 802-297-4211; stratton.com). Located atop a 4-mile

access road from Rt. 30 in Bondville, Stratton is a popular, well-groomed mountain. It was here that Jake Burton invented the snowboard, and today Stratton is noted for its terrain parks, for both skiers and snowboarders. Stratton keeps a loyal following by harvesting a steady crop of snow for what are predominantly intermediate-level runs, but there are also plenty of opportunities for advanced skiers along its 97 trails, including some good moguls and long top-to-bottom runs of 2,000 vertical feet. As one of Vermont's youngest ski areas (it was established in 1961, a year after Killington and five after Mount Snow), it is among the most modern, with a vibrant après-ski scene in winter and a well-known golf and tennis school. During the off-season, the slope-side population shrinks to 150 (although in 1960, its residents numbered a mere 24). Acquired by the Canadian resort company Intrawest in 1994, Stratton is respected statewide for its environmental policies; it has relinquished development rights on nearly a third of its acreage to protect bear, deer, and thrush habitat.

The mountain itself rises to 3,936 feet, with two separate areas: the original North Face, otherwise known as Stratton Village, and the distinctly sunnier Sun Bowl, the newer of the two. Thanks to the quantity of lifts, skiers are generally dispersed over the trail network. Stratton Village includes a variety of shops, restaurants, and spas; the resort offers a range of accommodations including two hotels, a 120-room lodge, the 90-room Liftline Lodge, and 300 condominiums, all within walking distance or a short shuttle ride from the slopes. A sports center includes a 25-yard-long pool, whirlpool, indoor tennis courts, cardio and weight rooms, and a schedule of classes such as Spin, yoga, and Zumba. Activities include cross-country skiing and snowshoeing at the Nordic Center, lift-served snowtubing, and snowmobiling.

A lot happens here in summer, too. There's a 27-hole golf course, hiking, mountain biking, hiking, paintball, fishing, kayaking, scenic gondola rides, and tennis and golf schools. Kids ages 6 weeks–12 years can attend KidsKamp for half or full days, late June–early Sept.

Lifts: 13: a 12-passenger gondola, four 6-passenger high-speed detachable, 3 quads, 1 triple, 1 double chair, and 3 Magic Carpets.

Trails and slopes: 97.

Terrain parks: Five, including a boardercross course designed with the help of Olympic medalists Ross Powers and Lindsey Jacobellis. Skiers and riders must earn access to Stratton's terrain parks by completing a safety awareness session.

Vertical drop: 2,003 feet.

Snowmaking: 95%.

Facilities: Restaurant and cafeteria in the base lodge; also cafeterias midmountain and in Sun Bowl. Chapel of the Snows at the parking lot, a little Bavarian-style church, has frequent nondenominational and Roman Catholic services. A shuttle bus brings skiers from inns on the mountain to the base lodge. You'll also find a clinic, sports center, and shops and restaurants in the base area Village Square.

Ski school: Ski and snowboard lessons.

For children: Childcare Center for ages 6 weeks–3 years including combined ski and play programs; slope-side meeting place for Kids-Kamp (ski and snowboard full-day programs for ages 4–12).

SKIING AT STRATTON
Stratton Mountain Resort

Rates: $84 per adult midweek, $98 weekends and holidays; less for young adults and seniors. Many special multiday packages. Ski and stay from $69.

🎿 ⚓ **Magic Mountain Ski Area** (802-824-5645; magicmtn.com), south of Londonderry off Rt. 11, 18 miles east of Manchester. Open Thurs.–Sun. along with "Powder Days" and holidays. It may not be the biggest of southern Vermont's ski areas, but Magic Mountain might be its most challenging. Its 42 trails are twisty and narrow, and almost half of the 1,700 vertical feet are steep drops. The 190-acre area was developed in 1960 by Swiss ski instructor Hans

Thorner, who hoped to re-create the atmosphere of a Swiss Alpine village. He chose this mountain for the sheer drama of its terrain. Magic remains relatively overlooked, making it a perfect destination for those out to escape the crowds (and expense) of the larger resorts. Though the advanced trails are the real draw here, there is still plenty of good, well-groomed terrain for beginners and intermediates. The two chairlifts, the bottom-to-top red double and the black triple, are long and comparatively slow, reminding you of what it was like to ski and socialize before high-speed detachable chairs were invented.

Beginners should turn left at the top and follow the Magic Carpet trail a third of the way down, then choose a blue or green route to the bottom. Intermediate-level skiers and riders would enjoy Whiteout, Betwixt, Trick, or Up Your Sleeve, all on the east side. Advanced skiers usually venture off the expert west side of the mountain, but can

STRATTON VILLAGE

Stratton Mountain Resort

also go straight down Red Line and turn a little right from the red chair to hit Twilight Zone and Goniff Glade, which are steep and dotted with numerous surprises, among them trees, rocks, bushes, and other natural obstacles. Magic Mountain is good for families, as the central base lodge is easy to find yet spacious enough to spread out in. The Black Line Brew Pub serves great food and is where this community hangs out for a little après-ski fun and music after a long day on the slopes. Though it lacks the indulgences and amenities of the larger resorts, the commercial hype and sprawling condos are refreshingly absent, too. Kids will enjoy the Ala Kazaam Tubing Park, which is illuminated Friday, Saturday, and holiday nights until 7; it's the only tubing park in the region with its own tow. Summer activities gear up at Magic Mountain with 4th of July fireworks and outdoor music events.

THE MAGIC RED CHAIR

Magic Mountain

Lifts: 4: 1 triple chair, 1 double, and 2 surface.

Trails and slopes: 42.

Vertical drop: 1,700 feet.

Facilities: Cafeteria on the main floor of the base lodge with bar, restaurant, and entertainment on the top floor of the lodge.

Ski school: Ski and snowboard lessons. Ask about special events and lift packages.

Tickets: $63 adults; multiday, teen, senior, student, and junior rates. Check the website.

ICE SKATING Riley Rink at Hunter Park (802-362-0150; 866-866-2086; rileyrink.com) is an Olympic-sized ice-skating rink on Rt. 7A, 1.4 miles north of its junction with Rt. 11/30. Check the website for public skating hours and fees; rentals available.

SLEIGH RIDES See *Horseback Riding, Etc.*

SNOWMOBILING A Winter Recreation Map, available free from the Green Mountain National Forest District Ranger Office (802-362-2307), Manchester, shows trails presently maintained in this area by the Vermont Association of Snow Travelers.

✿ **Stratton Snowmobile Tours** (802-379-1483; stratton.com). Nighttime snowmobile tours by the hour are offered at Stratton Mountain after skiing is done. Mini Snowmobile Tours are also offered for kids on weekends in the daylight.

❋ Green Space

✿ **Equinox Preservation Trust** (802-366-1400; equinoxpreservationtrust.org), Manchester Village. A nonprofit organization created in 1996 to oversee 914 acres of protected lands on and surrounding Mount Equinox, now a user-friendly preserve. Secure a map/guide to the trail system for hiking, mountain biking, and skiing/snowshoeing and inquire about the nature walks and seminars offered year-round, some geared to children. Horseback riding is permitted on the lower levels of the mountain. Be sure at least to walk the 1.2-mile loop through the hardwoods around Equinox Pond. *Note:* All parking for access to the trust property is at the parking lot of the Equinox Resort.

❂ ✾ ✿ *✿* **Merck Forest and Farmland Center** (802-394-7836; merckforest.org), 3270 Rt. 315, Rupert. Open year-round, dawn to dusk; free. This 3,160-acre forest and farming area, set aside in the 1950s to serve as a model for conservation and sustainable land use, is a nonprofit environmental education organization reliant solely on donations. Nature programs are offered year-round, and there is an organic farm, an organic sugarbush, and gift shop/online store selling farm products. The forest contains two mountains surrounded by more than 28 miles of trails for walking, hiking, skiing, snowshoeing, and horseback riding, and a spring-fed swimming pond at the end of a 2-mile hike. Eight rustic but fully enclosed cabins accommodating anywhere from 6 to 15 campers are available year-round (by reservation) for a modest fee, each with a wood-burning stove, wooden bunks, and a nearby outhouse. Shelters and tent sites are also available. Educational day programs and camping trips for children ages 4–20 as well as all-ages workshops.

✾ **Grout Pond Recreation Area** (802-362-2307; fs.usda.gov), west of the village of Stratton, marked from Kelley Stand Rd. Deep in the Green Mountain National Forest, this remote, forest-encircled lake is a great spot to bird-watch or picnic, complete with grills and a small beach. Tables and fireplaces overlook the shore, and there is a launch for canoes. Short hikes lead around the pond; one wanders 2 miles through the Green Mountain National Forest, emerging at the Somerset Reservoir. Campsites available on a first-come, first-served basis.

✾ **Lowell Lake State Park** (802-824-4035; vtstateparks.com), Londonderry, off Rt. 11 east of Magic Mountain. More than 460 acres surround this pristine lake with a 3.5-mile loop hiking trail. A former summer camp with a rustic lodge, it's currently undeveloped with no facilities. Entry is free and anything carried in must be carried out—leave-no-trace day use.

Also see *Hiking* (above), and Emerald Lake State Park and Hapgood Pond under *Lodging—Campgrounds*.

❋ Lodging

RESORTS ♂ ✾ *✿* ♿ **The Equinox Resort & Spa** (802-362-4700; 800-362-4747; equinox resort.com), 3567 Main St., Manchester Village 05254. This is Vermont's most historic hotel. It's grown incrementally over the centuries, beginning as a pre–Revolutionary War tavern and becoming a premier summer resort by 1863, the first year that Mrs. Abraham Lincoln vacationed here. It's the white-columned centerpiece of an aristocratic village that includes a domed courthouse and lineup of 19th-century clapboard mansions. Placed on the National Register of Historic Places in the 1980s, it was renovated from the foundations up. In the 1990s it received another infusion of life from British investors who also added off-road Land Rover Driving School (see *Bushwhacking*) to its exceptional choice of resort activities—which include the internationally known Orvis fly-fishing school (see *Fishing*) and the 18-hole golf

course. **The Equinox Preservation Trust** was formed to preserve the trout pond and nearly 900 acres on and around Mount Equinox, which rises majestically behind the hotel.

In 2008 another $20 million makeover by current owners HEI Hotels & Resorts revamped the spa and dramatically altered the interior look of the hotel. Replacing the old, low-beamed lobby as its focal entry, designer Geoffrey Bradfield has created an imposing "Great Room" featuring sculpture by Diego Giacometti and a contemporary feel. There are now a total of 195 rooms in four buildings, which together comprise the Inns at Equinox: the hotel; the cosmopolitan resort rooms and suites in the neighboring Charles Orvis Inn (built in the 19th century as a residence for the founder of the Orvis fly-fishing empire); The Townhomes; and the historic 1811 House, a magnificent building dating from the American Revolution and an inn since 1811, except for the few years when it was owned by President Lincoln's granddaughter, Mary Lincoln Isham. Until recently this was an independent bed & breakfast. It now has 13 traditionally furnished rooms, many with wood-burning fireplaces.

The hotel offers several dining options. **The Chop House** is decorated in browns, burgundies, and reds with leather banquettes. It features high-temperature, flash-broiled steaks. **The Marsh Tavern**, occupying the shell of the 1769 tavern by the same name, is open for lunch and dinner daily with live music on weekends. The elegant **Colonnade Room** serves breakfast daily as well as dramatic holiday buffets.

The superb **Spa at Equinox** is in a separate building with a fitness center, indoor pool, outdoor hot tub, and a full menu of services featuring Swedish and therapeutic massage, body scrubs, wraps, facials, manicures, and pedicures. You'll also find touring bikes, a 14-acre stocked trout pond, and tennis courts. Guests enjoy a full concierge service. Rates are $149–799 EP per night. Pets accepted for a hefty fee.

CONDOMINIUMS AND SKI LODGES

At Stratton Mountain Resort 05155

Stratton Mountain maintains a reservation and information service (866-814-8767; stratton .com) and serves over 20 lodges, condo clusters, and inns on and around Stratton.

Long Trail House. Condo lodge is a five-minute walk from the lifts. Amenities include a concierge desk, heated year-round outdoor pool, hot tubs, and a sauna. Winter rates: from $110 for a weekday in a studio to $749 for a two-bedroom unit during peak season.

Black Bear Lodge. All 122 rooms and suites have private bath, phone, and TV, and facilities include a large dining room, saunas, whirlpools, and an outdoor pool. Winter rates are $69–279 per night, including continental breakfast.

Stratton condominiums. The number of the resort's privately owned condominium units in the rental pool varies at any given time, as do the ranges of sizes and shapes. All resort guests have access to the sports center and its indoor pool, exercise machines, and racquetball and tennis courts (a fee is charged).

Liftline Lodge. This older, Austrian-style 70-room lodge is close to Stratton's lifts and village shops and restaurants. This is the best deal at Stratton and handy to the lifts. Don't expect to find a staffed front desk, however, and note that the walls are thin, carpets worn, and so on.

Rachel Carter

THE EQUINOX RESORT

Once upon a time it was privately owned, well tended.

INNS AND BED & BREAKFASTS

In Manchester

The Inn at Ormsby Hill (802-362-1163; 800-670-2841; ormsbyhill.com), 1842 Main St., Manchester Center 05255. The inn is 2 miles southwest of Manchester Village on Rt. 7A, set in 2.5 acres of rolling lawns with spectacular mountain views. For a century this elegant manor was the summer home of Edward Isham, Robert Todd Lincoln's law partner. The connections to Hildene are strong, and thanks to the warmth and sophistication of innkeepers Yoshio and Diane Endo, guests feel welcomed to a similar gracious summer home. The eight guest rooms and two suites have queen or king four-poster bed, fireplace, and two-person whirlpool tubs. The Frances Suite is over the top with its private second-floor deck, wood-burning fireplace, and two bathrooms. The Taft Suite, also with wood-burning fireplace and huge four-poster, has a separate sitting room. Common space includes a serene living room with Japanese touches, an inviting library, and an informal gathering room with a massive fireplace original to the 1764 house. The huge, many-windowed dining room resembles a ship's prow. Diane is a professional gardener, and there are patio rocking chairs and porch swings from which to enjoy the gardens and mountain views. Room rates ($340–535 in peak season, $240–425 in regular, $220–395 off-season) include breakfast and gratuities.

♂ **The Inn at Manchester** (802-362-1793; 800-273-1793; innatmanchester.com), 3967 Main St., Rt. 7A, Manchester Village 05254.

This gracious old home is set back from Main Street with a front porch, big windows, gables, and three floors. Its Celebration Barn, accommodating up to 150 guests, makes it one of the town's top venues for weddings. Longtime hosts Frank and Julie Hanes provide 21 rooms, which include 3 suites (4 rooms are in the restored, vintage-1867 carriage house out back). All have full private bath, TV, and air-conditioning, and four have gas fireplace. The dining room and parlors are comfortably furnished with a mix of modern and 19th-century tapestries and Oriental carpets. There is a fully licensed bar, a secluded pool in the back meadow, and plenty of rocking chairs on the rear porch. Breakfasts are full and hearty, including homemade breads and such treats as cottage cakes—a cottage cheese concoction served with hot apricot sauce. Rates are $175–315 per room, including a full breakfast and self-service pantry with drinks and fresh-baked goods.

♂ 🐾 ✿ ♿ **Reluctant Panther Inn & Restaurant** (802-362-2568; 800-822-2331; reluctant panther.com), 17–39 West Rd., Manchester 05254. Styling itself as Vermont's premier small luxury hotel, with 20 rooms that range from superior and deluxe, to junior and deluxe suites. All have fireplace, and suites feature two wood-burning hearths—one in front of the two-person whirlpool bath and a second in the bedroom. Dining options include the Panther Restaurant and the Marble Terrace for alfresco dining in warmer months. Open year-round; $199–549 per room, depending on season and room, includes breakfast. Pets are welcome for $50 per night, as are well-behaved children of all ages.

○ ♂ 🐾 ✿ ♿ **Wilburton Inn** (802-362-2500; 800-648-4944; wilburton.com), River Rd., Manchester 05254. This 30-acre secluded hillside estate is Manchester's most unusual option: a find for weddings, families, or groups as well as B&B guests—all with plenty of room to spare. The centerpiece brick, Tudor-style mansion offers paneled common spaces and comfortable, spacious upstairs suites and bedrooms. Seven additional, widely scattered buildings range from a two-bedroom innkeepers cottage to the Battenkill Valley Mansion, with a ballroom as well as multiple sitting rooms, accommodating 34 people. Guests can cook for themselves or sign on for catering or just breakfast at the inn. Obviously there's a story here. Short version: Psychiatrist Albert Levis and his late wife Georgette (sister of playwright Wendy Wasserstein) bought the property in 1987, and their four children are currently reenergizing it. Singer-songwriter Melissa Levis is now

innkeeper and with her sister Tajlei, a playwright, helps produce theatrical events, including murder mystery weekends. Brother Oliver manages the property's Sky Time Community Farm, known for its bread as well as produce showcased in Wed.-night Farm Night Dinners (June–Sept.), open to the public. The grounds include a pool, tennis court, a number of striking sculptures, and the Museum of the Creative Process, founded by Dr. Levis as a center of creative discovery and research. Rooms are $150–380 (for a suite) B&B; house rentals begin at $500 per night.

♂ 🐾 ✿ ♿ **The Inn at Willow Pond** (802-362-4733; 800-533-3533; innatwillowpond.com), Rt. 7A, Manchester Center 05255. Located 2.3 miles north of town on Rt. 7A and owned by the Bauer family, this inn offers 40 spacious guest rooms and suites in three separate, contemporary condo-like buildings on a hillside overlooking the Manchester Country Club's golf course. The 18th-century Meeting House reception building contains the lofty main lounge, conference facilities, a fitness center with exercise equipment, two saunas, a library, and an outdoor lap pool. The suites feature a living room with a wood-burning fireplace. $198–218 for a standard room, $248–268 for a one-bedroom fireplace suite, $428–488 for a two-bedroom fireplace suite. One entire building is ADA compliant, offering wheelchair-accessible rooms of all types. Children of all ages are welcome; pets are charged an additional $20 per night. Rates include continental breakfast.

THE INN AT ORMSBY HILL IS SPACIOUS INSIDE AND OUT.
Christina Tree

🍴 🛏 **The Barnstead Inn** (802-362-1619; 800-331-1619; barnsteadinn.com), Box 998, 349 Bonnet St., Manchester Center 05255. Just up Bonnet St. (Rt. 30), two blocks from the amenities of town, Vermonter Neil Humphrey has converted an 1830s hay barn into 15 attractive rooms with cable TV, A/C, individual thermostats, and lovely baths. It's all been done with consummate grace and charm, with many small touches like braided rugs, rockers, bedside lighting, and exposed old beams. There is also an attractive, secluded outdoor pool and a pond, plus an attractive "pub" (no food or drink but a nice place to socialize; BYOB). $99–275, higher during foliage. The high-end rates are for spacious suites with fireplace and Jacuzzi. No meals, but an easy walk to good breakfast places.

🍴 **Seth Warner Inn** (802-362-3830; seth warnerinn.com), 2353 Main St., Manchester Center 05255. This vintage-1800 house is set back from Rt. 7A southwest of Manchester Village. Ask Stasia Tetreault and Richard Carter to see the thank-you note that Robert Todd Lincoln wrote after staying here in 1911. Rooms with open beams and stenciling are furnished in antiques and curtained in lace. Five bright guest rooms have country quilts, queen canopy bed, and private bath. Common space includes a gracious living room, a small library, and the dining room, in which guests gather for a full breakfast. There is also a deck outside overlooking the brook-fed duck pond. $145–155 per room includes breakfast. Children 13 and over.

🍴 🛏 **Ira Allen House** (802-362-2284; 877-362-2284; iraallenhouse.com), 6311 Rt. 7A, Sunderland 05250. Maria and Ed Jones are the

LILIES AT THE WILBURTON INN

Wilburton Inn

innkeepers in this roadside tavern built by Ethan Allen (his brother Ira was the surveyor) in 1779 with a "new" wing added in 1846. There are five suites, some set up for families. It's a mile south of Manchester and 3 miles north of Arlington, near the entrance to the Mount Equinox toll road. Across Rt. 7A, the property includes lovely river frontage with Adirondack chairs set out under a big willow tree. The Battenkill is good for trout fishing; for the warmblooded, there's a 10-foot-deep swimming hole here. $110–160 per room with full breakfast. Children under 5 are free.

In Arlington 05250

🛏 **The Arlington Inn** (802-375-6532; 800-443-9442; arlingtoninn.com), 3904 Rt. 7A. This stunning 1848 Greek Revival mansion was built by Martin Chester Deming, a Vermont railroad magnate. Owners Eric (a noted chef) and Elizabeth Berger offer 18 rooms: 6 suites in the main house, 6 in the carriage house, and 6 in the adjacent 1830 parsonage. Most are spacious and furnished with Victorian antiques, and there's a formal parlor. Sylvester's Study on the ground floor of the main building is particularly impressive. The units in the parsonage have Drexel cherry four-posters and sleigh beds, TV, and air-conditioning. The inn is also a popular spot for dinner (see *Dining Out*), and the gardens make this a great spot for weddings. Rates per room are $149–319, including a full breakfast. Children ages 6 and up.

🛏 🛏 ♿ **West Mountain Inn** (802-375-6516; westmountaininn.com), 144 West Mountain Inn Rd. Open year-round. Overlooking splendid views of Mount Equinox and the Battenkill Valley, the Carlson family has presided over this rambling, century-old white-clapboard hillside

THE ARLINGTON INN

Rachel Carter

Rachel Carter

THE HILL FARM INN

home since 1978. The 22 attractive rooms, 9 of which are suites, are country elegant, named for famous people associated with Arlington; a copy of Dorothy Canfield Fisher's *Vermont Tradition* is in every room. There are also 3 two-bedroom town houses with cooking facilities at the Historic Mill on the property. There are paneled, many-windowed common rooms with fireplaces and a children's playroom. Breakfast and dinner are served daily (see *Dining Out*). The inn's 150-acre property includes walking and snow-shoeing trails, gardens, and llamas in residence. Inquire about special events. $165–340 B&B for two, more with MAP.

♂ ♪ ㊓ **Hill Farm Inn** (802-375-2269; 800-882-2545; hillfarminn.com), 458 Hill Farm Rd., Sunderland. Located off Rt. 7A north of the village, this historic farmstead is set on 50 acres of land with walking trails bordering the Battenkill. The 1830 main building and farmhouse underwent a major renovation in 2012 with an emphasis on energy-efficient luxury, the farming aspects of the property, and outdoor recreation. Cuddle up to goats, sheep, and potbellied pigs in the barn before enjoying breakfast prepared by the on-site chef. Double rooms are $185–295, including full country breakfast. The whole farmhouse is $550 each night. Children are welcome at special rates.

㊛ ♪ **The Inn on Covered Bridge Green** (802-375-9489; 800-726-9480; coveredbridge green.com), 3587 River Rd. Clint and Julia Dickens invite fans of Norman Rockwell to stay in his former home, built in 1792 across from a red covered bridge and the village green where Ethan Allen mustered his Green Mountain Boys. The inn offers four guest rooms, all with private bath, gas fireplace, and air-conditioning. Pets are accepted in the two housekeeping cottages, one of which was the studio where

Rockwell painted. There's swimming, canoeing, and fly-fishing in the Battenkill just a few hundred feet from the inn, and the setting is quintessentially Vermont. $160–225 includes a full country breakfast.

In Dorset 05251

✪ ♂ ㊛ ♪ ㊓ **The Barrows House** (802-867-4455; 800-639-1620; barrowshouse.com), 3156 Main St. In the heart of the village, this petite resort became a member of the Dorset Inn family in 2012. The property features a pool, two tennis courts, and 6 acres of manicured grounds and gardens, along with a newly renovated restaurant, bar, and outdoor dining terrace. The 27 guest rooms, suites, and cottages are a great fit for wedding parties, families, or special events. The central building is Dorset's first parsonage, built in 1796. Walk to town along marble sidewalks, but return for dinner at the exquisite gastropub, southern Vermont's first. $165–465 per couple; rates include elegant breakfast at the Dorset Inn. Pets and well-behaved children are welcome.

㊛ ㊛ **Dovetail Inn** (802-867-5747; 888-867-5747; dovetailinn.com), 3370 Rt. 30. This unpretentiously gracious 1800s inn faces Dorset's green. The 11 guest rooms (all with private bath) range from cozy to luxurious (Hearthside has a fireplace, wet bar, and deck), all with private bath and A/C. Guests have access to a butler's pantry with a fridge, microwave, and sink. An expanded continental breakfast is served in the Keeping Room or in guest rooms. From $99 midweek in spring to $265 for a foliage weekend, includes continental breakfast. Pets welcome for $30 per room.

㊓ **Inn at West View Farm** (802-867-5715; 800-769-4903; innatwestviewfarm.com), 2928

THE DOVETAIL INN

Rachel Carter

Rt. 30, just south of Dorset, is a small, well-groomed lodge with an appealing personality, once the focus of a 200-acre farm, now known especially for its exceptional cuisine (see *Dining Out*). The inn has a large, cozy living room with a wood-burning fireplace; common space also includes an inviting, wicker-filled sunporch. One downstairs room has been fitted for handicapped access, and the nine upstairs rooms are all furnished comfortably with cheerful paper, private bath, and bright, crisp fabrics; all rooms are air-conditioned. Rates are $135–205, including full breakfast. Children over 12.

❂ ☀ ♿ **The Dorset Inn** (802-867-5500; dorsetinn.com), 8 Church St. A national historic site and the state's most venerable hostelry (in continuous operation since 1796) faces Dorset's pristine town green. Known for its cuisine (see *Dining Out*) and relaxing atmosphere, the inn has 25 guest rooms, including six two-room luxury suites. It's within walking distance of the theater and offers a fireplace in the parlor as well as a lineup of front-porch rockers from which you might not want to stir. One more reason not to leave the property: the petite Studio day spa offers facials and massages. $165–425 includes breakfast. Pets are allowed in most rooms for a refundable deposit; older, well-behaved children are welcome, too.

In Landgrove 05148

✿ ❂ ♥ ☀ ♪ ♿ **The Landgrove Inn** (802-824-6673; 800-669-8466; landgroveinn.com), 132 Landgrove Rd. Off the beaten track, down a birch-lined dirt road in the Green Mountain National Forest, this inn is a winner. The red, mostly clapboard building rambles back and around, beginning with the 1810 house, ending an acre or two away. The "Vermont continuous architecture" draws guests through a handsome lobby, past 18 air-conditioned rooms (16 with private bath) that meander off in all directions, through the inviting Rafter Room Lounge (huge, filled with games and books), to the attractive dining room in the original house. Down by the pond innkeepers Tom and Maureen Checchia have added the In View Center for the Arts, a post-and-beam studio, expanding on the inn's tradition of workshops in art, writing, and dance. Check the website for current programs. Our favorite rooms are tucked up under the eaves in the oldest part of the inn, papered in floral prints and furnished with carefully chosen antiques but with new baths. Many rooms are well suited to families, who also will appreciate the heated pool, the stocked trout pond (catch and release), lawn games, and the two tennis courts. In winter you can take a sleigh ride or step out onto the 10 km groomed

Christina Tree

THE DORSET INN

cross-country trail system that leads to the picturesque village of Landgrove (just a church, a former school, and a salting of homes cupped in a hollow). You can ski on into the surrounding national forest. Bromley Ski Area is just 6 miles away, and Stratton is a 20-minute drive. Breakfast is an event here, served on oak tables in the wood-beamed dining room with a many-windowed wall overlooking the garden. The dining room is open to the public five nights a week (see *Dining Out*). $100–120 economy (shared bath), $160–189 for standard rooms, and $200–250 for a king-sized bed, fireplace, sitting area, Jacuzzi, and deck. Rates include full breakfast; pets may be considered.

In South Londonderry 05155

♥ ♪ ♿ **The Londonderry Inn** (802-824-5226; londonderryinn.com), 8 Melendy Hill Rd. On a knoll overlooking the West River, this large historic home has been a country inn since 1941. Innkeeper Maya Drummond has decorated the 27 guest rooms with folk-art-painted furniture and walls, private baths. The bright common rooms include a huge stone fireplace, billiards room, movie room, and Maya's antique bell collection. Fresh-baked cookies are served every afternoon. Maya has won state recognition for running an environmentally conscious inn. Children will enjoy the resident corgis, the thriving gardens, and the many nooks to explore. $129–156 for double rooms includes hot breakfast.

MOTELS ♿ **Palmer House Resort** (802-362-3600; 800-917-6245; palmerhouse.com), 5383 Main St., Manchester Center 05255. A family-owned motel with 50 rooms/suites: some with fireplace and Jacuzzi, all with cable TV, refrigerator, in-room coffee, and phone. Facilities include indoor and outdoor pools, fitness center, stocked trout pond, tennis courts, and nine-hole golf course, all on 22 acres adjacent to the Green Mountain National Forest. The venerable Ye Olde Tavern restaurant (see *Dining Out*) is right next door. Rooms $110–190, suites $220–330, depending on season. Children 12 and over.

✪ ♂ ♞ ♪ **Olympia Lodge** (802-362-1700; olympia-vt.com), Rt. 7A, Manchester Center 05255. The motto is "the motel that feels like an inn," and we can second that. Trish and Sal Asciutto have pretty much turned this 24-room lodge into an extension of their home and family. Accommodations are basic motel rooms, but the mostly returning guests don't come for the rooms; they come to ski and play, and when they're through to spend time in the fireplace lounge, which is more like Sal and Trish's friendly living room. Always decorated for the seasons with a roaring fire in winter and a full bar; children and adults alike gather to meet, socialize, share stories, and play games. Pool and tennis in summer, and a hot breakfast cooked by the family (who live upstairs) year-round. Rates of $89–185 include breakfast. They'll even help you throw a wedding.

♞ ♪ **The Weathervane Motel** (802-362-2444; 800-262-1317; weathervanemotel.com), Rt. 7A, 2212 Main St., Manchester 05254. Set back from the road with two picture windows in each of its 22 large units, this is a motel with class. Each air-conditioned room has TV, free coffee, and full or queen-sized beds, many with linens as fine as any upscale inn. Some of the rooms connect. There is a common area with Oriental carpets, antiques, and an outdoor deck. Out back you'll find a volleyball court, a trampoline, and a heated pool. Kids are welcome, pets not. $75–200 includes continental breakfast.

CAMPGROUNDS ✪ **Green Mountain National Forest** (802-362-2307; fs.usda.gov /greenmountain), District Ranger Office, Manchester. A public information office serving the southern half of the 400,000-acre Green Mountain National Forest is located on Rt. 30/11 east of Manchester at 2538 Depot St.; open year-round, Mon.–Fri. 8–4:30. Maps and details are available about where to fish, hike, cross-country ski, and camp. All national forest campsites are available on a first-come, first-served basis.

✪ ♪ **Emerald Lake State Park** (802-362-1655; vtstateparks.com), 65 Emerald Lake Lane, East Dorset, just off Rt. 7. Open Memorial Day–Columbus Day weekend. This 430-ace

park surrounds the 20-acre Emerald Lake, named for the color of its water. There's a beach, snack bar, and two hillside and one riverside picnic areas; also paddle- and pedal-boat rentals. There's good fishing, and 67 campsites and 37 lean-tos are sited on a heavily wooded ridge about the lake. Facilities include flush toilets, hot showers, and a dump station. Hiking and nature trails.

🏕 **Hapgood Pond Recreation Area** (802-362-2307; recreation.gov), Hapgood Pond Rd. (off Rt. 11), Peru. Acquired in 1931, this was the beginning of the Green Mountain National Forest. There is swimming, fishing, and boating on the 7-acre pond. Removed from the picnic ground and beach are 28 campsites (first come, first served). A pleasant 8-mile forest trail threads through the woods.

🏕 **Merck Forest & Farmland Center** (802-394-7836; merckforest.org), 3270 Rt. 315, Rupert. Rustic cabins, lean-tos, and tent sites in this 3,160-acre forest in the Taconic Mountains west of Dorset. See also *Green Space*.

✳ Where to Eat

DINING OUT

Tops

Silver Fork (802-768-8444; thesilverforkvt .com), 4201 Main St., Manchester. Open Mon.– Sat. from 5. Reservations are needed far in advance for this six-table restaurant with a large following. Menu choices are surprisingly large

SWIMMING HOLE AT THE DORSET QUARRY
Alice Levitt

too. Chef Mark is originally from Baltimore, and you'll usually find oysters on the menu here, maybe pan fried with homemade tartar sauce, and crabcakes with housemade shoestring potatoes. His training was under a German chef and there are dishes like veal sautéed with onions and mushrooms, served with housemade spaetzle. For 13 years he and his wife, Melody, who runs everything but the kitchen, had a restaurant in Puerto Rico, perhaps explaining the imaginative seafood. We haven't been able to eat here yet but we hear raves from everyone who has. Entrées $25–34.

✪ **Verdé** (802-297-9200; verdestratton.com), 19 Village Lodge Rd., Stratton Mountain. Open Wed.–Mon. for dinner. Reservations recommended. The region's most modern restaurant is a taste of New York sophistication made from Vermont ingredients. The house charcuterie has attracted a devoted following, but there are pizzas, pastas, and steaks for simpler tastes. Whatever you choose, it will be made from local ingredients with exceptional craft. Come in Wed. or Thurs. night for a three-course dinner for $25.

Mistral's at Toll Gate (802-362-1779), off Rt. 11/30, 10 Tollgate Rd., Manchester. Open for dinner daily except Tues., Wed. Reservations recommended. Chef Dana Markey and his wife, Cheryl, maintain this longtime dining landmark, housed in the old tollhouse once serving the Boston-to-Saratoga road. During warm-weather months a brook rushes along just under the windows. The menu is French, from the pâté maison, escargots, and frog legs through the roast duckling or stuffed châteaubriand. All are accompanied by a *Wine Spectator*–recognized wine list. Entrées $28–40.

The Chantecleer Restaurant (802-362-1616), Rt. 7A, East Dorset. Open for dinner Wed.–Sun. Long regarded as one of Vermont's top restaurants, Swiss chef Michael Baumann's establishment is known for nightly game specials and roast rack of lamb ($48). Leave room for profiteroles. The setting is an elegantly remodeled old dairy barn with a massive fieldstone fireplace. There is an extensive wine list. Inquire about the three-course meal for $35, available Wed., Thurs., and Fri. Reservations essential.

SoLo Farm & Table (802-824-6327; solo farmandtable.com), 95 Middletown Rd., South Londonderry. Open nightly for dinner, closed Wed. Chloe and Wesley Genovart have transferred their new family and East Village culinary prowess to the former Three Clock Inn location, creating the newest gastro rave in the farm-to-table movement in Vermont and bringing one of New York City's most celebrated chefs with it. At Degustation Restaurant, Chef Wesley earned stars and Zagat's mention, while maître d' Chloe was recognized by the James Beard Foundation for best service at Thomas Keller's Per Se Restaurant. Entrées $21–33.

More fine dining

The Perfect Wife Restaurant & Tavern (802-362-2817; perfectwife.com), Rt. 11/30, 1 mile east of the Rt. 7 overpass, Manchester. Open Tues.–Sat. for dinner; tavern open later. Manchester native Amy Chamberlain credits her stint at Arrows in Ogunquit, Maine, for two of her specialties, sautéed crabcakes served with rémoulade on mixed greens as an appetizer and sesame-crusted yellowfin tuna, seared medium rare and served over stir-fried vegetables as an entrée. Others range from Howling Wolf (steamed veggies with brown rice pilaf and sweet potato hash) to grilled filet mignon with a wild mushroom, roasted garlic, and Guinness Stout demiglaze. Dining is in either the cobblewalled dining room or the nicely lit greenhouse terrace. It's also possible to dine as we did on two appetizers (those crabcakes and the yummy Peking duck with Mandarin pancakes). **The Other Woman Tavern** is a totally different and equally inviting scene, a lively local gathering place with music on weekends and a pub menu ranging from salads, sandwiches, and burgers to grilled strip steak. Entrées $22–32.

Reluctant Panther (802-362-2568; reluctant panther.com), 39 West Rd. (Rt. 7A), Manchester Village. Open for dinner Tues.–Sat. The relatively formal, sleek Main House Dining Room of the inn features two fireplaces and many

STEAK FRITES AT BARROWS HOUSE, DORSET
Alice Levitt

windows with views of Mount Equinox and a landscaped backyard with a pond, gardens, and a gazebo. The cuisine is seasonal with an ever-changing menu, and the wine list is extensive. You might dine on braised stuffed cabbage or grilled Northeast Family Farms sirloin. Entrées $28–36.

🍴 **Ye Olde Tavern** (802-362-0611; yeolde tavern.net), 214 N. Main St., Manchester Center. Open daily for dinner from 5. A genuine 1790 tavern theoretically specializing in "authentic American" dinner dishes like roast tom turkey and pot roast, but sirloin and bouillabaisse are also on the menu. One of the better values in town with Yankee entrées from $17 (for chicken potpie) to $31 for the filet mignon with lobster. Early-bird menu before 6, Sun.–Thurs.

Brasserie L'Oustau de Provence (802-768-8538), 1716 Depot St., Rt. 11/30, Manchester Center. Open for lunch (11–3), dinner from 5 PM, and brunch 11:30–3 Sat., Sun. Francophiles take note: Here you can lunch on a goat cheese tapenade *et* roasted pesto panini or a "croque madame"; dine on a $38 three-course prix fixe menu beginning with onion soup, featuring steak frites, and ending with crème brûlée. Rated the number five French restaurant in the United States by *Travel + Leisure* in 2013.

Bistro Henry (802-362-4982; bistrohenry.com), 1942 Depot St., Manchester Center. Open for dinner daily except Mon. Dina and Henry Bronson run this Italian- and French-inspired dining room with a casual atmosphere and a full bar. Mixed reviews are consistent: People either love it or hate it. We think that's due to the outdated atmosphere in the posh landscape of Manchester combined with unconventional serving methods for such upscale cuisine. Maybe it's weird, maybe just the style. Worth examining for yourself, entrées $22–36. Great wine selection, and Dina's desserts have enjoyed a following ever since she concocted her own hot fudge recipe.

In Dorset

Inn at West View Farm (802-867-5715; inn atwestviewfarm.com), 2928 Rt. 30. Open for dinner Thurs.–Mon. Chef Raymond Chen describes his cuisine as contemporary American with French and Asian influences. Salads on a given night might include classic Vermont beets with goat cheese right next to sesame-dressed seaweed. There are smaller plates such as pork belly sliders or dumplings for around $10, but others—including coriander-flavored, braised short ribs—can run more than $30.

✪ **The Barrows House** (802-867-4455; barrowshouse.com), 3156 Rt. 30. Open for dinner nightly from 5:30. In 2013 the Barrows House replaced its fusty dining room with southern Vermont's first gastropub. But don't expect simple—this is still Dorset, after all. Start with tuna tartare nachos with seaweed salad and sambal aioli, a local cheese plate, or $10 duck wings worthy of legend. If it's available, be sure to save room for the s'mores pie, complete with blow-torched marshmallows on top. Cocktails made from local spirits are key, too. In summer, sit outside by the fire pit. Sunday brunch.

The Dorset Inn (802-867-5500; dorsetinn .com), 8 Church St. Breakfast, lunch, and dinner served daily. Popular for pre-theater dining, within walking distance of the Dorset Playhouse. Along with younger brother Barrows House, this restaurant's locavore menu recently enjoyed an updating. There are still tavern classics such as turkey croquettes, and liver with bacon and onions, but they're offered beside short rib poutine and rainbow beet salad these days.

Mio Bistro (802-231-2530; miobistro.net), 3229 Rt. 30. Open for dinner Tues.–Sat. The name implies Mediterranean cuisine, but what's served here with carefully chosen wine is far more eclectic. Red snapper in Thai green curry is a menu staple, but so is fettuccine in a sauce of Parmesan and local cheddar. Everything is made from scratch with emphasis on fish and organic products.

Elsewhere

🍴 **The Landgrove Inn** (802-824-6673; landgroveinn.com), 132 Landgrove Rd., Landgrove. Dinner by reservation Wed.–Sun. Meals are served by candlelight, overlooking the garden at this country inn. Dinners are on the old-school end, with starters such as shrimp cocktail, followed by steak au poivre. Still, the kitchen is happy to accommodate vegetarians and vegans.

The Arlington Inn (802-375-6532; arlington inn.com), 3904 Rt. 7A in the center of Arlington. Chef Eric Berger has a reputation for serving reliably fine food in his magnificent 1848 mansion. There's a mauve-walled formal dining room, or you can dine in the more casual Deming Tavern. The Arlington Inn mixed grill, with petit mignon, duck breast, and loin lamb chop, is the house special, famous for its goat cheese mashed potatoes served on the side in the form of an egg roll. There's always a vegetarian dish, perhaps porcini mushroom ravioli. Entrées $26–32.

West Mountain Inn (802-375-6516; west mountaininn.com), West Mountain Inn Rd. at the junction of Rt. 313 and River Rd. west of

Arlington. Open daily for breakfast and dinner. Hidden away up on a hillside, overlooking the Battenkill Valley and Mount Equinox, this is a gracious inn that's well worth seeking out. Fruit and cheese are served in the bar, followed by upscale, chef-driven meals that accentuate the beautiful food grown nearby, particularly local cheeses.

EATING OUT

In and around Manchester

❂ Depot Bistro Café (802-366-8181; depot62 .us), 515 Depot St., Manchester. The surroundings at this furniture store can best be described as futuristic Turkish shabby chic. But the wonderful secret (other than the eclectic furnishings) is the woodfired oven, which turns out pita, flatbreads, and kebabs straight from the fire. Ingredients are all organic, even those in the nutty, honey-rich baklava.

The Dormy Grill (802-362-7870; playequinox .com), in the Golf Club at the Equinox on Union St., serves lunch and dinner daily May–Oct. (dinner only through Labor Day) with outdoor deck seating overlooking the ninth green. Enjoy tasty soups, salads, burgers, and wraps while feasting your eyes on the spectacular mountain vistas here at one of the best views in town. Reservations are wise, as the best seats fill up fast.

❀ Gringo Jack's (802-362-0836; gringojacks .com), Main St., Manchester Center, is a southwestern bar and grill with its own barbecue smokehouse on premise. Open daily for lunch and dinner. Chips and salsa when you sit down, over 40 tequilas, children's menu, and a pleasant outdoor patio in summer. Margaritas are half price on Thurs.; seasonal specials. Check out their extensive product line.

❀ Mulligan's Manchester (802-362-3663), Rt. 7A, Manchester Village. Open daily for lunch and dinner. A convenient, moderately priced, family-geared place featuring flame-grilled steaks, seafood, and pastas. Children's menu.

❀ ☖ Bob's Diner (802-362-4681), Rt. 11/30, 2279 Depot St., Manchester Depot. Open daily for breakfast, lunch, and dinner (closing at 3 PM Sun. and Mon.). A shining chrome diner with very good food (the milk shakes are the best). Give it a try, especially with kids.

☙ ❀ ☖ Zoey's Double Hex Restaurant (802-362-4600), Rt. 11/30, Manchester. Open daily for lunch and dinner, closed Tues. Just what you may be looking for: a cheery informal atmosphere with roomy booths, a screened porch, and famous burgers—but plenty of other choices as well, from meatloaf and chicken

potpie to sage-rubbed grilled rib eye. Full liquor license. Kids' menu.

Seasons Restaurant (802-362-7272), 4566 Main St., Manchester Center. Open daily for lunch and dinner. A local favorite for basics from pizza, a Reuben, or a fish taco to a rib-eye steak. Fri.-evening music, mid-June–mid-Aug.

In Arlington

Jonathon's Table (802-375-1021), 29 Sugar Shack Lane. Open for dinner May–Dec. Keep your eyes peeled for the sign; the place is worth your trouble. This is the kind of place where Norman Rockwell paintings adorn the walls, and you can purchase Vermont maple syrup products. If you can handle the twee Vermonty-ness of it all, the reward is equally comforting food such as sherry-and-mushroom-sauced Veal Jonathon or Vermont maple pork chops.

Elsewhere

☙ ❀ The Barn (802-325-3088; barnrestaurant .com) 5581 Rt. 30, Pawlet. Open for dinner Wed.–Sun. We can't help but admit we're confused. The barn's menu lists prices for its entrées, but above those, we're told to disregard them: Everything is actually $14, from filet mignon with house Madeira sauce to scallops crusted in bread crumbs. This is a genuine old barn with a huge stone hearth and a view of the Mettawee River. There's a salad bar and children's menu.

❀ Mulligan's at Stratton Mountain (802-362-3663). This spacious restaurant (same ownership as the Manchester place) is open daily for dinner, lunch on weekends; good for burgers, sandwiches, salads, and dinner options. Children's specials include a Ninja Turtle Burger and Gorilla Cheese.

THE BARN RESTAURANT

Rachel Carter

In Londonderry

✪ 🍴 ✈ **The New American Grill** (802-824-9844; newamericangrill.com), Mountain Marketplace. Open daily for all three meals (dinner 4:30–9). Chef-owner Max Turner has put this cheerful, booth-filled eatery with friendly service and decent prices on the culinary map. It's a big, varied, reasonably priced menu with the area's best burger. Starters includes venison chili and mussels steamed in lemon broth, white wine, and lemon. There are salads, pastas, and barbecue, roast duck and steak poutine, jambalaya (seafood, sausage, and veggies in a Cajun broth), veggie stir-fry, grilled sandwiches (available at dinner), a kids' menu, and desserts. Daily specials.

Gran'ma Frisby's (802-824-5931), Rt. 11 east of Londonderry. Open daily except Tues. for lunch and dinner. When Magic Mountain Ski Area is open, you're lucky to get in the door. Known for its fries and fresh-dough pizza, this is a friendly, reasonably priced find any time of year.

Swiss Inn (802-824-3442; swissinn.com), Rt. 11. Open to the public for dinner nightly during ski season, less in other seasons. Raclette and fondues complement Swiss and German entrées ($13–23) such as Geschnetzeltes (veal à la Swiss), beef fondue, and chicken Lugano (chicken breast dipped in a Gruyère cheese batter); also Continental dishes like pasta with marinara and veal Marsala.

BREAKFAST & LUNCH

In and around Manchester

✈ ♿ **Little Rooster Cafe** (802-362-3496), Rt. 7A south, 4645 Main St., Manchester Center. Breakfast and lunch 7:30–2:30; closed Wed. This cheerful chef-owned café is one of the hottest lunch spots in town. Daily specials. The ultimate corned beef hash, signature Maine crabcakes served on watercress with French bread, delicious tuna Niçoise. Full liquor license (spicy Bloody Marys). If you come at noon, be prepared to wait. No credit cards.

Up for Breakfast (802-362-4202), 4935 Main St. Open Mon.–Fri. 7–12:30, Sat., Sun. 7–1:30. A cheerful, small upstairs eatery with a huge menu and reputation. Be prepared for fanciful omelets with avocado crabcakes and salmon, wild turkey hash, or Belgian waffles. The orange juice is fresh squeezed and the coffee can be cappuccino or latte.

📶 **Spiral Press Café** (802-362-9944; spiralpresscafe.com), 15 Bonnet St., at the Northshire Bookstore (see *Selective Shopping*). Open daily 7:30–6:30 (at 8 on Sun.). A pleasant oasis for book lovers with teas and specialty coffees, good sandwiches, and fresh-baked cookies and treats.

♿ 📶 **Al Ducci's Italian Pantry** (802-362-4449; alduccis.com), 133 Elm St., one block up Highland Ave. from Rt. 11/30, Manchester Center. Open daily 8–8, Sun. 9–4. Eat in or take out at this authentic Italian deli, pizza. Daily specials, plus the best supply of specialty cheeses and artisan breads in the region.

Gourmet Café and Deli (802-362-1254; manchestergourmetdeli.com), Rt. 7A, Manchester Center. Open daily for breakfast and lunch. Tucked back into Manchester Center's Green Mountain Village shopping center, this café is a real find, with a pleasant atmosphere and service, reasonable prices, great salads and sandwiches. A pleasant terrace in warm weather; beer, wine, and mimosas.

In South Londonderry

The Pantry (802-824-9800; thepantryvt.com), 1 Main St. Open daily. Owners Suzanne Fontain and Kevin Chapman offer a mouthwatering deli showcasing local produce, wines, and cheese. At this writing seating is limited but expands seasonally to the porch, which overlooks the village. Breakfast and lunch daily.

MORE FOOD AND DRINK ✪ ✈ Wilcox

Dairy (802-362-1223), 6354 Rt. 7A, Sunderland. Some of the creamiest, most delectable flavors (try maple gingersnap) in Vermont are made by Howard and Chris Wilcox, available in retail sizes at grocery stores and served in a variety of local restaurants. The ice cream stand is open in summer.

✈ **Mother Myrick's Confectionary** (802-362-1560; mothermyricks.com), 4367 Main St. (Rt. 7A), Manchester Center. Open daily 10–5:30. Sumptuous baked goods, handmade chocolates, and fudge.

✈ **Village Peddler Chocolate Shop** (802-375-6037; villagepeddlervt.com), 261 Old Mill Rd., East Arlington. In the middle of a picturesque village just off Rt. 7A, this is a colorful as well as tasty shop, known for a "Chocolatorium" in which visitors, for a small fee, can sample chocolate in its many forms, learn its history and processing. Demonstrations as well as tastings plus the world's largest chocolate teddy bear. Open year-round, closed Tues.–Wed.

GENERAL STORES ✪ H. N. Williams Gen-

eral Store (802-867-5353; hnwilliams.com), 2732 Rt. 30, about 2 miles south of Dorset. Open daily: 6–6 weekdays, 6:30–5 Sat., 8–4 Sun. A large white barn of a store housed in what started out as an 1840 harness shop, said to be

Vermont's oldest family-run business (six generations). The deli/café here is one of the best places around for a sandwich (hot or cold), panini, soup, pie, or daily special; eat in or take out. The store is also a popular source of clothing, specializing in U.S.-made apparel, and everything from yard equipment to toys, fertilizer, tools, and pet food and supplies. Dorset Farmers Market is held here Sun. 10–2.

Dorset Union Store (802-867-4400; dorset unionstore.com), Dorset Village, opposite the Dorset Inn. Open 7–7 daily. A village landmark since 1816, general provisions and then some, including baking to order, and an extensive selection of wines, cheeses, and Vermont products.

J. J. Hapgood General Store and Eatery (802-824-4800; jjhapgoodgeneralstore.com), 305 Main St., Peru. Open daily 7–7, serving breakfast and lunch. The center of the village of Peru since 1827, it has been transformed by owners Juliette and Tim Britton into a gathering space with tables, an open kitchen, and a full deli. Breakfast on organic oatmeal, corned beef hash, or mung beans with poached eggs, crème fraîche, and Vermont-made kimchi. Sandwiches on are housemade wheat bread, soups are made daily, and all meat and produce is locally sourced; specialty pizzas, Vermont products, fresh-baked goods, and more.

Mach's General Store (802-325-3405), Rt. 30, Pawlet Village. Open daily. The focal point of this genuine old emporium is described under Pawlet (see *Villages*), but the charm of this family-run place goes beyond its water view.

J.J. HAPGOOD GENERAL STORE & EATERY, PERU

Alice Levitt

Built as a hotel in 1818, it's filled with a wide variety of locally useful merchandise.

✳ Entertainment

Dorset Playhouse (802-867-5777; 802-867-5777; dorsetplayers.org). The Dorset Players, a community theater group formed in 1927, actually owns the beautiful playhouse in the center of Dorset and produces winter performances there. In summer the Dorset Theatre Festival stages new plays as well as classics, performed by big names and resident professionals six days a week, June–early Sept.

Manchester Music Festival (802-362-1956; mmfvt.org), early July–mid-Aug. with performances at the Southern Vermont Arts Center, Northshire Bookstore, Riley Center for the Performing Arts, and Burr and Burton Academy. A seven-week series of evening chamber music concerts. Also fall and winter performances in Manchester and Dorset.

Village Picture Shows (802-362-4771; village pictureshows.com), 263 Depot St., Rt. 30/11, Manchester Center. Mainstream and art films.

Also see the Weston Playhouse (westonplay house.org) in "Okemo Valley Region."

✳ Selective Shopping

LOCAL LANDMARKS Orvis Retail Store (802-362-3750; orvis.com), 4200 Rt. 7A, Manchester Center, supplying the needs of anglers and other sportsmen since 1856. Known widely for its mail-order catalog and retail shops throughout the United States and UK, the Orvis flagship store is styled as a luxury country lodge but still specializes in the fishing rods made in the factory out back. There's also fishing tackle and gear, country clothes, and other small luxury items—from silk underwear to welcome mats—that make the difference in country, or would-be country, living. Open daily, year-round. Note the **Orvis Outlet** at 4382 Main St.

✪ ✔ ((ᵠ)) The Northshire Bookstore (802-362-2200; 800-437-3700; northshire.com), 4869 Main St., Manchester Center. Open Sun.–Wed. 10–7, Thurs.–Sat. 10–9. One of Vermont's most browse-worthy bookstores. The Morrows have stocked the venerable Colburn House with a wide range of volumes, including used and antiquarian. A broad selection of adult titles, children's books, and DVDs, along with current hits and classics. They schedule frequent author lectures, book signings, and co-sponsored events, and offer breakfast, lunch,

Christina Tree
DAN LASSER MAKES NATIONALLY FAMOUS
POTTERY IN HIS LONDONDERRY STUDIO.

and snacks in their Spiral Press Café (see *Eating Out*).

ART GALLERIES & CRAFTS STUDIOS *Note:* Memorial Day weekend is Open Studio Weekend, vermontcrafts.com; see *Special Events.* Southern Vermont Arts Center (see *Must See*) hosts multiple exhibits.

In the Manchester area
Tilting at Windmills Gallery (802-362-3022; tilting.com), 24 Highland Ave., Rt. 11/30, Manchester Center. Open daily 10–5, Sun. 10–4. An unusually large gallery with national and international works in oils and egg tempera, mostly realism and impressionism.

✪ **Epoch** (802-768-9711; epochvermont.com), 4927 Main St., Manchester Center. This is a standout cooperative gallery, showcasing works by 18 top-tier members that include glass, wooden creations, furniture, and jewelry (Lucy Bergamini's glass necklaces!), paintings, sculpture and woven work, painted floor mats, and much more.

Manchester Hot Glass (302-362-5050; 79 Elm St.) is a full service glassblowing studio and gallery.

3 Pears Gallery (802-770-8820), 41 Church St., Dorset. Sited on Dorset's green, a well-curated showcase for the work of 30 local artists and artisans in media ranging from jewelry to furniture and clothing. Definitely worth a stop.

Gallery on the Marsh (802-867-5565), 2237 Rt. 30, Dorset. Open most days, 10–dark. The gallery beside the artists' home displays realistic wildlife paintings by John Pitcher and farm life landscapes and portraits by Sue Westin.

Flower Brook Pottery (802-867-2409; flower brookpottery.com), 3210 Rt. 30, Dorset. Open daily 10–5 except Tues. A showroom for hand-painted pottery, baby clothes, candles, cards, whimsical slippers, and more.

Elsewhere
✪ **Lake's Lampshades** (802-325-6308; lakes lampshades.com), School St., Pawlet. Open Mon.–Sat. 9–4. Judy Sawyer Lake's studio/shop is a riot of fabrics and colors, all shaped into lamp shades. If you can't find something here to brighten a corner of your life, Judy will make it to order.

Bob Gasperetti Furniture Maker (802-293-5195; gasperetti.com), 848 South End Rd., Mount Tabor. Shaker-, Mission-, and Arts & Crafts–inspired furniture; call for appointment.

Vermont Windsor Chairs & Fine Furniture (802-824-4550; vermontwindsorchairs.com), Landgrove Rd., Londonderry. David Spero's workshop features Windsor chairs, Queen Anne highboys, Shaker pieces, chests, and more. Call ahead.

✪ **D. Lasser Ceramics** (802-824-6183; 888-824-6183; lasserceramics.com), 6405 Rt. 100, Londonderry. Open daily 9–6. South of Weston, well worth a detour. A studio showroom with potters doing their thing, and shelves—inside and out—filled with bright pitchers and platters, bowls and vases, mugs and plates, all highly original and affordable.

FACTORY OUTLETS The contemporary cluster of designer discount stores in Manchester Center evokes mixed feelings from Vermonters. Some chafe at what they consider corporate

MANCHESTER OUTLETS
Lee Krohn

intrusion into a once quiet village. Others welcome the increased exposure, not to mention the acres of quality goods. In general, the prices are not rock bottom but better than you'd find in the city. Most are open 10–6 daily, later in summer.

Manchester Designer Outlets (manchester designeroutlets.com). The glass-and-wood anchor complex at and near the junction of Rts. 7A and 11/30 in Manchester Center presently houses Ann Taylor, Armani, J. Crew, Brooks Brothers, Coach, Crabtree & Evelyn, Polo Ralph Lauren, Eileen Fisher, Marimekko, Eddie Bauer, and many more.

Equinox Square (Rt. 11/30) includes Coldwater Creek.

J. K. Adams Co. and The Kitchen Store (802-362-4422; jkadams.com), Rt. 30, Dorset. Open daily 9–5:30. A three-floor cornucopia of top-quality kitchen gear, from butcher blocks to knife racks, tableware, and cookbooks, with an observation deck over the woodworking factory. Everything a foodie could want.

SPECIALTY SHOPS Long Ago & Far Away (802-362-3435; longagoandfaraway.com), Green Mountain Village Shops, Manchester Center. This is an extensive shop showcasing Native American craftsmanship, specializing in Canadian Inuit and Native Alaskan sculpture. Open daily.

CONSIDER BARDWELL FARM, WEST PAWLET
Alice Levitt

The Mountain Goat (802-362-5159; mountain goat.com), 4886 Main St., Manchester Center. Quality outdoor clothing and gear are the hallmarks of this and other Mountain Goats (in Williamstown and Northampton, Massachusetts). Owner Ron Houser really knows what shoe is good for your foot. Houser specializes in orthotics "for athletes, hikers and everyday victims of gravity." Open Mon.–Sat. 10–6, Sun. 10–5.

ANTIQUES SHOPS Marie Miller Antique Quilts (802-867-5969; antiquequilts.com), 1489 Rt. 30, Dorset. Over 300 antique quilts, all in superb condition, plus hooked rugs, Quimper, and other faience. Open daily 10–5.

Comollo Antiques (802-362-7188; vtantiques .com), 4686 Main St., Manchester Center. Open Tues.–Sat. 10–6, Sun.–Mon. 10–5, closed Wed. Furniture, fine art, estate jewelry, and international wines.

Brewster Antiques (802-362-1579), 152 Bonnet St., Manchester Center. Just off Rt. 7A, a wide assortment of antiques; open Mon.–Sat. 10–5.

In Arlington
East Arlington Antiques Center (802-375-6144), 1223 East Arlington Rd. Open daily 10–5. In a vintage former movie theater on a scenic byway, John Maynard maintains this space with 70 dealers selling everything from linens to silver, furniture, and art. Continue along this road to the Chiselville Covered Bridge, built in 1870 and named for the chisel factory that once stood nearby. It spans Roaring Branch brook. The road eventually crosses the Battenkill in Sunderland, joining Rt. 7A near the base of the Mount Equinox toll road.

Gristmill Antiques at Candlemill Village (802-375-2500), 316 Old Mill Rd., East Arlington. Open year-round, weekends in winter, daily in summer, best to call ahead. Ethan Allen's cousin, Remember Baker, built a gristmill on Peter's Brook in 1764. Two hundred years later it became a candle factory. Now the building on Peter's Brook is an inviting shop representing several area dealers with an emphasis on 1800s and early-1900s period antiques.

In Danby
1820 House of Antiques (802-293-2820), 82 S. Main St. Open year-round, daily 10–5 in summer, closed Tues.–Wed. in winter. A multidealer shop featuring American country and formal furniture and accessories. The proprietor is Carol Wehner; eight dealers.

FARMS *Note:* The last weekend in March is Maple Open House Weekend (vermontmaple .org). See *Special Events.*

✪ ✔ **Consider Bardwell Farm** (802-645-9928; considerbardwellfarm.com), 1333 Rt. 153, West Pawlet. Consider Stebbins Bardwell opened Vermont's first cheesemaking co-op here in 1864. More than a century later, this revived farm produces some of Vermont's best cheeses. Stay at the cottage overlooking a pond (they'll stock the fridge with cheese for you) or just visit to grab some Rupert, Dorset, or Pawlet and the goats and cows who make it. Check the website for on-farm events.

✔ **Dutton Berry Farm** (362-3083; dutton berryfarm.com), Rt. 11/30, Manchester. This is one of three super farm stands (the original is in Newfane) featuring local produce, much it grown in 14 greenhouses on Paul Dutton's farms in the West River Valley. In winter it's a good spot for locally grown Christmas trees and wreaths. The farm stand is open daily, year-round. Pick your own in summer.

✔ **Taylor Farm** (802-824-5690; taylorfarm vermont.com), 825 Rt. 11 west of Bromley Mountain (1 mile east of Londonderry). Some 40 Holstein and Jersey milk cows provide the milk for the farm's famous Gouda cheeses and baked goods. Wagon and sleigh rides, farm animal visits. Open daily 10–6.

Equinox Nursery (802-362-2610; equinox valleynursery.com), Rt. 7A, south of Manchester. Open daily, closed Thurs. in winter. An outstanding farm stand and nursery managed by three generations of the Preuss family; good for picking vegetables, berries in-season. Especially famous in fall for the 100,000 pounds of pumpkins it produces, also for its display of scarecrows and pumpkin faces. Sells pumpkin bread, pie, ice cream, and marmalade, along with other farm stand staples, annuals, perennials, and shrubs. In Jan. and Feb. the family cultivates a tropical conservatory with birds and indoor flowering plants.

✔ **Mad Tom Orchard** (802-366-8107; mad tomorhard.com), 2615 Mad Tom Rd., East Dorset. Raspberries in July and Sept., apples mid-Sept.–mid-Oct. Farm stand and pick your own seasonally.

✱ Special Events

March: **US Open Snowboarding Championships** (stratton.com), held first weekend of March. **Spring skiing** at area ski resorts. **Vermont Maple Open House Weekend**, last weekend, at area sugarhouses (vermont maple.org).

April: **Trout season** opens; Easter parades and egg hunts at ski areas. Whitewater canoeing on the West River.

Memorial Day weekend: **Vermont Open Studio Weekend**. See vermontcrafts.com for open studio tours of area art and crafts galleries.

June: **Manchester Antique & Classic Car Show** (manchestercarshow.com) held at Dorr Farm with a vintage sports car climb to Equinox Summit. **Wanderlust** (wanderlustfestival.com), Stratton Mountain, combining yoga and music.

Mid-June–early September: **Dorset Theatre Festival** summer season (dorsettheatrefestival .org).

✔ *July 4 :* Manchester and Dorset host an old-fashioned Fourth, a daylong celebration that culminates in fireworks (visitmanchestervt.com).

July–mid-August: The **Vermont Summer Festival Horse Show** comes to Manchester for six weeks (vt-summerfestival.com). **Manchester Music Festival**—a series of concerts at the Southern Vermont Art Center (mmfvt.org) with multiple productions. **Strattonfest** at Stratton Mountain Resort (stratton.com) features several weeks of folk, jazz, classical, and country music. **Summer concerts** on the Manchester town green, Tues. evenings 6–8 in July and Aug. (visitmanchestervt.com).

August: **Southern Vermont Crafts Fair** (craftproducers.com)—juried exhibitors, entertainment, food, and music at Riley Rink. **Norman's Attic** (stjamesarlingtonvt.org) in Arlington is a townwide tag sale. **Manchester Sidewalk Sale** (visitmanchestervt.com) is a garage sale of designer goods. ✔ **Annual Bondville Fair** (bondvillefair.org), one of Vermont's oldest and most colorful country fairs.

✔ *September:* **Peru Fair**—just one day (fourth Sat.; parking is at Bromley; perufair.org). Considered one of Vermont's most colorful fairs, it includes a pig roast, crafts, food, and entertainment.

October: **Foliage Art & Craft Festival** (craft producers.com) at Riley Rink. **Antiques in Vermont** (carlsonandstevenson.com) show (with around 80 exhibitors) at Riley Rink, Manchester Center.

December: **Manchester Merriment** (visit manchestervt.com)—a tour of the historic inns, tree lighting, Annual Lighted Tractor Parade, horse and wagon rides, wine tastings, and more Thanksgiving weekend through New Year's. Hildene Holiday Tours (hildene.org) through the mansion, decorated for Christmas Dec.–Jan. 1.

OKEMO VALLEY REGION

INCLUDING LUDLOW, CHESTER, CAVENDISH, MOUNT HOLLY, ANDOVER, PLYMOUTH, AND WESTON

O kemo is the name of the major ski resort that anchors this area. Its trails streak a massive mountain face above the lively village of Ludlow. The Black River rises in the chain of ponds and lakes north of town and joins Jewell Brook, forming the power source for the 19th-century mills around which the town was built.

East of town Rt. 131 follows the Black River through the smaller mill villages of Proctorsville and Cavendish. Rt. 103 branches south, following the Williams River to Chester, a handsome old cross-roads community at the confluence of five roads and comprising three distinctive villages, all within walking distance. It offers an exceptional choice of lodging, dining, and shopping as well as easy access to much of southern and central Vermont.

Given its central location and lodging both on and off the mountain, Ludlow is a good base from which to explore in all directions. Rt. 103 climbs west into hill towns and down into the Lower Champlain Valley. Rt. 100 climbs south up Terrible Mountain and down into Weston. North of town Rt. 100 follows the river and ponds to Plymouth, birthplace of Calvin Coolidge. His village of Plymouth Notch, preserved as a state historic site, looks much the way it did on August 3, 1923, when he was sworn in as the 30th president of the United States by his father in his kerosene-lit home. Coolidge had attended Ludlow's Black River Academy in a building that's now a great little museum.

GUIDANCE Okemo Valley Regional Chamber of Commerce (802-228-5830; 866-216-8722; yourplaceinvermont.com), P.O. Box 333, Ludlow 05149. Open except Sun. This walk-in information office in the Marketplace, across from Okemo Mountain Access Rd. on Rt. 103 (look for the clock tower), has regional menus, events listings, and lodging brochures. The chamber also publishes the *Okemo Valley Regional Guide*.

GETTING THERE *By air*: The Albany, Hartford, and Burlington airports are all a two-hour drive. **Cape Air** from Boston flies to Rutland (20 minutes).

By car: From points southeast, take I-91 to Vermont Exit 6 to Rt. 103 north, which leads you to Chester and on to Ludlow. The area can also be accessed from I-91, Exits 7 and 8. From New York and western Massachusetts, take I-87 north to New York Exit 23 then follow I-787 to Troy to Exit 9 toward Bennington.

GETTING AROUND Okemo Mountain Resort (802-228-4041) offers a free shuttle to the village during peak times in ski season.

Ludlow Transport is a free shuttle service that runs several routes throughout Ludlow and the surrounding area. The service operates Mon.–Fri. Pick up the schedule at the chamber of commerce.

WHEN TO GO The chain of lakes north of Ludlow and the classic countryside around Chester draw summer and fall visitors. In winter Okemo is the big draw; cross-country skiing and snowmobile trails crisscross the region. The Weston Playhouse draws patrons July until mid-September.

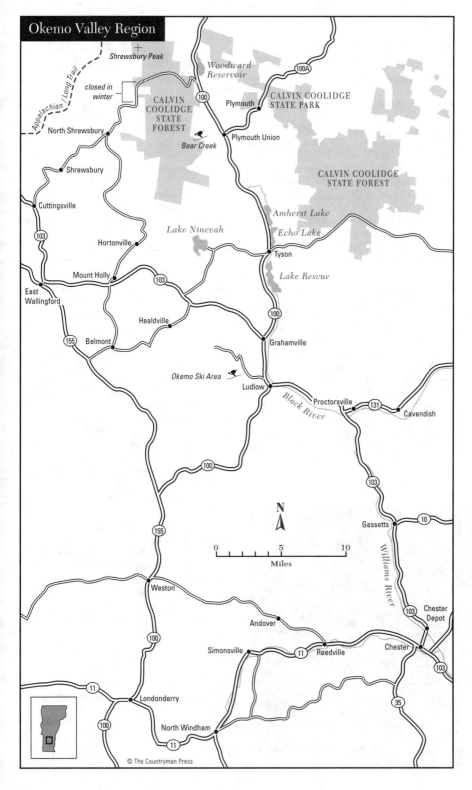

Okemo Valley Region

Shrewsbury Peak

Appalachian/Long Trail

Woodward Reservoir

100A

closed in winter

CALVIN COOLIDGE STATE FOREST

100

Plymouth

CALVIN COOLIDGE STATE PARK

North Shrewsbury

Bear Creek

Plymouth Union

Shrewsbury

CALVIN COOLIDGE STATE FOREST

Cuttingsville

103

Amherst Lake

Lake Ninevah

Echo Lake

Hortonville

Tyson

Mount Holly

103

Lake Rescue

East Wallingford

100

Healdville

155 Belmont

Grahamville

Okemo Ski Area

Ludlow

Black River

Proctorsville

131

Cavendish

100

103

N

103

10

Gassetts

0   5   10

Miles

Williams River

155

Weston

Andover

100

Chester Depot

103

Simonsville

11 Reedville

Chester

103

11

Londonderry

35

100

North Windham

11

© The Countryman Press

SOUTHERN VERMONT

✳ Towns and Villages

Ludlow (population 2,640) boomed with the production of "shoddy" (fabric made from reworked wool) after the Civil War, a period frozen in the red brick of its commercial block, Victorian mansions, magnificent library, and academy (now the Black River Museum). In the wake of the wool boom, the General Electric Company moved into the picturesque mill at the heart of town and kept people employed making small-aircraft engine parts until 1977. Okemo, opened in 1956, was a sleeper—a big mountain with antiquated lifts—until 1982 when Tim and Diane Mueller bought it and began transforming it into one of New England's most popular ski resorts, known for the quality of its snowmaking, grooming, and on-mountain lodging. An 18-hole golf course doubles as a full-service cross-country ski center. The old General Electric plant has been turned into condominiums. Other lodging options as well as shops and restaurants have multiplied. For a sense of Ludlow in its pre-skiing era, visit the **Fletcher Library** (802-228-8921) with its reading rooms with fireplaces; old-style, green-shaded lights; and 19th-century paintings of local landscapes. The **Black River Academy Museum** (802-228-5050), 14 High St., is open Memorial Day–Columbus Day, Tues.–Sat. noon–4. Built in 1889, the academy's reputation drew students from throughout New England. President Calvin Coolidge was a member of the class of 1890. Exhibits about "Main Street" circa 1900 and the third-floor classroom offer a sense of what it meant (and still means) to live in the Black River Valley. North of town off Rt. 100, rental cottages can be found on all four lakes.

Chester (population 2,997) is sited at the confluence of three branches of the Williams River and of five major roads. Its string-bean-shaped village green is lined with shops, restaurants, and the centerpiece Fullerton Inn. Across the street (Rt. 11) is the early-19th-century brick Academy building is now occupied by the **Chester Historical Society** (802-875-5459; chesterhistory.org), open May–Columbus Day, Sat.–Sun. 2–4. It presents the town's colorful history, including the story of Clarence Adams, a prominent citizen who broke into more than 50 businesses and homes between 1886 and 1902 before being apprehended. Rt. 103 forks north from the village center to **Chester Depot**, a cluster of homes and public buildings around the well-kept Victorian depot, the town hall, and Lisai's Market. Follow Rt. 103 up past the vintage-1879 red wooden Yosemite Fire House with its two towers (one for the bell and the tall one for drying hoses) to the **Stone Village**, a double line of early-19th-century houses built from locally quarried granite. Cool in summer, warm in winter, stone houses are a rarity in New England. All of these are said to have been built by two brothers in the pre–Civil War decade, with hiding spaces enough to make them a significant stop on the Underground Railroad. Chester offers more than its share of local lodging, dining, and shopping. It's handy to skiing at Magic Mountain and Bromley as well as Okemo, and to cross-country skiing and biking at Grafton Ponds.

WESTON VILLAGE GREEN
Christina Tree

Weston (weston-vermont.com). A mountain crossroads that's a logical hub for exploring southern Vermont, this village of just 630 souls looms large on tourist maps. It's the home of the **Weston Playhouse**, one of the country's oldest and best summer theaters, and the original **Vermont Country Store**. The oval common is shaded with majestic maples, and a band plays regularly in the bandstand. Weston was actually one of the first villages in Vermont to be consciously preserved. Like the theater, the unusually fine historical collection in the **Farrar Mansur House** and (indirectly) the Vermont Country Store all date from the "Weston Revival" of the 1930s. Even if you have never set foot inside a historic house, make an exception for this one, built in 1797 as a tavern with a classic old taproom. (Open for tours and demonstrations late June–mid-Oct., Sat. and Sun.

WESTON PRIORY

Christina Tree

afternoons, also Wed. through mid-Aug.) Thanks to 1930s Work Progress Administration (WPA) artists, murals of Weston in its prime cover the living room walls, and a number of primitive portraits hang in the adjacent rooms over period furniture and furnishings donated by Weston families. The upstairs ballroom displays 1820s stenciling. In the attic a rendition of townspeople dancing—each face is painted to resemble a specific resident—conjures the spirit of a town that knew how to have fun. Next door the reproduction 1780 **Old Mill** stands by a dam and waterfall. Grain is ground, and there are many vintage tools and demonstrations. The village also offers lodging and dining. Visitors are very welcome at **Weston Priory** (802-824-5409; westonpriory.org), a community of Benedictine monks, nationally known for the Gregorian chant in their daily common prayer and other music sung and played at Sunday liturgies; there's also a gift shop, retreat house, and rare sense of peace both in and outside the monastery. Free summer concerts are presented by the **Kinhaven Music School**.

✳ To See

SCENIC DRIVES Okemo Mountain Road in downtown Ludlow (off Rt. 100/103) follows the Okemo Mountain Access Rd. beyond the base lodge (stay left). This is a ski trail in winter, but in summer and fall it offers a hard-topped 2.5-mile route to the summit. There's a small parking lot and a half-mile trail through the woods to a former fire tower that boasts (on a clear day) 360-degree views.

Shrewsbury Loop. From Ludlow head north 2 miles on Rt. 100, then northwest on Rt. 103 for 5 miles to Healdville and the sign for the **Crowley Cheese Factory**. In the 1880s every Vermont town had its cheese factory to process surplus milk, but Crowley Cheese, which the family had begun making in the 1820s, was distributed up and down the East Coast. The three-story wooden building, built in 1882 by Winfield Crowley, is now billed as America's oldest cheese factory. It's a 2-mile detour down a side road but well worth the effort. Visitors are welcome weekdays 8–4, but cheese is actually made Tues.–Fri., and the best time to come is around 1 PM when the cheese is being "drained." The shower-capped employees also hand cut and rake the curd, rinsing it with springwater, draining 75 percent of the whey. This is a Colby cheese, which is moister and ages more quickly than cheddar. It takes 5,000 pounds of fresh milk to make 500 pounds of Crowley Cheese. Needless to say, you can pick up samples and reasonably priced "ends." Rt. 103 climbs on to Mount Holly, then continues another 5 miles to Cuttingsville. Turn up the road ("Town Hill") posted for **Shrewsbury**, and right again at the T. Shrewsbury Center is marked by a white wooden church set back on a knoll beside two face-to-face old taverns, now both B&Bs. One of these, **Maple Crest Farm**, remains in the same family that built it in 1808 and has been taking in guests since the 1860s. Although the dairy herd is gone, this is still a working farm with more than 30 head of beef cattle and some 300 acres in hay. Stop to buy some prizewinning maple syrup and take in the view. In North Shrewsbury, 2 more miles up the hill, the 19th-century **W. E. Pierce General Store** (802-492-3326; piercesstorevt.com) has been restored by the Preservation Trust of Vermont and is a community cooperative selling soups, sandwiches and freshly prepared foods, baked goods, and local produce and products as well as groceries. Check out the signs tacked to the big old fir tree nearby. They point west to Rutland and east to Plymouth Union, confirming the impression that you are standing on the peaked roof of this entire region. Fasten your seat belt and (conditions permitting) plunge east down the vintage-1930s CCC Road, one of Vermont's steepest and most scenic routes. It's 6 miles seemingly straight down—with superlative mountain and valley views—to Rt. 100 in Plymouth. Note the pullout for Shrewsbury Peak, the trailhead for a steep 1.2-mile path connecting with the Long Trail here. Remarkably enough, this was the site of Vermont's second rope tow, installed in 1935 by the Rutland Ski Club. According to the write-up, some 2,400 spectators came up this road (brand-new then, it's closed now in snow season) to watch the skiers come down. Continue down to Rt. 100A to Plymouth Union,

CALVIN COOLIDGE AND PLYMOUTH NOTCH

Calvin Coolidge (1872–1933) is best remembered for his dry wit and thrift, his integrity and common sense, all famously Vermont virtues. The village of Plymouth Notch—in which Coolidge was born, assumed the presidency, briefly governed the country (in the summer of 1924), and is buried—is said to be the best-preserved presidential birthplace in the nation. It may also be the best-preserved Vermont village, offering an in-depth sense of the people who lived there. In the **President Calvin Coolidge Museum & Education Center**, the main entrance to the village, the permanent exhibit *"More Than Two Words": The Life & Legacy of Calvin Coolidge* dramatizes the story of how a boy from Plymouth Notch became president, using Coolidge's own words and interactive media.

The village itself remains low-key. The **cheese factory** built by the president's father, John Coolidge, showcases the history of Vermont cheesemaking and produces its own exceptional 19th-century granular-curd cheese (plymouthartisancheese.com). The general store sells, among other things, cold cans of Moxie, the president's favorite soft drink; its upstairs hall is restored to look just as it did as the office of the Summer White House. The square-steepled Union Christian Church, with its acoustically superb interior, is the setting for frequent concerts and lectures. The general store also sells maple syrup, penny candy, and Coolidge memorabilia. "Colonel" John Coolidge became storekeeper here in 1868, and his son Calvin was born on the Fourth of July, 1872, in the modest attached house. The family moved across the street to the larger Coolidge Homestead when he was four years old, and it was there, because he happened to be home helping with the haying, that Vice President Calvin Coolidge learned of President Warren Harding's unexpected death. At 2:47 AM on August 3, 1923, he was sworn in, by his father, as 30th president of the United States.

"I didn't know I couldn't" was the reply Coolidge Sr. gave when reporters asked how he knew he could administer the presidential oath of office. "Colonel John" was a former state senator, a notary public, and the village sheriff as well as shopkeeper. His terse response typifies the dry wit for which his son would later become known.

It should come as no surprise that in this classic Vermont village you encounter a classic Vermont family. The Coolidges were hardworking (up before dawn for chores), self-sufficient (you see an intricate quilt that was stitched by Cal at age 10 and a graceful carriage built by his father), and closely linked to the land. Coolidge is buried with seven generations of his family in the small graveyard across the road from the village. Residents numbered 29 during Coolidge's presidency, and a high percentage of these formed the Old-Time Dance Orchestra, which played in the dance hall above the general store. This same room served as the office of the Summer White House for a dozen days in 1924. At the time Calvin and his wife, Grace, were grieving the death of their son Calvin Jr., a promising 16-year-old who had died due to a complication from an infected blister he acquired while playing tennis at the White House.

Plymouth resident Ruth ("Midge") Aldrich opened several tourist cabins (prefab jobs brought up from Boston) to accommodate the Secret Service and a Top of the Notch Tea Room to serve a steady stream of the Coolidge-curious. Plymouth Notch, however, never really hit the big time as a tourist attraction, perhaps because, while he continued to visit "The Notch," President Coolidge himself retired to private life not here but in his adopted home, Northampton,

perhaps the first rural Vermont village to appear in publications throughout the world—on August 3, 1923. (See the box.) Make your way back to Rt. 100; from Plymouth it's a scenic 9-mile ride south past a chain of lakes to Ludlow.

Route 100 Scenic Byway and loop. Officially 31 miles of Rt. 100 from Andover to Plymouth have recently been added to the Rt. 100 Scenic Byway. This stretch includes Plymouth Union (see above) and extends south through Ludlow. We suggest you follow over Terrible Mountain to Weston (see *Villages*), then follow the Andover Rd. 11 miles west to Chester (*Villages*) and loop back to Ludlow (12 miles) on Rt. 103, detouring into the village of Proctorsville. Be sure to stop at Singleton's Store.

Massachusetts. After graduating from nearby Amherst College, Coolidge had opened a law practice in Northampton, and it was there that he met his wife (fellow Vermonter Grace Anna Goodhue, who was teaching there at the Clarke School for the Deaf) and served as mayor. He represented Northampton in the Massachusetts Legislature before becoming governor of the Bay State, and he died in Northampton.

It was Aurora Pierce, the family housekeeper, who fiercely preserved the Coolidge Homestead, adamantly opposing even minor changes, like plumbing and electricity. Not until Aurora's death in 1956 did Vermont's Historic Sites Commission assume management of the house and its contents.

The President Calvin Coolidge State Historic Site presently encompasses 25 buildings, the majority of the village, including the 1870s **Wilder Barn**, housing farm implements, horse-drawn vehicles, and the **Wilder House Restaurant** (open daily 9–4:30 for breakfast and lunch)—a pine-walled café with exposed beams in what was once the home of Calvin Coolidge's mother. Power lines have been buried (electricity actually didn't reach Plymouth until after Calvin's death), and roads have been paved. Otherwise the village looks about as it did in the 1920s, sitting quietly at the foot of East Mountain. It's set in 580 acres presently owned by the Vermont Division for Historic Preservation, surrounded by the 500-acre Coolidge State Park, in turn abutting the 16,000-acre Calvin Coolidge State Forest. The **President Coolidge State Historic Site** (802-672-3773; historicsites.vermont.gov/directory/coolidge) is open late May–mid-Oct., daily 9:30–5. $9 adults, $2 ages 6–14; 5 and under are free; $25 family ticket. During the off-season the Aldrich House, which doubles as an office and exhibit space, is open weekdays (no charge but call ahead).

THE VISITORS CENTER AT CALVIN COOLIDGE STATE HISTORIC SITE
Vermont Division of Historic Preservation

✳ To Do

ADVENTURE ZONE ✿ **Okemo Mountain Resort** (802-228-4041; okemo.com) offers a summer/fall play center (for all ages) at Jackson Gore, Rt. 103 just northwest of Ludlow. The big attraction here is **Timber Ripper Mountain Coaster**, which operates in ski season as well. Riders can control the speed of the sledlike cars that travel along 3,100 feet of track following the contours of the mountain, looping along down a 375-vertical-foot descent (single ride: $13 per driver, $9 per rider). There's also the **Haulback Challenge Course**, **Sawyer's Sweep Zipline Tours**, **Segway Personal Transport Tours**, the **Maples at Okemo Disc Golf Course**, the **Lumberin' Cal** 18-hole miniature golf

Okemo Mountain

OKEMO'S TIMBER RIPPER IS A WAY DOWN THE MOUNTAIN IN SUMMER AS WELL AS WINTER.

course, and the **Stump Jumper Bungee Trampoline**. The timber theme commemorates one of the town's oldest industries.

ARTS AND CRAFTS Fletcher Farm School for the Arts and Crafts (802-228-8770; fletcher farm.org), 611 Rt. 103 south, Ludlow. Operated since 1947 by the Society of Vermont Craftsmen, headquartered in an old farmstead on the eastern edge of town. More than 200 courses are offered in summer and more than 100 in fall and winter in traditional crafts, contemporary crafts, and fine art. In summer lodging and meals are available on campus; fall through spring, multiday workshops are offered at area inns. Crafts include fiber arts, basketry, theorem painting, glass, weaving, woodcarving, quilting, oil and watercolor painting, spinning, rug hooking and braiding, and more. Open to all ages.

BIKING The Spring House at Jackson Gore at Okemo Resort (802-228-1419) offers seasonal hybrid bike rentals with map guides to Buttermilk Falls and to the Red Bridge Swimming Hole on Lake Rescue. **Mountain Cycology** (802-228-2722), Teen Center, Rt. 103, Ludlow. No rentals but equipment, repair, guidebooks, and local advice as well as sales.

BOATING Echo Lake Inn (802-228-8602), Rt. 100, Tyson, rents canoes and other boats to guests only. **Camp Plymouth State** Park (802-228-2025) off Rt. 100 in Tyson also offers seasonal canoe, kayak, and rowboat rentals (see *Swimming* for directions). Nearby **Lake Ninevah** is quieter, with some beautiful marshes and woods.

FISHING Public access has been provided to Lake Rescue, Echo Lake, Lake Ninevah, Woodward Reservoir, and Amherst Lake. Fishing licenses are required except under age 16. The catch includes rainbow trout, bass, and pickerel. There is also fly-fishing in the Black River along Rt. 131 in Cavendish, and the 6-mile stretch from the covered bridge in Downers down to a second covered bridge is a trophy-trout section, stocked each spring with 1.5-pound brown trout and 18-inch rainbows.

FITNESS CENTERS AND SPAS Castle Hill Spa (802-226-7419; castlehillresortandspa.com) junction of Rts. 103 and 131, Cavendish. An aesthetically pleasing center set apart from the inn and open to the public. The outdoor pool and whirlpool are heated for year-round use, the workout room offers aerobics classes as well as Nautilus equipment, and the Aveda spa offers a variety of wraps and massages; there's also a salon and Har-Tru tennis courts.

The Spring House at Okemo Mountain Resort (802-228-1418; okemo.com), Rt. 103, Ludlow. At Jackson Gore Lodge, a two-level fitness and aquatic center offers year-round swimming, racquetball, fitness classes, weights and cardio equipment, hot tub, and sauna. The Ice House sports pavilion transitions from a winter skating rink to a warm-weather complex with tennis courts, basketball courts, and jogging track. A full massage menu is offered. Day passes available.

GOLF The **Okemo Valley Golf Club** (802-228-1396; golf.okemo.com), Fox Lane, Ludlow. An 18-hole championship "heathland-style" course featuring wide fairways with dips, ripples, rolls, and hollows said to suggest Scottish links. Facilities include an 18-acre outdoor Golf Learning Center with a 370-yard-long driving range, four practice greens, a 6,000-square-foot indoor practice area, a computerized virtual golf program, classrooms, and changing rooms with showers; also a pro shop and Willie Dunne's Grille (see *Eating Out*).

Tater Hill Golf Club (802-875-2517), 6802 Popple Dungeon Rd., North Windham (off Rt. 11, not far from Chester). A recently renovated 18-hole course with a pro shop and practice range, now owned by Okemo.

SWIMMING ✸ **West Hill Recreation Area** (802-228-2849), West Hill off Rt. 103 in Ludlow, includes a beach and a small, spring-fed reservoir.

Buttermilk Falls, near the junction of Rts. 100 and 103. This is a swimming hole and a series of small but beautiful falls (turn at the VFW post just west of the intersection).

✸ **Camp Plymouth State Park** (802-228-2025). Turn east over the bridge off Rt. 100 across from the Echo Lake Inn at Tyson. Continue 1 mile to the crossroads, then turn left onto Boy Scout Camp Rd. There's a sandy beach on Echo Lake, picnic area, boat rentals, volleyball, horseshoes, and a playground. **Star Lake** in the village of Belmont in Mount Holly is also a great place for a swim.

WALKING Vermont Inn to Inn Walking, Hiking & Biking (800-728-0842; vermontinntoinn walking.com). Four-night, inn-to-inn walking tours (3–10 miles per day) are offered among four area inns. Luggage is transported for you and a trail snack is provided, along with lodging, breakfast, and dinner.

✴ Winter Sports

DOWNHILL SKIING ✸ **Okemo** (information 802-228-1600; snow report 802-228-5222; reservations 800-78-OKEMO; okemo.com). A big mountain with southern Vermont's highest vertical drop, Okemo is a destination ski and snowboard resort with a small-resort, family feel. This is a ski area of many parts—in fact five distinct areas: Jackson Gore Peak, Solitude Peak, South Face, Glades Peak, and South Ridge. Jackson Gore, added in 2006, brought a whole new face to the resort, one with its own entrance, base area, lodging, and restaurants. Off around the corner of the mountain from the main access, Jackson Gore is a useful rear entry to the slopes on busy weekends.

Family owned and operated since 1982 by Tim and Diane Mueller, Okemo is far larger than it looks from its base. Surprises begin at the top of the initial chairlifts, where you meet a wall of three-story condominiums and find your way down to the spacious Sugar House base lodge—from which the true size of the mountain becomes apparent. From the summit, beginners can actually run a full 4.5 miles to the base; there are also a number of wide, central fall-line runs down the face of the mountain. World Cup is a long and steep but forgiving run with sweeping views down the Black River Valley to the Connecticut River.

Lifts: 19, including 5 high-speed quads (one of which is a 6-passenger bubble chair with heated seats—the first of its kind in the U.S.).

Trails and slopes: 120 slopes trails and glades—32% novice, 37% intermediate, 31% advanced expert. 5 mountain areas: Jackson Gore Peak, Solitude Peak, South Face, Glades Peak, South Ridge.

Vertical drop: 2,200 feet (highest in southern Vermont).

Snowmaking: Covers 96% of trails (655 acres).

Facilities: **Base lodge** with cafeteria, Sitting Bull, and Vermont Pizza; midmountain Sugar House base lodge with café, Smokey Jo's BBQ, deli; **Summit Lodge** with café, Sky Bar, Jump (Asian specialties); Solitude Day Lodge with **Epic restaurant**, snack bar (open 11–3). At **Jackson Gore** you'll find the Roundhouse, Siena, and Coleman Brook Tavern (see *Dining Out*); Waffle House is at the bottom of the

BOARDING IS BIG AT OKEMO.

Okemo Mountain

140   Black Ridge Triple and at Jackson Gore base area.

Tip: **Epic** is the mountain's coolest lunch spot and the area's ultimate dining option Sat. nights in winter, the setting for 5-course candlelit dinners; $125 includes the ride up and down via snowcat.

Ski school: Okemo's Ski + Ride School is staffed by 450 instructors. Children's programs include Mini Stars (ages 3–4), Snow Stars (4–7), Mountain Explorers (7–14). Ski and snowboard programs include Women's Alpine Adventures (2- to 5-day intensive programs). Senior discounts are available on group lessons. The state-approved Penguin Day Care Center serves children 6 months to 6 years and offers supervised indoor and outdoor activities. Inquire about Kids' Night Out programs, available 6–9 PM in-season.

Lift tickets: Adults $82 midweek, $92 weekend and holiday, also young adult, junior, half-day, multiday tickets and online discounts. Kids 6 and under ski free. Savings on multiday tickets when packaged into stays at area inns and B&Bs as well as slope-side lodging.

SUN BEACH AT OKEMO

Okemo Mountain

CROSS-COUNTRY SKIING AND SNOWSHOEING Okemo **Valley Nordic Center** (802-228-1396; okemo.com), junction of Rts. 100 and 103, Ludlow. A café and a rental shop are surrounded by the open roll of the golf course; there are also wooded and mountain trails adding up to 22 km (including 22 km of skating lanes), plus 10 km of dedicated snowshoe trails. The clubhouse offers a fireplace, changing rooms, rentals, and showers.

Also see **Grafton Ponds Recreation Center** in Grafton (in "Lower Connecticut River Valley").

SNOWMOBILE RIDES Okemo Snowmobile Tours (802-422-2121; 800-FAT-TRAK; snowmobile vermont.com). The "Mountain Tour" is a one-hour tour through the woods, while the "Back Country Tour" is a 25-mile ride into the Calvin Coolidge State Forest for beginner through expert.

JACKSON GORE BASE AND LODGES

Okemo Mountain

✴ Lodging

RESORTS Okemo Mountain Resort (802-228-5571; 800-78-OKEMO; okemo.com), Ludlow 05149. Open year-round, featuring winter skiing and summer golf, with lodging options that include nearly 700 condominium units, along with **Jackson Gore Inn**, with 245 condo-style units at the Jackson Gore Base Area including restaurants, a reception area, health club, and underground parking. This complex includes the Adams and Bixby lodging annexes and the Spring House, a two-level fitness and aquatic center with year-round swimming, racquetball, fitness classes, weights and cardio equipment, hot tub, and sauna. The Ice House sports pavilion transitions from a winter skating rink to a warm-weather complex with tennis courts, basketball courts, and jogging track.

There is also **Okemo Mountain Lodge**, a three-story hotel at the entrance to the resort that's really a cluster of 55 one-bedroom condos, each with a sleeping couch in the living room. There's a compact kitchen with eating counter and a fireplace; enough space for a couple and two children. **Kettle Brook** has one-, two-, and three-bedroom units, all nicely built, salted along trails. **Winterplace**, set high on a mountain shelf, consists of 17 buildings with a total of 250 units ranging in size from two bedrooms to three bedrooms plus a loft. Residents have access to a fitness center with indoor pool. **Solitude Village** is a ski-in/ski-out complex of one- to five-unit condos and town houses plus a lodge with indoor/outdoor heated pool and a service area with a restaurant, ski shop, and children's learning center. **Ledgewood Condominiums** are three- and four-bedroom units with garages accessed by their own trail.

⚷ **The Castle Hill Resort and Spa** (802-226-7361; 800-438-7908; castlehillresortvt.com), 2910 Rt. 103, Proctorsville 05149. Quarry and timber baron Allen Fletcher, elected governor of Vermont in 1913, built this imposing neo-Jacobean stone manor on a knoll, importing European artisans in 1901 for the oak and mahogany woodwork and detailed cast-plaster ceilings. The 10 rooms are regal ($299–349); ask about spa, ski, and a variety of other packages. One- to three-bedroom condo units on the property run $399–700. See the day spa under *To Do*. Weddings and civil union celebrations for up to 200 are a specialty, with facilities to accommodate many guests in the neighboring resort homes and The Pointe motor inn (see *Motels*). The richly paneled dining room features a three-course prix fixe menu ($47–65) and is open to the public by reservation.

INNS

In the Ludlow area

⚷ ✿ ⚷ **The Andrie Rose Inn** (802-228-4846; 800-223-4846; andrieroseinn.com), 13 Pleasant St., Ludlow 05149. Michael and Irene Maston preside over this hospitable haven on a quiet street with unexpectedly luxurious rooms and suites and a reputation for fine dining. The inn itself is a 19th-century house in which the old detailing has been carefully preserved, but the feel—thanks to skillful decor and skylights—is light-filled, cheerful, and informal. Guests check in at the kitchen counter. Five of the nine upstairs guest rooms have whirlpool tub, and all are furnished with antiques and designer linens. Summit View features a skylight framing the summit of the mountain. Next door is Solitude (named for an express quad at Okemo), an 1840s Greek Revival building with seven luxury suites; two feature a bedside whirlpool tub for two facing a gas fireplace. See *Dining Out* for details about dinner. Amenities include shuttle service to and from Okemo. Irene is nationally recognized for the beauty of her wedding cakes, and weddings for up to 100 can be accommodated; inquire about the elopement package. The inn is fully licensed (wine and beer available), handy both to Okemo and to village shops. $119–275 summer, $140–350 in winter includes a full breakfast.

⚷ **Echo Lake Inn** (802-228-8602; 800-356-6844; echolakeinn.com), Rt. 100 in Tyson, but the mailing address is P.O. Box 154, Ludlow 05149. This white-clapboard, four-story inn rambles from its 1820 core through the 1840s, finishing with Victorian-style dormers and a long porch, lined in summer with pink geraniums and vintage red rockers. Year-round it offers 23 rooms, all with private bath, and eight condo units in the adjacent Cheese Factory and Carriage House. With good taste and carpentry skills, innkeeper Laurence Jeffery has brought it back up a notch or two. The living room with its hearth and upholstered couches is elegant as well as comfortable, and there's an inviting pub along with a low-beamed dining room that's been outstanding (see *Dining Out*). Guest rooms vary far more widely than in most inns, from country traditional (iron bedstead, small-print wallpaper, and genuine 19th-century cottage furnishings), to romantic come-ons with king-sized beds and jetted tubs in the room, to family suites. Amenities include a spa room, tennis courts, an outdoor pool, and a dock on Echo Lake across the road, with rowboats and canoes. Rates also vary widely: $119–249 per couple in summer, $129–259 in fall, $220–650 in winter, from $89 off-season. Inquire about MAP rates and special packages.

♿ **The Inn at Water's Edge** (802-228-8143; 800-706-9736; innatwatersedge.com), 45 Kingdom Rd., Ludlow 05149. The aforementioned water is Echo Lake, and Bruce and Tina Verdrager have taken full advantage of the location, offering canoeing and fly-fishing as well as bicycles for guests. The expansive, 150-year-old home has 11 well-appointed rooms and suites with jetted tubs and gas fireplaces. Doc's English Pub is a good spot for lounging, and amenities include an outdoor hot tub. Guests sit down to a four-course candlelit dinner. $175–300 plus 15 percent gratuity, including dinner as well as breakfast midweek; from $100 for B&B; many special packages.

⚑ ♥ ☯ **Combes Family Inn** (802-228-8799; 800-822-8799; combesfamilyinn.com), 953 East Lake Rd., Ludlow 05149. Ruth and Bill Combes have been welcoming families to their peaceful 1891 former dairy farm home since 1978. Many are now second-generation repeats. Sequestered up a back road near Lake Rescue, it's surrounded by meadows. The homey, comfortable common rooms include a real hearth and plenty of space to relax. The 11 guest rooms, all with private bath, are divided among the farmhouse and 5 attached motel-style units (where pets are allowed). "They are what they are," Ruth will tell you. No complaints from guests. B&B double rates are $86 spring, $100 summer, $134–196 winter. Ruth's delicious Vermont country dinners are available nightly by reservation at $20 per adult and $10 for kids. Inquire about inn-to-inn walking tours.

In Chester 05143
The Fullerton Inn (802-875-2444; 866-884-8578; fullertoninn.com), 40 the Common, P.O. Box 968. Bret and Nancy Rugg are the innkeepers of this big, old-fashioned inn on the Chester green. The Ruggs have renovated all 20 guest rooms (private baths), decorating each individually, adding country quilts and fabrics, sitting rooms, and ceiling fans. Common space includes the inviting seating in the handsome lobby around the stone hearth, a tavern with its own hearth, a formal, consistently good dining room (see *Dining Out*), and a sunny breakfast room. $114–164 per couple for rooms in summer and fall, $129–169 during ski season; suites are $169–209; rates include continental breakfast.

In Weston 05161
♀ ⚑ ♥ ♿ **Inn at Weston** (802-824-6789; innweston.com), P.O. Box 66, Rt. 100. Innkeepers Bob and Linda Aldrich have made this truly one

of Vermont's outstanding inns. Enthusiastic gardeners, they oversee the fabulous flowering of the 6 acres surrounding this vintage-1848 inn on the edge of Weston Village. The 13 guest rooms are divided among the main inn, the Coleman House (with its own library/sitting room) across the road, and the Carriage House, with the most luxurious suites. All have private bath and are delightfully furnished in antiques, fitted with phone, A/C, and TV; some have deck, whirlpool tub, and fireplace. The dining room (see *Dining Out*) is open to the public and justifiably popular, especially in summer when the Weston Playhouse is a big draw. The common room here is the library, inviting guests to relax by the hearth with a well-chosen book. Given the landscaped grounds, fine dining, and luxurious lodging, this is a popular place for weddings. $225–285 in the main inn, $185–205 in the Coleman House, $325 in the Carriage House. Add $50 per room on holidays.

⚑ ♥ ☯ ♿ **Colonial House Inn & Motel** (802-824-6286; 800-639-5033; cohoinn.com), 287 Rt. 100. A rare and delightful combination of nine motel units and five traditional inn rooms (shared baths), connected by a pleasant dining room, a comfortable, sunken sitting room with dried flowers hanging from the rafters, and a solarium overlooking the lawn. Second-generation innkeepers Kim and Jeff Seymour make all ages feel welcome, and most guests are repeats. Rates include multicourse breakfasts. A soup-to-nuts dinner is served family-style ($26.95) on weekends. The inn is 2 miles south of the village, with lawn chairs facing a classic farmscape across the road; most guest rooms overlook a meadow. Rooms are $60–130 double occupancy (B&B); extra charges for children, singles, pets ($10 per day), and service. Ramp available for wheelchairs.

BED & BREAKFASTS
In the Ludlow area
The Governor's Inn (802-228-8830; 800-GOVERNOR; thegovernorsinn.com), 86 Main St., Ludlow 05149. Open year-round except Dec. 23–26. William Wallace Stickney, governor of Vermont 1900–02, built this Victorian house with its ornate slate, hand-painted fireplaces. Now it's owned by Jim and Cathy Kubec. The seven upstairs guest rooms are furnished with antiques, and an inviting suite in the rear of the third floor features a jetted tub for two and a sitting room. Jessica's Room has a jetted tub for two; six rooms have gas fireplace. The living room is small but elegant. Beer and wine are available to guests in the den. A three-course breakfast is served in a cheery back room, warmed by the sun and a woodstove. A

serious tea is served in the front parlor. On request Cathy also prepares multicourse dinners, offers cooking classes, and will pack picnic baskets with a little prior notice. $184–294 B&B during ski and foliage seasons, otherwise $144–239; less for two-day and longer stays.

& **Golden Stage Inn** (802-226-7744; 800-253-8226; goldenstageinn.com), P.O. Box 218, 399 Depot St., Proctorsville 05153. Michael and Julie-Lynn Wood bring fresh energy to this handsome historic house. An inn in the 18th century, it belonged to the Skinner family for 100 years, beginning in 1830. There are six bright, comfortable guest rooms and two suites, one named for the writer and performer Cornelia Otis Skinner. Dining areas include the solarium and the inn's greenhouse. The inn is centrally air-conditioned and wheelchair accessible; a swimming pool is set in gardens. Rooms are $129–249; family suites sleeping up to five are $249–299, including a full breakfast, afternoon treats, and a bottomless cookie jar. Eggs are from the house chickens and honey from the house hives (giving new meaning to *golden*). The inn sits on the edge of the village of Proctorsville, 4 miles from Okemo Mountain. Inquire about the September honey harvest and ski packages.

The Okemo Inn (802-228-8834; out of state 800-328-8834; okemoinn.com), 61 Locust Hill Rd., near the junction of Rts. 100 north and 103, Ludlow 05149. Open year-round except for two weeks in Apr. and Nov. Ron Parry has been the innkeeper here since 1972, and his 1810 home has the feeling of a well-kept lodge, effortlessly welcoming. There are 11 nicely furnished guest rooms, 2 on the ground level, most with kings and queens, all with private bath. In the living room a table in front of the hearth is made from an old bellows, and the dining room has low, notched beams; there's also a TV room, a sauna, and in summertime a pool. $120–150 per day B&B per couple includes a full breakfast. Single rates and discounts for longer stays; two-night minimum, weekends. Inquire about ski, golf, and crafts packages.

In Chester 05143

♂ & **Inn Victoria** (802-875-4288; innvictoria .com), 321 Main St. With its mansard roof, and columned porch, this is a showy Victorian on the Chester green. All the rooms are named for Victoria's children. Six rooms have queen-sized bed, two have kings, three have a Jacuzzi, and the first-floor garden room is handicapped accessible. The Princess Victoria Room fills almost the entire third floor and features a queen-sized bed in front of a gas fireplace, a separate sitting room, a mini fridge, and a

deluxe bath with the works. Innkeepers Dan and Penny Cote stock a guest fridge, serve a three-course breakfast at the dining room table, and offer high teas (see *Tea* under *Where to Eat*). Request a room with access to hot tub on the back deck. From $150 for a small room off-season to $199 for the suite, a three-course breakfast included. Packages include inn-to-inn walks as well as biking and/or dinner.

♥ ❀ ✿ **Henry Farm Inn** (802-875-2674; 800-723-8213; henryfarminn.com), 2206 Green Mountain Tpk. We love this place! There's a nice out-in-the-country feel to the old tavern, set in 56 rolling acres. Larger than other farmhouses of the period, it was built in 1760 as a stagecoach stop on the Green Mountain Turnpike, which is now a quiet dirt road but minutes from the edge of the Chester green. It retains its pine floors, beehive oven, paneling, and sense of pleasant, uncluttered comfort. The nine rooms are large, with private bath. Two of the rooms are suites with kitchen, accommodating three or four. What you notice are the quilts and the views. A path leads to the spring-fed pond up the hill, and a swimming hole in the Williams River is just across the road. In winter you can ski out the back door and up around through the woods and meadow. Inquire about frequent quilting workshop weekends. Your hosts are Patricia and Paul Dexter. Children welcome. $100–145 per couple for rooms, up to $170 for three people in suites. Rates include a full country breakfast, served in the country dining room.

& **Chester House Inn** (888-875-2205; chester houseinn.com), 266 Main St. A gracious village house dating from 1780, now with seven guest rooms, including a handicapped-accessible first-floor room with a canopy bed; five have gas fireplace, another front room has a two-person Jacuzzi, and a family suite can sleep six. Many thoughtful touches and phones in every room. Hosts Bob and Jan Francis include a full breakfast, $129–189.

In Weston 05161

Apple Knoll Inn (802-824-0051; appleknollinn .com), 815 Rt. 100. Architecturally, 1830 was a good year, judging from the graceful lines of this farmhouse. Interior detailing includes Indian shutters, paneling, and wide-plank floors; there's a wood-burning Rumford fireplace and a piano in the parlor, also a library with a wood-stove and a pool in the garden. The old farmhouse looks at home in its surrounding of river, meadows, and woods, conservation land just north of the village. Known for many years as the Darling Inn, it's been given a new name and new life by hosts Wes and Lisa Hupp. The four rooms vary in size and bed choice (from twins to king) but all are comfortably furnished with antiques. $110–155 includes a full breakfast. Inquire about the cabin.

MOTELS ♂ ♿ **The Pointe at Castle Hill Resort & Spa** (802-226-7688; 800-438-7908; cavendishpointe.com), Rt. 103, Cavendish 05142. This contemporary motor inn has a lobby with fireplace. Facilities include an indoor pool, hot tub/spa room, business and fitness centers, and game room. The 70 fairly large rooms come equipped with cable TV, speakerphone, fridge, and coffeemaker; there are also 26 suites, some with full kitchen and sitting room with gas fireplace. This is also the check-in point for Castle Hill (see *Inns*), and guests have easy access (for a fee) to its full-service spa. Breakfast year-round ($199–279).

Brandmeyer's Mountainside Lodge (802-824-5851; brandmeyerslodge.com), 913 Rt. 100, Weston 05161. Located north of Weston, as Rt. 100 begins its climb up heavily wooded Terrible Mountain to Ludlow. Bob and Lisa Brandmeyer operate a cheery, 10-unit motor lodge with a comfortable pub at its center, serving a hot breakfast daily and dinner Fri., Sat., grinders Thurs. Rooms are large and nicely decorated, with individual thermostats, fridge, and TV. Family units have double beds plus bunks. $109–139 includes breakfast. $109 midweek, $139 weekends (two-night minimum), more during foliage and holiday weekends; ski-season specials and ski packages.

♥ ♂ **Timber Inn Motel** (802-228-8666), 112 Rt. 103, Ludlow 05149. This 18-room cedar and

IRENE MASTON OF ANDRIE ROSE INN IS A RESPECTED CHEF, NATIONALLY RECOGNIZED FOR HER WEDDING CAKES.

Christina Tree

knotty-pine motel (ground-floor units have been rebuilt since Hurricane Irene) on the Black River is on the eastern fringe of town and has surprisingly good views; a winter shuttle bus stop for Okemo. Hot tub and sauna in winter, heated outdoor pool in summer, rooms with phone, A/C, and cable TV; there's a two-bedroom unit as well as a two-bedroom apartment with full kitchen. Dogs are accepted by reservation ($15 per night). $69–239 includes morning coffee and teas.

♥ ♥ ♂ **Motel in the Meadow** (802-875-2626; motelinthemeadow.com), 936 Rt. 11 west, Chester 05143. Pat Budnick offers nine rooms with country quilts and decor. Two have kitchenette, another pair feature two queen-sized beds, and one room has two queens and two bunk beds. $75–89 for rooms, $115–125 for the big family room, includes a continental breakfast. A former nurse, Pat is accustomed to caring for people—as guests will attest. Inquire about Music in the Meadow, held on a Saturday in July.

✳ Where to Eat

DINING OUT The Andrie Rose Inn (802-228-4846; andrieroseinn.com), 13 Pleasant St., Ludlow. Open to the public by reservation (before 3 PM) Fri.–Sat. for à la carte casual fine dining in a 20-seat dining area. Chef-owner Irene Maston's locally sourced menu changes seasonally. On a winter night "small plates" included a Vermont Butter & Cheese Co. chèvre tart with crisp prosciutto; our large-plate choice was housemade confit of duck with mashed sweet potato and a fresh fig and port glaze, followed by lavender raspberry cheesecake. Entrées $21–28.

○ **The Downtown Grocery** (802-228-7566; thedowntowngrocery.com), 41 S. Depot St., Ludlow. Open except stick and mud seasons, nightly except Tues., Wed. Weston native chef Rogan Lechthaler and wife Abby have created the town's deservedly popular dining venue (formerly Cappuccino's). The blackboard menu lists the night's specials, but the printed menu is also as locally sourced as possible. On a winter's night, begin with celeriac soup (Maine lobster, squash seeds, pumpkin oil, $15), then dine on roasted eggplant with housemade herb ricotta and pomodoro sauce or Northeast Family Farms rib eye au poivre with garlicky mustard greens. All pasta is made and meats cured in-house. Entrées $14–36.

Inn at Weston (802-824-6789; innweston .com), Rt. 100, Weston. Open from 5:30 nightly but best to call ahead. The candlelit dining room (with live piano music) and adjacent pub are delightful in any season—and in summer there is dining on the deck and orchid-filled gazebo. Chef Craig Cornell uses local ingredients whenever possible. In winter you might begin with a duck confit tart ($11). Entrées range $24–35 (for a porcini-dusted petit filet).

❂ 🍄 ✦ **Harry's Cafe** (802-228-2996; harryscafe .com), 68 Rt. 100 N., Ludlow. Open daily 5–10; usually closed Mon.–Tues. Trip Pearce has been the area's most colorful chef since 1988 when he opened his café ("Harry" is his father) 3.5 miles up Rt. 103 in Mount Holly. The present venue (formerly Bella Luna) is far more expansive (140 seats) and central (junction of Rts. 103 and 100) but retains the light, airy, friendly, informal feel. There are still the same wide and zany choices. You might dine on a mix of appetizers—hand-rolled spring rolls and grilled Caesar salad or split an antipasto with Harry's smoked seafood chowder. A former lobsterman, Pearce is serious as well as creative with fish. Entrées range from $17 for fish-and-chips (dipped in beer batter) to $34 for a 12-ounce New York sirloin; pad Thai ($18, more with shrimp or chicken) is a signature dish. Try the grilled jerk scallops.

Echo Lake Inn (802-228-8602; 800-356-6844; echolakeinn.com), Rt. 100 north of Ludlow in Tyson. Open to the public for dinner. The dining room, with print wallpaper and shades of mauve, is attractive. Chef Kevin Barnes has established an enviable reputation over more than 20 years. The à la carte menu offers genuine choices and usually includes a freshly made vegetarian pasta dish such as roasted pumpkin ravioli. Specialties include pan-seared then roasted boneless duck breast served with the day's sauce; and sautéed veal tenderloin medallions. Entrées $19–29.

❂ **Tokai-Tei Japanese Restaurant at the Old Town Farm Inn** (802-875-2346; 888-232-1089), 665 Vermont Rt. 10. Open Wed.–Sun. 5–9 by reservation. Halfway between Chester and Ludlow isn't exactly where you expect to find a first-rate Japanese restaurant, but that's where Michiko Hunter presides over the kitchen of this old family-geared lodge, turning out tantalizing and reasonably priced sushi and such entrées as "gyu-aspara maki" (beef asparagus roll), "buta niku no shoga yaki" (gingered pork), and a choice of tempura dishes. It's BYOB, and desserts include green tea or red bean ice cream, made in-house. Entrées $23–33, including miso soup and garden salad.

Coleman Brook Tavern (802-228-1435), Jackson Gore Inn, Rt. 103, Ludlow. This is the signature restaurant in Okemo's base complex and

it's sleekly comfortable, with sofas, wing chairs, and dim lighting to mitigate its size. The cherrywood-paneled Wine Room is the most intimate setting. The menu ranges from vegetarian strudel to steak, pan-seared with a green peppercorn sauce. Entrées $12–35.

Sam's Steakhouse (802-228-2087), 91 Rt. 103, Ludlow. Open for dinner nightly with midweek specials. Known for filet mignon you can cut with a butter knife, excellent seafood, a good salad bar, and sinful desserts. Entrées $16–38. Children's menu.

Note: During ski season **Epic** at Okemo is the mountain's coolest lunch spot and the area's ultimate dining option on Saturday night in winter, the setting for five-course candlelit dinners; $125 includes the ride up and down via snowcat.

In Chester

Fullerton Inn (802-875-2444; fullertoninn .com), 40 the Common. Open nightly except Sun. This classic old inn's dining room is surprisingly casual with a varied menu and reliably good food, ranging from ravioli to orange-scented roasted half duck and pan-seared veal chop with marinated apples. Entrées $10–30. Also see *Eating Out*.

EATING OUT

In and around Ludlow

✦ **D. J.'s Restaurant** (802-228-5374), 146 Main St., Ludlow. Open daily 4–9:30. A first-rate family restaurant; a separate lounge has booths for diners. The burger with hand-cut fries and fixings in the pub is probably the best value in town. The menu is large; the crispy roast duckling is a house favorite. Nightly specials.

Mojo Café (802-228-7767), 106 Main St., Ludlow. Literally the hot place to eat in town. John and Judy Seward offer a huge blackboard choice of Mexican, Cajun, and southern specialties. Go for the poblano rings.

Willie Dunne's Grille (802-228-1387), at the Okemo Valley Golf Club and Nordic Center, Rt. 100. Open summer and fall for lunch and dinner. Chef Craig Cornell is known as one of the best around. A great lunch bet. Two windowed walls are open to views of the pond and the 18th green; patio dining, too. All entrées are served with greens.

✦ **Pot Belly Restaurant and Pub** (802-228-8989), 130 Main St., Ludlow. Open lunch through dinner daily. Since 1974, a pleasant atmosphere with live music on busy weekends. At lunch try a Belly Burger or the Cajun chicken sandwich. The dinner menu is large.

(ᵂ) **Java Baba's Slow Food Café** (802-228-7810; javababas.com), Okemo Marketplace, Rt. 100 across from the Okemo Access Rd. Open daily 6 AM–10 PM. An all-day oasis, good for breakfast bagels through creative sandwiches, salads, and wraps, housemade quiche, pizza, soups, fresh-baked muffins and pastries. Space to chill with a latte and computer.

Stemwinder (802-228-5200), 46 Depot St., Ludlow. Open Tues.–Sat. 5–close. Hidden behind the Wine & Cheese, this attractive new wine bar serves small plates, soup, greens, lettuce wraps. You'll also find beef sliders, an inspired taco with braised beef mole, seasonal ravioli, housemade thin-crust pizzas, and a cheese and meat board.

❂ **Crows Bakery and Opera House Café** (802-226-7007), 73 Depot St., Proctorsville. Off Rt. 103. Open Tues.–Sat. 6–6, Sun. 6–5. An attractive café serving full breakfasts and exotic wraps such as Veggie Wrapsody and Tuna Kahuna, plus a choice of veggie sandwiches as well as ham and Swiss. Known for its from-scratch pastries and breads.

The Hatchery (802-228-2311), 164 Main St., Ludlow. Open daily 7–2. Cash only! In the more than 25 years we've stopped here, not much has changed except the vegetarian lunch options and the prices. Breads are all housemade and the home fries are outstanding.

Vermont Apple Pies (802-554-0040), 265 Depot St., Proctorsville. Open daily 8–2. A homey, authentic eatery in the middle of the village, best known for apple pie but also a great breakfast spot, good for soup, quiche, and salads.

In Chester

✐ **Heritage Deli & Bakery** (802-875-3550; heritagedeliandbakery.com), Rt. 103 south of the green. Open daily 7–5:30. A warmly attractive café/gourmet food shop. Owner Michele Wilcox is the baker, and soups are from scratch, too. The café has Provençal-print tablecloths, bright colors, booths, and fresh flowers whenever possible. At lunch try a soup or salad combo with one of more than a dozen signature sandwiches named for folks like Grandma Moses (tarragon turkey salad on a croissant) and Ira Allen (turkey, sun-dried tomato cream cheese, and lettuce on a baguette). Box lunches.

🍴 ✐ **Country Girl Diner** (802-875-1003), 46 Rt. 103 south of Chester Village. Open 6:30–2:30 Mon.–Fri., 7–2 Sun. A local favorite; freshly made soups, a foot-long hot dog platter, and smashburger with caramelized onions and Swiss cheese.

(ᵂ) **Moon Dog Café** (802-875-4966), 287 S. Main St., on the green. Open 10–6 daily. Healthy food is cooked up in the middle of this combination health food store, crafts shop, and café, with plenty of comfortable seating. On a winter day we lunched at a deal table in the sunny, plant-filled dining area in the rear of the shop. The Turkish lentil soup was steaming hot, served in a china bowl.

Bradford Tavern (802-875-2444), at the Fullerton Inn, 40 the Common. Open for lunch Wed.–Sat. Yet another middle-of-the-village source of ciabatta and flatbread sandwiches, also wraps and pizzas. This is a casual lounge (full bar) with a fire.

✐ **Stone Hearth Inn** (802-875-2525; stone hearthinnvermont.com), 698 Rt. 11, west of the village. Open Thurs.–Mon., tavern from 4, restaurant from 5. Inquire about lunch on weekends. The feel here is of a classic, old-style ski lodge with a large, inviting family-geared lounge including a woodfired hearth and plenty to keep kids happy. There's also a smaller, more formal dining area. Begin with baked Brie or house-cured gravlax salmon and dine on a hearty beef stew, an eggplant stack layered with homemade pesto, or the "tart du jour." Sandwiches and burgers always available. Ask about Thai night and kids-eat-free nights. Fully licensed, beers on tap.

MacLaomainn's Scottish Pub in Chester (802-722-4855), 52 Main St. Open for lunch and dinner, closed Tues. Scotsman Alan Brown and Chester resident Deb Brown first met playing cribbage online, then physically met, built this cozy pub, and were married in it. Haggis, a dish so peculiarly Scottish it's a national symbol, has been a surprising big hit (don't ask what's in it besides oatmeal!), along with steak and fish pies. Late-night bites. The bar is fully licensed and offers a wide choice of beers, including Scottish, also whiskies.

❂ (ᵂ) **Baba-À-Louis Bakery** (802-875-4666), Rt. 11 west, Chester. Closed Apr. and the first part of Nov., as well as Sun. and Mon., but otherwise open 7 AM–6 PM. John McClure's sticky buns, croissants, French loaves, and peasant breads (including gluten-free) are distributed throughout New England, but here you'll also find his French pastries. The octagonal building, which McLure designed and built, features arches soaring 30 feet. There's a delightful dining area with lunch featuring soups and quiche, daily 11–3.

The Free Range (802-875-3346; thefreerange vt.com), 90 on the Common, Chester. Open Wed.–Sat. for lunch (11–4) and dinner (5–9) and for Sun. brunch (10–2). New in the fall of 2014, this is the right restaurant in the right place—imaginative comfort food in a Victorian house on the common. Anne and Rick Paterno had owned a home in Chester for some years before chucking their corporate jobs to open Free Range, partnering with well-known chef Michael Kennedy. *Free Range* refers not only to the locally raised chicken but to "Ranger Rick," as Paterno is known. Lunch on crispy calamari flatbread and dine on a maple-brined pork chop. Dinner entrées $14.95–19.95.

Also see *High Tea in Chester.*

In Weston

The Bryant House (802-824-6287), 657 Main St. Open daily for lunch 11–3:30, dinner Thurs.–Sat. until 9. Breakfast/brunch Sat., Sun. Owned by the neighboring Vermont Country Store, this fine old house dates from 1827, with an 1885 tavern. Lunch features "traditional sandwiches," freshly made soups with sides of Vermont Common Crackers, and the house johnnycake. Dinner entrées include Yankee pot roast and chicken pie. The signature dessert is Indian pudding. The bar is a beauty, solid mahogany with a brass rail, transported from the Hudson Valley and a perfect fit. Check out the Bryant family's 19th-century-style bedroom, preserved upstairs.

Café at the Falls (802-824-5288), Weston Playhouse, on the green. Open for dinner on theater nights beginning at 5:30; 5 on Sun. Currently run by the Inn at Weston, this is a pleasant dining room with windows overlooking a waterfall. It's less formal dining than at the inn; full bar, extensive wine list, and cabaret performances with light fare and dessert after the performance. Pre-theater dinner reservations can be made when booking tickets. (See also *Entertainment.*)

(◦) **The Village Green Gallery** (802-824-3669), 661 Main St. A delightful coffee bar with comfortable seating to gather your thoughts and/or check email surrounded by art and fine crafts. See *Selective Shopping—Art Galleries.*

HIGH TEA IN CHESTER Rose Arbour Tea Room (802-875-4767), 55 School St., just off the green. Open seasonally 11–5, closed most Tuesdays. This combination lunch spot, gift store, and tearoom has been specializing in multicourse high teas for 20 years. Chef Suzanne Nielson is known for her scones and pastries; tea also includes finger sandwiches, petits fours, and a choice of sandwiches. The lunch menu features soups, sandwiches, salads, and quiche.

Inn Victoria (802-875-4288; innvictoria.com), 321 Main St. High tea featuring pastries, scones, sweets, clotted cream, and a choice of 30 teas is served by reservation in the inn's elegant Victorian guest parlor or dining room. Inquire about special tea tastings.

✳ Entertainment

✪ **Weston Playhouse Theatre Company** (802-824-5288; westonplayhouse.org), 703 Main St., Weston. Not long after the Civil War, townspeople built a second floor in their oldest church on the green and turned the lower level into a theater, producing ambitious plays such as Richard Sheridan's *The Rivals*. Theatrics remained a part of community life, and in the 1930s a summer resident financed the remodeling of the defunct church into a real theater. Now billed as "the oldest professional theater in Vermont," the Weston Playhouse has a company composed largely of professional Equity actors and routinely draws rave reviews. Quality aside, Weston couldn't be more off-Broadway. The pillared theater (the facade is that of the old church) fronts on a classic village common and backs on the West River, complete with a waterfall and Holsteins grazing in the meadow beyond. Many patrons come early to dine at **Café at the Falls** and linger after the show to join cast members at the **Weston Playhouse's Act IV Cabaret** (reservations required). Performances are every night except Mon. (plus Wed. and Sat. matinees), late June–Labor Day weekend, plus a fall production. Main stage tickets run $28–55. Inquire about the campaign to transform nearby Walker Farm into a year-round campus for the development of theater arts; plans include a 140-seat studio theater.

Kinhaven Music School (kinhaven.org), Lawrence Hill Rd., Weston, a nationally recognized summer camp for musicians ages 10–19, presents free concerts by students in July, usually Fridays at 4 and on selected Sundays at 2:30. Faculty perform Saturdays at 8 PM. Performances are in the Concert Hall, high in the meadow of the school's 31-acre campus. It still looks more like a farm than a school. Picnics are encouraged.

Sundays on the Hill Concerts (vtchurchon thehill.org), Lawrence Hill Rd., Weston. On summer Sundays through mid-Sept., 4–5 PM, mostly chamber music concerts are held in a vintage-1838 church, now nondenominational.

Summer Music Series at Jackson Gore, Okemo Resort, Ludlow. Summerlong series of varied free concerts on the lawn.

✱ Selective Shopping

ANTIQUES SHOPS William Austin's Antiques (802-875-3032; wmaustin.com), 42 Maple St., Chester. A full line (more than 500 pieces) of antique country furniture and collectibles.

ART GALLERIES

In Chester

Crow Hill Gallery (802-875-3763), 729 Flamstead Rd. Open Wed.–Sat. 10–5, Sun. by appointment. Watercolorist Jeanne Carbonetti welcomes visitors to the many-windowed home and studio/gallery that she and her husband designed and built on a rise above the meadows, a great setting for the richly colored paintings. The author of several books, she also offers group and private instruction in painting and the creative process.

Chasse Fine Art Gallery (chasseart.com), 558 Main St. Open daily. Showcasing New England paintings and photography.

In Weston

The Village Green Gallery (802-824-3669), 661 Main St. The walls are hung with original art, with a corner devoted to children's book illustrations. The newly renovated space also features fine locally crafted items. Coffee bar, seating space.

BOOKS ○ Misty Valley Books (802-875-3400; mvbooks.com), on the green, Chester. Open daily. Lynne and Bill Reed maintain an unusually friendly, well-stocked bookshop; browsing is encouraged, and author readings are frequent. Their "New Voices" weekend in January features first-time novelists drawn from throughout

MISTY VALLEY BOOKS IS A COMMUNITY GATHERING SPOT.

Christina Tree

the country. Past flyers for this event paper the store's "archives" (the bathroom), and they picture a number of current best-selling authors. The store also sells Persian carpets and offers French classes (Bill Reed has taught in Africa and France as well as Vermont schools).

The Book Nook (802-228-3238), 136 Main St., Ludlow. An owner-operated independent bookstore with a wide selection of books. Frequent authors' readings.

CRAFTS

In the Ludlow area

Depot Street Gallery, Home of the Silver Spoon (802-228-4753), 44 Depot St., Ludlow. Steve Manning fashions an amazing variety of things—from bracelets (including watches) to decorative trees and fish. Local artists and sculptors are also featured in the first-rate adjoining gallery.

Six Loose Ladies (802-226-7373; fiberarts invermont.org), 7 Depot St., Proctorsville. Open Wed.–Sun. 10–6, Tues. until 9. The unlikely name for this totally wholesome store comes from the 19th-century practice of teaching streetwalkers to spin, weave, and knit as an alternative to their lifestyles. Local fleece, yarns, and woven products, pottery, and more are carried on consignment.

Craft Shop at Fletcher Farm (802-228-4348), 611 Rt. 103, east of Ludlow. Open late June–early Sept., 9:30–5, and weekends from Memorial Day. Work by members of the Society of Vermont Craftsmen (see *To Do*).

Clearlake Furniture (802-228-8395; clearlake furniture.com), 322 Rt. 100 north, Ludlow. Artisan-crafted hardwood furniture, also upholstered pieces and decorative accents.

In Chester

103 Artisan Marketplace (802-875-7400), Rt. 103. Open except Tues. 10–5. Just east of town, this sizable gallery is easy to miss. Don't. Turn around if you pass it by. The wrought iron and fanciful metalwork are by owners Elise and Payne Junker, who also showcase crafted pottery, blown glass, jewelry, prints, clothing, chocolate, and more.

○ Bonnie's Bundles (802-875-2114; bonnies bundlesdolls.com), Stone Village, 250 Rt. 103. Look for the OPEN flag in this 1814 house in the middle of Chester's Stone Village. It's usually out. Bonnie Waters doesn't like to sell her handmade cloth dolls to retail shops. "I want to meet the people who buy my dolls," explains Waters, who welcomes visitors to her parlor, home to roughly 100 one-of-a-kind dolls. Many people

Christina Tree

ELISE JUNKER SHOWCASES HER OWN WORK
AND THAT OF MANY OTHERS IN GALLERY 103.

request monogrammed portrait dolls, supplying
a photo of a child or friend. Over more than 40
years Bonnie has stitched more than 14,000
dolls. For many families these are now a multi-
generation tradition.

DeVallia Arts & Accents (802-875-1203;
thedavallia.com), 78 the Common. Michael and
Jessie Alon showcase the work of 65 Vermont
and nationally recognized artists. Great stuff:
From jewelry to furniture, this is a gem of a
shop. Also see **DeVallia at 39 North Street**
(802-895-8900), Rt. 103 in the Stone Village.

In the Weston area
CHEESE ✪ **Crowley Cheese Factory** (802-
259-2340; 800-683-2606; crowleycheese.com),
1.8 miles up the Healdville Rd., a left off Rt.
103, 5 miles northwest of the junction with Rt.
100 in Ludlow. Open Mon.–Sat. 8–4. Check for
hours. See *Scenic Drives* for the history of Vermont's oldest cheese factory and this exceptional cheese, sharper and creamier than
cheddar.

Plymouth Artisan Cheese (802-672-3650;
plymouthartisancheese.com), 106 Messer Hill
Rd., in the Coolidge State Historic Site in Plymouth Notch, off Rt. 100A. The cheese factory
was built by John Coolidge, father of the president. The equipment is modern, but traditional
methods produce a distinctive granular-curd
cheese, available here in waxed blocks and
rounds.

Wine & Cheese Depot (802-228-4128), 46
Depot St., Ludlow. A serious wine store. Owner
Leslie Stuart knows Vermont cheese, too, showcasing many, including both Crowley and Plymouth. See Stemwinder, the store's new wine
bar, under *Eating Out*.

**COUNTRY STORES The Vermont Country
Store** (802-824-3184; vermontcountrystore
.com), 657 Main St., Weston Village. Open
year-round, daily 8:30–6. Established by Vrest
Orton in 1946, this was a pioneer nostalgia
venue. The original store (actually an old
Masonic temple) has since quintupled in size
and spilled into four adjacent buildings. The
specialty of both the store and its catalog (which
accounts for most of the company's business) is
practical items that make life easy, especially
anything that's difficult to find nowadays—
rubber hot-water bottles, dial desk phones,
hardwood coat hangers, slippery-elm throat loz-
enges, garter belts, and old-school health aids,
to name a few. Lyman, the present Orton patri-
arch (sons Gardner, Cabot, and Eliot are all
now involved), has a penchant for newfangled
gadgets, such as a plastic frame to hold baseball
caps in dishwashers. He's a zealot when it
comes to basics that seem to have disappeared,
and he frequently finds someone to replicate
them, as in the case of the perfect potato
masher. The store's own line of edibles features
the Vermont Common Cracker, unchanged
since 1812, still stamped out in a patented 19th-
century machine. For most patrons this is destination shopping, and they stay to eat at the
store's Bryant House next door.

✪ **Singletons' General Store** (802-226-
7666; singeltonsvt.com), Main St. (Rt. 131),

IN CHESTER, BONNIE WATERS HANDCRAFTS
PORTRAIT DOLLS.

Christina Tree

Proctorsville. Best known for its smoked meats. This much-expanded family-run (for three generations) grocery store has kept abreast of the demands of the area's condo owners while continuing to cover the basics: great wine selection as well as a Vermont liquor store, fishing and hunting licenses, rods and reels, guns and ammo, sporting goods, Johnson Woolen Mills and other sturdy outdoor wear and boots, choice meats, a standout deli, and Vermont products. An average of 350 pounds of meat is sold per day. Note the antique guns running like a frieze above the shelves, and the stuffed trophies. But why the camel?

The Weston Village Store (802-824-5477), 660 Main St., Weston Open daily. A frankly tourist-geared emporium, boasting the state's largest collection of weather vanes, it's also known for its many varieties of fudge and a great Vermont cheese selection. And puzzles. Upstairs is a great array of toys and stocking stuffers.

Belmont General Store (802-259-2292; belmontgeneralstore.com), 2400 Belmont Rd., Belmont. Open Mon.–Thurs., Sat. 7–7, Sun. 8–7. An old-fashioned store but known for what you can eat right there, from breakfast sandwiches through burgers to potpies and seafood fettuccine.

FARMS AND FARMERS MARKETS
WAAWWE Farms Market (802-875-3663; waawwe.com), 32 Rt. 10 (junction with Rt. 103), Gassetts. Open Thurs.–Sun. selling local family farm produce, natural products.

Christina Tree
VERMONT COUNTRY STORE IN WESTON

Chester Farmers Market (802-875-2703; chesterfarmersmarket.ning.com). Memorial Day–Columbus Day weekends, Sun. 11–3, Rt. 103 south. **Ludlow** (ludlowfarmersmarket.org), Fri. 4–7 summer, 53 Main St. **Mount Holly Farmers Market** (802-259-2386), Belmont Green, Belmont.

SPECIAL SHOPS Next Chapter (802-975-0197), 126 Main St., Ludlow. Creative women's clothing and more.

✪ **Country on the Common** (802-875-3000), countryonthecommon.com; 80 the Common), Chester. A great selection of reasonably priced craft items and clothing by regional artists.

Conrad Delia, Windsor Chair Maker (802-875-4219), Popple Dungeon Rd., Chester. After a long career as a home builder on Long Island, Conrad Delia studied with several New England chair makers before opening his own shop. Call to schedule a visit.

MORE FOOD Green Mountain Sugar House (802-228-7151), Rt. 100, 4 miles north of Ludlow. You can watch syrup being produced in March and April; maple candy is made throughout the year on a weekly basis. This is also a place to find freshly pressed cider in September. The gift and produce shop is open daily 9–6 "most of the time."

✳ Special Events

February: **Chester Winter Carnival**, genuine old-fashioned fun.

Last weekend of March: **Vermont Maple Open House Weekend** (vermontmaple.org).

VERMONT COUNTRY STORE IN WESTON
Christina Tree

April: Okemo's annual **Slush Cup Wacky Spring Celebration** (okemo.com).

Memorial Day weekend: Open Studio tour.

July 1: **Fletcher Farm Arts and Crafts Fair**, Rt. 103, Ludlow; **St. Joseph's Carnival**; horse show and community picnic, Chester.

July 4: Fireworks, West Hill Park, Ludlow. **Calvin Coolidge Birthday Memorial**, Plymouth.

Late July: Annual **Music in the Meadow Festival**, Chester. **Plymouth Old Home Day** (historicvermont.org).

Late July–August: **Okemo Valley Music Festival**—free concerts in Ludlow, Cavendish, and Chester (yourplaceinvermont.org).

August 2: **Plymouth Old Home Day** at Calvin Coolidge Historic Site (historicsites.vermont .gov)—a long-standing tradition: wagon rides, sheep shearing, music, crafts, games.

August: **Chester Outdoor Art Show**. Thursday-evening concerts on the Chester green all month. **Kinhaven Music School concert series**.

Late September: **Civil War Expo Chester** (18thvt.com), Chester. **Fall Fair on the Green**, Chester. **Plymouth Cheese and Harvest Festival** (historicvermont.org).

October: The **Weston Antiques Show**, first weekend, one of the state's oldest and most respected, staged in the Weston Playhouse, features more than 200 dealers.

Columbus Day weekend: The **Weston Crafts Fair** (westoncraftsshow.com). **Cider Days in Mount Holly** features a 100-year old cider press, open studio tours, a community supper.

November–January: **Green Mountain Festival Series** of performances in Chester (green mountainfestivalseries.com).

December: **Overture to Christmas**, first and second Saturdays (see okemovalleyvt.org), Chester. Events include a Children's Day the first Saturday, with Santa and Mrs. Claus arriving by fire engine; tree lighting and candlelight caroling the second. **Torchlight Parade and Fireworks Display** at Okemo.

The Connecticut River Valley

2

THE CONNECTICUT RIVER VALLEY

THE LOWER CONNECTICUT
RIVER VALLEY
Including Bellows Falls, Saxtons River,
Grafton, Springfield, and Weathersfield

UPPER VALLEY RIVER TOWNS
Including Windsor, Hartford, Norwich,
Thetford, Fairlee, and Hanover,
New Hampshire

COHASE
Including Bradford, Newbury,
and Wells River , Vermont;
Piermont, Haverhill, and Woodsville,
New Hampshire

THE CONNECTICUT
RIVER VALLEY

The Connecticut River flows 410 miles from its high source on the New Hampshire–Quebec border to Long Island Sound in the state of Connecticut. What concerns us here are its 270 miles as a boundary—and bond—between the states of New Hampshire and Vermont. Defying state lines, it forms one of New England's most beautiful and distinctive regions, shaped by a shared history.

Judging from more than 130 archaeological sites along this stretch of the river, its banks have been peopled for many thousands of years. Evidence of Western Abenaki villages has been found at New-bury, at Claremont (New Hampshire), and at the Great Falls at present-day Bellows Falls. Unfortu-nately, these people were decimated by disease contracted from English traders.

By the late 17th century English settlements had spread from the mouth of the Connecticut up to Deerfield, Massachusetts, just below the present New Hampshire–Vermont border. Fort Dummer was built in 1724 in what, at the time, was Massachusetts (now Vernon, Vermont); Fort at No. 4 was built 50 miles upriver in 1743 in present Charlestown, New Hampshire. Settlers and Indians lived side by side. However, during this period former friends and neighbors also frequently faced each other in battles to the death.

At the reconstructed Fort at No. 4 you learn that five adults and three children were abducted by a band of Abenaki in 1754 (all survived), and that in 1759 Major Robert Rodgers and his Rangers retaliated for the many raids from the Indian village of St. Francis (near Montreal) by killing many more than 100 residents, including many women and children. The suffering of "Rodgers' Rangers" on their winter return home is legendary. A historic marker on Rt. 10 in Haverhill (New Hampshire) offers a sobering description.

After the 1763 Peace of Paris, France withdrew its claims to New France and English settlers surged up the Connecticut River, naming their new communities for their old towns in Connecticut and Massachusetts: Walpole, Haverhill, Windsor, Norwich, and more. This was, however, no-man's-land.

In 1749 New Hampshire governor Benning Wentworth had begun granting land on both sides of the river (present-day Vermont was known as "The New Hampshire Grants"), a policy that New York's Governor George Clinton refused to recognize. In 1777, when Vermont declared itself a republic, 16 towns on the New Hampshire side opted to join it. In December 1778, at a meeting in Cornish, New Hampshire, towns from both sides of the river voted to form their own state of "New Connecticut," but neither burgeoning state was about to lose so rich a region. In 1779 New Hamp-shire claimed all Vermont.

In 1781 delegates from both sides of the river met in Charlestown (New Hampshire) and agreed to stick together. Vermont's Governor Chittenden wrote to General Washington asking to be admitted to the Union, incorporating towns contested both by New Hampshire and New York. Washington replied: Yes, but without the contested baggage.

In 1782 New Hampshire sent 1,000 soldiers to enforce their jurisdiction. Not long thereafter Washington asked Vermont to give in—and it did. Needless to say, the river towns were unhappy about this verdict.

The Valley itself prospered in the late 18th and early 19th centuries, as evidenced by the exquisite Federal-era (1790s–1830s) meetinghouses and mansions still to be seen in river towns. With New

Hampshire's Dartmouth College, established in 1769, at its heart, and rich floodplain farmland stretching its length, this valley differed far more dramatically than today from the unsettled mountainous regions walling it in on either side.

The river remained the Valley's highway in the early 19th century. A transportation canal was built to circumvent the Great Falls at present-day Bellows Falls, and Samuel Morey of Orford (New Hampshire) built a steamboat in 1793. Unfortunately Robert Fulton scooped his invention, but the upshot was increased river transport—at least until the 1840s, when railroads changed everything.

"It is an extraordinary era in which we live," Daniel Webster remarked in 1847, watching the first train roll into Lebanon, New Hampshire, the first rail link between the Connecticut River and the Atlantic. "It is altogether new," he continued. "The world has seen nothing like it before."

In this "anything's possible" era, the Valley boomed. At the Robbins, Kendall & Lawrence Armory in Windsor, gun makers developed machines to do the repetitive tasks required to produce each part of a gun. This meant that for the first time an army could buy a shipment of guns and know that if one was damaged, it could be repaired with similar parts. In the vintage-1846 armory, now the **American Precision Museum**, you learn that this novel production of interchangeable parts became known as the American System of precision manufacturing. Springfield too became known for precision toolmaking. Until recently this area was known as Precision Valley.

In places the railroad totally transformed the landscape, creating towns where there had been none, shifting populations from high old town centers like Rockingham and Walpole (New Hampshire) to the riverside. This shift was most dramatic in the town of Hartford, where White River Junction became the hub of north–south and east–west rail traffic.

The river itself was put to new uses. It became a sluiceway down which logs were floated from the northern forest to paper mills in Bellows Falls and farther downriver. Its falls had long powered small mills, but now a series of hydro dams were constructed, including the massive dam between Barnet, Vermont, and Monroe, New Hampshire, in 1930. This flooded several communities to create both Comerford Reservoir—and the visual illusion that the Connecticut River stops there. At present 16 dams stagger the river's flow between the Second Connecticut Lake above Pittsburg, New Hampshire, and Enfield, Connecticut, harnessing the river to provide power for much of the Northeast.

By the 1950s the river was compared to an open sewer and towns turned their backs to it, depositing refuse along its banks.

Still, beyond towns, the river slid by fields of corn and meadows filled with cows. In 1952 the non-profit Connecticut River Watershed Council was founded to "promote and protect wise use of the

THE FORT AT NO. 4 IN CHARLESTOWN, NH

Connecticut Valley's resources." Thanks to the 1970s Clean Water Act and to acquisitions, green-ups, and cleanups by numerous conservation groups, the river itself began to enjoy a genuine renewal. Visitors and residents alike discovered its beauty; campsites for canoeists were spaced along the shore. At present kayaks as well as canoes can be rented along several stretches.

The cultural fabric of towns on either side of the river has remained close knit. Although many bridges were destroyed by the hurricane of 1927, the 21 that survive include one of the longest covered bridges in the United States (connecting Windsor, Vermont, and Cornish, New Hampshire). It's only because tourism promotional budgets are financed by individual state taxes that this stretch of the river valley itself has not, until recently, been recognized as a destination by either New Hampshire or Vermont.

The Connecticut River corridor is now officially "the Connecticut River National Scenic Byway." We are proud to note that for more than 30 years both our *New Hampshire* and *Vermont Explorer's Guides* have included both sides of the river.

Visually visitors see a river, not state lines. Interstate 91 on the Vermont side has back-roaded Rt. 5, as it has Rt. 10 on the New Hampshire side. Following these "byways" travelers can explore historic towns, farm stands, and local scenic spots, finding their way to quiet river roads along both riverbanks. Access to the river via canoe and kayak has increased in recent years, thanks to both outfitters and conservation groups that maintain launch areas and campsites.

Within each chapter prime sights to see shift from one side of the river to the other; the same holds true for places to eat, stay, hike, and generally explore this very distinctive region. See **ctriver byway.org** for excellent coverage of the cultural history as well as present attractions in towns along both sides of the Connecticut River.

THE LOWER CONNECTICUT RIVER VALLEY

INCLUDING BELLOWS FALLS, SAXTONS RIVER, GRAFTON, SPRINGFIELD, AND WEATHERSFIELD

I n Westminster I-91 cuts through magnificent old farms and apple orchards as it divides them from the valley's original highway, the Connecticut River. The village of Bellows Falls, sited at one of the largest drops in the entire length of the river, itself cascades down glacial terraces so steep that steps connect the brick downtown with Victorian homes above and with riverside mill buildings below. Above the dam here both the river and landscape resume a placid pace. Leafy roads follow the Connecticut and its tributaries to hauntingly still spots like the Rockingham Meeting House and Weathersfield Center, visitor-friendly villages like Saxtons River and Grafton—an entire village eerily preserved, complete with inn, cheese factory, museums, shops and galleries, and covered bridge. Today I-91 is the quick way up and down the river, but it's a stretch worth savoring as slowly as possible, preferably from the center of the river on a kayak or canoe.

GUIDANCE Great Falls Regional Chamber of Commerce (802-463-4280; gfrcc.org), 5 Westminster St., Bellows Falls. Open Mon.–Fri. varying hours. Nicely sited at the center of Bellows Falls, this chamber serves the town of Rockingham, including the villages of Bellows Falls and Saxtons River, and surrounding towns on both sides of the river.

The **Springfield Area Chamber Commerce** (802-885-2779), 56 Main St., answers phone queries year-round (weekdays 9–5) and maintains the 18th-century Eureka Schoolhouse (Rt. 11, near I-91) as a seasonal information booth.

GETTING THERE *By bus:* **Greyhound** (800-552-8737; greyhound.com) buses from points in Connecticut and Massachusetts stop in Bellows Falls at the rail station, 54 Depot St.

By train: **Amtrak** (800-USA-RAIL; amtrak.com). The *Vermonter* stops at Bellows Falls en route from New York City and Washington to Essex Junction and St. Albans.

GETTING AROUND I-91 provides a quick way north and south with exits at Putney, Westminster, Rockingham, and Springfield. Vermont Rt. 5 and New Hampshire Rt. 12 are the old, mostly scenic river highways, but connecting bridges are fewer than they once were. Note the bridge from Walpole, New Hampshire, to North Westminster at I-91, Exit 5. In Bellows Fall the Vilas Bridge from the square to Rt. 12 is closed indefinitely, but the Arch Bridge at the northern end of the village connects with North Walpole. A bridge also links Springfield and Charlestown at I-91, Exit 7.

MEDICAL EMERGENCY Call 911.

✳ Villages and Towns

Bellows Falls (a village, population 2,915, within the town of Rockingham—total population 5,309). The Bellows Falls Canal Co. was the first in the country to obtain a charter, and it was an amazing feat easing flatboats through a series of locks, substantially expanding navigation up the Connecticut. The

157

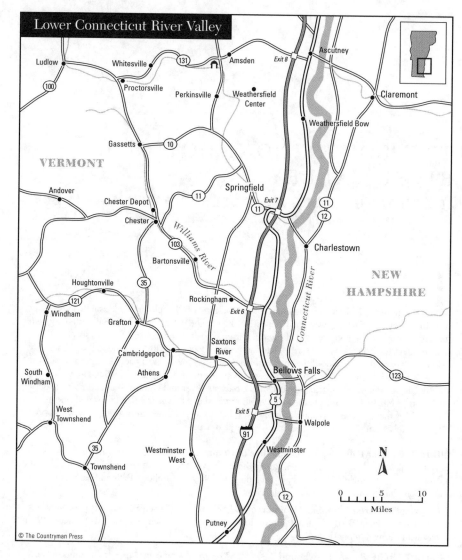

Lower Connecticut River Valley

© The Countryman Press

creation of the canal also formed the island (site of the **Amtrak** station) separating the village from the river, which for much of the year is now reduced to a modest cascade, dropping through the half-mile gorge beneath the dam.

Geologists tell us that 400 to 600 million years ago two continents collided and separated at this site, one of the narrowest points with one of the greatest single drops in the entire length of the Connecticut River. This has long been a sacred place for Native Americans, as evidenced by petroglyphs visible from the Vilas Bridge (although it's closed to traffic, you can walk out on it): a series of round heads, said to date in age anywhere from 300 to 2,000 years ago. Eroded by logging and railroad blasting, years ago they were painted bright yellow to make them easier to see.

In 1869 William Russell developed a way of making paper from wood pulp, using logs floated down from both sides of the river. He went on to found International Paper. The canal was put to work powering mills, and it still powers turbines generating electricity. Rockingham Town Hall, with its Florentine-style tower, includes a restored, town-owned 500-seat **Opera House** used for frequent live performances as well as films. The surrounding square is lined with a lively mix of shops and restaurants. Just off the square the cheerily yellow-painted **Exner Block** now houses studios and shops for artists and craftspeople thanks to the Rockingham Arts and Museum Project (RAMP).

The **Bellows Falls Historical Society, Inc.** (802-376-6789), operates the vintage-1831 **Adams Grist Mill** (open June–Oct., weekends 1–4) and has developed the **Bellows Falls Historic Riverfront Park and Historic Interpretive Trail** (see *Hiking/Walking*). The **Rockingham Free Public Library** (802-463-4270), 65 Westminster St., has archival photos and genealogical archives. Bellows Falls is also known as the home of Hetty Green (1835–1916), who parlayed a substantial inheritance into a $100 million fortune; she was called the Witch of Wall Street, to which she traveled by day coach, looking like a bag lady.

Saxtons River (population 480), like Bellows Falls, is a village in the town of Rockingham. Said to be named for a surveyor who fell into the river and drowned, it's best known as the home of the **Vermont Academy**, founded in 1876, a private prep school since 1932, with some 200 students from throughout the country and world. The handsome main street is home to **Maine Street Arts** (main streetarts.org) and the seasonal **River Artisans** cooperative, showcasing local arts and crafts. There's also the striking **Saxtons River Inn** (see *Lodging, Dining*) and other food options. The **Saxtons River Historical Museum** (802-869-2566; open summer Sundays 2–4:30) is housed in a former Congregational church built in 1836 at the western end of the village. Its collection includes art, tinware, toys, Civil War memorabilia, and a furnished Victorian parlor and kitchen.

Grafton (population circa 600; graftonvermont.org). Prior to the Civil War, Grafton boasted more than 1,480 residents and 10,000 sheep. Wool was turned into 75,000 yards of Grafton cloth annually; soapstone from 13 local quarries left town in the shape of sinks, stoves, inkwells, and foot warmers. But then one in three of Grafton's men marched off to the Civil War, and few returned. Sheep farming, too, "went west." An 1869 flood destroyed the town's six dams and its road. The new highway bypassed Grafton. The town's tavern, however, built in 1801, entered a golden era. Innkeeper Harlan Phelps invested his entire California gold rush fortune in adding a third floor and double porches, and his brother Francis organized a still-extant cornet band. Guests included Emerson, Thoreau, and Kipling; later both Woodrow Wilson and Teddy Roosevelt visited. However, the tavern was sagging, and nearly all the 80-some houses in town were selling cheap with plenty of acreage in the 1960s when the Windham Foundation, funded by a resident summer family, bought much of the town and set about restoring it. **The Grafton Inn** itself was renovated, cheesemaking was revived, the village wiring was buried, and **Grafton Ponds**, a cross-country ski center, was established, doubling as a mountain biking center in warm-weather months.

In **Mack's Place Café** behind The Grafton Inn, pick up a pamphlet *Walking Tour of Grafton*. The **Nature Museum**, **Vermont Museum of Mining & Minerals** (both open weekends), and **Grafton Village Cheese Company** are all worth a detour. Within its few streets, Grafton can pleasantly fill a day. The vintage-1811 Butterfield House is now the inviting **Grafton Public Library** (open daily except Sun.); and the **Grafton History Museum** (802-843-2584; graftonhistory.org; open varying days and hours) has an extensive collection of memorabilia as well as changing exhibits. The Windham Foundation continues to own nearly half the buildings in the central village and has

ROCKINGHAM TOWN HALL, BELLOWS FALLS

made a number available to craftspeople for use as studios. See *Art & Crafts Galleries* under *Selective Shopping*.

The foundation also owns 1,500 acres, which include walking trails, meadows to pasture its flock of sheep, vegetable gardens for the inn, and a greenhouse that, among other things, furnishes some 250 wreaths and 2,000 yards of evergreen roping to decorate the town for Christmas. The largest foundation chartered in Vermont, it funds a variety of philanthropic programs across the state and a series of conferences based at the inn. The town's cornet band, founded in 1867, performs on the village green in good weather and in the White Church if it's raining.

Springfield (population 11,707; springfieldvt.com). Sited near the confluence of the Connecticut and Black Rivers, Springfield boomed with Vermont's tool industry in the 19th and first half of the 20th centuries—and has suffered as that industry has atrophied. Beyond the defunct factories and the powerful falls, the town's compact downtown offers several places to eat and shop. Gracious 19th-century mansions in residential neighborhoods terraced above the historic district include the **Springfield Historical Society** and **Miller Art Center** at 9 Elm St. (802-885-2415; millerartcenter.org). It's open May–Oct., Wed.–Sat., with collections of pewter, Bennington Pottery, toys and dolls, primitive paintings, and costumes as well as changing art exhibits. Straight uphill from the village square, **Hartness House** is well known to astronomers. An inventor, James Hartness patented 120 machines. An aviator, he held one of the first 100 pilot's licenses in the United States and built Vermont's first airport. President of Jones Lamson, the town's leading tool company, and a Vermont governor (1920–22), Hartness was also an astronomer who installed one of the first tracking telescopes in the country (tours by reservation). It was designed by fellow Springfield native Russell W. Porter and sits at the end of an underground corridor connected to the mansion. Porter also organized the country's first group of amateur telescope makers, and his **Stellafane Observatory** on Breezy Hill is home base for an annual convention during the week of the July/August new moon. It routinely attracts 3,000 amateur astronomers (stellafane.com). See *Biking* for the **Toonerville Trail** along the Black River. The 18th-century Eureka School House on Rt. 11 exhibits vintage books and school materials, and serves as a seasonal information center.

Weathersfield (weathersfield.org). **Weathersfield Center**, sited on a scenic old north–south road between Springfield and Rt. 131, is a gem of a hamlet with its brick 1821 Meeting House and Civil War memorial, a particularly sobering reminder of how many young Vermonters served and died (12 boys from just this small village) in that war. The **Weathersfield Historical Society** (802-263-5230; housed in the Reverend Dan Foster House, 2656 Weathersfield Center Rd., and open by appointment) displays Civil War memorabilia, archival photos, an old forge, and the last wildcat killed in Weathersfield (1867). It was Weathersfield native William Jarvis who transformed the economy of Vermont—and the rest of northern New England—by smuggling 4,000 sheep out of Spain during his term as U.S. consul in Lisbon. That was in 1811. By 1840 there were upward of two million sheep in Vermont.

Across the river

Walpole, New Hampshire (population 3,697). Along the length of the Connecticut River, few communities are more closely historically and physically linked (by two bridges, one now closed to cars but open to pedestrians), yet more different, than Walpole and Bellows Falls. Walpole's village is a white wooden New England classic, set high above Rt. 12, graced by fine old churches and dozens of mansions, some dating from the late 18th century, more from the early and mid-19th century, when it was a popular summer haven with several large inns. Louisa May Alcott summered here; Emily Dickinson visited. In the 20th century James Michener came here to research the opening chapter of *Hawaii*—the one about the New England–born missionaries and their families. Current creative residents include filmmaker Ken Burns and chocolate maker Lawrence Burdick. Together they have transformed the Post Office Block in the middle of town into destination dining and shopping. **Burdick Chocolate Shop and Café** draws day-trippers from Boston. The **Walpole Historical Society** (603-756-3308; open May–Sept., Wed. and Sat. 2–4) displays a significant collection of paintings, photographs, furniture, and other local memorabilia. It's housed on three floors of the tower-topped Academy Building in the middle of the village and includes a large research library. Walpole's big hotels have vanished, but a vintage golf course remain. The town offers some of the area's best lodging.

Charlestown, New Hampshire (population 4,929), was a stockaded outpost during the French and Indian Wars. Its Main Street was laid out in 1763, 200 feet wide and a mile long, with more than five dozen structures that now make up a National Historic District; 10 buildings predate 1800. Note the

1840s Congregational church; the former Charlestown Inn (1817), now a commercial building; the
vintage-1800 Stephen Hassam House, built by the great-grandfather of impressionist painter Childe
Hassam; and the Foundation for Biblical Research, housed in a 1770s mansion. *Historic Charlestown
Walkabout*, a nominally priced guide, is available in most town stores. Also see the Fort at No. 4
under *To See*.

Claremont, New Hampshire (population 13,344). Massive textile mills and machine shops line the
Sugar River as it drops 300 feet from the city's compact core around Tremont Square, which retains
some fine 1890s buildings, notably the massive Italian Renaissance Revival–style city hall with its magnificent and well-used second-floor Opera House, and the Moody Building, built originally as a hotel
in 1892. The mammoth brick Monadnock Mills on Water Street (off Broad and Main) on the Sugar
River are among the best-preserved small 19th-century urban mills in New Hampshire. A walking
tour is available from the **Greater Claremont Chamber of Commerce** (603-543-1296), 24 Opera
House Square, open weekdays 10–2.

✳ To See
Listed from south to north
🦅 **Fort at No. 4** (603-826-5700; fortat4.org), 267 Springfield Rd. (Rt. 11), 1 mile north of Charlestown Village, New Hampshire. Open May–late Oct., Mon.–Sat. 10–4:30, Sun. 10–4. $10 adults, $7
seniors (55-plus), $5 ages 6 and up. Check the website for special events. This living history museum,
set in 20 acres on the Connecticut River, conjures an otherwise almost forgotten chapter in New England history. The stockaded village replicates the way the settlement looked in the 1740s. It served
first as a trading post in which Natives and newcomers lived together peaceably until the outbreak of
the French and Indian Wars. A full 50 miles north of any other town on the Connecticut River, the
original fort withstood repeated attacks. The complex includes the Great Hall, cow barns, and furnished living quarters; there is also an audiovisual program, and costumed interpreters demonstrate
18th-century life. Inquire about frequent battle reenactments and special programs throughout summer. A small museum displays locally found settler and Native American artifacts, and the gift store
carries historical books for all ages

SCENIC DRIVES Connecticut River Scenic Byway (ctrivertravel.net). From I-91 take either Exit
4 (**Putney**) or Exit 5 (**Westminster**). Just south of Exit 5 cross the river to **Walpole** (see *Villages*) and
turn at the sign for the village center. Back on New Hampshire's Rt. 12 head north to **Charlestown**
to see reconstructed **Fort at No. 4** (see *To See*). Cross back to Vermont on Rt. 11 at **Hoyt's Landing**
(just off I-91, Exit 7), picnicking and birding. Zip back down I-91 to Exit 6 and follow Rt. 103 for 1
mile to the turnoff for the **Rockingham Meeting House** (see the sidebar). Return to Rt. 5 south to
Bellows Falls (see *Villages*).

Westminster West Road. The scenic alternative to Rt. 5 or I-91 from Putney to Bellows Falls: From
Putney Village head up Kimball Hill Rd. and bear right at the top of the hill. This is a favorite bicycle
route for obvious reasons, as it winds past crafts studios and farmsteads.

✳ To Do
BICYCLING Road biking is popular in this area thanks to many interlinking back roads and river
roads.

Grafton Ponds (802-843-2400; graftonponds.com) rents mountain bikes and offers mountain biking
on its cross-country trails, along with guided tours and lessons.

In Springfield the **Toonerville Trail**, a 10-foot-wide, paved recreation path good for bicycling and
walking, follows the Black River along an old trolley line from the trailhead on Rt. 11 (behind the

Rockingham Meeting House, Meetinghouse Rd., off Rt. 103, roughly 1 mile west of I-91 Exit 6,
north of Bellows Falls. Open Memorial Day–Columbus Day, 10–4. Free but donations appreciated. Vermont's oldest unchanged public building was constructed as a combination church and
town hall in 1787. The Federal-style structure, standing quietly above its graveyard, is striking
inside and out. Inside, "pigpen"-style pews each accommodate 10 to 15 people, some with their
backs to the minister. The old burying ground is filled with thin markers bearing readable epi-
taphs. An annual pilgrimage is held the first Sunday in August, with a 3 PM historical program.

✎ GRAFTON VILLAGE MUSEUMS

Much of the village of Grafton has been preserved by the Windham Foundation (see *Villages*), with several buildings now housing museums and crafts shops as well making and showcasing Grafton Cheese. **The Nature Museum** (802-843-2111; nature-museum.org), 186 Townshend Rd. Open select days year-round 10–4. $4 adults, $2 children. Housed in the town Grange, the exhibits here are extensive and fascinating, focusing on local flora and fauna. Stuffed animals include such elusive forest residents as a catamount, a fox, a bobcat, and a fisher. Children can dig for fossils and explore a simulated underground tunnel; also family programs during vacation periods. Nature trails lead from here through meadow and woods to the green up to Rocky Cliff Junction, where you'll find the **Vermont Museum of Mining and Minerals** (802-875-3582), 55 Pleasant St. Open May 30–mid-Oct., Sat.–Sun. and by appointment. Exhibits include a miniature village made of Vermont marble. At the **Grafton Village Cheese Company** (graftonvillage cheese.com), 533 Townshend Rd., you can watch cheesemaking most weekdays through a viewing window. This is the original source of some of Vermont's best prizewinning cheddars. The window and a video convey a sense of cheesemaking, but the major production is now at the company's larger plant (see the Brattleboro chapter). The **Specialty Cheese & Wine Shop** (802-843-1062), 56 Townshend Rd., behind the Grafton Inn, showcases Grafton and other Vermont cheese, also wines, gifts, and gourmet foods.

GRAFTON CHEESE FACTORY

Windham Foundation

Robert Jones Industrial Center) 3 miles to another parking area on Rt. 5, just north of the Cheshire Bridge across the Connecticut.

BOATING

Boat access to the Connecticut River

Herricks Cove. Picnic area, boat landing, and bird sanctuary, a good picnic spot off Rt. 5 near I-91, Exit 6, in Rockingham, above Bellows Falls.

Hoyt's Landing. Off Rt. 11 and I-91, Exit 7, in Springfield, a recently upgraded put-in that's also good for fishing and picnicking.

Ashley Ferry Boat Landing. Off River Rd. (parallel to Rt. 11/12), about 2 miles south of Claremont, New Hampshire. A boat landing and park at a bend in the river.

Also see "Upper Valley River Towns."

CROSS-COUNTRY SKIING AT GRAFTON PONDS

Windham Foundation

Other boat access
North Springfield Lake and **Stoughton Recreation Area**, Reservoir Rd. between Springfield and Weathersfield, are maintained by the U.S. Army Corps of Engineers and offer boat launches.

FISHING You can eat the fish you catch in the Connecticut River. See *Boating* for put-in spots.

GOLF Bellows Falls Country Club (802-463-9809), Rt. 103, Rockingham. Scenic nine-hole course; clubhouse with bar and lunchroom.

Crown Point Country Club (802-885-1010), Weathersfield Center Rd., Springfield. A gem of an 18-hole course with pro shop, golf lessons, driving range, restaurant, and banquet facilities.

Hooper Golf Club (603-756-4020) Prospect Hill, Walpole. This vintage course offers nine holes and a clubhouse serving lunch.

HIKING/WALKING Bellows Falls Historic Riverfront Park and Trail System. This trail will run from the Bellows Falls Historical Society property on Mill St. along the Connecticut River. Phased plans include construction of a "Poet's Seat" river overlook, a riverside performing space, and fishing and kayak access. This trail will connect with the **Windham Hill Pinnacle Association** (windhamhillpinnacle.org) trail system in Westminster. Check the website for a map and access points for this well-maintained ridge trail running south to connect with Putney Mountain.

Also see **Ascutney Mountain** in the next chapter.

SWIMMING *Grafton Swimming Pond*, Rt. 121, 1 mile west of the village, is an oasis for children. The pond behind the lodge at **Grafton Ponds** (Rt. 35 south of the village) is also open for swimming in summer, complete with a swim-to wooden float.

Stoughton Pond Recreation Area (802-886-2775), Stoughton Pond Rd. off Rt. 106 in Weathersfield, offers pond swimming, and in the village of Perkinsville the **Black River** cascades into delicious pools at an old power site.

✳ Winter Sports

CROSS-COUNTRY SKIING AND SNOWSHOEING Grafton Ponds Outdoor Center (802-843-2400; graftonponds.com), Townshend Rd., Grafton. Fifteen km of trails groomed both for skating and classic strides, meandering off from a log cabin warming hut, over meadows, and into the woods on Bear Hill. Snowmaking on 5 km, rentals, and instruction, snowtubing, and 10 km of trails specifically for snowshoeing. Wine & Cheese snowshoe tours and sleigh rides are offered on selected weekends.

✳ Lodging

INNS *The Inn at Weathersfield** (802-263-9217; weathersfieldinn.com), 1342 Rt. 106, Weathersfield 05151. This is one of Vermont's most distinctive inns, best known for fine dining, styling itself "New England's premier culinary inn." Richard and Marilee Spanjian are the innkeepers and the chef is native Vermonter Jean-Luc Matecat. Each of the 12 guest rooms and suites is thoughtfully, comfortably furnished. All have phone and private bath (ranging from powerful shower to Jacuzzi) and amenities such as slippers and plush robes; most have fireplace. Set back from quiet Rt. 106, just south of the village of Perkinsville, the inn dates in part from 1792, but columns give it an antebellum facade. The setting is 21 wooded acres with hiking/snowshoeing trails and an amphitheater used as a wedding venue. The inn is handy to Okemo for winter skiing; in summer and fall there are hiking trails on Mount Ascutney, a web of back roads good for biking, and a glorious swimming hole up the road. See *Dining Out* for more about the inn's locally sourced dining and check the website for current classes with Jean-Luc, guest chefs, and cookbook authors, held at the inn's new Hidden Kitchen in the former loft of the barn. Room rates are $179–299 in high seasons, $149–238 in low, including full breakfast. Check the website for special dining packages.

♂ 🐾 🐈 ♿ **Grafton Inn** (802-843-2231; 800-843-1801; graftoninnvermont.com), 92 Main St., Grafton 05146, at the junction of Rts. 35 and 121. The brick core of this splendid building dates from 1801, but the double-porched facade is mid-19th century. The early-19th-century-style interior is country elegant but unstuffy and comfortable (a discreet elevator accesses the second and third floors). In recent years more than $1 million has been invested in reducing the number of rooms from 66 to 45, 11 (including 3 suites) in the old inn itself, the remainder divided between the Windham and Homestead cottages. Four rental houses with full kitchens and common space, some with working fireplace, sleep between 6 and 10 people apiece. In total the inn can accommodate 90. All guest rooms have private bath, many have air-conditioning, and all are individually decorated with antiques and country papers and fabrics. Candlelit dining is in The Old Tavern Restaurant (see *Dining Out*). **Phelps Barn Pub** offers a pub menu Thurs.–Sun. with a fireplace—and weekly live music. And you'll find a Ping-Pong table and game room in a neighboring house. Heated platform tennis courts, cross-country

THE GRAFTON INN REMAINS THE CENTERPIECE OF TOWN.

Windham Foundation

THE INN AT WEATHERSFIELD

biking trails, and a sand-bottomed swimming pond are all nearby; in winter there's cross-country skiing, tubing, and snowshoeing at Grafton Ponds. Youngsters ages 8 and older are welcome in all rooms, younger in some cottages. Well-behaved cats and dogs are welcome in select rooms and guest cottages, and you can bring your horse (there's a stable). $155–245 for rooms, up to $340 for suites. $45 for a third person, depending on the room, day (weekends are more expensive than weekdays), and season. Inquire about houses ($750–950). A full country breakfast and afternoon tea are included. Guests also receive Grafton Village Cheese and crackers on check-in.

Saxtons River Inn (802-869-2110; innsaxtons river.com), 27 Main St., Saxtons River 05154. There's some good news here. The vintage-1903 village inn with a distinctive square, five-story tower once more belongs to the family who restored it in the 1970s, ran it for 15 years, and put it on the culinary map. Innkeeper Averill Larson has freshened the 16 pleasant rooms (all with private bath and phone) and is once more the chef (see *Dining Out*). $99–159 per couple includes continental breakfast. The cheery pub at the front of the house is a popular gathering place.

BED & BREAKFASTS Listed from south to north.

In Grafton 05146

⚓ **The Inn at Woodchuck Hill Farm** (802-843-2398; woodchuckhill.com), Woodchuck Hill Rd. Open May–Nov. This is a 1780s farmhouse, high on a hill, off a back road. The porch, well stocked with comfortable wicker, has a peaceful, top-of-the-world feel, and there are views from the living room and dining room, too. The

Christina Tree

THE SAXTONS RIVER INN

innkeepers are Mark and Marilyn Gabriel and it's been operated by the Gabriel family for more than 30 years. There are eight guest rooms, six with private bath. By the pond, the old barn has been revamped to offer three suites, one with two bedrooms, bath, kitchen, and living/dining area with fireplace; also a one- and a two-bedroom unit. Spruce Cottage ($450 per night) is furnished in antiques and fully equipped; it sleeps up to seven people. The inn's recent addition is a light-filled yoga studio in which Marilyn, a certified Kundalini yoga instructor, teaches a morning class on weekends (guests welcome); inquire about weekend yoga retreats, all meals included. There's a sauna in the woods next to the pond, which is good for swimming, fishing, and canoeing, and the 200 rolling acres are laced with walking trails. $129–290 B&B for rooms, $200–290 for suites.

In Bellows Falls/Saxtons River
Readmore Bed, Breakfast & Books (802-463-9415; readmoreinn.com), 1 Hapgood St., Bellows Falls 05101. The most elegant B&B in the area, this was also the town's first certified "Green Hotel." It's a 19th-century mansion on the National Register with five guest rooms, each themed with appropriate books (for sale), most with fireplace and whirlpool bath, all with Bose radios and flat-screen TV. The Great Hall is a beauty, with a three-story atrium and comfortable parlors once designated for ladies and gentlemen (now the library). The garden is

planted with 50 different kinds of roses, and there's a wraparound front porch. $150–250 includes a full, locally sourced breakfast and afternoon tea.

Halladays Harvest Barn Inn (802-732-8254; harvestbarninn.com), 16 Webb Terrace, Bellows Falls 05101. Sited high on a steep hillside north of the village, this is a casual, comfortable place with river views and an expansive back meadow with a pond. Check the website for views of the seven rooms, all cheerful and comfortable with private bath, sharing sunny common space in the front of the house. A full breakfast is served at the harvest table. $99–159 includes breakfast and afternoon snacks featuring Halladays Harvest Barn dips.

Moore's Inn (802-869-2020; mooresinn .com), P.O. Box 424, 57 Main St. (Rt. 121), Saxtons River 05154. Dave Moore is a sixth-generation Vermonter who grew up in this Victorian house with its fine woodwork and spacious veranda. It remains very much Dave and Carol's family home and a guesthouse. The spacious guest rooms—six on the second floor and three on the third—are all self-contained, six with private bath, TV, fridge, coffeemaker, and breakfast cereals. The three third-floor guest rooms share a living room and can, of course, be rented as a whole. $109 per room (several can easily accommodate three people). The kitchen, living room, and bath are shared. Coffee and breakfast cereals provided. Bicyclists are especially welcome and will find maps and plenty of advice.

THE GREAT HALL AT READMORE BED, BREAKFAST & BOOKS, BELLOWS FALLS

Across the river

○ ♪ **The Inn at Valley Farms** (603-756-2855; 877-327-2855), 633 Wentworth Rd., Walpole, NH 03608. Set in 105 acres bordering an apple orchard, this circa-1774 house offers exceptionally handsome, antiques-filled guest rooms along with lovely common rooms, including a formal parlor and dining room, and a sunroom overlooking a lovely perennial garden. Upstairs in the main house there is a two-bedroom suite with bath, along with two other bedrooms, each with four-poster bed, private bath, phone, and dataport. Niceties include fresh flowers, plush robes, and Burdick chocolates. Families can choose one of two cottages, each with three bedrooms, kitchen, and living area. Innkeeper Jacqueline Caserta is a serious organic farmer/gardener; she uses fresh eggs as well as her organic vegetable harvest creatively to make a breakfast that's both good and good for you. Inn rates: $195–250 per couple with full breakfast. Cottages, which sleep six, are $195–250 for two, $35 per extra person. Cottages are stocked with the farm eggs and other breakfast basics, and a basket of homemade breads and muffins is delivered each morning to the door. Sunnyside, a renovated, three-bedroom, three-bath farmhouse a short walk from the inn, is available by the week, $1,500–1,850.

✳ Where to Eat

DINING OUT ♣ **The Inn at Weathersfield** (802-263-9217; weathersfieldinn.com), 1342 Rt. 106, just south of Perkinsville. Open for dinner Wed.–Sun. Reservations suggested. The dining room is a former carriage house, candlelit with windows overlooking the garden. A fall à la carte menu included Maine white mussels in cider with Red Hen crostini ($13 "small plate," $23 "large plate"); braised beef shortrib in spiced red wine with stone-ground polenta and red kale ($27); and a foliage risotto with delicata squash, leeks, caramelized onions, and mascarpone cheese ($17). Light fare is available in the Tavern; a seven-course tasting menu is offered ($100 per person) with paired wines ($59 per person) in the private wine cellar. The inn's prominent position on New England's culinary map was established by previous chef Joseph Tostrup (presently at Okemo). When it came time to replace him, innkeepers Marilee and Richard Spanjian interviewed 80 candidates before choosing Jean-Luc Matecat, son of a well-known Vermont chef who has earned his own reputation for blending French traditions with fusion flavors, innovative cooking methods, and local ingredients. Check the website for reasonably priced three-course midweek

dinners and many special events as well as cooking classes and programs at the inn's Hidden Kitchen.

♪ **Leslie's** (802-463-4929; leslistavern.com), Rockingham, Rt. 5 just south of I-91, Exit 6. Open nightly except Mon.–Tues. Reservations appreciated. John Marston opened his restaurant in a 1790s tavern back in 1986 and continues to create new and eclectic dishes, fusing many influences with experience and using as much homegrown produce as possible. Certified Black Angus beef and free-range chicken are served a variety of ways, and there's always a vegetarian plate and seafood—maybe Maine jumbo sea scallops with butternut squash ravioli and cauliflower puree. Leave room for dessert. Entrées $18–30; children's menu. Check the website for details about cooking classes.

The Old Tavern (802-843-2231; graftoninn vermont.com), Main St., Grafton, serves breakfast and dinner daily. Candlelit dinner is served in the formal old dining room amid fine portraits and Chippendale chairs. A winter menu might begin with a sweet potato and Brie tart with a crispy shallot garnish, and feature BBQ short ribs served with parsnip puree and root vegetable ragout or a classic lobster Newburg pie. Entrées $24–30. The menu in the informal Phelps Barn Pub (Thurs.–Sun.) might include pizza and beef stew.

○ **Popolo** (802-460-7676; popolomeanspeople .com), 36 the Square, Bellows Falls. Open Tues.–Fri. for lunch (11:30–2:30) and dinner (5–9:30), Sun. brunch 1–2, bar open until 11. *Popolo* means "people" in Italian, and the spirit of this place is bringing people together for good food, drink, and live entertainment at the heart of town. Housed in the recently renovated ground floor of the Windham Hotel, the casually elegant streetside space offers a choice of booths and nicely spaced tables. It's hung with full-sized copies of 1930s Federal Arts Program murals depicting Vermont farm scenes (the originals are in the former St. Albans post office). The limited but nicely varied menu is Italian-inspired farm to table. We lunched on an overflowing smoked turkey Cobb sandwich and a tasty tagliata (tender, marinated flank steak on a bed of arugula with roasted shiitakes). Dinner entrées run around $14–25, and pizza is always an option. Check the website for frequent live music and other performances. Be aware that this gets crowded before films at the Opera House across the square, upstairs in the town hall.

Saxtons River Inn (802-869-2110; innsaxtons river.com), 27 Main St., Saxtons River. Open for dinner except Mon. Averill Thomson is once more the popular chef-owner here. A winter menu in her cheery, old-fashioned dining room offers a choice of a dozen entrées, from a burger or fish-and-chips to smoked maple chipotle barbecue ribs with sweet potato fries to steak au poivre. $9–29.

Worth crossing the river for

& **Burdick's Bistro and Café** (603-756-2882; burdickchocolate.com), 47 Main St. (next to the post office), Walpole, NH. Open Tues.–Sat. 11:30–2:30 for lunch; 5:30–9 for dinner; Sun. brunch 10–2. Chocolatier extraordinaire Larry Burdick and his friend, filmmaker Ken Burns, have transformed the town's former IGA into a chic dining spot. With its warm yellow walls, soft lighting, and artfully placed mirrors and paintings, this is as close to a Paris brasserie as you can get in New Hampshire. You order from the same menu all day, but around 5 PM the ambience shifts. White tablecloths appear, and the café morphs into a more formal restaurant. You might lunch or dine on house sausage, Provençal beef stew, sole meunière, or oven-roasted chicken. The bread is crusty; the wine list, top-notch; the chocolate desserts, to die for. Entrées are $13–23; for two, figure $50 with wine.

EATING OUT Listed from south to north.

In and around Bellows Falls

Café Loco at Harlow Farm Stand (802-376-9626), Rt. 5 north of I-91, Exit 5, Westminster. Open Mon.–Sat., 7–5, Sun. 8–4, May–Dec. The farm stand is a standout, but it's easy to miss this delightful café orchestrated by Michael Lenox, featuring fresh-made soups, sandwiches, homemade pies, and daily specials. Try the corn crêpes or a grouper wrap.

♦ **Father's Restaurant** (802-463-3909), 7079 Rt. 5, 1 mile south of Bellows Falls. Open Sun. 7–3, Tues.–Sat. 6 AM–8 PM. An attractive family restaurant with a salad bar, kids' menu, wine and beer.

♨ (ⁿ) **Vermont Pretzel & Cookie** (802-460-2424), 24 Rockingham St., Bellows Falls. Christine Holtz, who founded Vermont Pretzel some years ago in nearby Saxtons River, supervises the large kitchen here, turning out daily-fresh soups and sandwiches on homemade bread and pretzels for those lucky enough to take advantage. We feasted on a pesto pretzel sandwich with stuffed with turkey, cheddar, and the works. Apple-stuffed pretzels are another specialty along with 20 kinds of cookies, brownies, bars, and biscotti. Definitely the preferred meeting/lunch spot in Bellows Falls.

Miss Bellows Falls Diner (802-463-9800), 90 Rockingham St., Bellows Falls. Open daily 6–2. Inside and out this Worcester Diner is still pure, unhokey 1920s.

Joy Wah (802-463-9761; joywah.com), 287 Rockingham St. (Rt. 5), Bellows Falls. Full-service Chinese fare in a Victorian farmhouse high on a hill north of downtown, overlooking the Connecticut River; all the usual dishes on its lengthy menu. Open daily for lunch and dinner. Sunday brunch is a local favorite.

Lisai's Corner Deli (802-732-8052; lisais .com), 92 Atkinson St. Open Mon.–Fri. 6 AM–6 PM, Sat. 7–3. Part of Lisai's Market, a local institution known for meats and fresh produce, this deli offers homemade soups, sandwiches, and a fresh salad bar.

(ⁿ) **Flat Iron Exchange** (802-460-0357; flat ironexchangevt.com), 51 the Square, Bellows Falls. Open 6 AM–9 PM. This attractive coffeehouse has quickly become the square's all-weather, all-day gathering spot. Owners Marc Kenney and Jana Bryan live upstairs and have created what amounts to a living room for the town—comfortable couches as well as tables, papers, a wide choice of coffees, teas, and home-baked pastries. The local art changes frequently, and there are Fri.-afternoon jam sessions and other frequent forms of live music.

Mack's Place Eatery (802-843-2255), Townshend Rd., Grafton. Just behind the Grafton Inn and attached to the Grafton Village Cheese retail shop. Open 7:30–4:30 daily for breakfast and lunch with soups, salads, wraps, and sandwiches.

Elsewhere

♦ **56 Main Street** (802-885-6987; fiftysixmain street.com), 56 Main St., Springfield. Open for lunch and dinner Tues.–Sat. Cozy, casual restaurant with a varied menu that includes Mexican, Italian, and vegetarian dishes as well as standard American fare. Entrées $7.99–18.99. Full liquor license.

Black Rock Steakhouse (802-885-2200), 284 River St., Springfield. Open Mon.–Sat. 11–9, Sun. 8–8 including Sun. brunch. Mixed reviews.

Country Creemee Restaurant (802-263-9327), Downers Corner, junction of Rts. 131 and 106, Perkinsville. Open Apr.–Oct. Locals will tell you that everything tastes good here; we always get the super-long hot dog to consume at a picnic table under the trees.

Pleasant Valley Brewery (802-869-4602), 16 Main St., Saxtons River. Open 4–11, from 2 Sun. Eight draft beers, a wide selection of mostly Vermont brews, pub food, and a welcoming pub atmosphere. Live music Fri., Sat.

✳ Entertainment

Bellows Falls Opera House (802-463-4766;), on the square in Bellows Falls, operated by the town of Rockingham. Formerly the New Falls Cinema, this vintage theater in the town hall has recently been refurbished with new seating, flooring, screen, and sound system. First-run movies are shown Fri.–Tues; classic films Wed. Tickets $5. Matinee concerts, too. This fine old vaudeville house is also the venue for live performances.

Stone Church Arts (802-463-3100), 20 Church St., Bellows Falls. Immanual Episcopal Church is the venue for a series of classical music performances.

More music and performance in Bellows Falls: Check the **Village Square Booksellers** website (villagesquarebooks.com). The store sells tickets and promotes musical performances staged at the Bellows Falls Opera House, including the Vermont Festival series, with concerts several times a rear.

There's also music during **Art Walk**, generally third Fridays (5–8).

Main Street Arts (802-869-2960; mainstreet arts.org), Main St., Saxtons River. This local arts council sponsors dance and musical performances, cabarets, recitals, as well as art classes.

Springfield Theater (802-885-2929), 26 Main St., downtown Springfield. First-run films.

The **Grafton Cornet Band** performs in either Grafton or Chester (sometimes in Townshend) on summer weekends. Grafton's **Phelps Barn Pub** (graftoninnvermont.com) features live music every Saturday night at 8; a monthly concert series with bigger acts is also offered free of charge.

✳ Selective Shopping

ANTIQUES SHOPS Windham Antique Center (802-732-8081), 5 the Square. Open 10–5 daily. A large new multigroup store in the heart of Bellows Falls.

S. B. & Company Antiques/Auctioneers (802-460-1190; sbauctioneers.com), 46 Canal St., Bellows Falls. Sharon Boccelli is well known in the antiques trade. Check the website for frequent auctions.

ART & CRAFTS GALLERIES *Note:* **Art Walk** (bf3f.org) is held in Bellows Falls the third Friday of every month.

Note: **The Putney Craft Tour** (putneycrafts .com), held for more than 30 years for three days after Thanksgiving, showcases the work of more than two dozen craftspeople within a dozen miles of Putney. Complementing rather than competing with Putney, **The Walpole Artisans Cooperative** also sponsors an open studio tour on Thanksgiving weekend (walpole artisans.org).

In Bellows Falls/Walpole
Coyote Moon Jewelry & Imports (802-463-9529), 22 Rockingham St., Bellows Falls. Open daily except Sun. Intriguing gifts from throughout the world with an emphasis on Mexico, and sterling-silver jewelry.

Sherwin Art Glass Studio/Gallery (802-376-5744; sherwinartglass.com), 33 Bridge St., Bellows Falls. Chris Sherwin usually can be found creating colored art glass; open house Fri.–Sun.

Walpole Artisans Cooperative (603-756-3020; walpoleartisans.org), 52 Main St., Walpole (across from Burdick's Café). Open Wed.–Sat. 11–6, Sun. 11–3. A lively cooperative showcasing local craftspeople.

In Grafton
Gallery North Star (802-843-2465; gnsgrafton .com), 151 Townshend Rd. Open daily except Tues. 10–5. Six rooms in this 19th-century Grafton Village house are hung with landscapes and graphic prints, oils, watercolors, and sculpture.

Jud Hartmann Gallery (802-843-2018; jud hartmanngallery.com), 6 Main St., by the Brick Church on Main St. Open mid-Sept.–Christmas holidays 10–5. Hartmann began his career as a sculptor in Grafton and has since won national acclaim for his bronze portrayals of Native Americans, specifically a series of limited-edition sculptures titled *The Woodland Tribes of the Northeast*. He is working on increasingly complex historical renditions. He divides his time among studios here and in Blue Hill, Maine. In winter you may find him teaching or skiing at Grafton Ponds, which he founded many years ago. The studio also displays paintings by various other artists.

Grafton Forge (windham-foundation.org; open Wed.–Sat. 10–5). Aaron Andersen demonstrates his craft.

My Mind's Design (802-842-1000; myminds design.com), 217 Main St. in the Old Fire Station, open Mon.–Sat. 10–5, showcases the work of fine furniture maker Jason Ballard.

In Saxtons River
River Artisans (802-869-2099), 26B Main St. Open weekdays noon–5, weekends 10–3.

May–Dec., daily noon–5. A crafts cooperative run by local artisans and carrying the work of many more on consignment: pottery, macramé, leather, weaving, batik, and hand-sewn, -knit, and -crocheted items.

In Springfield
Gallery at the Vault (802-885-7111; gallery vault.org), 65 Main St. This quality crafts store is all about Visual Art Using Local Talent (hence its name) and is definitely worth checking out, showcasing work by some 165 local artists and craftspeople.

Great Hall, 100 River St. A magnificent atrium space, a venue for public art and frequent special exhibits in the former Fellows Gear Sharper Factory building.

BOOKSTORES (•) **Village Square Booksellers and Wireless Café** (802-463-9404; village squarebooks.com), 32 the Square, Bellows Falls. Open Mon.–Thurs. 9–5, Fri. 9–6, Sat. 9–4, and Sun. 10–3. Patricia and Alan Fowler's independent, full-service bookstore also carries music, card, toys, local photography by Alan, and changing work by local artists. A café in the rear of the store makes an inviting place to linger with coffee and a laptop; it's also the venue for authors' readings and special programs. This is a source of tickets for performances at the Opera House (see *Entertainment*) and other local events.

Ray Boas, Bookseller (603-756-9900; rayboas bookseller.com), 44 Elm St., Walpole, NH. Open most days, but it's best to call ahead if you're traveling a distance. More than 13,000 titles with an emphasis on nonfiction in a lovely old Colonial home. Decorative arts and antiques a specialty.

FOOD, FLOWERS, AND FARM STANDS
Allen Brothers Farms & Orchards (802-722-3395), 6–23 Rt. 5, 2 miles south of Bellows Falls. Open year-round, daily, 6 AM–9 PM. Offers pick-your-own apples and potatoes in-season, also sells vegetables, plants and seeds, honey, syrup, and Vermont gifts.

Harlow Farmstand (802-722-3515), Rt. 5, less than a mile north of I-91, Exit 5. Open May–Dec., daily 9–6. Organic produce, bedding plants, flowers, and baked goods. Also see Café Loco under *Eating Out*.

Plummer's Sugar House (802-843-2207; plummerssugarhouse.com), 3 miles south of Grafton Village on Townshend Rd. Open all year. A third-generation maple producer, making pure syrup for more than 30 years; also maple candy, sugar, and more. Will ship anywhere in the United States.

Morning Star Perennials (802-463-3433; morningstarflowers.com), 221 Darby Hill Rd., Rockingham (off Rt. 5). More than 300 varieties of organically grown perennials, including many rare ones.

Wellwood Orchards (802-263-5200), 529 Wellwood Orchard Rd., Springfield. Pick your own strawberries (June and July), then raspberries and blueberries (mid- to late July), and finally apples (mid-Aug.–Oct.). Farm tours, farm stand.

Vermont Shepherd (802-387-4473; vermont shepherd.com), Patch Rd., Westminster West. Vermont Shepherd holds one of the country's top awards for its distinctive, hand-pressed, sweet creamy sheep's-milk cheese. It's made Apr.–Oct., then aged four to eight months and available mid-Aug. until the year's supply runs out in spring. Call for appropriate visiting times. A self-serve shop is open daily.

Halladay's Flowers & Harvest Barn (802-463-3331; halladays.com), 59 the Square, Bellows Falls. A village flower store that's also an outlet for herb blends, dip mixes, and cake mixes all made in town from natural ingredients.

In Walpole, New Hampshire
Boggy Meadow Farm (877-541-3953; boggy meadowfarm.com), 13 Boggy Meadow Lane; location marked from Rt. 12. The 620-acre Boggy Meadow Farm has been in the Cabot

BELLA PRESIDES AT VILLAGE SQUARE BOOKS IN BELLOWS FALLS

Alan Fowler

family since 1820. Powell Cabot produces Fanny Mason Farmstead Swiss Cheeses, all made with raw milk and vegetable rennet that pasteurizes naturally during the 60-day curing process. Their most recent product is "Switchel" (70-proof cider vodka!). Call to make sure the retail shop and cheese plant are open. The drive along the river to the shop is a treat in itself.

Walpole Mountain Winery (603-756-3948; bhvineyard.com), 114 Barnett Hill Rd. Open Memorial Day–Christmas, Fri.–Sun. Call for hours. More than 1,000 hardy grapevines are producing wines that can be sampled and purchased here in the tasting room. It's a glorious spot, high on a hillside with long views.

♂ **Alyson's Orchard** (603-756-9800; 800-856-0549; alysonsorchard.com), Wentworth Rd. Some 28,000 trees cover this beautiful hilltop overlooking the Connecticut River Valley. Heritage-variety apples, peaches, pears, blueberries, raspberries, hops. This is also a popular wedding venue.

FARMERS MARKETS In **Bellows Falls** (bffarmersmarket.com) on Fri. 4–7, Memorial Day–Oct. at the Waypoint Center (beside the railroad station). **Walpole, New Hampshire** (walpolefarmersmarket.com) Fri. 4–7 on the town common. **Springfield**, Wed. 3–6.

SPECIAL SHOPS Vermont Country Store (vermontcountrystore.com), Rt. 103, Rockingham Village. An offshoot of the famous Vermont Country Store in Weston, this is also owned by Lyman Orton and sells the familiar Vermont Common Crackers along with many flavors of the popular store-baked Cookie Buttons. You'll also find large selections of toys, bulk candies, flannel sleepwear, beauty products, and all the hard-to-find old-timey gadgets for which the

Vermont Country Store is famous. Frequent sales, excellent service.

J&H Hardware (802-463-4140; jandhhardware .com), 20 the Square, Bellows Falls. An old-style hardware store that has recently doubled its space to fill the need left when Brattleboro-based Sam's Department Store closed its store here. Now there are full sporting goods, men's and women's clothing departments.

✱ Special Events

Note: Check bellowsfallsvt.org for current happenings, and see Art Walk under *Art Galleries.*

May: **Herrick's Cover Wildlife Festival**, first Sunday.

June: **Roots on the River**, second weekend (rootsontheriver.com).

July 3: **Annual VSO Concert Under the Stars and Fireworks** at Grafton Ponds Outdoor Center, part of the Grafton Music Festival (graftonmusicfestival.com).

July 4 weekend: A big **parade** in Saxtons River and fireworks. **Windsor County Agricultural Fair** (802-886-1322), Barlow's Field, Eureka Rd., Springfield.

August: **Rockingham Old Home Days**, Bellows Falls (gfrcc.org). A full weekend of events—railroad excursions, live entertainment, art show, Rockingham Meeting House Pilgrimage, fireworks. Annual **Stellafane Convention of Amateur Telescope Makers** (stellafane .com), Springfield.

Thanksgiving weekend: **Putney Craft Tour** (putneycrafts.com) and the **Walpole Artisan Open Studios Tour** (walpoleartisans.com) add up to a great way to explore back roads and take care of holiday shopping.

UPPER VALLEY RIVER TOWNS

INCLUDING WINDSOR, HARTFORD, NORWICH, THETFORD, FAIRLEE, AND HANOVER, NEW HAMPSHIRE

T he Upper Valley ignores state lines to form one of New England's most rewarding and distinctive regions.

Upper Valley is a name coined in the 1950s by a local daily, the *Valley News*, to define its two-state circulation area. The label has stuck to a group of towns that in the 1770s tried to form the state of "New Connecticut" (see the introduction to "The Connecticut River Valley").

In 1769 Eleazar Wheelock moved his Indian school—which had been funded through appeals made by Mohegan preacher Samson Occum in England and Scotland to "spread Christian knowledge among the Savages"—from Lebanon, Connecticut, to Hanover, New Hampshire. Initially Dartmouth College recruited Indian students, but the school also served white students and the percentage of Indians quickly dwindled.

The Valley itself prospered in the late 18th and early 19th centuries, as evidenced by the exquisite Federal-era meetinghouses and mansions still salted throughout this area. The river was the area's only highway in the 18th and early 19th centuries and was still a popular steamboat route in the years before the Civil War.

The river remains more a bond than a boundary. The Upper Valley phone book includes towns on both sides of the river, and Hanover's Dresden School District reaches into Vermont (this was the first bistate school district in the United States). The Rivendell School District to the north stretches from Vershire, Vermont, on the west to Orford, New Hampshire.

Several Independence Day parades start in one state and finish across the bridge in the other. The Montshire Museum, founded in Hanover, New Hampshire, but now in Norwich, combines the two states in its very name.

Dartmouth College remains the cultural center of the Upper Valley. With the nearby Dartmouth-Hitchcock medical complex and West Lebanon shopping strip, this area also forms the region's commercial hub, handy to the highways radiating, the way rail lines once did, from White River Junction.

The Connecticut and White Rivers converge at White River Junction, an obvious stop for the area's first travelers, who arrived by canoe, then by raft and steamboat. Like an evolving species, they continued on land here with the advent of the railroad, which spawned a brick village. In the mid-19th century, some 100 steam locomotives chugged into this station each day. However, like a noose looping loosely around White River Junction, the interstates (I-89 and I-91) have since channeled traffic away from this 19th-century village, slowly draining its lifeblood. Happily, the downtown commercial blocks here are presently evolving as an arts and dining center, still with the vintage rail depot—now a visitors center—at its core.

In the town of Windsor, 12 miles south of White River Junction, the layerings of history are compressed along a Main Street that includes the 18th-century "Constitution House" (the official birthplace of Vermont), a 1950s diner, and a white-pillared 1790s Asher Benjamin–designed church. South of the covered bridge is an 1846 brick armory credited with introducing the concept of interchangeable parts, a process that revolutionized the gun and tool industry globally. Locally it spawned some significant tool companies, the reason this area was known as Precision Valley.

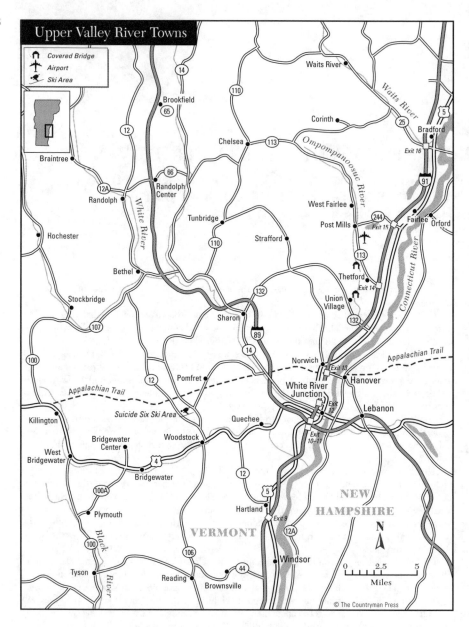

Upper Valley River Towns

New England's longest and most famous covered bridge links the communities of Windsor and Cornish, New Hampshire, site of the 19th-century summer home of sculptor Augustus Saint-Gaudens. Now a national historic site, the estate evokes the era (1885–1935) in which prominent artists, with the help of pioneering landscape architects, transformed many of the Valley's oldest farms into summer homes. They commuted from New York on the train line that still stops in Windsor.

GUIDANCE White River Junction Welcome Center (802-281-5050), 100 Railroad Row in the Amtrak station, White River Junction. Open 10–5 daily. This information-packed center offers friendly, knowledgeable advice, and restrooms. From I-91 and I-89 exits to Rt. 5, follow the blue WELCOME CENTER signs.

Windsor Welcome Center (802-674-5910), 3 Railroad Ave., Windsor. Open 9–2 but volunteer-operated. Down by the railroad station (marked from Main St. in the middle of downtown), this nicely restored building offers area information.

GETTING THERE *By car:* Interstates 91 and 89 intersect in the White River Junction (Vermont)–Lebanon (New Hampshire) area, where they also meet Rt. 5 north and south on the Vermont side; and Rt. 4, the main east–west highway through central Vermont.

By bus: White River Junction is a hub for **Greyhound** (800-552-8737; greyhound.com) with service to Boston, Burlington, New York, and Montreal. **Dartmouth Coach** (603-228-3300; concordcoach lines.com) offers aggressively competitive service from Boston and Logan Airport to Hanover, New Hampshire.

By air: The **Lebanon Regional Airport** (603-298-8878; flyleb.com), West Lebanon (marked from the junction of I-89 and Rt. 10), has frequent service to Boston via Cape Air (flycapeair.com). Rental cars are available, and the airport is also served by **Big Yellow Taxi** (603-643-8294).

By train: **Amtrak** (800-872-7245) serves Windsor and White River Junction, en route to and from New York/Washington and St. Albans, Vermont.

GETTING AROUND Visitors can easily explore both sides of the river. I-91, set high above the Vermont bank, offers a quick route up and down the Valley, but the old highways—New Hampshire Rts. 10 and 12 and Rt. 5 in Vermont—thread fields and villages, which are twinned at intervals along the river. Many of the bridges that once linked them are long gone but they survive between Windsor and Cornish, White River Junction and West Lebanon, Norwich and Hanover, Thetford and Lyme, Fairlee and Orford.

MEDICAL EMERGENCY Call **911**. **Dartmouth-Hitchcock Medical Center** (603-650-5000), off Rt. 120 between Hanover and Lebanon, is generally considered the best hospital in northern New England. However, in the course of researching this edition, we landed in the emergency room at **Mt. Ascutney Hospital** in Windsor (802-674-6711; mtascutneyhospital.org) and have to give this small friendly and efficient resource a plug.

✳ Communities

Listed from south to north

Windsor (population 4,979; windsorvt.com). In *Roadside History of Vermont*, Peter Jennison notes that while it is known as the "Birthplace of Vermont," Windsor can also claim to be the midwife of the state's machine tool industry. Windsor resident Lemuel Hedge devised a machine for ruling paper in 1815 and dividing scales in 1827. Asahel Hubbard produced a revolving pump in 1828, and Niconar Kendall in the 1830s designed an "under hammer" rifle, the first use of interchangeable parts, in the picturesque old mill that's now the **American Precision Museum**. Windsor's mid-19th-century prosperity is reflected in the handsome lines of the columned Windsor House, once considered the best public house between Boston and Montreal. The Italianate building across the street was designed in 1850 by Ammi Young as a post office (the oldest federal post office in continuous use in the United States) with an upstairs courthouse that served as Woodrow Wilson's summer White House from 1913 to 1915; the president spent his summers in Cornish, just across the **Windsor–Cornish Covered Bridge**. Cornish was at the time an artists' and writers' colony that had evolved around sculptor Augustus Saint-Gaudens. The colony nurtured artist Maxfield Parrish; his painting *Templed Hills* hangs in the Peoples United Bank, 50 Main St. (Parrish left it in perpetuity to the bank's tellers for "keeping my account balanced"). It depicts a mountain that resembles Mount Ascutney, towering above

DOWNTOWN WINDSOR

Christina Tree

water that resembles Lake Runnemede. The lake is now the town-owned conservation area **Paradise Park**. The 1798 **Old South Congregational Church** was designed by Asher Benjamin. Also worth noting: the contemporary St. Francis of Assisi Roman Catholic Church and its panels depicting the Seven Sacraments, donated by noted American painter George Tooker. On the common (off Main St.), St. Paul's, built in 1832, is Vermont's oldest Episcopal church. Townsend Cottage, across the common, is a striking example of 1840s Carpenter Gothic style. Several miles north of downtown a 34-acre riverside, visitor-geared complex has **Artisans Park**, a destination anchored by **Simon Pearce Glass**, the **Harpoon Brewery**, and local food purveyors as well as local sports outfitters and the **Path of Life Garden**.

White River Junction (population 2,569; whiteriverjunction.org) is one of five villages within the town of Hartford. As noted in this chapter's introduction, downtown White River—which at its peak saw 100 steam locomotives chug into the station daily—is now a bit of a cul-de-sac. Still, it's well worth finding. **Northern Stage**, a professional theater company, performs Oct.–May in the old Briggs Opera House. The Tip Top building, a former commercial bakery, is honeycombed with artists' studios. You'll also find a natural food co-op, some interesting shops, a choice of restaurants, and the groundbreaking **Center for Cartoon Studies** (a two-year program with a library endowed by Charles M. Schulz, creator of *Peanuts*). There are also several shops worth a detour in their own right. Museum exhibits span the Valley's river and air history as well as rail. Follow the walkway along the tracks to the free **Main Street Museum** (802-356-2776; mainstreetmuseum.org). Housed in a former firehouse, this "cabinet of curiosities" seems a parody of the museum genre. Owner David Fairbanks (as in St. Johnsbury's Fairbanks Museum) Ford's exhibits include Elvis Presley's gallstones and an eclectic range of stuffed and "found" objects. At the center of the village is the **Hotel Coolidge**, one of the last of New England's railroad hotels. In its former incarnation as the Junction House, the hotel's clientele included Lillian Gish and President Calvin Coolidge, for whose father it is named. Ask to see the hand-painted murals in the Vermont Room, depicting the state's history from wilderness to the 1940s. Lovingly preserved by its present owners, the Coolidge is rich in character, something conspicuously absent from the interstate-geared, brand-name motels and fast-food stops along the village periphery. Horace Wells of White River Junction was, incidentally, the first person to use laughing gas as an anesthetic for pulling teeth. The other villages in the town of Hartford are Quechee (see the Woodstock/Quechee chapter), Hartford Village, Wilder, and West Hartford.

Norwich (population 3,844; norwichvt.us), one of the prettiest towns in Vermont, was settled in 1761 by a group from Marshfield, Connecticut. It has always had close ties to Hanover (just across the bridge) and was itself the original home of Norwich University (founded 1819), which moved to Northfield after the Civil War. The village is an architectural showcase for fine brick and frame Federal homes. Note the Seven Nations House, built in 1832 as a commercial "tenement." **The Norwich Historical Society** (802-649-0124), housed in the renovated vintage-1807 Lewis House, 277 Main St., is open Wed., Thurs., and Sat.; check norwichhistory.org for times and current exhibits. The **Norwich Inn**, with its popular brewpub and dining room, is the hospitable heart of town. Hidden down between I-91 and the river, the **Montshire Museum** offers insights into ways the world and universe go 'round as well as into how the river shapes the immediate environment; also riverside walking trails. **King Arthur Flour Company**'s flagship Baker's Store and Baking Education Center on Rt. 5, south of town, draw devotees from throughout the county.

Hanover, New Hampshire (population 11,266), is synonymous with Ivy League **Dartmouth College** (dartmouth.edu), chartered in 1769 and one of the most prestigious colleges in the country. Few college towns are as visitor-friendly. Maple and elm-shaded Dartmouth Green doubles as the town common and includes a staffed information kiosk (open June–Sept.). Its frame of historic and architecturally striking Dartmouth College buildings include a hospitable hotel, a major performance center, and an outstanding art museum. Campus tours are offered. **Baker Memorial Library**, a 1920s version of Philadelphia's Independence Hall, dominates the northern side of the green. Visitors are welcome to see a set of murals, *The Epic of American Civilization*, by José Clemente Orozco, painted between 1932 and 1934 while he was teaching at Dartmouth. (Some alumni once demanded these be removed or covered because of the Mexican artist's left-wing politics.) In the Treasure Room (near the western stair hall on the main floor), Daniel Webster's copies of the double elephant folio first edition of John Audubon's *Birds of America* are permanently displayed. The **Hopkins Center for the Arts** (see *Entertainment*) was designed by Wallace Harrison a few years before he designed New York's Lincoln Center (which it resembles). It contains three theaters, a recital hall, and art galleries for permanent and year-round programs of plays, concerts, and films. The adjacent **Hood Museum of Art** (see the sidebar) is one of the oldest, largest college museums in the country; the neighboring

Black Family Visual Arts Center has changing exhibits. **Dartmouth Row**, a file of four striking white Colonial buildings on the rise along the eastern side of the green, represents all there was to Dartmouth College until 1845. You might also want to find **Webster Cottage**, maintained as a museum by the Hanover Historical Society, and the vintage-1843 **Shattuck Observatory** (open for observations at various times during the year; for schedules call 603-646-9100 or visit Dartmouth.edu /physics).

Lyme, New Hampshire (population 1,716) is known for its splendid **Congregational church**, completed in 1812, a Federal-style meetinghouse with a Palladian window, an unusual tower (three cubical stages and an octagonal dome), and no fewer than 27 numbered horse stalls. The gathering of buildings, including the **Lyme Inn**, fine old houses, and shops, is one of New Hampshire's most stately. Take **River Road** north by old farms and cemeteries, through an 1880s covered bridge.

Thetford (population 2,784). Thetford Center has a friendly general store and handsome brick Methodist church. Thetford Hill is a beauty, the site of Thetford Academy, the Parish Players, and the **Thetford Historical Society** (open Aug., Sun. 2–5) and its **Historic Library** (open year-round, Mon. and Thurs. 2–4, Tues. 10–noon).

Fairlee Village, shelved between the Palisades and a bend in the Connecticut River, is a plain cousin to aristocratic Orford, New Hampshire (well known for its lineup of elegant Federal-era houses), just across the river. But we like it better. Check out Chapman's, a 19th-century pharmacy that has expanded in unusual directions. Summer camps and inns line nearby **Lake Morey**. Samuel Morey, a resident of Orford and a lumberman in Fairlee, was the inventor of the first steamboat: In 1793, 14 years before Robert Fulton launched his craft, Morey was puffing up and down the river in a primitive vessel barely big enough to hold him and his firewood. The remains of the little steamer are believed to lie at the bottom of Lake Morey, scuttled by its builder when the $100,000 in stock offered him by Fulton turned out to be worthless. Morey also patented an internal combustion engine in 1825. Lake Fairlee, lined with children's camps and with a public swim beach, straddles the town line and is best accessed from Rt. 244 west of Ely.

Orford, New Hampshire (population 1,044), is known for its **Ridge Houses**, a center-of-town lineup of seven houses so strikingly handsome that Charles Bulfinch has been (erroneously) credited as their architect. They were built instead by skilled local craftsmen using designs from Connecticut Valley architect Asher Benjamin's do-it-yourself guide to Federal styles, "The Country Builder's Apprentice." These houses testify to the prosperity of this valley in the post–Revolutionary War era. Each was built by an Orford resident—with money earned in Orford—between 1773 and 1839. The **Samuel Morey House** is the oldest of the seven, a centerpiece for the others. Its owner, credited with inventing the steamboat, heated and lighted his house with gas, and in 1826 he patented a gas-powered internal combustion engine.

✳ Also See

View from Mount Ascutney in Mount Ascutney State Park, Windsor. Open late May–mid-Oct.; day-use fee. A well-surfaced 3.8-mile "parkway" spirals gently up through hardwoods from Rt. 44A (off Rt. 5) between Ascutney and Weathersfield. Note the pullout with picnic facilities and a great view up the valley. A parking lot in the saddle between the mountain's south peak and summit accesses an 0.8-mile foot trail that takes you the additional 344 vertical feet to the summit. It's well worth the effort for a 360-degree panorama, sweeping from the White Mountains to the northeast and west across Vermont farms and forests rolling into the Green Mountains. A former fire tower has been shortened and transformed into an observation platform. Local history traces the road to a trail cleared in 1825 for the Marquis de Lafayette's visit—but the marquis was a day behind schedule and came no closer than a coffee shop on Main Street. The present road was built in the '30s by the Civilian Conservation Corps. This is one of Vermont's first state parks, good for camping, mountain

LAKE FAIRLEE INVITES A SWIM OR PADDLE.
Christina Tree

MUST SEE

The Saint-Gaudens National Historic Site

(603-675-2175; nps.gov/saga), Rt. 12A, Cornish, NH. Grounds open daily, dawn–dusk. Buildings open 9–4:30 daily late Memorial Day–late Oct.; a modest admission fee is good for a week; free under age 16. This glorious property with a view of Mount Ascutney includes the sculptor's summer home and studio, sculpture galleries, and formal gardens, which he developed and occupied between 1885 and his death in 1907. A visitors center features a 15-minute orientation film about the artist and his work. Augustus Saint-Gaudens (1848–1907) is remembered primarily for public pieces: the Shaw Memorial on Boston Common, the

"LITTLE STUDIO" IN THE GARDENS AT SAINT-GAUDENS NATIONAL HISTORIC SITE

statue of Admiral Farragut in New York's Madison Park, the equestrian statue of General William T. Sherman at the Fifth Avenue entrance to Central Park, and the Abraham Lincoln in Chicago's Lincoln Park. He was also the first sculptor to design an American coin (the $10 and $20 gold pieces of 1907). His home, Aspet, is furnished much as it was when he lived there. Copies of some of the most famous works such as the Shaw Memorial, cast with the original molds, are displayed around the grounds. Augustus Saint-Gaudens loved the Ravine Trail, a quarter-mile cart path to his swimming hole along Blow-Me-Up Brook, now marked for visitors, and other walks laid out through the woodlands and wetlands of the Blow-Me-Down Natural Area. Saint-Gaudens was the center of the "Cornish Colony," a group of poets, artists, landscape designers, actors, architects, and writers who included Ethel Barrymore, Charles Dana Gibson, Finley Peter Dunne, and Maxfield Parrish; President Woodrow Wilson's first wife, Ellen, a painter, was drawn into this circle, and the president summered at a nearby home from 1913 to 1915. *Note:* Bring a picnic lunch for Sunday-afternoon chamber music concerts, at 2 PM in July and August.

Hood Museum of Art (603-646-2808; hoodmuseum.dartmouth.edu), Dartmouth green, Hanover, NH. Open Tues.–Sat. 10–5, until 9 on Wed.; Sun. noon–5. Free. An outstanding collection of world-class art from almost every geographic area of the world and historical period. Featuring ninth-century Assyrian reliefs from the Palace of Ashurnarsipal II at Nimrod (present-day Iraq); European Old Master prints and paintings; two centuries of American paintings, portraits, drawings, and watercolors; American decorative arts; ancient and Asian objects; traditional and contemporary African, Oceanic, and Native American collections; cutting-edge contemporary art; and a stunning set of murals by José Clemente Orozco. Two floors of galleries, permanent collections, traveling exhibitions. Explore on your own or arrange for a tour by calling 603-646-1469. The Hood Museum of Art Shop has something for all ages and budgets.

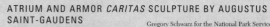

ATRIUM AND ARMOR *CARITAS* SCULPTURE BY AUGUSTUS SAINT-GAUDENS
Gregory Schwarz for the National Park Service

THE MONTSHIRE OFFERS PLENTY FOR VISITORS OF ALL AGES.

Montshire Museum

Montshire Museum of Science (802-649-2200; montshire.org), Exit 13, I-9, 1 Montshire Rd., Norwich. Open daily 10–5 except Thanksgiving and Christmas; June–Labor Day, $16 adults, $13 ages 2–17; otherwise $14 adults, $11 kids; members and children under 2 are free. Two-day passes are also available. Parking is free. Use of the outdoor exhibit areas, Woodland Garden, and trails is included with admission. Few cities have a science museum of this quality. This award-winning, hands-on science center with more than 140 exhibits is sited on 110 trail-webbed acres beside the Connecticut River. The name *Montshire* derives from blending *Vermont* and *New Hampshire*. The focus is on demystifying scientific phenomena, engaging your senses, and learning about the world around you. The elaborate 2.5-acre Science Park features water bubbling from a 7-foot Barre granite boulder, and from this "headwater" a 250-foot "rill" flows downhill, snaking over a series of terraces, inviting you to manipulate dams and sluices to change its flow and direction (visitors are advised to bring bathing suits and towels). You can also shape fountains, cast shadows to tell time, and push a button to identify the call of birds and insects. Note Ed Kahn's *Wind Wall*, an outdoor sculpture attached to the museum's tower, composed of thousands of silver flutter discs that shimmer in the breeze, resembling patterns on a pond riffled by wind. In the Hughes Pavilion overlooking Science Park, visitors may enjoy their picnic lunch or purchase lunch and snacks at the outdoor café (summer only).

The Montshire also serves as a visitors information center for the Silvio O. Conte National Fish and Wildlife Refuge; exhibits include a giant moose and tanks of gleaming local fish and turtles. Some of our favorite exhibits: the fog machine up in the tower, the see-through beehive, leaf-cutter ants, the physics of bubbles, and the planet walk. There are also astounding displays on moths, insects, and birds. Most exhibits are hands-on. While there's a corner for toddlers and many demonstrations geared to youngsters, this is as stimulating a place for adults as for their offspring. The Museum Store alone is worth stopping for. Inquire about special events, programs, summer camp, and visiting exhibitions. Check the website for events, programs, and special exhibits.

American Precision Museum (802-674-5781; americanprecision.org), 196 Main St., Windsor. Open Memorial Day weekend–Oct., 10–5 daily; $8 admission, $5 student, $20 family, free on Sun. The 1846 Robbins & Lawrence Armory, a National Historic Landmark, holds the largest collection of historically significant machine tools in the nation. In 1987 the American Society of Mechanical Engineers designated the museum an International Mechanical Engineering Heritage Site and Collection. At the 1851 Great Exposition in London's Crystal Palace, the firm demonstrated rifles made with interchangeable parts, the concept perfected at the Windsor armory. Based on that presentation, the British government ordered 25,000 rifles and 141 metal-working machines and coined the term *American System* for this revolutionary approach to gunmaking. Excellent special exhibits feature machine tools from the collection, tracing their impact on today's world.

THE AMERICAN PRECISION MUSEUM IN WINDSOR HOLDS THE NATION'S LARGEST COLLECTION OF HISTORICALLY SIGNIFICANT MACHINE TOOLS.

First Light Studios

biking, and hiking, and a popular launch spot for hang gliders.

Old Constitution House (802-674-6628; historicvermont.org), 16 N. Main St., Windsor. Open Memorial Day–Columbus Day, weekends and Mon. holidays 11–5. Nominal admission. This is Elijah West's tavern (but not in its original location), where delegates gathered on July 2, 1777, to adopt Vermont's constitution, America's first to prohibit slavery, establish universal voting rights for all males, and authorize a public school system. Excellent first-floor displays trace the history of the formation of the Republic of Vermont; upstairs is the town's collection of antiques, prints, documents, tools and cooking utensils, tableware, toys, and early fabrics. Special exhibits vary each year. A path out the back door leads to Lake Runnemede.

Christina Tree

OLD CONSTITUTION HOUSE, WINDSOR

COVERED BRIDGES At 460 feet the **Cornish– Windsor covered bridge**, linking Rt. 5, Windsor, and Rt. 12A, Cornish, is the country's longest two-span covered bridge and is certainly the most photographed in New England. A lattice truss design, built in 1866, it was rebuilt in 1989. There are three more covered bridges in Cornish, all dating from the early 1880s: Two span Mill Brook—one in Cornish City and the other in Cornish Mills between Rts. 12A and 120—and the third spans Blow-Me-Down Brook (off Rt. 12A). For the best view, turn left on Rt. 12A and look for the marked boat launch area a short way upstream.

✳ To Do

BALLOONING ✪ **Boland Balloons** (802-333-9254), Post Mills Airport, West Fairlee. Mid-May– mid-Nov., Brian Boland offers morning and sunset balloon rides. Boland builds as well as flies hot-air balloons (he's known internationally as a hot-air balloon designer) and maintains a museum with more than 150 balloons and airships—one of the largest collections in the world of flying contraptions you might never believe could fly—along with antique cars. Boland also maintains rustic cabins on the premises for patrons ($77 per night) and offers packages in conjunction with nearby Silver Maple Lodge (see *Bed & Breakfasts*). On the summer evening we last signed on, we floated above Lake Fairlee, over green shores and kids' summer camps and down over woods patched with cornfields, on toward the Connecticut River. On the Vermont bank, a dozen or so small figures were saluting the sunset with tai chi. We hovered briefly above an iron bridge and drifted southwest over New Hampshire woods, settling gently down in a Lyme hollow. Balloon rides are $260 per person. Even if you don't go for a ride it's worth taking a drive out Rt. 244 to Post Mills to see *Vermontasaurus*, a 122-foot-long, 25-foothigh dinosaur fashioned by Brian Boland, with the help of local students, using wood from his collapsed barn roof; a smaller dino beside him was born with the blowdown from the larger sculpture delivered by Hurricane Irene in 2011. When Boland is around, he permits visitors to tour the neighboring museum.

BRIAN BOLAND AND *VERMONTASAURUS* IN POST MILLS

Christina Tree

Also see **Balloons of Vermont** (balloonsof vermont.com) in "Woodstock/Quechee Area."

ROAD BIKING Given its unusually flat and scenic roads and well-spaced inns, this area is beloved by bicyclists. Search out the river roads: from Rt. 12A (just north of the Saint-Gaudens site) on through Plainfield, New Hampshire, until it rejoins Rt. 12A; from Rt. 10 north of Hanover, New Hampshire (just north of the Chieftain Motel), through Lyme, New Hampshire, rejoining Rt. 10 in Orford, New Hampshire. A classic, 36-mile loop is Hanover to Orford on Rt. 10 and back on the river road. The loop to Lyme and back is 22 miles. For inn-to-inn guided tours in this area, contact **Bike Vermont** (802-457-3553; 800-257-2226; bikevermont.com).

MOUNTAIN BIKING Sport Trails at Ascutney. The Sport Trails of the Ascutney Basin (STAB) volunteer organization maintains an evolving network of trails—also good for hiking, snowshoeing, and cross-country skiing—that is gaining an avid following among mountain bikers from Boston to Montreal. The 30-plus-mile network includes trails, with the prime access adjacent to the activity center at Ascutney Resort. Maps are available at the **Brownsville General Store** (see *Eating Out*) as well as around Windsor.

Paradise Sports (802-674-6742; paradisesportsshop.com), 38 Park Rd., Windsor. Bikes sold and fixed; some for rent.

BOATING With its usually placid water and scenery, the Connecticut River through much of the Upper Valley is ideal for easygoing canoeists and kayakers.

✎ **North Star Livery** (603-542-6929; kayak-canoe.com), Rt. 12A in Cornish, NH, will shuttle patrons to put-ins either 3 or 12 miles above the Cornish–Windsor covered bridge. North Star itself is New England's most picturesque canoe and kayak livery: The check-in desk is in the barn of a working farm. Full-day, half-day, and multiday trips are offered. This is the largest, oldest, and best-loved commercial rental service on the Connecticut River. Tubes, too.

Great River Outfitters (802-674-9944), 36 Park Rd. at the entrance to the Path of Life Sculpture Garden in the Simon Pearce/Harpoon complex north of the village of Windsor. Open daily, offering self-guided and guided canoe and kayak trips, shuttle service to Sumner Falls for a 4-mile paddle back down, also rafting, camping, and fishing.

The Ledyard Canoe Club (603-643-6709) in Hanover, NH, is Dartmouth's mellow, student-run canoeing and kayaking center. Rentals but no shuttle service.

Fairlee Marine (802-333-9745), Rt. 5 in Fairlee, rents pontoons, canoes, rowboats, and small motors for use on the Connecticut and two local lakes.

Information on seven primitive campsites along this stretch of the Connecticut River can be found on the **Upper Valley Land Trust**'s website: uvlt.org.

CAMPING See Wilgus and Mount Ascutney State Parks under *Green Space*. The Vermont State Parks reservation line operates weekdays: 888-409-7549.

FISHING You can eat the fish you catch in the Connecticut River—it yields brown and rainbow trout above Orford. There's a boat launch on the Vermont side at the Wilder Dam, another just north of Hanover, New Hampshire, and another across the river in North Thetford. Lake Mascoma (look for boat launches along Rt. 4A in Enfield, New Hampshire) and Post Pond in Lyme, New Hampshire, are other popular angling spots.

FITNESS CENTER Upper Valley Aquatic Center (802-296-2850; uvac-swim.org), 100 Arboretum Lane, junction of Rts. 89 and 91, White River Junction. Featuring a 25-meter competition training pool, three-lane lap pool, splash park with children's area, fitness center, and café. Open to the public.

GOLF Hanover Country Club (603-646-2000), Rope Ferry Rd., off Rt. 10, Hanover. Open May–Oct. Founded in 1899, an 18-hole facility with 4 practice holes, pro shop, PGA instructors.

Lake Morey Country Club (802-333-4800; 800-423-1211), Fairlee, has 18 holes.

HANG GLIDING Mount Ascutney State Park, Rt. 44A off Rt. 5, Windsor. Brownsville Rock, less than a mile by trail northwest of the Mount Ascutney summit, is a popular launch site. Note that a paved summit road accesses the trail.

HIKING Mount Ascutney offers the area's most dramatic hiking. Of the four trails to the summit, we recommend the 2.9-mile ascent from Weathersfield with an 84-foot waterfall about halfway (the trailhead is on Cascade Falls Rd., 3.5 miles north off Rt. 131). The 3.2-mile Brownsville Trail begins on

Rt. 44 between Windsor and Brownsville; the 2.7-mile Windsor Trail starts on Rt. 44A in Windsor. The 4.4-mile Futures Trail begins in Windsor State Park and links up with the Windsor Trail.

Also see **Sport Trails at Ascutney** (stabvt.org) under *Mountain Biking*.

Cross Rivendell Trail (crossrivendelltrail.org). Check the website for details and a map of this 36-mile trail across the Connecticut River Valley, from the Vermont hills above Vershire, running through West Fairlee, Fairlee, and Orford, New Hampshire, four towns that compose the bistate Rivendell School District. Pick up a map at Chapman's in Fairlee (see *Selective Shopping*).

Smarts Mountain via the Appalachian Trail. It's a roughly 3.5-mile hike to the summit from the parking area on Dorchester Rd in Lyme, New Hampshire. The parking area is just before the iron bridge. From the trailhead (marked in orange) follow the white blazes up the Lambert Ridge Trail (the AT) or the more gradual blue-blazed Ranger Trail. Both bring you to a spectacular view out across the valley. You can do a loop.

Fairlee Forest Trails. Fairlee boats over 35 miles of public trails with stunning mountain views, rushing streams, and an 80-plus-acre network of wetlands, many songbirds. Trail maps are available at Chapman's Country Store, Fairlee (see *Selective Shopping*).

HORSEBACK RIDING ❀ **Open Acre Ranch** (802-333-9196; openacreranch.com), 1478 Blood Brook Rd., Fairlee. Rebecca Guilette offers the increasingly rare chance to ride out through rolling farmland and back roads. Reasonably priced one-, two-, and four-hour trails rides are offered for riders of varying abilities; small children and beginner riders can ride in the ring. Private and group lessons. Trails web the 400-acre ranch and adjacent town forest.

SWIMMING Ask locally about swimming holes in the Connecticut River.

Kennedy Pond (Rt. 44 west) in Windsor has a small beach, great for kids. Inquire locally about numerous other swimming holes in the Black and Williams Rivers and about Twenty-Foot Hole (a series of cataracts and pools in a wooded gorge) in Reading.

❀ **Storrs Pond Recreation Area** (603-643-2134), off Rt. 10 north of Hanover, New Hampshire (Reservoir Rd., then left). Open June–Labor Day, 10–8. Bathhouse with showers and lockers, lifeguards at both the (unheated) Olympic-sized pool and 15-acre pond. Fee for nonmembers.

❀ ❀ **Treasure Island** (802-333-9615), on Lake Fairlee, Thetford. This fabulous town swimming area is on Rt. 244 (follow Rt. 113 north of town). Open late June–Labor Day, 10–8 weekends, noon–8 weekdays. Sand beach, picnic tables, playground, tennis. Nominal admission.

Union Village Dam Recreation Area (802-649-1606), Thetford. Open Memorial Day–mid-Sept.; five swimming areas along the Ompompanoosuc River. Also walking and cross-country skiing trails, picnic tables, and grills.

Also see *Fitness Center*.

✳ Winter Sports

CROSS-COUNTRY SKIING AND SNOWSHOEING Dartmouth Cross Country Ski Center (603-643-6534), Rope Ferry Rd. (off Rt. 10 just before the country club), Hanover, NH. Open in snow season Wed. 9–5, Tues.–Fri. 10–6, weekends 9–5. Twenty-five km of varied trails, some geared to skating, through the Storrs Pond and Oak Hill areas; rental skis, skates, and snowshoes.

Great River Outfitters (802-674-9944), 36 Park Rd. at the entrance to the Path of Life Sculpture Garden in the Simon Pearce/Harpoon complex north of the village of Windsor. A source of cross-country skis and snowshoe rentals with a 2.5-mile cross-country loop tracked for both classic and skating behind the shop in the riverside Path of Life Garden. Total access to trails on 100 neighboring acres with 45-minute dogsledding rides with or without snow; sleigh and wagon rides too. Inquire about winter tepee camping.

DOWNHILL SKIING ❀ **Dartmouth Skiway** (603-795-2143; skiway.dartmouth.edu), 39 Grafton Turnpike, Lyme Center, NH. An amenity for families as well as the college, with a snazzy 16,000-square-foot timber base lodge. Open 9–4 daily in-season; rentals and ski school. More than 100 skiable acres spread over two mountains, 30 trails: 1 quad chair, 1 double chair, a beginners' J-bar. Vertical drop: 968 feet. Snowmaking: 70 percent. Reasonable rates.

SKATING Lake Morey Resort (802-333-4311; lakemoreyresort.com), Club House Rd., Fairlee, The Upper Valley Trails Association, the Hulbert Outdoor Center, and the resort share maintenance of a

4.5-mile skate and broom trail; the resort rents skates and also maintains smaller rinks for recreation and hockey games.

✳ Green Space

✍ **Wilgus State Park** (802-674-5422; 802-773-2657), 1.5 miles south of I-91, Exit 8, Rt. 5, Windsor. Open Memorial Day–Columbus Day. This small, quiet campground on the Connecticut River is ideal for canoeists—the 17 tent sites, six lean-tos, and two cabins are on the riverbank. Car shuttle service available (see *Boating*); playground, picnic tables, hiking trails, also canoe, kayak, and rowboat rentals.

Ascutney State Park (802-674-2060). Open mid-May–mid-Oct., Windsor. Rising out of the Valley to an elevation of 3,144 feet, Mount Ascutney represents some 3,000 acres of woodland. The 3.8-mile paved Summit Road begins on Rt. 44A, off Rt. 5, between Ascutney and Windsor (see View from Mount Ascutney, above). Granite was quarried here as early as 1808. A total of 49 tent sites, trailer sites, and lean-tos can be reserved. Also see *Hiking*.

Paradise Park. Lake Runnemede in the heart of Windsor is circled by a 5.5-mile path set in this 177-acre preserve. It's best accessed from the Old Constitution House (see *To See*).

Path of Life Garden (pathoflifegarden.com), 36 Park Way, Windsor. Open year-round. $6 adults, $2 ages 4–12. Walk from the visitor-geared industrial park that's home to Simon Pearce and Harpoon Brewery—through a tunnel beneath the railroad tracks—and you are in a 14-acre meadow like no other. The path leads you through 18 distinct "rooms"—some resembling sculpture gardens but including a maze lined with 800 hemlock trees and a 90-foot rock labyrinth, huge dream catchers, a driftwood band, a granite Buddha, and more. A natural amphitheater is used for summer bonfires and drumming. A side path leads to the Connecticut River. Inquire about spending the night in one of the tepees. The creation of Norwich therapist Terry McDonnell, the garden is all about the circle of life and making life's decisions.

Pine Park, just north of the Dartmouth campus between the Hanover Country Club and the Connecticut River, Hanover, NH. Take N. Main St. to Rope Ferry Rd. Park at the trail sign above the clubhouse. These tall pines are one of the beauty spots of the Valley. The 125-year-old trees were saved from the Diamond Match Company in 1900 by a group of local citizens. The walk is 1.5 miles.

ġ **Montshire Museum of Science Trails,** Norwich. The museum's 110 acres include a 12-acre promontory between the Connecticut River and the marshy bay at the mouth of Bloody Brook. The 0.25-mile trail leading down through tall white pines to the bay is quite magical. The 1.5-mile Hazen Trail runs all the way to Wilder Village. These trails are hard packed, accessible to strollers and wheelchairs. See the museum sidebar for details about admission.

Thetford Hill State Park (802-785-2266; vtstateparks.com), 622 Academy Rd., Thetford Center. Open Memorial Day–Labor Day. Developed by the Civilian Conservation Corps in the 1930s, 177 acres with a campground (14 tent/trailer sites, two lean-tos, hot showers), hiking and cross-country trails (maintained by Thetford Academy).

See also **Quechee Gorge State Park** in "Woodstock/Quechee Area."

✳ Lodging

INNS AND HOTELS ◐ ☂ ✍ ġ **Norwich Inn** (802-649-1143; norwichinn.com), 325 Main St., Norwich 05055. Just across the river from Hanover and less formal and expensive than the Hanover Inn (below), this is very much a gathering place for Dartmouth parents, faculty, and students. The present three-story, tower-topped inn dates from 1889 (when its predecessor burned). Joe and Jill Lavin are the current owners. The 38 guest rooms are divided among the main inn and two clapboard annexes in the rear. The 16 in the inn retain the antiques and charm of an old inn. Those in the annexes are individually, tastefully, and traditionally decorated but add current luxuries: gas fireplaces, spacious baths, and central air. Walker House, with 16 rooms, has an elevator to access the second floor. In Ivy Lodge, two of the four luxurious suites are pet-friendly. The inn's Jasper Murdock's Alehouse features 15 varieties of inn-made brews (see *Eating Out*). The dining rooms are open for breakfast, lunch, and dinner. Rates run $129–249. All three meals are served but not included. There is a $25 pet fee.

ġ **Hanover Inn** (603-643-4300; hanoverinn .com), 2 E. Wheelock St., Hanover, NH 03755. The 108-room brick Dartmouth-owned hotel on the green has been recently renovated down to its 1902 studs, the decor transformed from neo-Colonial to sleekly, comfortably contemporary, featuring locally made furniture, furnishings, and art. It represents the ultimate luxury in Upper

Valley lodging. Rates are roughly $265–315, with honeymoon, ski, golf, and honeymoon packages. Handicapped accessible. See *Dining Out* for Pine, the inn's streetside restaurant.

Six South Street (603-643-0600; sixsouth.com), 6 South St., Hanover, NH 03755, is an attractive, 69-room hotel, a short walk from Dartmouth Green. Rooms from $169.

& **The Lyme Inn** (603-795-4824; thelymeinn .com), 1 Market St., Lyme, NH 03768. This classic inn has been rehabbed from top to bottom. An elevator now accesses nine rooms and five suites on the top three floors. Amenities include central air, gas fireplaces, and jetted tubs. There's a parlor on the first floor as well as **The Tavern** and the more formal **Garden Dining Room**. $225–400 includes a full breakfast.

& ✱ **The Hotel Coolidge** (802-295-3118; 800-622-1124; hotelcoolidge.com), White River Junction 05001. A beloved icon as New England's last railroad hotel, the Coolidge is also comfortable, clean, and reasonably priced. The hotel sits across from the Welcome Center/ Amtrak station, adjacent to the Briggs Opera House with shops and restaurants within walking distance. Local buses to Hanover and Lebanon stop at the door, and rental cars can be arranged. All 30 elevator-served guest rooms have private bath, phone, and TV and have been tastefully furnished. Some back rooms are dark, but others are quite roomy and attractive, and the family suites (two rooms connected by a bath) are a terrific value. The large, inviting lobby offers a guest computer. Search out the splendid Peter Michael Gish murals in the Vermont Room, painted in 1949 in exchange for room and board while the artist was studying with Paul Sample at Dartmouth. Owner-manager David Briggs, a seventh-generation Vermonter, takes his role as innkeeper seriously and will arrange for special needs. From $99–119 for most double rooms, $139–169 for two-room suites. Also see *Hostel*.

♂ ✱ & **Lake Morey Resort** (802-333-4311; 800-423-1211; lakemoreyresort.com), Club House Rd., Fairlee 05045. On the shore of Lake Morey, this sprawling, lakeside landmark best known for its golf course is also a winter destination for ice skaters. In summer supervised children's programs are included with MAP. Landscaped grounds and reception areas add up to a wedding venue. The resort dates from the early 1900s and was owned by the Avery family for some 20 years beginning in the 1970s, then sold but since reclaimed. The 130 rooms and suites vary from cozy and old-fashioned in the original building to spacious and balconied in the newest wing. The splendid lake view remains key, along with a player-friendly 18-hole golf course. Facilities include an indoor swimming pool, Jacuzzi, sauna, fitness center, and spa. There are also tennis courts. All three

VIEW FROM A ROOM AT THE LAKE MOREY RESORT

Christina Tree

Christina Tree

THE SNAPDRAGON INN IS A B&B IN A
HISTORIC WINDSOR HOME.

meals are served. Winter EP rates include up to two children sharing a room with parent: $105–149 per room and $179–270 for suites. MAP per-person summer and fall rates are $192–259 with a $35–54 charge for children, depending on age. Inquire about golf and other packages, and about cottage rentals.

BED & BREAKFASTS

Listed from south to north

🍃 **Snapdragon Inn** (802-227-0008; snap dragoninn.com), 26 Main St., Windsor 05089. This graceful brick mansion was built in 1815 and eventually formed the core of an estate that included several homes and 1,000 acres. Its best-remembered owner was Max Perkins, legendary editor to Thomas Wolfe, Ernest Hemingway, and F. Scott Fitzgerald. You can read their work in the library, a spacious, comfortable fireplace-centered room that's also stocked with board games. The nine second- and third-floor guest rooms are spacious and sparely furnished with an eye to light and comfort; the king or queen beds are fitted with feather comforters, and there are desks and fresh flowers. Baths feature heated tile floors and L'Occitane amenities. A European-style buffet breakfast is set out in the rose-colored dining room, included in the rates: $269–319. A path leads from the garden to Lake Runnemede (see Paradise Park in *Green Space*).

🐾 **The Pond House at Shattuck Hill Farm** (802-484-0011; pondhouseinn.com), P.O. Box 234, Brownsville 05037. This 1830s Cape sits beside its barn on a steeply rising back road near Mount Ascutney, with views across its pond and fields to mountains. There are three guest rooms, sparely, tastefully furnished, each with private bath. Gretel Schuck is an avid cook

with a passion for northern Italian; breakfast is full, and dinner is three courses. Guests dine together in the square dining room with its pumpkin pine floors and original six-over-six window. Gretel is also a cyclist and directs guests to back roads, also good for horseback riding. Horses and polite dogs can be accommodated. $150 includes breakfast and dinner.

♂ **Sumner House** (802-222-3366; sumner mansioninn.com), 4 Station Rd., Hartland 05048. This is a splendid brick mansion, built in 1807 with a wing housing spacious, bright common space added in the 1970s. It's recently been totally renovated and refurnished with antiques. The space seems designed for weddings and receptions, also for small groups of a dozen or less who want to get together for an event (as a group recently did for the Super Bowl), but it also works as a great place for a couple to stay. $175–245 per room with a full breakfast; $1,000 for the whole inn.

🍃 **Butternut Lane Bed and Breakfast** (802-649-1549; butternutbnb.com), 32 Butternut Lane, Norwich 05055. This splendid Federal-style yellow-brick home stands on a bluff overlooking the Connecticut River. Set in 38 acres that include flower and veggie gardens, it was built in 1821 by George and John Loveland. Your hosts are Carol and George Loveland. Still in the same family, the house with its wide-pine floors, 12-over-12-pane windows (many with original glass), and extensive paneling has been lovingly preserved. The two spacious front upstairs guest rooms, each with a private bath, command river views; the third ground-floor guest room also has a private bath. There are two parlors to relax in (one with TV/DVD) and a library. $120–140 per couple includes a generous breakfast. The grounds offer canoe or kayak access to the river.

Breakfast-on-the-Connecticut (603-353-444; breakfastonthect.com), 651 River Rd., Lyme, NH 03768. Built in the 1990s as a B&B with 15 rooms and suites, on a leafy knoll above the river but with access, kayaks, and canoes for guests. $115–186 for rooms, $199–250 for suites.

♂ 🐾 🍃 **Loch Lyme Lodge** (603-795-2141; lochlymelodge.com), 70 Orford Rd., Lyme, NH 03768. Location! Location. This grouping of 21 very rustic cabins on 120 acres has its loyal following of longtime patrons but, judging from online reviews, the appeal is primarily for families with young children, given the outdoor space and Post Pond with its grassy beach. There are 11 B&B and 11 efficiency cabins. The roadside home here is a venue for breakfast, a lunch bar, and dinner served late June–Labor Day. From $190 per night in-season with breakfast for two; weekly rates. The property is owned by a group who hope to transform it into a co-housing site; see pinnacleproject.info.

🦆 🐾 ♪ ⅙ **Silver Maple Lodge & Cottages** (802-333-4326; 800-666-1946; silvermaplelodge .com), 520 Rt. 5 south, Fairlee 05045. Just south of the village on Rt. 5, Silver Maple was built as a farmhouse in 1855 and has been welcoming travelers for more than 80 years. Innkeepers and Vermont natives Scott and Sharon Wright have seven nicely appointed guest rooms in the lodge and eight separate, pine-paneled, shaded cottages. The farmhouse has exposed hand-hewn beams in the living room and dining room, where fresh breads appear with other continental breakfast goodies. The newest cottages come with kitchenette and working fireplace. Play horseshoes, croquet, badminton, or shuffleboard on the lawn, or rent a bike or canoe. Scott will also arrange a ride in a hot-air balloon for you at neighboring Post Mills Airport. $89–119 per couple includes a continental breakfast. Pets are accepted in the cottages.

HOSTEL 🦆 ♪ **The Hotel Coolidge** (802-295-3118). A wing of the Coolidge, described under *Hotels*, is a Hostelling International facility with dorm-style beds and access to a self-service kitchen and laundry. Private family rooms are also available by reservation. $35–55 per person for non-HI-members.

✳ Where to Eat

DINING OUT Carpenter and Main (802-649-2922; carpenterandmain.com), 326 Main St., Norwich. Open for dinner except Tues. and Wed.; tavern 5:30–10, dining room 6–9; reservations suggested. An 1820s building at the heart of this village is the venue for chef-owner Bruce MacLeod's celebrated, locally sourced food. On a winter's night you might begin with a house pâté with cornichons or house-cured salmon, then dine on braised rabbit with sweet potato spaetzle and sautéed apples. Entrées $12–19 in the bistro and $25–38 in the formal dining rooms.

Jasper Murdock's Alehouse at the Norwich Inn (802-649-1143), 225 Main St., Norwich. Open for breakfast, lunch, and dinner except no breakfast, Mon.–Tues.; no lunch Mon. The same menu is available both in the inn's formal dining room and in the green-walled, comfortable pub, with seating that expands seasonally onto the flowery deck. The dinner menu might range from a smoked trout salad or vegetable strudel to ale-braised lamb shank with hazelnut

bread pudding and grilled Delmonico with Whistling Pig red ale demiglaze. The varied and widely respected house brews are available nowhere else. Dinner entrées $13–26.

Tip Top Café (802-295-3312; tiptopcafe vermont.com), 85 N. Main St., White River Junction. Open Tues.–Sat. 11:30–2:30 and 5–9. Reserve on theater nights (see Northern Stage under *Entertainment*). This is an elegantly casual glass-fronted bistro with an open kitchen on the ground floor of a former commercial bakery. Food is nicely plated with attention to veggies A fall menu might include ricotta fried dumplings and shrimp sausage gumbo. Lunch options might include creamy spinach crêpes and a turkey BLT. Entrées $16.95–23.85.

Elixir Restaurant and Lounge (802-281-7009; elixirrestaurant.com), 188 S. Main St., White River Junction. Tues.–Sat. 5–10:30. A casual but "night out" kind of place known for both cocktails and food, handy to Northern Stage and housed in the opposite end of a renovated railroad warehouse from Tupelo Music Hall. Dine on a butternut squash napoleon or cocoa-dusted petit filet mignon. Entrées $17–22. Patrons are also welcome to simply sip wine, beer, or cocktails.

○ **Canoe Club Bistro and Music** (603-643-9660; canoeclub.us), 27 S. Main St., Hanover, NH. Open daily for lunch and dinner with light fare between meals (2–5) and a bistro menu until 11:30, a real rarity in these parts. Reservations suggested for dinner. Acoustic music nightly, also Sunday jazz brunch. A must for decor alone, festooned with vintage canoes and Dartmouth memorabilia, and the food is dependably delectable. Lunch choices might include wild mushroom stroganoff, pulled pork quesadilla, and warm smoked sausage with port-braised cabbage. The dinner menu might offer "freeform lasagna" with housemade pasta and locally sourced veggies and cheese, or crispy pork schnitzel with porcini spaetzle, apple slaw, and Calvados sauce (both $16). Dinner entrées $13–26.

Pine (603-643-4300; hanoverinn.com), 2 E. Wheelock St., Hanover. Open daily for all three meals. Named for the lone tree in the Dartmouth College logo, this casually elegant streetside restaurant has quickly become a popular rendezvous. There's an inviting bar just inside the door, a leather sofa and armchairs by the open hearth at its center, and large Palladian-style windows overlooking both the green and South Main Street. The wide-ranging menu, orchestrated by locally rooted Justin Dane, ranges from sandwiches to memorable examples of flavor and texture such as locally raised chicken, basted with lemon thyme, serve with broccoli rabe, crispy pancetta, and potatoes. Dinner entrées $22–35.

Peyton Place (603-353-9100; peytonplace restaurant.com), 454 Main St. (Rt. 10), Orford, NH. Open for dinner Wed.–Sun. 5:30–10:30; in the off-season, Wed.–Sat. Reservations a must. Destination dining, this restaurant (named for owners Jim and Heidi Peyton) is housed in a 1773 tavern with a genuine old pub room—and a genuinely interesting pub menu—as well as more formal dining rooms. Dinner entrées might range from housemade vegetarian ravioli, Asian shrimp stir-fry, and steak fritters to rack of lamb with wild mushrooms. Ice creams and sorbets are handmade. Full bar. The pub menu might include housemade duck and chorizo dumplings, and quesadillas with tortillas made in-house. Dinner entrées $12–24. Inquire about cooking classes.

The Lyme Inn (603-795-4828; thelymeinn .com), 1 Market St., Lyme, NH. The tavern is open Wed.–Sun., 5 to close, Sun. brunch 11:30–2:20. The tavern fills much of the 18th-century part of this newly rehabbed old inn. The look and à la carte menu are traditional New England, from chicken potpie ($16) to center-cut pork loin chops ($26). Inquire about hours and menu for the more formal Garden Restaurant.

✪ ❀ ♪ **Ariana's Restaurant at Bunten Farm** (603-353-4405; arianasrestaurant.com), 1322 Rt. 10, Orford, NH. Open Mon., Wed., Thurs.–Sat. 5–9:30; Sun. brunch 10–1. Reservations suggested, a must on weekends, although chef-owner Martin Murphy tries to keep a table and sit-up bar at the open kitchen open for walk-ins. This is a small restaurant in the barn attached to one of the early brick farmhouses you see spaced along the Connecticut. The menu ranges from shepherd's pie (with local veal and cheddar), vegan curried rice, and a choice of pastas, to veal cassoulet (local veal osso buco and sausage), roasted dry sea scallops, and sirloin steak. Entrées $15–27.

EATING OUT

In and around Windsor

Windsor Stations and Barroom (802-674-4130; windsorstationvt.com), 27 Depot Ave., Windsor. Open for dinner except Mon. The town's handsome 1902 railroad station is back again as its go-to dining spot. The darkly paneled interior is brightened with art, divided between the "Lounge Car" with pub food, local beer and cocktails made with Vermont spirits, and the "Dining Car" with a more formal look and Italian-accented menu, from pastas (some

gluten-free) and chicken piccata to pan-seared tenderloin.

(ᵞ) **Red Barn Café** (802-674-677; redbarncafe .com), just off I-91, Exit 8, Ascutney. Open Tues.–Sat. 6–3. Family owned and locally popular with daily house-baked muffins, pies, cookies, and bread; also daily quiche, frittata, or strata. Daily specials and soups, the place for a sandwich or half sandwich and cup of soup. Save room for dessert.

Brownsville General Store (802-484-7450), Rt. 44 just west of the entrance to Ascutney Mountain Resort. Open Mon.–Sat. 6 AM–8 PM, Sun. 7–5. A general store with busy gas pumps but also with a big red Aga cookstove behind the lunch counter, a clue to the quality of Amy Yaten's soups and daily specials like chicken and biscuits. Bread is fresh baked, and there's a full deli. Note the solar-powered model train at the far end of the store.

♪ **Windsor Diner** (802-674-5555), 135 Main St., Windsor. Open daily 6 AM–8 PM. This spiffed-up 1952 classic Worcester diner (#835) serves good, honest diner food: meatloaf, liver and onions, and macaroni and cheese, along with omelets, burger baskets, pies, and more.

Riverbend Taps and Beer Garden (802-674-4591, ext. 221; harpoonbrewery.com), 336 Ruth Carney Dr., off Rt. 5 between Exit 9 and downtown Windsor. Open daily May–Oct., Sun.–Wed. 10–6, Thurs.–Sat. 10–9; Nov.–Apr., Tues., Wed. 10–6, Thurs.–Sat. 10–9, Sun. 10–6. Founded in Boston and still Boston based, Harpoon has transformed the former Catamount

RIVERBEND TAPS AND BEER GARDEN, WINDSOR

Christina Tree

Brewery into the town's largest and liveliest gathering place/informal restaurant. In summer it expands with outside tables. Brews on tap change with the season. The menu is basic pub with daily specials. Patrons (over 21 years) are welcome to sample up to four kinds. It's an attractive space with a glass wall overlooking the lawn and picnic tables, a two-sided hearth, and table as well as bar seating. Check the website or inquire about frequent music, special events, and hour-long brewery tours Fri.–Sun.

✿ **Skunk Hollow Tavern** (802-436-2139; skunkhollowtavern.com), 12 Brownsville Rd., Hartland Four Corners (off Rt. 12 south of Rt. 4, north of I-91, Exit 9). Dinner Wed.–Sun., more days during peak periods. Reservations suggested. This split-personality restaurant, hidden away in a small village, is a local favorite. Patrons gather downstairs in the pub to play darts and to munch on fish-and-chips or pizza; the more formal dining is upstairs in the inn's original parlor. The menu changes every few months, but staples include Chicken Carlos. Variables might be red pepper shrimp with Oriental pasta, or shiitake chicken; always salad of the day and homemade soups. Open-mike night Wed. and entertainment Fri. nights. Entrées $12.75–29.

In White River Junction

✿ ♪ ♿ ((ᵧ)) **Tuckerbox** (802-359-4041; tuckerbox vermont.com), 1 S. Main St. Open Tues.–Sat. 7 AM–10 PM, Mon. 7–5. Closed Sun. A great little oasis with Turkish and Mediterranean specialties, traditional kebabs, falafels, meze platters, and delectable hot appetizers like crispy pastry rolls filled with Turkish white cheese or sausage and cheese. $14–21; $28 for the mixed grill kebab made for sharing.

Also see **Tip Top Café** under *Dining Out*; it's a pleasant, reasonably priced lunch option.

((ᵧ)) **BoHo Café & Market** (802-296-2227), 39 Main St. Open 8–5 weekdays. A cheerful deli/café in the Hotel Coolidge, good for coffee, chai, freshly made soups, sandwiches, salads, and take-home casseroles.

Big Fatty's BBQ (802-295-5513), 186 S. Main St. Open except Tues. 11–9. Wide choice of BBQ plus a welcome salad bar; try the Piggy Sampler Platter, which comes with coleslaw, baked beans, and mac-and-cheese ($13).

In Norwich

King Arthur Flour Baker's Store (802-649-3361; kingarthurflour.com) 135 Rt. 5. Open daily 7:30–6. Inside this flagship campus, best known for its store and baking classes, a

spacious café is filled with the aroma of warm fresh breads, pizza, and tasty pastry pickings. Hot breakfast choices and a full lunch that includes soups and salads; espresso bar and kids' menu.

Note: **The Norwich Farmers Market** (norwichfarmersmarket.org) is Sat. 10–1, May–Oct., on Rt. 5, 1 mile south of the village. It's unusually big and colorful with 50 vendors, many baked goods. Winter markets are indoors at Tracy Hall, the first Sat. of each month. Check the website.

In Hanover, New Hampshire

✿ ♞ ♪ **Lou's Restaurant and Bakery** (603-643-3321; lousrestaurant.net), 30 S. Main St. Open for breakfast weekdays from 6 AM, Sat. and Sun. from 7. Lunch Mon.–Sat. until 3 PM. Since 1947 this has been a student and local hangout, and it's great: a long Formica counter, tables and booths, fast, friendly service, good soups, sandwiches, pies, daily specials, and irresistible peanut butter cookies at the register. At breakfast go for artery cloggers like poached eggs on corned beef hash or a virtuous egg white and goat cheese omelet. Lots of choices here.

♞ ♪ **Molly's Restaurant & Bar** (603-643-2570), 43 Main St. Open daily for lunch and dinner. The greenhouse up front shelters a big, inviting bar that encourages single dining. The menu is immense and reasonably priced: big salads, enchiladas, elaborate burgers at lunch, pasta to steak at dinner.

Sushiya (603-643-4000), 72–73 S. Main St. A bright lime-and-tangerine venue for authentic Korean bibimbap and kimchi and better-than-average sushi.

Morano Gelato (603-643-4233; moranogelato.com). 56 S. Main St. The creation of Morgan Morano, who grew up in Hanover but perfected her skills over years of working in Italian gelaterias, this has been hailed in *Forbes* magazine as the best gelato in America.

Umpleby's Bakery & Café (603-643-3030; umplebys.com), 3 South St. A Vermont migrant from the Bridgewater Mill, still offering the Valley's best croissants; also from-scratch soups and sandwiches on housemade bread.

Also see the **Canoe Club** under *Dining Out*, a great spot for lunch.

In East Thetford

♪ **Isabell's Café** (802-785-4300), 3052 Rt. 5. Open Tues.–Sat. 7–2. Beverly and Don Hogdon work together in this bright and cheery breakfast/lunch oasis just off I-91, Exit 14. A shelf of toys keeps young diners happy.

In Lyme, New Hampshire

Stella's Kitchen & Market (603-795-4302; stellaslyme.com), 5 Main St. Lunch and dinner except Mon. A spacious and sleek dining room hung with local art, a great, reasonably priced find for both meals. Check the menu online.

In Fairlee

Whippi Dip (802-333-3730), 158 Rt. 5. Open seasonally 6 AM–9 PM. A take-out known for BBQ and generally good food as well as hard and soft ice cream. Try the World's Fair Sundae: fried dough topped with vanilla ice cream, maple syrup, mixed nuts, and whipped cream. Inquire about outdoor barbecues, first Saturdays, noon–6.

Fairlee Diner (802-333-3569), Rt. 5. Closed Tues., otherwise 5:30 AM–2 PM; until 7 PM Thurs. and 8 PM Fri. Turn left (north) on Rt. 5 if you are coming off I-91. This is a classic wooden diner built in the 1930s (across the road from where it stands), with wooden booths, worn-shiny wooden stool tops, and good food. The mashed potato doughnuts are special, and both the soup and the pie are dependably good. Daily specials. No credit cards.

Leda's Restaurant & Pizza (802-333-4773), Rt. 5. Open daily for lunch and dinner. This is a friendly standby for Greek specialties like moussaka, gyros, and feta cheese pie along with burgers, pizza, and even rib-eye steak.

Note: See the **Fairlee Drive-In** under *Entertainment* for the best burgers in town.

COFFEE PLUS ((y)) **Boston Dreams** (802-230-4107), 7 State St., Windsor. A "sports gallery," with walls hung with mostly Red Sox photos and

THE FAIRLEE DINER

Christina Tree

memorabilia (for sale), also espresso, smoothies, Gifford's ice cream, more. Try the maple latte.

♪ ((y)) **Cedar Circle Farm** (802-785-4737; cedarcirclefarm.org), 225 Pavillion Rd., just off Rt. 5, East Thetford, offers coffee and more.

✳ Entertainment

MUSIC AND THEATER Hopkins Center for the Arts (box office 603-646-2422; hop .dartmouth.eduperformances), on the Dartmouth green, Hanover, NH. Sponsors musical and theater productions and films, all open to the public.

Lebanon Opera House (603-448-0400), town hall, Coburn Park, Lebanon, NH. This 800-seat, turn-of-the-20th-century theater hosts frequent concerts, lectures, and performances by the North Country Community Players. Throughout the month of August, **Opera North** (opera north.org) stages excellent performances featuring soloists from major opera companies.

♪ **Northern Stage** (802-296-7000; northern stage.org), Briggs Opera House, 12 N. Main St., White River Junction. Northern Stage is a professional nonprofit regional theater company that produces six main-stage shows Oct.–May in a theater with a three-quarter-thrust stage and 245 seats. Productions include dramas, comedies, musicals, as well as brilliant, lesser-known works and new plays fresh from Broadway and London's West End.

Tupelo Music Hall (803-698-8341; tupelohall vermont.com), 88 S. Main St., White River Junction. An intimate venue for a variety of music events and many nationally known musicians. Check the website for schedule, seating arrangements, and tickets.

The Parish Players (802-785-4344), based in the Eclipse Grange Hall on Thetford Hill, is the oldest community theater company in the Upper Valley. Its Sept.–May repertoire includes classic pieces and original works; summer presentations vary.

FILM *♪* **Fairlee Drive-In** (802-333-9192), Rt. 5, Fairlee. Summer only; check local papers for listings. This is a beloved icon, the last of the Valley's seasonal drive-ins. It's attached to the Fairlee Motel and has a famously good snack bar featuring "thunderburgers," made from beef on the family's farm across the river in Piermont. The gates open nightly at 7; films begin at dusk.

Dartmouth Film Society at the Hopkins Center (603-646-2576), Hanover, NH. Frequent showings of classic, contemporary, and experimental films in two theaters.

Nugget Theaters (603-643-2769), S. Main St., Hanover, NH. Four current films nightly, surround sound.

The Main Street Museum (mainstreet museum.org), 58 Bridge St., White River Junction, is a venue for film, music, and lectures. Check its website.

✳ Selective Shopping

Note: First Fridays of every month, galleries and a number of other venues in White River Junction and Lebanon, New Hampshire, host music, refreshments.

Cider Hill Gardens & Art Gallery (802-674-5293; ciderhillgardens.com), 1747 Hunt Rd., 2.5 miles west of State St., Windsor. Open May–June, daily 10–6; July–Oct., Thurs.–Sun. 10–6. Sarah Milek's commercial display garden is the setting for Gary Milek's studio, featuring his striking Vermont landscapes done in egg tempera, botanically correct floral prints, and stunning cards made from them. Check the website for special events—talks, tours, and exhibits—held every month May–July.

Simon Pearce Glass (802-674-6280; simon pearce.com), 109 Park Rd., off Rt. 5, north of Windsor. Open daily 10–5. Pearce operated his own glassworks in Ireland for a decade and moved here in 1981, acquiring the venerable Downer's Mill in Quechee and harnessing the dam's hydropower for the glass furnace (see "Woodstock/Quechee Area"). He subsequently

built this additional, 32,000-square-foot facility down by the Connecticut River. Designed to be visitor-friendly, it includes a catwalk above the factory floor—a fascinating place from which you can watch glass being blown and shaped. Of course there's a big showroom/shop featuring seconds as well as first-quality glass and pottery. The pottery shed next door is also open to visitors.

Sustainable Farmer (802-674-4260; my sustainablefarmer.com), 71 Artisans Way, Windsor. This large barn of a store features locally made honey, cheeses, and syrup, also Walpole Creamery ice cream. This space is the prime outlet for **Farmstead Cheese Company** (vermontfarmstead.com), crafted in nearby South Woodstock. A wide selection of Vermont cheeses and products with tastings; woodfired pizza (Fri.–Sun. 11–8)

Silo Distillery (silodistillery.com), 3 Artisans Way, Windsor. Open daily 1–5. The signature spirit is Silo Vodka, made from Vermont grain. There's also Silo Whiskey from a fusion of Vermont corn, barley, and rye, gin, elderberry vodka, and bourbon. This is an attractive space with a fully licensed bar.

In White River Junction

○ ✿ **Lampscapes** (802-295-8044; lampscapes .net), 77 Gates St., White River Junction. Open Tues.–Sat. 10–5. Kenneth Blaisdell is a former engineer and a serious landscape artist whose combination studio/shop is one of the more

Artisans Park (artisanspark.net), Rt. 5 between downtown Windsor and 1-91, Exit 9. This former dairy farm has been transformed into the area's leading commercial attraction, the brainchild of Norwich therapist Terry McDonnell, who created the riverside **Path of Life Garden** (see *Green Space*). It's currently a clustering of locally based enterprises—currently eight—anchored by the **Simon Pearce Glass Factory Outlet** (see *Selective Shopping*) and **Harpoon Brewery**, which moved here after absorbing local Catamount beer and maintains

ARTISANS PARK OFFERS PLAY SPACE AS WELL AS SHOPPING, DINING, KAYAKING, MORE

Christina Tree

the popular **Riverbend Taps and Beer Garden**. Other establishments include **Great River Outfitters** (see *To Do*) as well as the **Sustainable Farmer** and **Silo Distillery** (described elsewhere in this section). In warm-weather months the property is hopping, with a children's play area and adult lawn games on landscaped grounds.

KENNETH BLAISDELL HAND-PAINTS
"LAMPSCAPES" IN WHITE RIVER JUNCTION

exciting shopping finds in town. The metal floor
and table lamps themselves are simple but artistic; the shades are definitely works of art, each
one-of-a-kind and ranging from luminescent lit-
eral to semi-abstract, truly striking landscapes,
priced within reasonable reach. Check out his
new "BreakLight" series.

❂ **Revolution, Vintage & Urban Used
Clothing** (802-295-6487; shoptherev.com), 25
N. Main St., White River Junction. The decor
alone is worth a visit. Kim Sousa offers an
exceptional mix of eclectic, funky vintage,
designer, and Vermont-made clothing plus footwear, jewelry, and accessories. Special events,
free espresso.

Tip Top Media & Arts Building, 85 North
St., White River Junction. A warren of 40 studios and changing galleries, worth a look.

In Norwich

❂ **King Arthur Flour Baker's Store** (802-
649-3361; 800-827-6836; kingarthurflour.com),
135 Rt. 5. Open daily 7:30–6. Home as well as
prime outlet for the country's oldest family-
owned flour company (since 1790), this store
draws serious bakers and would-be bakers from
several time zones. The vast store is a marvel, its
shelves stocked with every conceivable kind of
flour, baking ingredient, and a selection of
equipment and cookbooks, not to mention
bread and pastries made in the adjacent bakery
(with a glass connector allowing visitors to watch
the hands and skills of the bakers). Next door,
too, is the **King Arthur Baking Education
Center**, offering baking classes ranging from
beginner to expert, from making piecrust to
braided breads and elegant pastries. Also see
the café under *Eating Out*.

Dan & Whit's General Store (802-649-1602),
319 Main St. The quintessential Vermont

country store. Hardware, groceries, housewares,
boots and clothing, farm and garden supplies,
and a great community bulletin board: If they
don't have it, you don't need it.

The Norwich Bookstore (802-649-1114), 291
Main St., next to the post office. This is a light,
airy store with well-selected titles and comfortable places to sit. Staff are very knowledgeable.
Frequent readings, and a good children's
section.

Heading north

Pompanoosuc Mills (802-785-4851; pompy
.com), 3184 Rt. 5, East Thetford. Showroom
open daily 9–6, Sat. 11–5, Sun. noon–5. Dartmouth graduate Dwight Sargeant began building furniture in this riverside house, a cottage
industry that has evolved into a riverside corporate headquarters/factory with showrooms
throughout New England.

❀ (ᵞ) **Cedar Circle Farm** (802-785-4737;
cedarcirclefarm.org), 225 Pavillion Rd., just off
Rt. 5, East Thetford. Sept.–Oct., closed Mon.;
otherwise open daily. A major farm stand selling
the farm's vegetables and flowers, offering PYO
strawberries in June, blueberries in July, herbs
June–Sept., pumpkins in Oct. The farm store
also carries local cheeses, honey, syrup, organic
milk, yogurt, and ice cream, books, note cards,
and more. Coffee and WiFi are available in its
Hello Café.

Flag Hill Farm/Vermont Hard Cyder (802-
685-7724; flaghillfarm.com), Vershire. Vermont
Hard Cyder is produced on this 250-acre hilltop, organic family farm with panoramic views.
Sabra and Sebastian Ewing welcome visitors but

KIM SOUSA'S HIP REVOLUTION CLOTHING
STORE IN WHITE RIVER JUNCTION

need warning to dispense directions (MapQuest seems to have it wrong). Check out their sparkling Hard Cyder, Still Cyder, and Pomme-de-Vie at stores throughout Vermont.

✪ **Chapman's Country Store** (802-333-9709; chapmanstore.com), Fairlee. Open daily 8–6, 7–5 on Sun. Since 1924 members of the Chapman family have expanded the stock of this old pharmacy to include 10,000 hand-tied flies, wines, Mexican silver and Indonesian jewelry, used books, maple syrup, and an unusual selection of toys. It also incorporates Lee's Sport Center selling fishing licenses, USGS maps, and stand-up paddleboards as well as dispensing information about local hiking trails.

Farmer Hodge's (802-333-4483), 2112 Rt. 5 north, Fairlee. Open daily, a working dairy farm with registered Holsteins, housemade jams, jellies, pickles, maple, beans, and pancake mix, plus seasonal produce, gifts. We took home corn picked that morning at their farm across the road.

Christina Tree

CHAPMAN'S STORE IN FAIRLEE IS A MUST-SEE.

✳ Special Events

For details about any of these events, phone the town clerk, listed with information.

Mid-February: **Dartmouth Winter Carnival**, Hanover, New Hampshire. Thurs.–Sun. Ice sculptures, sports events, ski jumping.

June–August: Free outdoor concerts at Lyman Point Park in White River Junction (Wed.) and Quechee Village Green, Quechee (Thurs.).

July–August: Sunday (2 PM) **lawn concerts** at the Saint-Gaudens National Historic Site (603-675-2175) in Cornish, New Hampshire; free with admission to the grounds. Bring a picnic.

Fourth of July: **Independence Day Open Fields Circus**, Thetford. A takeoff on a real circus by the Parish Players. **Fourth of July celebration**, Plainfield, New Hampshire. Community breakfast, footraces, parade, firemen's roast beef dinner. Lebanon, New Hampshire,

stages the largest fireworks display in the area. Hartland has a wonderful Fourth of July parade with all-day activities on the town's recreation field. **Windsor Heritage Days** (weekend following July 4) celebrate Vermont's birthplace as a republic.

Early August: **Thetford Hill Fair**, Thetford Hill. Small but special: a rummage sale, food and plant booths, barbecue. **Cornish Fair** (cornishfair.org), midmonth, is an old-fashioned country fair with horse and oxen pulls, 4-H judging, midway, and live entertainment.

Saturday after Labor Day: **Glory Days of Railroad celebration** in White River.

Saturday of Columbus Day weekend: **Horse Sheds Crafts Fair**, at the Lyme Congregational Church, Lyme, New Hampshire, 10–4; also a **Fall Festival** lunch at the church.

Mid-December–Christmas: **Christmas Pageants** in Norwich and Lyme, New Hampshire.

COHASE

INCLUDING BRADFORD, NEWBURY, AND WELLS RIVER, VERMONT; PIERMONT, HAVERHILL, AND WOODSVILLE, NEW HAMPSHIRE

Cohase is an Abenaki word meaning "wide valley." That's according to the chamber of commerce by that name that now embraces this gloriously little-touristed 15-mile stretch on both sides of the Connecticut River, north of the Upper Valley.

Its southernmost towns are sleepy Piermont, New Hampshire, and (relatively) bustling Bradford, Vermont, built on terraced land at the confluence of the Waits River and the Connecticut. Bradford is a 19th-century mill village that produced plows, paper, and James Wilson, an ingenious farmer who made America's first geographic globes. Low's Grist Mill survives across from the falls, now housing a popular restaurant; a golf course spreads below the business block across the floodplain. From Bradford the view across the river encompasses Mount Moosilauke, easternmost of the White Mountains.

Moving upriver, Haverhill, New Hampshire, and Newbury, two of northern New England's most handsome and historic towns, face each other across the river.

Haverhill is immense, comprising seven very distinct villages, including classic examples of both Federal-era and railroad villages. Thanks to a fertile floodplain, this is an old and still prosperous farming community. Haverhill Corner, New Hampshire, was founded in 1763 at the western terminus of the Coos Turnpike that wound its way up the Baker Valley and over the mountains from Plymouth. It became the Grafton County seat in 1773; a graceful 19th-century courthouse has recently been restored as a performance and information center. The village itself is a gem: a grouping of Federal-era and Greek Revival homes and public buildings around a double, white-fenced common.

Just north of Haverhill Corner (but south of the junction of Rts. 10 and 25) a sign points the way down through a cornfield and along the river to the site of the Bedell Bridge. Built in 1866, this was one of the largest surviving examples of a two-span covered bridge, until it was destroyed by a violent September windstorm in 1979. The site is still worth finding because it's a peaceful riverside spot, ideal for a picnic.

In North Haverhill, New Hampshire, you come unexpectedly to a lineup of modern county buildings—the courthouse, a county home, and a jail—and then you are in downtown Woodsville, New Hampshire, a 19th-century rail hub with an ornate 1890s brick Opera Block and three-story, mustard-colored railroad station. The Haverhill–Bath covered bridge, built in 1829 and billed as the oldest covered bridge in New England, is just beyond the railroad underpass (Rt. 135 north).

Newbury is one of Vermont's oldest towns, founded in 1761 by Jacob Bayley, a Revolutionary War general still remembered as the force behind the Bayley-Hazen Road, conceived as an invasion route northwest to Canada. It was abandoned two-thirds of the way along, but after the Revolution it served as a prime settlement route. A plaque at the northern end of the business block in Wells River (a village in Newbury) notes the beginning of the trail, while another in Hazen's Notch marks its terminus. Newbury was the site of a Native American village for many thousands of years, and its mineral springs drew travelers as early as 1800. Wells River marked the head of navigation on the Connecticut through the 1830s. In the 1840s river traffic was upstaged by the railroad, which transformed

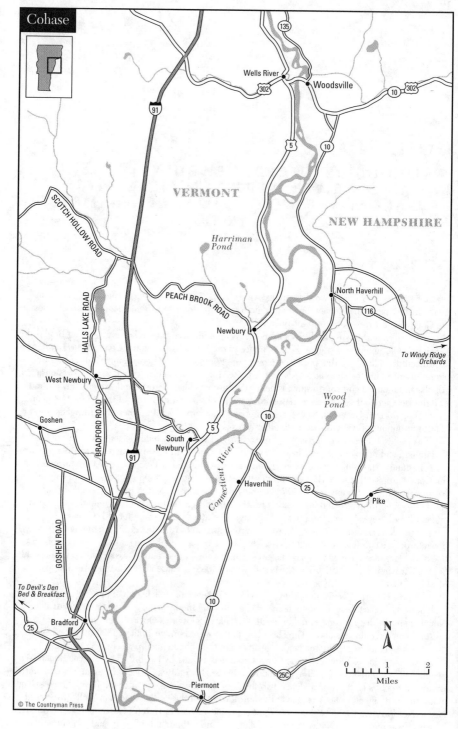

Cohase

© The Countryman Press

Woodsville. Wells River and Woodsville (the two are linked by a brief bridge) still represent a major highway junction (east–west Rt. 302 meets north–south Rt. 5, Rt. 10, and I-91), and some seriously good road food.

GUIDANCE Cohase Regional Chamber of Commerce (802-439-3797; cohase.org) publishes a helpful map/guide and maintains a seasonal welcome center in Wells River, just west of the bridge on Rt. 302.

GETTING AROUND Familiar as we are with both sides of the river here, it's difficult to decide whether Rt. 5 in Vermont or Rt. 10 in New Hampshire is prettier. The local slogan is "Take 5 (north) and Hang 10 (back south)." The bridges along this reach of the river are between Piermont, NH, and Bradford, VT; Haverhill, NH, and Newbury, VT; and Woodsville, NH, and Wells River, VT.

✹ To Do

BALLOONING See **Boland Balloons** in "Upper Valley River Towns."

BICYCLING Given the beauty of the landscape and the little-trafficked, level nature of Rt. 10 and of this stretch of Rt. 5, the appeal to bicyclists is obvious. It was cyclists who came up with the local slogan "Take 5, Hang 10," suggesting that you take Rt. 5 up the valley and Rt. 10 down. Less obvious are the long-distance routes that draw serious cyclists up over the White Mountains on Rts. 116 and 25.

BOATING Hemlock Pete's Canoes & Kayaks (603-667-5112; hpcanpes.com), Rt. 10, North Haverhill, NH. Scott Edwards teaches at the local high school and actually makes as well as sells and rents canoes and kayaks; guided tours, too. His shop is across from the fairgrounds.

GOLF Bradford Golf Club (802-222-5207), Bradford. Nine holes down by the river. **Blackmount Country Club** (603-787-6564; blackmountcountryclub.com), 400 Clark Rd., North Haverhill, NH. Cart rentals, driving range, practice green. A par-36, nine-hole golf course.

SWIMMING Lake Tarleton State Park, Rt. 25C in Piermont, Warren, and Benton, NH. More than 5,000 acres surrounding Lake Tarleton, smaller Lakes Katherine and Constance, and much of Lake Armington are now public land divided between White Mountain National Forest conservation trusts and a state park featuring the sand beach on Lake Tarleton (part of a onetime resort). The property was slated for major development in 1994 when preservation forces, spearheaded by the Trust for Public Land, raised more than $7 million to preserve this magnificent woodland with its views of Mount Moosilauke. The lake is stocked with trout and also beautiful for canoeing and kayaking (public boat launch). Hiking trails are taking shape, including a connector to the Appalachian Trail, which passes through the property half a mile from the lake.

✹ Lodging

Listed from south to north

🛏 ♂ ♿ **Piermont Inn** (603-272-4820; piermontinn.com), 1 Old Church St., Piermont, NH 03779. Open mid-May–early Sept. and for foliage. A 1790s stagecoach stop with six rooms, four in the adjacent carriage house (only the two in the inn are available year-round), all with private bath. The two in the main house are outstanding rooms, both carved from the tavern's original ballroom, high ceilinged and spacious, with writing desks and appropriate antiques. The carriage house rooms are simple but cheery; one is handicapped accessible. Common space includes a living room with a fireplace, TV, wing chairs, and a nifty grandfather clock. Charlie and Karen Brown are longtime Piermont residents who enjoy tuning guests in to the many ways of exploring this upper (less touristed) part of the Valley, especially canoeing the river. Rooms in the main

house are $139, and in the carriage house $99. A full breakfast is available in winter for $9. Small dogs welcome for a $20 fee.

♂ ♂ **The Gibson House** (603-989-3125; gibsonhousebb.com), 341 Dartmouth College Hwy. (Rt. 10), Haverhill, NH 03765. Open June–Oct. Innkeepers Susie Klein and Marty Cohen offer imaginatively decorated rooms in one of the Valley's finest Greek Revival homes, built in 1850 on the green in Haverhill Corner. The eight guest rooms, especially the four big second-floor rooms, are artistic creations, each very different from the next. Taj North is the most opulent and exotic with its faux balcony, rich colors, and glowing stained-glass moon. We enjoyed the golden, Asian-themed Bamboo Room, but our favorite is "A Day on the Beach," sunny, blue and white with a garden view. While the house fronts on Rt. 10, the 50-foot-long sunny back porch with wicker seats and swing takes full advantage of the splendid view west across the terraced garden and the Connecticut River. A full breakfast is served in the fanciful dining room. $145 weekdays, $175 weekends includes a full breakfast.

🐾 🍽 ♿ **Nootka Lodge** (603-747-2418; nootka lodge.com), 4982 Dartmouth College Hwy. (junction of Rts. 10 and 302), Woodsville, NH 03785. This attractive 34-unit log motor inn offers efficiencies, connecting rooms for families, and two-bedroom suites with Jacuzzi and fireplace. Amenities include TV, A/C, a pool, indoor whirlpool, and game room.

Also see **Lake Morey Resort** and **Silver Maple Lodge** in "Upper Valley River Towns," and **South Road Pottery** under *Selective Shopping*.

✴ Where to Eat

🍽 **Stone Mill Tavern** (802-222-3366; stone milltavern.com), 48 Main St., Bradford. Open daily, Mon.–Sat. 11–9, Sun. 2–9. Tavern 11–11. Housed in a historic brick mill by the falls (formerly The Perfect Pear) in the Waits River as you approach Bradford from the south. There are several venues here. The most appealing are overlooking the falls—on the deck in summer or beside a window inside upstairs. There is also a pubby, stone-walled tavern below. The menu includes soups, sandwiches, and burgers, also basic pub fare and reasonably priced entrées ranging from Thai veggie stir-fry to seared sea scallops Provençal. Dinner entrées $7.50–20.

The Hungry Bear Pub & Grill (802-222-5288), 776 Lower Plain, Bradford (Rt. 5 and

NEWBURY VILLAGE STORE

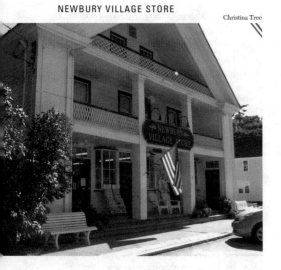

Christina Tree

I-91, Exit 16). Open for lunch through dinner daily. A lively sports bar and a casual dining room known for its burgers and steaks—but it's a big menu.

Colatina Exit (802-222-9008), Main St., Bradford. Open daily from 11. An expansive trattoria with a woodfired pizza oven and a choice of dining rooms; a few tables have a view of the river. The big menu offers plenty of antipasto, insalata, and pasta choices as well as traditional Italian dishes like chicken Marsala. Try the Robie Farm veal cannelloni and sausage served with fresh pasta. Plenty of pizza choices, panini, and calzones. There's also an upstairs pub with river views.

Bliss Village Store and Deli (802-222-4617), Main St., Bradford. Open 6 AM–7 PM. Housed in a former 19th-century hotel, this is a classic general store but with Crock-Pots full of soup, chili, or stew-fried chicken and a deli with daily specials. Tables are in the back—including a booth with the best river view in town.

Newbury Village Store (802-866-5681), 4991 Rt. 5, Newbury. Open 6 AM–8 PM weekdays, Sat. 6–9, Sun. 7–5. This is the new breed of general store with comfortable seating near the periodicals and a deli that features hot breakfast as well as other sandwiches. There are staple groceries, also a selection of wine and Vermont products. Note the **Thistle Café** in back, overlooking the Connecticut. Order sandwiches at the deli counter at lunch; burgers, creative pizzas, cheese steak, and supper menu from 5:30 most nights.

🍽 **The Happy Hour Restaurant** (802-757-3466), 42 Main St. (Rt. 5), Wells River. Open daily 11:30–8, later in summer. This large, pine-paneled family restaurant in the middle of town has been lightened and brightened in recent years and hums with a sense of friendly service and satisfied patrons. Most specials include the salad bar—and servings are generous. We couldn't finish a tender sirloin topped with red wine mushroom sauce, with baked potato and good coleslaw. Children's menu.

Saltwater Bar & Bistro (603-747-2365), 85 Central St., Woodsville, NH. Open Wed.–Thurs. 11–7, Fri.–Sat. until 9. Fairlee's loss (the owners ran the Holy Mackerel there) is Woodsville's gain. This attractive restaurant features fresh fish from lobster rolls to blackened swordfish. Entrées $11–21.

Shiloh's Cabin Cooking (603-747-2525), 202 Central St., Woodsville, NH. Open 7 AM–9 PM, closing Sun. at 2 PM. Nicole and Miranda Fenoff fill the need for good road food in Woodsville.

The beef and as many ingredients as possible are local. Great breakfasts.

P&H Truck Stop (802-429-2141), just off I-91, Exit 17, on Rt. 302, Wells River. Now open just 6 AM–10 PM for hot meals but still 24 hours for to-go premade sandwiches, pies, and the like. Dozens of rigs are usually parked on one side, and the range of license plates on cars in the other lot is often broad. This is a classic truck stop with speedy service, friendly waitresses, and heaping portions at amazing prices. Plus, the bread is homemade; ATM and phone are available (cell phones don't tend to work around here, and pay phones are scarce).

✳ Entertainment

Old Church Community Theater (802-222-3322; oldchurchtheater.org), 137 Main St., Bradford. For more than 20 years this community theater has presented seasonal, family-geared productions.

Alumni Hall (603-989-5500; alumnihall.org), 75 Court St., Haverhill Corner, NH. Open mid-June–mid-Oct., 10–4. Built gracefully in brick in 1846 as the Grafton County courthouse, later part of Haverhill Academy, it has been restored as a venue for concerts, lectures, performances, art shows, and the like. Check the website for upcoming programs and performances.

Summer band concerts can be found in Bradford, Woodsville, and Haverhill; for details see cohase.org.

✳ Selective Shopping

SPECIAL SHOPS ✪ Farm-Way, Inc. (800-222-9316), Rt. 25, Bradford. One mile east of I-91, Exit 16. Open Mon.–Sat. 8:30–5:30, until 8 PM Fri. Billed as "complete outfitters for man and beast," this is a phenomenon: a family-run source of work boots and rugged clothing that now includes a stock of more than two million products spread over 11 acres: tack, furniture, pet supplies, syrup, whatever. Now substantially solar-powered. Shoes and boots remain a specialty, from size 4E to 16; 25,000 shoes, boots, clogs, sandals, and sneakers in stock; also kayaks, sporting equipment, furnishings, and gifts.

Copeland Furniture (802-222-5300; copeland furniture.com), 64 Main St., Bradford. Open Mon.–Fri. 10–6, Sat. 10–5. Contemporary, cleanly lined, locally made furniture in native hardwoods displayed in a handsome showroom in the converted 19th-century brick mill across from Bradford Falls. Seconds.

Round Barn Shoppe (603-272-9026), 430 Rt. 10, Piermont, NH. Open June–Jan. 1, Thurs.–

Sun. 10–5; Jan. 2–June, Sat.–Sun. 10–5. This 1990s post-and-beam round barn replicates the authentic 1906 barn across the road. It houses a shop selling New England products ranging from baskets and dolls to smoked products and cheese plus ice cream, gelato, and fudge made on the farm.

North of the Falls (802-222-3500; north-of-the-falls.com), 148 Main St., Bradford. Open daily except Sun. An 1860s building houses this trove of primarily northern New England–made clothing, crafts, pottery, toys, and specialty foods.

Star Cat Books (802-222-5826), 157 Main St., Bradford. A browsing-friendly bookstore, both new and used titles.

South Road Pottery (802-222-5798; bruce murraypotter.com), 3458 South Rd., Bradford. Open May–Oct., 10–5. Bruce Murray is an established, nationally known potter whose studio/showroom is in a timber-frame 18th-century barn surrounded by farm fields. It's well worth the scenic drive to this exceptional, longtime studio with its wide variety of handmade and hand-decorated stoneware, both functional (lamps, vases, unusual butter dishes—really mini crocks that keep butter soft) and decorative (wall tiles and plaques). Inquire about workshops and about the **Barn Bridge Guest Room**, an attractive guest unit with a private deck, bath, and galley kitchen ($125 per night).

Note: This area is studded with artists and craftspeople who keep irregular studio hours but open for the Memorial Day state-wide crafts tour and again the first weekend in October (see *Special Events*).

FARMS Robie Farm & Store (603-272-4872; robiefarm.com), 25 Rt. 10, Piermont, NH. Six

BRUCE MURRAY IS A POTTER IN BRADFORD.
Christina Tree

generations of Robies have farmed this property. The farm store sells dairy beef, free from antibiotics and hormones; also low-fat and skim raw milk as well as pints of cream, plus eggs from free-range chickens. There's a variety of cheese, including Toma from their own raw milk, and ice cream made in small batches. Check the website for farm tours, hiking trails, and pontoon boat cruises.

Four Corners Farm (802-866-3342; 4corners farm.com), 306 Doe Hill Rd., just off Rt. 5, South Newbury. Bob and Kim Gray sell their own produce and flowers. An exceptionally pretty farm, just off but up above the highway, with a big farm stand. Known for strawberries, but always a trove of seasonal fruits and vegetables with year-round produce from their greenhouses, Christmas trees, PYO berries in-season.

Christina Tree
FOUR CORNERS FARM IN SOUTH NEWBURY

✔ **Windy Ridge Orchard** (603-787-6377; windyridgeorchard.com), Rt. 116, North Haverhill, NH. Open daily Labor Day–Thanksgiving, 9–6; weekends Thanksgiving to Christmas, 9–4. Pick your own apples and pumpkins, farm animals, kids corral playground, nature trails, picnic tables, **Cider House Café**, gift shop. Apple picking begins in mid-August and lasts through mid-October depending on the variety. There are 3,500 apple trees on 20 acres, overlooking the Valley and Green Mountains; also cut-your-own Christmas trees.

Look for seasonal **farmers markets** in **Bradford** (Sat. 9–1), **Piermont** (Tues. 3–6), and **Woodsville** (Fri. 4–7).

✳ Special Events

Memorial Day weekend: Open studio tours (cohase.org and vermontcrafts.com).

July: **Fourth of July Parade and celebration** in Woodsville and Wells River—marching bands, floats, horses, chicken barbecue, dancing, fireworks. **Connecticut Valley Fair**, mid-month, Bradford. Ox and horse pulling, sheep show, midway, demolition derby. **Cracker Barrel Bazaar**, third or final weekend, Newbury, includes fiddlers' contest, antiques show, quilt show, sheepdog trials, church suppers. The **North Haverhill (New Hampshire) Fair**, last weekend, is an old-style fair with ox and tractor pulls, pig races, and more.

October: First weekend: **Vermont North By Hand** (byhand.org). More than two dozen studios open, outstanding arts and crafts, a great excuse to explore back roads during peak foliage season in this area.

Central Vermont

3

WOODSTOCK/QUECHEE AREA

THE WHITE RIVER VALLEYS
Including the Towns of Randolph,
Sharon, Royalton, Bethel, Rochester,
Hancock, Braintree, Brookfield, Chelsea,
Tunbridge, and Strafford

SUGARBUSH/MAD RIVER VALLEY

BARRE/MONTPELIER AREA

KILLINGTON/RUTLAND AREA

Christina Tree

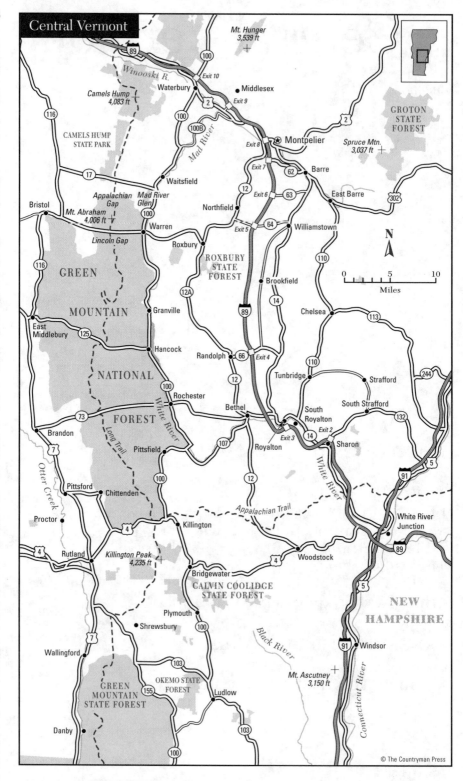

Central Vermont

Mt. Hunger
3,539 ft

Winooski R.
Waterbury
Exit 10
Middlesex

Camels Hump
4,083 ft
116

CAMELS HUMP
STATE PARK
100
100B

Mad River
Exit 9
Exit 8
Montpelier

Spruce Mtn.
3,037 ft

GROTON
STATE
FOREST

17
Waitsfield
Exit 7
62
Barre

302

Appalachian
Gap
Mad River
Glen
Northfield
12
Exit 6
63
East Barre

Bristol
Mt. Abraham
4,006 ft
100
Warren
Exit 5
64
Williamstown

Lincoln Gap
Roxbury
110

116
GREEN
ROXBURY
STATE
FOREST
Brookfield

MOUNTAIN
12A
Granville
89
14
Chelsea
113

East
Middlebury
125

NATIONAL
110

Hancock
Randolph
66
Exit 4
Tunbridge
Strafford
244

Rochester
12
100

White River
FOREST
73
Bethel
South
Royalton
South Strafford
132

Brandon
Long Trail
Pittsfield
107
Exit 3
Royalton
14
Exit 2
Sharon

7
Pittsford
Chittenden
100

Otter Creek
12
White River
91

Proctor
4
Appalachian Trail
White River
Junction

Killington
89

4
Rutland
Killington Peak
4,235 ft
4
Woodstock

Bridgewater
5
NEW
HAMPSHIRE

CALVIN COOLIDGE
STATE FOREST

Plymouth
Shrewsbury
100
Black River

91
Windsor

Wallingford
7
103

Mt. Ascutney
3,150 ft

GREEN
MOUNTAIN
STATE FOREST
155
OKEMO STATE
FOREST
Ludlow

Danby
103
100

Connecticut River

N

0   5   10
Miles

© The Countryman Press

WOODSTOCK/QUECHEE AREA

C radled between Mount Peg and Mount Tom and moated by the Ottauquechee (pronounced *otto-KWEE-chee*) River, Woodstock is repeatedly named among the prettiest towns in America. The story behind its good looks, which include the surrounding landscape as well as historic buildings, is told at the Marsh-Billings-Rockefeller National Historical Park, the country's only national park to focus on the concept of conservation.

The Ottauquechee River flows east through Woodstock along Rt. 4 toward the Connecticut River, generating electricity as it tumbles over falls beneath the covered bridge at Taftsville and powering Simon Pearce's glass factory a few miles downstream in Quechee Village. Below Quechee the river has carved Vermont's "Grand Canyon," Quechee Gorge, spanned by Rt. 4.

The Woodstock Railroad carried passengers and freight the 20 miles between Woodstock and White River Junction between 1875 and 1933. How to ease current traffic congestion, which includes 18-wheelers headed for Rutland as well as tour buses and tourists in summer and fall and skiers in winter, remains a very real challenge. Rt. 4 is the shortest way across "Vermont's waist," and an ever-growing stream of vehicles continues to wind up the valley, filing through the middle of Woodstock, around its exquisite green, and on through the village of West Woodstock, following the river west into Bridgewater.

Our advice: Walk. Park at the picnic area just beyond Quechee Gorge and savor the view of the river churning far below between 163-foot-high walls. Walk the path down to the water's edge or around VINS, the neighboring raptor and nature sanctuary. In Woodstock Village stroll the streets, then walk Mountain Avenue through Faulkner Park, on up to the top of Mount Tom, then back down the Pogue Carriage Road to Billings Farm.

Like most of the world's famously beautiful and heavily touristed areas, especially those that are also home to sophisticated people who could live anywhere, the Ottauquechee River Valley offers visitors plenty to see and do superficially and still more, the more you explore.

GUIDANCE The Woodstock Area Chamber of Commerce (802-457-3555; 888-496-6378; woodstockvt.com) maintains a friendly, staffed information center (802-432-1100) with restrooms on Mechanic St., marked from Central St. (the main shopping block), open weekdays, year-round, 9–5, 9–4 in winter. The chamber publishes *Window on Woodstock*, a useful free pamphlet guide. Lodging places post available rooms on the website of the chamber, which has been known to find beds during foliage season for stranded leaf-peepers. Restrooms are also available weekdays in the town hall, west of the green. Check the **Town Crier** blackboard at the corner of Elm and Central Sts. for current happenings.

The Quechee Gorge Visitors Information Center (802-295-6852; 800-295-5451; hartfordvt chamber.com) is maintained by the Hartford Area Chamber of Commerce, Rt. 4 at Quechee Gorge. Open year-round, 9–5 May–Oct., 10–4 off-season. This is a nice, well-stocked center with helpful staff and restrooms.

GETTING THERE *By car:* Rt. 4 west from I-91 and I-89.

For details about train, bus, and air, see *Getting There* in "Upper Valley River Towns."

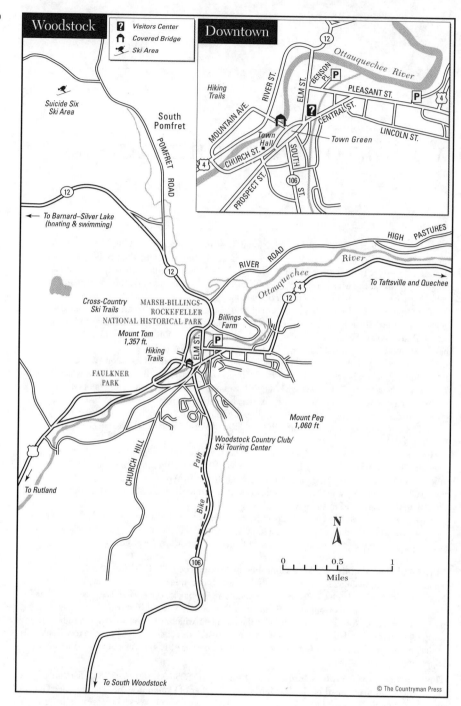

Woodstock

Legend:
- ? Visitors Center
- ⌂ Covered Bridge
- 🎿 Ski Area

Downtown

Suicide Six Ski Area

South Pomfret

POMFRET ROAD

12

To Barnard–Silver Lake (boating & swimming)

Hiking Trails

RIVER ST.

ELM ST.

BENSON PL.

P

Ottauquechee River

PLEASANT ST.

P

4

MOUNTAIN AVE.

Town Hall

? Town Green

CENTRAL ST.

LINCOLN ST.

SOUTH ST.

4 CHURCH ST.

PROSPECT ST.

106

HIGH PASTURES

RIVER ROAD

River

Ottauquechee River

4

12

To Taftsville and Quechee

Cross-Country Ski Trails

MARSH-BILLINGS-ROCKEFELLER NATIONAL HISTORICAL PARK

Billings Farm

Mount Tom 1,357 ft.

Hiking Trails

P

FAULKNER PARK

ELM ST.

CHURCH HILL

Mount Peg 1,060 ft

Woodstock Country Club/ Ski Touring Center

Bike Path

106

To Rutland

N

0   0.5   1
Miles

To South Woodstock

© The Countryman Press

PARKING This is a walk-around town in which the first thing you do is park. Two-hour meters on Central and Elm Sts. and four-hour meters on Mechanic off Central are closely monitored 10–4, Mon.–Sat.: 25¢ per half hour. Red drop boxes in front of the town's two pharmacies are provided to pay fines—but you can also bring a ticket to a merchant or restaurant in town and they will validate it (no fine!). There are free lots by the river on Pleasant St., behind the Norman Williams Public Library, and—on weekends only—at the elementary school on Rt. 106 south of the green.

WHEN TO GO This area is as genuinely year-round as Vermont gets. Marsh-Billings-Rockefeller National Historical Park and the Billings Farm & Museum are open May through mid-October, but Woodstock's early-December Wassail Weekend is its most colorful happening, and January through March bring cross-country and alpine skiing. The Quechee Hot Air Balloon Festival in June is the area's most famous event.

MEDICAL EMERGENCY Emergency service is available by calling **911**.

✳ Villages

Woodstock (population 3,048, including the village of South Woodstock and Taftsville). In the 1790s, when it became the shire town of Windsor County, Woodstock began attracting prosperous professionals, who, with local merchants and bankers, built the concentration of distinguished Federal houses that surround the elliptical green, forming an architectural showcase that has been meticulously preserved. In the 19th century it produced more than its share of celebrities, including Hiram Powers, the sculptor whose nude *Greek Slave* scandalized the nation in 1847, and Senator Jacob Collamer (1791–1865), President Lincoln's confidant, who declared, "The good people of Woodstock have less incentive than others to yearn for heaven."

Three eminent residents in particular—all of whom lived in the same house but in different eras—helped shape the current Woodstock (see the box in *Must See*).

"Innkeeping has always been the backbone of Woodstock's economy, most importantly since 1892 when the town's business leaders and bankers decided to build a new hotel grand enough to rival the White Mountain resorts," according to local historian Peter Jennison. By the turn of the 20th century, in addition to several inns, Woodstock had an elaborate mineral water spa and golf links, and it had become Vermont's first winter resort, drawing guests from Boston and New York for snowshoeing and skating. In 1934 America's first rope tow was installed here, marking the real advent of downhill skiing.

By the early 1960s, however, the beloved Woodstock Inn was creaky, the town's ski areas had been upstaged, and the hills were sprouting condos. Laurance Rockefeller acquired the two ski areas (upgrading Suicide Six and closing Mount Tom) and had the 18-hole golf course redesigned by Robert Trent Jones Sr. In 1969 he replaced the old inn. In 1992 his Woodstock Foundation opened the **Billings Farm & Museum. The Marsh-Billings-Rockefeller National Historical Park**, which includes the neighboring Rockefeller mansion and the 550 surrounding forested acres on Mount Tom, opened in 1998.

DOWNTOWN WOODSTOCK'S BUSIEST CORNER

Christina Tree

Woodstock itself remains a real town with a lot going on. Events chalked on the Town Crier blackboard at the corner of Elm and Central Sts. are likely to include a supper at one of the town's several churches (four boast Paul Revere bells), the current film at the theater in the town hall, as well as events at the historical society and guided walks.

Note: The Woodstock Historical Society has published detailed pamphlets and guides available at **Dana House** (see *Also See*).

Quechee (population 2,500) on Rt. 4, some 6 miles east of Woodstock, is one of five villages in the township of Hartford. In the mid- and late 19th century life revolved around the J. C.

Parker and Co. mill, which produced a soft baby flannel made from "shoddy" (reworked rags). A neighboring mill village surrounded the Deweys Mill, which made baseball uniforms for the Boston Red Sox and the New York Yankees. In the 1950s, however, both mills shut down. In the '60s the Deweys Mill virtually disappeared beneath a flood-control project, and 6,000 acres straddling both villages were acquired by the Quechee Lakes Corporation, the largest second-home and condominium development in the state. Thanks in good part to Act 250, Vermont's land-use statute, the end result is unobtrusive. Most homes are sequestered in woods; open space includes two (private) 18-hole golf courses. In Quechee Village the mill is now **Simon Pearce**'s famous glass factory and restaurant, and the former mill owner's mansion is the Parker House Inn. Dramatic **Quechee Gorge** is visible from Rt. 4 but is best appreciated if you follow the trail to the bottom. The **VINS Quechee Nature Center** is also here. Tourist-geared shops and eateries continue to proliferate along Rt. 4, but, along back roads, so does village conservation land.

Christina Tree

DAILY HAPPENINGS ARE POSTED ON THE TOWN CRIER IN DOWNTOWN WOODSTOCK.

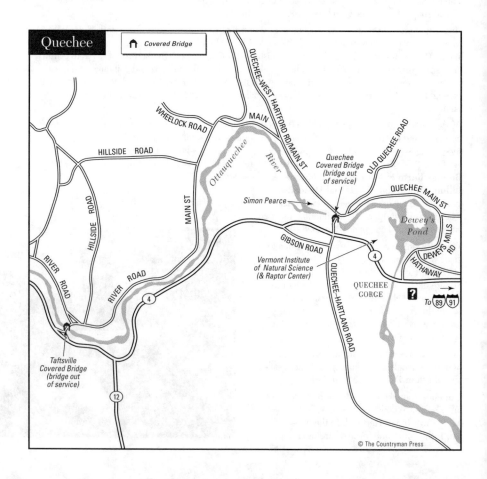

✳ Must See

Listed from east to west

Quechee Gorge, Rt. 4, is one of Vermont's natural wonders, a 3,000-foot-long, 163-foot-deep chasm sculpted 13,000 years ago. Visible from the highway, it is now encompassed by a state park that includes hiking trails along the rim and down into the gorge. See *Green Space*.

The Vermont Institute of Natural Science/Vermont Raptor Center (802-359-5000; vinsweb .org), 6565 Woodstock Rd. (Rt. 4), Quechee. Open 9:30–5 Apr.–Oct., 10–4 the rest of the year; also open holidays and school vacations. $13 adults, $12 seniors, $11 ages 4–17. A beloved institution devoted to rehabilitating birds of prey, VINS occupies 47 acres of rolling forestland just west of Quechee Gorge. Resident raptors include bald eagles, peregrine falcons, snowy owls, hawks, and other birds of prey that have been injured. They are displayed in huge outdoor flight enclosures. There are outdoor interpretive exhibits, nature trails, and a nature shop. Inquire about naturalist-led

GEORGE PERKINS MARSH (1801–82), FREDERICK BILLINGS (1823–90), AND LAURANCE ROCKEFELLER (1910–2005)

Three men in particular have helped shape Woodstock's landscape. The first, George Perkins Marsh, born and raised here, had damaged his eyesight by age 7 by devouring encyclopedias and books on Greek and Latin. Sent outdoors, he studied the woods, fields, birds, and animals with equal intensity. As a man he noted the effects of logging on the landscape (60 percent of Vermont's virgin forest was harvested in the first half of the 19th century) and the resulting floods and destruction of fisheries. Later, traveling in the Middle East as the U.S. ambassador to Turkey, Marsh noted how once fertile land had become desert. He wrote: "I fear man has brought the face of the earth to a devastation almost as complete as that of the moon."

Marsh wrote *Man and Nature* at age 63, while U.S. ambassador to Italy. Published in 1864, it is widely recognized as the first book to acknowledge civilization's effect on the environment, and the first to suggest solutions. In contrast with Henry David Thoreau (*Walden* appeared in 1854), Marsh doesn't idealize wilderness. Instead, he attempts to address the interdependence of the environment and society as a whole.

Man and Nature isn't an easy read, but it greatly influenced this country's nascent sciences of forestry and agriculture as well as many of the era's movers and shakers, among them Frederick Billings. Raised in Woodstock, Billings departed at age 25 for San Francisco. That city's first lawyer, he made a fortune registering land claims and speculating in land during the gold rush. As a returning son who had "made good," Billings spoke at the 1864 Windsor County Fair, remarking on the rawness of the local landscape, the hills denuded by logging and sheep grazing. In 1869 he bought the old Marsh farm and transformed the vintage-1805 house into a mansion. On Mount Tom he planted more than 100,000 trees, turned a bog into Pogue Pond, and created the carriage roads. Billings's primary home was in New York, and as president of the Northern Pacific Railroad (the reason Billings, Montana, is named for him) he toured the country extensively. He continued, however, to retreat to Woodstock, creating a model dairy farm on his property, a project sustained after his death, through thick and thin, by his wife and two successive generations of Billings women.

In 1934 Frederick Billings's granddaughter Mary French (1910–97) married Laurance Rockefeller in Woodstock. John D. Rockefeller Jr. had been largely responsible for creating more than 20 state and national parks and historic sites; Laurance inherited his father's commitment to conservation and quickly became an effective advocate of ecotourism. In the 1950s Mary Rockefeller inherited the Billings estate in Woodstock and in the 1960s Laurance bought and replaced the old Woodstock Inn, incorporating the golf course and Suicide Six ski area into one resort. Rockefeller also created the Woodstock Foundation, a nonprofit umbrella for such village projects as acquiring and restoring dozens of historic homes, burying power lines, building a new covered bridge by the green, and collecting local antique farm tools and oral histories, opening and maintaining the **Billings Farm & Museum** in 1983. The **Marsh-Billings-Rockefeller National Historical Park** opened in 1998.

walks and flight demonstration programs. Nominally priced snowshoe rentals for use on the trails.

Visitor Center for Billings Farm & Museum and the Marsh-Billings-Rockefeller National Historical Park, Rt. 12 north of Woodstock Village. Open May–Oct., daily 10–5. The parking lot and visitors center at Billings Farm serve both the farm and national park with displays on Marsh, Billings, and Rockefeller and a theater showing *A Place in the Land*, Charles Guggenheim's award-winning documentary dramatizing the story of all three men. (There's no admission fee for the restrooms and gift shop, but a nominal fee is charged to see the film if you aren't visiting the farm or museum.) *Note:* A combination ticket to the Billings Farm & Museum and programs at Marsh-Billings-Rockefeller National Historical Park is $16 adults, $12 seniors.

Christina Tree

TOURS OF THE ROCKEFELLER MANSION FEATURE THE COLLECTION OF AMERICAN LANDSCAPE ART

Marsh-Billings-Rockefeller National Historical Park (802-457-3368; nps.gov/mabi), Rt. 12 north of Woodstock Village. Mount Tom carriage roads and forest trails (see *Green Space*) are open year-round, free in summer (for winter use see *Cross-Country Skiing*). The Queen Anne mansion, the centerpiece of this estate, is notable for its antiques, Tiffany glass, and especially for its American landscape art, as well as a sense of the amazing individuals who lived there. Guided hour-plus tours, offered Memorial Day–Oct., are limited to a dozen visitors at a time; reservations are advised ($8 adults, $4 seniors and ages 6–15). These depart from the **Carriage Barn** (open late May–Oct., 10–5; free), an inviting space with dark bead-board walls and the feel of a library, with exhibits that position Marsh, Billings, and Rockefeller within the time line of America's conservation history. A multimedia exhibit, *People Taking Care of Places*, profiles individuals practicing conservation around the world. Visitors are invited to take advantage of the reading area with its conference-sized table (crafted from wood harvested on Mount Tom) and relevant books, including children's stories.

♂ ⑤ **Billings Farm & Museum** (802-457-2355; billingsfarm.org). Open May–Oct., daily 10–5; weekends Nov.–Feb. 10–4. Christmas and Feb. vacation weeks, open 10–4. $14 adults, $13 seniors 62 and over, $8 ages 5–15, $4 ages 3–4; 2 and under, free. Billed as the "Gateway to Vermont's Rural Heritage," this is one of the finest Jersey farms in America and a museum dedicated to telling the story of Vermont's rural past. Established as a model farm by Frederick Billings in 1871, it became a museum under the stewardship of his granddaughter Mary French Rockefeller and her husband, Laurance Rockefeller. Exhibits demonstrate traditional ways of plowing, seeding, cultivating, harvesting, and storing crops; making cheese and butter; woodcutting and sugaring. The restored 1890 farm manager's house reflects the farm as it was in Billings's day. Visitors can also observe what happens on a modern dairy farm with a prizewinning Jersey herd. The farm's Percheron workhorses—Jim, Joe, Sue, and Lynn—welcome visitors. Almost every day activities are geared to kids, from toddlers on up. Cows are milked daily at 3:30 PM. Inquire about special events, like Pumpkin & Apple Celebration and Harvest Weekend in fall; Thanksgiving weekend and Christmas week celebrations; sleigh ride weekends in Jan. and Feb.;

WAGON RIDE AT BILLINGS FARM & MUSEUM, WOODSTOCK

Christina Tree

and periodic demonstrations and crafts exhibits. Their annual quilt exhibit in Aug.–Sept. is worth a special trip.

The Dana House (home of the Woodstock Historical Society, 802-457-1822; woodstockhistorical.org), 26 Elm St., Woodstock. Open May–Oct., Tues.–Sat, varying hours. Office and research library open year-round. Admission $5 (free under age 6); 40-minute tours on the hour. John Cotton Dana was an eminent early-20th-century librarian and museum director whose innovations made books and art more accessible to the public. Completed in 1807 and occupied for the next 140 years by the Dana family, this historic house has an interesting permanent exhibit portraying the town's economic heritage and an admirable collection of antiques, locally wrought coin silver, portraits, porcelains, fabrics, costumes, and toys. The John Cotton Dana Library is a research and reference center. There is also an exhibit gallery.

🖊 ((•)) **The Norman Williams Public Library** (802-457-2295), on the Woodstock green. Open daily 10–5 except Sun. and holidays. A Romanesque gem, donated and endowed in 1883 by Dr. Edward H. Williams, general manager of the Pennsylvania Railroad and later head of Baldwin Locomotives. It offers children's story hours, poetry readings, and brown-bag summer concerts on the lawn; also Internet access for a small fee.

✳ Also See

COVERED BRIDGES There are three in the town of Woodstock. The **Lincoln Bridge** (1865), Rt. 4, West Woodstock, is Vermont's only Pratt-type truss; the **Middle Bridge**, in the center of the village, was built in 1969 by Milton Graton, "last of the covered-bridge builders," in the Town lattice style (partially destroyed by vandalism and rebuilt). The **Taftsville Bridge** (1836), Rt. 4 east, the second oldest bridge in Vermont, was disabled in 2011 by Hurricane Irene, rebuilt and reopened in 2014.

SCENIC DRIVES The whole area offers delightful vistas; one of the most scenic shortcuts is North Rd., which leaves Rt. 12 next to Silver Lake in Barnard and leads to Bethel. Also be sure to drive Rt. 106 to South Woodstock. This section of Rt. 4 is now a part of the Vermont Crossroads Scenic Byway.

✳ To Do

BALLOONING Balloons of Vermont (802-291-4887; balloonsofvermont.com), based in Quechee, operates year-round (the two-person basket has a seat) and will launch from your home or inn (conditions permitting). **Balloons Over New England** (800-788-5562; balloonsovernewengland.com) operates seasonally from Quechee, which is also the scene of the **Quechee Hot Air Balloon Festival** on Father's Day weekend in June, New England's premier balloon festival, featuring rides as well as live entertainment and crafts (see *Special Events*).

BICYCLING Discovery Bicycling Tours (802-457-3553; 800-257-2226; bikevt.com), Box 207, Woodstock. Vermont's most experienced, most personalized, and altogether best inn-to-inn tour service, offering weekend, five-, and seven-day trips through much of Vermont. Twenty-one-speed Trek and Cannondale hybrids are available for rent.

Wilderness Trails (802-295-7620), Clubhouse Rd. at the Quechee Inn. Bike rentals for the whole family, plus maps.

Woodstock Sports (802-457-1568), 30 Central St., Woodstock, has mountain and hybrid bike rentals; offers repairs and clothing; and rents snowshoes and skates.

Mountain as well as touring bikes are available at **The Woodstock Inn**, and there are (single- and doubletrack) trails on neighboring Mount Peg.

BOATING Wilderness Trails (802-295-7620), Clubhouse Rd. at the Quechee Inn, offers guided canoe and kayak trips; also rentals and shuttle service on the Connecticut, White, and Ottauquechee Rivers, as well as in the Deweys Mills Waterfowl Sanctuary. Inquire about island camping.

Silver Lake State Park (802-234-9451) in Barnard rents rowboats, canoes, and kayaks.

FISHING Vermont Fly Fishing School (802-295-7620), the Quechee Inn at Marshland Farm. Marty Banak offers lessons as well as providing tackle and guided fishing on Deweys Pond and the Connecticut, White, and Ottauquechee Rivers.

FITNESS CENTER AND TENNIS Woodstock Resort Racquet & Fitness Center (802-457-6656), part of the Woodstock Inn and Resort, Rt. 106. Indoor tennis and racquetball, lap pool, whirlpool, aerobic and state-of-the-art fitness equipment; spa treatments, facials, massage, manicure and pedicure; flexible memberships and day-use options; pro shop. There are 10 outdoor courts (4 DecoTurf and 6 clay) that can be rented; also lessons and equipment rental.

ℱ **Vail Field**, Woodstock. Two public tennis courts and a children's playground.

GOLF Woodstock Inn and Resort Golf Club (802-457-2114; woodstockinn.com), part of the Woodstock Inn and Resort, offers one of Vermont's oldest (1895) and most prestigious 18-hole golf courses, scenic and compact, redesigned by Robert Trent Jones Sr. in 1961. Be warned that it crosses water 11 times. Tee times can be reserved just 24 hours in advance of play. Facilities include a pro shop, putting green and practice range, lessons, electric carts, restaurant, and lounge.

HORSEBACK RIDING Woodstock has been an equestrian center for generations, especially for the hardy Morgans, which are making a local comeback in South Woodstock. **Kedron Valley Stables** (802-457-1480; kedron.com), Rt. 106, South Woodstock. Lessons, plus carriage, wagon, and sleigh rides. **The Green Mountain Horse Association** (802-457-1509; gmhainc.org), Rt. 106, South Woodstock, sponsors events throughout the year including sleigh rallies, long-distance rides, and jumping and dressage competitions. Visitors are welcome at shows and other events.

Note: **Open Acre Ranch** (openacreranch.com) in Fairlee (see the previous chapter) offers trail rides of varying lengths for most ability levels.

POLO Quechee Polo Club (quecheeclub.com). Matches are held most Saturdays at 2 PM in July and Aug. on the field near Quechee Gorge.

SPA The Spa at The Woodstock Inn & Resort (802-457-6697; woodstockinn.com), 14 the Green, Woodstock. This is a major new spa with a light-filled poolside Great Room in which to luxuriate after treatments, which include many kinds of massage, body polishes and wraps, facials, and skin care.

SWIMMING Silver Lake State Park (802-234-9451; vermontstateparks.com), 10 miles north on Rt. 12 in Barnard, has a nice beach. Open Memorial Day weekend–Labor Day weekend. Another smaller beach is right next to the general store.

ℱ **The Woodstock Recreation Center** (802-457-1502), 54 River St., has two public pools, mostly for youngsters.

For **indoor pools** see *Fitness Center* above and in "Upper Valley River Towns."

✳ Winter Sports

CROSS-COUNTRY SKIING AND SNOWSHOEING Woodstock Inn and Resort Tubbs Snowshoe Adventure Center & Fischer Skis Adventure Center (802-457-6674; woodstockinn.com), Rt. 106. A total of 60 km of some of the most varied and scenic trails for skiing and snowshoeing in New England. The network utilizes 30 km of 1880s carriage roads on Mount Tom, climbing gently from the valley floor (700 feet) to the summit (1,250 feet), skirting a pond, and finally commanding a view of the village below and down the Ottauquechee Valley. The center itself, source of tickets, a map, ski (skating and classic stride) and Tubbs snowshoe rentals (also poles), lockers, and lessons, is at the Woodstock Racquet & Fitness Center, with 10 km of gentle, meadow skiing out the door on the golf course, connecting with woodland trails on Mount Peg as well as snowshoe trails. Lessons, salesroom, lockers, soup and sandwiches.

Wilderness Trails (802-295-7620; quecheeinn.com), Clubhouse Rd. at the Quechee Inn, has 18 km of track-set trails, including easy loops through the woods and meadows around Quechee Gorge, offering fine views of its waterfalls, also harder trails down into the gorge. Snowshoe rentals are offered.

DOWNHILL SKIING *ℱ* **Suicide Six Ski Area** (802-457-6661; woodstockinn.com), South Pomfret, 5 miles north of Woodstock on Pomfret Rd. Heir to the first ski tow in the United States, which was cranked up in 1934 but on the other side of this hill, Suicide Six is now part of the Woodstock Inn and Resort complex and has a base lodge finished with native woodwork. Its beginners' area has a J-bar; two double chairlifts climb 655 vertical feet to reach 23 trails ranging from easy to the Show Off and Pomfret Plunge, plus a half-pipe for snowboarders. Lessons, rentals, retail shop, and restaurant/lounge.

ICE SKATING Silver Lake, by the general store in Barnard. **Union Arena**, at Woodstock Union High School, Rt. 4 west, Fri.-night skating for families. **Woodstock Sports** (802-457-1568), 30 Central St., Woodstock, offers skate and ski rentals. **Wilderness Trails** (see *Cross-Country Skiing*) in Quechee also rents skates and clears the pond on its property and across the road.

✳ Green Space

Mount Tom's 1,250-foot summit towers above the village of Woodstock. It's one of Vermont's most walked and walkable mountains. From Mountain Ave. in the village itself, **Faulkner Park** (donated by Mrs. Edward Faulkner, one of Woodstock's most thoughtful philanthropists) features a trail patterned on Baden-Baden's "cardiac" walks. A marked, 1.6-mile path zigzags up to the summit (bring a picnic; a bench overlooks the village). The **Marsh-Billings-Rockefeller National Historical Park** encompasses more than 500 acres on the backside of Mount Tom, with 30 miles of footpaths that were originally carriage roads, including a trail to Pogue Pond. Enter on Rt. 12 at the park (follow signs) or at the trailhead on Prosper Rd., just off Rt. 12. Inquire about frequent seasonal programs offered by the national park (802-457-3368). Also see *Cross-Country Skiing* for winter use.

Mount Peg Trails begin on Golf Ave. behind the Woodstock Inn. Open May–Oct. One is roughly 5 miles round-trip, a peaceful walk up along easy switchbacks beneath pines with a picnic bench at the summit, with views west down the valley to Killington.

Quechee Gorge State Park (802-295-2990; vtstateparks.com), off Rt. 4, Quechee. This 611-acre preserve encompasses the gorge (see *Must See*), and trails from the rim lead gently down (south of Rt. 4) into the gorge, which should be approached carefully. On a hot day it's tempting to wade into the shallow water at the south end of the gorge—but beware sudden water releases that have been known to sweep swimmers away. Ditto for the rockbound swimming hole at the north end of the gorge under the spillway. Look for picnic tables under the pines on Deweys Mills Rd. The campground (open mid-May–Oct. 15) offers 47 tent/trailer sites, seven lean-tos, and a dump station. This property belonged to a local woolen mill until the 1950s when it was acquired by the U.S. Army Corps of Engineers as part of the Hartland Dam flood-control project.

North Hartland Lake Recreation Area (802-295-2855) is a 1,711-acre preserve created by the U.S. Army Corps of Engineers to control the confluence of the Ottauquechee and Connecticut Rivers. It offers a sandy beach, wooded picnic area with grills, and nature trail. Access is poorly marked, so ask directions at the Quechee information booth.

Silver Lake State Park (802-234-9451; Jan.–May 800-299-3071; vtstateparks.com), Rt. 12, Barnard. Campground open Memorial Day–Labor Day. Silver Lake is good for fishing, swimming, and boating (rentals available). The park offers a snack bar and wooded campground with 40 tent/trailer sites and seven lean-tos. Hot showers.

Teagle Landing is Woodstock's vest-pocket park, a magical oasis below the bridge in the middle of town (Central St.). Landscaping and benches invite sitting a spell by the river, a tribute to Frank Teagle (1914–97), one of Woodstock's most dedicated residents.

Dewey Pond Wildlife Sanctuary, Deweys Mills Rd., Quechee. Originally a millpond, this is a beautiful spot with nature trails and a boat launch, good for bird-watching and fishing.

Hurricane Forest, Rt. 5, White River Junction. This 500-acre town forest harbors a pond and many miles of trails. Ask directions at the Quechee information booth.

Eshqua Bog, off Hartland Hill Rd., Woodstock. A 40-acre sanctuary managed by the New England Wild Flower Society and The Nature Conservancy with a white-blazed loop trail circling through 8 acres of wetlands, with orchids blooming in summer. Ask directions locally.

Also see Vermont Institute of Natural Science under *Must See*.

THE PAUSE THAT REFRESHES BY SILVER LAKE, BARNARD VILLAGE

Christina Tree

✳ Lodging

RESORTS Twin Farms (802-234-9999; 800-894-6327; fax 802-234-9990; twinfarms.com), Barnard 05031. There's luxury and then there's luxury. Twin Farms is Vermont's premier resort. Peter Jennison, for many years this book's coauthor, noted how ironic it is that the former country home of Sinclair Lewis, whose novels satirize the materialism of American, and Dorothy Thompson, the acerbic foreign correspondent, is now a 325-acre Shangri-La for "corporate CEOs, heads of government, royalty, and celebrities . . . to unwind, frolic, and be rich together in sybaritic privacy." That said, this is authentically a place apart, with each of the rooms and 10 sequestered "cottages" amazing creations. There's also a sense of place here, and the Vermont landscape is front and center. Instead of formal gardens or a golf course, paths wind through woods, orchards, and meadows. In winter there's cross-country and downhill skiing. Instead of an elaborate spa there's a 3,000-gallon Japanese-style soaking pool.

In design and detail each of the cottages is a space so special that we can't imagine wanting to leave it. The Studio, set beyond a meadow on the edge of the woods, features a two-story window and sitting room decorated with original art by the likes of Frank Stella and David Hockney. The Treehouse is squirreled in the pines and decorated in amazing twig furniture; hand-carved birds peer down on you from the top of the spiral-posted ebony bed. The contemporary glass-walled, two-story aviary blurs the sense of inside/outside; a sunken, jetted bath resembles a pool below a cave-like stone hearth.

For us a part of the fascination of this Shangri-La is its creator, Thurston Twigg-Smith, descended from Hawaii's pioneer missionaries. Known in his home state as the publisher who turned the *Honolulu Advertiser* into a successful newspaper, and as a patron of the arts, his free financial rein permitted architects, interior designers, and local craftsmen to create what they have. Twigg-Smith's own art collection on display here includes works by Milton Avery, Jasper Johns, and Roy Lichtenstein as well as Hockney and Stella.

Before dinner guests gather for cocktails in the living room of the Main House and dine off a set menu in the rustic dining room. The tone throughout the resort is casual, relaxed, and friendly. Of the four stylish rooms in the main house, Red's is only $1,440 a day; the cottages range $1,850–3,000, including meals, two bars, and the use of all recreational amenities: a fully equipped fitness center, croquet, tennis, a pond,

and mountain bikes. There are minimum stays on weekends and holidays, and an 18 percent service charge. There is a staff of 42 here for 20 rooms. The average stay is four to five days. Check the website for current rates—which, given the economy, may include almost affordable specials.

✍ **The Woodstock Inn and Resort** (802-457-1100; 800-448-7900; woodstockinn.com), 14 the Green, Woodstock 05091, is the lineal descendant of the 18th-century Eagle Tavern and the famous "old" Woodstock Inn that flourished between 1893 and 1969, putting the town on the year-round resort map. Today's 142-room, air-conditioned, Colonial-style 1970s edition was created by Laurance Rockefeller and has been recently, thoroughly, and tastefully remodeled. The comfortably furnished main lobby is dominated by a stone hearth where 5-foot birch logs blaze late fall through spring, the glowing heart of this sociable town. A book-lined library with games of chest and a beautiful Conservatory invites guests to sit back and enjoy their time away.

Vermont's best-known craftspeople have contributed to the most recent remake of guest rooms, which vary substantially in look and feel but are all fitted with marble bathrooms, down comforters, and flat-screen TVs. Among the more moderately priced rooms we prefer those in the front of the inn, overlooking the green. The most luxurious are the Tavern Rooms, with fireplace or sunroom overlooking inner garden, and two-room suites with one full bath and one half bath (sleeping two to four).

The grounds include a landscaped swimming pool and a full-service **spa**. Resort facilities are also spread around town. See *To Do* for details about the outstanding 18-hole **Golf Club**, the

WOODSTOCK INN

Christina Tree

Racquet and Fitness Club, **Suicide Six Ski Area**, and the **Nordic Center** with 60 km of trails meandering out over the golf course and on Mount Tom.

The Red Rooster off the lobby is the inn's casually elegant restaurant. Beyond a small, sleek bar, the bright space is nicely divided. Windows overlook the garden, and a there's a soothing fountain in the middle (see *Dining Out*). The formal main dining room is reserved for breakfast and functions while richly paneled **Richardson's Tavern** with its deep leather chairs is open evenings for drinks and pub fare.

All in all, this is one of Vermont's premier places to stay and play. Current regular-season rates, depending on room and season, are roughly $150–$820; children 12 and under are free when staying in the same room with an adult. MAP available. Check out the many packages.

❄ ✿ **The Quechee Inn at Marshland Farm** (802-295-3133; 800-235-3133; quecheeinn .com), P.O. Box 747, Quechee Main St., Quechee 05059. Off by itself on a quiet side road east of Quechee Village, just up from Deweys Mills Pond and Quechee Gorge, this historic farm is a comfortable and attractive inn with 25 guest rooms. Look closely in the oldest rooms and you'll see the rough-hewn beams of the original Georgian-style house built here by Colonel Joseph Marsh in 1793. With successive centuries and owners it expanded to include a distinctive, two-story, double-porched ell. In 1954 it was actually forced to move to higher ground to escape the rising waters created by the Hartland Dam. In 1968 it became the first headquarters and accommodations for the Quechee Lakes Corporation; a decade later it was acquired by an energetic couple who established its present looks and reputation, which subsequent owners have preserved.

Rooms vary in size and feel. Three are suites; all have private bath and phone and are furnished with antiques. The brick-floored, raftered lounge with its piano, books, and games opens onto a big, sunny dining room in which breakfast and dinner (see *Dining Out*) are served. The inn is home to the **Vermont Fly Fishing School** and also offers canoeing and kayaking tours on the Connecticut, White, and Ottauquechee Rivers, along with mountain bike rentals. In winter it maintains 18 km of groomed cross-country ski trails. Guests also enjoy privileges at the nearby **Quechee Club** with its 18-hole golf course, tennis courts, health center, and pools. Rates range $90–250 and include full breakfast. Inquire about packages.

INNS ♂ ✿ ✿ **The Kedron Valley Inn** (802-457-1473; 800-836-1193; kedronvalleyinn.com), P.O. Box 145, Rt. 106, South Woodstock 05071. This mellow brick centerpiece of South Woodstock has been welcoming visitors since 1828 and served as a stop on the Underground Railroad. There are 27 varied guest rooms divided among the main inn, the Tavern Building (vintage 1822), and the log lodge motel. The 12-acre property includes a 2-acre swim pond with sandy beach. All guest rooms have TV, A/C, and private bath; most have a fireplace. Both the pub-style Tavern and the inn dining room are gathering places for local residents as well as guests. Room rates are $159–359 B&B, $219–359 for a two-bedroom suite with full kitchen. The inn can host receptions for up to 200. Also see *Dining Out*.

✿ **Parker House Inn** (802-295-6077; the parkerhouseinn.com), 1792 Main St., Quechee 05059. A redbrick mansion built in 1857 by Vermont senator Joseph Parker beside his flannel mill on the Ottauquechee River, this inn is best known for food (see *Dining Out*) but is also a comfortable place to stay. Since acquiring it, chef Alexandra Adler and husband, Adam, have installed new baths and revamped the rooms. The downstairs parlors are now dining rooms, but there is a small second-floor sitting room with a TV, a sunny downstairs reading nook, a breakfast room, and a riverside deck. Dine and Stay packages from $349. Add 15 percent gratuity. Guests have access to Quechee Club facilities.

✿ **506 On the River Inn** (802-457-5000; ontheriverwoodstock.com), 1653 West Woodstock Rd. (Rt. 4) 05091. This two-story, 38-room contemporary inn opened in 2014 on the 6-acre site of a former riverside motel. Spacious guest rooms have balconies or patios; upper-floor rooms overlook the Ottauquechee. Rooms and suite have king beds, armchairs, mini bars, and many more amenities. There's also plenty of common space. A large, nicely decorated open room is divided into open, casual kick-back space at one end and the **506 Bistro & Bar**, with its antique bar, at the other. There's also a game room, toddlers' playroom, library, and gym. In warm weather relax in Adirondack chairs by the river or pond. $189–479 includes a full breakfast. In case you're wondering: "506" was the address on West Woodstock Rd. in a simpler not-so-long-ago era, the one in which a family-run gem of a motel on this spot was a reasonably priced find.

Lincoln Inn & Restaurant (802-457-7052; lincolninn.com), 2709 West Woodstock Rd. (Rt.

4), West Woodstock. Reopened in 2014, this 1870s farmhouse has been reincarnated as an English-style "restaurant with rooms." Along with the neighboring Lincoln Covered Bridge, it's named for Abraham, a cousin of a previous owner. Innkeeper Mara Mehlman has a culinary background but it's her partner, Jevgenija Saromova, who has the serious credentials. Rooms are comfortable and the inn is sited on 7 riverside acres. $145–205 includes breakfast.

BED & BREAKFASTS

In Woodstock 05091

Note: Parking can be tough, hence the advantage of the many in-town B&Bs described below. All face major thoroughfares, however; you might want to request back- or side-facing rooms.

❧ **Ardmore Inn** (802-457-3887; ardmoreinn .com), 23 Pleasant St. One of the most convenient B&Bs to downtown shops, this is a cheery, comfortable, meticulously restored 1867 Greek Revival village house with five spacious guest rooms, each with private marble bath. Back in Southern California innkeeper Charlotte Hollingsworth managed a bookstore; here she has named each of the rooms for a Vermont author or illustrator, fitting it with appropriate volumes. Our favorite is the spacious Archer Mayor Room, named for Brattleboro's detective novelist. It's in the rear of the house, with a queen bed, handy reading lamps, rockers to read by the gas fireplace, and a writing desk. There's also a well-stocked downstairs library with fireplace and a many-windowed sunroom with rockers. In the dining room guests gather around the antique Nantucket dining room

ARDMORE INN IS A HOSPITABLE B&B CONVENIENT TO SHOPS AND RESTAURANTS.
Christina Tree

table for a multicourse breakfast—which can carry you through much of the day. Both Charlotte and husband Gary offer helpful advice about local sights and dining. $209–259, from $199 off-season, includes the three-course breakfast and afternoon refreshments.

The Charleston House (802-457-3843; charlestonhouse.com), 21 Pleasant St. This luxurious Federal brick town house (vintage 1835) in the middle of the village is especially appealing, with period furniture in nine guest rooms, all with private bath and air-conditioning, several with fireplace and Jacuzzi. Five rooms are in the original part of the house, four in the more contemporary back. Rates are $135–290 (higher during foliage season) and include full breakfast in the dining room. Your genial hosts are Willa and Dieter (Dixi) Nohl. For many years Dixi managed Burke Mountain ski area in the Northeast Kingdom.

♂ **The Jackson House Inn** (802-457-2065; 800-448-1890; jacksonhouse.com), 43 Senior Lane (just off Rt. 4), West Woodstock 05091. This luxuriously appointed and equipped 1890 farmhouse has been expanded to include five queen guest rooms and six spacious single-room suites furnished in period antiques, several with French doors. Our favorites are the two second-floor suites in the main house with gas fireplace and French doors opening onto a balcony over the landscaped grounds with gardens and a spring-fed pond. Common space in the inn is ample and elegant: library, dining room and living room, and a fully licensed lounge with fireplace. Current innkeepers Kathy and Rick Terwelp reserve the large, sunny dining area, formerly a restaurant, for guests and for special events. Rates, which include a full breakfast, begin at $185 for a classic room; suites begin at $259 on weekends.

The Woodstocker (802-457-3896; 866-662-1439; woodstockervt.com), 61 River St. (corner of Rt. 4). Brits Dora Foschi and David Livesley have painted the exterior of this 1830s house neon yellow. Much of the interior is decorated equally boldly, with contemporary flair. The eight guest rooms and one suite are pictured on the website, but the bathrooms deserve closer coverage. Westminster features two clawfoot slipper tubs; Chelsea's sink and tub are both a luminous ruby color that's illuminated from within. There are also traditional rooms and baths. Common space includes a well-stocked library and attractive dining room with a woodstove, the setting for generous organic breakfasts. The inn fronts on busy Rt. 4 but rambles back along quiet River St. and is near the entrance to Faulkner Park with its walking trails up Mount Tom. Rates are $130–275 in low season, $210–375 in peak periods.

Beyond the village

✿ ☻ ♪ **Deer Brook Inn** (802-672-3713; deerbrookinn.com), 4548 West Woodstock Rd. (Rt. 4), Woodstock 05091. Five miles west of Woodstock and 10 miles east of Killington's Skyeship Gondola, George DeFina and David Kanal have added some great decorating touches to this restored 1820 farmhouse, set back in fields across the road from the Ottauquechee River. The floors are wide honey-colored pine, and each of the five rooms has a full bath and climate-controlled heat, radio/CD player, and air-conditioning. A ground-floor two-room suite with a sitting room is a delight and good for families. Our favorite of the four second-floor rooms is Room 1, with skylights above the bed and in the bathroom. $135–210 includes a full breakfast served either at a common or an individual table in the light-filled dining room or on the stone patio overlooking the grounds.

♂ ☻ ♪ ♿ **Apple Hill Inn Bed & Breakfast** (802-457-9135; applehillinn.com), P.O. Box 24, 2301 Hartwood Way, Woodstock 05091. The 30-mile view of the Ottauquechee and surrounding hills is spectacular in any season, and the spacious, many-windowed house has been designed to maximize it. Longtime innkeepers Beverlee Cook and husband Andy have furnished the contemporary interior with Oriental rugs and authentic 18th-century antiques, an elegant counterpoint to the large, light-filled rooms. The effect is rich but airy and uncluttered. An avid (organic-geared) cook and baker, Beverlee Cook caters receptions and serves afternoon teas in the solarium. The vintage barn down the hill adds to wedding option venues. $135–285 depending on room and season; $10 per extra person includes a full, healthy buffet breakfast. Pets are welcome—as are young children—in the Paradise Room (with a 360-degree view) above the garage.

Applebutter Inn (802-457-4158; 800-486-1734; applebutterinn.com), P.O. Box 395, Happy Valley Rd., Woodstock 05091. This is a graceful 1850s Federal with gables and wide-pine floors, a bright, spacious dining area/library, a music room with grand piano, and an elegantly comfortable living room with a fireplace. The six guest rooms, each named for a different variety of apple, have private bath and A/C; four have a gas fireplace or stove, and two are kings. Just off Rt. 4 on a quiet road, set in gardens. Your hosts are Barbara Barry and Michael Pacht. $100–195 per couple includes a three-course breakfast and afternoon refreshments.

☻ ☻ ♪ **Bailey's Mills Bed & Breakfast** (802-484-7809; 800-639-3437; baileysmills.com), 1347 Bailey's Mills Rd., Reading 05062. As happens so often in Vermont, surprises lurk at the end of a back road, especially in the case of this venerable guest house, a few miles west of Rt. 106. With a two-story porch and fluted columns, Bailey's Mills resembles a southern antebellum mansion. The 17-room brick home includes 11 fireplaces, two beehive ovens, a dance hall, and an 1829 general store, all part of an ambitious manufacturing complex established by Levi Bailey (1766–1850) and operated by his family for a century. Today Barbara Thaeder offers several comfortable rooms, two with working fireplace, each with a cozy sitting area and private bath, tastefully furnished with antiques. A spacious solarium makes the Honeymoon Suite especially appealing. The library with its Rumford fireplace has a large collection of fascinating books and is furnished, as is the dining room, with family antiques and "old stuff." Paths lead off across the meadows into the woods and to a swim pond. Barbara is an avid conservationist, a member of Green Hotels of Vermont. $135–199 with breakfast. (Ask about the adjacent Spite Cemetery.) The justly popular Keepers Cafe (see *Dining Out*) is minutes away.

Fan House (802-234-6704; thefanhouse.com), P.O. Box 294, Rt. 12 north, Barnard 05031. This distinguished, 1840s clapboard house is filled with light, decorated with heirloom tapestries, antique furnishings, and interesting art and books, creating the feel of an Italian villa. The three artfully furnished guest rooms have

PATIO AT THE FAN HOUSE IN BARNARD
Christina Tree

private bath and are fitted with high-thread-count linens. Our favorite is the fireplace suite with its cathedral ceiling, skylight, king four-poster, great linens, and hearth. On a summer morning you can grab a beach towel from the porch and head down the road to Silver Lake for a swim before breakfast. Bring a book to the bench in the flower garden with afternoon tea. From $185 includes a full breakfast; less for multiple days and midweek. Inquire about a family suite.

👓 **Maple Leaf Inn** (802-234-5342; 800-516-2753; mapleleafinn.com), P.O. Box 273, 5890 Rt. 12, Barnard 05031. Mike and Nancy Boyle are the innkeepers in this Victorian-style farm-house, designed specifically as a B&B. Stencil-ing, stitchery, and Nancy's handmade quilts decorate the seven air-conditioned guest rooms, each with a capacious private bath, king-sized bed, sitting area, telephone, and TV/VCR. Most guest rooms have wood-burning fireplaces and whirlpool baths. The parlor, library, and dining room are bright and inviting. $155–275 per room includes a full breakfast. The Country Garden Room on the main floor has easy access for anyone who needs special assistance.

Farmhouse Inn (802-672-5433; farmhouse innvt.com), 543 Woodstock Rd., Woodstock 05091. Six miles west of Woodstock Village, this imposing white-clapboard farmhouse sits back from the road, across the river from the Ottau-quechee River and backed by a striking five-story red barn. Barry and Tory Milstone offer five second- and third-floor guest rooms with private bath and temperature control, furnished in antiques. Children are welcome, and there's a family suite with a sitting room. $145–225 per couple for rooms, $180–265 for a suite sleeping up to four, includes a full breakfast.

Also see the **October Country Inn** in "Killing-ton/Rutland Region."

OTHER ✪ 🐾 🐕 👓 Shire Riverview Motel (802-457-2211; shiremotel.com), 46 Pleasant St., Woodstock 05091. Location, location. This two-story, independently owned 42-unit motel is within walking distance of downtown, and while it fronts on Pleasant St. (Rt. 4), it backs on the river; most rooms have river views and many have deck access. A contemporary building with six upscale suites is also in back; another recently refurbished building houses three more high-end rooms. All rooms are comfortable with phone and computer hookup, furnished with two queens, two doubles, or a king. All have a fridge, and some have gas fireplace and Jacuzzi. Rates are $118–178 in winter and spring, $158–228 (for a luxury river-view room with a gas fire-place and/or Jacuzzi) in summer and fall.

🐕 **Shepherd's Hill Farm** (802-457-3087; shepherdshillfarm.com), P.O. Box 34, 25 Hart-wood Way, Taftsville 05073. High on the hill above the Taftsville General Store, Ellen Terie raises sheep. This contemporary house on 36 acres features an open kitchen and eclectically furnished two-story living room overlooking the valley and its hemming hills. Ellen, an artist and psychotherapist, has covered the walls with var-ied art. Two guest rooms share a bath. Guests are invited to collect eggs from the henhouse for their breakfast and to help with as many farm chores as they wish. These include herding sheep, picking vegetables, and feeding farm animals.

OTHER LODGING 🐕 At **Quechee Lakes Resort** (quecheelakes.com), rental units range from small condos to six-bedroom houses, all with access to resort facilities, which include a small ski mountain, golf courses, and clubhouse with its indoor pool and squash courts. These can be rented through local Realtors, such as **Quechee Lakes Rentals** (802-295-1970; 800-745-0042; quecheelakesrentals.com) and **Care-free Quechee** (802-295-9500; carefreequechee vacations.com).

Note: For camping at the area's two state parks, see *Green Space.*

✱ Where to Eat

DINING OUT ✪ 🐾 🐕 Simon Pearce Restau-rant (802-295-1470; simonpearce.com), The Mill, Quechee. Open for lunch (11:30–2:45) and dinner (5–9; reservations advised), Sun. brunch (11–2:45). This is a cheerful, contemporary place for consistently superior food, served on its own pottery and glass, overlooking the

THE DINING ROOM AT SIMON PEARCE OVERLOOKS THE NEW QUECHEE COVERED BRIDGE.

Christina Tree

waterfall and covered bridge that's been rebuilt since Hurricane Irene. This is a high-profile tourist stop with a recently expanded viewing area to watch glass being blown in the stone mill below or to shop in the original store that remains open through the dinner hours. But the Ballymaloe brown bread alone is worth a lunch visit, especially savored with Vermont cheddar soup or Guinness stew on a fall day. Dinner choices might include maple-and-herb-glazed pork chop with caramelized parsnips, roasted pear onions, porcini mushrooms, and braised kale. Dinner entrées $23–38.

The Prince and the Pauper (802-457-1818; princeandpauper.com), 24 Elm St., Woodstock. Open nightly for dinner (reservations advised on weekends). Since 1981, owner-chef Chris Balcer's Continental cuisine has been consistently considered superior by regular patrons. The $49 prix fixe changes nightly, but there are always half a dozen appetizers and entrées from which to choose. You might begin with house-smoked salmon followed by grilled Tuscan lamb or veal Dijonnaise. The dining room is candlelit, elegantly rustic. In the more casual wine bar a bistro menu might include hickory-smoked baby back ribs and herbed chicken, and there's always a pasta and hearth-baked pizzas.

🖋 **The Barnard Inn Restaurant & Max's Tavern** (802-234-9961; barnardinn.com), 10 miles north of Woodstock on Rt. 12, Barnard. Max's Tavern is open Tues.–Sat. from 5, the dining room Thurs.–Sat. from 6. Reservations advised. Will Dodson grew up in St. Louis, graduated from the Culinary Institute of America, in 2000 acquired this 1796 brick house, and has been known ever since for his exceptional, locally sourced fare. He grows 80 percent of summer veggies and keeps chickens and ducks for their eggs. A three-course $65 prix fixe menu in winter might include (chosen from multiple options) curried carrot soup, a goat cheese, asparagus, and leek tartlet, and braised beef short ribs or winter vegetable gnocchi. In the less formal Max's Tavern, the menu changes nightly but you might begin with an order of seasoned sweet potato fries and dine on chicken "Wienerschnitzel." Entrées $17–34. A large selection of wines and beers is available by the glass. Desserts are irresistible in both venues.

The Red Rooster at The Woodstock Inn and Resort (802-457-1100; woodstockinn.com), 14 the Green, Woodstock. Open daily noon–10. This casually elegant restaurant is airy and inviting, decorated in light woods and bright fabrics, divided in a way that permits privacy. A wall of windows overlooks the garden, a small fountain provides a soothing undertone,

and a sleek bar divides the dining area from the lobby. The menu stresses locally sourced products and produce. Lunch options feature specialty sandwiches and salads. The à la carte dinner menu includes a plate of regional cheeses. Entrées range from pasta to filet mignon ($23–34). There's a reasonably priced children's menu. Pub fare is available in Richardson's Tavern (see *Eating Out*).

Lincoln Inn & Restaurant (802-457-7052; lincolninn.com), 2709 West Woodstock Rd. (Rt. 4), West Woodstock. Open for dinner, by reservation only. Latvian-born Jevgenija Saromova is the chef orchestrating this serious new dining option. The venue is an 1870s farmhouse by the river. $55 for a five-course set daily-changing menu.

💿 🖋 **Melaza Caribbean Bistro** (802-457-7110; melazabistro.com), 71 Central St., Woodstock. Open for dinner Wed.–Sun., also lunch in summer and fall. On a gray winter's night we felt as if we had stumbled into Old San Juan in the middle of Woodstock. The menu extends this illusion beautifully. We heartily recommend the vegetarian "piononos," a timbal of sweet plantain stuffed with eggplant ragout, served on a bed of arugula ($17). We also split an order of delicious pan-seared scallops, served with coco rice, curry, coconut lime sauce, pineapple chutney, and tamarind glaze. Entrées are $17–25. There's also a wide selection of small plates and tapas, and a full bar.

💿 🖋 **The Meadows at the Quechee Inn at Marshland Farm** (802-295-3133; 800-235-3133; quecheeinn.com), Clubhouse Rd., Quechee. Open nightly at 6, this country-elegant dining room is just enough off the beaten track to be a discovery, the quiet setting for dependably fine food. Dutch-bred chef Ed Kroes offers a traditional menu. The signature dish is slow-roasted crispy duck with orange apricot demiglaze. Entrées $24–29. At this writing Wednesday features a three-course prix fixe menu for $24.50 per person; Friday multicourse dinner for two is $50 with a glass of wine.

Parker House Inn (802-295-6077; theparkerhouseinn.com), 1792 Main St., Quechee. Open for dinner daily (reservations, please); also for lunch summer weekends. Chef Alexandra Adler continues to get good reviews for her French-accented bistro in a classic brick Victorian mill owner's mansion. You might begin with classic escargots or a goat cheese caramelized onion tart, followed by *moules frites* with field greens or roasted New Zealand rack of lamb. Entrées $20–30. Light fare and cocktails are served in the riverside back bar. Lunch, when served, is on the riverside deck.

✍ **The Kedron Valley Inn** (802-457-1473; kedronvalleyinn.com), Rt. 106, 5 miles south of Woodstock. Open for dinner Thurs.–Mon. 5:30–9. The large, low-beamed dining room is country elegant and casual. Entrées from $14 for a (Cloudland Farm beef) burger to $29 for New York strip steak.

✪ ✍ **Keepers Cafe** (802-484-9090; keepers cafe.com), Rt. 106 at Baileys Mill Rd., Reading. Open Tues.–Sat. for dinner, Sun. too in summer. The former Hammondsville Store offers three connecting rooms in a warm green with finished wood floors, good-sized pedestal tables, and hardy wooden office chairs. The feel is Shaker and the food is fresh. It's a limited menu. Entrées include an oven-roasted bird du jour with options like grilled sirloin, and char-grilled house kielbasa with porcini sauerkraut and fingerling potatoes—and there's also always a burger. $19–25. Children's menu. No reservations for fewer than six people.

Cloudland Farm (802-457-2599; cloudland farm.com), 1101 Cloudland Rd., Woodstock. Open by reservation for dinner Thurs., Fri., and Sat. Closed in mud season. This is a new twist on farm-to-table: The tables are at the farm. Drive 3.8 miles up and up and up Cloudland Road and you come to a many-windowed post-and-beam building constructed from wood harvested on this farm. Come on a Thursday night and you sit down to an informal dinner featuring the farm's own meat. On the day we stopped by it included BBQ chicken wings with Vermont blue cheese sauce followed by an Angus burger served with a choice of local cheeses, with housemade chocolate and peanut butter sundaes for dessert ($31). Fridays and Saturdays are more formal, with tables draped

THE KEDRON VALLEY INN

in linen. The three-course menu, still family-style, is $46. Prices vary slightly with the menu, which you can check online before reserving. It's BYOB, and in summer you can savor the view before dinner from a rocking chair on the porch. There's also a big woodfired hearth. Children are half price.

Also see **Norwich Inn**, **Carpenter and Main**, and **Skunk Hollow Tavern** in "Upper Valley River Towns."

EATING OUT

In Woodstock

Bentley's Restaurant (802-457-3232), 1 Elm St., Woodstock. Open daily for lunch and dinner. The 1970s restaurant here, an oasis of Victoriana and plants, has been expanded and updated by new owners and both service and quality have improved. A lifesaver in the middle of town, good for burgers or specialty sandwiches and flatbreads at lunch; dinner choices range from fish-and-chips to crispy roasted duck ($28). Frequent live music.

Worthy Kitchen (802-457-7281), 442 East Woodstock Rd. This companion piece to the Worthy Burger in South Royalton is Woodstock's current hot spot. Craft beers (18 and counting) and hard ciders are the big draw, along with a blackboard menu and good-vibes atmosphere. You order and wait to be buzzed. Fresh, local ingredients, gluten-free, all the right things and delicious. Try the fried chicken.

Fairways Grille (802-457-6672), Woodstock Inn and Resort Golf Club, Rt. 106 south. Open in summer for lunch 11:30–3. This is a Woodstock insider's meeting spot for lunch but open to the public, especially appealing on sunny days when you can dine on the deck. Designer sandwiches and salads, burgers, a good grilled Reuben. During ski season hot chili and snacks are available for cross-country skiers in the fireside lounge.

Mon Vert Café (802-457-7143), 69 Central St. Open 7:30–11:30 for breakfast, until 4 for lunch. This bright, attractive café fills the need for a light, locally sourced, imaginative café in the middle of the village. The yogurt and pesto are homemade. Breads are from Red Hen, and even the chicken in the chicken salad sandwich has its provenance noted.

✍ **Melaza Caribbean Bistro** (802-457-7110; melazabistro.com), 71 Central St. Open summer through foliage for lunch, good for a black bean burger, Jamaican jerk chicken sandwich, or fish taco. See *Dining Out* for more.

✍ **Mountain Creamery** (802-457-1715), 33 Central St., serves breakfast daily 7–11:30, lunch until 3, pastry and espresso until 6. Soups, sandwiches, salads, daily specials, and their own handmade ice cream as well as apple pie. Pies and cakes are also for sale.

♠ Richardson's Tavern at the Woodstock Inn (802-457-1100; woodstockinn.com), 14 the Green. Usually open evenings for pub fare in a casual dining and tavern setting, but check. This is a delightful find, a richly paneled tavern room with a woodfired hearth, wing chairs, and all the accoutrements of an exclusive club, including reading lights beside tables. Entrées include reasonably priced comfort food and burgers, $12–30.

White Cottage (802-457-3455), 863 Woodstock Rd. Open May–Oct., 11–10. Hurricane Irene did a job on this local legend but it's back, better than ever. The classic 1950s take-out has reopened with expanded indoor as well as outdoor seating overlooking the river. The lobster bisque and chowder (Ipswich clams are delivered daily) are housemade. We recommend the Jamaican pulled pork. The menu is large. Gifford's ice cream.

♪ River Stones Tavern (802-295-1600), Rt. 4, Waterman Place., Quechee. Open daily for dinner, lunch Wed.–Sun. Formerly Firestones, under new ownership since 2013. A rustic, lodge-like restaurant, with a big woodfired oven as its centerpiece, featuring made-to-order flatbreads. You'll also find pastas, salads, and pub-food-like fish (dipped in Long Trail beer batter) and chips.

The Quechee Club (802-295-9356; quechee club.com), 1119 Quechee Main St. Open to the public Thurs.–Sat. for dinner. The Grille Room offers a pleasant ambience and reasonably priced menu.

Barnard General Store (802-234-9688), 6134 Rt. 12, Barnard. Open 7–7. Sited beside Silver Lake and in the middle of a small village, this is a beloved landmark. When it closed in 2013, the community raised funds and, with the help of the Preservation Trust of Vermont, bought it back. It continues to be a great spot for breakfast and lunch as well as milk shakes and coffee, sandwiches to take to the lake across the street. This is also a full general store selling ethanol-free gas and groceries.

South Woodstock General Store (802-457-3050), Rt. 106, middle of South Woodstock. Open daily for staples, great breakfast, lunch (order and grab a table), take-out foods, freshly baked bread, Vermont gifts.

Out of Bounds—Suicide Six Ski Area (802-457-6661; woodstockinn.com), South Pomfret, 5 miles north of Woodstock on Pomfret Rd.

During the winter months, enjoy savory homemade soups, hearty sandwiches, fresh salads—and don't forget the bar for a warm-up hot chocolate or hot toddy. Located slope-slide at Suicide Six.

PICNICS On a beautiful summer or fall day the best place to lunch is outside. In Woodstock itself there's Teagle's Landing, right on Central St. by the river, and Faulkner Park on Monument Ave. See *Green Space* for other ideas.

♠ Woodstock Farmers Market (802-47-3678; woodstockfarmersmarket.com), 468 Woodstock Rd. (Rt. 4), West Woodstock. Deli hours: Tues.–Sun. 10–4. Rebuilt after a hit from Hurricane Irene, this is the town's standout place for locally sourced organic produce. It also has soups, sandwiches, and salads to go and lots of veggie options. (We recommend The Garden of Eden on multigrain bread.) The store also sells fresh fish, free-range chicken, local produce, meals to go, and Baba À Louis bread.

The Village Butcher (802-457-2756), 18 Elm St., Woodstock. A superb butcher and a deli with sandwiches, soups, and specials to go, along with its top-flight meats, wines, and baked goods, plus homemade fudge.

✳ Entertainment

Pentangle Arts (802-457-3981; pentanglearts .org), Town Hall Theater, 31 the Green, Woodstock. First-run films are shown Fri.–Mon. evenings at 7:30 in the Town Hall Theater. Live presentations at town hall and at the Woodstock Union High School include a variety of musical

WOODSTOCK FARMERS MARKET IS KNOWN FOR LOCAL PRODUCE AND A STELLAR DELI.
Christina Tree

and other live entertainment. Check the **Town Crier** blackboard at the corner of Elm and Central Sts. for current happenings. Inquire about the Woodstock Film Society.

Also see *Entertainment* in "Upper Valley River Towns."

✷ Selective Shopping

ANTIQUES SHOPS The Woodstock area is a mecca for antiques buffs. There are two big group galleries. **Quechee Gorge Village Antique Mall** (802-295-1550), Rt. 4, east of Quechee Gorge, open daily, is one of New England's largest antiques collectives, with two floors full of dealers. The **Antiques Collaborative** (802-296-5858; antiquescollaborative.com), Waterman Place, Rt. 4 at the blinking light in Quechee, is also open daily (10–5) and shows representative stock from more than 150 dealers: period furniture usually in good condition, silver, Oriental rugs, and more.

Among the more than dozen individual dealers: **Wigren & Barlow** (802-457-2453; wigren andbarlow.com), 29 Pleasant St., is Woodstock's most elegant antiques shop, with a large selection of fine country and formal furniture, decorative accessories, and garden appointments (open daily 10–5); **Pleasant Street Books** (802-457-4050; pleasantstreetbooks .com), 48 Pleasant St., Woodstock, carries 10,000 selected old and rare titles in all fields (open daily 11–5 in summer and fall, by appointment off-season).

Note: **The Vermont Antique Dealer's Association** (vermontada.com) holds its annual show in July at Woodstock's Union High School. A pamphlet guide to *Antiquing In and Around Woodstock* is available from the information center (see *Guidance*).

ART GALLERIES The following are all in Woodstock: **Woodstock Gallery** (802-457-2012), 8 Elm St., specializes in contemporary carvings, prints, and antiquities. **Gallery on the Green** (802-457-4956), corner of Elm St., features original art, limited-edition prints, photography, and occasionally sculpture, from New England artists. **The Fox Gallery** (802-457-1250; thefoxgallery.com), 5 the Green. Neil and Janice Drevitson have maintained this gallery in their house for more than 40 years, exhibiting primarily their own traditional, highly realistic landscapes, portraits, and still lifes, also a select number of sculptors and other artists.

The Collective (802-457-1298), 47 Central St., Woodstock. An outstanding artisan-run gallery showcasing a mix of contemporary art and fine craft in the old riverside linseed mill.

Christina Tree

A FORMER LINSEED FACTORY IN WOODSTOCK HOUSES MULTIPLE GALLERIES.

Artemus Global Art (802-547-7199), 23 Elm St. Open 11–5. Woodstock's newest gallery, worth a look.

ARTISANS ✪ ✧ Simon Pearce Glass (802-295-14470; simonpearce.com), The Mill, 1760 Main St., Quechee. The shop (802-295-2711) is open 10–9 daily. The brick mill by the falls in the Ottauquechee was the 19th-century home of J. C. Parker and Co., producing "shoddy": wool reworked from soft rags. Parker was known for fine baby flannel. In 1981 Simon Pearce opened it as a glass factory, harnessing the dam's hydropower for his glass furnace. Pearce had already been making his original glass for a decade in Ireland, and here he established a national reputation for his distinctive production pieces: tableware, vases, lamps, candlesticks, and more. In the rebuild after Hurricane Irene, the glass-blowing viewing from the Simon Pearce Restaurant (see *Dining Out*) has been expanded and is a must-see. Simon Pearce now also operates a large, visitor-friendly glass and pottery factory in nearby Windsor (see "Upper Valley River Towns").

Charles Shackleton Furniture and **Miranda Thomas Pottery** (802-672-5175; shackleton thomas.com), 102 Mill Rd., The Mill, Rt. 4, Bridgewater. Open daily 10–5. This couple met at art school in England and again at Simon Pearce Glass. Charles was an apprentice glassblower before he switched to furniture making; Miranda founded the pottery studio there. They have since acquired much of the Bridgewater Mill, and Charles works with fellow crafters to produce exquisite furniture. It's made to order, but models are displayed (along with seconds at the mill), complemented by Miranda's distinctive pottery, hand thrown and carved with traditional designs, such as rabbits, fish, and trees.

Her pottery is housed in a former worker's cottage in the mill's parking lot. Inquire about furniture workshops and pottery studios.

Farmhouse Pottery (802-774-8873; farmhouse pottery.com), 1837 West Woodstock Rd. (Rt. 4), Woodstock. Open Wed.–Sun. The store showcases partially rough-finished, elegantly simple tableware, vases, and small useful pieces that you can watch being crafted in the adjoining workshop. Zoe and James Zilian see their distinctive work as expressing "Farm to Table Values." James, with a long background at Simon Pearce, is obviously a skilled marketer. Prices are high, and Farmhouse Pottery is already a hot gift item.

Danforth Pewter (802-457-7269; danforth pewter.com), 9 Central St., Woodstock. Now nationally known and distributed, known for pewter work that includes lamps, jewelry, kitchen items, and much more, Danforth was founded in Woodstock in 1975 but its workshop has long since moved to Middlebury. This new store is a trove of likely gifts.

BOOKSTORES The Yankee Bookshop (802-457-2411; yankeebookshop.com), 12 Central St., Woodstock. Established in 1935, this is Vermont's oldest continuously operated independent bookshop. It carries an unusually large stock of hardbound and paperback books for adults and children, plus cards; it features the work of local authors and publishers. It also carries toys and learning tools, kites and spinners.

SPECIAL SHOPS
In Woodstock Village

F. H. Gillingham & Sons (802-457-2100; 800-344-6668), Elm St., owned and run by the same family since 1886, is something of an institution, retaining a lot of its old-fashioned general store flavor. You'll find plain and fancy groceries, wine, housewares, hardware for home, garden, and farm, books, Vermont products, and much more.

⚓ **Woodstock Pharmacy** (802-457-1306), Central St. Open daily 8–6, Sun. until 1 PM. Another Woodstock institution that has branched out well beyond the basics, especially good for stationery and (downstairs) for children's toys and books.

Who Is Sylvia? (802-457-1110), 26 Central St., in the old village firehouse, houses two floors of great vintage clothing and accessories for men as well as women.

Red Wagon Toy Co. Children's Shop (802-457-9300), 41 Central St., specializes in creative toys and children's clothing, from infant to size 16.

Whippletree Yarn Shop (802-457-1325), 7 Central St., has yarns, knitting patterns, sample sweaters, and gifts. Inquire about knitting classes.

In and near Quechee

F. H. Clothing Co. (802-296-6646; fathat .com), 1 Quechee Main St. (corner of Rt. 4). A business that has evolved over more than 30 years from making floppy "fat hats" to a variety of comfortable, colorful clothing, most designed and made right here. Check out the markdowns upstairs.

⚓ **Quechee Gorge Village** (802-295-1550; quecheegorge.com), Rt. 4 at Quechee Gorge. A long, weather-proofed shopping complex housing a number of quality enterprises, among them the vast **Antique Center** (see *Antiques Shops*); **Vermont Spirits Distilling** (vodka); the **Quechee Country Store**, a Cabot Cheese outlet with Putney Mountain Winery tastings; and the **Vermont Toy & Train Museum and Gift Shop**, with seasonal rides on a miniature train and carousel.

Taftsville Country Store (802-457-1135; taftsville.com), Rt. 4 east, Taftsville. This 1840 landmark is also still the post office and carries Vermont products; cheeses, maple products, jams, jellies, smoked ham, and bacon, plus staples, wine, and books, more. Mail-order catalog.

Scotland by the Yard (802-295-5351; scotland bytheyard.com), Rt. 4 in Quechee, 3 miles east of Woodstock, open year-round daily, 9–5. This is a trove of quality things Celtic: Irish tweed caps as well as Scottish tartans and tweeds, kilts,

THE VINTAGE-1840 TAFTSVILLE COUNTRY STORE SPECIALIZES IN VERMONT PRODUCTS.
Christina Tree

capes, coats, sweaters, skirts, canes, books, records, oatcakes and shortbreads, Irish and Cornish jewelry, more.

Elsewhere

FARMS Sugarbush Farm (802-457-1757; 800-281-1757; sugarbushfarm.com), RR 1, Box 568, Woodstock, but located in Pomfret: Take Rt. 4 to Taftsville, cross the covered bridge, go up the hill, turn left onto Hillside Rd., then follow signs. Warning: It's steep. Beware in mud season, but it's well worth the effort: Sample seven Vermont cheeses, all packaged here along with gift boxes, geared to sending products to far corners of the world. In-season you can watch maple sugaring, walk the maple and nature trail, or visit with their farm animals.

On the Edge Farm (802-457-4510), 49 Rt. 12, Woodstock (2.5 miles north of Woodstock Village). An outstanding farm stand open year-round but just Fri.–Sun. in Jan. Locally raised and smoked meat as well as seasonal fruit and veggies, fresh eggs, jams, pickles, pies, and flowers.

Seasonal farmers markets in Woodstock are Wed. (3–6) on the village green.

✳ Special Events

Note: Check the **Town Crier** blackboard on Elm St. for Woodstock weekly happenings.

Washington's birthday: **Winter Carnival** events sponsored by the Woodstock Recreation Center (802-457-1502).

March: **Home Grown Vermont**—sugaring and a festival of Vermont foods. **Maple Madness**, sponsored by the Woodstock Area Chamber of Commerce.

May: **Plowing Match**, first weekend, among dozens of teamsters and draft horses and oxen at Billings Farm & Museum, also the scene of **Sheep Shearing**. In downtown Woodstock the **Memorial Day Parade** is worth a trip to see.

First Sunday of June: **Covered Bridge Quechee/Woodstock Half Marathon.**

Father's Day weekend: **Quechee Hot Air Balloon Festival** (802-295-7900)—a gathering of

Christina Tree

FARMERS MARKET ON THE WOODSTOCK GREEN

more than two dozen balloons with ascensions, flights, races, crafts show, entertainment.

July: **An Old Fashioned 4th** at Billings Farm & Museum includes a noon reading of the Declaration of Independence, 19th-century-style debates, games, and wagon rides. **Bookstock**, last weekend.

August: **Quechee Scottish Festival**, third Saturday—pipe bands, sheepdog trials, Highland dancing, more than 50 clans. **Billings Farm Quilt Show**, all month. Also at Billings Farm: **Antique Tractor Parade**, first Sunday. **Taste of Woodstock**, second Saturday.

September: **Annual Vermont Fine Furniture & Woodworking Festival** at Woodstock's Union Arena (vermontwoodfestival.org). **Woodstock Art Festival**, weekend after Labor Day.

Mid-October: Quechee **antiques and crafts festivals**. **Apple & Crafts Fair**, Columbus Day weekend, Woodstock—more than 100 juried craftspeople and specialty food producers.

Second weekend of December: **Christmas Wassail Weekend** includes a grand parade of carriages around the Woodstock green, Yule log lighting, concerts.

THE WHITE RIVER VALLEYS

INCLUDING THE TOWNS OF RANDOLPH, SHARON, ROYALTON, BETHEL, ROCHESTER, HANCOCK, BRAINTREE, BROOKFIELD, CHELSEA, TUNBRIDGE, AND STRAFFORD

A s I-89 sweeps up through central Vermont in a grand 52-mile arc—from White River Junction to Montpelier—it yields a series of panoramas. Motorists see the high wall of the Green Mountains beyond the Braintree Range on the west and catch glimpses of an occasional valley village. What they don't see is one of Vermont's best-kept secrets: the classic old villages, abrupt valleys, and hill farms along the White River and its three branches.

The White River rises high in the Green Mountains in Granville Gulf and rushes down through Hancock, widening and slowing among farms in Rochester, keeping company with Rt. 100 until Stockbridge, where its course dictates a dogleg in the highway. Turning sharply east, it carves a narrow valley for Rt. 107. At Bethel the river begins to parallel Rt. 14 and I-89. As it courses through the Royaltons and Sharon, it's joined by the three northern branches.

Each of these streams, rising some 20 miles north of the main stem of the river, has carved its own valley. The First Branch, shadowed by Rt. 110, threads six covered bridges, lush farmland, and the unself-consciously beautiful villages of Chelsea and Tunbridge. The Second Branch begins above picturesque Pond Village in Brookfield, known for its floating bridge, and flows south along Rt. 14. The Third Branch rises in Roxbury, conveniently near a fish hatchery, and flows south through a lonely valley (along Rt. 12A) to Randolph, one of the area's few I-89 exits and an Amtrak stop as well as the only commercial center of any size in this entire area.

Beautiful as these valleys are, the high east–west roads that connect them, climbing up over hills and down into the next valley, are more rewarding still. To begin exploring this back-roaded and unresortified heart of Vermont, you might exit in Sharon and climb through the Straffords to Tunbridge and north to Chelsea, west to Brookfield, then south to Randolph, on down Rt. 12, and west over Rochester Mountain. See *Scenic Drives* for tours that can pleasantly fill many days.

In the absence of any major resort hub, a variety of widely scattered farms and B&Bs offer lodging and many good reasons to explore this rural region, genuinely as well as geographically the heart of Vermont.

In 2011 Hurricane Irene dealt a heavy blow to towns along the main stem of the White River. Rain-swollen brooks surged down hillsides and into the river. Farms, homes, and businesses were flooded; coffins from a cemetery floated downstream. Stretches of Rts. 100 and 107 were wiped out, isolating the towns of Rochester and Stockbridge. The roads have since been rebuilt and the riverbed widened, incidentally improving access for picnicking and swimming, fishing and tubing.

GUIDANCE White River Valley Area Chamber of Commerce (802-728-9027; whiteriver valleychamber.com), 31 Rt. 66, Randolph 05060. Phone answered and office open year-round, Mon., Wed., Fri. 9–1; information center maintained Memorial Day–mid-Oct. at State Plaza just off I-89, Exit 4. This Randolph-based chamber website also serves 10 smaller, surrounding towns covered in this chapter.

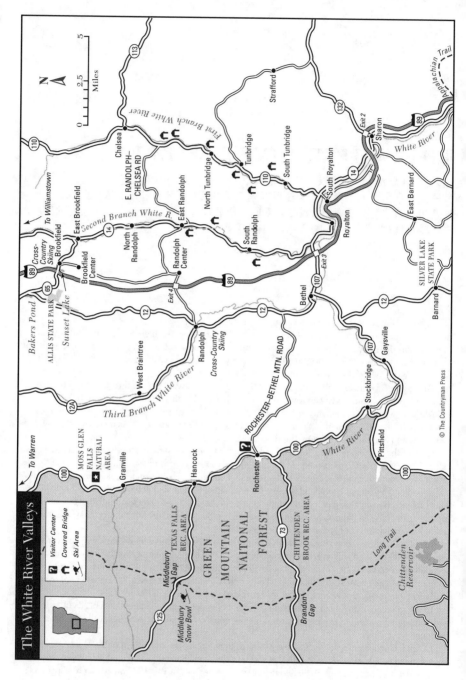

The White River Valleys

Visitor Center
Covered Bridge
Ski Area

© The Countryman Press

& **Sharon Northbound Information Center and Vermont Vietnam Veterans' Memorial** (802-281-5216), I-89, Sharon. Open 7 AM–11 PM. Not what you expect to find at a roadside rest area. The 7,000 names on the memorial itself represent all the Vermonters who served in the Vietnam War, which is recalled through exhibits that include a time line and film clips. Also unexpected here: a "living greenhouse" filled with plants and descriptions of how they recycle waste. The center is staffed, a good source of local information. The restrooms, incidentally, are outstanding.

Green Mountain National Forest Ranger District Office and Visitor Center (802-767-4261), Rt. 100 in Rochester. Open 8–4 daily (except Sun.) Memorial Day–Columbus Day, weekdays off-season. A magnificent center (restrooms) with detailed information on hiking, biking, picnicking, bird-watching, camping, and other recreation in this part of the GMNF.

Herald of Randolph (802-728-3232; ourherald.com). The Randolph weekly, published on Thursday, carries local news and events for Orange and northern Windsor Counties.

GETTING THERE *By train:* **Amtrak's Vermonter** (800-USA-RAIL; amtrak.com). Randolph and White River Junction (see "Upper Valley River Towns") are stops for trains from Washington, DC, and New York City via Springfield, Massachusetts.

By car: This area covers a wide, hilly swath of Vermont. I-89 runs diagonally across it, but with only three exits (Sharon, Bethel/Royalton, and Randolph).

GETTING AROUND Stagecoach (802-728-3773).

WHEN TO GO Rochester offers winter cross-country skiing, and Tunbridge draws Vermonters for the World's Fair in September and many more events. March brings sugaring; in May there's kayaking and in summer, tubing along the lower reaches of the White River. In July there are old-fashioned Independence Day parades, the biggest one in Randolph. Labor Day weekend, that same town is the site of the New World Festival, with performances by more than 100 old-time northern New England and Canadian musicians. Given its scattering of appealing places to stay, its farms, and its back-road scenery, this is a rewarding getaway area anytime except mud season (April and early May).

MEDICAL EMERGENCY Call **911. Gifford Medical Center** (802-728-7000), 44 S. Main St., Randolph.

✴ Villages

Sharon Village. An old commercial center at the junction of the river road (Rt. 14) and the high road (to Strafford), this remains a cluster of services just off I-89. The columned **Sharon Trading Post** is a classic general store with a serious meat department, also selling local maple products. The **Sharon Historical Society**, also at this crossroads, is open summer Sundays 1–3.

South Royalton Village. On a bend in the river and off Rt. 14, this classic railroad village frames an outsized green with two bandstands and a Civil War cannon. A granite arch recalls the 1780 raid on Royalton by more than 300 Native Americans commanded by an English lieutenant. The railroad hotel, an 1887 brick Queen Anne–style commercial block, the train depot, and many of the clapboard buildings within eyeshot have all received a new lease on life thanks to the presence of the **Vermont Law School**. Founded in 1973 and headquartered in a tower-topped old school building, this draws students from around the country. In the village of Royalton, north on Rt. 14, most buildings predate the Civil War.

Tunbridge. Some 20,000 people jam into this village of 400 over four days each September. They come for the Tunbridge World's Fair, first held in 1867. Sited in a grassy, natural bowl by a bend in the river, it has everything an agricultural fair should have: a midway, livestock displays and contests, a Floral Hall, collections of old-time relics, dancing, sulky racing, a fiddling contest, horse pulls, a grandstand, and more. Known as "the Drunkards Reunion" during a prolonged era when it was claimed that anyone found sober after 3 PM was expelled as a nuisance, it's now a family event. Biannually in June the fairgrounds are also the site of the wonderfully colorful annual Vermont History Expo, showcasing Vermont historical societies from around the state with displays, reenactments, music, and much more. Tunbridge boasts four covered bridges (see our map), a fishing hole, and a photogenic brick Methodist church (in South Tunbridge).

Strafford. If it were any nearer a highway, this quietly spectacular village would be mobbed with tourists. Happily, it's 9 miles north of I-89, and not on the way to anywhere except Tunbridge. Coming from Tunbridge, the road climbs steeply through woods and fields, finally cresting and beginning its downhill run through beautifully restored farms with ponds out back (pools would be too garish), stables, and other signs of wealth not evident on the western side of the mountain. Aristocratic homes—which include the Gothic Revival Justin Morrill Homestead—cluster near the common, at the head of which stands the churchlike white-clapboard Town House, built in 1799, so classic it's a staple of New England photo books.

Chelsea. A village with not just one but two picturesque commons and twin brick 1818 general stores. Noteworthy buildings also include a steepled church, the Orange County Courthouse, a brick library, a bank (since 1822), and many Federal-era homes. An amazing number of services—post office, restaurants, barber, and fish and wildlife office—are compressed into a small space.

Brookfield. "Pond Village," as it's known, easily ranks among the most picturesque four-corners in all New England. It boasts the state's oldest continuously operating library (established in 1791) and Sunset Lake, traversed by a floating bridge, buoyed by barrels (the lake is too deep to

Christina Tree

STRAFFORD'S 1799 TOWN HOUSE IS A BEAUTY.

support a pillared span), currently closed to traffic. Soon as it's warm enough, someone is always fishing here. On the last Saturday in January it's a coveted viewing point for one of New England's last ice-harvest festivals. At the center of the village seasonal **Ariel's Restaurant** draws diners from 50 miles around. Chef Lee Duberman offers seasonal Farm Suppers that are sourced totally from within a 10-mile radius, a clue to the variety of local farms, many of which welcome visitors, some with lodging (floatingbridgefoodandfarms.com). Both **Green Trails Inn** and **Brookfield Bed & Breakfast** offer lodging in the village. **Allis State Park**, a few miles west, offers camping, picnicking, and a sweeping view. The **Marvin Newton House**, Ridge Rd., is an eight-room home built in 1835, now housing local historical exhibits (open Sun. in July and Aug.).

Bethel (population 1,968). At the confluence of the White River and its Third Branch as well as of Rts. 107 (east–west) and 12 (north–south), with access to I-89. This was once a major source of white granite used to face such buildings as Washington, DC's Union Station. An eight-sided former school, now a community center, stands on Rt. 12 in West Bethel.

WILL'S STORE IN CHELSEA IS A SOURCE OF HOMEMADE ICE CREAM.

Christina Tree

Randolph (population 4,800). **Randolph Center** (east on Rt. 66 from I-89, Exit 4) is clearly the oldest of the town's five villages. It's a lineup of brick and clapboard Federal-era mansions along a main street that was cut unusually wide with the idea that this might be the state capital. Instead it's now a quiet village, home to **Vermont Technical College**, grown from the grammar school built here in 1806. According to a historical marker, musician and schoolmaster Justin Morgan brought a young stallion from Massachusetts to his home here in 1789 (Morgan the man lies buried in the nearby cemetery; the grave of the horse—progenitor of the beloved breed—is marked by a simple stone off Rt. 110 in Chelsea). Randolph remains a horsey community, but with the arrival of the railroad in the mid-19th century, population shifted from

Christina Tree

SUNSET LAKE IN BROOKFIELD

the center down to the valley, 3 miles west (now the other side of I-89). It's here that Amtrak now stops, at the station steps from the **Chandler Center for the Arts**, a lively town-owned performance center. The **Randolph Historical Society Museum**, upstairs in the police station, exhibits memorabilia, with the emphasis on railroading; three rooms are furnished in circa-1900 style. (Open third Sun. in May–Oct., 2–4; also July 4.) On Main Street check out **Belmains**, a well-stocked representative of that vanishing breed: "the five-and-dime." Randolph's Independence Day parade is one of the biggest around.

Rochester (population 1,200) straddles Rt. 100 in a quiet valley between the Green Mountains and the Braintree Range. The village centerpiece is 4-acre Rochester Park, a classic green with a bandstand, the scene of Sunday concerts. Just north of the park, a walkable lineup of mismatched buildings is full of surprises. There's a locally owned supermarket (Mac's), a heavy-duty hardware store/laundry, a serious bike shop, two major galleries, a bookstore, plus your choice of cafés and dining options.

Lodging ranges from an upscale inn and luxurious hideaways to a family-geared working dairy, **Liberty Hill Farm** (see the sidebar). The approach over Rochester Mountain provides panoramic views and a delightful alternation of field and forest. North of the village on Rt. 100 the **Green Mountain National Forest Visitor Center** orients sportsmen, picnickers, and hikers to the largely uninhabited western portion of the town that lies within the GMNF. The Bingo area, in particular, offers swimming holes, abandoned town roads, cellar holes, and Civil War–era cemeteries. Rochester also has a nine-hole golf course and serves as a center for mountain biking and for backcountry cross-country skiing. The **Rochester Historical Society** (rochesterhistorical.org) is upstairs in the library, open seasonally on Sat. 10–2. Summer brings a variety of music, inside and out, but everything about Rochester is very low-key. In summer the **Rochester Chamber Music**

BANDSTAND IN DOWNTOWN RANDOLPH

Christina Tree

Society (rcmmsvt.org) sponsors a series of chamber music concerts at the Federated Church as well as the **Green Mountain Suzuki Institute**.

✳ To See

Justin Morrill Homestead (802-828-3051; morrillhomestead.org), 214 Rt. 132, Strafford Village. Open Memorial Day–Columbus Day, Wed.–Sun. 11–5; tours $6. Justin Morrill never went to college but is remembered as the congressman who sponsored the Land Grant Colleges Acts (one in 1862 and another in 1890) that created more than 76 present institutions, currently enrolling some 2.9 million students. Many have evolved into state universities. The son of a Strafford blacksmith, Morrill made enough money as a country storekeeper (which he parlayed into a chain of stores) to retire at age 38 and enter politics on an antislavery and temperance platform. He served in Congress for 44 years (1855–98), never finding much time to spend in his striking, 17-room Gothic Revival mansion because he kept getting reelected. A man who was instrumental in the design and construction of the Washington Monument and the Library of Congress, Justin Morrill helped design his own house and now restored gardens and orchard. The icehouse and carriage barn are fitted with interpretive panels about Morrill and the many national events in which he played a role. Inside and out, this is a fascinating house, well maintained by the Vermont Division for Historic Preservation and Friends of the Morrill Homestead. Check the website for frequent programs and events.

Floating Bridge at Sunset Lake, Pond Village. First built in 1820, the bridge is buoyed up on barrels. It's been replaced seven times since and is presently closed except for foot traffic. It's quite picturesque, a popular place to fish. See Brookfield under *Villages*.

Joseph Smith Memorial and Birthplace (802-763-7742), 357 LDS Lane (off Dairy Hill Rd.), South Royalton. Open year-round: May–Oct., 9–7 daily, 1:30–7 Sun.; otherwise closing at 5. A marker on Rt. 14 (1 mile southeast of the village) points you up a steep, 2-mile hill to a complex maintained by the Church of Jesus Christ of the Latter-day Saints. The property itself begins with a steep hill of maples leading to a hilltop visitors center with paintings, sculpture, exhibits, and a film housed in two buildings. A 38.5-foot-high shaft, cut from Barre granite in 1908, marks the site of the farm on which the founder of the Church of Jesus Christ of Latter-day Saints was born in 1805 and lived until he was 10. Each foot on the shaft marks a year in the life of the prophet, who was murdered by a mob in Carthage, Illinois, in 1844. The 360 well-maintained acres include picnic tables.

Texas Falls, Hancock. On Rt. 125 west of Rt. 100 in Hancock; a Green Mountain National Forest sign points to the road to the falls. It's a quarter mile. The falls are an exceptional series of shoots and pools, rimmed by interesting rock formations. A short, steep (be careful) trail still leads down to the falls. A quarter mile farther up the road is a pleasant riverside picnic area with grills and outhouses.

SCENIC DRIVES The Quickie Tour: Sharon to South Royalton via Strafford and Tunbridge (22 miles). Take I-89 to Exit 2, Sharon, and climb Rt. 132 to Strafford, site of the **Justin Morrill Homestead** and the Town House. Continue up and over the hills and down into **Tunbridge**. If time permits, turn north on Rt. 110 for 5 miles and past three **covered bridges** (see the sidebar) to **Chelsea**. Otherwise turn south on Rt. 110 for the 5 scenic miles back (past one covered bridge) to Rt. 14 at South Royalton and pick up I-89 again at Exit 3 in Royalton, or turn back down Rt. 14 to Sharon. En route you pass the turnoff for the **Joseph Smith Memorial**.

Randolph Center, Brookfield, Chelsea (27 miles). Take I-89 to Exit 4 and turn east into Randolph Center, then north along a glorious ridge road (marked TO BROOKFIELD) to Pond Village with its floating bridge across Sunset Lake (see *Villages*). Addicted as we are to shortcuts, we still recommend passing up the gravel road from East Brookfield to Chelsea; go around through East Randolph (6 miles south on Rt. 14, then turn onto the road marked for Chelsea; it's 6 more miles). Return on Rt. 110 and Rt. 14 to I-89, passing six covered bridges.

COVERED BRIDGES There are five covered bridges in Tunbridge: the **Cilley Bridge**, south of the junction of Rt. 110 with Strafford Rd. and built in 1883; the **Howe Bridge** (1879), east off Rt. 110 in South Tunbridge; and in North Tunbridge, the 1845 **Flint Bridge** and 1902 **Larkin Bridge**, both east of Rt. 110. The **Mill Bridge** (1883), crushed by ice in the winter of 1999, has been rebuilt. In Randolph two multiple kingpost bridges, both built in 1904, are just off Rt. 14 between East Randolph and South Randolph. In Chelsea there is the **Moxley** or **Guy Bridge**, an 1886 queenpost truss wooden bridge, east off Rt. 110.

BIKING Green Mountain Bikes (802-767-4464; 800-767-7882; greenmountainbikes.com), Rt. 100 in Rochester Village. Doon Hinderyckx is a font of information about local trails in and beyond the national forest. He offers guided tours and rents and sells mountain and cross bikes.

Also check with the **Green Mountain National Forest Visitor Center** (*Guidance*), and see *Scenic Drives.*

BOATING AND TUBING While most of the White River is navigable in high water (May–Aug.), the 20-mile stretch from Rochester to Stockbridge and Bethel is especially popular with canoeists, tubers, and kayakers. A good place to put in is at the cement bridge just south of Rochester. In Stockbridge, **Vermont River Tubing** (802-746-8106; vermontrivertubing.net), Rt. 100, just below the junction with Rt. 107, offers rentals, organized tubing trips, and shuttle service. Phone for river conditions. In 2011 Hurricane Irene hit Stockbridge hard, stranding the town and washing out much of Rt. 107, which took three years to rebuild with an eye to future flood control. The result is a wider riverbed with more pullouts and access. The **Sharon Trading Post** (802-763-7404) just off I-89 at the junction of Rts. 14 and 132, also rents tubes. The stretch between North Royalton and South Royalton is favored for canoes and kayaks.

FISHING Trout abound at the junction of the Tweed and White Rivers, downstream of Bethel, above Randolph, and below Royalton. Fly-fishing enthusiasts find the Bethel area good for large rainbow and brown trout, while below Royalton there are bass, spring walleye, and trout. Fishing licenses are available at Tracy's Midway, a convenience store and gas station on N. Main St. in Sharon; at Hubbard's General Store in Hancock; and elsewhere.

Bakers Pond on Rt. 12 in Brookfield has a parking area and boat launch, good for trout fishing. There is a boat access on Rood Pond in Williamstown and a canoe access on **Sunset Lake** in Brookfield, also stocked with trout. The floating bridge is a popular fishing spot.

White River National Fish Hatchery, (802-234-5241) in Bethel, Rt. 107 near the jct. of Rt. 12, raises salmon for the Connecticut River restoration program. Visitors welcome.

Roxbury State Fish Hatchery, Rt. 12A in Roxbury, raises brookies and Atlantic salmon, over 350,000 fish per year. It abuts the Third Branch of the White River, and the fishing downstream can be amazing.

GOLF Montague Golf Club (802-728-3806), Randolph. One of the oldest courses in Vermont, 18 holes. The Second Branch of the White River winds through it. Light fare is served in the clubhouse; lessons offered. *Note:* A driving range is maintained by the Three Stallion Inn just off I-89, Exit 4, on Rt. 66.

The White River Golf Club (802-767-GOLF), Rt. 100, Rochester. Nine holes, clubhouse with a restaurant serving lunch (dinner by arrangement). Open May–Oct. Affordable, great for families, a historic and beautiful course. Next to it is a driving range (802-767-3211).

HIKING The Green Mountain National Forest (see *Guidance*) harbors numerous trails. On Rt. 100 itself in Granville Gulf there are two short nature trails. At Moss Glen Falls, the 0.5-mile loop on the west side of the road is more rugged than the 1-mile loop on the east side.

Allis State Park, Brookfield (off Rt. 12; see *Green Space*). A 2.5-mile trail circles down through meadows and back up through woods. A trail leads from the picnic area to a fire tower with one of the best views in central Vermont

VERMONT RIVER TUBING ORGANIZES FLOAT TRIPS DOWN THE WHITE RIVER.
Christina Tree

(on a clear day, from Killington–Pico to Mount Mansfield to Ascutney). The Bear Hill Nature Trail is another reason for finding this special place.

PICNICKING Brookfield Gulf, Rt. 12 west of Brookfield. Picnic facility, nature trail.

Braintree Hill, Braintree Hill Rd. (off Rt. 12A just west of downtown Randolph). A great picnic spot with an early cemetery and sweeping views to the White Mountains. The handsome Braintree Meeting House here is open by appointment and on Old Home Day (first Sun. in Aug.).

Bingo Brook in Rochester off Rt. 73 in the national forest. Picnic sites with grills by a mountain stream, good for fishing and swimming.

Rt. 100 picnic sites in Rochester beckon down by the White River; check at the GMNF visitors center.

& **Texas Falls** (see *To See*), off Rt. 125, Hancock, offers picnic sites. Handicapped accessible.

SWIMMING Ask locally about various swimming holes in the First, Second, and Third Branches and the main stem of the White River. In Randolph Center there is a manmade beach, bathhouse, and picnic area. Downtown Randolph also offers a pool at its recreational field off School St. One of the deepest swimming holes is under the bridge on Blackmer Blvd. in Stockbridge; just off Rt. 107, look for parking and a trail that takes you down.

✳ Winter Sports

CROSS-COUNTRY SKIING AND SNOWSHOEING Three Stallion Inn Ski Touring Center (802-728-5656; threestallioninn.com), Stock Farm Rd., off Rt. 66, Randolph. Twenty km of groomed skating and touring trails weave through woods and meadows; there are also trails and equipment for snowshoeing. Rentals and instruction are available.

✪ **Nordic Adventures** (802-767-3272; vt-nordicadventures.com), Rt. 100, Rochester Village. Dean Mendell offers a full line of cross-country equipment and snowshoes, lessons, rentals, and guided tours into the heart of the Green Mountain National Forest and from inn to inn. His slogan is "Ski everywhere."

Green Mountain National Forest (see *Guidance*) maintains trails in Rochester on Liberty Hill and at Chittenden Brook.

✳ Green Space

Allis State Park (802-276-3175), Brookfield. Open May 30–Sept. 15. A camping area with 18 tent sites, 8 with lean-tos (no hookups), each on a wooded loop road separate from the picnic area, in which you can choose tables on a windy hilltop or under a pavilion. A hiking trail (see *To Do*) accesses a fire tower with an outstanding view.

Green Mountain National Forest (GMNF). Among the highlights of the Rochester district of the GMNF are the Long Trail and the Texas Falls Recreation Area. Because of the abundance of other things to do in this area, be sure to drop in the GMNF visitors center 2 miles north of the Rochester green on Rt. 100 (802-767-4261).

✳ Lodging

INNS Huntington House Inn (802-767-9140; huntingtonhouseinn.com), 19 Huntington Place, Rochester 05767. Sited on Rochester's large, leafy Central Park, this handsome home has been an inn for many years. From 1819 until 1964, however, it served as a combination home and office for four generations of Huntingtons, all of them doctors—hence the pub known as Doc's Tavern. Six guest rooms are comfortably, unfussily furnished with crafted beds, quilts, and simple window treatments; they're equipped with private bath, air-conditioning, phones, and TV. $129–169 includes a full country breakfast. Next door a former general store

has been transformed into three luxurious two-bedroom condo units accessed by elevator, each with a full kitchen, two baths, and a living room furnished with Oriental rugs and antiques, gas fireplace, and large-screen TV ($255 per night for two, $299 for four). See *Dining Out* and *Eating Out*.

♪ **Three Stallion Inn** (802-728-5575; 800-424-5575; threestallioninn.com), 665 Lower Stock Farm Rd., off Rt. 66, Randolph 05060. From 1927 to 1962 this was the 1,300-acre Green Mountain Stock Farm, one of Vermont's major centers for Morgan horses. Since 1971 it has been owned by real estate developer Sam

Sammis and it's been up for sale for several years. Reviews are mixed. The property adjoins the 18-hole Montague Golf Club, and the inn maintains a driving range. There's also swimming and fishing in the Third Branch of the White River, which runs through the property; a trout pond invites catch-and-release. Facilities include a fitness room, a whirlpool and sauna, two tennis courts, and an outdoor lap pool. Rooms are divided between the main house and the Morgan House across the road. From $125–150 in the main house, but posted rates from $98. Its restaurant is closed at this writing. Thurs.–Sun., the inn's **Willy B's Tavern** (www .willy-b.com) is open, frequently with live music.

BED & BREAKFASTS ✪ ✿ ✎ **Green Trails Inn and Fork Shop** (802-276-3412; green trailsinn.com), P.O. Box 494, Brookfield 05036. Open May–Jan. This handsome house at the heart of Pond Village has welcomed visitors since Jessie Fiske, a Brookfield native who became one of the first women professors at Rutgers University, began renting rooms to her students and associates. Jane Doerfer, the present innkeeper, is an accomplished cook and cookbook author. She offers eight attractive rooms; three work well as a family suite ($100 discount if rented together) with its own entrance. Beds have high-quality mattresses and linens, and the guest rooms all have well-chosen antiques and books. A buffet-style breakfast usually includes fresh fruit, smoked salmon, local cheeses, and a hot dish such as sausage apple cobbler. It's served either in the dining room or in the big, sunny kitchen area with a stone hearth, both with views of Sunset Lake across the road. Guests have access to a grassy beach across the way on the pond. $84–140, $25 per extra person. Inquire about cooking classes,

GREEN TRAILS INN

Christina Tree

solo rates, and whole-house rental (it sleeps 18) as well as **The Fork Shop**, built as a 19th-century pitchfork factory at the edge of the lake, with a waterfall churning musically down along one side. It offers five bedrooms and features a common room walled in windows; also a private patio on the lake. Ariel's Restaurant (see *Dining Out*) is across the street.

✪ **Brookfield Bed & Breakfast** (802-276-3146; brookfieldbandb.com), 2152 Rt. 65, Brookfield 05036. A handsome 19th-century house set back on the edge of Pond Village with views of Sunset Lake. Carrie and George Karal's comfortable, imaginatively furnished one-bedroom apartment with kitchen facilities is a gem ($165); also two more nicely designed rooms in a recent addition. Books and art are everywhere, and a full breakfast is served in the gracious dining room. Both the porch and gardens invite you to relax ($125 per couple).

✪ **Cobble House Inn** (802-234-5458; cobble houseinn.com), 47 Cobble House Rd., Gaysville 05746. Off Rt. 107 between Bethel and Stockbridge. This handsome 1860s Italianate mansion with floor-to-ceiling parlor windows, a widow's walk, and a wide veranda is the only historic building that has survived the series of floods between 1913 and 2011 that have virtually obliterated this village on the main stem of the White River. Built on a ledge high above and back from the river, this is a beauty, sensitively restored by innkeeper Tony Caparis—who, with his amazing mother, Frances, offers a warm welcome. The four guest rooms are comfortably furnished with antiques; the baths, along with the state-of-the-art kitchen, showcase Tony's handiwork. A full breakfast is included in $129 per room. Check the website for local activities.

FARMS *Note:* **Liberty Hill Farm**, described in the sidebar, is our best farmstay pick.

Green Mountain Girls Farm (802-505-1767), 923 Loop Rd., Northfield 05663 (just off I-89, Exit 5). Mari Omland and Laura Olsen are the enterprising hands-on owners of this 20-acre hill farm. Aside from raising pigs, goats, lambs, chickens, and turkeys for organic meat and a wide variety of vegetables and herbs for their farm store, they offer a spacious bedroom with a loft upstairs in the back of their rehabbed 19th-century barn, which also includes a large ground-floor eating and meeting space with a kitchen and bath (composting toilet). $240 for the first night, $200 after for up to six people. The New Farmhouse, completed in 2012, offers three bedrooms, comfortably sleeping six people ($450 per night plus $150 cleaning fee). Grounds include a pond with a swim channel.

✪ ❀ ✿ **Liberty Hill Farm** (802-767-3926; libertyhillfarm.com), 511 Liberty Hill, Rochester 05767. Liberty Hill is the oldest surviving and most authentic farmstay in New England. It's the real thing: a working dairy farm—more than 100 cows—set in a broad meadow, backed by mountains. Its 1890s red barn with cupola, one of the most photographed and painted in Vermont, was built by Dr. Charles Wesley Emerson, founder of Boston's Emerson College. There's a capacious white-clapboard 1825 farmhouse and, best of all, there is farmwife-host par excellence Beth Kennett (Vermont's Innkeeper of the Year in 2013). Beth's own family's farming history dates back to the 17th century in Maine, and "farmer" Bob Kennett's roots run deep into New Hampshire soil. Both families were horrified when Beth and Bob moved "west" in 1979 to this 230-acre spread in a magnificent Vermont valley. Since 1984 they've been welcoming guests. Visitors of all ages are treated to a sense of how much fun (and work if they so desire) living on a farm can be. Kids quickly get to know the cows (black-and-white registered Robeth Holsteins—for Robert and Beth), each with a name tag in her ear. They can help milk, bottle-feed the calves, and collect eggs. It's also a rare chance to meet an authentic Vermont farm family. Sons Tom (with an agriculture business degree) and David (with a degree from UVM in animal science) are now totally involved in the farm, which—among its numerous distinctions—was recognized as Vermont's first Green Agritourism Enterprise. In the barn a transfer unit takes heat from the cows' milk and warms water used to feed the baby calves their milk as well as washing the milking equipment.

Meals are served family-style, and Beth makes everything from scratch. Dinner is at 6 (BYOB) and as delicious as it is prodigious—maybe incredibly moist sliced turkey, a zucchini casserole, cucumber salad, a garden salad with tomatoes, pumpkin muffins, mashed potatoes or a carrot soufflé, fresh-picked sweet corn, a choice of homemade dressings and stuffings—all set in the middle of a table seating eight adults and at least as many children. The kids disappear after the main course, and adults linger over blueberry pie with homemade (from the farm's own milk) raspberry ice cream. Usually guests number a dozen or so, but our last (July) visit coincided with the Rochester-based Green Mountain Suzuki Institute, with parents and children around the long dinner table numbering upward of 30. Beth's warmth as well as her table expanded to embrace every kid as well as grown-up, making us all feel smart enough to be there.

Difficult as it is to believe today, this was one of the farms hardest hit by Hurricane Irene in August 2011. The lower fields and barn were flooded and, with a house full of guests, Liberty Hill was isolated for five days. Beth can't say enough about the volunteers who poured over the hills and down the streambeds on ATVs, initial responders to help with the animals and clearing the detritus from the soil. Cabot Creamery Cooperative, of which the Kennetts are members, not only

Elsewhere

❀ ✿ **Devil's Den Farm Homestay Bed & Breakfast** (802-685-458), 296 Rt. 110, Chelsea 05038. Rhoda and Bill Ackerman offer a warm welcome to their rambling farmhouse, built by Rhoda's grandparents. Both sides of the family are rooted six generations deep in Chelsea. There's plenty of sitting space inside and out (on the flower- and rocker-lined porch). There's a downstairs guest room off the sitting room; upstairs are two double-bedded rooms and a suite. All are furnished with family antiques, quilts, and handwoven rag rugs on polished hardwood floors. Note the many woodcarvings by Rhoda's mother, Clara Gilman. You'll also enjoy 65 acres of fields, pastures, and woods, access to the First Branch of the White River, and a trail to downtown Chelsea, a mile back

beyond the bend. $90 includes breakfast; inquire about discounts. Maple syrup sold year-round. The entire five-bedroom house can be rented for $500 per night.

❀ ✿ **Marge's B&B at Round Robin Farm** (802-763-7025), RR 1, Box 52, Fay Brook Rd., Strafford 05072. This is a 395-acre farm with one of Vermont's famous 10-sided barns (built in 1917). It's been in the family for seven generations. What's offered is the homey, clean, and cheerful farmhouse with its Mission-style dining room and sitting room with a TV/VCR, or rooms therein (two rooms with double bed and two with twins, sharing one bath), plus a fridge with the fixings for making your own breakfast in the big country kitchen. Marge Robinson lives within call in the adjacent house. Cross-country skiing. No smoking and no pets, please. A supplied volunteers but reimbursed them for the week's worth of milk they had to dump. (The farm produces 8,000 pounds' worth of milk a day).

There's plenty of common space, including two sitting rooms with pianos, but in summer adults seem to congregate on the porch. There are seven guest rooms (five with queen beds, one with two single beds, and a room with four single beds) and four shared baths; families can spread into two rooms sharing a sitting room and bath. In summer you can hear the gurgle of the White River (good for trout fishing as well as swimming and tubing), and in winter you can ski or snowshoe up into the adjacent Green Mountain National Forest or off into the village across the meadows. This is also a handy location for exploring the Champlain Valley to the west via the Middlebury Gap, as well as much of central Vermont to the east via Rochester Gap or Rt. 100 heading north and south. $120 per adult, $60 per child under 12, MAP.

THE HOUSE AT LIBERTY HILL FARM

double room is $45 per person per night. Inquire about the price for the whole house. Snowmobile trails run through the property.

Grand View Farm (802-685-4693; grandview farmvt.net), 1628 Scales Hill Rd., Washington 05675. This is a hilltop fiber farm. Kim Goodling and her husband, Chuck, raise sheep, llamas, and angora goats, as well as rabbits, hens, and pigs. The B&B part of the farmhouse is divided from the family house by the kitchen. Dating from the 1700s, it consists of a sitting room and two bedrooms, one with twins and the other with a four-poster queen. Breakfast can be full or continental. $220 per night for both rooms, $150 for one. Inquire about fiber workshops.

Four Springs Farm, Campground and Learning Center (802-763-7296; foursprings farm.com), 776 Gee Rd., Royalton 05068. Jinny

Cleland raises organic vegetables, chickens, and flowers on her 70-acre farm and invites visitors to tag along on chores. Programs are also offered to the families and groups who stay here, taking advantage of either eight secluded campsites ($25) or the four-bunk cabin with mountain views ($50). There's a central washhouse and a picnic pavilion.

SECOND HOMES ✿ **Hawk North**, Vermont's Mountain Hideaway (800-832-8007). Two- to four-bedroom contemporary hilltop chalets with superb mountain and valley views in the Stockbridge/Rochester area, privately owned but splendidly built by the same developer, all with signature fieldstone fireplace, living room deck, and fully equipped kitchen. Rates vary with the season: $200–375 per night, third night free. Weekly, monthly rentals.

CAMPGROUNDS Lake Champagne Campground (802-728-5298), P.O. Box C, Randolph 05061. Open Memorial Day weekend–mid-Oct. A 150-acre property with fields, a 3-acre swim lake, hot showers, mountain views, and facilities for tents through full-sized RVs.

Abel Mountain Campground (802-728-5548; abelmountain.com), 354 Mobile Acres Rd., Braintree 05060. Sited on 270 acres by the Third Branch of the White River, 131 grassy RV and tent sites, two shower houses, swimming pool, hiking trails, river tubing.

Limehurst Lake Campground (802-433-6662; limehurstlake.com), 4101 Rt. 14, Williamstown 05679. This family-geared campground offers 76 sites with full hookups for RVs, a separate area for lean-tos and tents, modern restrooms, hot showers, a waterslide, a sandy swim beach, boat rentals and fishing (no license required), and a game room.

Chittenden Brook Campground in the Green Mountain National Forest (802-767-4261), 5.3 miles west of Rochester on Rt. 73. The 17 campsites are fitted with picnic tables and grills; there are hand-operated water pumps and vault toilets. The surrounding forest provides good fishing, hiking, and birding. No trailers over 18 feet. No hookups or showers.

Note: Primitive camping is permitted almost everywhere in the Green Mountain National Forest.

Allis State Park (802-276-3175; vtstateparks .com). Open mid-May–Labor Day. Named for Wallace Allis, who deeded his Bear Mountain Farm to the state as a campground and recreational area. Sited on the summit of Bear Mountain, it includes a picnic area and trail to the fire tower, as well as 18 tent and 8 lean-to sites, each with a picnic table and fireplace. Hot showers but no hookups. Handy to several good fishing ponds.

✱ Where to Eat

DINING OUT

In Randolph/Brookfield

✪ ✿ **Ariel's Restaurant** (802-276-3939; ariel srestaurant.com), 29 Stone Rd., Brookfield. Open late Apr.–Oct., Wed.–Sun. 5:30–9:30. Reserve. Overlooking Sunset Lake in the middle of Pond Village, this destination dining room is known as one of the best places to eat in Vermont. Lee Duberman and Richard Fink are longtime chef-owners who specialize in Mediterranean and Pacific Rim dishes, using local ingredients whenever possible and offering a choice of small, medium, and large plates. On a summer's day you might begin with a crabcake in kataify pastry, then dine on grilled boneless Cavendish Farm quail with fig, honey, and balsamic vinaigrette, topped off with a lemon napoleon with raspberry coulis. Entrées $22–28. Children are welcome. Don't pass up dessert, maybe a seasonal fruit crisp with buttermilk sorbet and caramel sauce or honey lavender crème brûlée with housemade cookies ($8). Inquire about cooking classes and seasonal three-course Farm Suppers ($29) that are sourced totally from within a 10-mile radius, a clue to the variety of local farms (floatingbridgefoodandfarms .com).

In Randolph

✪ **One Main Tap & Grill** (802-431-3772; one maintg.com), 1 Main St. Open daily from 3, Thurs.–Sat. until midnight. A great addition! An attractive space with seasonal sidewalk table. Local beers are a specialty, with more than a dozen on tap, as well as other not-so-local brews plus Citizen Hill (hard) Cider and a thoughtful choice of wines. The food isn't an afterthought either: from burgers and panini to rabbit with an apricot demiglaze roasted in Bent Hill (brewed in Braintree) red ale. Entrées $12–15.

✪ **Black Krim Tavern** (802-728-6776; the blackkrimtavern.com), 21 Merchants Row. Open for dinner Tues.–Sat. Named for a variety of tomato, this is a small, colorful restaurant that draws diners from a distance. The menu changes each week, but the focus is on fresh and creative combinations of local. You might dine on a fava bean patty in peanut sauce and roasted rabbit with a yam cake and toasted walnuts. The reasonably priced menu features Asian and vegetarian dishes with a stress on fresh and local. Cocktails, local brews on tap.

In Rochester

School Street Bistro (802-767-3126; school streetbistro.net) 13 School St., corner of Main St. (Rt. 100). Open Tues.–Sat. 5–9. Eugene and Brent Smith's small bistro is a winner with a constantly changing, imaginative, and reasonably priced menu. It includes a choice of burgers served with root veggies and a choice of vegetarian and meat dishes—maybe pork tenderloin in a Dijon mustard and cider cream sauce. $9–20.

Doc's Chop House at the Huntington House Inn (802-767-9140; huntingtonhouse inn.com), 19 Huntington Place. Open Wed.–Sun. 5–9. This attractive inn dining room overlooks the green. Chef Bobby Cheshire uses local ingredients as much as possible. Entrées from $16 for rosemary-encrusted pork to $22 for rib eye. Soup and salad bar for $12. Also see Doc's Tavern under *Eating Out*.

WORTHY BURGER IS HOUSED IN A FORMER
FREIGHT HOUSE IN SOUTH ROYALTON.

Elsewhere

Inn at Idlewood Restaurant (802-763-5236), 54 Steele Rd. (Rt. 132), Sharon. Theoretically open for dinner Wed.–Sat. but call. Minutes from the I-89 Sharon exit. Well-spaced tables in this bright, deftly decorated, century-old barn are the setting for locally sourced, fairly basic dishes like fish-and-chips and soft pulled pork tacos—but obviously chef-owners Alex Roupunican and Marcy Marceau would rather be showcasing their French training. Pass up the all-natural burger and go for the bistro tenderloin steak with frites and flourless chocolate torte or crème brûlée. Entrées $14–29.

Stone Soup Restaurant (802-765-4301), 7 Brook Rd., Strafford. Reservations requested. Open Thurs.–Sun. 6–9. No credit cards. There is no sign outside this distinguished old house in Strafford Village, just down from the striking 1799 Town House. The chef-owners continue to earn rave reviews for signature dishes ranging from quail to scallops to Burmese stew.

EATING OUT Road food, listed geographically from south to north, off I-89.

In South Strafford

Café 232 (802-765-9232; cafe232.com), 232 Rt. 132. Open for breakfast and lunch daily except Mon., also for dinner Thurs., Fri. A great roadside oasis delivering local comfort food "with a twist." Dinner the evening we stopped by included crabcakes on a bed of greens and pulled pork with potato salad and coleslaw. Both $14.95.

In South Royalton

Worthy Burger (802-763-2575), 56 Rainbow St. Open for lunch and dinner. Styled as "a craft beer and burger bar" and housed in the former railroad freight house, this is the hot spot for this town full of law students, who simply walk across the tracks from the green. More than a dozen microbrews were on tap when we stopped by.

#5 Olde Tavern & Grill (802-763-8600), 192 Chelsea St. Open daily 11–11. The original eatery by this name is at 5 Olde Nugget Alley (hence the name) in Hanover, New Hampshire; a sleek, student-geared coffeehouse/pub, good for pizza, burgers, and quesadillas along with veggie stir-fry and ribs.

Chelsea Station Restaurant (802-763-8685), 108 Chelsea St. Open 6–3. A folksy place with a counter and booths. Most people know one another, but visitors feel welcome. Better-than-average diner food, freshly baked bread, good soups.

((ᵂ)) South Royalton Market (802-763-2400; soromarket.com), 222 Chelsea St. Open daily. A co-op style store featuring local and organic foods and Equal Grounds Café.

Along Route 110 in Chelsea

Dixie's II (802-685-7802), Main St. (Rt. 110), Chelsea Village. Open 6–3, closing at 1:30 Mon.–Wed. The same menu all day with blackboard specials. This is a 19th-century brick bank building with a nice atmosphere, standard menu.

At I-89, Exit 3

✪ Eaton's Sugar House, Inc. (802-763-8809). Located at the junction of Rts. 14 and 107 in Royalton, just off I-89, Exit 3. Open daily 7–3. A good old-fashioned family restaurant featuring pancakes and local syrup, sandwiches, burgers, and reasonably priced daily specials. Try the turkey club made with fresh-carved turkey on homemade bread. Vermont maple syrup, cheese, and other products are also sold.

In Bethel

Bethel Village Sandwich Shop (802-234-9910), 269 Main St. Open 7–late afternoon. David Sambor's pleasant café now offers full breakfast and lunch with special house-baked muffins—maybe raspberry cheesecake—each morning and hot lunch specials. On an October morning it was pumpkin ginger soup with a steak, avocado, and cheese wrap.

Cockadoodle Pizza Café (802-234-9666; cockadoodlepizza.com), 269 Main St. Open Mon.–Thurs. 11–8, Fri.–Sat. 11–9, Sun. noon–8. A wide choice of mouthwatering signature pizzas plus panini and sandwiches on "rustic rolls," each named for a different Vermont town.

CENTRAL VERMONT

Along Route 107

Tozier's Restaurant (802-234-9400), Rt. 107 west of Bethel. Open May–Oct., in summer 11–8, Thurs.–Sun. in shoulder seasons. A classic road-food stop with pine paneling and a river view. Seafood (mostly fried, some broiled) is a dinner specialty, along with turkey dinner. Take-out window for ice cream and basics.

❂ ✿ **Creek House Diner** (802-234-9191), junction of Rts. 107 and 12, Locust Creek. Open year-round, daily 7 AM–8 PM. A clean, handy road-food stop with booths, a salad bar, liver and onions, prime rib, friendly service, beer and wine. We dined happily on a grilled chicken salad. Great daily specials. Children's menu.

At I-89, Exit 4, Randolph

Three Bean Café (802-728-3533), 22 Pleasant St. Open 6:30–5. Closed Sun. The in gathering place for many miles around offers from-scratch croissants and baked goods, then nourishing soups and veggie sandwiches plus a variety of coffees and teas, the day's papers, and comfortable seating.

((ᵧ)) **Randolph Depot** (728-3333), 2 Salisbury St. Open Mon.–Sat. 7–4. Housed in the town's Victorian-style brick train depot (an Amtrak stop), this attractive restaurant features an unusual choice of salads as well as panini sandwiches and wraps.

Randolph Village Pizza (802-728-9677), 1 S. Main St. Open daily 11–9, until 10 in summer

THE SODA FOUNTAIN AT THE ROCHESTER CAFÉ

Christina Tree

and on weekends year-round. A wide variety of pizzas and calzones; also salads, grinders, and pasta.

Chef's Market (802-728-4202), 839 Rt. 12 south. Open weekdays 9–6, Sat. 9–5, Sun. 10–3. Featuring local and organic produce, this is also a source of great sandwiches, from organic PB&J on oatmeal bread ($3.99) to a Gobbler Grill or Roast Beef & Bleu.

Along Route 100

Doc's Tavern at the Huntington House Inn (802-767-9140; huntingtonhouseinn.com), 19 Huntington Place, Rochester. Open except Tues. Housed in a newly renovated barn, this is an informal sports bar with booths and a pool table, a pub menu, and a dozen local beers on tap. Seasonal outdoor seating.

Rochester Café & Country Store (802-767-4302), Rt. 100, Rochester Village. Breakfast 7–11:30, lunch until 5. Good fries and burgers, pleasant atmosphere. Great soda fountain, booths, the town gathering place. Try the maple cream pie.

✿ **Sandy's Books and Bakery** (802-767-4258), 30 N. Main St. (Rt. 100), Rochester. Open 7:30–6. Just north of the gas pumps. Good in the morning for espresso, fresh-made whole-grain breads and muffins, and at lunch for soups, salads, and sandwiches, vegetarian choices, cookies all day, beer and wine. Light dinner served but only until 6.

✳ Entertainment

Chandler Center for the Arts (802-728-6464; chandler-arts.org), 71–73 Main St., Randolph. This community-based arts organization, housed in **Chandler Music Hall** (built in 1907), includes a 575-seat theater with outstanding acoustics and handsome stenciling. Facilities were recently renovated and expanded to mark the building's centennial. It's open year-round for performances that include chamber music, traditional and heritage music, folksingers, family performances, and the Vermont Symphony Orchestra, as well as several self-produced events, including the annual Mud Season Variety Show, Mini Mud Show for youth, and annual July 4 youth musical. In addition to main stage events, the **Live & Upstairs** series in the renovated Upper Gallery includes a curated film series and intimate performances. **Chandler Gallery** is a venue for changing exhibits featuring outstanding regional artists, as well as local student and adult artists. Regular gallery hours are Thurs. 4–6 and Sat.–Sun. 1–3, as well as during performances or by appointment.

YOUNG ARTISTS AT CHANDLER CENTER FOR THE ARTS

The Music Hall also stages three annual festivals: The **Summer Pride Festival** highlights stories of parenting, marriage, faith, and love with the goal of deepening cultural understanding of gay and lesbian themes; the **Central Vermont Chamber Music Festival** features performances by outstanding classical musicians; and the annual **New World Festival** on Labor Day Sunday celebrates the region's Celtic and French Canadian heritage with performances by more than 70 musicians in Chandler and all-weather tents. Check the website for current programming.

In August the **Central Vermont Chamber Music Festival** (centralvtchambermusicfest .org) includes performances in the area.

Rochester Chamber Music Society Concert Series (802-767-9234; rcmsvt.org) during June and July in Rochester and Hancock Village venues.

Summer Park Concert Series, Rochester, summer Sunday evenings.

The Playhouse Movie Theatre (playhouse flicks.webplus.net), Main St., Randolph, is the oldest movie house in the state. Shows first-run flicks most of the week and old favorites a few nights per week. The schedule varies a lot.

Randall Drive-In Movie Theatre, Rt. 12 in Bethel, operates weekends in summer.

The White River Valley Players (wrvp.org), a major community theater in Rochester, performs a spring musical and fall production in the high school.

✷ Selective Shopping

ART/CRAFTS STUDIOS AND GALLERIES
❦ **Green Mountain Glassworks** (802-767-4547), 5523 Rt. 100, Granville. Open Wed.–

Mon. 9–5 most of the year. Don't pass up this exceptional roadside studio and gallery. Vermont natives Michael and Angela Egan shape Venetian-style freehand blown glass into spectacular vases, pitchers, and a variety of art glass, reasonably priced glass earrings.

Judy Jensen Clay Studio (802-767-3271), 61 N. Main St., Rt. 100 back behind the Rochester Café. Open daily. Jensen's pottery ranges from tiny vases to large urns, tiles to chess sets, sculpture, handmade cards, and plenty of highly decorative functional ware. She also displays work in fiber.

BigTown Gallery (802-767-9670; bigtown gallery.com), 99 N. Main St., Rochester Village. Open Wed.–Sat. 10–5, Sun. 11–4. Anni Mackay designs and makes wearable art, but her studio showcases an eclectic mix of paintings, sculpture, and furniture as well as yarns and one-of-a-kind hats and scarves. The gallery features local artists with exhibits changing monthly. It's also a setting for piano rehearsals and plays performed in the backyard amphitheater.

Art of Vermont (802-565-8296; artofvt.com), 27 N. Main St., Randolph. Open Wed.–Sat. 3–7. New in the winter of 2014–15, this upscale gallery represents Vermont artists in a variety of media. The gift shop showcases pottery, jewelry, and more.

SPECIAL STORES Sandy's Books & Bakery (802-767-4258; seasonedbooks.com), 30 N. Main St., Rochester. Librarian Sandy Lincoln specializes in sustainable lifestyles, wilderness tales, and renewable energy; the store is also a café (see *Eating Out*) and sells a full line of Vermont Soap Organics (Sandy's husband's venture) as well as crafted items, fresh flowers, and more.

MICHAEL EGAN AT WORK AT GREEN MOUNTAIN GLASSWORKS, HANCOCK

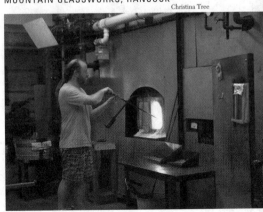

FLOATING BRIDGE FOOD AND FARMS

The beauty of this region is best appreciated by following back roads to the many farms that welcome visitors. Call ahead for tours, workshops, lodging, and to check on pick-your-own offerings, farm stands, and stores. In and around Brookfield's Pond Village a dozen or so farms, Ariel's Restaurant, and Green Trails B&Bs have joined forces in a common website: **floatingbridgefoodandfarms.com**. Their logo is the work of local resident—and nationally recognized *New Yorker* cartoonist—Ed Koren. Members include **Green Mountain Girls Farm** (802-505-1767), 923 Loop Rd., Northfield (just off I-89, Exit 5). Mari Omland and Laura Olsen are the enterprising hands-on owners of this 20-acre hill farm. Their farm store sells organic meat (they raise pigs, goats, lambs, chickens, and turkeys) and a wide variety of vegetables and herbs (also see *Lodging*). **Fat Toad Farm** (802-279-0098; fattoadfarm.com), 787 Kibbee Rd., Brookfield, is a family-run goat farm producing goat's-milk caramel sauces, handcrafted in small batches. **Brookfield Bees** (802-276-3808), 1148 Kibbee Rd., Brookfield. From their apiary Dan Childs and Marda Donner offer raw honey and make candles and soap. **L. H. Stowell & Son Christmas Trees** (802-276-3392), 1591 Twin Pond Rd., Brookfield. A 200-acre Christmas tree farm offering choose & cut trees. Inquire about cottage rental.

Floating Bridge Food & Farms Cooperative

Ed Koren

FLOATING BRIDGE FOOD & FARMS COOPERATIVE INVITES VISITORS TO EAT, SLEEP, AND SHOP AT ITS MEMBER FARMS, RESTAURANT, AND B&BS

The Bowl Mill (802-767-4711; outside Vermont 800-828-1005), Rt. 100, Granville. Open 9–5 daily, year-round. Decorative wooden bowls are no longer made here but still sold at this writing, along with toys, crafts, baskets, maple products.

GENERAL STORES The Tunbridge Store (802-889-5525), Rt. 110, Tunbridge. Open daily 7–7, the 1830s village store is now owned by Kathi and Scott Terami. They offer coffee and ice cream as well as staples and Vermont products. There's a full deli, a sandwich source.

Snowsville General Store (802-728-5252; snowsville.com), Rt. 12, East Braintree. Owner Gene Booska, an avid hunter, stocks more than 400 guns, from handguns to rifles, new and used, and U.S.-manufactured outdoor clothing such as Johnson Woolen Mill jackets and pants; wood and used cars are also sold along with groceries and a selection of papers, just not *The New York Times*. The Round Oak stove here burns away most of the year, the centerpiece for this village gathering spot.

FARMS ⚘ Neighborly Farms of Vermont (802-728-4700; 888-212-6898; neighborlyfarms .com), 1362 Curtis Rd., Randolph Center. Open Mon.–Sat. 9–4. Rob and Linda Dimmick and their three children run an organic dairy and make organic cheeses that they sell at the farm store and through area stores. Visitors are welcome to see the cows and watch cheesemaking (call ahead for days/hours) through the viewing window in the store, which also features honey products from Brookfield (the bees are raised on several local farms) and fresh goat cheese, lamb, eggs, four flavors of goat's-milk caramel from Fat Toad Farm in Brookfield, and floral wreaths and baskets from Spruce Lake Farm (also in Brookfield).

⚘ Vermont Technical College Farm (802-728-3395), Rt. 66 east off I-89, Exit 4. Tour the sugarhouse, apple orchard (pick your own in-season), and dairy barn.

Maple Ridge Sheep Farm (802-728-3081; mrsf.com) in Braintree, said to be the oldest and largest Shetland sheep farm in the country, produces fleece, machine-washable sheepskin, yarn, knit and woven items, meat. Call first.

Lincoln Farm (802-728-9333), 3075 Rt. 66, Randolph Center. A seasonal farm stand with produce, flowers, bakery, maple products, and honey.

✪ **Sunshine Valley Berry Farm** (802-767-3989), Rt. 100 north. Organic blueberries and raspberries, pre-picked or PYO, open in-season daily 10–6.

Redrock Farm (802-685-2282; 866-685-4343; christmastrees.net), 2 Redrock Lane (off Jenkins Brook Rd., which is off Rt. 110), Chelsea. Pick out your Christmas tree any time of year and have it shipped to you—anywhere in the contiguous 48 states—at Christmas. You can also order by mail, but you miss half the fun.

✳ Special Events

Last Saturday of January: **Brookfield Ice Harvest Festival**—ice cutting, ice sculpting, hot food, sledding, skating, skiing.

March: **Maple Open House Weekend** (vermontmaple.org), local sugarhouses.

Mid-June: Held biannually, **Vermont History Expo** is a two-day gathering of Vermont historical societies from throughout the state, bringing their exhibits to fill the Tunbridge Fairgrounds. Historic reenactments and demonstrations, music, grandstand, and many varied events. See vermonthistory.org/expo.

July: July 4 parades in Strafford and Rochester, a bigger one in Randolph (usually over 5,000 spectators), with food and crafts. **Family Farm**

Festival, Randolph Center. Chandler Players perform at Chandler Center for the Arts, Randolph. **Chelsea Flea Market**—150 dealers cover both greens. **Summer Night**, a community-wide celebration in Rochester.

July–August: **Randolph Gazebo Series** (802-728-3010)—Tuesday-evening music. Summer music school workshops at the Mountain School, Vershire. **Huntington Farm Show**, Strafford. **Brookfield Blues Festival** (August), off Rt. 65 in Brookfield. The **South Royalton Town Band**, in business for more than a century, gives free concerts on the green Thursday evenings. The **Tweed River Music Festival** (tweedriverfestival.com) is a mix of music, camping, midmonth in Stockbridge.

September: **New World Festival** (newworldfestival.com), Sunday before Labor Day at the Chandler Music Hall in Randolph, features northern New England and Celtic music, in addition to food and crafts. **White River Valley Festival**, Bethel. **Tunbridge World's Fair** (tunbridgefair.com), Tunbridge, four days at midmonth, ongoing for more than 130 years in a superb setting, definitely one of the country's most colorful agricultural fairs with horse and oxen pulling, contra dancing, sheepdog trials, livestock and produce judging, horse racing, amusement rides, pig races, pony rides, and more. **Harvest Fair** on the park in Rochester.

October: **Vermont Sheep and Wool Festival**, first weekend, at the Tunbridge Fairgrounds.

November: **Annual Hunters' Supper**, Barrett Hall, Strafford.

SUGARBUSH/MAD RIVER VALLEY

Seven miles wide and named for the river down its center, the Mad River Valley is magnificent, walled on the west by some of the highest peaks in the Green Mountains, with meadows stretching to the Roxbury Range in the east. In summer and fall there is hiking on the Long Trail, soaring in gliders above the Valley, mountain biking on ski trails and high woods roads, horseback riding, fishing and swimming in the Mad River, plus outstanding golf and tennis. In August the monthlong Vermont Festival of the Arts offers daily happenings.

There were farms and lumber mills in this valley before Mad River Glen began attracting skiers in 1948, but the look and lifestyle of the present community center on its ski areas. The '60s brought an influx of ski-struck urbanites to Sugarbush, Glen Ellen (the two have long since merged), and Mad River Glen. They played polo, built an airport, a gliding school, specialty shops, and fine restaurants. Young architects eager to test new theories of solar heating and cluster housing designed New England's first trailside homes and condominiums. This early commitment to design is still evidenced by the fact that several thousand visitors can bed down here on any given night, but it's far from obvious where.

Physically just 4 miles apart, Sugarbush and Mad River Glen are diametrically different. By the 1990s it had become painfully clear that northern New England's natural snow is too fickle a base for the big business that skiing had become. To make snow you need water, a challenge the two ski areas faced in their own ways. Mad River Glen, the "ski it if you can" mountain, kept its demands and lift prices modest, becoming the country's first cooperatively owned ski area (divided among some 2,000 shareholders). It also remains the only area in the East that bars snowboarders, featuring telemarking and animal tracking instead.

Sugarbush installed a snowmaking pond and now offers manmade cover on the majority of its 111 trails, but remains one of the most ecologically and community-sensitive of the East's mega ski resorts. Back in the '90s when its multi-resort-owner proposed building one of its signature "grand" hotels at the base of Lincoln Peak, the community balked. Sugarbush Resort has now been owned by a locally based partnership for more than a decade and has undergone a major revitalization. Snowmaking has been improved, and a there's a new slope-side Vermont-themed village with a condo hotel and two new base lodges.

With direct links to the Champlain Valley via the scenic roads through the Appalachian and Lincoln Gaps on the west, this is a logical lodging and dining hub from which to explore some of Vermont's most magnificent and varied landscapes. Dining and shopping are outstanding but uncrowded.

GUIDANCE Mad River Valley Chamber of Commerce (802-496-3409; 800-82-VISIT; madriver valley.com), Box 173, Waitsfield 05673. A walk-in visitors center in the General Wait House, 4061 Main St., Waitsfield, is open year-round weekdays 9–5, though the lobby is open 24 hours with brochures, lodging vacancies, courtesy phone, and clean restrooms. Request the helpful, free guide from their website or by phone.

Green Mountain National Forest Ranger District Office and Visitor Center (802-767-4261), Rt. 100 in Rochester. Open 8–4. While this excellent information center is 25 miles south of Warren, it's worth knowing it's there (see "White River Valleys") as a resource for exploring much of the area immediately west and south of the Valley.

GETTING THERE *By bus and train:* Montpelier is the nearest Vermont Transit/Greyhound stop. Waterbury, 12 miles north of Waitsfield, is the closest Amtrak station.

By air: Burlington International Airport is 45 miles away; see "Burlington Region" for carriers.

By car: Valley residents will tell you that the quickest route from points south is I-89 to Randolph, 15 miles up Rt. 12A to Roxbury, then 8 miles over the Roxbury Gap to Warren. This is also the most scenic way (the view from the top of the gap is spectacular), but be forewarned: This high road can be treacherous in winter. In snow, play it safe and take I-89 to Middlesex, Exit 9, then Rt. 100B the 13 miles south to Waitsfield.

GETTING AROUND During ski season the **Mad Bus** fleet circles among condos at the top of the access road and restaurants and nightspots. These are free 26-passenger buses that link the Valley floor to all three mountain base areas, running daily and until 1:30 AM on Saturday night.

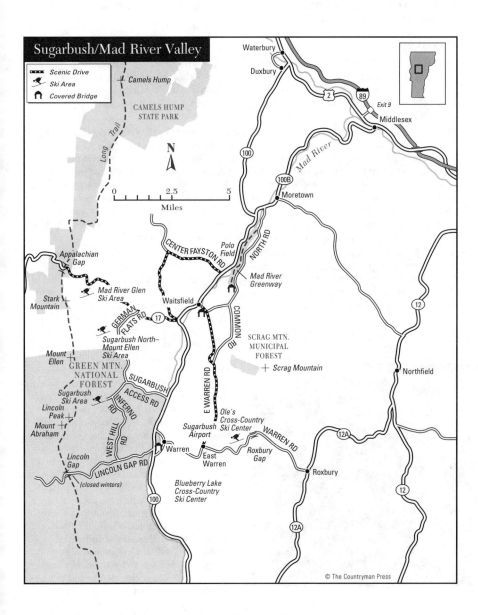

Alpine Limo (802-793-3543), **C&L Taxi** (802-496-4056), and **Morf Transit** (802-864-5588; 800-696-7433) offer local and long-distance service.

Note: Waitsfield–Champlain Valley Telecom offers free local calls on some phones (but not all, so check) scattered around the Valley. Wireless Internet service is widely available in local lodgings and coffee shops.

WHEN TO GO Christmas week through February is high season, high volume, especially in a snowy season when Mad River Glen is wide open. Midweek during this same period is cheaper and far quieter. Ditto for March, when the manmade snow base at Sugarbush is deep and weekend crowds have eased. By mid-April it's all over. May and June appeal to birders (spring migration before trees are in full leaf). Warren's Fourth of July parade, small but famous, kicks off a series of summer events. As noted above, thanks to the gap roads this is an ideal hub for foliage. After the leaves fall it's dead until mid-December.

MEDICAL EMERGENCY Call **911**. **Ambulance** (802-496-3600). **Mad River Valley Health Center** (802-496-3838), Rt. 100, Waitsfield.

✳ Villages

The Mad River Valley includes **Moretown** (population 1,653) to the north and **Fayston** (population 1,141), an elusive town (it's easy to get to, just hard to find!) without a center that was an important lumbering presence into the early 20th century. It's home to the former Mount Ellen (now part of Sugarbush Resort) and Mad River Glen ski areas, and to inns and restaurants along Rt. 17 and the German Flats Rd.

Warren Village. The village center of the long-established farm town of Warren (population 1,700) is a compact clapboard cluster of town hall, historic meetinghouse, bandstand, and general store across from an inn. At first glance the village doesn't look much different from the way it did in the 1950s when Rt. 100 passed through its center, but the effect of Sugarbush, the ski resort that's way up an access road at the other end of town, has been total. The **Pitcher Inn**'s self-consciously plain face masks an elegant restaurant and some of the most elaborate (and expensive) themed rooms in Vermont; the **Warren Store** (once a stagecoach inn itself) stocks a mix of gourmet food and upscale clothing and gifts. Arts, antiques, crafts, are within an easy walk, and a covered bridge spans the Mad River. The village is the setting for one of Vermont's most colorful July 4 parades.

Waitsfield (population 1,659; historicwaitsfieldvillage.com) is the Valley's commercial center, with two small, well-designed shopping centers flanking Rt. 100 on land that was farmed until the 1960s. This area is also known as Irasville, but don't let the highway signs confuse you: It's still the center of Waitsfield. The historic district is half a mile north on Rt. 100, a gathering of 17th- and 18th-century buildings, including a library and steepled church, on and around Bridge St. (leading to the Great Eddy Covered Bridge). Much larger and denser than it first looks, the village offers a sophisticated mix of boutiques and services and several first-rate restaurants. Changing historical exhibits from the Waitsfield Historical Society (waitsfieldhistoricalsociety.com) are displayed in the General Wait House Visitor Center. Benjamin Wait, you learn, had been a member of Vermont's famed Rodgers' Rangers and weathered dozens of French and Indian Wars battles, as well as serving in the Revolution before founding the town at age 53 in 1789. He later was pitted against his fellow settlers on the question of where to put the town common. He wanted it just about where the commercial center is today (the original common has been left high and dry out on Joslin Hill Rd.). Check out the **Madsonian Museum of Industrial Design** (802-496-2787; madsonian.org), 45 Bridge St. Open Sat. 2–6, with exhibits ranging from cars to toasters, the latest project of Valley architect David Sellers.

WAITSFIELD'S COVERED BRIDGE SPANS A POPULAR SWIMMING HOLE.

Christina Tree

In winter the Valley's magnets are its alpine and cross-country ski areas, but in summer there are an unusual number of activities to pursue. Check the following list and find details and updates at **madrivervalley.com/activities.**

BICYCLING—ROAD & MOUNTAIN The area's outstanding scenery and variety of hard-topped roads have long drawn serious cyclists. Recently a quickly expanding network of technical singletrack trails—a total of 60 miles over a vertical variance of 3,000 feet—has been gaining traction in mountain biking circles. Sugarbush Resort's lift-serviced trails now connect with a Valley-wide network. **Mad River Riders**, a local organization with both mountain and roadie members, has mapped and connected about 30 miles of trails through a mix of public forest and private farmland. Their 5-mile network at **Blueberry Lake** opened in 2013, has been hailed as a model design that's banked and pitched for beginners as well as experienced riders. (This is also a local favorite because you can ride and then cool off in the lake.) Another fave is the **Revolution Trail**, looping from Lareau Farm into the Camel's Hump State Forest. For maps and events, check madriverriders.com. **Sugarbush Adventure Center** (sugarbush.com) offers rentals with pads and helmets as well as clinics, kids' and adult mountain bike camps, and lift service to its trails. For questions and repairs, check with **Clearwater Sports** (802-496-2708), **Infinite Sports** (802-496-3343), or **Stark Mountain Bike Works** (802-496-4800), which offers Thurs.-evening bike rides (junction of Rts. 100 and 17). The possible tours for road cyclists are spectacularly varied—from quiet river roads to two of the highest gaps (mountain passes) in Vermont. This is the hub of the four-day Labor Day weekend **Green Mountain Stage Race** (gmsr.info), attracting some of the country's most serious cyclists. Check **madriver valley.com** for suggested routes, along with those listed here under *Scenic Drives*. **Fit Werx** (fitwerx .com), 4312 Main St., Waitsfield, is nationally famed for fitting serious cyclists to their bikes.

CANOEING AND KAYAKING Clearwater Sports (802-496-2708; clearwatersports.com), Rt. 100, Waitsfield. Barry Bender offers rentals and learn-to-canoe, -kayak and -stand-up programs including guided river trips and paddleboard yoga. Tubing rentals are available, as are put-ins and pickups. The local paddling pond is manmade Blueberry Lake in Warren.

FISHING Numerous streams offer good fly-fishing. The chamber of commerce keeps a list of half a dozen guide services. Vermont fishing licenses are required and can be obtained at the Village Grocery (802-496-4477), Rt. 100, Waitsfield; Moretown Store (802-496-6580); and Bisbee Hardware (802-496-3635). **Fly Fish Vermont Service** (802-253-3964). Rob Shannon, based at the Fly Rod Shop in Stowe (flyrodshop.com), offers year-round instructional, guided tours.

FITNESS CENTERS Sugarbush Health & Racquet Club (802-583-6700; sugarbush.com), Sugarbush Village, Warren. An outstanding complex with indoor and outdoor pools, indoor and outdoor Jacuzzis, whirlpool, sauna, steam room, exercise room, indoor squash, tennis, and racquetball courts, massage room, aerobics studio, 11-station Nautilus, and a full range of cardiovascular equipment. Massage also available.

Bridges Family Resort and Tennis Club (802-583-2922; bridgesresort.com), Sugarbush Access Rd., Warren. A year-round health and tennis club with indoor and outdoor tennis, heated pools, fitness center, hot tub, and sauna.

FOR FAMILIES ✐ Sugarbush Summer Adventure Center (802-583-6300; sugarbush .com), Lincoln Peak Village, top of the Access Rd. Open seasonally. An 800-foot zipline; two disc-golf courses, including the Peak Course (chairlift access); and mountain biking with kids' programs and instruction for all ages. There's also a four-station bungee trampoline that can send you soaring. The **Sugarbush Health & Racquet Club** (802-583-6700) has a state-of-the-art indoor climbing wall, open to anyone

LIFT-ASSISTED MOUNTAIN BIKING AT SUGARBUSH RESORT

John Atkinson

over 6 years old (instruction available). Summer day camps are offered at the **Bridges Family Resort and Tennis Club** (802-583-2922; 800-453-2922) in Warren. For ages 13 and up there's even a weeklong **Junior Soaring Camp** (802-492-2708) at the Sugarbush Airport (see *Soaring*). **Mad River Glen** offers nature-geared day camps in summer.

GOLF **Sugarbush Resort Golf Club** (802-583-6725), 1091 Golf Rd., Warren. An 18-hole, Robert Trent Jones Sr. course, PGA rated 42, par 72; cart and club rentals, lessons, practice range, café. Inquire about golf/lodging packages.

HIKING Pick up a copy of *Trails, Paths & Long Trail Hikes Guide*, available at the chamber of commerce, which unlocks the area's many superb hiking secrets.

Sandy Macy

SUGARBUSH GOLF CLUB OFFERS 18 HOLES, DESIGNED BY ROBERT TRENT JONES.

The **Long Trail** runs along the ridge of the Green Mountains here and is easily accessible from three places: the two gap roads and the Sugarbush Bravo chairlift. From the Lincoln Gap Rd. (the gap itself is 4.7 miles west of Rt. 100) you can hike a short way south to Sunset Ledge for a view of the Champlain Valley and Adirondacks. The more popular hike, however, is north from the gap (be advised to start early; parking is limited) to the Battell Shelter and on to Mount Abraham (5 miles round-trip), a 4,052-foot summit with spectacular views west, south as far as Killington Peak, and north as far as Belvidere Mountain. From Mount Abraham north to Lincoln Peak (accessible by Sugarbush chairlift) and on to Mount Ellen (4,135 feet) is largely above tree line; 3,600-foot General Stark Mountain to the north is best accessed (still a steep 2.6-mile hike) from Rt. 17 at Appalachian Gap. For details about the two shelters, contact the **Green Mountain Club** (802-244-7037; green mountainclub.org). Mill Brook Inn's Joan Gorman also recommends beginning 2.1 miles up Tucker Hill Rd. at the small parking area (on the left) at the CAMEL'S HUMP STATE FOREST sign. Follow the blue blazes through the stand of pines known as "the Enchanted Forest" to the top of Dana Hill Rd. (approximately a one-hour round-trip, good for skiing and snowshoeing).

Mad River Glen (802-496-3551; madriverglen.com) offers a full schedule of guided backcountry trips and bird-watching tours. The ski trails are a popular route up to the summit of Stark Mountain, with spectacular views west to Lake Champlain and the Adirondacks. Also see *Walking and Running* for the Mad River Path Association trails.

HORSEBACK RIDING **Vermont Icelandic Horse Farm** (802-496-7141; icelandichorses.com), 3061 N. Fayston Rd., Waitsfield. Year-round. These strong, pony-sized mounts were brought to Iceland by the Vikings, but are still relatively rare in this country. Karen Winhold uses her stable of around 20 mounts for one- and two-hour, half- and full-day trail rides and (seasonal) inn-to-inn treks from her stable. The horses have an unusually smooth gait (faster than a walk, gentler than a trot).

ROCK CLIMBING The **Valley Rock Gym** (802-583-6754), part of the Sugarbush Health & Racquet Club, Sugarbush Village, features an indoor climbing wall. Open to anyone over age 6 but no experience necessary. Instruction offered.

SCENIC DRIVES **East Warren Road**. If you miss this road, you miss the heart of the Valley. From Bridge St. in Waitsfield Village, cross the covered bridge, bear right onto East Warren Rd., and continue the 6 miles to East Warren. The views are of the Green Mountains set back across open farmland. For an overview of the Valley, take the Roxbury Gap Rd. up to the pullout (be careful, because there aren't many places to turn around). From East Warren, loop back the 2 miles through Warren Village to Rt. 100.

Bragg Hill Road. The views from this peerless old farm road are magnificent: down across pastures and the narrow valley cut by the Mill Brook to Mount Ellen. Begin at Bragg Hill Rd. (off Rt. 100 just north of the Rt. 17 junction) and drive uphill, continue as it turns to dirt, and follow it around (bearing left); it turns into Number 9 Rd. and rejoins Rt. 17.

Granville Gulf (see the map in "The White River Valleys"). Drive Rt. 100 south from Warren and the Valley quickly disappears, replaced by a dark, narrow, and twisty pass, part of the Granville Gulf State Reservation. At the height-of-land, the Mad River begins its north-flowing course toward the Gulf of St. Lawrence and the White River rises, flowing south to eventually empty into Long Island Sound. A few miles south **Moss Glen Falls** spill down a steep cliff by the road. To turn this 20-mile drive into a day trip, continue to Hancock and across the Middlebury Gap to Middlebury, then back across Appalachian or Lincoln Gap (see the box) to the Mad River Valley.

Mad River Byway. Rt. 100 from Granville Gulf to Middlesex Village has been designated the "Mad River Byway"; pick up a pamphlet guide at the chamber office or check it out on the website mad rivervalley.com.

SOARING Sugarbush-Warren Airport (802-496-2290; sugarbush.org), Warren. Open daily May–Oct. Respected as one of the East's prime spots for riding thermal and ridge waves. Solo and private glider lessons, rides, vacations available for all ages. Come just to see who's gliding in and out. Thurs.–Sun. seasonal **Sugar Mamma's** (802-496-7841) offers soups, sandwiches, salads, and Sun. brunch in the pleasant airport café.

SPAS MadRiver Massage (802-496-5638; madrivermassage.com), Starch House overlooking the Mill Brook, Rt. 100, Waitsfield (just north of the Rt. 17 junction). Open daily 10–5, Sun. seasonally. A full range of massage, also shiatsu, reflexology, Reiki, and "stress-diffuser," plus body and bath products.

SWIMMING South of Warren Village, the Mad River becomes a series of dramatic falls and whirl-pools cascading through a gorge. The most secluded swimming hole is by the **Bobbin Mill** (the first right off Rt. 100 after Lincoln Gap Rd., heading south); park by the gravel pit and follow the path through the pines to a series of pools, all icy cold. Ask locally about **Warren Falls** and the best spot for skinny-dipping. The **Lareau Farm swimming hole** (now a town park) in the Mad River, south of Waitsfield on Rt. 100, is best for kids. **Blueberry Lake** in Warren is now owned by the Green Mountain National Forest; the **Ward Fishing Access area** on Rt. 100B in Moretown is another good bet. **Bristol Falls** is just about 10 miles from Warren via the Lincoln Gap Rd. The **Sugarbush Sports Center** features a large, L-shaped outdoor pool with adjacent changing facilities, café, bar, and Jacuzzi; the **Bridges Family Resort and Tennis Club** offers indoor and outdoor pools and swimming lessons. Many inns also have outdoor pools. The **Punch Bowl** swimming hole off Rt. 100 south of Warren is clothing-optional; inquire.

TENNIS The **Bridges Family Resort and Tennis Club** (802-583-2922; 800-453-2922), Sugarbush Access Rd., Warren, offers indoor and outdoor courts and year-round tennis clinics for both adults and juniors.

Sugarbush Health and Racquet Club (802-583-6700; 800-53-SUGAR) is open to the public and is the venue for **New England Tennis Holidays** (netennisholidays.com), a top-rated tennis instruction program.

WALKING AND RUNNING The **Mad River Path Association** (madriverpath.com) maintains several evolving recreation paths in the Valley, namely: the **Warren Path**, beginning near Brooks Field at Warren Elementary School (Brook Rd., Warren); the **Millbrook Path** in Fayston, running along the hill through the woods (blue blazes) between Millbrook Inn and Tucker Hill Lodge, on up across German Flats Rd. to the Inn at Mad River Barn; the **Mad River Greenway**, following the Mad

MOSS GLEN FALLS IN GRANVILLE GULF ON RT. 100 SOUTH OF WARREN

Christina Tree

River from a parking area on Meadow Rd.; and the **Village Path**, which begins at Fiddlers' Green and heads south to the Irasville Cemetery and beyond. See also *Hiking* and *Scenic Drives*.

WEDDINGS ♂ Many inns and resorts throughout Vermont specialize in weddings—but those in the Valley were among the first to do so. Indeed, the area probably still represents the state's single largest concentration of venues and related services. Begin with the chamber—vermontweddings .com/MadRiverValley—and look for our weddings symbol throughout this chapter.

✳ Winter Sports

CROSS-COUNTRY, TELEMARK SKIING, AND SNOWSHOEING Ole's Cross-Country Center (802-496-3430; olesxc.com), 2355 Airport Rd., Warren. More than 30 miles of groomed trails radiate out across the meadows and into the woods with elevations ranging from 1,120 to 1,640 feet. Reservations requested for lessons and tours. The center is downstairs in a small airport building; upstairs **Sugar Mamma's** (802-496-78420) offers breakfast, lunch, and Sun. brunch in a many-windowed space with views of fields and mountains.

🐾 **Blueberry Lake Cross-Country Ski Center** (802-496-6687), 424 Plunkton Rd., East Warren. A hidden treasure, not far from Ole's on the scenic east side of the Valley, this is a homey, old-style touring center with snacks, drinks, and a woodfired hearth as well as rentals and some 30 km of secluded and protected trails with elevations of 1,300–1,500 feet, groomed to skating width, set single track.

Clearwater Sports (802-496-2708), Rt. 100, Waitsfield, offers rentals, along with custom and group tours, backcountry skis, and "skins" for attempting local stretches of the Catamount Trail (below).

Local trails

Puddledock in Granville Gulf State Reservation on Rt. 100, south of Warren, has 3.5 miles of ungroomed trails marked with red metal triangles; a map is available at the registration box.

Catamount Trail (catamounttrail.org). Check the guidebook (see "What's Where") and website for stretches of the trail in the Valley. The most popular begins at the Battleground (see *Lodging*) on Rt. 17 and climbs steadily uphill to the Beaver Ponds in the Phenn Basin Wilderness area.

DOWNHILL SKIING ♂ **Sugarbush Resort** (802-583-6300; 800-53-SUGAR; sugarbush.com), 1840 Sugarbush Access Rd., Warren. Skiers and boarders of all abilities find plenty to please here. Six peaks and two separate trail systems on two major mountains—3,975-foot Lincoln Peak at Sugarbush South and 4,135-foot Mount Ellen at Sugarbush North—are linked by a 2-mile (9½-minute) quad chair. It traverses the 2,000-acre Slide Brook Basin (also accessible to backcountry skiers via a 12-passenger Pisten Bully cat), which separates these formerly distinct ski areas. Sugarbush skiers will tell you how fortunate their resort was to be sidelined during the era in which a large percentage of New England's best ski trails were smoothed, widened, and generally homogenized. In particular they are thankful that the Castle Rock trails, recognized throughout the country as some of the meanest, most natural, and most interesting expert terrain at any major American ski resort, survive. Intermediates will also find classic, wide cruising runs as well as wide, open trails.

The primary base area for the resort is Lincoln Peak Village at Sugarbush South. It's evolved over the years, with the newest additions all Vermont themed and named. The barn-red Claybrook Hotel Ski sports a silo and round barn-shaped restaurant. Ski services are in the Farmhouse and kids' programs, in the Schoolhouse. The Mount Ellen base area is less extensive but user-friendly, a good place to begin on a busy weekend. Mount Ellen is the resort's highest lift-accessed peak and offers varied terrain, expansive views, and the Reimergasse Terrain Park (for riders and freestyle skiers). The two base areas are connected by frequent shuttle service.

Lifts: 16: 7 quads, 3 triples, 4 doubles, and 2 surface. All operate 9–4, 8:30–4 weekends and holidays.

Trails: 111: 20 acres of patrolled tree skiing; 508 skiable acres.

Vertical drop: 2,650 feet.

Snowmaking: 285.5 acres overall.

Facilities: At the Lincoln Peak base, the Gate House, Schoolhouse (children's programs), and Farmhouse lodges offer cafeterias, lounges, ski shops, rentals, and restaurants; the centerpiece here is the slope-side Clay Brook Hotel and Residences, condominiums. Pisten Bully access to Allyn's Lodge on Lincoln Peak for specialty dinners and Powder Morning First Tracks.

Sugarbush Ski and Snowboarding School: Headed by Olympian extreme skier John Egan, the emphasis is on learning by doing. Clinics, special teen program; women's clinics, guided backcountry skiing are offered.

Snowboarding: Rentals, lessons, terrain parks.

For children: Nursery from infancy; the curbside accessible Schoolhouse houses a Children's Adventure Leaning Center with Micro, Mini, and SugarBear programs.

Rates: In 2014–15: $84 weekdays, $91 weekends and holidays adults; $65/71 ages 7–18 and 70-plus; there are also substantial savings with multiday rates and lodging packages.

Tips: Favorite intermediate runs are Jester and Snowball (upper and lower).

✍ **Mad River Glen** (802-496-3551; in-state snow reports 802-406-3551, ext. 150; outstanding website: madriverglen.com). The ubiquitous red-and-white bumper sticker challenges MAD RIVER GLEN: SKI IT IF YOU CAN, but the mountain is one of the friendliest as well as the most challenging places to ski. It's also the only one in New England to prohibit snowboarding. One of the region's oldest major ski areas (the first to offer slope-side lodging), in 1995 it became the first to be owned cooperatively by its skiers, who are dedicated to preserving its narrow, continuously vertical trails, cut to the contours of the mountain. Access to the summit of Stark Mountain (3,637 feet) is via the vintage-1948 single chair, the only one left in the country, rehabbed rather than replaced in 2007. All trails funnel into the central base lodge area, the better for families, many of whom are now third-generation Mad River skiers. Another matter of Mad River fact: Some long-popular woods trails are off the ski map, a phenomenon that has since been aped by many other ski areas. This is also a favored place for telemarking and the only major ski mountain with a serious snowshoe trail system and full program of snowshoeing/nature treks. On a good snow day it's the region's best ski buy.

Lifts: 4 chairs, including the single (see above), plus the Callie's Corner Handle Tow.

Trails and slopes: 21 expert, 8 intermediate, 16 novice, a total of 800 skiable acres.

Vertical drop: 2,037 feet.

Snowmaking: 15%, which includes top-to-bottom on the Practice Slope, also other high-volume, low-elevation areas.

Facilities: Base lodge, cafeteria, and pub; also the newly restored Birdcage, halfway up the mountain, serving sandwiches, drinks; ski shop, rentals, ski school.

For children: Cricket Club Nursery for 6 weeks–6 years; programs for ages 3–17 include Junior Racing and Junior Mogul.

Rates: $66 adults, $70 holidays, $45 midweek; less for juniors (14 and under) and seniors (65–69); half-day, multiday rates. Under 6 and over 70 ski free.

Tip: According to frequent MRG skier Joan Gorman, intermediates can experience the same kind of terrain the experts enjoy without the steepness or the large moguls. Joan's favorite is Porcupine, a wide trail with some pitch and length to it. It is often groomed, but with moguls allowed to build up along the edges. Snail, a long, winding, almost cross-country-ski-type trail, is entirely different, lined with trees and with twists and turns that keep you paying attention. Off the single chair, intermediates can enjoy the narrow, beautiful cruiser Antelope to the mid-station and then cross over to continue down the mountain on Bunny, not quite as benign as its name implies. Back off the double, Quacky can be enjoyed by skiers of differing abilities, the more expert skiers entering from the very top and the more intermediate skiers, from one of the two lower entrances. Joining this trail with Periwinkle creates a very long top-to-bottom intermediate run.

ICE SKATING The Skatium at Mad River Green Shopping Center in Waitsfield (lighted) offers rentals, also available from neighboring **Inverness Ski Shop** (802-496-3343); free day and night skating on the groomed hockey rink at Brooks Recreation Field off Brook Rd. in Warren. Also see the **Ice Center** in Waterbury (icecenter.org).

Stark Mountain by Snowshoe (Mad River Glen 802-496-3551; madriverglen.com), Warren. Half a dozen trails ranging in length from a short spur to 2.2 miles are marked, and Mad River's resident naturalist Sean Lawson offers a full program of guided **tracking treks**, 10:30 weekend days, also monthly full moon. An on-mountain nature center has been recently rehabbed and expanded. **Telemarking** is also a longtime specialty at **Mad River Glen**. Inquire about rentals, lesson and lift packages, and special events.

SNOWMOBILING Eighty miles of local trails are maintained by the Mad River Ridge Runners; snowmobile registration can be purchased at **Kenyon's Store**, Rt. 100,Waitsfield. No rentals.

SUGARBUSH/MAD RIVER VALLEY

✳ Lodging

Note: The website madrivervalley.com offers overviews of Valley lodging. Inquire about Ski The Valley Passport with discounted tickets at both ski areas as well as cross-country and other perks.

Note also: Many Valley lodgings request a two-night minimum stay on winter and other popular weekends.

RESORTS Sugarbush Resort (800-53-SUGAR; sugarbush.com), 1840 Sugarbush Access Rd., Warren 05674, maintains the two following properties.

🐾 ♂ **Claybrook at Sugarbush**, 104 Forest Dr., Warren 05674. This new, full-service, 110-room condo-hotel lies at the hub of the Sugarbush lifts. Red with a central silver silo, it's an improvement on the standard box hotels built recently at many ski mountains, with units ranging from studios to five rooms, all with Shaker-style decor, fireplace, and granite-topped kitchen. Sixty-one units are in the rental pool; those in the South Wing are pet-friendly. Facilities include an outdoor pool and whirlpools, a fitness room, a garage, and Timbers Restaurant (see *Dining Out*). In winter you are steps from the lifts; in summer there is golf, mountain biking, and more.

Sugarbush Inn (802-583-6100; 800-537-8427; sugarbush.com), Warren 05674. Handy (via shuttle and car) to lifts at both Lincoln Peak and Sugarbush North and across the road from the golf course, this is an inviting 42-room inn, owned by the same company that owns the mountain. Amenities include use of the Sports

CLAYBROOK AT SUGARBUSH IN THE EVENING SNOW

Sugarbush Resort

and Racket Club, room phones, air-conditioning, a library and sitting room, and an outdoor pool.

♂ **The Bridges Family Resort and Tennis Club** (802-583-2922; 800-453-2922; bridges resort.com), 202 Bridges Circle, Warren 05674. A self-contained, family-geared resort just down the access road from the Sugarbush main lifts and base lodge. Tennis is the name of the game here. Facilities include indoor tennis and outdoor courts, an indoor pool, saunas, hot tub and fitness room, and 100 attractive condo-style units ranging from one to three bedrooms, each with fireplace, sundeck, TV, and phone, some with washer/dryer. $165 for a one-bedroom midweek to $710 for two nights (the minimum) for a three-bedroom on a weekend. Cheaper off-season and the longer you stay; inquire about ski and tennis packages.

INNS The inns listed below serve dinner as a matter of course; B&Bs may serve dinner on occasion.

🐾 **Pitcher Inn** (802-496-6350; pitcherinn .com), 275 Main St., Warren 05674. Designed by architect David Sellers to look like it's been sitting in the middle of Warren Village for a century, the white-clapboard inn opened in the 1997–98 winter season, replacing a building that had burned. A member of Relais & Châteaux, this is the Valley's most luxurious inn. Common spaces include a small library, a hearth, an elegant dining room (see *Dining Out*), and the downstairs pub. Each of the nine guest rooms in the inn itself was designed by a different architect to convey a different aspect of local history. The Lodges suggests a Masonic lodge (once a major social force in the Valley), with a ceiling painted midnight blue and delicately studded with stars, and obelisk-shaped posts on the king-sized bed. From a bedside switch in the Mountain Room, you can make the sun rise and set over the mountains painted on the facing wall. Bathrooms are splendid. $325–650 for rooms, $825 for each of the two suites in the neighboring annex, includes breakfast and afternoon tea (Sun.–Thurs. is $100 less); a 13 percent service charge is added. Deduct $75 for single occupancy but add $75 per extra person. Dogs are permitted in the Stable Suite. Inquire about packages.

♂ ♂ **Mad River Barn** (802-496-3310; mad riverbarn.com), 2849 Mill Brook Rd., Waitsfield 05673. Heather and Andrew Lynds have taken the Valley's most legendary lodge down to the studs and put it back together with new plumbing, wiring, central air, and an ambience that's just as appealing to families and sports-minded singles and couples as ever, also just as

MILLBROOK INN IS KNOWN FOR ITS GOOD FOOD

distinctive as the old icon. The large game room and bar as well as the rooms are all brighter and cleanly lined but with furnishings and detailing creatively recycled, much of it from the old lodge. The 18 rooms are divided between the main Barn (built originally as lodging for the CCC in the '30s and a ski lodge since the '40s) and the adjoining small "Farmhouse," now housing two amazing-looking bunk rooms, each with six beds and one bath. Each can be rented as a whole (minimum four people) or per bed. In the old (1980s) Annex, the family-sized rooms are clean and comfortable, a pre-makeover sampling. From $120 midweek, $175 weekends, breakfast included. For more about the bar and restaurant, both open to the public, see *Eating Out*.

The Waitsfield Inn (800-758-2801; 800-758-3801; waitsfieldinn.com), P.O. Box 969, Rt. 100, Waitsfield 05673. Innkeepers Jon and Vickie Walluck seem equal to the task of managing this middle-of-the-village inn, an 1825 parsonage with a "great room"—offering plenty of space to relax in front of the hearth—in the attached (former) carriage and horse barn. The dining rooms (serving buffet dinners to the public Thurs.–Sun.) are well away from the several comfortable spaces reserved for guests. The 14 guest rooms (all with private bath) vary from cozy doubles to family rooms with lofts. Appropriate for children ages 6 and older. $99–229 during regular summer and winter seasons includes a full breakfast.

🏕 **Weathertop Mountain Inn** (802-496-4909; 800-800-3625; weathertopmountaininn.com), 755 Mill Brook Rd., Waitsfield 05673. Deceptively plain on the outside, inside Weathertop is filled with light—and also with Asian art, Persian carpets, and souvenirs from the several

years innkeepers Lisa and Michael Lang spent traveling while based in Singapore. More surprises: In addition to a full breakfast, they offer guests an optional full dinner menu with a dozen entrée choices, such as spiced minced lamb with yogurt and mint sauce, or venison medallions in black pepper. Common space includes a large, comfortable living room with fieldstone fireplace and piano as well as TV with DVD/video player and a library of old movies, plus a fourth-floor game room with a fireplace. Down off the patio there's a hot tub and sauna. The eight air-conditioned rooms have either two quilt-covered double beds, a queen, or a king. All have fridge and full bath. $119–179 per room includes breakfast; add $32 for dinner.

BED & BREAKFASTS 🗡 **The Inn at Round Barn Farm** (802-496-2276; theroundbarn .com), East Warren Rd., Waitsfield 05673. Named for its remarkable round (12-sided) barn built in 1910 and now housing the Green Mountain Cultural Center (see *Entertainment*), with a lap pool and greenhouse on its ground floor, this old farmhouse is one of New England's most elegant bed & breakfasts. There are 12 antiques-furnished rooms, 7 with gas fireplace, several with steam shower and/or Jacuzzi, all overlooking the meadows and mountains. Guests who come in winter are asked to leave their shoes at the door and don slippers to protect the hardwood floors. Common space includes a sun-filled breakfast room, a stone terrace, a book-lined library, and a lower-level game room with pool table, TV, VCR, and a fridge stocked with complimentary soda and juices. From $175 midweek off-season for a double room with a regular shower to $330 on weekends in high season for a suite with marble fireplace, canopy king bed, Jacuzzi, and steam shower. Prices include gourmet breakfast and afternoon edibles. Weddings are a specialty of the barn, which also serves as a venue for summer concerts and opera. In winter the inn maintains extensive snowshoe trails (snowshoes are complimentary to guests). Appropriate for children 15 and older. The inn hosts an Opera Festival in June, a photo exhibit in August, and a juried art show in foliage season.

❂ ❀ 🏕 🗡 **Millbrook Inn** (802-496-2405; 800-477-2809; millbrookinn.com), 533 Mill Brook Rd. (Rt. 17), Waitsfield 05673. Open year-round except Apr., May, and mid-Oct.–mid-Dec. This 19th-century farmhouse is a gem. The two living rooms, one with a fireplace, invite you to sit down. Each of the seven guest rooms is different enough to deserve its own name, but all have stenciled walls, bureaus, antique beds with firm twin, queen-, or king-sized mattresses, and private bath. One of the Valley's first ski lodges, Millbrook is open in summer as well. Longtime innkeeper Joan Gorman, a serious chef, offers an optional four-course dinner to guests ($37 per person), and a full breakfast is included in $120–140 per couple. Pets by prior arrangement, no charge. Inquire about the two-bedroom, two-bath Octagon House where children are welcome (there's a crib). It's a short walk but on the wooded hillside behind the inn (minimum two days).

Wilder Farm Inn (800-496-8878; wilderfarm inn.com), 1460 Main St., Waitsfield 05673. A handsome yellow 1850s farmhouse north of the village, across the road from the Mad River and one of its better swimming holes. Inside and out there's plenty to please here: a parlor with a TV, appropriate but comfortable seating, floor-to-ceiling windows, and a library with even more comfortable seating and a big stone hearth that, like the one in the dining room, burns real logs. Breakfast is a serious, organic production with ingredients from the garden or otherwise as local as possible. The eight rooms are tastefully decorated, and innkeepers Luke and Linda offer extras like snowshoes to use on the grounds, as well as tubes for the river. Luke is an avid beer connoisseur and offers tours—guided or otherwise—of Vermont's best micro-breweries, also an avid mountain biker with advice about the area's best singletrack tours. He's the Naked Potter, too, well known for the "naked raku" pottery produced in the full-service studio next door. From $125 per room, weekdays in August, to $172 on winter weekends.

The Mad River Inn (802-496-7900; 800-832-8278; madriverinn.com), P.O. Box 75, Tremblay Rd. off Rt. 100, Waitsfield 05673. An 1860s house with fine woodwork and large picture windows overlooking meadows that invite snowshoeing in winter. It is also steps from the recreation path and a good swimming hole and serves as lodging base for the Vermont Icelandic Horse Farm. The seven guest rooms and a single two-bedroom suite all have featherbed and private bath. Facilities include an outdoor hot tub and a downstairs game room with a pool table. Rates from $105 for the smallest room with a private but hall bath, to $160 for the largest with private bath on a weekend; a three-course breakfast and afternoon tea are included. Children 5 years and older are welcome. Inquire about two- to five-day riding packages.

1824 House (802-496-7555; 800-426-3986; 1824house.com), 2150 Main St. (Rt. 100), Waitsfield 05673. North of the village, the gabled house is decorated with an eye to room colors, and comfort. The eight guest rooms vary, but all have private bath. There are gracious drawing and dining rooms with fireplaces. The 15-acre property invites walking, and there's a good swimming hole in the Mad River just across the road. The 1870s post-and-beam barn is a frequent wedding venue. $125–175 per room includes a full breakfast. Two-day minimum on weekends, three on winter holidays.

West Hill House (802-496-7162; 800-898-1427; westhillbb.com), 1496 West Hill Rd., Warren 05674. A gabled farmhouse off in a far corner of the golf course but convenient both to the Sugarbush lifts and to the village of Warren. Susan and Peter MacLaren offer nine guest rooms, including two suites, some Scottish themed, all with private bath with either a Jacuzzi tub and shower or steam bath/tub/shower combo, and all with gas fireplace and direct phone. The house offers an unusual amount of common space: a living room, library with fireplace and pool table, and sunroom with views to the mountains and spectacular gardens. Step out the front door to cross-country ski or play golf, out the back into 9 wooded acres. $140–280 per couple.

Mountain View Inn (802-496-2426; vtmountainviewinn.com), 1912 Mill Brook Rd. (Rt. 17), Waitsfield 05673. This very Vermont house is bigger than it looks, with seven nicely decorated guest rooms (private baths). It's been geared to guests since it became one of the Valley's first ski lodges in 1948. Since 1978, under ownership by Fred and Susan Spencer, its year-round feel has been that of an unusually hospitable small country inn. Rooms are furnished with antiques (our favorite is the 1840s "rolling pin" tiger maple bed) and bright quilts. Guests gather around the wood-burning stove in the living room and at the long, three-century-old pumpkin pine harvest table for breakfast. Handy to Sugarbush, Mad River Glen, and the Mill Brook Path. $100–150 per couple B&B.

The Featherbed Inn (802-496-7151; feather bedinn.com), 5864 Main St. (Rt. 100), Waitsfield 05673. Tom and Linda Gardner are the innkeepers in this nicely restored 1806 inn, with exposed beams, pine floors, and a formal living room as well as an informal "lodge room" with a fieldstone fireplace, games, and books. It's set far back from Rt. 100, overlooking flower gardens and fields. Ten guest rooms are divided between the main house, which includes two family-friendly suites, and a garden cottage with three more rooms, all with featherbed mattresses. $130–184 (depending on room and season) includes a full breakfast; the cottage is $249.

Beaver Pond Farm (800-685-8285; beaver pondfarminn.com), 1225 Golf Course Rd., Warren 05674. There's a welcoming feel to Kim and Bob Sexton's beautifully renovated 1840s farmhouse, overlooking a beaver pond and set in the rolling expanse of the Sugarbush Golf Course. The four guest rooms all have private bath, fine linens, and down comforters; also spa robes to ease your way to the outside hot tub. Breakfast is an event, and the 24-hour wet bar includes complimentary coffee and tea, honor-system wine and beer. $159–204. Check Ski & Stay packages.

The Sugartree Inn (802-583-3211; 800-666-8907; sugartree.com), 2440 Sugarbush Access Rd., Warren 05674. This contemporary ski lodge, with a country inn interior, stands near the very top of the access road. Brits Graham Hewison and Maxine Longmuir offer nine attractive rooms; there's a fireplace in the comfortable living room, a hot tub outside. In the dining room a two-course (sweet or savory) breakfast, with specials like stuffed pears and three-cheese soufflé, is included in the $120–195 per couple; so is afternoon tea.

Yellow Farmhouse Inn (802-496-4263; 800-400-5169; yellowfarmhouseinn.com), P.O. Box 345, 550 Old County Rd., Waitsfield 05673. This 1850s farmhouse sits off above meadows, minutes from the middle of Waitsfield. Mike and Sandra Anastos offer seven comfortable guest rooms and a suite (all with private bath); several rooms have gas or electric Vermont Castings stove, some a whirlpool tub. $109–239 (the high end is for the two-room suite with Jacuzzi and kitchenette, sleeping four).

&. **Tucker Hill Inn** (phone/fax 802-496-3983; 800-543-7841; tuckerhill.com), 65 Marble Hill Rd., Waitsfield 05673. A classic 1940s ski lodge with a fieldstone hearth in the pine-paneled living room. Phil and Alison Truckle offer 15 rooms and suites, all with private bath, phone, TV. Most rooms have queen or king bed and are accessed off one hall in the main house. Most suites are in the newer Courtyard Building, but a two-room on the lower level of the main house—with a Jacuzzi, gas fireplace, and private entrance—can accommodate a family (no children under 6, please). From $139 per room to $329 per suite includes a full breakfast.

♂ **Inn at Lareau Farm** (802-496-4949; 800-833-0766; lareaufarminn.com), 48 Lareau Road at Rt. 100, Waitsfield 05673. This classic old farm adjoins the American Flatbread (pizza) Company, which now owns it. The 13-room inn has spacious grounds stretching to a swimming hole and back to a wooded hill and including an outdoor pavilion, a popular site for weddings. $90–135 per couple.

♀ ☸ ♪ **Hyde Away Inn** (802-496-2322; hyde awayinn.com), 1428 Mill Brook Rd. (Rt. 17), Waitsfield 05673. One of Mad River's original ski lodges, the Hyde Away offers reasonably priced accommodations geared to families and hard-skiing singles alike. The tavern (see *Après-Ski*) is literally tucked away at the back with a separate entrance from the inn. Guests have their own living room with a fireplace; there's also a family-geared restaurant (see *Eating Out*). Rooms range from two "over the bar" with shared bath ($89), to recently added suites with whirlpool bath or fireplace, to family rooms sleeping up to five, $109–199 during ski season. Cheaper in summer. Request a quiet room.

Hostel Tevere (802-496-9222; hosteltevere .com), 203 Powderhound Rd., off Rt. 100, Warren 05674. An attractive hostel, the creation of Sarah (from Cape Cod) and Giles (from Milwaukee), who met in Rome. A UVM grad who grew up skiing at Sugarbush, Sarah saw the need for reasonably priced, hostel-style lodging in the Valley—and felt they needed to include a bar as well (not approved by Hostelling International). There are four coed bunkrooms with featherbeds (towels are extra): $35 per adult, less for students and kids. Breakfast is so good that it draws locals. Sarah is surprised by the number of older (20s-plus) folks and families who are frequent repeaters.

Also see **Mountain Valley Farm** under *Selective Shopping—Farms*.

CONDOMINIUMS The Valley harbors upward of 1,000 condominium units, but only 350 or so are available for rental. Many are clustered around Sugarbush South (Lincoln Peak), more are scattered along the access road, and some are squirreled away in the woods. No one reservation service represents them all.

Sugarbush Resort Condos (802-583-6160; sugarbush.com). The number of resort-managed units available varies and usually averages around 100—some slope-side, most walk-to-the-slopes—with health club access. From $115 for a one-bedroom to $2,176 for a four-bedroom at Claybrook Hotel. Prices vary with season. **Sugarbush Village Condominiums** (800-451-4326; sugarbushvillage.com) represents a similar range of condos and homes around Sugarbush. **Sugarbush Real Estate Rentals** (802-496-2591; sugarbushrentals.com) offers nightly, weekly, and monthly rentals in a variety of local condos and homes.

♪ **The Battleground** (802-496-2288; 800-248-2102; battlegroundcondos.com), Rt. 17, Fayston

05673. An attractive cluster of town houses handy to Mad River Glen and Mount Ellen, each designed to face the brook or a piece of greenery, backing into one another and thus preserving most of the 60 acres for walking or snowshoeing. In summer there's a pool, tennis and paddle tennis courts, and a play area for children. Rates (two-night minimum) for two-, three-, and four-bedroom units from $190 per night off-season to $374 for a two-bedroom; weekly and monthly rates.

✳ Where to Eat

DINING OUT *Note:* The Valley restaurants are unusual in both quality and longevity. Most have been around for quite some time and, like most culinary landmarks, have their good and bad days.

275 Main at the Pitcher Inn (802-496-6350; pitcherinn.com), 275 Main St., Warren Village. Open for dinner Wed.–Mon. Reservations essential. The elegant inn dining room features an à la carte menu orchestrated by chef Sue Schickler. The bill of fare leans toward the rich and comforting, but is dictated by the local ingredients available that day. On a January evening you might begin a roasted butternut squash soup ($9) or seared foie gras ($24). Entrées $26–36. The choice of wines by the glass is large, and the wine list itself is long and widely priced.

ℰ **Chez Henri** (802-583-2600), Sugarbush Village. Open only during ski season from 11:30 for a bistro/bar menu and from 5:30 for dinner. A genuine bistro, opened in 1964 by Henri Borel, former food controller for Air France. You're paying more for his coddling and a room full of antiques than the high-priced, fusty fare, including fondue, French onion soup, and steak au poivre. Children's menu.

❂ **The Common Man Restaurant** (802-583-2800; commonmanrestaurant.com), 3209 German Flats Rd., Warren. Dinner only. Reservations recommended. The ultramodern cuisine from Gotham Bar & Grill alum Adam Longworth, a Vermont native, is at delicious odds with the chandelier-bedecked, mid-19th-century barn in which it's served. Thursday is pasta night, featuring dinners that are less expensive but no less impressive. Whatever soup is on the menu, we say order that! Longworth is a wizard with them, layering flavors and textures for a one-of-a-kind experience. Look for the Common Kitchen Meatball Co. truck out front for a less formal treat.

Sandy Macy

TIMBERS RESTAURANT AT SUGARBUSH IS OPEN YEAR-ROUND.

Timbers Restaurant (802-583-6800) at Lincoln Peak Village, Sugarbush Resort, Warren. Vermont's newest post-and-beam round barn at the base of the Sugarbush lifts is a full-service restaurant serving three squares including a serious dinner menu with a commitment to fresh and local. Whole animals are butchered in-house, so dinner might include an empanada filled with homemade chorizo, pork belly tacos, and a porcine entrée, all originating from the same pig.

Allyn's Lodge (802-583-6590), midmountain at Lincoln Peak. By day (10–2 in ski season) this is a pleasant enough eating spot, but on winter weekend evenings it's literally the height of dining out in the Valley. Reservations are required and limited. Access is via the Lincoln Limo (snowcat). There's candle and firelight, a four-course, locally sourced meal, and wine. Guests can don headlamps and ski down, conditions permitting, or take the cat, all included in $175 per person.

Peasant (802-496-6856, peasantvt.com), 40 Bridge St., Waitsfield. Dinner Thurs.–Mon. The name tells you what you need to know about the aesthetic here. Owner Chris Alberti walked out of his World Trade Center office 20 minutes before the first plane hit on 9/11. His well-earned joie de vivre is palpable in his simple food. Pastas, meatballs, and a hearty cassoulet are typical of his rustic, pan-European menu.

EATING OUT ❂ **American Flatbread Restaurant** (802-496-8856), 40 Lareau Rd., Rt. 100, Waitsfield. Open Thurs.–Sun. 5–9:30, year-round (more or less). George Schenk's distinctive pizza is baked in a primitive, wood-fired oven heated to 800 degrees; the results are distributed to stores from Florida to Chicago. On dining nights, the kitchen becomes an informal seating area featuring flatbread (toppings include cheese and herbs, sun-dried tomatoes, homemade sausage with mushrooms) and salads whose dressing boasts homemade fruit vinegar. Also specials such as grilled vegetables with garlic-herb sauce and oven-roasted chicken.

🍴 **Big Picture Café** (802-496-8996; bigpicture theater.info), 48 Carroll Rd., off Rt. 100, Waitsfield. Open Wed.–Sun. 7 AM–10 PM. Eat and drink while you take in a film, or enjoy your meal in the adjacent space that's become an all-day community gathering spot. The international menu spans from huevos rancheros through croque monsieur to homemade shepherd's pie. There's also an espresso bar with Italian and French sodas, a Biergarten in summer, a full bar, and an authentic soda fountain.

ALLYN'S LODGE, MIDMOUNTAIN AT LINCOLN PEAK, IS THE ULTIMATE IN WINTER DINING.
Sugarbush Resort

🍴 **Mad River Barn and Pub** (802-496-3310; madriverbarn.com), 2849 Mill Brook Rd., Waitsfield. Open from 4 nightly. We miss the funky old pub with its stuffed moose above the hearth and authentic ash can art in the dining room. That said, this lighter, brighter, totally renovated version is beautifully designed, admittedly more open and inviting. Families, skiers, hikers, and cyclists all fit comfortably and mingle in the pub and adjacent game room with its classic pinball and hand shuffleboard. You can always build your own burger or dine on truffle mac-and-cheese or on a duo of crispy duck breast and duck confit leg ($23). The extensive $7.50 kids' menu comes with sides and applesauce.

Elusive Moose Pub & Eatery (802-496-6444), 6163 Main St., Waitsfield. This restaurant in the former Purple Moon Pub spot gets top marks for creative, tasty "comfort food with a twist" from breakfast through dinner. A $25 diner menu might begin with a seven-veggie salad followed by curried veggie strudel, topped off by "chocolate moose." Daily specials.

🍴 **MINT Restaurant** (802-496-5514; mint vermont.com), 4404 Main St. (enter from Bridge St.), Waitsfield. Open Wed.–Sun. for lunch (11:30–2:30); Fri.–Sun. for dinner (5:30–8:30). Vegetarians and carnivores alike rave about the taste of everything here. Lunch on a toasted cheese quesadilla with soy mozzarella, sweet corn, avocado, salsa fresca, and salad greens tossed in lavender herb vinaigrette. The tea selection is the best in the Valley (and beyond). A winter dinner might begin with lemongrass ginger soup, then continue to home-made fettuccine with mascarpone crème, shallots, and grilled asparagus or a savory veggie and feta cheese tart. Wine and beer at dinner. Chef Iliyan is from Bulgaria and his wife, Savitri (your server), from Budapest. The couple met in California.

🍴 **Localfolk Smokehouse** (802-496-5623), jct. of Rt. 17 and Rt. 100. Open Tues.–Sat. from 5 for food. Trusted local foodies rave about the hickory-smoked barbecued ribs and chicken, also Tex-Mex staples. A wide choice of draft beers, funky atmosphere, a pool table and outdoor deck, frequent live music.

Hostel Tevere (802-496-9222) 203 Powderhound Rd, just off Rt. 100, Warren. Breakfast daily, dinner Wed.–Sat. 6–10:30. Breakfasts like gingerbread pancakes and French toast stuffed with fruit and cream cheese, finished in a crunchy coating, have an enthusiastic local following (most choices are $5 or under). Dinner choices might include a cassoulet of chicken,

Italian sausage, cannellini beans, and creamy polenta; Thursdays feature sushi.

⊘ **The Mad Taco** (802-496-3832), 2 Village Square, Waitsfield. Open 11–8 daily. Don't ask for nachos here—they don't have them at this authentic Mexican eatery. House-smoked, local meats find their way into tacos, tortas, and burritos that taste more Oaxaca than Waitsfield, especially when doused with one of the colorful homemade hot sauces.

Warren Store (802-496-3864; warrenstore .com), Warren Village. Open daily 8–7; on Sun. and in winter until 6. Year-round the bakery produces French and health breads, plus croissants and great deli food and sandwiches, panini specials, breakfast till noon, daily specials; inside tables plus (in summer) a deck overlooking the small waterfall.

❸ Maynard's Snack Bar, Rt. 100B just north of the Rt. 100 split, Moretown. Open May–Labor Day, 11:30–8:30. Closed Wed. A classic old family-run roadside stand with great hand-cut fries, burgers and corn dogs, creemees and homemade pies. Picnic tables overlook Maynard's Farm.

❋ Entertainment

The Big Picture Theater & Café (802-496-8994; bigpicturetheater.info), Rt. 100, Waitsfield. Mainstream and independent films.

Green Mountain Cultural Center (802-496-7722; theroundbarn.com/gmcc.htm) at the Joslyn Round Barn, East Warren Rd., Waitsfield. This concert and exhibit space in a classic round barn is the setting for a series of summer concerts and operas, along with workshops and a major foliage-season art exhibit.

The **Valley Players** (802-583-1674; valley players.com), a community theater company housed in the Waitsfield Odd Fellows Building, produces three or four plays a year in its own theater in Waitsfield Village, Rt. 100.

The **Phantom Theater** (802-496-5997 in summer), a local group with New York City theater community members, presents original plays and improvisational performances for children and adults at Edgecomb Barn in Warren.

The Commons Group (802-496-4422; the skinnerbarn.com), the Skinner Barn, 609 Common Rd., Waitsfield. Founded by Broadway and TV performer Peer Boynton, presenting theater, concerts, and a cabaret series.

Also note **Mad River Chorale** performances in June and December (check with the chamber of commerce: 802-496-7907).

APRÈS-SKI The Hyde Away (802-496-2322) is the hot spot near Mad River Glen (Rt. 17). Literally hidden away behind the inn (see *Lodging*), **Zach's Tavern** offers a fireplace, big friendly bar, and pool table, as well as dimly lit corners for pub food or the inn's full menu; many microbrews and nightly specials (see *Eating Out*).

Castlerock Pub at Gatehouse Lodge, Lincoln Peak base area, is the Sugarbush gathering spot at the base of the lifts. Also see **Localfolk Smokehouse** in *Eating Out*.

❋ Selective Shopping

ART GALLERIES Artisans' Gallery (802-496-6256), 20 Bridge St., Waitsfield. Open daily 11–6. A selective collection of crafted items from throughout Vermont: clothing, pottery, baskets, rugs, glass, decoys, ornaments, photography, and much more. The adjoining **Bridge Street Emporium** (802-496-4556) is an outlet for more than two dozen artists and artisans.

Parade Gallery (802-496-5445) in Warren Village is a long-standing and widely respected source of affordable prints and original art, sculpture, and photography, featuring Gary Eckhart watercolors and Sabra Field prints.

CRAFTS SHOPS AND GALLERIES Mad River Glass Gallery (802-496-9388), 4237 Main St. (Rt. 100), Waitsfield Village. Melanie and Dave Leppia's handsome gallery is a must-stop. The glass is deeply colored, highly original, and created (blown and cast) on the premises.

Waitsfield Pottery (802-496-7155; waitsfield pottery.com), Rt. 100 across from Bridge St. Ulrike Tesmer makes functional, hand-thrown stoneware pieces, well worth a stop.

Luminosity Stained Glass Studio (802-496-2231; luminositystudios.com), the Old Church, Rt. 100, Waitsfield. Open except Tues. This is a very special shop. Since 1975 this former church has served as the studio in which Barry Friedman fashions Tiffany lamp shades and a variety of designs in leaded and stained glass. Now he devotes most of his time to custom work but keeps a selection of opulent lighting, also showcases Arroyo craftsmen and mica lamps.

Mad River Quilting (802-496-6770), 4412 Main St. (Rt. 100), Waitsfield. Open daily July–Oct.; Nov.–June, open Wed.–Sun. Quilter Lisa Thierren doubles as a middle school teacher, hence the longer summer hours. Quilting supplies and finished quilts, classes.

Also see **Green Mountain Glassworks** (egan glass.com) studio in Granville, south of Warren on Rt. 100 (the sign outside still says PLUSH QUARTZ ART GLASS). Michael Egan's hand-blown glass creations are worth the short, scenic trip; we describe it in "The White River Valleys."

SPECIAL SHOPS **The Warren Store** (802-496-3864), Warren Village. Open 8–6 in winter, until 7 in summer. Staples, good wine selection, Vermont specialty items, and the deli and bakery are downstairs (see *Eating Out*). Upstairs the More Store is one of Vermont's best-kept secrets, an eclectic selection of clothing, jewelry, hardware, and gifts. We treasure everything we have bought here, from earrings to a winter coat.

All Things Bright and Beautiful (802-496-3397), Bridge St., Waitsfield. You'll find an incredible number of stuffed animals and unusual toys on two floors of this old village house.

The Store (802-496-4465; vermontstore.com), Rt. 100, Waitsfield. Since its 1965 opening, this shop has grown 10-fold, now filling two floors of an 1834 former Methodist meetinghouse with antiques, cookware, tabletop gifts, collectibles, lifestyle books, Vermont gourmet products, and children's toys and books from around the world. Inquire about cooking in the test kitchen out back.

Tempest Book Shop (802-496-2022), Village Square, Waitsfield. Model trains circle above in this bookstore, a trove of titles in most categories, including children's books. We like their motto: "A house without books is like a room without windows" (Horace Mann). CDs, cassettes, posters.

Alpine Options (802-583-1763; 888-888-9131), with locations at Sugarbush (on the Access Road) and at Mad River Glen. Open daily, Fri. until 11 during ski season. Ski and snowboard rentals, demos, and repair: the best-quality all-around service, according to locals.

East Warren Community Market (802-496-6758), 42 Roxbury Mountain Rd. Open daily 7–7. Housed in the former East Warren schoolhouse, a market and food co-op specializing in local and organic, staples, wines, baked goods.

FARMS AND A FARMERS MARKET *Note:* Of all Vermont's ski resort areas, the Mad River Valley remains the most visually and genuinely committed to preserving its farms, some 50 of which are listed and located on a map in the 2012 Mad River Valley Guide, free from the chamber (see *Guidance*); also see vermont localvore.org.

Waitsfield Farmers Market (802-472-8027; waitsfieldfarmersmarket.com), mid-May–mid-Oct. at the Mad River Green, Sat. 9–1. A real standout with a wide selection of herbs, veggies, fruits and flowers, breads, cheese, syrup, meats, also crafts, music.

Year-round
Mountain Valley Farm (802-496-9255; mountainvalleyfarm.com), 1719 Common Rd., Waitsfield 05673. Set high on an open shoulder of the Valley with a classic red cupolaed barn, the farm welcomes visitors for wagon and sleigh rides, weddings, birthday parties, or simply to meet the barnyard animals and walk or cross-country ski. Inquire about the guest suite.

Kingsbury Market Garden (802-496-6815; kingsburymarketgarden.com), 248 Rt. 100. Vermont Foodbank Farm. Summer Thurs.–Sun. 11–6, winter Fri., Sat. 11–6. Owned by the Vermont Land Trust with 7 tillable acres, this farm supplies many of the Valley's best restaurants.

Gaylord Farm (802-496-5054; gaylordfarm .com), 8405 Main St., Waitsfield. The farm store is open year-round. Call for hours. A longtime family farm, formerly dairy, presently 600 acres with 250 belted Angus beef, 400 laying hens, 600 meat birds, plus seasonal produce. Look for Hap's Garage (also part of the family).

SUGARHOUSES **Eastman Long & Sons** (802-496-3448), 1188 Tucker Hill Rd., Fayston. "Sonny" Long sets 6,000 taps on 100 high wooded acres that have been in his family for generations. He maintains that the higher the elevation, the better the syrup, and he welcomes visitors to his roadside sugarhouse during sugaring season.

Palmer's Maple Products (802-496-3696), East Warren Rd., Waitsfield. Delbert and Sharlia Palmer sell syrup from their farm on this scenic road.

Also check with the chamber of commerce (see *Guidance*).

✻ Special Events

Note: Check with the chamber of commerce (see *Guidance*) and its website (madrivervalley .com) for weekly listings of special events.

March: **Annual New England Telemark Festival**, Mad River Glen.

May–June: Guided bird walks. Baked Beads annual wholesale tent event, Memorial Day weekend.

Mid-May–early October: **Farmers Market**, Sat. 9–1 at Mad River Green, Rt. 100, Waitsfield (waitsfieldfarmersmarket.com).

June: **Green Mountain Opera Festival** (greenmountainoperafestival.com)—open rehearsals, Green Mountain Cultural Center (the round barn), Warren.

July 4: Outstanding **parade**, Warren Village. **Mad Marathon**.

July–August: **Summer productions** by the Valley Players and by the Phantom Theater (see *Entertainment*).

August: **Vermont Festival of the Arts** (vermontartfest.com) throughout the Valley: daily happenings. **Century Ride** (third Saturday; mrvcenturyride.com). **Mad Marathon**, part of the **Vermont Festival of the Great Outdoors**. Live theater at the Skinner Barn in Waitsfield.

Labor Day weekend: Two-day **crafts exhibits**. **Green Mountain Stage Race** (gmsr.org).

Early October: **Soaring Encampment** throughout the Valley. **Peak Foliage Celebration Day**, weekend chairlifts. **Juried Art Show** at the Round Barn Farm, late September to mid-October.

November: Waitsfield PTO's Ski & Skate Sale is huge.

December: First Saturday in December is **Country Christmas Open House and Holiday Paint-In**—shopping specials, prizes, and artists painting holiday scenes in local stores. **Holiday events** throughout the Valley.

BARRE/MONTPELIER AREA

Any serious attempt to understand the character of Vermont entails a visit to Montpelier: a stroll through the exceptional Vermont Historical Society Museum and into the ornate but informal statehouse built of Vermont granite and marble, and still heated with wood. Montpelier itself is a disarmingly small, bohemian college town with colorful shops and restaurants along State and Main Streets, which are as charming as the Hollywood film they inspired (*State and Main*). The back streets are a jumble of bridges, narrow lanes, and mansard roofs.

An exit on I-89, Montpelier is also at the hub of old roads radiating off into the hills, including Rt. 2, which runs all the way to Bangor, Maine, and Rt. 302 to Portland, which begins here as central Vermont's big commercial strip, "the Barre–Montpelier Road."

Billed as "the granite capital of the world," Barre (pronounced *Berry*) continues to quarry, cut, and sculpt its high-quality gray granite, now used primarily for memorial stones. The big attraction is the Rock of Ages Quarry in Graniteville, southeast of town, but its two large cemeteries are the prime showcase for the work—ranging from quirky to spectacular—of generations of mostly Italian stone carvers. The Vermont History Center (headquarters of the Vermont Historical Society) and the Barre Opera House, one of Vermont's most beautiful historic theaters, are right downtown.

Southwest of Montpelier is the proud old town of Northfield, home of Norwich University—the oldest private military college in the United States, more recently known for its hard-to-beat criminal justice major—and of no fewer than five covered bridges. East Barre and East Montpelier are both spread thick with rural charm. As Rt. 2 climbs northeast through Plainfield and Marshfield, it accesses country-chic lodging, shopping, and dining, spin-offs from liberal (writ large) Goddard College.

GUIDANCE The Capital Region Visitor Center (802-828-5981), 134 State St., Montpelier, is open 6:30–6 weekdays, 9–5 weekends May–Oct.; 6:30–5 weekdays, 8–4 weekends Oct.–May. Housed in a redbrick house across the street from the capitol with a flag out front, it has knowledgeable, friendly staff and a restroom.

IN BARRE

Central Vermont Chamber of Commerce

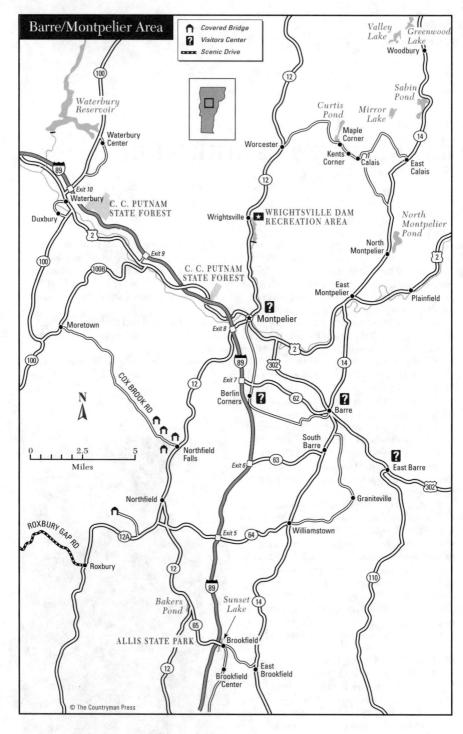

Barre/Montpelier Area

	Covered Bridge
?	Visitors Center
▪▪▪▪	Scenic Drive

Central Vermont Chamber of Commerce (877-887-3678; central-vt.com) publishes several helpful booklet guides to the area.

Montpelier Alive (802-223-9604; montpelieralive.com) is Montpelier's Downtown Association and has a useful website specific to downtown Montpelier, including many art, music, and food events.

Downtown Barre Partnership (802-476-0267; thebarrepartnership.com) is Barre's Downtown Association and a useful source for local business information as well as the area's history.

GETTING THERE *By bus:* **Greyhound** (800-552-8737; greyhound.com) from Boston to Montreal, connecting with New York and Connecticut service, stops in Montpelier in front of city hall on Main St.

By train: **Amtrak** (800-USA-RAIL; amtrak.com) stops in Montpelier Junction, a mile west of town on the other side of I-89.

By car: For **Montpelier** take I-89, Exit 8. At the second traffic light, make a left, crossing the river on Bailey Ave. At the light, turn right onto State St. Paid parking is available on the street and in several lots behind shops. The capitol and Vermont Historical Society are a short way up across the street.

To reach **Barre** take I-89 to Exit 7 and follow signs for Rt. 62, a divided highway, to Main St.

WHEN TO GO Never come on a Monday when the Vermont Historical Society Museum is closed. Otherwise this is a rare corner of Vermont that varies little from season to season. Come Jan.–Apr. to see the Vermont Legislature in action. The chocolate chip cookies upstairs at the State House are worth a trip on their own.

MEDICAL EMERGENCY Call **911**. **Central Vermont Medical Center** (802-371-4100; cvmc.org) is in Berlin off Rt. 62; Exit 7 off I-89.

✳ Towns

Montpelier. The smallest and possibly the most livable of the nation's state capitals, Montpelier is a town of fewer than 8,000 people, with a popular farmers market on Saturdays and legislative-session Wednesdays, along with high school playing fields and tennis courts just a few blocks from the capitol. The gold dome of the State House itself is appropriately crowned by a green hill rising steeply behind it. A path leads right up that hill into **Hubbard Park**, 185 leafy acres with winding roads, good for

A VIEW OF MONTPELIER

Capitol Plaza Hotel

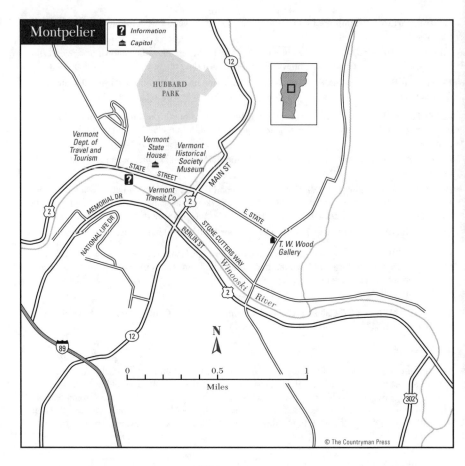

Montpelier

? Information
🏛 Capitol

HUBBARD PARK

Vermont Dept. of Travel and Tourism

Vermont State House

Vermont Historical Society Museum

STATE STREET

MAIN ST

Vermont Transit Co.

E. STATE

MEMORIAL DR

NATIONAL LIFE DR

BERLIN ST

STONE CUTTERS WAY

Winooski River

T. W. Wood Gallery

N

0   0.5   1
Miles

89

12

302

© The Countryman Press

biking and jogging. Stone Cutters Way down along the Winooski River is also a pleasant bike or jog. The **State House**, the **Vermont Historical Society Museum**, and the **T. W. Wood Art Gallery** are all must-see sights, as is **Morse Farm Maple Sugarworks** just northeast of town. Montpelier is also the home base for the New England Culinary Institute (NECI).

Precisely why this narrow floodplain of the Winooski was chosen in favor of Burlington or the more central Randolph as Vermont's capital in 1805 is uncertain, as is why it was named for a small city in the Languedoc region of France. The fact is, however, that Vermont's first legislators picked a town noted for its unusual number of whiskey distilleries (it's still famous for its legislative watering holes) and named it for a town known for its wine and brandy. It's also true that Montpelier is unusually accessible, by roads both old and new, from every corner of central and northern Vermont.

THE CAPITAL CITY FARMERS MARKET
Rachel Carter

Barre. This is a city of just less than 9,000 people, surrounded by a town of almost 8,000. Motorists caught in Main Street's perpetual traffic may ponder the facades of the commercial buildings. Most date from 1880–1910, during which the community's population jumped from 2,000 to 12,000, swollen by stonecutters and craftsmen from Scotland, Eastern Europe, Italy,

Central Vermont Chamber of Commerce
THE STATE HOUSE IN MONTPELIER

and French Canada, not to mention England, Scandinavia, Spain, Germany, and the Middle East. This volatile mix of largely underpaid workers who elected a socialist mayor were not afraid to strike for their rights or to shelter victims of strikes elsewhere. In the World War I era, many famous anarchists and socialists spoke here. The **Old Labor Hall** (vintage 1900) at 46 Granite St. (off N. Main), the focal point of this struggle, has been partially restored and currently houses the city's best historical exhibits; it's also a popular event space (oldlaborhall.com). The quarries continue to employ some 2,000 people to produce one-third of the country's memorial stones—for which **Hope Cemetery** and **Elmwood Cemetery** serve as museums of stonecarving virtuosity. A formal **Vermont Granite Museum and Stone Arts School** (802-476-4605; stoneartsschool.org) offers tours and workshops.

The quarries themselves are southeast of town, in an area known, appropriately, as Graniteville, where Millstone Hill has been chipped and chiseled since 1812. The memorial stone business escalated after 1888, when the branch railroad finally linked the quarries to finishing sheds in the valley and to outlets beyond. All but one of the major quarries is now owned by **Rock of Ages**. This company has long made its operations a showcase for visitors, who can view the unforgettable, surrealistic landscape of the quarries themselves, hear the roar of the drills, and watch ant-sized men chip away at the giant pits.

Northfield (population 5,748). This town's mid-19th-century commercial blocks suggest the prosperity that it enjoyed while native son Charles Paine served as governor. Paine actually railroaded the Vermont Central through his hometown instead of the more logical Barre. The old depot, now a bank, stands at one end of the handsome common. Today the town's pride is Norwich University, a private, coed college of 1,000 cadets, which bills itself as "the oldest private military college in the United States." In the Norwich University Museum in White Memorial Chapel, you learn that this institution sent more than 300 officers into the Civil War. It wasn't until 1867, however, that the college moved to Northfield from its original site in Norwich. More Northfield memorabilia as well as changing exhibits can be seen in the **Northfield Historical Society Museum** (see *Historical Attractions*). Northfield also boasts six covered bridges, five of which are in publicly accessible areas.

✴ Must See

✎ ♿ **The Vermont Historical Society Museum** (802-828-2291; vermonthistory.org), 109 State St., Montpelier. Open year-round, Tues.–Sat. 10–4; $5 adults, $3 ages 6–17, students with ID cards, and seniors. This outstanding state museum, maintained by the Vermont Historical Society, occupies the ground floor of the replica of the Pavilion Hotel, a five-story, mansard-roofed landmark that occupied this site between 1870 and 1966. *Freedom & Unity: One Ideal Many Stories*—the permanent exhibition—chronicles Vermont from the year 1600 to the present time. ("Freedom in Unity" is the state motto.) It dramatizes Abenaki Indian life; draws visitors into Bennington's Catamount Tavern to explore the state's beginnings; and explores life in the 19th century through interactive exhibits and re-created buildings.

✎ **Rock of Ages Visitor Center and Tours** (802-476-3119; 877-870-9057; rockofages.com), 558 Graniteville Rd., Graniteville. The visitors center is open May–Oct., Mon.–Sat. 9–5 and fall Sundays; factory tours year-round Mon.–Fri. 9–3:30. There's also a narrated shuttle tour May–Oct. to a working, 50-acre, 600-foot-deep quarry farther up the hill. Self-guided factory tours are free; listen to a narrated tour on your phone for $5. From the observation deck of the Manufacturing Division, you'll see the granite being polished and sculpted by master sculptors. The center features interactive exhibits and a retail store with granite gifts. But many visitors come with a different type of purchase in mind: their gravestones.

⚷ **Morse Farm Maple Sugarworks** (802-223-2740; 800-242-2740; morsefarm.com), 1168 County Rd., Montpelier. (Go up Main St., turn right at the roundabout onto Country Rd., continue up the hill 2.7 miles.) Open year-round, daily except holidays. Sugar-on-snow parties Mar.–Apr., cross-country skiing all winter long, antiques and crafts fairs in summer, and foliage walks and farm market in fall. The farm has been in the same family for eight generations, and the ice cream is so legendary it was memorialized in the song "Oh, Maple Creemee," by regional musician Lewis Franco. The store features its own syrup and maple products; Vermont crafts; and a sugarhouse tour with tastings and an outdoor museum devoted to Vermont farm life. Also see *Cross-Country Skiing*.

ROCK OF AGES QUARRY

Central Vermont Chamber of Commerce

✳ To Do

BIKING Check out the Central Vermont Chamber of Commerce website (central-vt.com) for extensive biking resources including a printable map, suggested routes through this area, mountain bike clubs, tours, and races. **Onion River Sports** (802-229-9409; onionriver.com), 20 Langdon St., Montpelier, is a source of local bike maps and rentals (mountain bikes and hybrids). The 2-mile **Montpelier Bike Path** runs from Stone Cutter's Way and Granite St. intersection to Junction and Dog River Rd. intersections.

A superb biking destination is the **Millstone Hill Touring & Recreation Center** (802-479-1000; millstonetrails.com), 34 Church Hill Rd., Websterville. Seventy miles of singletrack trail web 1,500 acres of wooded terrain, spotted with dozens of abandoned quarries. A century ago this resembled a harsh moonscape, but the quarries have since filled with water; birch, maple, and aspen have sprouted between cast-off granite boulders. Trails are clearly marked and also open for hiking. Open seasonally, check ahead when weather prevails; yearly, seasonal, or day fees apply. The Millstone Hill Trail Association maintains this fine example of Vermont's working landscape turned to recreation and offers bike rentals and repair. Accommodations available in the converted barn that serves as the center, in a group rental cottage, and in the primitive campground. See *Lodging*.

BOATING AND FISHING ⚷ **Wrightsville Beach Recreation Area** (802-223-1938; wrightsville beachvt.com), created by the **Wrightsville Dam**, just north of Montpelier on rural Rt. 12, is popular for swimming, boating, fishing, and picnicking with a rugged landscape that is refreshing for being so close to civilization. Canoe and kayak rentals available. See the Mad River Valley and Waterbury/Stowe chapters for boat tours.

The area is sprinkled with dozens of ponds, making for a variety of fishing spots, including **North Montpelier Pond**, with a fishing access off Rt. 14; and **Curtis Pond** and **Mirror Lake** in Calais (pronounced *CAL-lus*). **Nelson Pond** and **Sabin Pond** in Woodbury are both accessible from Rt. 14, as are **Valley Lake** and **Greenwood Lake** (good for bass and pike). The **Stevens Branch** south of Barre and the **Dog River** in Northfield offer brook trout. Fishing licenses are required; more info at vtfishandwildlife.com. **R&L Archery** (802-479-9151; 800-269-9151; randlarchery.com) in Barre is the best local source for fishing and hunting, as well as bird-watching, archery, kayaking, geocaching, paintballing, even gold prospecting gear. Also sells licenses.

MOUNTAIN BIKING AT MILLSTONE HILL

Central Vermont Chamber of Commerce

Hope Cemetery, 201 Maple Ave., Barre, 802-476-6245. When Italian immigrants flooded Barre at the turn of the 20th century, the craft of carving Rock of Ages granite took on a bold, beautiful, and decidedly weird new shape. Because those craftsmen were tasked with taking care of their own, the graves of simple artisans and their families often surpass anything Shelley's mythical tyrant Ozymandias could have wished for.

The over-the-top monuments may owe to the difficulty of the craftsmen's lives. Many expired slowly and torturously from silicosis before achieving old age. Known by a variety of colorful nicknames based on profession (potters' rot, anyone?), the lung disease is the result of inhaling silica dust. After the introduction of mechanized equipment and with little knowledge of how to protect themselves, early-20th-century Barre carvers were a prime target for the disease's wrath.

Perhaps the most touching artwork on the grounds is the grave of Louis Brusa. An activist for himself and other granite carvers, Brusa—whose work can be seen throughout the cemetery—made it his life's mission to make ventilation systems mandatory in granite sheds. He himself died of silicosis.

When he took ill, he commissioned fellow carver Don Colletti to carve him a gravestone. The result is Brusa's chilling prediction of his final moments in three dimensions: his wife, Mary, cradling him as he sits lifeless or near death in an armchair. Brusa posed for the sculpture himself. It's rumored that his mistress's image replaced Mary's. But she triumphed in the end: Mary Brusa was buried beneath the stone in 1957, 20 years after her husband's passing at the age of 51.

Around the corner, pajama-sporting couple William and Gwendolyn Halvosa hold hands in bed eternally—a less unsettling portrait of marital bliss.

While older stones lean toward Italian-tinged fine art, including a scale model of Michelangelo's *Pietà*, newer graves are more lighthearted but no less skillfully crafted.

The fun continues past this mortal coil with a giant soccer ball, a three-dimensional racecar in tribute to local racer Joey Laquerre, and a couple square-dancing together into the great beyond. One stone, emblazoned with a baseball bat, glove, and ball, stands over the resting places of three family members, informing visitors, THEIR BASEBALL MEMORY WILL LIVE ON.

More than 10,000 monuments stand silently in the friendly memorial park, all carved from the local granite. Hope Cemetery is a vibrant museum of art and culture that's enjoyed equally by the living and the dead. Whether it's to visit or stay, there's always room for one more.

COVERED BRIDGES Off Rt. 12 in Northfield Falls (turn at the general store) stand three covered bridges: The **Station Bridge**, spanning 100 feet, and the **Newell Bridge** are within sight of each other; farther along Cox Brook Rd. is the **Upper Bridge**, with a span of 42 feet. Another bridge is just south off Rt. 12 on Slaughter House Rd.

DISC GOLF Two disc-golf courses are in the area, one at **Wrightsville Beach Recreation Area** and the other in **North Calais**. Details at gmdgc.org.

GOLF Montpelier Elks Country Club (802-223-7457), 203 Country Club Rd., Montpelier. Nine holes at an active country club of the local Elks Club.

🐾 **Barre Country Club** (802-476-7658; ccofbarre.net), 142 Drake Rd., Plainfield. A hilly, affordable 18-hole course with some excellent views; restaurant with views is run by the restaurateurs behind Cornerstone Pub & Kitchen (see *Eating Out*); reservations recommended.

Northfield Country Club (802-485-4515; northfieldcountryclub.com), 2066 Roxbury Rd., Northfield. Nine holes and the Clubhouse Café serving deli-style grub.

HIKING/WALKING *Guidance:* **The Green Mountain Club** (802-244-7037; greenmountainclub .org), RR 1, Box 650, Rt. 100, Waterbury Center 05677. The club encourages general inquiries and trail description updates (see *Hiking and Walking* in "What's Where").

Spruce Mountain, Plainfield. An unusually undeveloped state holding of 500 acres, rich in bird life. The trail begins in Jones State Forest, 4.2 miles south of the village; the three-hour hike is described in *50 Hikes in Vermont* (The Countryman Press) and in *Day Hiker's Guide to Vermont* (Green Mountain Club).

Worcester Range, north of Montpelier. There are several popular hikes described in the books listed under Spruce Mountain (above), notably **Elmore Mountain** in Elmore State Park (a 3-mile trek yielding a panorama of lakes, farms, and rolling hills—see "North of the Notch"), **Mount Worcester** (approached from the village of Worcester), and **Mount Hunger**.

Allis State Park (vtstateparks.com). See "The White River Valleys."

Groton State Forest, east of Montpelier. This 25,000-acre forest offers an extensive year-round trail system. See "St. Johnsbury and Burke Mountain."

⚡ **Hubbard Park** and **North Branch River Park** in Montpelier are both accessible from **North Branch Nature Center** (802-229-6206; northbranchnaturecenter.org), 713 Elm St. (Rt. 12 north). Hubbard Park, also accessible from the State House, is 200 acres webbed with trails and a stone observation tower; North Branch offers gentle trails along this fork of the Winooski as well as more challenging, higher-altitude trails. Both parks are used for cross-country skiing and snowshoeing. The nature center offers year-round birding programs and other events, several for children.

Also see **Millstone Hill** under *Biking*.

HISTORICAL ATTRACTIONS ⚡ & **USS** *Montpelier* **Museum** (802 223-9502, montpelier-vt.org), 39 Main St. Tucked upstairs in a few back rooms of the city hall is this unexpected display of ship models, uniforms, medals, and diaries documenting the life of Admiral George Dewey, a native son who inspired the christening of at least three U.S. Navy ships after his hometown, the most recent a 1993 nuclear attack submarine. Open weekdays when city hall is. Free.

⚡ & **Kellogg-Hubbard Library** (802-223-3338; kellogghubbard.org), 135 Main St., Montpelier. Open Mon.–Sat., hours vary; check website in advance. This lovely Italianate structure, built in 1895 of rough granite blocks, is as palatial inside as out. Behind its two-story columned entrance you'll find a second-floor balcony, ornate fireplaces, a fine oak-and-marble staircase, classical friezes, and a central skylight that fills the hall with light. New York City real estate tycoon Martin Kellogg and his wife, Montpelier native Fanny Hubbard, both died in 1889, leaving their estate to the town for the construction of cemetery gates and a public library. But Fanny's nephew contested the will. The probate court ruled in his favor, and the town countersued in a battle that lasted three years and left Montpelier split in two. The nephew offered a truce, to build the library if the town would drop the dispute. He paid dearly: The structure cost $30,000 more than the amount set aside in the will.

& **Vermont History Center** (802-479-8500; vermonthistory.org), 60 Washington St., Barre. Open Tues.–Fri. 9–4 (Wed. until 8), second Sat. 9–4. $5 research fee. Housed in the splendid Spaulding School, designed in 1891 by Lambert Packard—the architect of St. Johnsbury's Fairbanks Museum—the Vermont Historical Society headquarters includes a gallery with changing exhibits and research library.

Northfield Historical Society Museum (802-485-4792; nhsvt.org), 75 S. Main St., Northfield. Housed in the former Governor Charles Paine House with collections of photographs, manuscripts, and scrapbooks of the town. Exhibits in summer. Call ahead for hours or to make appointment.

HORSEBACK RIDING T-N-T Stables (802-476-3097; freewebs.com/tntstables1), 75 Pine Hill Rd., Barre. Tina and Tiffany Poulin offer hour-long trail rides, pony rides, and instruction for those 8 years and over.

SCENIC DRIVES Roxbury to Warren. The road through Roxbury Gap, while not recommended in winter, is spectacular in summer and fall, commanding a breathtaking view of the Green Mountains from the crest of the Roxbury Range. Do not resist the urge to stop, get out, and enjoy this panorama. Ask locally about the hiking trail that follows the ridgeline from the road's highest point.

Northfield to Moretown. Cox Brook Rd. (marked on our map) connects Northfield Falls with the village of Moretown. It's dirt part of the way, offering views in both directions near the crest and passing through three covered bridges at the Northfield Falls end. In Northfield, Turkey Hill Rd. begins across from Depot Square and climbs up to panoramic views.

STOCK CAR RACING Thunder Road International Speed Bowl (thunderroadspeedbowl.com), marked from Quarry St., Barre. Check the website for frequent races and other events.

SWIMMING ⚡ **Wrightsville Beach Recreation Area** (802-223-1938; wrightsvillebeachvt.com), Rt. 12, Middlesex—5 miles north of Montpelier. There are also numerous swimming holes in the Kents Corner area of Calais. Inquire about local swimming holes.

✳ Winter Sports

CROSS-COUNTRY SKIING ✍ **Morse Farm Ski Touring Center** (802-223-0560; skimorsefarm .com), 1168 County Rd., Montpelier. Open daily, weather-dependent. At an elevation of 1,200 feet, the farm offers a series of loops ranging from 0.7 to 3.9 km—more than 25 km of trails in all. Rentals, lessons, and a warming hut hitched to the gift shop with snacks available. Separate snowshoe trails.

Millstone Hill Touring & Recreation Center (802-277-0144; millstonetrails.com), 34 Church Hill Rd., Websterville, has 40 km of groomed cross-country and snowshoe trails that weave around some 30 old quarries. The touring center is located in a restored general store, around the corner from Millstone Hill Lodge (see *Lodging*), with trail maps and rentals; open daily, weather dependent.

Onion River Sports (802-229-9409; onionriver.com), 20 Langdon St., Montpelier, rents cross-country skis, snowshoes, and backcountry skis. Open daily, year-round; hours vary, check website.

ICE SKATING ✍ **The Central Vermont Civic Center** (802-229-5900; cvmcc.org) at 268 Gallison Hill Rd., Montpelier, off Rt. 302. Public skating and rentals; public skating hours vary, check website.

✍ **Barre City BOR Ice Arena** (802-476-0258; barrecity.org), 25 Auditorium Hill, Barre, in the Civic Center. Open for public skating mid-Oct.–mid-Mar., call ahead for days/hours. Rentals available.

SNOWMOBILING A large number of **VAST trails** (Vermont Association of Snow Travelers—in other words, snowmobile trails) are in parts of Washington and Orange Counties extending through the Barre/Montpelier area. The Central Vermont Chamber of Commerce hosts the best information at central-vt.com. VAST trails are mostly on private land and are open to responsible snowmobilers mid-Dec. (after hunting season) to mid-Apr. (snow depending).

Note: For more on winter sports, see "Sugarbush/Mad River Valley" and "Stowe/Waterbury."

✳ Lodging

In Montpelier 05602

○ ✍ **The Inn at Montpelier** (802-223-2727; innatmontpelier.com), 147 Main St. Two of the town's most stately (adjacent) Federal-style manses, renovated and furnished with antiques and Oriental carpets. Both belonged to James Langdon, a prominent local businessman. A marvelous Greek Revival porch, added around 1900, wraps around the yellow-clapboard Lamb-Langdon house, its wicker chairs a perfect place to rest after an afternoon stroll. Nineteen rooms, from standard to deluxe, are the most handsome in town. Number 27 has a huge private deck. Each comes with private bath and a homemade continental breakfast. Innkeepers John and Karol Underwood offer a downstairs guest pantry for coffee, tea, and freshly baked cookies at any hour. A beautifully appointed parlor and living room boast comfortable period furnishings. $175–290. Children under 6 free.

♂ **Capitol Plaza** (802-223-5252; 800-274-5252; capitolplaza.com), 100 State St. The former landmark tavern is now a four-story downtown hotel with 65 guest rooms including traditional doubles, Colonial "inn-style," mini suites, and 3 two-room suites. Jet hot tubs or spa showers in some suites. Amenities include a fitness room, golf privileges to the Country Club of Vermont (private course), and room service from J. Morgan's Steakhouse (see *Dining Out*). Located almost across the street from the Vermont Statehouse, the hotel is often booked for state-related conferences and events as well as weddings. $133–348.

✍ **Betsy's Bed & Breakfast** (802-229-0466; betsysbnb.com), 74 E. State St. Betsy and Jon Anderson are warm, helpful hosts who offer 12 attractive rooms and suites (9 of the rooms are suites) in adjacent Queen Anne and Victorian houses and a carriage house in a quiet hillside neighborhood, a short walk from Vermont College and the middle of town. Rooms have

CAPITOL PLAZA HOTEL

Capitol Plaza Hotel

private bath and satellite TV; eight rooms share full kitchen. Seasonal rates range $85–190 per room, including a generous breakfast with both Vermont and southern flavors.

In Barre 05641

Maplecroft Bed & Breakfast (802-477-5050; maplecroftvermont.com), 70 Washington St. Convenient for anyone researching Vermont history or genealogy next door at the Vermont History Center, this striking Victorian house is on Rt. 302 just above downtown and the small city park. Built by a Scottish granite shed owner in 1887 to resemble castles at home, it's now occupied by Dan Jones, Yasunari Ishii, and their West Highland white terrier, Barney. There are five guest rooms, all with private bath. Rates range $100–175 per room, double occupancy, and vary depending on weekdays, weekends, and holiday/foliage season. Children 12 and over welcome. Rates include a hearty breakfast. English and Japanese spoken.

♥ ❦ ✿ **The Lodge at Millstone Hill** (802-479-1000; millstonehill.com), 59 Little John Rd., East Barre. About 4 miles east of downtown Barre, this contemporary lodge is a converted barn, moved here from Warren. Owner Pierre Couture is a walking encyclopedia when it comes to the 70 historic granite quarries that stretch from one a few yards away to Millstone Hill a mile or so above, now part of a trail-webbed recreation area he has developed for mountain biking and cross-country skiing (see To Do). The interior is all open lofts, barnboard walls, exposed beams, and views. There are five guest rooms, three with private bath, full breakfast included. Luxury suites and apartments include full kitchens and therefore no breakfast. Common spaces include multilevel living rooms and a secluded game room, all with Oriental carpets, mounted trophies, and leather armchairs. Dog-friendly options. Lodge room rates are $95–400 with breakfast. Cottage, Studio, and Loft range $60–250.

Beyond

The Comstock House (802-272-2693; comstockhousebb.com), 1620 Middle Rd., Plainfield 05667. A beautifully restored 1891 home on 175 acres with large-windowed, immaculate rooms, utter quiet, and spectacular mountain views on a dirt road 2 miles southwest of Plainfield, handy to Goddard College. Innkeepers Warren Hathaway, a social worker, and journalist Ross Sneyd offer three comfortable rooms, each with private bath; one on the ground floor and two upstairs, both with option of expanding to a suite. There is an antiques-filled parlor where guests can mingle, and the dining room table overlooks a mountain panorama (and sunsets). Afternoon tea, full breakfast included; outdoor patio in warmer months. No pets; children over 12 welcome. $125–264 depending on room/season; two-night minimum June–Oct.

✪ ❦ ✿ **The Northfield Inn** (802-485-8558; thenorthfieldinn.com), 228 Highland Ave., Northfield 05663. This 1901 hillside mansion has been restored to reflect its Victorian vintage, complete with a gazebo overlooking the village. There are 10 spacious and comfortable guest rooms, 8 with private bath (several combine into family suites), furnished with antiques, brass or carved-wood beds, and European feather bedding. It's delightfully easy to get lost in this rambling old house with its scattered common spaces, including a library, parlor, game room, fitness room, and comfy third-floor TV room. $95–238, including a formal multicourse breakfast, snacks throughout the day, and an evening nightcap. Well-behaved children welcome.

♥ ❦ ✿ **Marshfield Inn & Motel** (802-426-3383; marshfieldinn.com), 5630 Rt. 2, Marshfield 05658. A Victorian, flat-roofed farmhouse set back and above Rt. 2, forms the centerpiece of this friendly complex. Lodging is in the 10 neighboring motel units with queen or two double beds, 2 with kitchenettes. A nominally priced breakfast (there's a full menu) is served in the main house. Halfway between Montpelier and St. Johnsbury, it's a good hub from which to explore in many directions, and there's a riverside path through the extensive property. $70 double in summer, $128 in foliage season, double occupancy; $10 for additional person per night. Pets welcome.

✿ **Hollister Hill Farm B&B** (802-454-7725; hollisterhillfarm.com), 2193 Hollister Hill Rd., Marshfield 05658. Technically in Marshfield but less than 2 miles uphill from Plainfield Village, this is a splendid 1825 farmhouse set in 204 acres with three guest rooms, all with private bath. Bob and Lee Light fled New Jersey for Vermont in 1972 and milked cows for 25 years, eventually replacing them with beefalo, pigs, chickens, and turkeys, all of which they sell from the farm store in the barn, along with honey from their hives and their own maple syrup. One guest room has a red cedar sauna; the other two have fireplaces (one can be a family suite by adding an adjoining room). In winter, guests are invited to bring cross-country skis, or borrow snowshoes; VAST trails also run through the property. The price range of $115–150, double occupancy ($170–190 for the family suite), includes a homegrown, home-laid, and homemade breakfast.

Rachel Carter

KISMET

Pie-in-the-Sky Farm Bed & Breakfast and Retreat (802-426-3777; pieinsky.com), Dwinell Rd., Marshfield 05658. This rambling Civil War–era farmhouse was home for a time to the Pie-in-Sky commune; it's since been a dairy and sheep farm and home for Jay Moore, Judy Sargent, and their cats for many years. Three upstairs rooms can be rented as a suite, with or without living room and kitchen facilities, or as individual double and single rooms, with shared bath. There's common space, a guest kitchen with fridge and snacks, a sunroom with a large tiled hot tub, and 120 acres with a beaver pond and a barn, as well as access to VAST trails on the property. Groton State Forest with hiking trails and swimming is nearby. From $95 (for a double), $155–185 for the full six-room apartment, breakfast included. Inquire about retreats and weekly rentals.

✳ Where to Eat

DINING OUT ✪ ♿ **Cornerstone Pub & Kitchen** (802-476-2121; cornerstonepk.com), 47 N. Main St., Barre. Barre natives Keith Paxman and Rich McSheffrey built this gastropub, literally on a busy corner, as one of the first shots fired in a slowly revitalizing Barre. Local beers are on tap at this spacious restaurant, but the ambience is local, too. The walls are decorated with 1930s signs from Barre's Magnet Theatre, advertising showings of films starring Mae West and Ginger Rogers. But hearty food is the main attraction. Try fish-and-chips with celeriac slaw or the caveman-esque barbecue pork shank with jalapeño mac-and-cheese and braised greens.

✪ ♿ **Kismet** (223-8646; kismetkitchens.com), 52 State St., Montpelier. Open for dinner Tues.–Sat. and brunch on weekends. Owner Crystal Maderia changes menus as the season's produce dictates. What doesn't budge is her brilliant palate and taste for innovation. Plates have varied from Lebanese tartare kibbeh and grilled octopus with peaches to an indulgent burger served with fries drizzled in truffle honey. Brunch is unapologetically hearty, with several takes on the Benedict alongside Portuguese baked eggs and bone-marrow bread pudding. Enjoy yours with a dandelion latte.

✐ ♿ **J. Morgan's Steakhouse** (802-223-5222; capitolplaza.com), 100 State St., Montpelier. Breakfast, lunch, dinner year-round, seven days a week; large Sun. brunch buffet. Model trains chugging their way around the dining room keep kids busy at this hotel restaurant. The "Millionaires Cake," a crabcake that also includes lobster and shrimp with a lemon-caper butter sauce, is a standard, as are the hand-cut steaks and steak burgers. Entrées $12–29.

NECI on Main (802-223-3188; neci.edu), 118 Main St., Montpelier. Open for lunch and dinner Tues.–Sat., and Sun. brunch. Culinary students pull out all the stops for an opulent Sunday buffet. There's always an action station in the dining room overlooking Main St., where guests can see chefs show off their chops. At lunch and dinner, a mix of Mediterranean and American fare is all ultra-handmade.

✪ **Salt** (802-229-6678; saltcafevt.com), 207 Barre St., Montpelier. Dinner Fri.–Sun. Former critic Suzanne Podhaizer put her money where mouth was with this petite restaurant—reservations a must. During the week, she offers culinary consulting and pop-up meals. Friday and Saturday, there are whimsical prix fixe meals using food she grows herself, including geese from her own farm. Podhaizer ends the week with a casual Sunday farm dinner. All of the above require reservations.

J. MORGAN'S STEAKHOUSE

Capitol Plaza Hotel

♠ ♂ ♿ **Sarducci's Restaurant & Bar** (802-223-0229; sarduccis.com), 3 Main St., Montpelier. Open for lunch Mon.–Sat.; dinner nightly. This spacious, yellow-walled restaurant with a woodfired oven is popular with legislators and families alike; reservations recommended, especially on weekends. There's always a view of the Winooski River, but it can be enjoyed outdoors in the warmer months.

EATING OUT

In Montpelier

✪ ♂ **Chill Gelato** (802-223-2445), 32 State St. Tues.–Sun. The gelato here is made in small batches using local milk. Making only a bit at a time allows owners Theo and Nora Kennedy freedom to explore quirky tastes. You're in luck if you arrive when the couple has been making creamy rose or chai flavors.

✪ ♂ **The Mad Taco** (802-225-6038; themadtaco.com), 72 Main St. Lunch and dinner every day. The menu changes daily at this tiny taco counter, which has a larger branch in Waitsfield. Just don't expect nachos. This locavore establishment is devoted to roasted or smoked meats and veggies, stuffed into tacos, burritos, and quesadillas. The rainbow of homemade hot sauces is worth a visit on its own.

Three Penny Taproom (802-223TAPS; threepennytaproom.com), 108 Main St. The hard-to-find beers on the 24-brew tap list make this an imbibable cabinet of delicious curiosities. Pair them with elevated versions of bar food, including Scotch eggs and *moules frites*.

♂ **Wilaiwan's Kitchen** (802-505-8111), 34 State St. Open Mon.–Fri. for lunch only. You'll feel like you stepped into a rough-and-tumble roadside eatery in Thailand when you fight for a seat at this popular restaurant. There are only three items on the weekly menu, but they burst with authentic fire.

Beyond

✪ ♠ ♂ **Wayside Restaurant and Bakery** (802-223-6611; waysiderestaurant.com), 1873 Rt. 302, Barre–Montpelier Rd., Berlin. Open daily for breakfast, lunch, and dinner. Vermont's ultimate family restaurant has been serving up comfort food since 1918. The menu hasn't changed much since then, including exquisite holdovers such as salt pork and milk gravy; pickled honeycomb tripe; and in-season, locally caught perch. For dessert, try the famous doughnuts or freshly baked pie—with a $3.50 margarita.

♂ **Positive Pie** (802-454-0133; positivepie.com), 65–69 Main St., Plainfield. Open daily for lunch and dinner; breakfast on weekends.

This is the place to gather in Plainfield. Twenty craft beers, ciders, and root beers on tap go down easy alongside locavore pizza, pasta, and eclectic sandwiches.

♂ **The Knotty Shamrock Irish Pub** (802-485-4857; knottyshamrock.com), 21 East St., Northfield. Dinner Wed.–Sun., weekend lunch, Sunday Irish breakfast. As headquarters of Paine Mtn. Brewing, the tipples at this Irish-themed pub include homemade IPAs, milk stout, and Bavarian wheat bear. The cottage pie is inspired by Edward Bourn, an early Irish-born president of nearby Norwich University.

BREAKFAST/LUNCH

In Montpelier

✪ ♿ ☏ **National Life Cafeteria** (802-229-3397; neci.edu), 1 National Life Dr. Open for breakfast 7–9, for lunch 11:30–1:30. The cafeteria here partners with the New England Culinary Institute (NECI). Views are through plate-glass windows to the mountains. Pick up a dining room pass at the lobby. There's a big salad bar, a choice of made-to-order sandwiches, grill items, specials like eggs Benedict with steak, locally raised barbecued pork over pasta with Cabot cheddar, and a wide choice of desserts.

La Brioche Bakery & Cafe (802-229-0443; neci.edu), 89 Main St. Open Mon.–Sat. for breakfast and lunch. New England Culinary Institute instructors and students bake everything here, right behind a large window—sort of like a pastry zoo. Pastries are an appealing mix of French-inspired classics and highly original experiments. At mealtime, get freshly made salads and made-to-order sandwiches. Eat in the dining room or on the patio. Even easier? Grab a bagged lunch to go.

♠ ♂ ♿ **Coffee Corner** (802-229-9060; coffeecorner.com), corner of Main and State. Open 6:30–3, daily. A lively little city diner in the thick of things that specializes in fresh produce, fresh-baked bread, cozy booths, and fast, friendly service. Breakfast all day.

♂ ♿ **Hunger Mountain Food Co-op** (802-223-8000; hungermountain.com), 623 Stone Cutters Way. Open daily 8–7:30. Hidden away in a corner of this cooperative market is a deli with many vegetarian choices and a very attractive glass-sided café area overlooking the river. There's a hot bar, too.

☏ **Capitol Grounds** (802-223-7800; capitolgrounds.com), 27 State St. Open breakfast, lunch, and late afternoons seven days a week. An inviting and lively coffeehouse with a wide selection of coffees, teas, and other drinks as well as soups, sandwiches (including breakfast ones), pastries, and other treats.

Birchgrove Baking Café (802-223-0200; birchgrovebaking.com), 279 Elm St. Breakfast and lunch daily. There are always savory pastries available for a meal, but you'll be tempted to skip them in favor of a s'mores tart, crackling caramel monkey bread, and a homemade floral soda. Planning a celebration? The bakers specialize in ornate cakes.

Beyond

&. (p) **Red Hen Bakery & Café** (802-223-5200; redhenbaking.com), 91B Rt. 2, Middlesex, right off I-89 Exit 9. Open seven days for breakfast and lunch. Husband-and-wife team Randy George and Liza Cain are Vermont bread barons, famous for their crusty, organic loaves. They're served with practically everything at this café and gourmet store. The blackboard menu lists soups and deli sandwiches; there are also sweet and savory pastries that crowd the cases and counter. For breakfast grab an espresso and maple-glazed bun. In the afternoon, pick up a pizza crust to make at home.

Rainbow Sweets (802-426-3531), 1689 Rt. 2, Plainfield. Open for breakfast and lunch daily except Tues., dinner on Fri.–Sat. Closed Mar.–May. This colorful café has been a destination for more than 30 years. Stop by in the morning for empanadas and espresso, or for a lunch of Moroccan bisteeya; homemade pizza nights on the weekends. The bakery is perhaps most famous for a pastry called "Johnny Depp on a Plate," a suggestive profiterole filled with custard and dipped in caramel.

✸ Entertainment

THEATER Barre Opera House (802-476-8188; barreoperahouse.org), 6 N. Main St., Barre. Built in 1899, after fire destroyed its predecessor, this elegant, acoustically outstanding, 650-seat theater occupies the second and third floors of city hall. It's open year-round; close to 100 productions are performed, from local theater and arts programming to international music, dance, and opera.

Lost Nation Theater Company (802-229-0492; lostnationtheater.org), Montpelier City Hall Arts Center, 128 Elm St., Montpelier. Black-box productions of contemporary plays, classics, and original works year-round by a professional troupe. The Winterfest Series features four different shows weekends in February.

MUSIC Farmer's Night Concert Series (802-828-2228; leg.state.vt.us). Free concerts given on Wednesdays at the State House

Jan.–Apr., when the legislature is in session. The series began in the 19th century for lawmakers who found themselves far from home with little to do in the evening after a day's session. At first the men performed for one another. Today the entertainment is a mix of talks and music by different Vermont performing groups.

Capital City Concerts (capitalcityconcerts .org), a classical chamber music series in Montpelier, stages five concerts per year at churches around town.

🎵 **Brown Bag Music Series** (802-2239604; montpelieralive.com). Free lunchtime concerts Thursdays in the summer at the Christ Church Courtyard, 64 State St.

Adamant Music School (802-223-3347; adamant.org), 1216 Haggett Rd., Adamant. Piano students perform concerts through the summer for $10 at this lovely spot between East Montpelier and Calais. Painting and sculpture exhibits can also be enjoyed; free theater productions in the QuarryWorks Theater.

FILM The Savoy (802-229-0598; savoytheater .com), 26 Main St., Montpelier. The capital's only theater for independent, international, and art films. Occasional speakers and special events.

🎵 **Capitol Showcase**, 93 State St., Montpelier, and **Paramount Twin Cinema,** 241 N. Main St., Barre, are both classic old movie houses showing first-run feature films (802-229-0343; http://fgbtheaters.com).

✸ Selective Shopping

ANTIQUES A drive starting on Rt. 2 in Montpelier and heading east all the way to Danville can bring forth many treasures from scattered antiques sheds and yard sales spring through fall weekends.

East Barre Antique Mall (802-479-5190; east barreantiquemall.com), 133 Mill St., East Barre. Open May–Oct.; call ahead for days/hours. A sprawling former furniture store housing central Vermont's largest group shop: some 400 consignees and dealers on three floors with plenty of furniture, glass, and china and a whole room of kitchenware.

ART GALLERIES AND CRAFTS STUDIOS
Note: Check the Montpelier Alive website (montpelieralive.com) for the scheduled **Art Walk** with music and art throughout downtown every other month.

T. W. Wood Art Gallery and Arts Center (802-262-6035; twoodgallery.org) at 46 Barre St., Montpelier. Open since 1896, but now

Rachel Carter

A VIEW OF MONTPELIER

relocated closer to downtown, this gallery houses one of the state's largest permanent art collections. Changing exhibits feature contemporary Vermont artists and craftspeople.

The Artisans' Hand (802-229-9492; artisan shand.com), 89 Main St., Montpelier. Open daily. An exceptional variety of Vermont craftwork by a cooperative of some 125 artisans in multiple media.

The Mud Studio (802-224-7000; themud studio.com), 961 Rt. 2, Middlesex. Open Tues.–Sun. year-round. Several dozen individual potters share this studio producing stoneware and porcelain, whimsical and functional. Classes and shop.

Green Mountain Hooked Rugs (802-223-1333; greenmountainhookedrugs.com), 2838 County Rd., Montpelier (near Morse Farm). Open Tues.–Sat. 10–5. Stephanie Allen-Krauss comes from four generations of rug hookers and sells colorful examples of the craft at this gallery. Inquire about the June Green Mountain Rug School, the nation's largest, and the Fall Foliage Fiesta of Rug Hooking.

SPA (Studio Place Arts) (802-479-7069; studioplacearts.com), 201 N. Main St., Barre. Open Tues.–Sat. This art center offers classes for both adults and children and maintains the Studio Place Arts Gallery.

Blackthorn Forge (802-426-3369; blackthorn forge.com), 247 Gilman Rd., Marshfield. Call ahead. Working in a red barn, Steve Bronstein makes functional and sculptural ironwork. Judaica is a focus—his Classic Curve menorah was featured on a 2013 USPS Hanukkah stamp.

Also see **vermontcrafts.com**. This area is particularly rich in studios that open to visitors over the Memorial Day Open Studio Weekend and may or may not be accessible on a regular basis.

BOOKSTORES *Bear Pond Books* (802-229-0774; bearpondbooks.com), 77 Main St., Montpelier. Open daily year-round; check website for times. One of the state's best bookstores, heavy on literature, art, and children's books; regular author readings.

Rivendell Books (802-223-3928; rivendell booksvt.com), 100 Main St., Montpelier. Open daily, year-round, but good to check ahead. Owned by Bear Pond Books, this is the official bookstore for the New England Culinary Institute, meaning lots of cooking textbooks and NECI swag. The selection leans toward used tomes but also new books, remainders, and bargain-priced best sellers. Some rare and signed books as well.

The Country Bookshop (802-454-8439; the countrybookshop.com), 35 Mill St. (off Rt. 2 at the blinker), Plainfield. Open daily 10–5, but it's wise to call ahead. Some 30,000 books, plus postcards and paper ephemera, are loaded into one floor at this aptly named oasis; owner Ben Koenig's specialties include books on folk music, folklore, and bells.

FARMERS MARKETS Local farmers markets include Plainfield Village Farmers Market, Northfield Farmers Market, Capital City (Montpelier) Farmers Market, and Barre Granite Center Farmers Market. Dates, times, details at vermontagriculture.com.

FARMS The area is dotted with maple sugaring farms, which get active once the sap starts flowing Feb.–Apr. Maple Open House Weekend is held annually at the end of March; participating farms can be found at vermontmaple.org.

See **Morse Farm Maple Sugarworks** under *Must See* and *Cross-Country Skiing*.

♪ **Bragg Farm Sugarhouse & Gift Shop** (802-223-5757; 800-376-5757; braggfarm.com), 1005 Rt. 14 north, East Montpelier. Open daily, year-round. Serving sugar-on-snow Mar.–Apr. weekends, noon–5. This fifth-generation farm still collects sap the traditional way (in 2,500 buckets) and boils it over wood fires. The shop carries a variety of maple and other Vermont crafts and specialty foods and includes a museum and a maple ice cream parlor.

Grand View Winery (802-456-7012; grandviewwinery.com), 2113 Max Gray Rd., East Calais. Open Memorial Day weekend–Oct.; call ahead. Take Rt. 14 north 4 miles from East Montpelier, turn right onto Max Gray Rd., continue 2.3 miles. The tasting room at the farm is set in gardens amid works by Vermont artists. The wine selection is extensive, from rhubarb, dandelion, and blueberry to French grape blends; hard cider, too. Winemaker Phil Tonks has been growing fruit here for 30 years and established the winery in 1997. Inquire about specialty events.

Fresh Tracks Farm (802-223-1151; freshtracksfarm.com), 4373 Rt. 12, Berlin. Christina Castegren and Kris Tootle grow seven varieties of grapes on 14 acres. Their hard work has paid off, as they have brought to fruition a variety of award-winning grape wines—and a few apple. Store and tasting room open Wed.–Sun. afternoons. Live music some evenings in summer—check website.

♪ **Knight's Spider Web Farm** (802-433-5568; spiderwebfarm.com), off Rt. 14 at 124 Spider Web Rd., at the south end of Williamstown Village. Open 9–6 daily June 15–Oct. 15, then weekends till Christmas. Aptly self-styled as the "original web site." Artist Will Knight encourages and harvests spiderwebs in his barn, then mounts them onto wood. Chat with Knight about the little critters, then buy a web to take home.

♂ ♪ **Eat. Stay. Farm.** (802-505-9840; eatstayfarm.com), 923 Loop Rd., Northfield. Open year-round. Laura Olsen and Mari Omland lead a dynamic charge and offer farm experiences from making goat cheese to caring for chickens; cooking classes that begin with picking farm produce and using it to create a culinary display; and the Omnivore Farm Stand, selling the farm's humanely raised and organically managed pork, chicken, lamb, turkey, goat; eggs and cheese; and a sweeping array of vegetables. Frequent community events, including farm yoga. **Farmstays** are available in the barn's loft and

can accommodate up to six people. Rates begin at $240 for the first night and are $200 for each night following and include a farm tour and breakfast starter basket as well as access to a private kitchen to make your own farm breakfast.

Note: Also see **Floating Bridge Food & Farms Cooperative** in "The White River Valleys."

SPECIAL SHOPS Zutano (802-223-2229; zutano.com), 79 Main St., Montpelier. Open Mon.–Sat. 10–6. With offices in nearby Cabot, Manhattan artists Uli and Michael Belenky, who didn't give a thought to baby clothes until their daughter Sophie arrived in 1989, produce a delightful collection of soft, whimsical onesies that defy the tired maxim that blue is for boys and pink for girls. Now known nationwide, this is the duo's flagship boutique.

♪ **Woodbury Mountain Toys** (802-223-4272; woodburymountaintoys.com), 24 State St., Montpelier. Open daily. The motto is "Come in and play with us." This independent toy store carries many locally made and hard-to-find items as well as major lines. Like a hands-on whimsical toy museum, but you can take the displays home.

Buch Spieler Music (802-229-0449; bsmusic.com), 27 Langdon St., Montpelier. Open daily. An independent music store specializing in cards, novelties, and all kinds of music from around the world, since 1973.

✴ Special Events

Mid-March: **Green Mountain Film Festival** (802-262-3423; gmffestival.org) brings artistic, interpretive, and thought-provoking films to four venues for two weekends and the week in between.

April: **Poem City** (802-223-9604; montpelieralive.com) celebrates National Poetry Month with poems, displays, events, readings slams, and more all month long.

♪ *March–April:* Vermont maple sugaring; see Bragg and Morse Farms and vermontmaple.org; second to last March weekend is **Maple Open House Weekend**.

♪ *Mid-May:* **Black Fly Festival** (802-223-5760; blackflyfestival.org) is a locals' self-consciously quirky celebration of the end of winter and start of blackfly season held at the Adamant Co-op. There are nature walks, live music, a pie-baking contest, and a fashion show—all devoted to the blood-sucking bugs.

Memorial Day weekend: **Open Studio Weekend** throughout Vermont (vermontcrafts.com) where artisans open their studios for tours and shopping.

May–October: **Farmers markets** (vermont agriculture.com).

❧ *June–July:* **Vermont Mountaineers Baseball** (802-223-5224; thevermontmountaineers .com), New England intercollegiate baseball games at the Recreation Field, Elm St., Montpelier. Check website for schedule.

❧ *July 3:* **Montpelier's Independence Day Celebration** (802-223-9604; montpelieralive .com)—live music, games, road race, parade, vendors, and a giant fireworks display.

❧ *Last weekend in July:* **Barre Heritage Festival & Homecoming Days** (802-476-3615; barreheritagefestival.org). This four-day downtown festival—with art exhibits, live music, sidewalk sales, vending, and street fair—brings together the history of Barre and the current culture into a vibrant event.

❧ *Labor Day weekend:* **Northfield Labor Day Weekend** (802-485-9206; northfieldlaborday .org) is a family fun weekend of events with a pageant, parade of floats, and Norwich cadets.

Mid-October: **Cabot Apple Pie Festival** (802-563-2526) is a daylong apple pie celebration with a serious apple pie contest, crafts fair, and auction.

Last weekend in November: **Winter Festival of Vermont Crafters** (greaterbarrecraftguild. com), a good-sized crafts fair bringing forth popular and obscure crafts.

KILLINGTON/RUTLAND AREA

K illington Resort is the largest ski area in the eastern United States. It boasts seven mountain areas, including Pico Mountain, and the region's most expansive lift network and snowmaking system. Killington Peak at 4,241 feet, the second highest summit in the state, is flanked by four other mountains and faces another big majestic range across Sherburne Pass.

Although the road through this upland village has been heavily traveled since the settling of Rutland (11 miles to the west) and Woodstock (20 miles to the east), there was never much of anything here. In 1924 an elaborate, rustic-style inn was built at the junction of Rt. 4, the Appalachian Trail, and the new Long Trail. A winter annex across the road was added in 1938, when Pico Mountain (now part of Killington) installed one of the country's first T-bars. But the logging village of Sherburne Center (now the town of Killington) was practically a ghost town on December 13, 1958, when Killington Basin Ski Area opened.

Condominiums currently cluster at higher elevations, while lodges, inns, and motels are strung along the 4.5-mile length of Killington Rd. and west along Rt. 4 as it slopes ever downward through Mendon to Rutland. Ski lodges are also salted along Rt. 100 north to the pleasant old town of Pittsfield, and in the village of Chittenden, sequestered up a back road from Rt. 4, near a mountain-backed reservoir. Forested mountains dominate the surrounding landscape in all directions. This is a major crossroads for foot traffic on the Appalachian and Long Trails as well for vehicles.

The big news at Killington Resort is the Peak Lodge, a state-of-the-art glass-walled summit lodge on Lincoln Peak, open year-round. It offers one of the most spectacular views in the Northeast, a destination in its own right. It's also symbol of resurgence for this major resort that peaked in popularity more than a decade ago. Hurricane Irene dealt a devastating blow by to the base area and town below in 2011. Killington's 840 residents plus 700 visitors were isolated for the 19 days that Rt. 4 was impassable.

It's taken several years to thoroughly recover. A major new master plan is in the works to merge Killington the town and Killington the resort in more visible ways. There's also more focus on the community as a major crossroads, both of Vermont's major east–west and north–south roads and of its hiking trails. A new visitors center has been positioned at the junctions of Rts. 4 and 100, stocked with information about local hikes and extensive mountain biking trails, both on and off the mountain. Summer and fall events have multiplied, and more restaurants are open year-round.

Home of the Vermont State Fair, Rutland is the business and shopping center for a large

KILLINGTON PEAK
Killington Resort

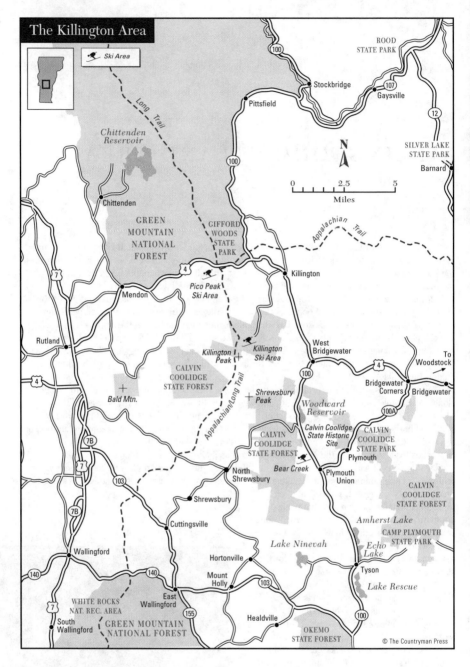

Ski Area

ROOD
STATE PARK

Stockbridge

Gaysville

Pittsfield

*Chittenden
Reservoir*

SILVER LAKE
STATE PARK

Barnard

0   2.5   5
Miles

Chittenden

GREEN
MOUNTAIN
NATIONAL
FOREST

GIFFORD
WOODS
STATE
PARK

Appalachian Trail

Mendon

*Pico Peak
Ski Area*

Killington

Rutland

*Killington
Peak*

*Killington
Ski Area*

West
Bridgewater

To
Woodstock

CALVIN
COOLIDGE
STATE FOREST

*Shrewsbury
Peak*

Bridgewater
Corners

Bridgewater

Bald Mtn.

Appalachian/Long Trail

*Woodward
Reservoir*

CALVIN
COOLIDGE
STATE FOREST

*Calvin Coolidge
State Historic
Site*

CALVIN
COOLIDGE
STATE PARK

Plymouth

North
Shrewsbury

Bear Creek

Plymouth
Union

CALVIN
COOLIDGE
STATE FOREST

Shrewsbury

Cuttingsville

Amherst Lake

CAMP PLYMOUTH
STATE PARK

*Echo
Lake*

Wallingford

Lake Ninevah

Hortonville

Tyson

Lake Rescue

Mount
Holly

WHITE ROCKS
NAT. REC. AREA

East
Wallingford

South
Wallingford

GREEN MOUNTAIN
NATIONAL FOREST

Healdville

OKEMO
STATE FOREST

© The Countryman Press

A VIEW OF RUTLAND

Scott Herdling

rural radius. Stolid, early-Victorian mansions and streets crisscrossed with railroad tracks testify to its 19th-century prosperity—when Rutland was known as "the marble city." The long-established shops along Merchants Row and Center Street, among the state's best-preserved commercial blocks, have held their own in recent years.

Rutland lies in a broad, gently rolling corridor between New York State and the Green Mountains. It's broad enough to require two major north–south routes. Rt. 7, the busier highway, hugs the Green Mountains and, with the exception of the heavily trafficked strip around Rutland, is a scenic ride. Rt. 30 to the west is a far quieter ride through farm country and by two major lakes, Lake Bomoseen and Lake St. Catherine, both popular summer meccas.

Rt. 4 is the major east–west road, a mountain-rimmed four-lane highway from Fair Haven, at the New York line, to Rutland, where it angles north through the middle of town before turning east again, heading uphill to Killington. In 2011 Rt. 4 from West Rutland east to Hartford was named the "Crossroads of Vermont Byway" by the Vermont Scenic Byway Program (byways.org). Rt. 140 from Wallingford to Poultney is the other old east–west road here, a scenic byway through Middletown Springs, where old mineral water springs form the core of a pleasant park. Bed & breakfasts are salted through this rolling farm country and the high hamlets of Shrewsbury and North Shrewsbury, tucked up on along the spine of the Green Mountains, still less than 10 miles from Rutland.

GUIDANCE The Rutland Region Chamber of Commerce (802-773-2747; 800-756-8880) maintains a website (rutlandvermont.com) and **visitors center** in Main Street Park at the junction of Rts. 7 and 4, open late daily May–mid-Oct., staffed on weekends. The chamber office downtown at 50 Merchants Row operates a year-round, staffed visitors center in the lobby Mon.–Sat.

A VIEW OF RUTLAND

Scott Herdling

Killington Chamber of Commerce (802-773-4181; 800-337-1928; killingtonchamber .com) is a source of year-round information about the area and maintains a visitor-geared office on Rt. 4 across from the Killington access road, staffed Mon.–Fri. 10–5, Sat. 10–1; restrooms.

The Fair Haven Welcome Center (802-265-4763) on Rt. 4 near the New York line is open every day 7–7.

GETTING THERE *By train:* **Amtrak** (800-USA-RAIL; amtrak.com). Daily service to and from New York City on the Ethan Allen Express to Rutland.

By air: **Rutland Southern Vermont Regional Airport** (flyrutlandvt.com) is served by Cape Air (800-352-0714) with frequent flights to Boston and Florida. Links to rental cars and taxis are on the website.

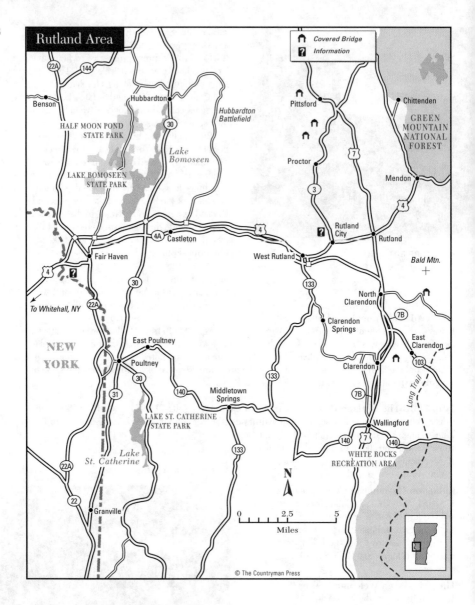

By bus: **Marble Valley Regional Transit District** (802-773-3244; thebus.com), operator of "**The Bus**," connects Rutland with Killington, the Rutland airport, Manchester, Fair Haven, and Middlebury as well as points within the city. In winter **shuttle buses** run from Marble Valley in Rutland to several Killington points, including Pico Mountain on Rt. 4, and up and down the length of Killington Rd. **Vermont Transit** (802-888-7267; vttranslines.com) stops at the Killington Chamber of Commerce, Rt. 4, en route from Hanover, New Hampshire, to Rutland.

Getting around: A **Free Shuttle** (802-422-FREE) operates nightly in ski season among lodging places and five restaurants along the access road.

MEDICAL EMERGENCY Call 911. **Rutland Regional Medical Center Fast Track Emergency Service** (802-747-3601; rrmc.org), 160 Allen St., Rutland.

✷ Villages

Poultney (population 3,600; poultneyvt.com), on Rt. 30 near the New York border and just north of Lake St. Catherine. Poultney is home to Green Mountain College, a four-year coed liberal arts college focusing on environmental studies. It also has significant journalistic associations: Horace Greeley, founder of the *New York Tribune*, lived at the venerable Eagle Tavern in East Poultney (now a private home) while he was learning the printing trade at the *East Poultney National Spectator* in the 1820s (and organizing a local temperance society). Working with him was George Jones, who helped found *The New York Times* in 1851. Attracted by the slate quarries, Vermont's first Jewish community settled here during the Civil War, and Welsh immigrants poured in to take up quarrymen jobs. Welsh was spoken here until the 1950s in what was one of the largest Welsh communities in the country. Green Mountain College has an extensive Welsh archive, teaches Welsh heritage, and maintains the only choir in the country that sings Welsh songs at each of its performances.

East Poultney is a picturesque hamlet worth detouring to see. The fine white Baptist church, built in 1805, is the centerpiece, standing on a small green surrounded by a cluster of historic buildings—the Melodeon Factory, Union Academy, and the Old School House. Tours are available for download at poultneyhistoricalsociety.org. **The Original Vermont Store** is located here, next to the fast-flowing Poultney River.

Castleton (population 4,372; castletonvt.com) at Rts. 4A and 30, is home to **Castleton College**, the oldest member of Vermont's state college system. It was also here in Remington Tavern that Ethan Allen and Seth Warner planned the capture of Ticonderoga. As an offshoot of this conspiratorial meeting, blacksmith Samuel Beach—Vermont's own Paul Revere—reputedly ran some 60 miles in 24 hours to recruit more men for the raid. The town itself grew rapidly after the Revolution and is a showcase of pillared Greek Revival houses, most designed by Thomas Royal Dake. Main Street is a showcase for his workmanship; note the **Ransom-Rehlen Mansion**, with its 17 Ionic columns, and Congregational Meeting House, now the **Federated Church**, with the lovely pulpit that Dake completed with his own funds. Between 1850 and 1870 the West Castleton Railroad and Slate Company was the largest marble plant in the country.

Fair Haven (population 2,952; fairhavenvt.org), located where Rts. 4, 4A, and 22A intersect, is at the core of Vermont's slate industry. One of its earliest developers in the 1780s was the controversial Matthew Lyon, who started an ironworks and published a newspaper called *The Scourge of Aristocracy*, in which he lambasted the Federalists. Elected to Congress in 1796, Lyon had scuffles on the floor of the House and criticized President Adams so vehemently that he was arrested and jailed under the Alien and Sedition Act. Lyon's case caused such a national uproar that this patently unconstitutional censorship law was soon rescinded. Lyon was reelected to Congress while still in jail and took his seat in time to cast the tie-breaking vote that made Thomas Jefferson president instead of Aaron Burr.

Around the spacious green are three Victorian mansions (two faced with marble) built by descendants of Ira Allen, founder of the University of Vermont.

Benson (population 1,039; benson-vt.com), west of Rt. 22A, 8 miles north of Fair Haven, is one of those tiny proverbial villages "that time forgot" except as a scenic photo op, but in recent years it has developed a creative personality with its artisans and special shops.

Pittsfield (population 546; pittsfieldvt.org) is almost completely enclosed in the Green Mountain National Forest on Rt. 100 north of Killington as you begin the scenic drive to the Mad River Valley. This route was one of the most severely damaged by 2011's Hurricane Irene, isolated for two weeks. Pittsfield is also known as the home of the running, biking, and snowshoe races and endurance competitions introduced by Joe De Sena, the town's major landholder, owner of the Amee Farm Lodge, the Trailside Inn, Amee Farm, and the Original General Store (see peak.com and spartanrace.com) and creator of a 20-mile trail system.

✷ Must See

✪ ⛷ **Peak Lodge** (killington.com). Open when the K-1 Express Gondola ($15 round-trip/$10 one-way) operates, daily during ski, foliage, and summer seasons. Check in shoulder seasons and to make sure it isn't closed for a function. In summer and fall many patrons hike up and take the gondola back down. At 4,214 feet, this is Vermont's most spectacular view for the least effort. On a clear day the view from the summit of the state's second highest summit encompasses five states. It sweeps northwest to the Adirondacks, east to the White Mountains, and north along the spine of the Green Mountains. It's the spot on which the Reverend Samuel Peters in 1763 is said to have christened all that he could see "Verd Monts." Even in winter nonskiers are welcome. On a clear summer day we could have curled up with a brew in one of the inviting leather armchairs, changing seats every hour or two to take in the view from another side of the lodge. The food is worthy of its setting: The frank is Boar's Head and the cheeseburger is from local Angus beef, with Cabot sharp cheddar.

✪ ♂ **Vermont Marble Exhibit** (800-427-1396; vermont-marble.com), 52 Main St., Proctor. From Business Rt. 4 in West Rutland follow Rt. 3 north. Open mid-May–Oct., daily 9–5. $7 adults, $5 seniors, $4 teens, children free. Reduced rates available online. The first commercial marble deposit was discovered and quarried in Vermont in 1784. This is a privately, superbly maintained museum housed in one of the vast old marble sheds on Otter Creek. The approach is across a multiarched marble bridge built in 1915 as a memorial to Fletcher D. Proctor, a scion of the family who formed The Vermont Marble Company in 1870. The entrance to the museum is through a monolithic marble arch and across railroad tracks, then up marble steps to a grand marble hall. An award-winning film relates the story of Vermont's part in the quarrying and carving of the Tomb of the Unknown Soldier at Arlington National Cemetery. Marble from Proctor and Danby was used for the U.S. Supreme Court building, the Lincoln Memorial, and the Beinecke Library at Yale. The Proctor family was Vermont's major political dynasty, filling state and national offices for nearly a century. The company continued to thrive until World War II, employing 5,000 workers at its height. The quarry has since been acquired by the Swiss-based Pleuss-Staufer Industries. Marble quarrying, however, continues in Vermont and includes a subterranean quarry in Danby. The museum includes a number of exhibits, notably a gallery of bas-reliefs of American presidents by local sculptor Renzo Palmerrini. You'll also find replicas of the *Pietà* and the *Last Supper*, a sculptor in residence, and a hands-on geology and fossil exhibit. There is an extensive gift shop. A quarter-mile walkway leads to the old Sutherland Falls Quarry. Pick up a sandwich or Vermont specialty treat at the Proctor Co-op or at the Museum's Cookie Barn.

Note: **The Carving Studio and Sculpture Center** (802-438-2097; carvingstudio.org), 636 Marble St., West Rutland. Sited at the head of a 200-acre former quarrying and manufacturing site, the center offers workshops, residencies, sculpture sales, a sculpture garden, and rotating exhibits and events. Check website for schedule.

ALSO SEE ♠ ♂ **The New England Maple Museum** (802-483-9414; maplemuseum.com), 4578 Rt. 7, Pittsford. Call for hours. $5 adults, $1 children over 6. Maple was originally a Native American sugar that was traded with European settlers; then the "art" of sugar making was shared. The settlers developed new processing methods, and reportedly a French missionary made the first maple syrup in 1690. This museum illustrates the history, production, and consumption of maple syrup and its byproducts. You can view the Danforth Collection of antique equipment, murals, and a 10-minute slide show. There's a tasting room, too, for education of another sense.

MAPLE SUGARING

Rutland Chamber of Commerce

Chaffee Art Center (802-775-0356; chaffeeartcenter.org), 16 S. Main St., Rutland. Open Tues.–Sat., 10–5. Galleries are housed in an 1896 Queen Anne Victorian listed on the National Register of Historic Places. Permanent and periodic exhibits and a youth gallery for school displays. Traditional and contemporary paintings, sculpture, crafts, graphics, and photography are included. Donation appreciated.

Slate Valley Museum (518-642-1417; slatevalleymuseum.org), 17 Water St., Granville, NY 12832. Open year-round, closed Sun.–Mon. Admission $5 per person; children 12 and under are free. Just across the New York border from Poultney in the heart of the slate industry's historic base, on a site where immigrant quarry workers once lived in tenements, this 19th-century Dutch barn reflects the many colors and shapes of slate. It includes a quarry shanty, tools, a mural, paintings, photographs, family artifacts, and a gift shop.

⚲ ♂ ♿ **Wilson Castle** (802-773-3284; wilsoncastle.com), 2970 W. Proctor Rd. between West Rutland and Proctor. open for guided tours daily, late May–late Oct., 9–5. $10 adults, $6 children. This 19th-century turreted mansion was built in 1867 for the English bride of a Vermont physician, John Johnson, no expense spared. Almost everything was imported, including the exterior brick. The opulent furnishings include Venetian tapestries, 400-year-old Chinese scrolls, a Louis XIV French onyx-covered table, and a gallery of classic sculpture, not to mention 84 stained-glass windows. But the seclusion was too much for the aristocratic Mrs. Johnson; she returned to England two years later, and the house was sold. In 1939 it was acquired by pioneering radio engineer Herbert Lee Wilson, who established AM radio towers around the world. Inquire about special Saturday-night murder mystery dinners and the Halloween Haunted House. The mansion can also be rented as a party or wedding venue.

♿ **The Hubbardton Battlefield** (802-273-2282; historicvermont.org/hubbardton), 5696 Monument Rd. in East Hubbardton, 7 miles north of the posted Rt. 4 exit. A hilltop visitors center is open late May–Columbus Day, Thurs.–Sun. 9:30–5. Admission $3. Battle buffs won't want to miss the diorama and narrated 3-D map of this 1777 Revolutionary War site, where Colonels Seth Warner, Ebenezer Francis, and Nathan Hale led Vermont, Massachusetts, and New Hampshire soldiers in a successful rear-guard action against British and German troops. They saved the main American army, which was retreating from Mount Independence and Fort Ticonderoga. Of all American battlefields, this one looks most the way it did on the day of the battle. Paths lead to signs describing the events that unfolded, and the views are spectacular, with sweeping vistas of the Taconic Mountains to the south, Pittsford Ridge to the east, and the Adirondacks to the west.

✳ To Do

AERIAL RIDES The **Killington K-1 Express Gondola** (800-621-MTNS; killington.com) runs ski season and late June–Columbus Day from K-1 Lodge to the Peak Lodge (see above) top of Killington Peak. Check in early September and off-season. $15 round-trip, $10 one-way. Recently repainted in bright designs, carrying mountain bikes in summer and fall as well as skis in winter.

BIKING There's a lot of great bike riding in this area; check for maps at voga.org. Little-trafficked roads wind through the gently rolling countryside around Lake St. Catherine and Middletown Springs. Rentals are available from the **Sports Peddler** (802-775-0101) at 158 N. Main St., Rutland. The **Bike Shop** at **Vermont Adventure Tours** (802-773-3343; vermontadventuretours.com), 223 Woodstock Ave., Rutland, rents mountain bikes and also offers a variety of touring options.

Mountain Bike Park at Killington Resort (800-621-MTNS; killington.com). The K-1 Express Gondola operates July–Columbus Day (weather permitting), hoisting bicyclists and their bikes from the K-1 Lodge up to Killington Peak, accessing 35 miles of trails and a 1,700-foot vertical drop spread across five mountain areas. The Snowshed Express Quad lift serves expanded beginner terrain on weekends. Guided tours, instruction, bike rentals, and packages available.

Pine Hill Park (pinehillpark.org), located entirely in the city of Rutland with its trailhead at the Giorgetti Athletic Complex, 2 Oak St. Ext., Rutland. The park offers a unique 300-acre, highly refined 16-mile singletrack trail system for mountain biking, running, hiking, walking, geocaching, and snowshoeing.

Green Mountain Trails (gmtrails.org), Rt. 100, Pittsfield. Accessible from Amee Farm, maps from the Original General Store. Twenty miles on 750 acres, a fast-growing network of multiuse singletrack trails geared to varied abilities; check the website for races and events.

Also see *Hiking*.

BOATING Speed, ski, pontoon, and fishing boat rentals as well as canoes and kayaks for **Lake Bomoseen** are available from **Woodard Marine, Inc.** (802-265-3690; woodardmarine.com).

♂ **Lake St. Catherine, Half Moon,** and **Bomoseen State Parks** (vtstateparks.com) each offer canoe, kayak, and rowboat rentals. See *Green Space.*

Chittenden Reservoir is a sublime place to canoe or kayak, an expansive 674 acres backed by mountains. Boat access is at the end of Chittenden Dam Rd. **Woodford Reservoir** on Rt. 100 south is another beautiful spot to paddle.

Base Camp Outfitters (802-775-0166; basecampvt.com) offers kayak rentals for use on **Kent Pond** in Killington.

Vermont Adventure Tours (802-773-3343; vermontadventuretours.com) offers canoe, kayak, and whitewater tours as well as canoe and kayak rentals.

COVERED BRIDGES There are six in the area: the 1836 **Kingsley** or **Mill River Bridge**, East Rd., off Airport Rd., East Clarendon; the 1880 **Brown Bridge**, off Cold River Rd., Shrewsbury; the 1840 **Depot Bridge**, off Rt. 7 north, Pittsford; the 1849 **Cooley Bridge**, Elm St., Pittsford; the 1843 **Gorham** or **Goodnough Bridge**, Gorham Bridge Rd., off Rt. 3, Pittsford; and the 1830 **Twin Bridge**, East Pittsford Rd., off Rt. 7 north, Rutland.

DISC GOLF Disc Killington Disc Golf Course (killington.com) begins at the K-1 Lodge and meanders its way through 18 holes on Snowden Mountain.

Scott Herdling

THE KINGSLEY COVERED BRIDGE

FISHING Licenses are available at vtfishand wildlife.com and additional resources at voga .org. Landlocked salmon and trout can be had in **Chittenden Reservoir**; trout are the catch in **Mendon Brook**. There also is fishing in **Kent** and **Colton** Ponds, and the **White**, **Tweed**, and **Ottauquechee** Rivers. **Woodward Reservoir** on Rt. 100 south and **Echo Lake** in Tyson (accessible from Plymouth Camp State Park) have good fishing.

Stream & Brook Fly-Fishing (802-989-0398; streamandbrook.com) offers beginners' programs and full- and half-day guided trips. Rod Start, a Vermonter with over 30 years' fishing experience, offers **Green Mountain Fishing Guide Service** (802-446-3375; greenmtnguide.com), based in Tinmouth.

✍ **Dwight D. Eisenhower National Fish Hatchery** (802-483-6618; fws.gov/r5pnfh), 4 Holden Rd., North Chittenden. Open 8–4 daily. The Fish and Wildlife Service raises landlocked salmon and lake trout here and children can feed the fish.

FITNESS CENTERS AND SPAS Pico Sports Center (802-747-0564; picomountain.com), 4763 Rt. 4, Killington. Open daily. A 75-foot lap pool, aerobics and fitness classes, cardio equipment, strength training machines, free weights, Jacuzzi, saunas, tanning, and fitness evaluations. Day passes and short-term memberships available.

Killington Grand Spa (802-422-1050), Killington Grand, 228 East Mountain Rd. Full menu of spa treatments.

New Life Hiking Spa (802-422-4302; newlifehikingspa.com), based at the Inn of the Six Mountains (see *Lodging*). Mid-May–Sept. Since 1978 Jimmy LeSage has been refining and fine-tuning weight loss fitness programs that combine sensible eating and moderate exercise. The daily regimen begins with a pre-breakfast walk and includes body conditioning, yoga, and hiking (all levels). Meals are varied, and the focus is on increasing energy and stamina (a good solo vacation).

The Gymnasium (802-773-5333; thegymnasium.net), 11 Cottage St., Rutland. Open daily. A complete wellness and cardiovascular center with full line of equipment and classes.

Vermont Sport & Fitness Club (802-775-9916; vermontsportandfitness.com), 40 Curtis Ave., Rutland. Open daily. Full-service health club with tennis and racquet sports, classes, cardio, strength, and training equipment, nutrition programming, personal training.

ENDURANCE RACES (peakraces.com), based at Amee Farm, Pittsfield. The latest craze in adventure sports, ultramarathons and mountain bike races on ever-expanding singletrack **Green Mountain Trails** (gmtrails.org) on 750 acres of woods and fields, some involving multiple obstacles and physical challenges, multiple days. It began with the **Death Race**; now the **Spartan Race** is a worldwide phenomenon, and there are bike and snowshoe races. All are the brainchild of Joe De Sena, Wall Street trader and author of the best-seller *Spartan Up*.

GOLF **Killington Golf Course** (802-422-6700; killingtongolf.com), Killington Rd. Killington Resort has its own 18-hole, 6,186-yard, par-72 course designed by Geoffrey Cornish. Clinics, league nights, packages, and restaurant. PGA professional instruction, rental clubs, and popular instructional programs through their Mountain Golf School.

Green Mountain National Golf Course (802-422-4653; gmngc.com), Barrows–Towne Rd. and Rt. 100, Killington. This highly rated 18-hole course includes a clubhouse, three practice teeing areas, four target greens, and an 8,000-square-foot putting green as well as pro shop, restaurant, and lessons.

The Rutland Country Club (802-773-3254; rutlandcountryclub.com), a mile north of the business section on N. Grove St., Rutland. An 18-hole golf course on rolling terrain; restaurant, pro shop, putting green.

Proctor-Pittsford Country Club (802-483-9379; proctor-pittsford.com), Cornhill Rd., Pittsford. Eighteen holes over very scenic countryside with a lounge and a small-town feel.

Lake St. Catherine Country Club (802-287-9341; lsccc.net), Rt. 30, south of Poultney. Eighteen holes over varied elevations; restaurant, pro shop, lessons.

Prospect Pointe Country Club (802-468-5581) in Castleton offers nine holes on Lake Bomoseen.

Stonehedge Golf (802-773-2666; stonehedgegolf.com), Rt. 103 west, North Clarendon, is a nine-hole, par-3 public course with great rates.

HIKING Pick up a copy of the widely available, free *Killington Region Hiking Guide* (discover killington.com).

The **Appalachian Trail** (appalachiantrail.org) and the **Long Trail** (greenmountainclub.org), accessed north and south from Rt. 4 in Killington, offer endless possibilities, and both websites offer access to maps and guidebooks. For guided hikes check out Killington-based Appalachian Trail Adventures (888-855-8655; appalachiantrailadventures.com).

Deer Leap Trail, off Rt. 4 behind the Inn at Long Trail, is the most popular short hike: a 45-minute one-way trek up a winding, moderately steep path that yields a southerly panoramic view from the top of a tall cliff. For a whole-day hike, you can continue along the Long Trail to Chittenden Reservoir or branch east at the Maine Junction onto the Appalachian Trail. This trail also connects with Gifford Woods State Park. Park a car at the other end and be sure to bring a hiking map.

◯ Bald Mountain. This 3-mile, three-hour round-trip hike is in Aitken State Forest, off Notch Rd. from Rt. 4 in Mendon. The blue-blazed circle trail begins just past the intersection with Wheelerville Rd. On the West Haven side is the **Helen W. Buckner Memorial Preserve** (nature.org) with hiking trails and nature exploration in this Nature Conservancy tract.

&. Thundering Falls Trail, Killington. Off River Rd., a 900-foot handicapped-accessible boardwalk and path through floodplain and forest lead to a platform at the base of Thundering Falls, a sheer rock face with water pouring down it, part of the Appalachian Trail.

Killington Hiking Center (800-621-MTNS; killington.com). The K-1 Express Gondola offers easy access to 15-plus miles of trails.

White Rocks Recreation Area, Rt. 140 off Rt. 7 in Wallingford. Follow signs from the White Rocks Picnic Area. The big feature here is a 2,600-foot, conical white peak surrounded by quartzite boulders that retain ice and snow into summer. We advise picking up a hiking guidebook (see *Hiking and Walking* in "What's Where") before starting out.

Delaware Hudson Rail Trail, Poultney–Castleton. A rail-trail enjoyed by hikers, snowmobilers, walkers, bikers, equestrians, and cross-country skiers.

HORSEBACK RIDING **Mountain Top Inn & Resort Equestrian Program** (802-483-2311; mountaintopinn.com) offers May–October horseback riding geared to every level from beginner to experienced, one- and two-hour guided trail rides, both English and Western. Jumping, dressage, cross-country, and children's instruction are available. Trail rides for ages 8 and up.

Pond Hill Ranch (802-468-2449; pondhillranch.com), 1683 Pond Hill Rd., Castleton, a 200-acre family-owned ranch offering trail rides, lessons, and pony rides for children. Saturday-night **rodeos** are also staged here all summer long and into fall.

Chipman Stables (802-293-5242; chipmanstables.com), Danby Four Corners. This family-run stable offers trail rides, hayrides, and pony rides.

ROCK CLIMBING ✑ **Green Mountain Rock Climbing Center** (802-773-3343; vermontclimbing .com). Based in Rutland at 223 Woodstock Ave., the center offers lessons and climbs for all abilities, from age 4 up. Inquire about winter ice climbing.

The **Pico Mountain Adventure Center** (800-621-MTNS; killington.com) operates several climbing walls during warmer months.

SWIMMING Elfin Lake Beach, off Rt. 140 west, 2 miles southeast of Wallingford, and **Crystal Beach**, a municipally owned white sand beach on the eastern shore of Lake Bomoseen. **Kent Pond** in Killington is town-owned, accessible from River and Thundering Brook Rds. near the town offices. Given its small size, it's warmer than most Vermont lakes. Also see state parks (vtstateparks.com) under *Green Space*. For pools, see *Fitness Centers & Spas*.

TENNIS Summit Lodge (802-422-3535; summitlodgevermont.com), Killington Rd., Killington. Four clay outdoor courts are available to the public if not in use by members. **Vermont Sport & Fitness**

SKIING AT KILLINGTON

Killington Resort

DOWNHILL SKIING AND SNOWBOARDING

Killington Resort (802-422-3333; killington.com), 4763 Killington Rd., Killington 05751. With more than 155 interconnected trails on six mountains plus 57 at its sister resort Pico Mountain (5 miles away and connected by shuttle service), Killington is unquestionably big, worthy of its title "Beast of the East." Thanks to five (counting Pico) entry points and a far-flung network of lifts and trails, skiers are dispersed throughout almost 2,000 skiable acres. Given its size and diversity, Killington attracts ski weekers in larger numbers than other eastern mountains, making for a lively midweek atmosphere. New England's first mountain to introduce high-quality snowmaking, it boasts the East's longest ski season, traditionally beginning in October and lasting into May. **Peak Lodge**, opened at 4,241 feet on Killington Peak's summit in December 2013, is itself an almost year-round destination, served by the K-1 Express Gondola (see *Must See*).

Club (802-775-9916; vermontsportandfitness.com) in Rutland has three indoor and eight outdoor courts.

Public courts are also maintained by the city of Rutland and the towns of Chittenden, Killington, Castleton, Fairhaven, Poultney, and Proctor.

✳ Winter Sports

CROSS-COUNTRY SKIING AND SNOWSHOEING ❄ ✐ Mountain Meadows Cross Country Ski and Snowshoe Area, operated by Base Camp Outfitters (802-775-7077; xcskiing.net), 2363 Rt. 4, Killington, just east of the main Killington access road. Open daily (conditions permitting) 9–4. Rentals and sales.

✐ **Mountain Top Nordic Ski & Snowshoe Center** (802-483-6089; mountaintopinn.com), Mountain Top Rd., Chittenden. Sixty km of trails, 40 km of which are groomed, begin at the Nordic Center, one of the country's oldest commercial cross-country ski centers and an ideal location at 1,495–2,165

Lifts: 22, including 9 quads (5 high-speed) plus the Skyeship and K-1 Express Gondolas, 2 doubles, 3 triples, 6 surface lifts (carrying 38,315 riders per hour).

Trails and slopes: 155, with 1,509 skiable acres including 73 miles of trails.

Vertical drop: 3,050 feet.

Snowmaking: 600 acres of terrain, with 1,500-plus snow guns, including 500-plus low-energy guns.

Snowboarding: Two half-pipes, 7 terrain parks, and The Stash, an "all-natural" terrain park with over 50 features such as rock-wall rides, log jibs, and cliff drops, designed to challenge intermediate and advanced riders.

Facilities: 6 base lodges, 5 ski rental shops, 1 mountaintop lodge, 5 lounges.

Special programs: **Ramshead Family Center** with a children's Snow Sports School divided into 5 levels of programs with a maximum of 3–5 student per instructor. More than 60 ski and snowboard school instructors hold the highest level of certification.

Rates: $92 adults weekend and peak or $84 midweek, nonpeak at the ticket window—but no one in their right mind pays that. Less for seniors and ages 7–18 (it's free ages 6 and under and 80-plus). Check the website or phone Killington's Central Reservations (800-621-MTNS; killington.com) for the many options. The best value is always the 5-day lifts/lodging package, available at most local inns, lodges, and condo rental offices.

Pico Mountain (802-422-3333; picomountain.com). One of Vermont's first mountain resorts, Pico opened in 1937 with a tow hooked up to the engine of a Hudson auto. Currently under the same ownership as Killington, the winter lifts at this family-friendly resort are only open Thurs.–Mon. and holiday weeks.

Vertical drop: 1,967 feet.

Skiable acres: 468, with 57 trails adding up to 19 miles, the largest percentage intermediate, all funneling to the base lodge.

Lifts: 2 express quads, 2 triples, and 2 doubles, 1 rope tow.

Snowmaking: 75% of trails have snowmaking.

Facilities: Rentals, instruction, sport center, and condo lodging (see killington.com).

Rates: $69 peak, $67 weekends, and $52 midweek for adults.

feet, with sweeping views of the mountains and of Chittenden Reservoir; rentals, lessons, and some snowmaking.

ICE SKATING ✍ In Rutland, Castleton State's **Spartan Arena** (802-775-3100) offers public ice skating, as does **Giorgetti Arena** (rutland rec.com).

SLEIGH RIDES ✍ Mountain Top Inn & **Resort** (802-483-6089; mountaintopinn .com). Thirty-minute horse-drawn sleigh rides in-season.

SNOWMOBILING ✍ Killington Snowmobile **Tours** (802-422-2121; snowmobilevermont .com). One- and two-hour mountain and back-country tours, plus snowcross track for kids ages 4–11. Rental helmets, clothing, and boots. This is also a source of info about local VAST clubs. **Mountain Top Inn & Resort** also offers guided snowmobile rides (mountaintopinn.com).

Vermont State Parks

GIFFORD WOODS STATE PARK

✳ Green Space

Note: For more information about the following, see **vtstateparks.com**.

Calvin Coolidge State Forest. This 16,000-acre preserve, which includes Killington and Shrewsbury Peaks, is scattered through seven local towns and divided by Rt. 100 into two districts. The recreational center is **Coolidge State Park** (802-672-3612), Rt. 100A east of Plymouth Notch. Open late May–mid-Oct., these 500 acres include a campground (62 campsites including 36 lean-tos, a dump station, picnic area, and restrooms with hot showers), picnic shelters (but no hookups), and hiking and snowmobile trails. In another part of the forest, **Camp Plymouth State Park** (802-228-2025), off Rt. 100 in Tyson, served as a served as a Boy Scout camp beginning in 1927, and was owned by the Boy Scouts of America until ownership was transferred to the state in 1984. It offers a beach on Echo Lake (picnic area, food concession), two open-air picnic pavilions, one enclosed shelter with a full kitchen, a group camping area, and four cottages. Inquire about gold panning and trails into the abandoned village of Plymouth Five Corners. North of the turnoff for Rt. 100A, the steep CCC Rd. (marked for Meadowsweet Farm) climbs away from Rt. 100 into the western swatch of the forest, with beautiful views back down the valley. It's unfortunate (but sensible) that this road is closed in winter, because it harbors some of the area's snowiest cross-country trails, accessible only by going the long way around through Shrewsbury (see *Scenic Drive* in "Okemo Valley Region").

HALF MOON STATE PARK

Vermont State Parks

⚙ **Gifford Woods State Park** (802-775-5354), half a mile north of Rt. 4 on Rt. 100, Killington. The campground (22 tent/trailer and 20 lean-to sites, four cabins, restrooms, and hot showers) is patronized by hikers on the Appalachian Trail, which runs through the park. Across the road is the Gifford Woods Natural Area, a 7-acre stand of virgin hardwoods (sugar maple, yellow birch, basswood, white ash, and hemlock). Trails lead up to Deer Leap Mountain and to the lovely waterfalls where Kent Brook enters Kent Pond. In winter cross-country trails connect with Mountain Meadows.

Lake Bomoseen, just north of Castleton, is a popular local summer colony. The lake gained notoriety in the 1930s because of Alexander Woollcott's summer retreat on Neshobe Island. The portly "Town Crier," a nationally known newspaper columnist, entertained such cronies as Harpo Marx, who was known to repel curious interlopers by capering along the shore naked and painted blue.

Bomoseen State Park (802-265-4242), Rt. 4 west of Rutland, Exit 3, 5 miles north on Town Rd. Its 66 campsites, including 10 lean-tos, are set in a lovely 3,576-acre wildlife refuge; beach, picnic area, nature program, trails, boat ramp, and rentals. A popular geocaching spot.

Half Moon State Park (802-273-2848), between Fair Haven and Rutland on Rt. 4; take Exit 4, go 6.5 miles north on Rt. 30, left on Hortonia Rd. and continue 2 miles, then go left on Black Pond Rd. for 2 miles. Wooded campsites (52 tent sites; 11 lean-tos; five cabins) around a secluded pond; boat rentals; hikes to **High Pond**, a remote body of water in the hills.

Lake St. Catherine State Park (802-287-9158), 3 miles south of Poultney on Rt. 30. Fifty tent or trailer campsites and 11 lean-tos, plus sandy beaches, fishing, boat rentals, nature trails.

✳ Lodging

At and around Killington

Killington Central Reservations (800-621-MTNS; killington.com). Open daily; the bureau keeps a tally on vacancies and makes reservations. A wide variety of two- to five-day ski and summer packages are available.

Note: Killington's Skyeship Gondola on Rt. 4 also puts the inns of Plymouth (to the southeast) within easy reach, and lodging in both Woodstock (see "Woodstock/Quechee Area") and Ludlow (see "Okemo Valley Region") is within 14 miles. See *Guidance* for central reservations numbers.

RESORTS ♂ ♦ ⅙ **The Killington Grand Resort Hotel** (888-64-GRAND; killington .com), 228 East Mountain Rd., Killington 05751. At the base of the lifts, this 200-room, newly renovated facility offers standard hotel rooms, also studios; one-, two-, and three-bedroom suites (with kitchen); and penthouse suites. It's immense, with endless corridors and Vermont's biggest meeting space (the Grand Ballroom)—ideal for conventions. The rooms are irreproachably comfortable. Amenities include an outdoor heated pool, outdoor hot tub, sauna, health club, game room, on-site day care, Ovations Restaurant (see *Dining Out*), a café, and walk-to-the-slopes convenience. It's close not only to the base lodge, but in summer to the golf course as well. $125–500. Best values year-round if combined with a sports package.

♂ 🐾 ♦ ⅙ **Mountain Top Inn & Resort** (802-483-2311; mountaintopinn.com), 195 Mountain Top Rd., Chittenden 05737. Set high on a hill with a spectacular view of Chittenden Reservoir against a mountain backdrop, this 350-acre self-contained resort has been operating as an inn since the 1940s. It hosted President Dwight Eisenhower and his entourage in 1955 when he arrived for a fishing expedition. Today it is one of the only Vermont resorts to offer both horseback riding and a cross-country skiing center (both open to the public). Thirty-two lodge rooms (breakfast included) from classic doubles to luxury rooms and suites, many with themes: Stags Run, for instance, features a huge rough-hewn log bed. Angler's Retreat has a balcony with a bird's-eye view of the surrounding Green Mountain National Forest. There are also four brand-new one-bedroom cabins with kitchenettes, four brand-new two- and three-bedroom cottages, and 19 chalet rentals, each different, all with at least two bedrooms, beginning at $350 per night. In addition to riding, summer activities include swimming in both the lake and a heated pool, tennis, lawn games, disc golf, canoeing, paddleboarding and kayaking, claybird shooting, archery, fly-fishing, and scenic pontoon boat rides on the lake, where moose sightings are not unusual. There's a horsemanship summer camp for kids, and any number of winter activities: 60 km of cross-country ski trails, snowshoeing, horse-drawn sleigh rides, ice skating, snowmobiling, and massage therapy. The events barn, a wedding and conference venue adjacent to the main lodge, includes yoga and massage rooms, a

MOUNTAIN TOP INN & RESORT
Christina Tree

theater, game room, and fitness center. The outdoor pool and hot tub are also here. Equestrian and Nordic programs are based at the nearby rustic Activities Center. Outdoor weddings are held on the knoll above the main lodge and at the lake. Dine at Highlands Dining Room (see *Dining Out*) or the **Mountain Top Tavern**. Rooms range $160–1,600 in low season, $265–1,800 in high, when double occupancy is required. Be sure to request a room with a lake view. Pets are $35 per night in the cabins (they receive a dog bed, bowls, and a welcome treat). Inquire about the many special offers.

INNS AND BED & BREAKFASTS

✪ ♂ ♿ **Red Clover Inn** (802-775-2290; 800-752-0571; redcloverinn.com), 54 Red Clover Lane, Mendon 05701. Open year-round. Set on 5 secluded acres, minutes from Pico and from the Killington access roads, this 1840s farmhouse has been transformed over the years, first into a 200-acre summer retreat and finally into a top-notch inn and restaurant (see *Dining Out*). The Inn and Carriage House combined offer 13 guest rooms, many with fireplace or Jacuzzi: uncluttered but bright, spacious and tastefully traditional, the kind you want to linger in. Ditto for common rooms. The welcome here is not only warm but helpful. $125–245 in low seasons, $195–340 in high, includes breakfast and afternoon tea. Tented weddings are available for up to 150 guests. Children age 8 and older are welcome. For family fun in summer, check out their sister property, **The Tyler Place**, in "The Northwest Corner."

✪ ♂ ♣ ♪ **The October Country Inn** (802-672-3412; octobercountryinn.com), junction of Rts. 4 and 100A, Bridgewater Corners 05035. Handy to Killington and Woodstock (8 miles) as well as most of the things to do and see in this chapter, just off Rt. 4 but on a back road. Hiking trails that lead past the swimming pool to the top of a hill for a sweeping, peaceful view. This old farmhouse has a large, comfortable living room with inviting places to sit around the hearth and at the big round table in the dining room—not to be confused with the other cheery dining room, in which guests gather around long tables for memorable meals. Seasoned innkeepers Edie and Chuck Janisse are as expansively hospitable as the house itself. Chuck is a great source of anything you ever wanted to know about Killington, where he teaches snowboarding. Check the website for more than a dozen well-researched bike tours from the inn (bring a bike or rent up the road); sag service offered. They offer gourmet candlelit dinners with wine and all-fresh local produce served family-style, prix fixe $40. Breakfasts are equally

Christina Tree

FOX CEEK INN, CHITTENDEN

creative and ambitious, geared to fuel bikers in summer and skiers in winter. The 10 guest rooms (with private bath) vary in size; most have queen-sized bed, many with Edie's handmade quilts. $145–245 includes breakfast; higher during foliage. Small weddings can be accommodated.

✪ ♿ **Fox Creek Inn** (802-483-6213; 800-707-0017; foxcreekinn.com), 49 Dam Rd., Chittenden 05737. Susan and Bob Smart bought this hidden gem of an inn in November 2012, and a month later Bob unexpectedly died. "But you can't lie in bed when guests need breakfast," Susan says, adding that all the work of getting the inn up to speed—which included replacing infrastructure as well as linens and furnishings—proved to be great therapy and that the community helped in ways she couldn't have dared dream. Sequestered up the back road leading from Chittenden Village to the reservoir, the inn offers an away-from-it-all feel but with easy access to both Killington and downtown Rutland. It was superbly built as a summer house for inventor William Barstow, who had managed to sell his various holdings for $40 million right before the 1929 stock market crash. Each of the eight guest rooms—three downstairs, five up—is different, but all are freshly furnished. Many are fitted with gas fireplace, most with Jacuzzi tub. A two-room suite has two baths. Guests gather around the big stone fireplace in the paneled den, in the comfortable living room, and at the cozy bar. There is swimming, canoeing, and fishing in the Chittenden Reservoir just down the road, and in winter you can cross-country ski or just lounge around. $195–305 includes full breakfast; higher during foliage. Children must be 12. Inquire about four-course candlelight dinners and seasonal inn-to-inn walking tours.

🍷 ♦ & **The Vermont Inn** (802-775-0708 vermontinn.com), 78 Cream Hill Rd., Mendon 05701. Set above Rt. 4 with a view of Killington and Pico, this 19th-century farmhouse has a homey feel to its public rooms—the living room with woodstove, the pub/lounge with fireplace, a game room, and an upstairs reading room, a sanctuary in the evening when the dining room is open to the public (see *Dining Out*). There's a sauna and hot tub; summer facilities include a pool. The 17 guest rooms range from smallish to spacious. Five have a gas fireplace; several are suites. Facilities include a fitness center, plus game and reading rooms. Rates vary widely depending on season, $95–305, breakfast included.

♂ **Casa Bella Inn** (802-746-8943; casabella inn.com), 3911 Rt. 100, Pittsfield 05762. Pittsfield is 8 miles north of Killington with a handsome green, which this double-porched old inn overlooks. It's been welcoming guests since 1835. Innkeeper Susan Cacozza is from Britain. Her husband, Franco, is a chef from Tuscany and offers a delicious and convenient order-ahead service in the restaurant. The feel is very much that of a village country inn in the center of this classic Vermont town far removed from the traffic around Killington. The eight comfortable guest rooms, all with private bath, are $115–155, including a delicious breakfast. Children 10 and over welcome.

LODGES ✪ 🍷 🐾 **The Inn at Long Trail** (802-775-7181; 800-325-2540; innatlongtrail .com), 709 Rt. 4, Killington 05751. This is the first building in New England specifically built

THE VERMONT INN OFFERS PATIO DINING WITH A VIEW.

Christina Tree

to serve as a ski lodge. It began in 1938 as an annex to a splendid summer inn that has since burned. Designed to resemble the inside of the forest as much as possible, the interior incorporates parts of trees and boulders in amazing ways, the furnishings are largely Adirondack-style, and the fire in the large stone hearth is real. Since 1977 the inn has been owned by Patty and Murray McGrath and their family. They cater to through-hikers on the Appalachian and Long Trails and to outdoorspeople of all sorts. The 22-foot-long bar is made from a single log, and a protruding toe of the backyard cliff can be seen in both the pub and the dining room. The 14 rooms are small but cheery (2 are family suites); there are 5 two-room suites with fireplace and some with whirlpools. The redwood hot tub soothes muscles after hiking or skiing. Dinner is served varying nights in the dining room, but you can usually count on **McGrath's Irish Pub** (see *Eating Out*). Rates begin at $89, from $110 for one of the five two-room fireplace suites, more weekends and holidays, and depending on how many breakfasts/dinners are included. Pets by advance arrangement. Inquire about rock-climbing packages.

& 🍷 ♦ **The Summit Lodge** (802-422-3535; 800-635-6343; summitlodgevermont.com), 200 Summit Rd., Killington 05751. Sited on a knoll just off Killington Road. Open year-round except for mud and stick seasons. This is an expansive lodge with fieldstone fireplaces, hand-hewn beams, a cozy library, and male and female Saint Bernard greeters—a 40-year tradition. Amenities include a large indoor hot tub, saunas, an outdoor heated pool, a game room, and massage therapy. In summer there are also red clay tennis courts, racquetball, bocce, horse-shoes, and the **Gazebo Bar**. The **Saint's Pub** is open nightly for dinner in winter, serving comfort food with flair; **Maxwell's** serves breakfast, included with your stay. The 45 guest rooms vary, all with private bath, cable TV, king and queen beds (the family rooms sleep up to six). $89–319 depending on season, midweek/weekend, room type.

♂ ♦ & **Mountain Meadows Lodge** (802-775-1010; mountainmeadowslodge.com), Thundering Brook Rd., Killington 05751. The main building is an 1856 barn, now a classic lodge with an informal dining room, a game room, and a spacious sunken living room with a lake view. Anne and Bill Mercier gear the year-round inn to families and Appalachian Trail hikers, catering to people who like the outdoors in warm-weather months as well as in winter. This is also the kind of place that lends itself to renting as a whole for weddings, family reunions, and retreats, which tend to fill the lodge every weekend in warm-weather months. There are 17 guest rooms and two suites, many of them great for families, all with private bath. A sauna and outdoor Jacuzzi are among the amenities. Kent Lake abuts the property and is good for fishing and canoeing as well as swimming. In winter it adjoins a ski-touring center. Continental breakfast included on weekdays, full breakfast on weekends; lunch can be arranged, and dinner is served in high season. A pettable assortment of farm animals live here and wildlife stop by frequently. $110–325, depending on season, includes a full breakfast.

♂ �& **Inn of the Six Mountains** (802-422-4302; 800-228-4676; sixmountains.com), 2617 Killington Rd , Killington 05751. This 99-room, four-story, Adirondack-style hotel has gabled ceilings, skylights, balconies, and a two-story lobby with a fieldstone fireplace. There is also a spa with lap pool, Jacuzzis, and exercise room; Cedars Pub serves light fare in winter. In summer $79–159 per room, fall $199–249, winter $149–309, depending on the day and week, continental breakfast included. In winter check on the two-day packages that include skiing, lodging, and breakfast. Children are free with two adults but $17 if over 12. Inquire about Jimmy LeSage's New Life Hiking Spa (newlifehikingspa.com), a program based here early May–Oct.

The Trailside Lodge (802-449-2553; trailside innvt.com), 115 Coffee House Rd., Killington 05751. A longtime Killington-area lodge, recently purchased and entirely renovated by Joe De Sena of Spartan Race fame. It now features wide-plank pine floors, handcrafted wooden headboards, a comfortable great room, family room, and pool. You have a choice of standard rooms ($125–145 per night), suites, bunkrooms, and self-contained spaces in the two-story Barn and Loft, sleeping 10, $615 per night. Handy to the Green Mountain National Golf Course as well as Killington.

♂ **Lodge** (802-746-8196; ameefarm.com), 4275 Rt. 100, Pittsfield 05762. This attractive, vintage-2009 log lodge with 16 guest rooms is geared to groups ranging from weddings and reunions to bike tours and competitors in owner Joe De Sena's legendary obstacle races. De Sena also owns the farm across the road as well as other properties (see *Endurance Races*). Singles and guests are, of course, welcome, and the many-windowed, post-and-beam rooms are frequently empty, especially midweek. Rooms have wide-plank pine floors and are sparely furnished with handcrafted furniture; 11 have private bath featuring a fabulous shower. $95–225 per night. Inquire about organized **bike tours**, based at

the lodge. It's now under the same ownership as Amee Farm Lodge; weddings are a specialty.

CONDOS/RENTALS Killington Resort's Central Reservations (800-621-MTNS; killington.com) serves many hundreds of condo units ranging from **Sunrise Condominiums**, high on the mountain, to **Pico Resort Hotel** on Rt. 4 beside the Pico base lodge. **The Woods Resort & Spa** (866-785-8904; woodsresortand spa.com) offers townhouse living with a fully developed spa on the premises. **The Killington Chamber** (killingtonchamber.com) lists local Realtors specializing in condo and private home rentals.

CAMPGROUNDS See *Green Space* for information on camping in Calvin Coolidge and Gifford Woods State Parks.

In Rutland and beyond
SUMMER RESORT ❀ ♂ �& **Edgewater Resort** (802-468-5251; 888-475-6664; edge watervermont.com), 2551 Rt. 30, Bomoseen 05732. Lake Bomoseen was a celebrity playground in the big-band era. There were five major hotels and a dance pavilion; Benny Goodman and Glenn Miller played. This resort—in the Rogers family for nearly 60 years—includes the more-than-150-year-old Edgewater Inn with its huge porch and pine paneling, as well as a chalet, motel, condo apartments, cottages, and lakeside efficiencies. Most have cooking facilities and lake views; some are right on the water. There is a beach, boating, fishing, an outdoor pool, an adjacent nine-hole golf course, a game room, a tavern with live entertainment, and a playground. This is not a luxurious destination, but guests return year after year. Rates for double occupancy only are $60–95; more with meals included. Some year-round lodging options.

INNS AND BED & BREAKFASTS
In Rutland 05071
Harvest Moon Bed & Breakfast (802-773-0889; harvestmoonvt.com), 1659 N. Grove St. Both of these comfortable rooms include a private bath with close proximity to downtown Rutland. The 1835 classic Vermont farmhouse is listed on the National Register of Historic Places. It's close to downtown Rutland, but also offers great views of Killington Peak and Pico Mountain. Rates are $95–130 and include a vegetarian continental breakfast.

Antique Mansion Bed & Breakfast (802-855-8372; antiquemansionbb.com), 85 Field Ave., located across the street from the Rutland Country Club (see *Golf*). The 1867 Proctor-Clement House includes three suites and one downstairs room, all with private bath. Rates ($119–169) include breakfast and afternoon tea.

In Shrewsbury 05738, up in the hills 10 miles southeast of Rutland

🍁 🍴 **Smith Maple Crest Farm** (802-492-3367; smithmaplecrestfarm.com), 2450 Lincoln Hill Rd. This handsome white-brick farmhouse sits high on a ridge in the old hilltop center of Shrewsbury. It was built in 1808 as Gleason's Tavern and is still in the same family—they began taking in guests in the 1860s and have done so off and on ever since. "Every piece of furniture has a story," says Donna Smith—and she knows each one. The family also raises beef cattle and maple syrup (see *Farms*). The sweeping views can be enjoyed in winter on cross-country skis. $50–95 per room, including breakfast.

♂ **Crisanver House** (802-492-3589; 800-492-8089; crisanver.com), 1434 Crown Point Rd. Set high on 120 acres of woods and meadows, this is a find—but it's frequently booked weekends for weddings. The 1802 portion of the house offers four attractive guest rooms and two suites, all with down comforters and pillows, exposed beams and original art. There are also three cottages. The living room, with a fireplace and grand piano, adjoins a spacious, sunny conservatory maximizing the panoramic view. A barn accommodates 120 people for weddings and parties. In summer there's a heated pool and an all-weather tennis court; in winter, cross-country skiing and snowshoeing. Dinner can be prearranged. Rates, including a full breakfast and tea, begin at $185.

🍴 **The Buckmaster Inn** (802-492-3720; buckmasterinn.com), 20 Lottery Rd. Built as the three-story Buckmaster Tavern beside the Shrewsbury church in 1801, the house includes four guest rooms, each with a private bath. There is a spacious living room, a library with fireplace and TV/DVD player, and a long, screened-in porch that's especially inviting in summer and fall. 109–139 double includes continental breakfast on weekdays and full breakfast on weekends; no credit cards.

In Fair Haven 05743

🍁 **The Haven Guest House Bed & Breakfast** (802-265-8882; havenguesthousevt.com), 1 4th St. Gisela and Werner Baumann are your hosts in this renovated Colonial with its wooden floors and expansive, curving porch. The four comfortable suites each has private bath. Guests can sit by a crackling fire in the living room, play chess at a dining room table, or sit in the parlor. There is a breakfast menu, and Gisela's hearty offerings include fresh breads and pastries.

$109–139 includes breakfast. Children over 6; no pets.

Elsewhere

🍁 **Twin Mountains Farm** (802-235-3700; twinmountainsfarmbb.com), 549 Coy Hill Rd., Middletown Springs 05757. This 1830 farmhouse with modern comforts is secluded on 150 acres stretching from the ridgeline of Coy Mountain on the north to Morgan Mountain on the south. There are three air-conditioned guest rooms with private bath and guest robes. Cross-country skiing, snowshoeing, and a mapped system of hiking trails are steps away, as is Lake St. Catherine. Breakfast is served by the woodstove in winter, on the patio in summer, and is included in the $95–125 rates.

MOTELS

In Rutland 05071

🍁 🐾 🍴 **Mendon Mountain Orchards** (802-775-5477; mendonorchards.com), 1894 Rt. 4, Mendon, isn't really a motel but rather a series of pleasant, very reasonably priced (under $100 per night) old-fashioned cabins, surrounded by orchards, with a pool and a shop for homemade goodies, apples in-season, cider, and flowers. **Holiday Inn Rutland/Killington** (802-775-1911; hivermont.com), 476 Holiday Dr., is a downtown landmark that includes **Greenfields Steak & Seafood**, an indoor pool, sauna and exercise room, and **Seven South Lounge**. The 112-room **Best Western Plus Inn & Suites** (802-773-3200; bestwestern-rutland.com) features one- and two-bedroom condo suites, an outdoor pool, tennis court, and game room.

CAMPGROUNDS See *Green Space* for information on campgrounds in Lake Bomoseen State Park, Half Moon Pond State Park, and Lake St. Catherine State Park.

✳ Where to Eat

DINING OUT

In the Killington area

✪ **Red Clover Inn Restaurant & Tavern** (802-775-2290; 800-752-0571; redcloverinn.com), 54 Red Clover Lane (off Rt. 4), Mendon. Open for dinner Thurs.–Mon., reservations appreciated. Destination dining for foodies. Chef Colin Arthur offers a blend of farm-to-table comfort food, fine dining, and elegant wines dinners. The venison-stuffed, juniper-and-cider-brined quail could be a meal in itself for smaller appetites. The lamb shank is richly braised in red wine, served with organic dates, mascarpone orzo, and toasted pine nuts. Entrées $25–35. Save room for desserts like almond chocolate galette. Inquire about monthly wine dinners and the chef's tasting menu.

✪ **The Countryman's Pleasure** (802-773-7141; countrymanspleasure.com), just off Rt. 4, Mendon. Open 5–9 Tues.–Sat. Chef-owner Hans Entinger, a native of Austria, is known for top-drawer Austrian-German specialties: veal schnitzel, Bavarian sauerbraten, veal à la Holstein, also classics like roast half duckling and rack of lamb. Vegetarian fare is available. The attractive dining rooms occupy the first floor of an 1824 red-shuttered farmhouse. There's a long wine list, and beers as well as international coffees and nonalcoholic wines and beers are served. The atmosphere is cozy and informal with an open fireplace. An early dinner menu is served with prices under $16. Otherwise entrées are $20–30.

& **The Vermont Inn** (802-236-3082; vermont inn.com), 78 Cream Hill Rd., Mendon; just off Rt. 4 in Killington. Open for dinner Tues.–Sat. The pleasant inn dining room with a huge field-stone fireplace also features a large pub-area patio with a view of the mountains. There's a solid menu with varied salads, appetizers, and desserts. Comfort-food main choices range $12–16, while the exquisite entrées range $9–30.

✔ & **Choices Restaurant & Rotisserie** (802-422-4030), Glazebrook Center, 3 miles up Killington Rd., Killington. Open for dinner nightly in winter, Wed.–Sun. in summer. Chef Claude Blais has an enthusiastic following at this combination bistro/brasserie/pub. The menu offers many choices indeed, including appetizers, salads, soups, raw bar, sandwiches, and pastas, not to mention entrées ranging from curried vegetables with couscous to filet mignon. Dinner entrées $18–28, children's menu.

✔ **Highlands Dining Room at the Mountain Top Inn and Resort** (802-483-2311; mountain topinn.com), 195 Mountain Top Rd., Chittenden. Open daily for breakfast, lunch, and dinner; reservations expected. The lower-level dining room is large and formal with a big stone fireplace and views of the lake and mountains. The menu changes seasonally. On a fall evening you might begin with sweet polenta cakes, then dine on maple-braised pork shoulder with broccolini, housemade johnnycakes, and chive crème fraîche. There's a choice of salads and desserts, an impressive wine list, and a kids' menu. Entrées $24–34. The adjacent, casual **Highlands Tavern** is open daily for lunch and dinner. The menu features wraps, salads, grilled sandwiches, burgers, and a full bar.

& **Peppino's Ristorante Italiano** (802-422-3293; peppinoskillington.com), 1 mile up

Killington Rd., Killington. Open nightly 5–10 in summer and ski season. A traditional and reliable Italian restaurant with dining-out decor, a large choice of pastas ($16–19), and all the classics, from linguine with clams to sirloin pizzaiola as well as staple house specialties ($20–30).

✔ & **Ovations Restaurant at the Killington Grand Resort** (802-422-6111; killington.com), 228 East Mountain Rd., Killington, is open for breakfast daily and nightly for dinner. This is a family-geared hotel dining room with plenty of kid-friendly plates, health and diet options, and good old hearty fare for a big appetite. Entrées $13–28.

& **The Garlic** (802-422-5055;), 1724 Killington Rd. (midway up). Open nightly, with a broad range of tapas at the bar. A cozy, informal setting for hearty Italian fare, with a choice of pasta dishes and entrées featuring the namesake ingredient. Entrées are $18–28 and are mouthwatering. Reservations not taken, but the place is popular so prepare to wait; full bar.

In Rutland and beyond

✔ & **Little Harry's** (802-747-4848; littleharrys .com), 121 West St. Open daily 5–10. This offspring of the popular Harry's Cafe in Mount Holly is romantically lit and decorated. Owners Trip Pearce and Jack Mangan share their own interpretations of international favorites: pad Thai, Jamaican jerk scallops, and cioppino, to name a few. Entrées $15.50–29.

✪ ✔ & **The Palms** (802-773-2367; palms vermont.com), 36 Strongs Ave. Open Mon.–Sat. for dinner. The Italian immigrants who flooded into Rutland at the turn of the 20th century are still alive in the many pizzerias and Italian organizations in town. The Palms opened its doors on Palm Sunday, 1933, and in 1948 it served the first pizza in Vermont. It was also likely the first restaurant in the state to have a television. Now operated by the fifth generation of the Sabataso family, it's a family-geared place that tastes like history. Neapolitan-style pizza remains a specialty, along with all the comfort food from the Boot that you expect. Entrées $12–22.

✔ & **Table 24** (802-775-2424; table24.net), 24 Wales St. Open Mon.–Sat. for lunch and dinner. Chef-owner Stephen Sawyer provides contemporary decor, and local ingredients and flavors. A woodfired rotisserie slow-roasts chicken. Prime rib, macaroni and cheese, and meatloaf are all on the menu, as are burgers and sandwiches. Entrées $10–30.

Elsewhere

✔ **Lakehouse Pub & Grill** (802-273-3000; lakehousevt.com), 3569 Rt. 30 north, on Lake

Bomoseen. Open daily for lunch and dinner and Sun. brunch. This popular place features a wooden hillside stairway leading down to umbrella-shaded waterside tables, spectacular sunset views from the air-conditioned indoor dining room, and a menu of seafood specials. The bar is just as active in winter, when ice fishing and snowmobiling are popular on and around Lake Bomoseen. Entrées from $11.

The Victorian Inn at Wallingford (802-446-2099; thevictorianinn.com), 55 N. Main St., Rt. 7, Wallingford, serves dinner Tues.–Sat., brunch Sun. Swiss-born chef-owner Konstantin Schonbachler, formerly executive chef at the Kennedy Center in Washington, DC, brought his European culinary talents with him when he moved to this French Second Empire home in the center of Wallingford. Guests eat in one of three downstairs rooms in a casually elegant ambience. Inquire about a wide variety of cooking classes. $30 prix fixe.

EATING OUT

In the Killington area

✪ **McGrath's Irish Pub at the Inn at Long Trail** (802-775-7181; innatlongtrail.com), Rt. 4 at the Inn at Long Trail, Killington. Open nightly for dinner and drinks. The 22-foot-long bar is made from a single log, and a protruding boulder can be seen in both the pub and the dining room. The first place to serve Guinness on tap in Vermont, the pub boasts the state's largest selection of Irish whiskey and features Irish country and folk music on weekends. The house specialties are Guinness stew and shepherd's pie. There's serious fare in the adjoining dining room, but it's the pub that's truly special.

✿ ✐ **Charity's 1887 Saloon-Restaurant** (802-422-3800), midway up Killington Rd., Killington. Open daily in-season for dinner, lunch on weekends. Happy hour (free wings) 3–6. Tiffany shades, 1880s saloon decor, and wooden booths—this is the place for French onion soup, a Reuben, or a vegetarian casserole at lunch. Steak is a good dinner choice. Informal and satisfying.

✐ **Back Behind Restaurant & BBQ Smokehouse** (802-422-9907; backbehind.com), junction of Rts. 4 and 100 south, Killington. Open Thurs.–Mon. for dinner year-round, lunch on weekends in summer, Thurs.–Mon. weekdays in winter. A zany museum-like atmosphere (look for the red caboose and antique Mobil gas pump), barnboard, stained glass, a big hearth. Specialties like venison and saloon roast duck augment a full BBQ menu; generous portions and children's menu.

✐ ✔ **The Foundry** (802-422-5335), Killington Rd. on the Summit Lodge grounds. Open for lunch and dinner daily, Sun. brunch. Formerly named The Gristmill and designed to look like one, it's sited on the pond in front of Summit Lodge and features a vintage waterwheel. The interior is airy and pleasing, dominated by a huge stone hearth. Unfortunately my most recent meal there was a downer. As a single diner, the wait was more than half an hour to order and as long to be served one of the smallest, driest burgers in memory. In fairness the place was packed, the menu is large and varied. Entrées $12–26.

✪ ✐ **The Original General Store** (802-746-8888; originalgeneralstore.com), Rt. 100, Pittsfield. Country store. Chef Kevin Lasko, a New York Times-starred chef, is behind the locavore breakfasts, sandwiches and wraps at this newly modernized store. On weekends, Lasko and partner Katie Stiles open their catering kitchen to guests for intimate prix-fixe dinners as well as classes and culinary events. It's known as the **Backroom** and is well worth a trip..

✪ **Swiss Farm Market** (802-746-9939), Rt. 100, Pittsfield Village. The town's genuine general store, part of the Pittstop of Pittsfield, is under the same ownership as Swiss Farm Inn, legendary for its breakfasts. The deli here is a standout, judging from the Harvest Chicken Salad ($5.99)—housemade chicken salad with apple and cranberry mayo on a fresh ciabatta roll.

BREAKFAST Sugar & Spice (802-773-7832; vtsugarandspice.com), Rt. 4, Mendon. Open daily 7–2 with breakfast all day. A pancake restaurant housed in a large replica of a classic sugarhouse surrounded by a 50-acre sugarbush. Besides dining on a variety of pancake, egg, and

SUGAR & SPICE

Rachel Carter

omelet dishes, along with soups and sandwiches, you can watch both maple candy and cheese being made several days a week. Gift shop.

♫ ((•)) **World's Best Breakfast at the Swiss Farm Inn** (800-245-5126; swissfarminn.com), Rt. 100, Pittsfield. The "world's best breakfast" of blueberry buttermilk pancakes, raspberry-rhubarb-stuffed French toast, eggs any style, home-fried potatoes, country smoked bacon, and home-baked muffins is served Thurs.–Sun. 6–10, until 11 on Sun. This is a local hot spot. Family-friendly lodging is also available.

Sunup Bakery (802-422-3865; sunupbakery .com), 2250 Killington Rd., Killington. Open daily, closed Tues. in summer. Located in an adorable A-frame chalet, breakfast is served all day. The menu is varied with several innovative vegetarian options (sometimes hard to find in the area). Local and organic as much as possible, no processed food. Excellent lunch sandwiches as well.

PIZZA Outback Pizza & Nightclub (802-422-9885; outbackpizza.com), on Killington Rd., Killington. Features woodfired brick-oven pizza with outdoor patio seating and live music.

♫ **iPIE Pizzeria & Lounge** (802-422-4111; ipiepizzeria.com), 1307 Killington Rd. Open daily from 11 on. Pleasant atmosphere and options like grilled chicken salad and specialty panini as well as a variety of fairly exotic specialty pizzas.

Picarello's Pizza (802-746-8331), 55 Lower Michigan Rd., Pittsfield. Just off Rt. 100 on the southern edge of the village. Open from 5 PM, except Mon., Wed. A long-established insider's spot with limited eat-in space and a signature eggplant Parmesan as well as a variety of great pizzas.

BREWS Long Trail Brewing Company (802-672-5011; longtrail.com), Rt. 4 west at Bridgewater Corners (near Rt. 100A), produces Long Trail Ale as well as Blackberry Wheat, IPA, Pale Ale, and Double Bag, plus seasonals and Brewmaster Limited Editions. Pub fare daily 11–6 with riverside seating (in summer); gift shop, taproom, and tours.

Liquid Art Coffeehouse & Gallery (802-422-2787; liquidartvt.com), 37 Miller Brook Rd., Killington. Open 8–8 Mon.–Thurs., 8–9 Fri.–Sat., 8–6 Sun. Closed Wed. July–Sept. Look for the blue A-frame on the rocks, 2 miles up Killington Access Rd. on the right. The gallery features local artists, the brews are espresso with variations like macchiato and rolo latte; also chai and loose teas. A pleasant, peaceful kind of place for a time-out from the rest of the road.

"Morning Nibbles" include housemade crêpes; all-day "Light Bites" could be an herb-roasted chicken sandwich or sweet Italian sausage polenta lasagna. Inquire about monthly wine dinners.

APRÈS-SKI Wobbly Barn (802-422-6171; wobblybarn.net), 2229 Killington Rd., Killington. A steak house offering national music and comedy acts, themed parties, dancing, blues, rock and roll. Ski season only.

McGrath's Irish Pub at the Inn at Long Trail (802-775-7181; innatlongtrail.com), Rt. 4, Killington. Live Irish music on weekends to go with the Gaelic atmosphere and Guinness on tap. It's a great pub with a 22-foot-long bar made from a single log and a boulder protruding from the back wall.

❂ **Pickle Barrel** (802-422-3035; picklebarrel nightclub.com), Killington Rd., Killington. Regional and national live music acts, best nightclub in Vermont next to Higher Ground in Burlington. Purchase tickets online.

Jax (802-422-5334), 1667 Killington Rd., Killington. A popular local hangout with deck dining in warm weather; jazzy interior, sports bar with "food and games." Boasting Killington's biggest burger and reasonably priced lobsters.

Lookout Tavern (802-422-5665), 2901 Killington Rd., Killington. Open from 3. Shuttle service offered. A lively venue with wide choice of reasonably priced food and drink.

Note: In our opinion the best après-ski happens right at the mountain, with ski boots and boards still on.

In Rutland

🍲 **Three Tomatoes Trattoria** (802-747-7747; threetomatoestrattoria.com), 88 Merchants Row, right near the Paramount Theater. The final Vermont link in the former chain, along with a location in Lebanon, New Hampshire—woodfired pizzas and all. Open for dinner nightly from 5. The authentically Italian pre-show dining here can't be beat.

The Yellow Deli (802-775-9800; yellowdeli .com), 23 Center St. Open Mon.–Thurs. 10–9, Fri. 10–3, closed weekends. Operated by the Twelve Tribes (see "Island Pond"), imaginatively decorated with wood slab tables and intimate booths, a sidewalk café in summer. The stress is on wholesome food: sandwiches on homemade bread, salads, soups, a smoothie bar plus coffees, herbal teas, and maté.

♿ **Roots the Restaurant** (802-747-7414; roots rutland.com), 51 Wales St. Serving lunch and dinner daily, closed Mon. A friendly local eatery featuring hearty local food and traditional specials like fish-and-chips as well as more innovative dinners, often made with local emu. Chef Donald Billings also owns The Bakery (122 West St., 802-775-3220), where sandwiches on homemade bread include meats from North Country Smokehouse alongside veggie fillings such as eggplant or pea-and-ricotta.

Gill's Delicatessen (802-773-7414; gillsdeli .com), 68 Strongs Ave. Open daily except Sun. Gill's is short for "Gilligan's," and Kathy Gilligan Phillips is the second generation to the oldest bakery/deli in Rutland. There are 10 tables, but most people take their sandwiches on hefty homemade rolls to go.

Ana's Empanadas (802-775-1988; ana empanadas.com), 54 Strongs Ave. Open for lunch Mon.–Fri. This farmers market staple opens up its bakery to guests during the workweek. Argentina native Ana DiTursi and her husband, Rob, craft her flaky meat and veggie pies here, crimped into uncommon shapes with unique designs. The flavors include classic beef, pork, and chicken, but also originals such as a Cubano pie.

🍴 ⎣ **Seward Family Restaurant** (802-773-2738), 224 N. Main St. Open daily for breakfast, lunch, and dinner; Sun. brunch. This diner and dairy bar has been in the Seward family since 1947. After downing a burger or fried chicken with "Freedom Fries," dig into the "Pig's Dinner," an extra-large banana split served in a trough.

Elsewhere

🍴 🍴 **Birdseye Diner** (802-468-5817; birdseye diner.com), 590 Main St., Castleton. This restored 1940s Silk City diner, open all day, is a justifiably popular spot for college students and local residents alike.

Perry's Main Street Eatery (802-287-5188) 253 Main Street, Poultney. Open daily for three meals, this family-run diner is renowned for its fluffy pancakes and big breakfasts. At dinner, comfort food reigns, including ribs and mac-and-cheese.

Wheel Inn (802-537-2755), 730 Lake Rd., Benson. Open for three meals daily. The Wed.-night chicken-and-biscuits is famous for miles, and there's liver-and-onions every day. This wagon-wheel-covered dining room is a delightful throwback.

✴ **Entertainment**

Also see *Special Events* and *Après-Ski*.

Paramount Theatre (802-775-0903; paramountvt.org), 30 Center St., Rutland. This theater is still vital at more than 100 years old. In fact, it's one of Vermont's best entertainment venues with international and national tours featuring music, dance, and theater. There are local dramatic groups and musicians, too, as well as a classic film series. Check website for tickets and schedules of events.

🎵 **Merchant's Hall** (802-855-8081; merchants hall.com), 40–42 Merchants Row, Rutland. A multipurpose event space. There are art installations and lectures here, but the raison d'être is theater and music, including acts from Vermont and New York City. Inquire online about renting the large, modern space.

🎬 **Flagship Premium Cinemas** (802-786-8003; flagshipcinemas.com), 143 Merchants Row, Rutland, shows first-run flicks.

Peak Races (peakraces.com) puts on hard-core adventure races year-round. Key events include a snowshoe challenge, ultramarathon, bike challenges, and the infamous summer and winter Death Races. For those fainter of heart (perhaps literally), the wild events are a spectacle to behold. Hey, maybe someone will die! Based at **Amee Farm** (see *Selective Shopping—Farms*) in Pittsfield.

Killington Music Festival (800-621-MTNS; killington.com), a series of mostly chamber music concerts in Ramshead Lodge and at a scattering of other local sites; weekends in July and Aug, also a series of Young Artist Concerts in July.

🎵 **Cooler in the Mountains** (discoverkillington .com), a free family-friendly, outdoor concert series during July and Aug. held at the Killington Resort Base Lodge featuring regional and national touring acts.

✴ **Selective Shopping**

ART GALLERIES & CRAFTS STUDIOS
Handmade in Vermont (802-446-2400; handmadeinvermont.com), 205 S. Main St., Wallingford. Open Mon.–Sat. Housed in America's first pitchfork factory (built 1791), this marble structure is now owned by White Rocks Land Trust and operated by a consortium of artists and craftspeople. Ironwork, especially lighting fixtures, is featured, along with Danforth Pewter and a wide selection of Vermont-crafted glass, pottery, furniture, and jewelry.

Farrow Gallery & Studio (802-468-5683; farrowgallery.com), Old Yellow Church, 835 Main St., Castleton. Call ahead to visit. The late Patrick Farrow's limited-edition, award-winning bronze sculptures and wearable artworks are featured, along with the metal works of Susan Farrow, who runs the gallery.

Peter Huntoon Studio (802-235-2328; peter huntoon.com), 17 Studio Lane, Middletown Springs. Open by appointment. Huntoon is one of Vermont's premier watercolorists, who also teaches and conducts workshops at his studio. His work is available for viewing and for sale online.

Note: See Open Studio Weekend under *Special Events* and vermontcrafts.com.

Killington Arts Guild (802-422-3852; killington artsguild.org), 2363 Rt. 4. Upstairs in the Base Camp and Fever Gifts building across from the Killington Access Rd. Check the website for opening receptions, changing exhibits, workshops in traditional and mixed media, photography.

Also see **Liquid Art Coffeehouse & Gallery** under *Brews*.

Note: See Open Studio Weekend under *Special Events* and vermontcrafts.com.

BOOKSTORES The Bookmobile (802-775-6993; anniesbooks.com), 58 Merchants Row, Rutland. Open Mon.–Sat., as well as Sun. Thanksgiving–Christmas. The stock here is mostly used books, with a few special new titles, too. Even if you're busy reading this book, there are also uncommon gifts and cards.

The Book Shed (802-537-2190; thebookshed .com), 733 Lake Rd., Benson. Open Apr.–Dec., Wed.–Sun. 10–6; Jan.–Mar., Fri.–Sun. 11–5.

Housed in what used to be the town clerk's office, this used- and antiquarian-book store with 15,000 volumes is one of the biggest things going in this tiny town.

FARMS ♂ Amee Farm (802-746-8196; ameefarm.com), 4275 Rt. 100, Pittsfield. Produce and livestock are raised, for a seasonal farm stand, but primarily for the lodging extension of Pittsfield's most distinguished wedding venue, Riverside Farm (riversidefarmweddings .com). The farm can also be rented as a retreat—bed & breakfast rooms are available in off-seasons, worth an inquiry.

Maple Crest Farm (802-492-2151; smith maplecrestfarm.com), 2450 Lincoln Hill Rd., Shrewsbury. Award-winning maple syrup and all-natural Vermont beef are the specialties on this working Vermont farm, which also offers an excellent-value bed & breakfast (see *Lodging*). Visit the sugarhouse or order online.

♂ Hathaway Farm & Corn Maze (802-775-2624; hathawayfarm.com), 741 Prospect Hill Rd., Rutland. The largest corn maze in Vermont, covering 12 acres, is cut to a different thematic shape each year. It operates July–Oct. daily (except Tues.) and some weekends during other seasons. A Sat.–evening "Moonlight Madness" includes glow sticks and a marshmallow roast. The farm offers wagon rides and an interactive livestock barn. $12 adults, $10 children and seniors, under 3 free. The farm also raises

AMEE FARM

Rachel Carter

grassfed beef and produces maple syrup, both available in the seasonal farm shop.

FARMERS MARKETS The region is rich in farmers markets, with four in Rutland alone, including one that is year-round based at the Rutland Co-op (rutlandcoop.com). Additional farmers markets can be found in Castleton, Fair Haven, Mount Holly, and Poultney.

SPECIAL SHOPS ❧ **Greenbrier Gift Shop** (802-775-1575; greenbriervt.com), junction of Rts 4 and 100, Killington. You can't miss this massive 7,000-square-foot barn gift shop stacked full with Vermont products, clothing, baby items, home decor, and even gads of wedding types of gifts.

Base Camp Outfitters (802-775-0166; base campvt.com), 2363 Rt. 4, Killington. In winter this is the area's best source of "free heel"— cross-country, snowshoes, telemark, et cetera— gear and clothing. Owner Mike Miller and his wife, Diane, also operate the Mountain Meadows Ski Touring Center. In summer hiking and disc golf have become hugely popular on the property. Also on the property is **Cabin Fever Gifts**, a year-round source of Vermont products, art, crafts, jewelry, and much more.

Norman Rockwell Museum (802-773-6095; 877-773-6095; normanrockwellvt.com), Rt. 4 east, Rutland. Open daily, more of a store than a museum, but for Rockwell buffs it offers thousands of Rockwell's magazine covers, ads, posters, portraits, and other published illustrations, displayed chronologically with small, almost unreadable typed captions. The gift shop, with its many Rockwell prints and cards, is large and portrays an interesting profile of the artist (1898–1978) and a documentary of changing American culture and graphic styles.

GENERAL STORES W. E. Pierce Store & Shrewsbury Co-op (802-492-3326; pierces storevt.com), 2658 Northam Rd., Shrewsbury. This traditional country store nestled up in the mountains is run as a community-managed cooperative. Besides the basics, there's a local artisan section, local wine and beer, chef-prepared food, and everything from community workshops to sing-alongs.

East Poultney General Store (802-287-4042), 11 On the Green, East Poultney. An old-fashioned general store with a difference: namely, a state liquor outlet. The baked goods have a better-than-average reputation, as does the savory food, which might include chicken wings, lobster bisque, or crabcakes.

Also see Pittsfield's two general stores under *Eating Out.*

WINERY Whaleback Vineyard (802-287-0730; whalebackvineyard.com), 202 Old Lake Rd., Poultney. Over 4,000 grapevines on 7 acres cover this old-farm-turned-vineyard between Lake St. Catherine and the Green Mountains. Tastings are Wed.–Sun. 11–5.

✳ **Special Events**

Also see *Entertainment.*

January–March: Frequent **alpine ski and snowboard events** at Killington Resort and Pico Mountain (killington.com).

Late February: **Great Benson Fishing Derby**, a small-town fishing derby. Info at iceshanty .com and benson-vt.com.

Memorial Day weekend: **Open Studio Weekend** (vermontcrafts.com) for artisan and crafts studios throughout the region.

June–August: Sunday- and Wednesday-evening **Concerts in the Park**, Rutland, 7:30 (802-773-1822; rutlandrec.com), and Tuesday **Castleton College's Concerts on the Green**, Castleton (rutlandvermont.com).

Late June–August: **Friday Night Live**, 6–10. Downtown Rutland streets become a stage for live entertainment, open-air shopping, and dining (rutlanddowntown.com). **Killington Music Festival** (killingtonmusicfestival.org), Saturdays at 7 at Rams Head Lodge—a series of classical music concerts.

July 4: **Rutland Fireworks Extravaganza**, Vermont State Fairgrounds, Rutland (rutland vermont.com); **Poultney Fourth of July Parade** and fireworks (poultneyvt.com); **Killington Independence Day Parade** (killingtontown.com).

Mid-July: **Annual Killington Wine Festival** (killingtonchamber.com).

Mid-July–mid-August: **River Road Summer Concert Series**, Killington village.

Early August: **Art in the Park Fine Art & Craft Festival**, Rutland, sponsored by the Chaffee Center (802-775-0356; chaffeeart center.org), in Main Street Park, junction of Rts 7 and 4 east. Also held Columbus Day weekend.

Early September: **Vermont State Fair** (802-775-5200; vermontstatefair.net)—midway, exhibits, races, demolition derby, and tractor pulls animate the old fairgrounds on Rt. 7 south, Rutland.

Labor Day–Columbus Day: **Killington Hay Festival** (killingtonchamber.com)—decorative hay sculptures adorn local businesses, fall-themed events on weekends.

First weekend of October: **Killington Resort's Annual Brewfest** (killington.com).

Columbus Day weekend: **Art in the Park Fine Art & Craft Festival**, Rutland, the second date of this two-date event.

Last Saturday in October: Rutland City's **Halloween Parade**, one of the oldest and best (rutlandhalloween.com).

Early December: **Vermont Holiday Festival** at Killington's Grand Resort Hotel—over 100 decorated trees, sleigh rides, workshops, and more (killingtonchamber.com).

Lake Champlain Valley

4

LAKE CHAMPLAIN VALLEY

LOWER CHAMPLAIN VALLEY
Including Middlebury, Vergennes,
Brandon, and Bristol

BURLINGTON REGION

THE NORTHWEST CORNER
Including the Islands, St. Albans,
and Swanton

Shelburne Farms

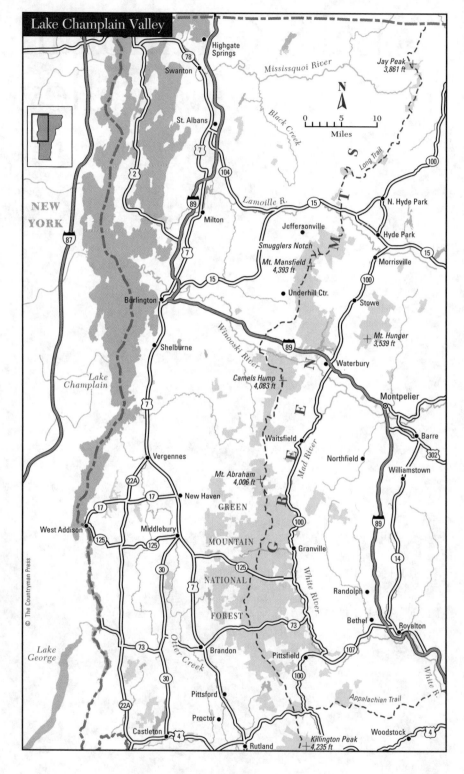

Lake Champlain Valley

Highgate Springs

Swanton

78

Mississquoi River

Jay Peak
3,861 ft

St. Albans

7

Black Creek

N

0   5   10
Miles

104

2

89

104

NEW
YORK

87

Milton

Lamoille R.

15

N. Hyde Park

100

Jeffersonville

Hyde Park

15

Smugglers Notch

Mt. Mansfield
4,393 ft

Morrisville

15

Underhill Ctr.

100

7

15

Burlington

Stowe

Winooski River

89

Mt. Hunger
3,539 ft

Shelburne

Waterbury

Lake
Champlain

Camels Hump
4,083 ft

Montpelier

7

Waitsfield

Barre

Vergennes

Mad River

Northfield

302

22A

Mt. Abraham
4,006 ft

Williamstown

17

17

New Haven

89

West Addison

125

Middlebury

GREEN

100

14

MOUNTAIN

Granville

125

125

30

NATIONAL

White River

Randolph

7

125

Bethel

Royalton

FOREST

73

107

Lake
George

73

Brandon

Pittsfield

White R.

Otter Creek

30

100

Pittsford

Appalachian Trail

22A

Proctor

Castleton

4

Woodstock

4

Rutland

Killington Peak
4,235 ft

GREEN MTS

Long Trail

© The Countryman Press

LAKE CHAMPLAIN VALLEY

Lake Champlain begins in New York and flows north to Canada. For much of its 110 miles, the New York–Vermont border runs down its center. Still, the country's sixth largest lake belongs to Vermont in all the important ways, beginning 20,000 years ago. That's when the glacial waters receded, revealing islands and a wide valley on its eastern shores as opposed to rocky hills rising to mountains—the Adirondacks—on the west.

Traces of human habitation in this fertile valley date back 7,500 years. Archaeological finds of pottery and trading beads suggest both domestic life and distant travel for valley residents by 1000 BC. But it's not the natives who give the lake its modern name. That honor went to Samuel de Champlain, the first European to set foot in present-day Vermont in 1609.

In the 18th and early 19th centuries Lake Champlain served as a strategic military corridor. Ethan Allen and the Green Mountain Boys captured Fort Ticonderoga on the New York shore from the British in 1775. During the following winter the fort's heavy cannons were dragged on sleds through thick snow and forest to Boston, where they were mounted above the harbor, ultimately forcing the British to evacuate the city.

THE VIEW FROM CAMELS HUMP
Rachel Carter

Early in the 19th century Burlington boomed into a metropolis as a lumbering port. It remains by far Vermont's largest and most dynamic city, one squarely facing Lake Champlain and offering access points for sailing, paddling, and swimming. Burlington is also home to several colleges, including the University of Vermont. In the Lower Valley, Middlebury—home to its own prestigious liberal arts school—is another cultural, dining, and lodging center.

Twelve miles wide at its widest, less than a mile at its narrows, Lake Champlain is 400 feet deep in places, deep enough to harbor the monster Champ (mascot of Burlington's minor-league baseball team, the Vermont Lake Monsters). Long and thin like the state itself, this is Vermont's West Coast.

LOWER CHAMPLAIN VALLEY

INCLUDING MIDDLEBURY, VERGENNES, BRANDON, AND BRISTOL

A ddison County packs as much contrasting scenery within its borders as any region in the country. Look east for a view of the high, western wall of the Green Mountains, laced with hiking trails and pierced by four of the state's highest, most dramatic "gaps" (passes). The mountains drop abruptly through widely scattered hill towns—Lincoln, Ripton, and Goshen—into a 30-mile-wide, farm-filled valley, a former ocean floor that now contains Vermont's largest concentration of dairy farms and orchards. Lake Champlain is far narrower here than up around Burlington, and the Adirondacks in New York close enough to touch, gracing the cows, barns, and apple trees with a spectacular backdrop.

Middlebury, the hub of Addison County, is among New England's most sophisticated towns, the home of one of its most prestigious private colleges, several museums, a world-class opera company, and restaurants. Brandon, a particularly spirited and visitor-friendly community 15 miles south of Middlebury, is the southern gateway to the Lower Champlain Valley.

Throughout the Valley, the Lake Champlain shoreline is notched at regular intervals with quiet and accessible bays, from Mount Independence across from Fort Ticonderoga to Chimney Point (across from New York's Crown Point) and on up to Basin Harbor and Kingsland Bay State Park. Thanks to widely scattered lodging, it's possible to stay in the heart of farm (Addison and Bridport) and orchard (Shoreham) country, in historic towns like Bristol and Vergennes (actually the country's smallest city), and up in the Green Mountain towns of Ripton and Goshen, close to wooded walking/biking and ski trails, with occasional but spectacular lake and valley views.

ADDISON COUNTY

Addison County Chamber of Commerce

GUIDANCE Addison County Chamber of Commerce (802-388-7951; 800-SEE-VERMONT; addisoncounty.com), 93 Court St., Middlebury, is open Mon.–Fri., 9–5. The staff at this walk-in information center offers help finding lodging, even in difficult foliage time. The chamber also maintains an unstaffed information booth on the common in Vergennes.

Brandon Area Chamber of Commerce (802-247-6401; brandon.org), 4 Grove St., Brandon, operates a self-service visitors center at the historic Stephen A. Douglas birthplace; open daily, year-round. It's well stocked with brochures, including an informative walking tour guide to the town's rich architectural heritage. The

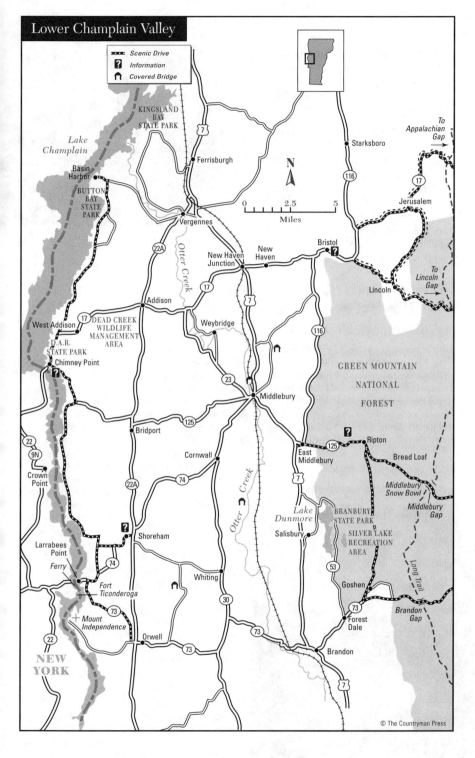

Lower Champlain Valley

- ▰▰▰ Scenic Drive
- ❓ Information
- ⌂ Covered Bridge

Lake Champlain

KINGSLAND BAY STATE PARK

Basin Harbor

BUTTON BAY STATE PARK

Ferrisburgh

Starksboro

To Appalachian Gap

N

0   2.5   5
Miles

Vergennes

Jerusalem

22A

Otter Creek

New Haven Junction

New Haven

Bristol

Lincoln

To Lincoln Gap

Addison

17

Weybridge

West Addison

17

DEAD CREEK WILDLIFE MANAGEMENT AREA

D.A.R. STATE PARK

Chimney Point

23

Middlebury

GREEN MOUNTAIN NATIONAL FOREST

Bridport

125

Ripton

Bread Loaf

22
9N

Cornwall

East Middlebury

Crown Point

22A

74

7

Middlebury Snow Bowl

Middlebury Gap

Lake Dunmore

BRANBURY STATE PARK

Larrabees Point

Ferry

Shoreham

Salisbury

SILVER LAKE RECREATION AREA

74

Whiting

53

Goshen

Long Trail

Fort Ticonderoga

30

Brandon Gap

Mount Independence

73

Orwell

73

Forest Dale

NEW YORK

22

73

Brandon

7

© The Countryman Press

seasonal **Brandon Museum** can also be toured at this location.

GETTING THERE *By car:* The major north–south highway is Rt. 7, but we advise anyone from Boston to approach through the Middlebury or Brandon Gaps (see *Scenic Drives*). From the west you can take the brand-new Champlain Bridge in Crown Point, New York, year-round, or the seasonal ferries described below.

By ferry: **Lake Champlain Ferry** (802-864-9804; ferries.com) from Essex, New York, to Charlotte operates spring through fall (longer when ice permits), takes 20 minutes, and puts you just above Vergennes.

Fort Ticonderoga Ferry (802-897-7999; forttiferry.com), Larrabees Point to Fort Ticonderoga. Mid-June–mid-Oct., making the crossing in seven minutes.

ADDISON COUNTY FARM

Rachel Carter

MEDICAL EMERGENCY Call **911**. **Porter Memorial Center** (802-388-4701; portermedical.org), 115 Porter Dr., Middlebury.

✳ Villages

Middlebury (population 8,496; middlebury.govoffice.com) is the county seat, the hub of Addison County, and home to one of the nation's most sought-after private colleges. Inns and restaurants serve visitors as well as potential students and their parents with a touch of liberal arts intellectualism. Middlebury College was founded in 1800 by Gamaliel Painter, a surveyor who settled here before the Revolution. Painter accompanied Ethan Allen on the Fort Ticonderoga raid and returned to Middlebury to become the town's principal landowner, sheriff, judge, and assemblyman. Another benefactor was Joseph Battell (see the box), who owned thousands of acres of forest and mountain land that he left to the college and the state when he died in 1915. He was the proprietor of the famous old summit house, the Bread Loaf Inn, now the nucleus of the summer Bread Loaf School of English and the Bread Loaf Writers Conference. Battell also owned a weekly newspaper in which he fulminated against the invasion of motorcars. Emma Hart Willard, who pioneered in the education of women, was another Middlebury luminary. The town's proudest buildings—the courthouse, the Middlebury Inn, the Battell House, and the fine Congregational church—are grouped, along with compact business blocks, around the green. It's a short walk down Main Street to the churning Otter Creek Falls, a centerpiece for dozens of shops in the old mills and marbleworks on both banks of the river, connected by a footbridge. The distinctive Middlebury College (middlebury.edu) campus rises impressively in tiers as you approach town from the west on Rt. 125.

OTTER CREEK FALLS, MIDDLEBURY

Addison County Chamber of Commerce

Brandon (population 3,966; brandon.org) is rich in historic architecture, from Federal style to Queen Anne; its entire center, some 240 buildings, is on the National Register of Historic Places. And lucky you, several Brandon manses are open to the public as bed & breakfasts, as is

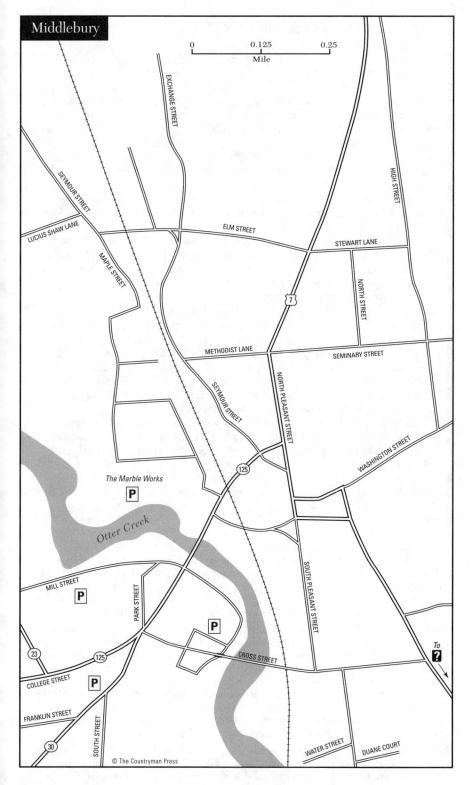

Middlebury

0   0.125   0.25
Mile

EXCHANGE STREET

HIGH STREET

SEYMOUR STREET

LUCIUS SHAW LANE

MAPLE STREET

ELM STREET

STEWART LANE

NORTH STREET

7

METHODIST LANE

SEMINARY STREET

SEYMOUR STREET

NORTH PLEASANT STREET

WASHINGTON STREET

125

The Marble Works

P

Otter Creek

MILL STREET

P

PARK STREET

P

SOUTH PLEASANT STREET

23

125

CROSS STREET

To
?

COLLEGE STREET

P

FRANKLIN STREET

30

SOUTH STREET

WATER STREET

DUANE COURT

© The Countryman Press

JOSEPH BATTELL AND MIDDLEBURY

The stone bridge that Joseph Battell built in downtown Middlebury is but one element of an enormous and enduring legacy of mountaintops and mortar that this eccentric bachelor left to the state of Vermont as a whole and to Middlebury College in particular.

Battell was born in 1839 to a wealthy and influential Vermont family. He attended Middlebury College, but ill health kept him from finishing his degree. Instead, he went off to travel the world; upon his return he bought land in the mountain town of Ripton, where he ran an inn, mainly for his friends. Today that land and those buildings house two of the college's most highly regarded summer programs: the Bread Loaf School of English and the Bread Loaf Writers Conference. In addition to being publisher of the *Middlebury Register*, a local newspaper, Battell was also an author. One of his oddest efforts was a book titled *Ellen, or, The Whisperings of an Old Pine*, a dense tome that is seldom read but much wondered about.

Battell was a man who loved mountains and woods and hated cars, so much so that he refused to allow cars on the road that ran up to his Ripton inn. Yet it was because of Battell that the stone bridge spanning Otter Creek in downtown Middlebury is still, a century later, a key to the transportation infrastructure in Addison County. The original wooden bridge that carried traffic across the creek burned down a century ago. Middlebury's town fathers, in a fit of economy, decided to build an iron bridge on the site, but Battell was opposed, arguing that a stone bridge would last significantly longer than an iron one. So determined was he that he is said to have paid the difference out of his own pocket.

A pioneering conservationist, Battell used to send his hired man into the woods, armed with blank deeds and instructions to buy as much acreage as he could from any farmer or logger he came across. Over time he acquired about 35,000 acres, including Camels Hump, which he donated to the state of Vermont for use as a state park. His landholdings also reached over Bread Loaf Mountain from East Middlebury to Hancock, Granville, and Rochester, along Rt. 100, and followed the spine of the Green Mountains from Mount Ellen south to Brandon Gap. When he died in 1915, most of this land was bequeathed to Middlebury College, which has sold off much of it over the years, keeping only a few hundred acres.

Battell is also the father of the University of Vermont's Morgan Horse Farm. He began breeding Morgans on his farm in the latter 1800s, an interest that would prove instrumental in saving America's first breed of horse from extinction. He hired architect Clinton Smith to build the beautiful white farm buildings that still stand in Weybridge. With typical Battell intensity, he spent years tracing out the pedigrees published in the first volume of the *Morgan Horse Register* in 1894. Then in 1906 he gave his farm and his Morgan horses to the U.S. government. It remains a working horse farm to this day, supplying stock to Morgan breeders across the country.

the municipal library. Sited in Rutland County (it's just over the southern border of Addison County) between Otter Creek and the Neshobe River, Brandon (and the adjacent town of Forest Dale) was the home of Thomas Davenport, who invented and patented an electric motor in 1838, and the birthplace of Stephen A. Douglas (1813–61), the "Little Giant" of the famous debates with Abraham Lincoln in 1858, when Douglas was a senator from Illinois. Brandon has blossomed in recent years with the addition of art galleries, antiques shops, bookstores, and some of the region's best dining.

Bristol (population 3,788; discoverbristolvt.com). Billing itself as the "Gateway to the Green Mountains," Bristol is nestled at the foot of Lincoln Gap, at the junctions of north–south Rt. 116 (less heavily trafficked than Rt. 7) and east–west Rt. 17. Its broad Main Street is lined with a delightful mix of stores and restaurants, housed in a western-style 19th-century block that leads to a square green, complete with fountain, park benches, and a gazebo. Its pride is the elaborately hand-painted stagecoach in front of the historical society at 19 West St. and the **Lord's Prayer Rock** (on the south side of Rt. 17 entering Bristol from the east), which is inscribed with the Lord's Prayer. A physician named Joseph C. Greene commissioned the inscription in 1891, presumably because he was thankful for having reached this point safely when, as a youth, he was hauling logs over steep, slippery roads.

Vergennes (population 2,588; vergennes.org) has long claimed to be the smallest city in the country and it's the oldest in Vermont, incorporated as a city in 1788. With a thriving francophone population, it's no surprise that Ethan Allen named it for Charles Gravier, comte de Vergennes, the French minister of foreign affairs who was a strong supporter of the American Revolutionary cause. Vergennes is sited on an impressive set of falls; its handsome, early-19th-century commercial buildings include the stained-glass dome upstairs in the **Bixby Memorial Library** (bixbylibrary.org) with its display of Plains Indian artifacts including baskets, clothing, and beadwork, along with local memorabilia and an outstanding archive of Vermontiana.

Shoreham (population 1,265; shorehamvt.org) is known for its orchards and farms. Shoreham Village is a beauty, with a classic Congregational church (1846), a Masonic temple (built in 1852 as the Universalist church), and the graceful St. Genevieve Catholic Church (1873), as well as the old inn. Follow Rt. 74 southwest from the village through the orchards; or continue straight on Witherell Rd. where 74 jogs south, then turn south (left) onto Smith St. along the lake. Either way, you get to Larrabees Point, the site of the small, car-carrying "Fort Ti" cable ferry. It has held the franchise from the Vermont and New York legislatures since 1799, but records indicate the service was initiated by Lord Jeffery Amherst in 1757 for use by his soldiers in the campaigns against the French. Next door is Teachout's Lakehouse Store & Wharf, built in 1836. Continue south on Rt. 73 to the turnoff for Mount Independence.

Orwell (population 1,250; town-of-orwell.org). Best known for Mount Independence, the small village at the center of this orchard and dairying community circles a long, sloping green with a brick Congregational church (1843) on a rise by the white-clapboard town hall (built in 1810 as the Baptist church). It all overlooks a brief line of shops with the First National Bank of Orwell, billed as "the world's smallest bank," in the middle. Chartered in 1863 (but known as the Farmers Bank for many years), the bank remains a real center of town, with notices of upcoming events tacked to the authentic old tellers' cages. The other village nerve center is **Buxton's General Store**, the genuine article.

✳ Must See

The Champlain Bridge (champlainbridgecommunity.org) connects Rt. 17 in Addison to Rt. 185 in Crown Point, New York, over a narrow span of Lake Champlain at **Chimney Point State Historic Site** on the Vermont side and **Crown Point State Historic Site** in New York. Originally built in 1929, the bridge was closed and then destroyed late in 2009 due to its deterioration over time. Local architect Ted Zoli was chosen to design the new bridge, which reopened in November 2011 with pedestrian and bicycle lanes on both sides. Additional historic sites, **Mount Independence** and **Fort Ticonderoga**, make for a pleasant loop tour. See details under *Historical Attractions*. During the two years when the bridge was under construction, archaeological digs unearthed artifacts revealing human habitation since glacial waters receded 9,000 years ago. Evidence was discovered of a 1731 French fort, as was 1790s redware of the early Vermont potter Moses Bradley, which you can view at Chimney Point.

🏛 ♿ **Lake Champlain Maritime Museum** (802-475-2022; lcmm.org), 4472 Basin Harbor Rd. Open late-May–mid-Oct., daily 10–5; $10 adults, $9 seniors, $6 ages 5–17. This museum began in a local schoolhouse constructed from native limestone in 1818, moved stone by stone (2,000 of them) and reconstructed to serve as an exhibit gallery. Today the museum's 14 buildings, spread over 3 acres, contain Native American and Revolutionary War artifacts, a working blacksmith shop, and dozens of small craft built around the lake over a period of 150 years. Exhibits reveal the lake's dramatic role in history, colorful characters, and the stories of hundreds of shipwrecks still beneath the surface. Attempts to raise them began in the 1930s but

THE NEW LAKE CHAMPLAIN BRIDGE
Rachel Carter

have been abandoned because wood that's been submerged in fresh water quickly disintegrates when exposed to air. Instead, watch nautical archaeologists in LCMM's conservation lab work to preserve artifacts and learn about the lake's Underwater Historic Preserves designated by Vermont and New York. Inquire about on-water shipwreck tours using ROV (remote-operated vehicle), special lectures, and boatbuilding and blacksmithing courses. A working replica of Benedict Arnold's 1776 gunboat *Philadelphia II*, built on the spot, is open to visitors, and LCMM's full-sized replica 1862 canal schooner *Lois McClure* can be explored at ports of call throughout the region—view her itinerary and Ship's Log at lcmm.org.

✍ **Moosalamoo National Recreation Area** (802-779-1731; moosalamoo.org), stretching from the western slopes of the Green Mountains to Lake Dunmore; a downloadable map is available on the website. For outdoor enthusiasts at all levels in all seasons, Moosalamoo is a 15,875-acre treasure deep in the Green Mountain National Forest. More than 70 miles of well-maintained trails, from rugged cliffs to gentle slopes, offer hiking, biking, wildlife- and bird-watching, cross-country skiing, and snow-shoeing. Multiple trailheads such as the Robert Frost Interpretive Trail present spectacular scenery, expansive mountain vistas, hardwood and softwood forests, waterfalls, and secluded lakes and streams. Visit the website for camping information as well as inns along the trails.

✳ To Do

BICYCLING It's no coincidence that the country's first bicycle touring company was founded in this area. The Champlain Valley, with its relatively flat terrain and mountain views, holds a wealth of back roads leading through covered bridges, connecting historic sites and comfortable inns with ample swimming holes, ice cream, and antiquing stops en route. But beware deceptively quiet but narrow, truck-trafficked roads like Rt. 22A and Rt. 30. The area's bicycling info clearinghouse is **champlain bikeways.org**.

Vermont Bicycle Touring (VBT) (800-245-3868; vbt.com), 614 Monkton Rd., Bristol, the state's oldest bike tour company, offers guided group inn-to-inn tours.

Country Inns Along the Trail (800-838-3301; inntoinn.com), 52 Park St., Brandon. Bike tours begin and end in Brandon, visiting a number of inns along the way. Hiking and skiing tours available as well.

Mountain Biking at Blueberry Hill (802-247-6735), Goshen. An extensive network of ski trails and woods roads that is well suited to mountain biking, including Moosalamoo access. **Green Mountain Bikes** (greenmountainbikes.com) out of Rochester offers a drop-off and pickup service.

BIRDING Otter Creek, near Lake Champlain in Vergennes, and the **Dead Creek Wildlife Management Area** in Addison (off Rt. 17) are particularly rich in bird life, especially during migration seasons in spring and fall. Mount Independence is another popular birding area. Birders should secure the free map/guide to the **Lake Champlain Birding Trail** (802-287-4284; lakechamplain region.com). **DAR State Park** is also an excellent lookout for bird-watching (vtstateparks.com). Also see *Green Space*.

BOATING Waterhouse's (802-352-4433; waterhouses.com), 937 West Shore Rd., Salisbury (Lake Dunmore), rents paddleboats, canoes, and motorboats; fuel station, fishing supplies, and a game room in the boathouse.

Champlain Houseboat Charters (802-948-2288; champlainhouseboatcharters.com) offers houseboat, trawler, and pontoon boat rentals located at **Chipman Point Marina** in Orwell.

DAR State Park in Addison offers some prime points from which to launch a boat into Lake Champlain. **Kingsland Bay** and **Button Bay State Parks** have canoe, kayak, row, and pedal-boat rentals in their bays, both in Ferrisburgh. **Branbury State Park** in Salisbury offers similar rentals on Lake Dunmore (vtstateparks.com).

COVERED BRIDGES ✍ *Note:* These bridges are marked on our Lower Champlain Valley map.

The **Pulp Mill Covered Bridge**, between Middlebury and Weybridge, spanning Otter Creek near the Morgan Horse Farm, is the oldest in the state (1808–20) and the last two-lane span still in use.

Halpin Bridge (1824), Middlebury, 2 miles east of Rt. 7, off Halpin Rd., is Vermont's highest bridge above the streambed.

Station (or Salisbury) Bridge, across Otter Creek in Cornwall (2 miles east of Rt. 30 on Swamp Rd.), is a 136-foot Town lattice bridge built in 1865.

Shoreham Covered Railroad Bridge, East Shoreham off the Whiting–Shoreham Rd. (turn south onto Shoreham Depot Rd.); the bridge is marked on area maps. A Howe bridge built in 1897 by the Rutland Railroad, spanning the Lemon Fair River, one of the few remaining railroad covered bridges left in Vermont. A designated state historic site.

Spade Farm Covered Bridge, located along Rt. 7 in Ferrisburgh, is now on the property of the Artisans Guild and Starry Night Café. It was built in 1824 and moved 3 miles to its present location in 1959.

CULTURAL ATTRACTIONS & **Middlebury College Museum of Art** (802-443-5007; museum .middlebury.edu), 72 Porter Field Rd. at the Mahaney Center for the Arts. Open Tues.–Sun., closed during holiday periods. Free. The college's distinguished permanent collection ranges from the decorative arts through modern painting, with emphasis on photography, 19th-century European and American sculpture, and contemporary prints. Permanent and changing exhibits are displayed in galleries within the multi-tiered arts center, which also includes a café and several performance areas.

○ **Vermont Folklife Center** (802-388-4964; vermontfolklifecenter.org), 88 Main St. Open Mon.– Sat. 10–5, Sun. 11–4. This growing organization (founded in 1984) collects and preserves the traditional arts and heritage of Vermont, primarily through taped interviews (its archive contains over 3,800). It mounts changing exhibits and maintains an excellent on-site gift shop.

○ ♪ **The UVM Morgan Horse Farm** (802-388-2011; uvm.edu/morgan), 74 Battell Dr., Weybridge. Open daily May 1–Oct. 31; small admission charged. The first "Morgan" was born in the late 1790s and is recognized as the sire of an entire breed of Vermont horse. Colonel Joseph Battell began breeding Morgans on this farm in the 1870s and is credited with saving the breed (America's first developed breed of horse) from extinction. The farm is now a breeding and training center operated by the University of Vermont. Guided tours of the stables and paddocks are available, along with an audiovisual presentation about the Morgan horse and farm.

♪ & **National Museum of the Morgan Horse** (802-388-1639; morganmuseum.org), 34 Main St. Middlebury. Open Wed.–Sat. 10–5. This quant museum depicts the history of the Morgan horse in America, with changing exhibits from original works of art to historical materials. Admission by donation.

DISC GOLF Currently the **Vergennes Community Disc Golf Course** serves the region (see gmdgc.org).

FISHING **Otter Creek** is a warm-water stream good for smallmouth bass and northern pike. The cooler **Neshobe River**, especially in Forest Dale, is better for trout, and rainbows can be found in the **Middlebury River** just below Ripton. The **New Haven River** between Lincoln and Bristol and south of New Haven Mills also offers good trout fishing. The Vermont Outdoor Guide Association maintains a very helpful website at voga.org and additional information as well as licenses at vtfishand wildlife.com.

Stream & Brook Fly-Fishing (802-989-0398; streamandbrook.com) offers beginners' programs and full- and half-day guided trips.

FITNESS CENTERS AND SPAS **Vermont Sun** (vermontsun.com) sports and fitness center has locations in Vergennes and Middlebury with training equipment, an Olympic-sized pool, and racquetball courts. **Middlebury Fitness** (middleburyfitness.com) in Middlebury features a wide variety of fitness and wellness classes. **Waterfalls Day Spa** (middleburyspa.com) offers a full menu of spa services.

GOLF **Ralph Myhre Golf Course** (802-443-5125; middlebury.edu), Rt. 30 just south of the Middlebury campus, is owned and operated by the college; 18 holes. Open mid-Apr.–Nov.

The Basin Harbor Club (802-475-2311; basinharbor.com), 4800 Basin Harbor Rd., Vergennes. Vermont's only Audubon-sanctioned course offers golfers 18 holes with some exceptional wildlife overlooking Lake Champlain. Open early May–mid-Oct. Dining at the Basin Harbor Club (see *Resort* and *Where to Eat*).

Neshobe Golf Club (802-247-3611; neshobe.com), 224 Town Farm Rd. (just off Rt. 73), Brandon. Open Apr.–Oct. Eighteen holes and a full-service club with restaurant, pro shop, and driving range.

HIKING **The Green Mountain National Forest District Office** (802-388-4362), 1007 Rt. 7 south, Middlebury, offers a free pamphlet guide to 28 day hikes. Open year-round, weekdays 8–4:30.

Country Inns Along the Trail (802-247-3300; 800-838-3301; inntoinn.com). Over a dozen inns collaborate to provide lodging along an 80-mile stretch of the Long Trail and some of its side trails, including back roads through the Green Mountain National Forest and trails through Moosalamoo National Recreation Area.

Trail Around Middlebury (802-388-1007; maltvt.org). The local Middlebury Area Land Trust has created this remarkable 16-mile loop that circles the town and strings together two parks and half a dozen woodland paths. The most scenic segment is the Otter Creek Gorge Trail, which runs riverside and traverses meadows, forests, and wilderness areas. The Land Trust publishes The Trail Around Middlebury (TAM), a free map/guide (see website), and organizes hikes and treks throughout the year.

Snake Mountain, Bridport. From Rt. 22A, take Rt. 17 east; turn right after a mile onto Mountain Rd. Park about 2 miles up on your right in the designated area. The trail begins on Mountain Rd., about 300 feet south. The first half of this popular hike used to be easy, but in recent years has gotten muddy due to overuse—hike carefully; insect repellent is a must. It gets steeper and rockier as you reach the summit with lovely lake and Adirondack views.

Mount Abraham, Lincoln. At over 4,000 feet above sea level, this is Vermont's fifth highest peak, its summit above the tree line, so the open views are magnificent. There are two trails, both strenuous. From the top of Lincoln Gap, you can park at the TV tower and follow the Long Trail (plan 3½ hours round-trip, and remember that the Lincoln Gap is not plowed in winter). You can also take the Battell Trail, a 5.8-mile loop that takes about four hours total. For this route, go to Lincoln Village and turn north onto Quaker St.; after 0.7 mile turn right onto Elder Hill Rd. The parking area is 2 miles ahead. Bring water, a detailed map, a sweater, and insect repellent.

Moosalamoo National Recreation Area (moosalamoo.org), an Abenaki word meaning "he trails the moose" or "the moose departs," is a 15,875-acre tract within the Green Mountain National Forest that is prime moose habitat. It is also crisscrossed with hiking routes and a 10-mile spur of the Long Trail, which begins at the parking area atop Brandon Gap on Rt. 73 and threads north for a steep 0.1 mile to a trail to Mount Horrid Cliffs, a rocky outcropping with memorable Adirondack views. The Long Trail stretch ends at a parking area on Rt. 125. See *Must See*, and visit the website for maps.

HISTORICAL ATTRACTIONS ✔ & **Mount Independence State Historic Site** (802-948-2000; historicsites.vermont.gov), 497 Mount Independence Rd., Orwell. Grounds open year-round with a handicapped-accessible trail; museum open Memorial Day weekend–Columbus Day, daily 9:30–5. $5; under 15, free. This National Historic Landmark is one of America's best-preserved Revolutionary War sites. A state-of-the-art visitors center tells the story of the 12,000 men who built a massive fort here in 1776 to fend off the British, many of them freezing to death the following winter. An exhibit displays the military trappings, clothing, and even food they left behind. Six miles of marked hiking trails start at the visitors center, weaving past the remains of the hospital, batteries, blockhouses, and barracks of this once bustling fort.

✔ **Fort Ticonderoga** (518-585-2821; fort-ticonderoga.org), 30 Fort Ti Rd., Ticonderoga, New York. Open mid-May–late Oct., daily 9:30–5. $17.50 adults, $15 ages 62 and up, $8 ages 5–12. Accessible via the Fort Ti Ferry from Larrabees Point in Shoreham (see *Getting There*). The 18th-century stone fort has been restored and includes a museum displaying weapons, uniforms, and historical artifacts. Built by the French (who named it Fort Carillon), it was captured by English general Jeffery Amherst and held by the British until 1775, when Ethan Allen and his Green Mountain Boys took the fort by surprise, capturing the guns that eventually helped free Boston. **America's Fort Café** serves burgers, sandwiches, and salads 11–5.

✔ **Crown Point State Historic Site** (518-597-4666; nysparks.com), 21 Grandview Dr., Crown Point, New York. Grounds open May–Oct. at no cost. Museum is $4 adults, $3 seniors and students, free ages 12 and under. Just across the Lake Champlain Bridge from Chimney Point, West Addison, Vermont. Fifteen miles north of Fort Ticonderoga, Crown Point started out as the French-built "Fort St. Frederic." The British captured it in 1759, but in 1775 American colonists overtook it and hauled its cannons and heavy ordnance off to Boston for use in fighting the British. The complex includes 18th-century ruins and a museum.

✔ & **Chimney Point State Historic Site** (802-759-2412; historicvermont.org), 8149 Rt. 17W, Addison, at the Vermont end of the Champlain Bridge. Open Memorial Day–Columbus Day, Wed.–Sun. 9:30–5. Adults $5; children under 14 free. The "chimney" here alludes to what was left of the houses the French settlers burned in 1759 on their way back to Canada after the arrival of British general

Amherst. The present late-1700s tavern on this site houses exhibits exploring Vermont's three earliest cultures—Native American, French, and early American—through archaeological artifacts from the site and region. Each settled at this lakeside spot, recognizing its strategic importance.

The Henry Sheldon Museum of Vermont History (802-388-2117; henrysheldonmuseum.org), 1 Park St., Middlebury. Open Tues.–Sun. in May–Oct.; closed Sun. in winter, check the website ahead and make appointments for research. $5 adults, $4.50 seniors, $3.50 students with ID, $3 ages 6–18, under 6 free. One of America's oldest history museums is located in an 1829 marble merchant's house with no fewer than six black marble mantels. Collections include furniture, art, clothing, and personal effects of Addison County residents.

Rokeby Museum (802-877-3406; rokeby.org), 4334 Rt. 7, Ferrisburgh. Open for guided tours Memorial Day–Columbus Day., Fri.–Mon. at 11 and 2. Property is open daily. $10 adults, $9 seniors, $8 for kids over 5. A period-furnished home and nine outbuildings evoke the lives of four generations of a Quaker abolitionist family whose members included pioneers, farmers, and Rowland E. Robinson, the 19th-century author, illustrator, and naturalist. Rokeby was one of several merino sheep farms that dotted the Vermont landscape in the early 19th century. More important, it was a destination for freedom-seeking slaves who took refuge here and worked in the open before the Civil War. The family occupied the property until 1961, when it became a museum. Frugal by nature, they kept every diary, receipt, and newspaper, which added up to an immense library (including close to 20,000 family letters), making this the best-documented Underground Railroad site in the country.

The John Strong DAR Mansion (802-759-2309; johnstrongmansion.org), 6656 Rt. 17 west, W. Addison. Open Memorial Day–Labor Day, weekends 10–5. $5 adults, $3 seniors and students. This is one of several historic structures built from stone taken from the ruins of Fort Crown Point and skidded across frozen Lake Champlain by oxen. General Strong, an early settler and Green Mountain Boy, built his residence here in 1796 with brick from his own clay pits on the "Salt Lick" where he first hunted deer. Furnishings reflect five generations of the family.

SWIMMING Middlebury Gorge, East Middlebury, off Rt. 125 just above the Waybury Inn, where the road suddenly steepens beyond the bridge. Paths lead down to the river.

Dog Team Tavern Hole, 3.1 miles north of Middlebury, off Dog Team Tavern Rd. Park by the site of the former restaurant and walk along the riverbank until you find an appealing spot in the bends of the New Haven River. Small beach area, gentle current.

Lake Pleiad, behind the Middlebury College Snow Bowl about 8 miles from Middlebury on Rt. 125 east. Park in the lot past the entrance near the Long Trail and walk it south for half a mile, turning right onto Lake Pleiad Trail. A truly idyllic setting, perfect for swimming and picnics. The large rocks on the western end provide a perfect perch from which to take in the pristine surroundings.

Bartlett Falls, Bristol. Near the beginning of Lincoln Gap Rd. (off Rt. 116 in Rocky Dale), there's a pull-off for this popular swimming hole with its 20-foot cliffs. A bronze plaque explains that the land is a gift from Irving Wesley Sr., in memory of his son who died at 19 fighting a 1943 forest fire in British Columbia. It's a beautiful spot by a stream with shallow falls dropping into pools. Swimming shoes are a good idea.

✔ **Lake Dunmore** (see *Green Space*), a scenic lake with a firm, sandy bottom and extensive sand beach, has plenty of space for running, game playing, and picnics.

✔ **Vermont State Parks** (vtstateparks.com). **Button Bay State Park** is the only state park with a swimming pool, **DAR State Park** has Lake Champlain swimming access, **Kingsland Bay State Park** offers a large grassy area with an old-fashioned concrete dock into Lake Champlain, and **Branbury State Park** gives popular beach access to Lake Dunmore. See also *Green Space*.

SCENIC DRIVES Middlebury Gap. This is our favorite approach to Addison County from the southeast, and this stretch of Rt. 125 is more dramatic driving east to west. Begin in Hancock and stop at Texas Falls (see the map in "White River Valleys"). The road quickly crests at its junction with the Long Trail, near the Middlebury Snow Bowl. Then it's all downhill through the woods until the huge, wooden Bread Loaf Inn (now part of Middlebury College) improbably appears. The Robert Frost Wayside Picnic Area and the Interpretive Trail are a short way beyond. We also like to stop in the small, 19th-century cemetery a bit farther down, where a wind chime strikes softly in a row of maples. The picturesque hill town of Ripton is just below, and as the road continues to plunge into the valley, you glimpse the Adirondacks in the distance.

Brandon Gap. Rt. 73 is a high road over Goshen Mountain and through Brandon Gap, also a Long Trail crossing. At the height-of-land, several wooded hiking trails are posted, and a rest area has been sited to catch the full majesty of Mount Horrid's Great Cliff. The road then rushes downhill with Brandon Brook, joining Rt. 100 and the White River below Rochester.

Note: A well-surfaced woods road (Goshen Rd.) runs south from Ripton through the national forest, past the turnoffs for Silver Lake and past Blueberry Hill to Rt. 73 in the Brandon Gap.

Appalachian Gap. East from Bristol, Rt. 17 climbs steadily for 4 miles (past the Jerusalem General Store), eases off for a couple of miles, and then zigzags steeply to crest at more than 3,000 feet, yielding some spectacular views before dropping into the Mad River Valley. It's even more spectacular heading west.

Lincoln/Appalachian Gap Loop. From Bristol, follow Rt. 17/116 to the turnoff for Lincoln 2 miles east of Bristol, past Bartlett Falls (be sure to stop) to Lincoln and out Downingsville Rd. to Jerusalem, back down on Rt. 116 to Rt. 17.

Lincoln Gap. Follow Rt. 17/116 east from Bristol, as above, but from Lincoln continue on the narrow Gap Rd., unpaved in sections. Again there are beautiful views, and you are quickly down in Warren. *Note:* Unsuitable for trailers and RVs. Closed in winter.

Along Lake Champlain. See *Villages* for Shoreham and Orwell.

✳ Winter Sports

CROSS-COUNTRY SKIING Rikert Nordic Center at the Bread Loaf Campus of Middlebury College (802-443-2744; middlebury.edu), 106 College Cross Rd., Ripton. This college-owned land has 50 km of groomed trails in the area of the Robert Frost Farm and the college ski bowl. Elevations range from 975 to 1,500 feet. Rentals, accessories, lessons, and repairs.

Blueberry Hill Inn (802-247-6735; blueberryhillinn.com), 1307 Goshen–Ripton Rd., Goshen, has 70 km of trails within 22,000 acres of the Green Mountain National Forest and Moosalamoo National Recreation Area reaching backcountry elevations of 1,400–3,100 feet. This is a surefire cross-country mecca during even marginal seasons. The ski center has ski and snowshoe rental equipment, waxing, and repairs; $10 trail-use fee gets you free soup noon–2.

DOWNHILL SKIING AND SNOWBOARDING Middlebury College Snow Bowl (802-443-SNOW; middleburysnowbowl.com), 6886 Vermont 125, Hancock. Middlebury's throwback to a less commercial era of skiing, with well-maintained and winding trails. Two triple chairs, one double, a total of 17 trails, 6 glades, and full access to all wooded terrain within ski area boundaries; 40 percent covered by snowmaking. It also offers a ski school, shop, rentals, and a cafeteria that boasts the least expensive ski food in the state.

✳ Green Space

Also see *Birding, Hiking, Swimming, Scenic Drives.*

On or near Lake Champlain

🦆 **Button Bay State Park** (802-475-2377; vtstateparks.com), 5 Button Bay State Park Rd., off Panton Rd. just below Basin Harbor. Open Memorial Day–Columbus Day weekends. Named for the unusual, button-like clay formations found in years past along its shore, this 253-acre area overlooks splendid scenery of the lake and Adirondacks; 73 campsites, 13 lean-tos, two cabins, picnic areas, swimming (in the state park pool only), fishing, boat rentals, nature museum, and trails. Rocky Point juts into Lake Champlain like the prow of a ship.

⊗ 🦆 🦆 **Kingsland Bay State Park** (802-877-3445; vtstateparks.com), 787 Kingsland Bay State Park Rd., Ferrisburgh. Marked from Rt. 7 off Little Chicago Rd. Facilities include a large grassy picnic area on Lake Champlain, swimming, boating, and hiking trails. This is a particularly lovely overlook of Kingsland Bay with lawns that roll down to the lakeside shaded by old maples. Weddings and summer get-togethers are very popular here.

Dead Creek Wildlife Management Area (vt.audubon.org), 1 mile west of Rt. 22A on Rt. 17, is a 2,800-acre, semi-wilderness tract with a parking area and posted visitors information about the many species of birds that congregate here, including herds of snow and Canada geese that can number up to 20,000 during spring and fall migrations.

Addison County Chamber of Commerce

SILVER LAKE

DAR State Park (802-759-2354; vtstateparks .com), 6750 Rt. 17 west, 8 miles west of Addison, a 95-acre park comprising the 1765 stone foundations of the area's first colonial structures (in the picnic area). A grassy field contains 70 campsites, including 24 lean-tos. Steps lead down to a smooth shale beach for swimming; Lake Champlain boat access; superb bird-watching.

In or near the Green Mountain National Forest

Lake Dunmore, in Salisbury between Brandon and Middlebury on Rt. 53 off Rt. 7, is a tranquil, 1,000-acre lake lined with summer cottages at the foot of Mount Moosalamoo and along its hiking trails. On the east shore road is **Branbury State Park** (802-247-5925; vtstate parks.com), with a natural sandy beach, vast grassy areas, 37 tent sites, seven lean-tos, boating, snack bar, picnic grove, nature trail, and hiking to the Falls of Lana. Pets allowed. The trail begins just south of the Branbury Park entrance, and it's just half a mile to the picnic area and falls. From Rt. 53 it's 1.6 miles past these falls up to secluded **Silver Lake**, once the site of religious camp meetings in the 1880s; a large hotel (actually constructed as a seminary) occupied the spot of the present picnic area and stood until around 1940, when it was destroyed by fire. About a mile long, it is now part of the Green Mountain National Forest, accessible only by foot and mountain bike (0.6 mile via the Goshen Trail from the second parking lot on Forest Rd. 27, off Goshen Rd.). There are first-come, first-served primitive no-fee campsites and a nature trail around the lake; swimming is permitted.

♿ **"Robert Frost Country"** in the Green Mountain National Forest is a title bestowed in 1983 on a wooded piece of the town of Ripton because it was here, in a log cabin, that the poet summered for 39 years. This section of Rt. 125, between the old Bread Loaf Inn (part of the Middlebury College campus) and the village, has been designated the Robert Frost Memorial Highway; there is also a wheelchair accessible Robert Frost Interpretive Trail and a Robert Frost Wayside picnic area near the road leading to the farm and cabin. The picnic area has grills and drinking water, and it's shaded by red pines that were pruned by Frost himself. Just east of the wayside, a dirt road leads to the Homer Noble Farm, which Frost bought in 1939. Park in the lot provided and walk past the farm to Frost's cabin (it's not open to the public). The Robert Frost Interpretive Trail, a bit west on the opposite side of Rt. 125, is an easy walk, just three-quarters of a mile. It begins with a bridge across Beaver Pond and winds through woods and meadow, past seven Frost poems mounted along the way. This trail is popular with cross-country skiers and snowshoers, and with July and August blueberry pickers.

♿ **Texas Falls**, in Hancock, is easily accessible from the marked road, 3 miles east of the Middlebury Gap. It's a short drive to the parking area, and the succession of falls is just across the road, visible from a series of paths and bridges that in 2012 was made wheelchair accessible. There's also a picnic area.

✷ Lodging

INNS

In the Middlebury area

♿ **Swift House Inn** (802-388-9925; 866-388-9925; swifthouseinn.com), 25 Stewart Lane, Middlebury 05753. Formerly the family estate of the legendary philanthropist Jessica Stewart Swift, the Swift House is now under the ownership of Dan and Michele Brown. Antiques, elaborately carved marble fireplaces, formal gardens, and extravagant wallpaper and upholstery add to the charm of this 1814 mansion. (Ask to see the vintage elevator.) Common space in the inn itself includes a cozy bar as well as two attractive living rooms. Meals (full breakfast included) are served in the cherry-paneled main dining room, the library, or the window-ringed sunporch. There are nine guest rooms in the main house, five in the Victorian gatehouse on Rt. 7, and six contemporary-styled ones in the renovated 1886 carriage house. One room is wheelchair accessible, as is the dining room. All Carriage House rooms have a sitting area, whirlpool tub, and a fireplace. $159–279 in high season, $139–239 in low. The dining room, Jessica's Restaurant, serves upscale meals (see *Dining Out*). Pets are welcome in Carriage House for $50 per dog per day.

♂ ☜ ♦ ♿ **The Middlebury Inn** (802-388-4961; 800-842-4666; middleburyinn.com), 14 Court Square, Middlebury 05753, has been the town's imposing chief hostelry since 1827. The vast, comfortable lobby with a formal check-in desk and portraits of the Battell family and Robert Frost is a firm reminder of the renovated inn's heritage. Breakfast, lunch, afternoon tea, and dinner are served in the comfortable tavern and on the front porch in summer and early fall. Waterfalls Day Spa (see *Fitness Centers and Spas*) has added wellness and spa amenities to this tasteful inn. The 71 guest rooms are divided among four adjoining buildings. Those in the main inn are on two floors (there's a 1926 Otis elevator) and are furnished in reproduction antiques. They have private bath, cable TV, air conditioner/heater, and direct-dial phone. The vintage-1825 Porter Mansion, with handsome architectural details and a lovely curved staircase, has been renovated with special care and an eye to housing wedding parties; it includes a luxury suite and eight rooms. The remaining rooms, in the motel-style Courtyard Annex, are also tastefully fitted with inn-style furnishings. Rates run $119–269 double, including afternoon tea. Children 17 and younger stay free in parent's room. Pets are welcome in the motel units for a daily fee.

♂ ☜ ♦ ♿ **Waybury Inn** (802-388-4015; 800-348-1810; wayburyinn.com), 457 E. Main St., East Middlebury 05740. A historic former stagecoach stop that exudes character in each of the 13 imaginatively furnished rooms. The Waybury was a favorite of Robert Frost's when he lived up the hill in Ripton, and its exterior gained fame on the TV series *Newhart*. There is a pub dining room and the more formal Pine Room restaurant (see *Dining Out*), and you can dine on the porch or terrace in warmer months. A swimming hole under the nearby bridge is a down-home way to cool off. In winter you can warm up by the fire in the pub downstairs. Dinner and Sunday brunch are served year-round. $105–285 double occupancy includes a full hot breakfast. Two-night minimum stay on busy weekends and holidays. Pets ($25 per night) and children welcome.

In Brandon 05733

♂ ☜ ♿ **Lilac Inn** (802-247-5463; 800-221-0720; lilacinn.com), 53 Park St. A Brandon-born financier built this romantic old mansion with an imposing five-arched facade in 1909.

Rachel Carter

THE SWIFT HOUSE INN

Splendid common spaces (a glassed-in ballroom with its crystal chandelier is the scene of wedding receptions), glorious antiques, and a wide entrance hallway with a grand staircase keep the grand historic feel alive. There is also a formal garden with a gazebo and cobbled patio, a small living room with a fireplace and floor-to-ceiling bookcases, and a copper-topped fully licensed bar with comfortable seating. The nine ample

RESORT

♂ ☜ ♦ ♿ **Basin Harbor Club** (802-475-2311; 800-622-4000; basinharbor.com), 4800 Basin Harbor Rd., Vergennes 05491. Open mid-May–mid-Oct. Vermont's premier lakeside resort is located on 700 acres and offers 145 rooms in the main lodge, three guest houses, and cottages scattered along the shore. Since 1886, when they first began taking in summer boarders, members of the Beach family have assiduously kept up with the times. Over the years a large swimming pool, an 18-hole golf course, a wellness center, and even an airstrip have been added. Those who like to dress for dinner have ample opportunity; at the main restaurant, men and boys over 12 must wear jackets and ties during the summer season. The casual Red Mill Restaurant and outdoor dining venues complete the menu. Daily rates per couple start at $279 for two adults. Daily rate extra for children 3 and older, depending on age. There are also seasonal packages; inquire about kayaking, waterskiing, horticultural workshops, crafts and cooking classes, and nature treks.

guest rooms all have luxurious bathrooms with deep, clawfoot tubs; each is furnished in antiques and has a hidden TV. The bridal suite (the original master bedroom) has a whirlpool bath, fireplace, and dressing area. There is one handicapped-accessible room. Weddings are a specialty. Rates include a three-course breakfast served in the sun-filled garden room; special-occasion dinners can be arranged for 10 or more. $175–295 midweek, $210–345 weekends, more during foliage. Children must be over 12, and pets must be arranged in advance with extra fee.

♂ ♞ ♥ ♪ ⅙ **The Brandon Inn** (802-247-5766; 800-639-8685; historicbrandoninn.com), 20 Park St. A large brick landmark overlooking the village green, this inn dates from 1892 and is on the National Register of Historic Places. Innkeepers since 1988, Sarah and Louis Pattis offer 39 rooms, 2 of them suites. There are TV rooms upstairs as well as large living rooms downstairs, and some of the 19th-century furniture and a good deal of the original atmosphere survive. The inn's 5 landscaped acres include a swimming pool (with Jacuzzi) and a stretch of the Neshobe River, good for trout fishing. An 18-hole golf course is just up the way. Rates include full breakfast and are $135–200; $150–220 in peak seasons. Pets welcome for $20 per visit.

Elsewhere

♞ ♥ ♪ **The Shoreham Inn** (802-897-5081; 800-255-5081; shorehaminn.com), 51 Inn Rd., Shoreham 05770. Dominic and Molly Francis present a friendly, comfortable place that's old-time Vermont with an English touch. The 10 private-bath guest rooms are furnished with include king beds as well as day beds for the many visiting families. The age of this 1790 structure is felt in the floorboards, exposed beams, and steep, creaking stairs. At the center of a quaint village surrounded by apple country, it is not far from Lake Champlain and Middlebury. The common rooms have plenty of sofas and easy chairs, along with chess and backgammon boards, a wood-burning fireplace, British antiques, and, frequently, the aroma of coffee or some other culinary temptation emanating from the pub (see *Eating Out*). Rates range $145–235, higher in peak seasons, including a full hot breakfast. Pets accepted with conditions.

✪ ♂ ♥ ♪ **Blueberry Hill Inn** (802-247-6735; 800-448-0707; blueberryhillinn.com), 1245 Goshen–Ripton Rd., Goshen 05733. Over the past four decades Tony Clark has turned this blue 1813 farmhouse on a high, remote back road into one of New England's most famous country inns. The lures are gourmet cuisine,

peace and quiet, hiking and mountain biking, and, in winter, cross-country skiing. But there is more to it: a sure touch. The 11 rooms—some with loft, all with full bath—have antiques, handmade botanicals, and fine decor, and the common areas are cozy and inviting, with roses and geraniums blooming in the indoor greenhouse off the kitchen, and a stone fireplace in the dining room. Guests tend to mingle, from morning coffee to evening hors d'oeuvres and dinner, served family-style at long wooden tables. This inn has long been known for its extraordinary food, and chef-owner Tony produces elaborate, creative dinners featuring fresh ingredients, many of them straight from the garden and included in most room rates (as well as breakfast). The cross-country ski center (see *Winter Sports*), with 70 km in the Moosalamoo National Recreation Area, tends to be snowy, thanks to its elevation. In midsummer the blueberry crop ripens and you can graze at leisure, provided half your take makes it to the kitchen. There's swimming in the pristine reflecting pond out back, gorgeous gardens, and a sauna. Rates include dinner and breakfast and are $299 double occupancy in summer ($199 option excludes dinner); $322–368 in winter (also including trail passes); and $414 during foliage. For those traveling with pets, inquire about the Moosalamoo Cottage.

✪ ♂ ♪ **The Inn at Baldwin Creek** (802-453-2432; 888-424-2432; innatbaldwincreek.com), 1868 N. Rt. 116, Bristol 05443. A classic 1797 Vermont farmhouse inn set on 25 acres including a perennial garden with paths down to Baldwin Creek for wading and fishing; garden tours available. Mary's Restaurant, attached to the inn, is a fine regional dining spot (see *Dining Out*), renowned as a farm-to-table innovator. Five guest rooms with private bath include a couple of two-room suites, which work well for families. Weddings and catered events for up to 200 people. Chef Doug Mack is a founding member of Vermont Fresh Network; in summer he hosts special farmhouse dinners featuring local farmers, cooking classes, and music and theater performances in the barn. $125–295 depending on room and season, including a three-course breakfast and afternoon refreshments; children 16 and under are free in the same room, $25 per extra adult.

BED & BREAKFASTS

In and around Middlebury 05753

♪ ⅙ **The Inn on the Green** (802-388-7512; 888-244-7512; innonthegreen.com), 71 S. Pleasant St. An attractive 1803 Federal town house has two colorfully decorated suites in the main house, plus nine other spacious rooms: Six sleep

LAKE CHAMPLAIN VALLEY

two, three have both a double and single bed, and all have private bath. Complimentary "breakfast-in-bed" baskets are delivered to your door, but afternoon tea service requires that you emerge from under the covers. Rates per room $129–299.

♂ ♂ ♿ **Cornwall Orchards Bed & Breakfast** (802-462-2272; cornwallorchards.com), 1364 Rt. 30, Cornwall. English-born Juliet Gerlin and her husband, Bob, a recovering lawyer, have turned this 1784 Cape into an airy, comfortable place with hardwood floors, antique linens, Oriental carpets, and a spacious living room with a wood-burning fireplace. There's an antique cast-iron cookstove in the open kitchen and an outdoor deck with orchard views and a large garden. Of the five guest rooms, four have queen-sized bed, and one has two twins tucked under the eaves; all have private bath. The ground-floor Governor Room is wheelchair accessible. $140–150 includes a fresh, full breakfast served family-style in the dining room. Two-day minimum during foliage season and on summer and holiday weekends.

♂ ❀ ♂ **Chipman Inn** (802-388-2390; 800-890-2390; chipmaninn.com), Rt. 125, Ripton 05766. On the way to or from Bread Loaf and the Middlebury College Snow Bowl, this 1828 inn sits in the center of the tiny village of Ripton, which consists of a schoolhouse, community meetinghouse, church, and general store. It's also within striking distance of Robert Frost's house and cabin and the Robert Frost Trail. The house has eight guest rooms of varying sizes, all with private bath. Guests can gather in the bar, around a very large old hearth, in the sunny sitting room near the woodstove, and elsewhere in this roomy house. There's a TV and plenty of books to peruse, as well as breakfast served around a large table. $139–249, less for a single, includes full breakfast. Children and pets welcome.

South and west of Middlebury

Quiet Valley Bed & Breakfast (802-897-7887; quietvalleybedandbreakfast.com), 1467 Quiet Valley Rd., Shoreham 05770. A new house whose stressed-pine floors make it feel old, this Cape is down a dirt road on 48 acres of hay fields along the Lemon Fair River. The living room includes a shallow, Rumford-style fireplace, and interesting antiques abound. One of the three guest rooms has a pair of four-poster double beds, woodstove, and private bath. The other two have twin singles and share a bath. Fortifying breakfasts are served at a table overlooking inspiring mountain views. Guests are welcome to hike the trails or take the canoe for a run up the river. Rates are $125–150, including breakfast.

♠ ❀ ♂ **Buckswood Bed & Breakfast** (802-948-2054; buckswoodbandb.com), 633 Rt. 73, Orwell 05760. Linda and Bob Martin offer two guest rooms (private baths) and ample common space in their 1814 home, located in a pleasant country setting just east of Orwell Village. Dinner by reservation. $85–95 per couple includes breakfast. Polite pets accepted as Bob and Linda's Airedale, Abby, enjoys company.

In and around Brandon 05733

Old Mill Inn (802-247-8002; 800-599-0341; oldmillbb.com), 79 Stone Mill Dam Rd. This attractive 1786 farmhouse set in 5 acres above the Neshobe River adjoins the 18-hole Neshobe Golf Club. Unusually helpful innkeepers Bob and Rhonda Foley offer four spacious, comfortable, and tastefully furnished guest rooms with private bath. Guests can lounge in the two art-filled living rooms, relax on the wicker porch chairs in warm weather, or stroll through the Neshobe River Winery (see *Wineries*) and Foley Brothers Brewing, famed for its Fair Maiden double IPA. The neighboring river contains a good swimming hole. $109–169 per couple (depending on room and season) includes a full breakfast. Children over 10; no pets.

♠ ❀ **The Inn on Park Street** (802-247-3843; 800-394-7239; theinnonparkstreet.com), 69 Park St. Park Street is Brandon's Park Avenue: It is lined with the town's finest homes, most of them on the National Historic Register. Judy Bunde, a professional pastry chef, offers six guest rooms in this delightful Queen Anne Victorian, five with private bath and the sixth part of a two-room suite. The Theresa Room comes with double sinks, and a two-person Jacuzzi on a marble floor. The bedding is down filled and hand pressed; rooms come with robes and fine toiletries. In winter months a fire crackles in the tastefully furnished parlor with its baby grand piano; in summer you can dine on the spacious porch. A masterful dessert buffet is prepared each evening, and Bunde's breakfasts are scrumptious. Dinner can be prearranged. The "Cooking with Chefs" program has become wildly popular—definitely inquire. One room offers a pet option, and children under 12 are considered. $100–185 include breakfast and dessert buffet, surcharge during foliage.

Rosebelle's Victorian Inn (802-247-0098; 888-767-3235; rosebelles.com), 31 Franklin St. This restored, mansard-roofed house has a high-ceilinged living room with fireplace and TV and a large dining room—the setting for afternoon tea and full breakfasts. Hostess Ginette Milot speaks French. Four elegantly decorated guest rooms each have private bath. $129–139 includes breakfast. Children must be over 12 and have a separate room. Two-night minimum stays are required on holiday weekends and during foliage season.

In and around Vergennes 05491

♂ � ♿ **Strong House Inn** (802-877-3337; stronghouseinn.com), 94 W. Main St. Built in the 1830s by Samuel Paddock Strong in the graceful Federal style, this roomy old house features fine detailing, such as curly maple railings on the freestanding main staircase. The 14 guest rooms all include a private bath, cable TV, and telephone. The rooms are in the main house as well as in Rabbit Ridge Country House, a newer building in back. Rates begin at $120 for most rooms, $350 for a suite with Adirondack furnishings—king-sized Adirondack canopied four-poster, private deck, wet bar, and double Jacuzzi tub—including full breakfast and afternoon refreshments. Inquire about quilting, crafting, and other special weekends. Dogs accepted on a limited basis.

♨ ✎ **Emerson Guest House** (802-877-3293; emersonhouse.com), 82 Main St. There are five bright, high-ceilinged guest rooms all with shared bath and a suite with private bath in this 1850 French Second Empire mansion once owned by a prominent local judge. Susan (an artist) and Bill (a musical theater pro with Broadway credits including *Les Misérables*) Carmichael serve breakfasts in a downstairs nook bordered by stained glass that looks over the backyard. On the edge of Vergennes, the house is set in 4 acres of land with walking trails, gardens, and apple trees. Common space includes a library (with TV) and a living room with a vintage-1927 Steinway. Rooms with shared bath, full breakfast $70–125; the Willard Suite, $140–160.

In Addison 05491

♂ � ✎ **Whitford House** (802-758-2704; 800-746-2704; whitfordhouseinn.com), 912 Grandey Rd. Situated east of the lake on rich farmland, this idyllic 1790 farmhouse is set among flower gardens on acres of fields with gorgeous views of the Adirondacks. Tranquility and warm hospitality are the hallmarks of Bruce and Barbara Carson's inn, which they share with a cat, a beagle, and a small flock of sheep The two cozy upstairs rooms have king or twin beds, and a first-floor room comes with a four-poster double bed. There's also a guest cottage ($275–300 per couple) with a king-sized bed, a sitting room with sofa bed, and a full bath (with radiant-heated floor) that can accommodate a family of

four. All have private bath. The great room, with its wood-burning fireplace made from local Panton stone, is a wonderful place to unwind. There's a book-lined library, plenty of art and antiques, wide-plank floors, and exposed beams. Rates run $175–250, $25 more in high season, breakfast included. Pets upon prior arrangement in the cottage ($10 per night). Children welcome, guests with younger children asked to reserve the cottage.

✎ **Barsen House Inn** (802-759-2646; 888-819-6103; barsenhouseinn.com), 53 TriTown Rd. Innkeeper Peter Jensen, a skilled woodworker, built this house and most of its furniture. He and his wife, Daphne, host guests in three rooms with private bath, one with a king-sized bed or two twins, and two with queen. Two of them form a suite with a sitting room, TV, and private bath. Kids will find plenty to do here: gathering eggs, picking berries, catching frogs, or roasting marshmallows in the fire pit. There's also swimming and boating at a 3-acre beach nearby. $115–135 includes full breakfast; more for the suite, $20 higher during foliage.

In the Bristol area 05443

♂ **Dream House Country Inn** (802-453-2805; 855-253-4600; dreamhousecountryinn .com), 382 Hewitt Rd., Bristol. This classic Gothic Revival cottage is set on 6 acres with three guest rooms, one a bridal suite, all with private bath, TV/DVD, temperature control, and luxury linens. The grounds include a gazebo, perennial gardens, and plenty of space for an event tent. $125–190 depending on room and season includes breakfast. Children over 8 welcome, no pets.

✎ **The Old Hotel** (802-453-2567; oldhotel.net), 233 East River Rd., Lincoln. This rambling 1840s gabled building, serving for many years as a hotel for the mill across the street, sits high in the small village near the height of Lincoln Gap. Owned by a local pastor (David) and teacher (Donna), it's funky and comfortable with an eat-in kitchen, common space with a gas fireplace and a screened porch. Rooms include two large suites ($130–155) and two rooms with shared bath ($65–105), breakfast included. The feel is that of a place geared to groups, good for family reunions. It can be rented as a guesthouse or as a private B&B for a group, beginning at $595 a night, $2,500 for the week.

OTHER LODGING ✎ ♿ **Courtyard Marriott** (802-388-7600; marriott.com), 309 Court St., Middlebury 05753. Just south of Middlebury Village, this is an 89-room clapboard, gabled New England–style structure with all the amenities. There are 11 suites with whirlpool tub and fireplace. Facilities include an indoor pool, exercise room, and the Courtyard Café, serving breakfast daily. $145–229 in low season, $165–259 in peak-demand periods.

🐾 🐾 🐾 **Cozy Cottages** (802-247-6644; cozy cottagesvermont.com), 1246 Franklin St., Brandon 05733. Open early May–mid-Oct. Located on Rt. 7, 1 mile south of Brandon, this is a shady campus of 20 well-spaced one- and two-room cottages well built in the 1930s by Ethan Allan Furniture Company. All have private bath, heat, TV, fridge, microwave, and coffeemaker; many have fireplace and A/C. Grounds include shuffleboard, a stocked trout pond, and a swimming pool. Owners Stephen and Ursula Zahn are also owners of their labor-of-love, the Otter Valley Winery (see *Wineries*). $89–149 includes continental breakfast.

North Cove Cottages (802-352-4236; north covecottages.com), 1958 Lake Dunmore Rd., Salisbury 05679. Eleven cottages, all with bath and fully equipped kitchen, several winterized. Open year-round. Sandy beach, free rowboats, additional watercraft rentals.

Note: The Addison County Chamber of Commerce (addisoncounty.com) lists rental cottages on both Lake Dunmore and Lake Champlain.

CAMPGROUNDS 🐾 DAR State Park in Addison, Branbury State Park in Salisbury, and Button Bay State Park in Ferrisburgh all offer popular Vermont State Park (vtstateparks.com) camping. See *Green Space*.

🐾 🐾 **Kampersville** (802-352-4501; kampers ville.com), located on Lake Dunmore in Salisbury. Open early May–late Oct. Weekly RV and cabin rentals and all the RV campground amenities from mini golf and heated pools to playing fields and courts to boat rentals.

SALAD PRESENTATION AT TOURTERELLE
Rachel Carter

✳ Where to Eat

DINING OUT

In the Middlebury area

🐾 ᕓ **Fire & Ice Restaurant** (802-388-7166; 800-367-7166; fireandicerestaurant.com), 26 Seymour St., Middlebury. Open for dinner daily, lunch served Fri.–Sun. This is not so much a restaurant as a dine-in museum, with its stained-glass and mahogany nooks, a library, and a 1921 Hackercraft motorboat that serves as a salad bar with more than 55 items. Since 1974 this has been a local favorite, specializing in steaks, prime rib, and chicken in champagne and mushroom cream sauce. The **Big Moose Pub** serves more casual fare with daily drink specials amid taxidermy and seven TVs.

ᕓ **Jessica's Restaurant at the Swift House Inn** (802-388-9925; jessicasvermont.com), 25 Stewart Lane, Middlebury. Dinner is served Wed.–Sun. in three atmospheric rooms: a dining area with a working fireplace, a book-filled library, and a converted porch. Menu items change regularly with the seasons, but always include a range of dishes ($14–29 for entrées) that span Europe, Asia, and New England. The bar is a regular *Wine Spectator* award winner, and beers from Otter Creek Brewery down the street are a staple.

✪ 🐾 ᕓ **The Lobby** (802-989-7463; lobby restaurantvt.com), 7 Bakery Lane, Middlebury. Open daily for lunch and dinner; brunch is served Sunday. Sit on the covered outside deck or by a wall-sized window overlooking Otter Creek at this hip eatery. Walls are covered with chalkboards—feel free to enjoy the quotes from culinary luminaries or add your own artistic touch. At lunch, try the Brie grilled cheese with housemade merguez (lamb sausage), raspberries, and balsamic vinaigrette ($10). Creative burgers ($11–16), each with its own unique bun, are served all day.

Morgan's Tavern at the Middlebury Inn (802-388-4961; middleburyinn.com), 14 Court Square, Middlebury. Breakfast and afternoon tea daily, lunch weekdays, dinner Wed.–Sun. Local ingredients are combined to create homey favorites such as meatloaf and chicken Cordon Bleu, but also more eclectic offerings including Korean barbecue beef shortribs. Entrées $14–29.

Tourterelle Restaurant (802-453-6309; tourterellevt.com), 3629 Ethan Allen Hwy. (Rt. 7), New Haven. Open for dinner Wed.–Sat.; also Sun. brunch. Reservations recommended. On a stretch of Rt. 7 dominated by farms and fields, this grand, cupola-topped stagecoach inn

WAYBURY INN SOUP

Rachel Carter

is an oasis of civility. New York chef Bill Snell and his wife, French event planner Christine, have transformed the former Roland's Place into an elegant French country estate best known for its bouillabaisse with an uncommon red curry broth ($13 for an appetizer portion; $25 for an entrée). Brunch leans on eggs and crêpe dishes. Weddings and events are a specialty. There are also three cozy **guest rooms** upstairs ($175–200).

& **Waybury Inn** (802-388-4015; wayburyinn .com), Rt. 125, East Middlebury. Open daily for dinner and Sunday brunch; lunch served in summer. This inn's claim to fame is its stand-in role as the Stratford Inn on Bob Newhart's eponymous 1980s TV show. Larry, Darryl, and Darryl would likely be fixtures at the pub (entrées $10.95–23). For a more elegant experience, hit the Pine Room for local venison or a mushroom Wellington (entrées $18–32). In summer lighter fare is also available on the porch and terrace.

In Brandon

Café Provence (802-247-9997; cafeprovencevt .com), 11 Center St. Open daily for lunch and dinner. On Sun., brunch replaces lunch. Chef-owner Robert Barral earned his stripes cooking for the Four Seasons hotel chain, subsequently teaching for several years at Vermont's New England Culinary Institute. Now he has a near monopoly on Brandon dining, with this upscale-casual restaurant as well as the **Center Street Bar** (802-465-8347, open daily) downstairs and **Gourmet Provence Bakery & Wine Shop** down the street (37 Center St., 802-247-3002).

At Barral's upstairs flagship, the open kitchen gleams with polished chrome and hanging pans. The fare produced there changes regularly, but always includes crave-worthy seafood such as

the chef's signature stew, a lobster-tarragon broth filled with shellfish and served over saffron risotto. Enjoy the outdoor terrace in summer and inquire about special events and Barral's famous cooking classes and his weekend culinary retreats. Dinner entrées $16–26, and hearth-baked pizzas $12.50.

In the Vergennes area

✪ **Black Sheep Bistro** (802-877-9991; black sheepbistrovt.com), 253 Main St., Vergennes. Open nightly 5–8:30, this intimate bistro has been wildly popular ever since chef Michel Mahe started serving his innovative French-inspired dishes more than a decade ago. You feel as if you're on a side street in Paris, except that the service is first-rate. All appetizers are $7, including Mahe's signature duck cigar rolls with apricot-tarragon dipping sauce. Entrées are $19, with regular options including bacon-and-Brie-stuffed chicken in balsamic cream and a seasonal take on duck confit. No matter what you order, it's accompanied by a creamy garlic mash and crisp, salty frites with addictive dipping sauces. Terrace seating in summer months. Reservations essential.

✪ 🍴 & **Basin Harbor Club Main Dining Room** (802-475-2311; basinharbor.com), Basin Harbor, off Panton Rd., 7 miles west of Vergennes. Open mid-May–mid-Oct. Jacket and tie are required July–Aug. for gentlemen over 12. That's just one of many throwbacks at this lakeside resort, which has changed little since its inception in 1886. The single exception is the creative cuisine from chef Christian Kruse.

CAFÉ PROVENCE

Rachel Carter

Formal, six-course dinners may include seared tuna with radish sorbet and avocado crema to start, followed by venison served with a date-tamarind puree. A buffet breakfast is served in the dining room daily. For casual fare, head to **Red Mill Restaurant at Basin Harbor**, also on-site.

In Bristol

& **Mary's Restaurant at Baldwin Creek** (802-453-2432; 888-424-2432; innatbaldwin creek.com), junction of Rts. 116 and 17. Open for dinner Wed.–Sun., brunch Sun. Daily breakfast for guests. The first president of the Vermont Fresh Network, chef Doug Mack has been using ultra-local ingredients at his inn since 1983. In fact, much of the restaurant's produce comes from gardens on the property. There's a choice of three dining rooms, but when it comes to starters, there's no reason to debate: Just order a cup or bowl of the deservedly famous creamy garlic soup. Other dishes range from lobster poutine to a simple pasta in ricotta-mint pesto. Inquire about cooking classes; reservations a must. Check the website for regular culinary events.

✢ **The Bobcat Café & Brewery** (802-453-3311; bobcatcafe.com), 5 Main St. Open daily, bar at 4, dinner at 5. This eatery began as a community effort and in 2008 came under the same ownership as the Black Sheep Bistro in Vergennes. A reclaimed wood bar sets the mood for handcrafted food and house-brewed beer. Hearty pub fare changes with the seasons, but there are always flavorful vegetarian options and the signature venison-chorizo meatloaf.

Elsewhere but worth the drive

Starry Night Café (802-877-6316; starrynight cafe.com), 5371 Rt. 7, North Ferrisburgh. Open Wed.–Sun. 5:30–9; reservations are essential. Chef Josh Krechel is a Culinary Institute of America grad known for his imaginative flavor combinations and colorful salads. The intimate front dining room with its art-covered walls is a former cider mill featuring an antique bar with locally crafted stools, tables, and chairs. There's a larger octagonal dining room, also with locally crafted furnishings, an outdoor deck, and changing art by local artists. Inquire about live music. Entrées $25–30.

✺ **Gastropub at The Shoreham Inn** (802-897-5081; shorehaminn.com), Rt. 74 west, Shoreham. Dinner served Thurs.–Mon. Dominic and Molly Francis have transformed the downstairs of this circa-1790 tavern into a British-style gastropub serving English standards such as bangers and mash with a pint of Guinness. They installed a copper-topped bar

Rachel Carter

THE DESSERT SPREAD AT MARY'S RESTAURANT, INN AT BALDWIN CREEK

and a mantel mirror from Greenwich, England. The menu changes daily, but entrées generally cost less than $25.

EATING OUT

In the Middlebury area

✢ & **A & W Drive-in** (802-388-2876), Rt. 7 south, a few miles from Middlebury. Vermont's (and possibly New England's) last surviving drive-in with carhop service, open in summer months. The 1960s roadside spot still dispenses its root beer the old-fashioned way, in frosted mugs. A hard-core bacon cheeseburger is the obvious choice, but save room for the fried cheese curds, too.

✺ ✢ & **American Flatbread Middlebury Hearth** (802-388-3300; americanflatbread .com), 137 Maple St., at the Marble Works. Serving Tues.–Sat. 5–9 year-round, with outdoor seating when possible. This company started in the Mad River Valley and remains the Middlebury area's only true craft pizzeria. The all-natural pies are made with organic flour and toppings and baked in a woodfired oven.

❂ ✺ ✢ & **Costello's Market** (802-388-3385; costellosmarket.com), 2 Maple St., at the Marble Works. Open from 10 AM Tues.–Sat. The freshest fish around and a slew of Italy's best meats and cheeses fill the case here. But the real attraction is the prepared food. If you're lucky, chef John Hamilton will be slow-roasting his heavenly porchetta for fennel-scented sandwiches. If not, there are still ample sandwich options, as well as popular fish tacos and inexpensive plated meals such as risotto or beef braciole.

& (ɣ) **Otter Creek Bakery** (802-388-3371; ottercreekbakery.com), 14 College St. Open

Mon.–Sat. 7–5:30, Sun. 7–3. Hugely popular at lunchtime for soups, salads, and deli sandwiches ranging from homemade hummus with veggies in a pita pocket to fresh crabmeat salad. Breads are the specialty, baked from scratch with no preservatives, in a dozen varieties, including wheat berry and onion Asiago. There are fresh, flaky croissants too, plus dozens of cookies, tarts, and cakes.

♦ ♂ & **Rosie's Restaurant** (802-388-7052; rosiesrestaurantvt.com), 1 mile south of Middlebury on Rt. 7, is open daily 6–9. This large family restaurant has a counter and three cheerful dining rooms. The pulled turkey is an uncommon take on a hot turkey sandwich, while the monkey bread is a sweet classic. Kids' menu and daily specials.

In Brandon
♦ ♂ & (ᵠ) **Cattails** (802-247-9300; cattailsvt .com), 2146 Grove St. (Rt. 7, just north of Brandon). Lunch and dinner daily, breakfast on weekends. Lance Chicoine and Stephanie Kellogg run this family eatery that serves up large portions of homestyle American fare with occasional touches of Asia, the American South, and the Southwest. Children's menu. Early-bird dinner specials.

♂ **Patricia's Restaurant** (802-247-3223), 18 Center St. Open daily for lunch and dinner; also a Sunday brunch. Also known as Sully's Place, this is a local gathering, eating, and drinking place with a whole lot of character. Traditional fare like grilled pork chops and fried haddock, as well as Italian-style dishes ranging from cheese ravioli to spaghetti with hot sausage.

In Vergennes
♦ ♦ ♂ & **3 Squares Café** (802-877-2772; 3squarescafe.com), 221 Main St. Open for three square meals daily. Chef-owner Matt Birong's restaurant is a Golden Barn member of the Vermont Fresh Network, but not all of his food is grown in the Green Mountains. As a proud owner of a cacao farm in the Dominican Republic, he also handpicks pods that become deep, dark chocolaty treats back home in Vergennes. Besides drinking chocolate and truffles, the plant is most likely to show up in his taqueria specials on Thurs.–Sat. evenings. But the exotic is just a small part of what makes 3 Squares beloved by locals. Breakfast is served until 3 PM each day, while lunch and dinner bring a roster of perfectly balanced panini, salads, and eclectic specials.

♂ & **Antidote** (802-877-2555; barantidote.com) 35C Green St. How locally focused is this bar and restaurant? Chef-owner Ian Huizenga's "13 Mile Burgers" are prepared entirely from ingredients sourced from within that distance. The pork in the "Pig Mac" comes from Huizenga's own farm. There are tacos, flatbreads, and charcuterie, too.

♂ & **Vergennes Laundry** (802-870-7157; vergenneslaundry.com) 247 Main St. Open Wed.–Sun. 7–6. This woodfired bakery inside a former Laundromat turns out intensely French breads and pastry. Be sure to grab a cheesy gougère or a sweet morning bun. The 24-seat café fills up quickly and doesn't take reservations, so keep in mind alternate locations in which to enjoy a tart or simple sandwich made from local produce.

In Bristol
& (ᵠ) **Bristol Bakery & Café** (802-453-3280; bristolbakeryandcafe.com), 16 Main St. Open at 6:30 weekdays, 7:30 weekends for breakfast and lunch; Sun. brunch. This inviting storefront is filled with the aroma of coffee and breads, hung with local art, and furnished with chairs by the coffeepot. Pause with a muffin and your paper or laptop or to sample the crabcakes, soups, and specialty salads or design your own sandwich. Breads are baked fresh each morning.

Elsewhere
♦ ♂ & **The Bridge** (802-759-2152; thebridge restaurantvt.com), 17 Rt. 17, West Addison. Open daily (except Tues.) at 6:30 for breakfast, plus lunch and dinner till 9 (8 in winter). The farm and lake country south of Vergennes and west of Middlebury is eatery-scarce, but here, the service is quick and friendly. The low prices reflect the throwback nature of the rib-sticking comfort food, including maple cream pie.

SCOOPS The Inside Scoop (802-247-6600), 22 Park St., Brandon. Open daily, year-round with the exception of holidays. There are more than 25 flavors at any given time at this combination antiques shop (Antiques by the Falls) and vintage-1950s soda fountain. Vermont's own Wilcox Ice Cream is served from a suitably vintage marble counter. The antiques are whimsical—and everywhere.

lu°lu (802-318-0883), 11 Main St., Bristol. Open daily. The small-batch scoops at this ice cream shop change daily and are all made from Vermont cream, produce, and candies. Try the Slumdog Millionaire, flavored with curry and peanut.

BREWS Otter Creek Brewing (800-473-0727; ottercreekbrewing.com), 793 Exchange St., Middlebury. Open daily 11–6. Self-guided tours, gift shop, tasting room, and pub fare served. See also the *Made in Middlebury* sidebar.

Two Brothers Tavern (802-388-0002; two brotherstavern.com), 86 Main St., Middlebury. Open daily for lunch, dinner, and late night. Local hangout with 15 Vermont microbrews on tap and continuous events and partnerships that benefit all aspects of the community.

((ŷ)) **51 Main at the Bridge** (802-388-8209; go51main.com), 51 Main St., Middlebury. Open for lunch, dinner, and late night Tues.–Sat. Lounge, social space, and live music venue with internationally flavored, locavore food.

COFFEEHOUSE ((ŷ)) **Carol's Hungry Mind Café** (802-388-0101; carolshungrymindcafe .com), 24 Merchants Row, Middlebury. Open daily until 5, later for special events. This riverside coffeehouse with yellow- and merlot-colored walls offers soft music, art, pastries, sandwiches, and plenty of spots to settle into with a book or a group of friends. Check the website for upcoming events.

TEAROOM ✪ **Brandon Music Café & Tearoom** (802-465-4071; brandonmusicvt.com), 62 Country Club Rd., Brandon. Open daily until 6, closed Tues. Housed in a barn once owned by artist Warren Kimble, this recording company, gallery, and tearoom is owned by Stephen and Edna Sutton, recent transplants from the UK. Stop in for teatime or a lunch of steak-and-ale pie.

✴ Entertainment

Mahaney Center for the Arts (802-443-3168; middlebury.edu), 72 Porter Field Rd., Middlebury College. The 370-seat concert hall in this dramatic building on the southern edge of the college campus offers a full series of concerts, recitals, plays, dance performances, and films.

MIDDLEBURY COLLEGE'S MAHANEY CENTER FOR THE ARTS
Addison County Chamber of Commerce

Addison County Chamber of Commerce

TOWN HALL THEATER

♂ **Town Hall Theater** (802-382-9222; town halltheater.org), 52 Main St., Middlebury. Performances throughout the year. This restored 1884 town hall on the green stages music, dramatic performances, and children's events. It's home to the nationally acclaimed, professional **Opera Company of Middlebury** (ocm vermont.org), the **Middlebury Actors Workshop** (middleburyactors.org), the **Middlebury Community Players** (middleburycommunity players.org), and the occasional **After Dark Music Series** (afterdarkmusicseries.com). Also a fun location for weddings and events.

Compass Music & Arts Center (802-247-4295; cmacvt.org), 333 Jones Dr., Brandon. The owners of Brandon Music are also behind this downtown gallery and performance space. Regular exhibits include a collection of historic phonographs, radios, and TVs, as well as a show detailing the building's history as the Brandon Training School. Local and emerging artists are represented in changing shows.

Vergennes Opera House (802-877-6737; vergennesoperahouse.org), 120 Main St., Vergennes. A renovated, century-old theater that once rang with the sounds of vaudeville now offers occasional music and theater. Check the website for an events schedule.

Bristol Band Concerts are held Wed. evenings, June 15–Labor Day, in Central Park.

Brandon Town Hall (brandontownhall.org), 49 Center St. This beautiful 1861 hall is open for movies, music, and community activities. Home to the Brandon Town Players.

See also *Brews, Coffeehouse, Tearoom,* and *Special Events.*

✳ Selective Shopping

ANTIQUES Middlebury Antique Center (802-388-6229; middantiques.com), 3255 Rt. 7, East Middlebury. Open daily, year-round. Furniture and furnishings representing 50 dealers at the same location for 25 years.

Branford House Antiques (802-483-2971; brandfordhouseantiques.com), 6691 Rt. 7, Brandon. A large, handsome farmhouse and barn filled with a variety of antiques, specializing in furniture.

Broughton Auctions (802-758-2494; tom broughtonauctions.com), 2250 Rt. 22A, Bridport. Throughout the summer, auctions are held under the blue and white tents (Broughton also rents tents) at the Auction Barn, once the home of the Bridport Cheese Factory and later a milk plant for H. P. Hood. Check the website for on-site auctions. Even if you aren't looking to buy

anything, it's worth coming just to hear Tom Broughton hold forth.

Antiques by the Falls in Brandon is several rooms full of antiques and collectibles in Brandon; see The Inside Scoop under *Scoops.*

ART GALLERIES & CRAFTS STUDIOS

In Middlebury

Sweet Cecily (802-388-3353; sweetcecily.com), 44 Main St. Open Mon.–Sat. Nancie Dunn bills her shop as "a country store for today," replete with folk art of every stripe from craftspeople worldwide. The shop's back porch offers a great view of Otter Creek Falls.

Vermont Folklife Center Heritage Shop (802-388-4964; vermontfolklifecenter.org), 88 Main St. Open Tues.–Sat. One-of-a-kind, handmade traditional art as well as a wide variety of visual art from Vermont creators, plus books and recordings.

Edgewater Gallery (802-458-0098; edge watergallery-vt.com), 1 Mill St. Open daily, year-round. Located in the former space for the Vermont State Craft Fair at Frog Hollow, Edgewater continues the tradition of showcasing Vermont-based artists and artisans with a

MADE IN MIDDLEBURY: FACTORY TOURS AND SHOPPING

Downtown Middlebury offers plenty of shopping/browsing, but a number of local ventures have outgrown their downtown digs, migrating to the northern fringe of town on and around Exchange St. (see the map), where they remain visitor-friendly. Here **Otter Creek Brewing** (800-473-0727; ottercreekbrewing.com), 793 Exchange St., is the big draw, open daily 11–6 for free guided tours, free samples, and sales of its Otter Creek craft beers and Wolaver's organic ales. Otter Creek first opened in 1991, in the plant presently occupied by **Vermont Country Soap** (616 Exchange St.; vermontsoap.com), now the largest manufacturer of natural handmade soaps in North America. Visitors can take a "Soap Tour," view the soap museum, and shop the factory outlet (open weekdays 9–5, Sat. 10–4). At **Maple Landmark Woodcraft** (802-388-0627; 800-897-7031), 1297 Exchange St., one of the country's largest wooden toy manufacturers—known for "Name Trains" and "Montgomery Schoolhouse" lines—visitors can view toymakers through plate-glass windows (call ahead for a factory tour; shop open weekdays 9–5, Sat. 9–4, Sun. seasonally). **Danforth Pewter** (802-388-8666; danforthpewter.com), Middlebury's best-known artisan brand, recently expanded into a workshop and store at 52 Seymour St. (same area) with a similar setup that permits visitors to view craftsmen spinning "holloware" and shaping pewter plates, jewelry, and ornaments, then purchase the results (Mon.–Sat. 10–5; May–Dec., also open Sun. 11–4). Turn off Exchange St. onto 38 Pond Lane to find **Geiger of Austria** (800-2-GEIGER; geigerfashion.com), known for its classic felted jackets. Middlebury has been the company's only American base, and the factory store (Mon., Wed., Fri. 10–5) is well worth checking for bargains. Around the corner is **Beau Ties Ltd.** (802-388-0108; 800-488-8437; beautiesltd.com), 69 Industrial Ave. This is a mainly catalog business but there's always someone on hand in the store to knot ties for novices. Choose from seemingly every fabric imaginable; also ascots, scarves, and accessories (open weekdays 10–4:30; tours by appointment). All of these companies, plus Lincoln Peak Vineyard (see *Wineries*), have formed "Made in Middlebury" (madeinmiddlebury.com).

318

varied collection of arts and fine crafts in many price ranges.

In Brandon

Brandon Artists Guild (802-247-4956; brandonartistsguild.org), 7 Center St. Open daily year-round. A standout nonprofit gallery representing more than 50 local artists and artisans. Year-round special events; see Art in the Snow under *Special Events*.

Warren Kimble Gallery & Studio (802-247-4280; warrenkimble.com), 10 Park St. Open by appointment for serious inquiries about purchasing original paintings by the "America's best-known living folk artist."

In Bristol

Art on Main (802-453-4032; artonmain.net), 25 Main St. Open daily, less in winter, check website for hours. This exceptional nonprofit community artists' cooperative gallery displays a changing selection of art, crafts, textiles, and jewelry from local craftspeople.

Robert Compton Pottery (802-453-3778; robertcomptonpottery.com), 2662 N. Rt. 116, just north of Bristol. Showroom open daily, but best to call ahead. A complex of kilns, studios, and gallery space has evolved out of a former farmhouse and now contains the work space of this seasoned potter, who uses salt glazes and Japanese wood-firing techniques to produce everything from water fountains to crockery to sinks.

Lincoln Pottery (802-453-2073; judithbryant pottery.com), 220 W. River Rd., Lincoln. Visitors welcome, call ahead. Judith Bryant creates wheel-thrown stoneware. Her studio and showroom are located in an old dairy barn.

Worth a detour

♦ **Norton's Gallery** (802-948-2552; nortons gallery.com), Rt. 73 in Shoreham, 1 mile south of the car ferry to Fort Ticonderoga. Call beforehand to make sure they're open. The small red gallery overlooking Lake Champlain houses a of menagerie of dogs, cats, rabbits, birds, and fish, along with flowers and vegetables—all the work of nature lover Norton Latourelle, sculpted from wood in unexpected sizes. Sculpted dog portraits are a specialty.

Be sure to visit vermontcrafts.com for complete artisan listings and for details on **Vermont Open Studio Weekends,** held each year in the spring and fall.

BOOKSTORES The **Vermont Book Shop** (802-388-2061; vermontbookshop.com), 38 Main St., Middlebury. Open Mon.–Sat. 9:30–5:30, Sun. 11–4. First opened in 1947 by Robert

Dike Blair, who retired as one of New England's best-known booksellers and the publisher of Vermont Books, an imprint for the poems of Walter Hard. Robert Frost was a frequent customer for more than two decades, and the shop has sold many autographed Frost poetry collections.

Otter Creek Used Books (802-388-3241; ottercreekusedbooks.com), 99 Maple St., Middlebury, follow Printers Alley behind the Marble Works. Open Mon.–Sat. Don't know what you want? You'll still find it here, among 25,000 titles.

♦ **Monroe Street Books** (802-398-2200; monroestreetbooks.com), 1485 Rt. 7, 2 miles north of downtown Middlebury. Open Mon.–Sat. 9–6, Sun. 11–6. Dick and Flanzy Chodkowski have some 80,000 volumes at Vermont's largest used-book store. Specialties include children's books, graphic novel, and Vermontiana.

& **Bulwagga Books & Gallery** (802-623-6800), 3 S. Main St., Whiting, at the Whiting Post Office. Open Tues.–Sat. More than 10,000 titles plus an art gallery, handcrafted furniture, and a reading room with mountain views and coffee.

FARMERS MARKETS Seasonal farmers markets are held throughout the Lower Champlain Valley, including Middlebury, Bristol, Brandon, Orwell, and Vergennes. The Middlebury Farmers Market is held year-round. Additional markets take place in smaller villages depending on harvest—check details for all at vermontagriculture.com.

FARMS ♂ ♦ **Champlain Orchards** (802-897-2777; champlainorchards.com), 3597 Rt. 74 W., Shoreham. There's far more than apples at this scenic orchard overlooking Lake Champlain. Seasonally, there are also pick-your-own berries, cherries, peaches, pears, and plums. Concerts and pig roasts are just some of the events that happen between spring and autumn. The diverse apples are crushed into both virgin cider and hard ice cider. Extensive farm market open 10–4 daily.

Douglas Orchard & Cider Mill (802-897-5043), 1050 Rt. 74, Shoreham. Pick your own strawberries, raspberries, and apples. There's also a small retail store selling hand-knit felt hats. Call ahead for opening times.

Monument Farms Dairy (802-545-2119), 2107 James Rd., Weybridge. Open for tours by appointment only. The store is open weekdays 8:30–5:30. One of the few surviving milk producer-handlers in Vermont. Try the chocolate milk.

Golden Russet Farm (802-897-7031; golden russetfarm.com), 1329 Lapham Bay Rd., Shoreham. A certified-organic farm raising a variety of animals, perennials, vegetables, and herbs, wholesaled to stores and restaurants, also sold at their farm stand, open Mon.–Sat. 9–5.

Maple View Farm (802-247-5412; mapleview farmalpacas.com), 185 Adams Rd., Brandon. Deb and Ed Bratton raise alpacas and invite tourists to see their animals; it's best to make an appointment. An on-site fiber mill supplies the farm store with clothing, teddy bears, and rugs, all made from the fuzzy camelidae.

Wood's Market Garden (802-247-6630; woodsmarketgarden.com), Rt. 7, just south of downtown Brandon. Open seven days a week in-season. A fruit, vegetable, and flower farm with a seasonal market that has sold fresh food for more than 100 years.

SPECIAL SHOPS Dakin Farm (800-99-DAKIN; dakinfarm.com), 5797 Rt. 7, Ferrisburgh. Open daily. Distributing nationally via stores and catalog, this is the original farm store selling cob-smoked ham, maple syrup, aged cheddar, and much more.

Daily Chocolate (802-877-0087; daily chocolate.net), 7 Green St., Vergennes. Open Tues.–Fri. 11–5:30, Sat. 11–4. Pick up these GMO-free, organic chocolates made from locally produced cream, butter, and maple syrup, packed into sumptuous gift boxes.

Vermont HoneyLights (802-453-3952; 800-322-2660; vermonthoneylights.com), 9 Main St., Bristol. Open daily. An assortment of hand-poured and rolled 100 percent beeswax candles are produced in this cute shop and workshop.

WINERIES Otter Valley Winery (802-247-6644; ottervalleywinery.com), 1246 Franklin St. (Rt. 7), Brandon. Since debuting their first vintage in 2011, the couple behind Cozy Cottages has expanded its line to seven different wines. Besides white, red, and rosé sips, bottles include the "Chocolate Mousse." Yes, it's what it sounds like. Tastings and gift shop open daily May–Oct., 10–7.

Lincoln Peak Vineyard (802-388-7368; lincoln peakvineyard.com), 142 River Rd., New Haven. This vineyard's 10 varieties of wine are all grown on this rocky New Haven hilltop. The Marquette, which won for best-in-show red at the International Cold Climate Wine Competition, is a local favorite. Open daily in-season, less frequently in winter.

Neshobe River Winery (802-247-8002; neshoberiverwinery.com), 79 Stone Mill Dam Rd., Brandon. Located at the Old Mill Inn (see

Lodging) and backed by the fifth hole of the Neshobe Golf Club with the Neshobe River running in front, this petite, picture-perfect winery operates a small vineyard and supplements with grapes from elsewhere in Vermont as well as California and the Finger Lakes. Visit Foley Brothers Brewing on-site, too. Open Fri.–Sun. in-season. Call ahead for hours.

✳ Special Events

Note: For current happenings check the *Addison Independent* (addisonindependent.com) or *Seven Days* (sevendaysvt.com) calendars of events.

Mid-February: **Art in the Snow** (802-247-6401; brandon.org), Brandon—winter arts and wine festival throughout the endearing village of Brandon.

Late February: **Middlebury College Winter Carnival** (802-443-3168; middlebury.edu), Middlebury College—ice show, concerts, snow sculpture; oldest student-run winter carnival in the country.

Mid-March: **Vermont Chili Festival** (better middleburypartnership.org), Middlebury. A Vermont Chamber of Commerce Top Ten Winter Event—the downtown overflows with restaurants and caterers from around the state competing for the best chili prize and the thousands of folks who come to watch and taste.

Late April/early May: **Middlebury Maple Run** (802-388-7951; middleburymaplerun.com), Middlebury. A popular half marathon, "The Sweetest Half" road race, followed by townwide food and events.

Memorial Day weekend: Middlebury's **Memorial Day Parade** is a popular annual event featuring lots of school marching bands, Scouts, Little Leaguers, politicians, floats, and fire trucks. It starts at 9—and you can catch a similar parade two hours later in **Vergennes** if you prefer to sleep in.

July 4: **Bristol** hosts one of the most colorful **Independence Day Parades** around with its comic Outhouse Race, crafts fair, and parade. **Brandon** also hosts a parade and fireworks the Sat. closest to the Fourth.

Early July: The weeklong **Festival on the Green** (802-462-3555; festivalonthegreen.com), Middlebury, features individual performers and groups such as the Bread & Puppet Theater as well as a potpourri of music from folk to jazz to exotic international talent. No charge for admission.

Mid-July: **French Heritage Day** (802-388-7951; frenchheritageday.com) in Vergennes—

Franco-American and French Canadian heritage celebration in Vermont's smallest city. **Annual Basin Bluegrass Festival** (802-247-3275; basinbluegrassfestival.com), Brandon—a weekend of food, music, and pickin'. **Moosalamoo Goshen Gallop** (802-247-6735; bluberryhillinn.com) is billed as "one of the toughest 10ks in New England." The race is held over rural roads and wilderness trails in Moosalamoo National Recreation Area.

Early August: **Town Wide Yard Sale Day** (802-247-6401; brandon.org), Brandon—yard sales, all over town. **Addison County Field Days** (802-545-2257; addisoncountyfielddays .com), New Haven—livestock and produce fair, horse pull, tractor pull, lumberjacks, demolition derby, and other events. There's also a **Taste of Vermont** dinner one night that requires reservations, but the food is worth the small effort.

Mid-August: **Annual Pie and Ice Cream Social** at the Rokeby Museum (802-877-3406; rokeby.org) in Ferrisburgh with music and house tours.

Fourth Saturday in August: **Vergennes Day** (802-475-2853; vergennesday.com)—pancake breakfast, road races, music, street fair, food, crafts.

Fourth Saturday in September: **Bristol Harvest Festival** (802-388-7951; addisoncounty .com)—fall farm harvest, crafts, and car show.

Early October: **Annual Ladies Car Rally** (802-877-6737; vergennesoperahouse.org), Vergennes—popular fund-raiser for the Vergennes Opera House. If you happen to have a wonderful antique car (the driver must be female), sign on up! If not, come catch the finish of the rally with festivities on the Vergennes green. **Dead Creek Wildlife Day** (802-241-

Brandon Chamber of Commerce

INDEPENDENCE DAY CELEBRATION IN BRANDON

3700)—wildlife demonstrations, nature walks, crafts, and food. **Brandon HarvestFest** (802-247-6401; brandon.org) is Brandon's fall harvest festival featuring "Make Your Own Leaf Person."

Late October: **Spooktacular** (802-388-8666; bettermiddleburypartnership.org), Middlebury—a daylong, family-friendly Halloween event. **Pumpkins in the Park** (802-388-7952; vergennes.org), Vergennes—all are invited to bring their carved pumpkins for an evening glow of orange.

Early December: **Vergennes Holiday Stroll** (vergennes.org), Vergennes—holiday activities and crafts fair. Monthlong holiday celebrations include **Bristol's Cool Yule Celebration** (schedule at addisoncounty.com) and **Very Merry Middlebury** (calendar at better middleburypartnership.org).

BURLINGTON REGION

Superbly sited on a slope overlooking Lake Champlain and the Adirondack Mountains, Burlington is Vermont's financial, educational, medical, and cultural center. While its fringes continue to spread over recent farmland (the core population hovers around 40,000, but the metro count is now more than 150,000), its heart beats ever faster. Few American cities this size offer as lively a downtown, as many interesting shops and excellent restaurants, or as easy an access to boats, bike paths, and ski trails. The city sits overlooking the widest portion of Lake Champlain with magnificent views of the Adirondacks beyond.

The community was chartered in 1763, four years after the French were evicted from the Champlain Valley. Ethan Allen, his three brothers, and a cousin were awarded large grants of choice lots along the Onion (now Winooski) River. In 1791 Ira Allen secured the legislative charter for the University of Vermont (UVM), from which the first class, of four, was graduated in 1804. UVM now enrolls more than 10,000; it's the largest of the city's three colleges.

Ethan and Ira would have little trouble finding their way around the city today, except the ravine that divided the city in their time has long since been filled in. Main streets run much as they did in the 1780s—from the waterfront uphill past shops to the school Ira founded and on to Winooski Falls, site of Ira's own grist- and sawmills.

Along the waterfront, Federal-style commercial buildings house shops, businesses, and restaurants. The ferry terminal and neighboring Union Station (now a part of Main Street Landing), built during the city's late-19th-century boom period as a lumbering port—when the lakeside trains connected with myriad steamers and barges—are now the summer venue for excursion trains, ferries, and cruise boats. The neo-Victorian Burlington Boathouse is everyone's window on Lake Champlain, a place to rent a row- or sailboat, to sit sipping a morning coffee or sunset aperitif, or to lunch or dine on the water. The adjacent Waterfront Park and promenade are linked by bike paths to a series of other lakeside parks (bike and in-line skate rentals abound), which include swimmable beaches.

Halfway up the hill, the graceful Unitarian Church, designed in 1815 by Peter Banner, stands at the head of Church Street—a bricked, traffic-free marketplace for four long blocks, a promenade that's become a 21st-century-style common, the place everyone comes to graze.

Today that waterfront includes several parks, such as Oakledge (formerly a General Electric property), just south of downtown, North Beach (with an urban campground), and Leddy (site of a former rendering plant) in the North End. The waterside green space is linked by a 12-mile recreational path that includes the

SAILING ON LAKE CHAMPLAIN

321

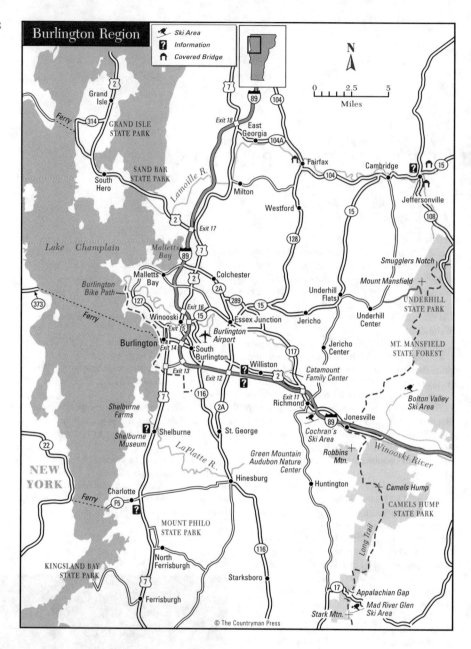

Burlington Bike Path extending across the Winooski River into Colchester and across Lake Champlain to the Champlain Islands, merging with the Missisquoi Valley Rail Trail (see "Northwest Corner").

Downtown lodging makes it possible to walk from high-rise hotels and several pleasant B&Bs to sights and water excursions, dining and shopping. Of course it's also appealing to bed down in the real countryside that's still within a quick drive of the city, so we have included B&Bs in nearby Jericho, Williston, Richmond, and Shelburne.

The Shelburne Museum, 6 miles south of the city, draws visitors like a magnet, with treasures ranging from a vintage Champlain Lake steamship and lighthouse to world-class paintings and folk art.

Neighboring Shelburne Farms is quite simply New England's most fabulous estate, with prizewinning cows (and cheese), miles of lakeside walks, and a mansion in which you should dine, sleep, or at least breakfast.

GUIDANCE The Lake Champlain Regional Chamber of Commerce (802-863-3489; 877-686-5253; vermont.org), 60 Main St., Burlington 05401. Open weekdays year-round, this welcome center is housed in the former motor vehicles building, halfway between Church St. and the waterfront. This site is augmented by a staffed information booth at the airport that is open daily.

The Burlington Parks & Recreation Department (802-864-0123; enjoyburlington.com) maintains much of the waterfront, bike path, parks, and activities as well as a useful website.

The Lake Champlain Byway connects Grand Isle County (see "Northwest Corner") and Addison County (see "Lower Champlain Valley") directly through the Burlington region (also known as Chittenden Country) via Lake Champlain. All associated activities and routes can be found at lake champlainbyway.com.

GETTING THERE *Note:* Burlington is Vermont's single most car-free destination, accessible by bus from Boston and Montreal and by train from New York City and Montreal, blessed with good local public transport and little need to use it.

By air: **Burlington International Airport** (802-863-1889; burlingtonintlairport.com) is just 3 miles from downtown, served by Continental, United, US Airways, Delta, and JetBlue. Six car rental agencies are available, as is taxi and bus service.

By bus: **Greyhound** (802-864-6811; 800-231-2222; greyhound.com) offers service to Albany, Boston, New York City, Montreal, Portland, and many points between. Buses depart from the Burlington International Airport.

By car: I-89, Rts. 7 and 2.

By ferry: **The Lake Champlain Transportation Company** (802-864-9804; ferries.com), King Street Dock, Burlington. Descended from the world's oldest steamboat company, LCTC offers three local car-ferry services. Between June and October the car ferries make the 75-minute crossing between Burlington and Port Kent, New York. Year-round depending on ice, they also ply between Charlotte, just south of Burlington, and Essex, New York. Year-round service is offered on the 15-minute run between Grand Isle (see "Northwest Corner") and Plattsburgh, New York.

By train: **Amtrak** (800-USA-RAIL; amtrak.com). The Vermonter (Washington to St. Albans via New York and Springfield, Massachusetts) stops at Essex Junction, 5 miles north of Burlington. (The station is served by taxis and Burlington CCTA buses; see *Getting Around.*) Faster, more scenic service from New York City is available via the Adirondack to Port Kent, New York, which connects with the ferry to Burlington.

GETTING AROUND *By bus:* **Chittenden County Transportation Authority** (802-864-2282, CCTAride.org). CCTA bus routes radiate from the corner of Cherry and Church Streets (hub of the Church Street Marketplace), serving all of Chittenden County and outward to St. Albans, Middlebury, and Montpelier with 19 bus routes seven days a week (Sunday is limited). The fleet of buses is now low-emission, clean diesel—a landmark environmental move for Burlington.

MEDICAL EMERGENCY Call **911.** **Fletcher Allen Health Care** (802-847-0000; 800-358-1144; fletcherallen.org) on the UVM campus, 111 Colchester Ave., Burlington, has a 24-hour emergency room.

FARM CART AT THE INN AT SHELBURNE FARMS

Alice Levitt

LAKE CHAMPLAIN VALLEY

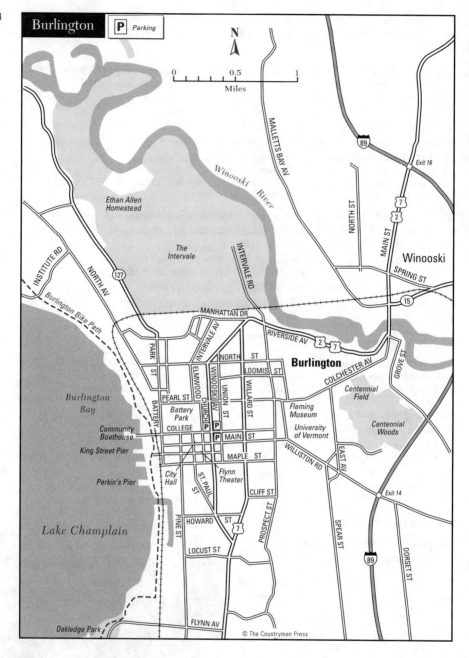

© The Countryman Press

✳ Nearby Villages

Jericho (jerichovt.gov). Northeast of Burlington, Jericho is best known for the **Old Red Mill** (jericho historicalsociety.org; 802-899-3225), on Rt. 15 at Jericho Corners (open daily, except Jan.–Mar., when it's open only Wed.–Sun.). This 19th-century red mill set above a gorge is one of the most photo-graphed buildings in Vermont and appropriately houses prints and mementos relating to one of the state's most famous photographers, Wilson A. "Snowflake" Bentley. The Jericho farmer was the first person in the world to photograph individual snowflakes and collected more than 5,000 micro photos.

Rachel Carter

OLD ROUND CHURCH IN RICHMOND

A basement museum also tells the story of the many mills that once lined six sets of falls. Sales from the crafts store benefit the preservation of the building, which is owned by the Jericho Historical Society. A 20-acre park behind the mill, along the river, offers picnic tables and hiking trails. Head to nearby Jericho Center on Rt. 15, with its oval village common and **Jericho Center Country Store** (802-899-3313; jericho countrystore.com), a genuine, old-fashioned market that's been operating since 1807. The museum-like shop trades in local products and produce as well as a fine selection of country store staples. A friendly ghost is said to help keep stock.

Richmond (richmondvt.com). East of Burlington on Rt. 2 (I-89, Exit 11) and the Winooski River, Richmond was badly damaged in the flood of 1927 and then again in Hurricane Irene, but the architecturally interesting downtown remains. Turn down Bridge St. and drive by the old Blue Seal grain store (now **Sonoma Station**; see *Eating Out*) and the library (a former church) to the **Old Round Church**. This 16-sided building, one of the most unusual in the state, was constructed in 1812–13 as a community meetinghouse to serve five denominations; in winter its illuminated windows are a vision of Christmas past (oldroundchurch.com).

Shelburne (shelburnevt.org). Beyond the commercial sprawl of Shelburne Rd. (Rt. 7 south from Burlington) lie two of Vermont's greatest treasures, both the legacy of 19th-century railroad heirs William and Lila Vanderbilt Webb. In the 1880s the couple hired Frederick Law Olmsted to landscape their 4,000-acre lakeside model farm, and in 1946 their daughter-in-law founded a major museum of Americana. Today 1,400 acres of the estate—**Shelburne Farms**—survive as a combination inn, demonstration, and working farm, complementing the exhibits in no fewer than 39 buildings in the nearby **Shelburne Museum**. Inevitably shops and attractions continue to multiply along Rt. 7, including the **Vermont Teddy Bear Company**. (See *Must See* and *To Do* for details about all three.)

Winooski (onioncity.com) is just across the 32-foot Winooski Falls from Burlington. Ira Allen was the first to harness the water that subsequently powered several mammoth brick 19th-century mills, attracting workers from Ireland, Canada, and Eastern Europe who settled in the cottages that line its streets. The falls, with an art deco bridge, and the common, framed by the vintage-1867 Winooski Block and the handsome Champlain Mill (now an office complex that's home to MyWebGrocer), still form the center of town, which gained a controversial roundabout in 2005 and a continuing sprawl of luxury condos overlooking the falls. St. Michael's College, with its summer-stock Playhouse (presenting a variety of professional theater performances—see *Entertainment*), is just up Allen St. (Rt. 15) into Colchester.

✳ Must See

✿ ✐ ✦ **Shelburne Museum** (802-985-3346; shelburnemuseum.org), 6000 Shelburne Rd., is open daily 10–5. $22 adults, $11 ages 5–18, family day pass $55. This fascinating "collection of collections" features American folk art but also includes paintings by Rembrandt, Degas, Monet, and Manet. Each of more than three dozen buildings—many of them historic transplants from around New England—houses a different collection. The 45 landscaped acres include flower and herb gardens, an apple orchard, and more than 90 varieties of lilacs.

An adequate description of the collections (more than 150,000 objects) would fill a separate chapter. Highlights include a 1915 steam locomotive and a vintage-1890 private Palace Car; the side-wheeler *Ticonderoga*, in her basin near the Colchester Reef Lighthouse; folk art; and paintings. Children will glory at the operational carousel and miniature circus.

Acquisitions continue, but this is still substantially the collection of one woman, gathered at a time when few people were interested in Americana. Electra Havemeyer was 18 in 1910 when she bought her first cigar-store figure. Three years later she married James Watson Webb of Shelburne (son of

SHELBURNE FARMS GARDENS

the wealthy couple who had built Shelburne Farms; see below). Over the next 30 years she raised five children, traveled widely, and managed homes on Long Island and in Manhattan and a 50,000-acre "camp" in the Adirondacks, as well as the Shelburne estate. Gradually she filled all her holdings (even her indoor tennis court) with her treasures, founding the museum in 1947 when her husband retired to Shelburne. Both died in 1960, but their vision for the museum was fulfilled by their son, the late J. Watson Webb Jr. Inquire about gallery talks and special events.

✪ ♂ ☜ ❀ ♫ **Shelburne Farms** (802-985-8686; shelburnefarms.org), at 1611 Harbor Rd., Shelburne, just west of Rt. 7. The Farm Store and Visitor Center (802-985-8442), with an exceptional introductory film, is open daily year-round, 9–5:30 (10–5 in the off-season). Mid-May–mid-Oct., general admission for the walking trails, children's farmyard, and cheesemaking operation on the 1,400-acre lakeside property costs $8 adults, $6 seniors, $5 ages 3–17; full 1½-hour open wagon tours are offered four times daily mid-May–mid-Oct. Guided tours cost $11 adults, $9 seniors, $7 ages 3–17. There is no charge to use the walking trails the rest of the year (leashed pets are welcome on the grounds Nov.–Apr.). Inquire about house and garden tea tours, Breeding Barn tours, and special events. This grand 1880s lakeside estate is now a nonprofit environmental education center and working farm whose mission is to cultivate a conservation ethic. Founded by railroad magnate William Seward Webb and his wife, Lila Vanderbilt Webb, who built it to be a model agricultural estate, it initially comprised 3,800 acres. Its magnificent setting was landscaped by Frederick Law Olmsted (who also designed New York's Central Park) with the help of America's pioneer forester Gifford Pinchot. Manhattan architect Robert Henderson Robertson designed the magnificent Norman-style barns and the 100-room summer "cottage," known then as Shelburne House, on a bluff overlooking Lake Champlain.

SHELBURNE FARMS VIEW

Shelburne Farms

SHELBURNE ORCHARDS

The mansion is now the Inn at Shelburne Farms (open mid-May–mid-Oct.; see *Lodging* and *Dining Out*). The immense, five-story, 416-foot **Farm Barn**, where livestock were kept, is now a place for children to collect eggs, learn to milk a cow, or enjoy a tractor-drawn wagon ride. It also houses the cheesemaking facility, education center, and **O Bread Bakery**. The **Coach Barn**, once the family stable, now hosts weddings, special events, art exhibits, and workshops. The massive **Breeding Barn**, where Dr. Webb's English Hackneys were bred, is now used for large-scale events; guided tours are given Mon. afternoons. The farm's prizewinning cheddar cheese, made from the milk of its own herd of Brown Swiss cows, is sold, along with other Vermont products, in the Farm Store.

Eight miles of walking trails wind from the Visitor Center, networking the farm and providing sweeping views of Lake Champlain and the Adirondacks. Inquire about naturalist-led bird walks and special events.

Tip: The Inn at Shelburne Farms is open to the public by reservation for breakfast as well as dinner. Enjoy the most elegant breakfast in New England, or dine on local delicacies as you watch the sun set over the lake. Before you go, get a glimpse of the spectacular library and stroll the lakeside perennial, herb, and rose gardens.

Burlington waterfront (enjoyburlington.com). As noted in the chapter introduction, Burlington's revived waterfront affords dramatic views and is accessible to the public. The handsome (vintage-1915) train station and nearby buildings make up **Main Street Landing** at the base of Main St., home to businesses and a new performing arts center. The King Street Dock remains home to the **Lake Champlain Transportation Company** (LCTC), established in 1826. At the base of College St. at the College Street Pier, the (1991) **Community Boathouse** echoes the design of the Lake Champlain Yacht Club, a prestigious gentlemen's domain built on this site in 1889. **The ECHO Lake Aquarium and Science Center**, operated by the Champlain Basin Science Program, doubles as a research facility and science museum. ECHO, which stands for "ecology, culture, history, and opportunity," is becoming a world-class museum irresistible to kids (see *For Families*). The **Burlington Bike Path** links these sites with the nearby **Waterfront Park** to the north (which includes a stroller-friendly fishing pier and a boardwalk promenade with swings) and with **Perkin's Pier** (parking, boat launch, picnic area, canal boat exhibit, and waterfront benches) just to the south. Farther south is **Oakledge Park** with two picnic shelters, a beach, and a wheelchair-accessible tree house. Several more beaches and parks stretch in both directions. Not surprisingly, shops and restaurants have proliferated along neighboring Battery St.; **Battery Park** is the visually majestic setting for free summer concerts and frequent special events.

✳ To Do

AIR RIDES Above Reality Hot Air Balloon Rides (802-899-4007; balloonvermont.com) offers balloon rides at launch locations near the base of Mount Mansfield near the company base in Jericho. **Mansfield Heliflight** (802-893-1003; mansfieldheliflight.com), 159 Catamount Dr., Milton. Hour-long flight tours are offered.

BICYCLING The **Burlington Bike Path** (802-864-0123; enjoyburlington.com) runs for 7.6 miles along the waterfront, connecting six different parks, beginning with Oakledge Park in the south and continuing into the Champlain Bikeway, making for a 12-mile trail. A bike bridge spans the Winooski River, continuing the path through Colchester to a bike ferry that links it with the Champlain Islands. Fun side trips include Ethan Allen Park with its stone lookout tower, the Ethan Allen Homestead, Intervale Community Farms, and the Salmon Hole Fishing Area near the Winooski bridge. **Rental bikes** (including tandems, trailers, and trail-a-bikes) are available from **Local Motion's Trailside Center** (802-652-2453; localmotion.org), on the Burlington waterfront stretch of the Bike Path at College St., as are maps and bike lockers. The path is used for walking, running, and in-line skating as well as biking. Note that CCTA buses have bicycle racks. For serious bicyclists, we recommend the Greater

Kim Grant

SUNSET AT PERKIN'S PIER IN BURLINGTON

Burlington Hiking and Biking Map, published by Map Adventures (mapadventures.com), which details several Burlington-area loops and longer tours on both sides of Lake Champlain, using ferries. You can also download a free Burlington biking map at localmotion.org.

Mountain bikers should check out the 500-acre **Catamount Family Center** (802-879-6001; catamountoutdoor.com), 592 Governor Chittenden Rd., Williston, for a variety of mountain bike events, workshops, and camps. **Sleepy Hollow Inn, Ski & Bike Center** (802-434-2283; skisleepy hollow.com), 1805 Sherman Hollow Rd., Huntington, features over 10 miles of singletrack plus another 20 miles of converted ski trails linking to the Catamount Family Center Mountain Bike Trail. Trail fees.

There is also the **Essex Transportation Trail**, a 3-mile rail-trail from the Essex Police Station to Rt. 15 (Lang Farm); the **Shelburne Recreation Trail**, from Bay Rd. through Shelburne Bay Park to Harbor Rd.; and the unpaved **Intervale Bikepath**, from Gardener's Supply on Intervale Ave. to the Ethan Allen Homestead. For bike parts and repairs as well as an interesting historic bike experience, visit **Old Spokes Home** (802-863-4475; oldspokeshome.com), 322 N. Winooski Ave., Burlington.

BIRDING ✍ **The Birds of Vermont Museum** (802-434-2167; birdsofvermont.org), adjacent to the **Green Mountain Audubon Center** (see *Green Space*) at 900 Sherman Hollow Rd., Huntington. Open May–Oct., daily 10–4; by appointment in winter. Amazingly life-like carvings of more than 200 species of birds by Robert Spear Jr.; also nature trails, recorded birdsongs. $6 adults, $5 seniors, $3 ages 3–17.

SHELBURNE ORCHARDS APPLE PIE CONTEST

Rachel Carter

BOATING Boats of all sizes abound in the Burlington Bay Harbor, which extends north to Mallet's Bay and south to Shelburne Bay. Most towns in the area also sport their own lake or pond (see *Swimming* and *Green Space*), and the **Winooski River** offers several access points for kayaking and even tubing.

Canoes and kayaks can be rented at **North Beach** in Burlington (enjoyburlington.com) from Canoe Imports (802-651-8760). **Lake Champlain Community Sailing Center** (802-864-2499; communitysailingcenter.org), located along the Burlington Bike Path, is a nonprofit, public-access sailing center with a host of learn-to-sail and learn-to-canoe programs for kids, adults, and families, as well as dinghy, keelboat, kayak, canoe, and paddleboard rentals. At **True North Kayak Tours** (802-238-7695; vermontkayak .com) mother-and-son team Jane and Dovid Yagoda offer instruction and guided tours from a variety of locations on Lake Champlain. Inquire about multiday paddles through the Champlain Islands with B&B lodging. **Waterfront Boat Rentals** (802-864-4858; waterfrontboatrentals.com) at Perkin's Pier, at the bottom of King St. in Burlington, rents canoes, kayaks, rowboats, skiffs, whalers. The popular and classic sloop *Friend Ship* located near the Burlington Community Boathouse offers daily cruises July–Sept. (802-598-6504; whistlingman.com).

♂ ♦ ⅄ *Spirit of Ethan Allen III* (802-862-8300; soea.com). Seasonal, daily scenic cruises as well as themed dinner cruises aboard a triple-deck, 500-passenger excursion boat, departing from the Burlington Community Boathouse mid-May–mid-Oct. Narrated sightseeing, plus sunset cruises, dinner, lunch, and brunch cruises, murder mystery cruises, live music cruises, and specialty food cruises. Check website for a complete list and pricing.

♂ *Moonlight Lady* (802-863-3350; vermontdiscoverycruises.com). Seasonal overnight cruises on a three-deck converted swamp yacht with open-air dining and eight staterooms, each with private bath. Destinations include Vergennes, Basin Harbor, and Montreal. Complete schedule and pricing available online.

♂ *Northern Lights* (802-864-9669; lakechamplaincruises.com). A 115-foot-long cruise boat built as an early-20th-century replica offers scenic, dinner, and concert cruises late June–Oct., departing from the King Street Dock, Burlington.

CULTURAL ATTRACTIONS ♦ **Shelburne Art Center** (802-985-3648; shelburneartcenter.org), 64 Harbor Rd., Shelburne. This nonprofit complex has been holding classes for children and adults for over 65 years. It offers year-round workshops of varying length in pottery, woodworking, fiber, metal, stained glass, and all the fine arts, and shows local work in the on-site gallery, a former library. Summer camp programs for children.

⅄ **Robert Hull Fleming Museum** (802-656-0750; uvm.edu/~fleming), 61 Colchester Ave., on the University of Vermont campus. Open daily (closed Mon.) year-round, hours vary winter to summer. Limited parking. $5 adults, $3 students and seniors, $10 per family. Varied collections of early to postmodern art, natural history, archaeology, and geology. Holdings include ancient primitive art from several cultures and continents, a collection of American portraits and landscapes (from the 18th century to contemporary works), a Native American collection, and frequent special exhibits showcasing everything from Picasso to the history of shoes. Gift shop and café. The building was designed by the renowned firm of McKim, Mead & White, which also designed UVM's Ira Allen Chapel (1927) and Burlington's City Hall.

♂ ♨ ♦ ⅄ **Burlington City Arts** (802-865-7166; burlingtoncityarts.org), 135 Church St., Burlington, next to City Hall. Open Tues.–Fri. 9–5, Sat. noon–5. Free to view exhibits. A nonprofit community space that began as a fine arts gallery showcasing innovative Vermont artists has blossomed into a multiuse contemporary art center featuring local and regional exhibitions, classes and programs, and special events including music, film, and performance.

♨ **South End Arts & Business Association** (802-859-9222; seaba.com), 404 Pine St., Burlington. Located in Burlington's industrial-turned-artistic South End, this group (known locally as SEABA) puts on the Annual Art Hop (see *Special Events*) and First Friday Art Walks year-round, showcasing the growing number of art galleries, crafts spaces, and interesting forms of artistic expression in the South End. SEABA also operates its own art gallery, open Mon.–Fri. 9–5, no charge.

DIVING Lake Champlain Historic Underwater Preserves (historicvermont.org). The Vermont Division for Historic Preservation (historicvermont.org) maintains seven

SOUTH END ART HOP

Steven Mease

shipwrecks, identified by yellow Coast Guard–approved buoys, at various points on Lake Champlain; all are open to scuba divers. The Horse Ferry, the Coal Barge, the O. J. Walker canal boat, and the General Butler are off Burlington. The Phoenix and the Diamond Island Stone Boat are in Colchester and Vergennes, respectively, and the *Champlain II*, a passenger ship, lies on the New York side across from Basin Harbor. Register at the **Waterfront Diving Center** (802-865-2771; waterfrontdiving .com), 214 Battery St., Burlington, which provides equipment rentals and repair; instruction in snorkeling, underwater archaeology, photography, and scuba; and charters to historic preserved shipwrecks.

FISHING Schirmer's Fly Shop (802-863-6105, schirmersflyshop.com), 34 Mills Ave., South Burlington, specializing in Ed Schirmer's own flies, tackle, accessories, guided trips, and instruction. **Pleasant Valley Fly Fishing Guides** (802-338-0649; pleasantvalleyflyfishing.com). Lawton Weber specializes in dry-fly wild trout fishing in his half- and full-day excursions. All expertise levels welcome; all equipment provided.

For more fishing guides, contact the Vermont Outdoor Guide Association (voga.org), and for licensing visit vtfishandwildlife.com. The **Salmon Hole fishing area** off Riverside Ave., just west of the Winooski bridge, is a popular local spot, as is the **Fishing Pier** on the Burlington waterfront behind the Water Department Building next to the Coast Guard station.

FOR FAMILIES *Note:* The best family resource in the area and probably all of northern Vermont is maintained at findandgoseek.net. For a print guide, look for *Kids VT*, a free monthly newspaper available around the state.

✪ ✍ ♿ **ECHO Lake Champlain Aquarium** (802-864-1848; echovermont.org), 1 College St., Burlington, open daily year-round, 10–5. Closed Thanksgiving, Christmas Eve, and Christmas Day. Admission is $12.50 adults, $10.50 for students and seniors 60 and over, and $9.50 ages 3–17 (ask about annual passes and group rates). This is the place to see (and handle) what's swimming in the lake (not only the fish, but a display on "Champ," the local Loch Ness monster) as well as what shouldn't be in the lake. Changing exhibits range from plastinated human remains to bloodsucking fauna; lots of hands-on programming. An environmental-themed café offers lunch, and the gift shop teems with science-minded toys and collectibles.

✍ **Vermont Teddy Bear Company Factory and Museum** (802-985-3001; 800-829-BEAR, vermontteddybear.com), 6655 Shelburne Rd., Rt. 7 at the south end of Shelburne Village. Open daily 9–5; later in summer. A phenomenon in its own right, the huge, fanciful birthplace of well over 100,000 teddy bears a year now includes a museum depicting teddy bear history and an entertaining 30-minute tour ($3 adults, free for children under 12). There is, of course, a huge teddy bear store; be prepared to make a purchase.

♦ ✍ **The Vermont Lake Monsters** (802-655-4200; vermontlakemonsters.com). Minor-league baseball team plays at Centennial Field (off Colchester Ave.) all summer. There is free parking at the Trinity Campus parking lot at the northern end of East Ave. The field is a few minutes' walk away. The season is mid-June–Sept. 1, tickets are cheap, the park is lovely, the concession food is pretty good, and there's a giant Day-Glo dancing Champ mascot for the kids. All in all, a great time—and the baseball isn't bad.

✍ **Ben & Jerry's** (802-862-9620; benjerrys.com), 36 Church St., Burlington. This scoop shop isn't the original location, but the world's legendary ice cream makers did get their start a few blocks away (on the southwest corner of St. Paul and College Sts.). Factory tours are at the Waterbury location (see "Stowe and Waterbury").

✍ **Catamount Outdoor Family Center** (802-879-6001; catamountoutdoor.com), 421 Governor Chittenden Rd., Williston, offers a growing number of camps and events geared toward youth.

GOLF Vermont National Country Club (802-864-7770; vnccgolf.com), 1227 Dorset St., South Burlington, an 18-hole, Jack Nicklaus–designed championship course; **Rocky Ridge Golf Club** (802-482-2191; rockyridge.com), St. George (5 miles south on Rt. 2A from Exit 12 off I-89), 18 holes; **Kwiniaska** (802-985-3672; kwiniaska.com), 5531 Spear St., Shelburne, 18 holes, Vermont's longest course; **Williston Golf Club** (802-878-3747; willistongolfclub.com), 424 Golf Course Rd., Williston, 18 holes; **Essex Country Club** (802-879-3232; essexccvt.com), 332 Old Stage Rd., Essex Junction, 18 holes; **Cedar Knoll Country Club** (802-482-3186; cedarknollgolf.com), 13020 Rt. 116, Hinesburg, 27 holes; **Links at the Lang Farm** (802-878-0298; linksatlangfarm.com), 39 Essex Way, Essex, 18 holes; **West Bolton Golf Club** (802-434-4321; westboltongolfclub.com), 5161 Stage Rd., W. Bolton, 18 holes; **Catamount Country Club** (802-878-7227; catamountcountryclub.com), 1400 Mountain

View Rd., Williston, 9 holes; **Arrowhead Golf Course** (802-893-0234; arrowheadvt.com), 350 Murray Ave., Milton, 9 holes.

HIKING See hiking options under *Green Space* including area state parks (vtstateparks.com). The Green Mountain Club (greenmountainclub.org) publishes *A Day Hiker's Guide to Vermont*, which offers numerous hikes in the area.

HISTORICAL ATTRACTIONS ✍ **The Ethan Allen Homestead** (802-865-4556; ethanallen homestead.org), off Rt. 127 just north of the downtown Burlington waterfront (take the North Avenue Beaches exit off Rt. 127, the Northern Connector). Open May–Oct., Thurs.–Mon. 10–4, closed Tues. and Wed. Vermont's godfather is memorialized here in the timber farmhouse in which he lived out the last years of his turbulent life; he died in 1789. The visitors center offers a film, interesting descriptive and multimedia exhibits, and a gift shop. The setting is a working garden and an extensive park with some 4 miles of walking trails along the Winooski River and wetlands. $7 adults, $5 seniors and Vermont residents, $3 ages 3–6.

ROCK CLIMBING Petra Cliffs (802-657-3872; petracliffs.com), 105 Briggs St., Burlington. Indoor climbing center with mountaineering guide tours. Petra Cliffs operates the programming at the Bolton Adventure Center.

✍ **Northern Lights Climbing** (802-316-3300; northernlightsvt.com), 14 Freeman Woods Rd., Essex Junction. Directly connected to The Essex (see *Resorts*), Northern Lights provides "the outback" experience of the area's premier resort and operates as a stand-alone with outdoor rock and ice climbing walls, zipline tours, geocaching, and a variety of team development programs, camps, and events.

SWIMMING North Beach (802-862-0942; enjoyburlington.com), off North Ave. at 60 Institute Rd., Burlington (turn at Burlington High School), is the city's longest (and most crowded), providing tent and trailer sites, picnic tables, a snack bar and change room, and swimming from a long, sandy beach, late May–mid-Sept.; vehicle charge, pedestrians and bicyclists free. A growing number of lakeside and music events take place throughout the season. **Leddy Park** (802-865-5399; enjoyburlington.com), a more secluded, tree-lined beach with picnic areas, grills, and tables (farther north off North Ave. from North Beach, turn left before the shopping mall onto Leddy Park Rd. and drive to the end). **Oakledge Park** (802-865-7247; enjoyburlington.com), a tiny yet cozy beach with a rocky spit, plus sheltered picnic area and numerous open-air picnic tables with grills, three tennis courts, a two softball fields, volleyball courts, and walking trails. It's located at the southern end of the bike path off Rt. 7, at the end of Flynn Ave. Fee for vehicles; pedestrians and bicyclists free. A trail leads to an extravagant tree house; handicapped accessible. **Red Rocks Park** (802-864-4108; sburlrecdept.com), Central Ave. South Burlington's small but serviceable public beach is valued mostly for its forested hiking trails, with a few picnic tables overlooking the lake. Fee for all users. **Sand Bar State Park** (802-983-2825; vtstateparks.com), in Milton as Rt. 2 heads into the Champlain Islands, offers sandy beach access for swimming and picnic areas, especially good for little kids; fee for all users. **Lake Iroquois** (town.williston.vt.us) south from Williston off Rt. 2 on Pond Rd. in St. George offers a surprisingly pristine lake with family-friendly beach for swimming, fee for all users.

✳ Winter Sports

CROSS-COUNTRY SKIING Northern Vermont Nordic Skiing and Snowshoe, a weatherproofed map detailing cross-country and snowshoeing trails throughout the region, is available at local outlets and from Map Adventures (mapadventures.com).

Bolton Valley (802-434-3444; boltonvalley.com), Bolton. Ranging in elevation from 1,600 to 3,200 feet, this 88 km network is Vermont's highest cross-country system, with snow that usually lasts well into April. About 26 km are machine groomed. There is a wide and gently sloping 1-mile Broadway and a few short trails for beginners, but most of the terrain is backwoods, much of it splendidly high wilderness country. You can take an alpine lift to the peak of Ricker Mountain and ski Old Turnpike, then keep going on cross-country trails for a total of 7 miles. There's a ski school, rentals are available in the cross-country center, and experienced skiers are welcome to stay in the area's high hut, the Bryant cabin, by reservation. Telemarking is a specialty here, along with guided tours. Trail fee.

The legendary 12-mile **Bolton-to-Trapp trail** originates here (this is by far the preferred direction to ski it), but requires spotting a car at the other end or on Moscow Rd. Inquire about the exciting new telemark/backcountry trail beginning at the top of Bolton's Wilderness Chair and meandering down into Little River State Park in Waterbury–Stowe. Again, a car needs to be spotted at the other end.

♲ ♣ Catamount Outdoor Family Center (802-879-6001; catamountoutdoor.com), 421 Governor Chittenden Rd., Williston. The 35 km of groomed trails at this 500-acre nonprofit, family-owned recreation area include a 3 km loop that's lit 5–8:30 for night skiing on select evenings, weather dependent. All of it radiates over rolling terrain, both wooded and open. Geared to families. Guided tours, rentals, instruction, sledding hill, snowshoe trails, and warming hut. Trail fee. A B&B and wedding venue also operates (see *Lodging*).

Sleepy Hollow Inn, Ski & Bike Center (802-434-2283; skisleepyhollow.com), 1805 Sherman Hollow Rd., Huntington. An 870-acre tract offers 35 km of well-groomed cross-country ski trails that weave up to the elevated Butternut Cabin (which can be rented all year) with its gorgeous views of Camels Hump. Another 20 km are good for snowshoeing, and there are rentals, lessons, and a warm-up lodge with accommodations (see *Lodging*). Popular with the locals, Sleepy Hollow also offers night skating on its pond, and skiing on a 2 km loop each Mon., Wed., and Fri.

Note: See *Green Space* for more about local parks with trails that lend themselves to cross-country skiing.

DOWNHILL SKIING AND SNOWBOARDING ♣ Bolton Valley Resort (802-434-3444; 877-926-5866; boltonvalley.com), Bolton. This mountain is smaller and less commercial than the state's better-known ski areas, but has advantages the others lack. For one thing, it has the highest base elevation of any winter resort in Vermont, meaning lots of natural snow. The mini village is cozy and Alpine-like, keeping everything within walking distance. A fitness center furnishes muscle-building (and muscle-soothing) facilities, including a sauna, pool, multiperson Jacuzzi, and more. Seventy trails cover 300 skiable acres, about a third of them geared to intermediate-level skiers, a third to beginners, and a third to experts. At night the lights go on over 10 trails and four lifts, making Bolton the state's largest night-skiing destination. There's something for everyone: snowshoeing, lots of Nordic trails, and three terrain parks with jumps and rails. Since Vermonters Larry Williams and Doug Nedde took over in 2007, some $2.3 million has been invested in snowmaking equipment. Bolton has a woodfired pizzeria, new glades and backcountry trails for the more adventuresome, and a quad chairlift that runs from the base lodge to Vista Mountain's 3,150-foot summit, the most ambitious improvements in 20 years. Set atop a winding, 4-mile road that is blissfully free of the junk-food and chain hotel establishments that plague other ski areas, the spot is refreshingly scenic while still being accessible to Richmond, a 10-minute drive, and to Burlington Airport, some 20 miles away. Prices are another attraction. Lift tickets are considerably lower than in southern Vermont, with plenty of enticements: Saturday-night and early-season ticket deals, plus ski packages that include overnights and breakfast at the resort's ski-in, ski-out hotel. In summer the trails fill with hikers and mountain bikers. Residents of the 200 private condos have the mountain largely to themselves much of the time. The Ponds has become a popular spot for scenic mountaintop weddings. The closest ski resort to Burlington, the area remains an unspoiled natural area teeming with wildlife and terrific alpine views. With its steep access road veering off a lonely stretch of Rt. 2 between Montpelier and Burlington, this is a genuinely self-contained resort whose atmosphere is guaranteed to make you want to stay put for a while.

AT BOLTON VALLEY

Justin Cash

Vertical drop: 1,704 feet.

Trails: 70; 6 lifts: 2 quads, 3 double chairlifts, 1 surface.

Base elevation: 2,100 feet.

Snowmaking: 60%.

Rates: Full-season, half-day, night-skiing, and package ticket options.

♣ Cochran Ski Area (802-434-2479; cochranskiarea.com), 910 Cochran Rd., Richmond. When Mickey and Ginny Cochran bought this hillside farm in 1961, little did they know that in 1998 it would become the nation's first nonprofit ski area and the incubator of Olympic champions. Two generations of Cochrans have joined the U.S. Ski Team; two have won top trophies. What started as a single backyard slope with a 400-foot rope tow has stretched into a good-sized racing mountain with six trails and three

Cochran Ski Area

COCHRAN SKI AREA RACE

lifts, including a rope tow, a T-bar, and a handle lift. This is the state's best children's and instructional spot. Olympic gold medalist Barbara Ann Cochran runs "Ski Tots," teaching parents to instruct their own 3- to 5-year-olds. The lodge serves hot snacks and rents equipment, there's a ski school, and free Lollipop races are held each Sunday; winners receive lollipops. Open Tues. and Thurs. 2:30–5, Fri. 2–8; weekends and school vacation weeks 9–4 (check ahead, as all school vacation weeks are not the same). Full-season family pass $365 if purchased before Dec. 1, $475 thereafter. Day passes $20 adults, $14 students; half days are $14 for adults, $12 for students.

Note: See also Smugglers' Notch Resort in "North of the Notch," "Stowe and Waterbury," and "Sugarbush/Mad River Valley." Five major alpine areas are within easy striking distance of Burlington.

ICE SKATING ✔ **Gordon H. Paquette Arena at Leddy Park** (802-862-8869; enjoyburlington .com), off North Ave., Burlington, offers an Olympic-sized rink with public skating as well as hockey and figure-skating instruction. Snack bar, rentals, skate sales. Check the website or call for the schedule.

✔ **C. Douglas Cairns Arena** (802-658-5577; cairnsarena.com), 600 Swift St., South Burlington, offers public skating, rentals, skate sharpening, and snack bar.

SLEIGH RIDES ✔ **Shelburne Farms** (802-985-8442; shelburnefarm.org) offers rides in 12-passenger sleighs through a 19th-century-esque landscape of sculpted forests and snow-covered fields, with visions of opulent barns in the distance. Daily late Dec.–Jan. 1 (except Christmas), then weekends through Feb. $8 adults, $6 ages 3–17.

✳ Green Space

🐾 ✔ ♿ **Burlington Parks and Recreation** (802-864-0123; enjoyburlington.com). Burlington's lakeside parks are superb. **Oakledge Park** (take Flynn Ave. off Pine St. or Rt. 7) offers swimming and picnicking, and sports a wheelchair-accessible tree house (parking fee, but you can bike or walk in). **Red Rocks Park** just south, occupying the peninsula that divides Burlington from South Burlington (take Queen City Park Rd. off Rt. 7), offers walking and cross-country ski trails as well as a beach. **Ethan Allen Park** (North Ave., past the high school) is a 67-acre preserve, once part of Ethan's farm (near the Homestead) and webbed with trails that climb to the Pinnacle and to a Norman-style stone tower built on Indian Rock in 1905; both high points offer panoramic views of Lake Champlain.

🐾 ✔ **Winooski Valley Park District** (802-863-5744; wvpd.org) consists of 13 parks, one a wetlands, one landlocked, and most maintained as nature preserves. A few contain canoe launches and bike paths. **The Intervale** (entrance on the corner of Riverside Ave. and N. Prospect St.) along the Winooski River offers walking as well as bike trails; it includes the Intervale Community Farm (inter valecommunityfarm.com) and Gardener's Supply (a retail and catalog outlet—gardeners.com). Also along the Winooski: a children's discovery garden, a museum in the 67-acre park around the Ethan Allen Homestead (ethanallenhomestead.org), and walking trails at **Macrea Farm Park** and **Half Moon Cove Park**. **Delta Park** at the mouth of the Winooski River is a magical place with a sandy trail traversing woods to a wetland observation platform. **Centennial Woods** offers nature trails; access is from East Ave.

✔ **Bayside Park** (colchestervt.gov), off Blakely Rd. in Colchester. The site of a 1920s resort, this 22-acre park now offers a playground, beach, shuffleboard and tennis courts, sports facilities, and walking trails. In winter this is also a popular spot for ice fishing, sailboarding, and ice skating.

✔ **Sand Bar State Park** (802-893-2825; vtstateparks.com) is part of the 1,000-acre Sand Bar Wildlife Refuge, a result of tens of thousands of years of sediment washing down from what is now the Lamoille River and most notably known for its sandy beach and water access that without the sandbar would be over 150 feet deep. Swimming and boat rentals.

To the east

🐾 **Underhill State Park** (802-899-3022, vtstateparks.com), on the western edge of 4,300-foot Mount Mansfield, the state's highest peak, lies within the 34,000-acre Mount Mansfield State Forest. Camping mid-May–mid-Oct., a Civilian Conservation Corps log picnic pavilion, and four trails to the summit ridge of Mount Mansfield. It's accessed from the Pleasant Valley Rd. west of Underhill Center.

The Green Mountain Audubon Nature Center (802-434-3068; vt.audubon.org/centers .html), Huntington. (Turn right at Round Church in Richmond; go 5 miles south to Sherman Hollow Rd.) Trails wind through 230 acres of representative habitats (beaver ponds, orchards, and woodlands). Interpretive classes offered. Groups are welcome to watch (and help in) the woodfired sugaring conducted each year. Open all year, but call ahead to confirm.

Rachel Carter

HIKING CAMELS HUMP

❂ 🐾 **Camels Hump State Park** provides access to Vermont's most distinctive and third highest mountain (4,083 feet). It's best accessed from Huntington via East St., then East St. to Camels Hump Rd. Request a free map and permission for primitive camping (at lower elevations) from the Vermont State Parks in Waterbury (802-241-3655; vtstateparks.com). The **Green Mountain Club** (802-244-7037; greenmountainclub.org) at 4711 Waterbury–Stowe Rd. (Rt. 100) in Waterbury Center also has maps and maintains shelters, lodging, and the Hump Brook Tenting Area. The name "Camel's Rump" was used on Ira Allen's map in 1798, but by 1830 it was known as "Camel's Hump." *Note:* All trails and roads within the park are closed during mud season in spring.

To the south

🐾 **LaPlatte River Marsh Natural Area**, Shelburne; parking on Bay Rd. Managed by The Nature Conservancy of Vermont, this 211-acre preserve at the mouth of the LaPlatte River is rich in bird life. It is traversed by an easy trail (45 minutes round-trip).

🐾 **Shelburne Bay Park** (nature.org), Shelburne. (Park on Bay Rd., across from the entrance to the Shelburne Farms Visitor Center.) The Shelburne Recreation Department maintains a blue-blazed trail along the bay through mixed woods.

MOUNT PHILO STATE PARK VIEW

Rachel Carter

Shelburne Farms. Eight miles of easy trails on 1,400 acres landscaped by Frederick Law Olmsted, who designed New York's Central Park. Check in at the visitors center—see *Must See*.

🐾 **H. Lawrence Achilles Natural Area** (nature.org), Shelburne, access off Pond Rd. A short hiking trail leads to Shelburne Pond.

🐾 ✇ **Mount Philo State Park** (802-425-2390; vtstateparks.com), 5425 Mount Philo Rd., Charlotte. Founded in 1924, Vermont's oldest state park has a small, intimate, mountaintop picnic area and campground, with spectacular views of the valley, lake, and Adirondacks. A short but steep ascent off Rt. 7 (not recommended for trailers or large RVs); 10 campsites; admission fee.

✳ Lodging

In Burlington 05401

HOTELS ❂ 🐾 🐕 ♿ **Hotel Vermont** (802-651-0080; hotelvt.com), 41 Cherry St. Burlington's first boutique hotel is resolutely a product of its home state. The modern lobby is crafted from Vermont granite, slate, and reclaimed wood. The 120 rooms and five suites keep up the Green Mountain vibe with flannel robes and Johnson Woolen Mill blankets; local, high-end toiletries; and Vermont books by the bed. Conference rooms are offered for those who work hard. For those playing hard, bikes are provided free of charge for two hours at a time. Yoga, massages, and regular cultural events, including concerts and trivia, are offered on-site. At standout restaurant **Juniper**, chef Douglas Paine serves breakfast, lunch, and dinner, all with local ingredients and eye-pleasing presentations. A sequel to Waterbury's landmark **Hen of the Wood** restaurant is accessible through a separate entry, just to the left of the hotel's lobby. There, chef Eric Warnstedt's crew cooks over a wood fire, ensuring nearly every dish is touched by flame. Reservations should be made well in advance, but there's often room at the bar for creative cocktails, oysters, and high-end ham. Rooms from $199. Entrées $14–29.

🐕 ♿ **Courtyard Burlington Harbor Hotel** (802-864-4700; 800-321-2211; marriott.com), 25 Cherry St. Before there was Hotel Vermont, the same owners greeted guests with this 161-room franchise location. Many rooms are graced with direct views of Lake Champlain and the Adirondacks. Some boast stone-lined walk-in showers. All feature flat-screen TVs and refrigerators, convenient for take-out from so many restaurants. Those might include **Bleu Northeast Seafood**, Burlington's first upscale seafood restaurant. Don't miss the seafood lasagna with uni béchamel or Sunday brunch, featuring a score of different Benedicts. A fitness center, indoor pool, and hot tub are on the ground level; exceptional business center and valet parking also available. Rooms start at $159.

🐕 🐾 🐕 ♿ **Hilton Burlington** (802-658-6500; burlington.hilton.com), 60 Battery St. This link in the big chain features a two-story lobby, room service, and a ballroom and convention center. Half the units boast lake views. Most of the 258 rooms contain the standard two double beds; three family-friendly rooms open onto the indoor pool. There's a fitness center and pool on the second floor with lake views, an attached parking garage, and a free airport shuttle. The lobby-level **Mounted Cat** hosts an outdoor, bike-in/bike-out "catio" with fire pit and pricy

but casual bistro grub such as steak frites. Rates run $149–189 in low season, $189–279 during peak and foliage. Twelve rooms are wheelchair accessible. Pets are welcome at $50 per night.

🐕 🐾 🐕 ♿ **The Sheraton-Burlington** (802-865-6600; 800-325-3535; sheraton.com), 870 Williston Rd. With 309 rooms, this behemoth is a regular destination for conventions and trade shows. It's set on campus-like grounds in South Burlington at the top of the hill by the UVM campus and Fletcher Allen Health Care. Pluses include an indoor pool, fitness center, 10 wheelchair-accessible rooms, conference rooms, free parking, and pet-friendly rooms. **G's Restaurant** serves three meals daily in a four-story atrium filled with plants and lots of natural light. **Tuckaways Pub** offers traditional pub eats. $129–329 per room, depending on season.

BED & BREAKFASTS

In Burlington 05401

Willard Street Inn (802-651-8710; 800-577-8712; willardstreetinn.com), 349 S. Willard St. Burlington's most elegant "green" inn, this 1881 brick mansion built grandly in the upscale hill section (a few blocks from Champlain College) offers 14 guest rooms, all with private bath. Guests enter an elaborate cherry-paneled foyer and are drawn to the many-windowed, palm-filled solarium with its checkered marble floor and baby grand piano. The living room has a hearth, a tiny gift shop, and vintage portraits. Mornings start with coffee in the dining room, followed by a chef-prepared breakfast served in the solarium. Guest rooms are decorated individually and range in size and detailing from

A WARM WELCOME AT HOTEL VERMONT, BURLINGTON

Alice Levitt

spacious master bedrooms and suites to smaller rooms on the third floor. $150–265 includes a full breakfast. Ask about off-season specials. Children 12 and over.

♂ ♂ ⚹ **Lang House on Main Street** (802-652-2500; 877-919-9799; langhouse.com), 360 Main St. There are nine rooms with private bath in this lovely Victorian home done in period and modern furnishings, antiques, and lush fabrics. Common areas include a comfortable living room, a sunroom, and a breakfast area with historic images of Burlington as it looked a century ago. City attractions are within walking distance. $139–289 includes full breakfast. Well-behaved children of all ages welcome, but Willoughby and Biba prefer to be the only pups in-house.

♂ **Howard Street Guest House** (802-864-4668; howardstreetguesthouse.com), 153 Howard St. Two bright, spacious suites in a detached carriage barn surrounded by a patio and flower beds. The one downstairs is colorful and contemporary with an airy, open living area and kitchenette, a queen, and a twin. The upstairs is similar, with skylights and gorgeous wooden floors, furnished with flair. Besides the queen bed, it has a pullout sofa and a "secret" closet cot for Harry Potter fans. No breakfast, though guests can help themselves to the coffee, tea, cereal, and juice. The house is on a quiet street, about a 15-minute walk from the waterfront and Church St. shopping. $170 per night for the first floor, $185 for the second, double occupancy. Two-night minimum.

⚘ **Sunset House** (802-864-3790, sunsethouse bb.com), 78 Main St. Paul and Nancy Boileau are your hosts at this 1854 Queen Anne–style home, a former boardinghouse, just two blocks from the waterfront. The four air-conditioned guest rooms share two baths and are decorated with family antiques; there's a kitchen nook and living room for visitors' use. $139–169 includes continental breakfast.

One of a Kind (802-862-5576; oneofakindbnb .com), 53 Lakeview Terrace. The flower garden of Maggie Sherman's modest 1910 house looks out over a stunning lake panorama. Her second-floor suite has a queen-sized bed, a private bath, and a sunny sitting room with a pantry that is stocked with local, organic foods she provides so you can take breakfast at your leisure. The Carpe Diem Cottage has one bed, a fully equipped kitchen stocked with breakfast foods, and a private bath. Rates are the same for either the suite or the cottage, $180 before tax. Children over 12. Two-night minimum; single-night and off-season rates upon request.

254 South Union Street Guesthouse (802-862-7843; 254southunion.com), 254 S. Union St. An 1887 gabled Queen Anne in an architecturally picturesque neighborhood about four blocks from Church St. with a tastefully furnished guest room and a suite, both with private entrance and bath. The suite, with its queen-sized bed and full-sized pull-out sofa, has a fully equipped kitchen, dining area, and sitting room. The smaller room, which sleeps two in a queen, has a gas fireplace. No breakfast, but owner Cindy Secondi provides snacks and fresh coffee each morning. $155–249.

⚘ **Made Inn Vermont** (802-658-9242; vermontbedandbreakfast.com), 170 Ferguson Ave. From the outside, this is an unassuming colonial home in a residential neighborhood. Inside is all retro-chic luxury, a "green" hotel with soaring ceilings and modern amenities. The three rooms are filled with an ever-changing assemblage of vintage toys, games, and musical instruments, but each room always has a chalkboard and colored chalk for late-night artistic inspiration. Lounging areas include a living room, outdoor pool, and breakfast nook. Rates starting at $225 including a continental breakfast.

Beyond Burlington
RESORTS ♂ ⚹ ♂ ⚹ **The Essex, Vermont's Culinary Resort & Spa** (802-878-1100; 800-727-4295; essexresortspa.com), 70 Essex Way, Essex 05452. Set on 18 acres in a suburban area 10 miles northeast of downtown Burlington, this contemporary, neo-Colonial complex has grown into the largest resort and spa this side of Stowe, and the only one with such a dedicated commitment to the culinary experience. A former partner with the New England Culinary Institute, the resort now operates as its own entity with multiple cooking classes and program at the Cook Academy. Restaurants include a tavern and the sophisticated Junction, a contemporary restaurant with an open kitchen and a creative prix fixe menu. Accommodations in the 120 rooms include spa or deluxe suites and fireplace rooms. Rooms range $179–319 per night; a $15 resort fee covers shuttles, unlimited coffee/tea in the lobby, multiple newspapers, spa access, and parking. Children of all ages are welcome, as are pets (additional fee).

Besides the first-rate food and lodging, the complex boasts conference and wedding facilities, a 22,000-square-foot, full-service spa with salon, 10 treatment rooms, indoor pool, saunas, steam rooms, outdoor hot tub, lounges, and a fitness center. The grounds include an 18-hole golf course, outdoor heated pool, hiking trails,

The Essex

THE ESSEX LAWN

bicycle rentals, snowshoeing, gardens, and hot-air balloon rides. Fly-fishing enthusiasts will appreciate its on-site casting pond with guides and instruction. Rock and ice climbing as well as ziplines can be found at Northern Lights Rock & Ice (see *Rock Climbing*). The resort also offers Vermont Tennis Vacations with accommodation packages. Additional amenities include a game room, gift shop, and library. The extensive Essex Shoppes & Cinema (see *Selective Shopping*) is right around the corner. Inquire about activity packages.

♂ ♂ **Bolton Valley Resort** (802-434-3444; 877-9-BOLTON; boltonvalley.com), Bolton 05477. A high mountain valley with a cluster of shops, condominiums, and an indoor sports center, this resort comprises 5,000 wooded acres that abound with birds and wildlife. In winter it's snow-minded with slope-side lodging and night skiing; in summer the focus is on hiking. Facilities include a five-floor, 60-room hotel, 20 suites, and condominium rentals. Some rooms come with fireplace and kitchenette; most have kings or multiple doubles and balconies with mountain views. The sports center houses an exercise room, pool, tennis courts, game room, and snack bar. The Ponds wedding facility overlooks the water as promised, as well as the Green Mountains. Rooms range $95–289 with continental breakfast; condos higher, depending on size.

INNS ♂ ♂ **Inn at Shelburne Farms** (802-985-8498; shelburnefarms.org), Shelburne 05482. Open mid-May–mid-Oct. Guests are treated to a peerless taste of Edwardian grandeur in this 100-room, Queen Anne–style mansion built by William Seward Webb and Lila Vanderbilt Webb on a spectacular bluff overlooking Lake Champlain. Completed in 1899,

the house is the centerpiece of a 1,400-acre estate (see *Must See*). Perhaps because its transition from mansion to inn in 1987 entailed a $1.6 million restoration but no sale (the Webb family has turned the estate into a nonprofit environmental education organization), there is a rare sense of a time as well as place here. Turn-of-the-20th-century furnishings predominate. Play billiards in the richly paneled game room, leaf through one of the 6,000 leather-bound books, or play the piano in the library. There's also an elegant tearoom (ask about the inn's special Tea Tours); the Marble Dining Room, a formal dining room with silk damask wall coverings, a marble floor; and long windows overlooking the formal gardens and lake. Don't miss the third-floor playroom, with its dollhouses.

Guest rooms vary in size and elegance—from the second-floor master bedroom to servants' quarters to the two secluded cottages and three-bedroom house—which means room prices also vary. Guests have access to tennis, boating, sumptuous gardens, and miles of splendid walking trails. Rates for the 24 individualized bedrooms (17 with private baths) run $155–480. There is a two-night minimum stay on weekends. Breakfast and dinner are extra, and memorable.

♂ ♣ ♂ ♿ **Sleepy Hollow Inn, Ski & Bike Center** (802-434-2283; skisleepyhollow.com), 427 Ski Lodge Dr., Huntington 05462. This family-owned lodge is the eco-friendly choice: It's heated with solar energy. The house is built on 870 private acres deep in the forest off a dirt road between Richmond and Hinesburg. Six of the eight guest rooms have a private bath, and most have a queen-sized bed; two are equipped

COOK ACADEMY AT THE ESSEX

The Essex

with two twins, one with four. There is a two-room suite, and a wheelchair-accessible unit with a wide shower, a full-sized Murphy bed, two twins, and a working fireplace. Common areas include two spacious living rooms with throbbing woodstoves, one upstairs, one down, and the fresh, hot breakfasts are served family-style featuring family-made maple syrup. A 17-sided event center and attached pavilion, built in 2006 to resemble Richmond's pictur-esque Old Round Church, can be rented for weddings. A woodfired sauna hut sits at the edge of a garden pond that ices over for skating in winter. Biking and ski trails lead through meadows and woods to views of Camels Hump (see *Biking* and *Cross-Country Skiing*). Closer to home you can wander the 35,000-volume Sleepy Hollow Books in the event center's base-ment, which specializes in used tomes on New England, Vermont, and railroads. The adven-turesome might choose to trek the mile uphill to the Butternut Cabin, a woodstove-heated cabin with mountain views that sleeps eight (no electricity or running water). $50 per night in summer, $100 in winter (for four), includes fire-wood and trail passes. Lodge rooms run $135–155, including breakfast.

BED & BREAKFASTS 🐾 ✑ ♿ **Barnhouse B&B** (802-985-3258; urpampered.com), 9 McDonald Farm Rd., Shelburne 05482. This 100-year-old dairy barn (on what was old McDonald's farm!) is now a light-filled haven of exposed beams, gardens, and in- and outdoor sitting areas. The wheelchair-accessible Water Garden Room has a queen bed and opens onto a private water-fountain garden that used to be the silo. A circular stairway leads to the Balcony Hayloft Suite (good for families) with a queen on one end, two twins on the other, a private bath, and an open balcony with a hanging chair under a skylight. Both rooms contain air filters, magnetic mattress pads, filtered water, and a free magnetic (hands-free) back massage. A hot homemade breakfast is included in rates that range $125–175.

🐾 🐾 ✑ **Homeplace B&B** (802-899-4694, homeplacebandb.com), 90 Old Pump Rd., Essex 05452. This intriguing, H-shaped house is secluded in a 100-acre wood at the end of a half-mile driveway. The interior is a maze of hidden nooks and corners filled with scholarly books and European antiques. There's a big, secluded swimming pond in the rear, a duck pond in the front, a screened-in terrace with bucolic views, and a bevy of animals: chickens, horses, sheep, dogs, a donkey, and a cat. The plant-filled living room is artful and eclectically furnished with marble floors, a wood-burning

fireplace, walls of books, and interesting knick-knacks. There are six guest rooms, four with pri-vate bath. Innkeeper Mariot Huessy serves up eggs from the hens for breakfast served in the hexagonal barn. $115 single, $125 double, including breakfast. Children and pets welcome; $25 for extra person and per pet, by prearrangement.

♂ 🐾 **Hidden Gardens B&B** (802-482-2118; thehiddengardens.com), 693 Lewis Creek Rd., Hinesburg 05461. This post-and-beam house is surrounded by 250 acres of land trust forest and bordered with gardens that cascade down the side of a hill to a trout-stocked pond and con-tinue the length of a small field. A sunken gar-den by the house is filled with water lilies, orchids, and large, exotic blossoms, and the grounds are laced with waterfalls, trails, and Japanese-like micro gardens. The two guest rooms, one a double and one a king, feature ele-gant linens and share a bath. Rates run $90–160 and include a sumptuous breakfast. The com-mon rooms are spacious and sunny with vaulted ceilings, fine art, a granite-countered kitchen, and a bevy of Labrador retrievers. Guests can build a bonfire by the pond, fish, swim, stay in the rustic pondside cabin, or hike wooded trails. Children over 8 welcome.

♿ **Heart of the Village Inn** (802-985-9060; 866-985-9060; heartofthevillage.com), 5347 Shelburne Rd., Shelburne 05482. A handsome 1886 home that's truly in the heart of town. All nine guest rooms have a private bath and new flat-screen TV. The most deluxe are in the car-riage house: the two-room honeymoon or Webb Suite, for example, has two skylights, sofas, and a two-person whirlpool bath. The Barstow Room has wheelchair access. Rates are $150–250, with breakfast and afternoon refreshments included.

✑ ♿ **Sinclair Inn Bed & Breakfast** (802-899-2234; 800-433-4658, sinclairinnbb.com), 389 Rt. 15, Jericho. This fully restored 1890 Queen Anne "painted lady" is located in a village set-ting within easy driving distance of Richmond and Burlington. Six guest rooms each have pri-vate bath, and one is fully handicapped accessi-ble. The lawns overflow with perennials and water lilies. $139–179 per couple includes a full breakfast, complimentary beverages, and after-noon treats.

♂ 🐾 ✑ **The Richmond Victorian Inn** (802-434-4410; 888-242-3362; richmondvictorianinn .com), 191 E. Main St., Richmond 05477. This classy house has five comfortable guest rooms, all with private bath, individually decorated with antiques, and equipped with down comforters, bathrobes, and good reading lights. Children over 6 welcome. Scottish-born Frank Stewart, a former chef and caterer, runs the place with his American wife, Joyce, serving up fresh homemade breads each morning, private dinner parties (advance reservations required), and, on Sunday 2–5, a three-course afternoon cream tea. $139–189 for a double includes a full gourmet breakfast.

❧ **Elliot House** (802-985-2727; 800-860-4405; elliothouse.com), 5779 Dorset St., Shelburne. This updated 1865 Greek Revival farmhouse adjoins 400 acres of Nature Conservancy land with hiking and cross-country ski trails and mountain views both east and west. All three graciously furnished guest rooms have a private bath. Common areas include a library and sitting room with piano. Guests can wander the extensive perennial gardens, relax on the patio, or take a dip in the secluded swimming pool. Rates are $120 per night, with homemade breakfast.

❧ **Inn at Charlotte** (802-425-2934; innat charlotte.com), 32 State Park Rd., Charlotte 05445. This contemporary home on the Rt. 7 turnoff to Mount Philo has four rooms, all with bath, private entrance, and TV. Two have king-sized beds and cathedral ceilings and open out onto an oval pool. There are tennis courts, a basketball net, and leather-sofa-filled common areas; breakfast is served family-style. $130–195 includes full breakfast.

♂ ☻ ❧ **Windekind Farm** (802-434-4455; windekindfarms.com), 1425 Bert White Rd., Huntington 05462. Hidden away in a 160-acre upland valley that's seen little development since it was last farmed around 1935, this expansive spot offers sweeping views and total quiet save the gurgling of a brook. Camels Hump State Park spreads for miles, providing space for an extensive network of upland trails. Mark Smith and his Dutch-born wife, Marijke, live in a restored farmhouse and accommodate guests in a flock of contemporary cottages. The Studio is an upstairs apartment with mountain views, and the Breidaclick Cottage is a converted post-and-beam blacksmith shop. Outside are numerous gardens and ponds, plus ducks, heifers, friendly dogs, endless hiking and cross-country skiing potential, and Mark's shop, where he builds historically accurate miniature steam locomotives that haul firewood, curious adults, and ecstatic children. The grounds are ideal for weddings and tented receptions. Rates range from $170 for the Studio, to $325 for the Campanula building, which sleeps six. Children and pets welcome.

♂ ☙ ❧ **Catamount Bed & Breakfast** (802-878-6001; catamountoutdoor.com), 592

Governor Chittenden Rd., Williston 05495. Built in 1796 by Thomas Chittenden, the state's first governor, this historic brick Federal has been in Lucy and Jim McCullough's family since 1873. Its antique furnishings, including 6-foot carved headboards and sepia photographs, are original to the house. Two guest rooms share a bath, and a suite has private bath and sitting room. $110–145, double occupancy, includes breakfast. Can be rented in entirety for weddings.

ADDITIONAL LODGING Numerous hotels, motor inns, and extended-stay suites are sprinkled throughout the area, but beware: Most are on the seedy side. These are options where you can stay without fear. On Rt. 2: **Best Western Windjammer Inn & Conference Center** (802-863-1125; 800-371-1125; bestwestern.com /windjammerinn) with steaks and a massive salad bar at both **The Windjammer** and **The Upper Deck Pub**, and the **Doubletree Hotel** (802-658-0250; burlington.doubletree.com) with on-site restaurant **Trader Duke's**—a great value. Rt. 7 in Colchester is the **Hampton Inn and Conference Center** (802-655-6177; 800-HAMPTON, hamptoninnburlington.com). The Burlington area is also exceptionally well populated with airbnb.com properties at reasonable prices.

CAMPING ❧ **North Beach Campground** (802-862-0942; 802-864-0123; enjoyburlington .com/campground.cfm), 60 Institute Rd., Burlington, has 137 shaded campsites for tents or RVs within 45 wooded acres a few minutes' walk from Burlington's largest sandy beach, with its snack bar, change rooms, and grill-equipped picnic tables. Open May 1–Columbus Day.

Note: See **Underhill State Park**, **Camel's Hump State Park**, and **Mount Philo State Park** at vtstateparks.com. Also **Maple Wind Farm** (maplewindfarm.com) for yurt rentals in Huntington.

✳ Where to Eat

Note: Burlington has the best restaurant scene between Boston and Montreal, though many of the choicest tables are out of the downtown area. Reservations are essential everywhere when dining in downtown Burlington. If reservations are not accepted, we suggest going early or after 8 PM.

DINING OUT Bluebird Tavern (802-540-1786; bluebirdvermont.com), 86 St. Paul St., Burlington. Open daily for dinner and late night. Reservations essential. What began in 2009 as an upscale place for a craft burger is now one of downtown's fine-dining destinations. There are still gloriously greasy local burgers, but today the menu is more focused on beautifully plated, creative takes on seafood and seasonal Vermont produce. Entrées $14–27.

& **Inn at Shelburne Farms** (802-985-8498; shelburnefarms.org), Shelburne. Open for daily breakfast and dinner, as well as Sun. brunch by reservation mid-May–late Oct. This turn-of-the-20th-century manor offers imaginative cuisine using ingredients grown at Shelburne Farms. The stunning view of the sun setting over Lake Champlain and the Adirondacks competes with walls covered in fin-de-siècle silk damask from Spain and a black-and-white marble floor. You might begin with a salad of market veggies or a homemade butcher board; entrées $27–31. Brunch is also an event and requires a reservation weeks in advance. Inquire about prix fixe Sunday suppers.

❂ & **The Kitchen Table Bistro** (802-434-8686; thekitchentablebistro.com), 1840 W. Main St., Richmond. Dinner Tues.–Sat. Steve and Lara Atkins operate this superlative bistro in a brick-walled home that once belonged to Vermont's first governor. They've been nominated for several James Beard Foundation awards, both together and separately. Steve's pastas are always worth the carb splurge, though meat dishes, such as mustard-crusted pork, are not to be missed. Lara's open-faced coffee-chocolate sundae with candied almonds is a signature, but look for her seasonal fruit ice creams and sorbets.

& **Leunig's Bistro** (802-863-3759; leunigs bistro.com), 115 Church St., Burlington. Open weekdays for lunch, dinner nightly, brunch on weekends. In classic bistro style, Leunig's has dark wood, gleaming coffee machines, romantic lighting, a full bar, and streetside tables for people-watching, all of which makes it Church Street's most popular establishment. Entrées $21–35 featuring Vermont twists on Gallic bistro fare. Not in the mood for a full meal? Head to the art deco upstairs lounge. Frequent live entertainment.

A Single Pebble (802-865-5200; asinglepebble .com), 133 Bank St., Burlington. Open nightly for dinner, weekdays for lunch; also dim sum Sundays. No fried rice, egg rolls, or MSG here. Instead you get Chop Your Head Off Soup, for example, a savory blend of ground pork, shredded cabbage, and rice cakes, or Ants Climbing a Tree, a smoky-tasting blend of cellophane noodles, ground pork, black mushrooms, scallions, and tree ear fungus. All is served on china placed on a lazy Susan to encourage sharing.

There are numerous small dishes to choose from, like dumplings and mock eel. Entrées $16–24. Reservations essential.

❂ Trattoria Delia (802-864-5253; trattoria delia.com), 152 St. Paul St., Burlington. Open nightly 5–10, reservations essential. Exposed wooden beams, a roaring fire, and Italian pottery make this one of Burlington's most romantic restaurants. Entrées range $16.50–24 for housemade pasta and $22.50–36.50 for proteins. Designer Karl Lagerfeld is a fan of the beef tenderloin in Barbera wine and white truffle butter. An excellent selection of digestivi and dolce to follow.

EATING OUT *Note:* Thanks to Burlington's huge student population and insatiable hunger for novel cuisine, the restaurant scene is a highly varied, ever-expanding thing. Stroll up and down Church St. for an eyeful of the many options or check out the restaurant listings on Burlington-based alternative weekly *Seven Days'* website (sevendaysvt.com).

In Burlington

🐾 & **The Farmhouse Tap & Grill** (802-859-0888; farmhousetg.com), 160 Bank St. How much do Burlingtonians love their local food? The only trace of a McDonald's downtown is this temple to homegrown burgers and brews—located on the former site of the Golden Arches. Besides the main dining room and bar, there's a basement lounge and outdoor biergarten. Any of which is fitting for a charcuterie plate, house-dry-aged burger or a cult beer from near or far. The same owners keep the farm-to-table aesthetic at the forefront just down the street at **El Cortijo Taqueria Y Cantina** (802-497-1668; cortijovt.com; 189 Bank St.), in a shiny metal diner car. Go early for both—first

DIM SUM AT A SINGLE PEBBLE, BURLINGTON
Alice Levitt

come, first served, as reservations are not accepted.

🍴 **Duino Duende** (802-660-9346; duino duende.com), 10 N. Winooski Ave. Between its sister properties, Radio Bean (see *Coffeehouses*) and Light Club Lamp Shop, this bohemian eatery blends the eclectic sounds of Radio Bean with the smells of international street food. Dishes globe hop from Belgium to Nepal, El Salvador to Korea, but the best dish is the all-American fried-chicken-and-waffles. Entrées run $9–15; lunch and dinner served daily. Open late.

🍴 ♿ **American Flatbread, Burlington Hearth** (802-861-2999; americanflatbread .com), 115 St. Paul St. Open daily for dinner; Mon.–Fri. lunch; Sat.–Sun. brunch. In the dead of winter, the woodfired oven radiates heat. The mostly organic pizzas are made to order and ideal for pairing with the in-house brews on tap. The weekend brunch eggs Benedict pizza is deservedly legendary. No reservations, so plan to wait or go early.

🍴 ♿ **August First Bakery & Café** (802-540-0060; augustfirstvt.com), 149 S. Champlain St. Open Mon.–Sat. for breakfast and dinner. Touring Burlington, you may see a youth delivering slow-leavened artisan bread on a bike. This spacious bakery is the source. For baked goods, head into the Main Street entrance for quick service. In the mood for a panini, soup, or salad made from local ingredients? Relax at the South Champlain café space next door without your computer. August First's screen-free policy has gotten it international press.

✪ 🍴 ♿ **Bluebird Barbecue** (802-448-3070; bluebirdbbq.com), 317 Riverside Ave. Open daily for dinner. The massive trays of regional barbecue served here are worth a trip off the beaten path to this road that connects Burlington to Winooski. You could settle for a plate of smoked tacos or ribs, but we recommend trying a little bit of everything with a family-style combo.

✪ 🍴 ♿ **Pascolo Ristorante** (802-862-9010; pascolovt.com), 83 Church St. Open for lunch and dinner daily. People watch on the pedestrian mall or descend into the brick-and-cork-bedecked basement for Italian classics handmade from Vermont ingredients. Watch a chef create the pasta from scratch before slurping up your pappardelle con funghi or tagliatelle Bolognese. Pizzas are woodfired and topped with local takes on Italian meats and cheeses.

✪ 🍴 **Pizzeria Verita** (802-489-5644; liveat nectars.com), 1156 St. Paul St. Diners at Burlington's only destination for authentic Neapolitan pizza sit among piles of split logs that power the 900-degree pizza oven. What emerges is chewy, soft, and covered in housemade mozzarella. From there, choose toppings such as fire-roasted corn and speck or fig and Gorgonzola. The salads and creative cocktails are as winning as the pies, but save room for ricotta-and-Nutella-filled dessert pizza, too.

🍴 🍴 ♿ **The Vermont Pub and Brewery** (802-865-0500; vermontbrewery.com), 144 College St. Open daily for lunch, dinner, and late night. Despite the modern building, there's an old beer-hall feel at this pub specializing in ales and lagers brewed on the premises. The menu isn't gourmet, but includes American bar standards as well as Brit favorites such as toad in the hole, and bangers and mash.

Penny Cluse Cafe (802-651-8834; pennycluse .com), 169 Cherry St. Open daily for breakfast and lunch. This breakfast spot is known as much for its long lines as its southwestern-tinged food. The flavorful Vermont ingredients make even an egg-and-cheese sandwich an event here, though picante egg dishes including huevos rancheros are the hallmark. Can't wait? Try sister restaurant **Lucky Next Door** (802-399-2121), which serves pressed sandwiches and salads for three meals daily.

♿ **Mirabelles** (802-658-3074; mirabellescafe .com), 198 Main St. A delightful bakery that serves eclectic, international breakfast and lunch daily. The mouthwatering Euro-style pastries are pricy, but worth every indulgent penny.

On the waterfront

✪ ♿ **San Sai Japanese Restaurant** (802-862-2777, sansaivt.com), 112 Lake St., Burlington. Open daily for lunch and dinner. Owners Kazutoshi Maeda and Chris Russo made a name for themselves with Tsuki in NYC. Uncommon sushi such as salmon tartare in carrot sauce or fluke with yuzu and tea salt is served in an appropriately austere setting complete with flower-filled alcove. The $35 chef's choice comprises four memorable courses of cooked specialties and sushi before a dessert of green tea ice cream.

🍴 **Shanty on the Shore** (802-864-0238; shanty ontheshore.com), 181 Battery St. Open daily for lunch and dinner for fish fry that's handy to the ferry. The building was once the home and general store of Isaac Nye, the 19th-century "Hermit of Burlington." Children's menu.

♂ ♿ **The Skinny Pancake** (802-540-0188; skinnypancake.com), 60 Lake St., at College St. Known as much as a music venue as a casual crêperie, this restaurant also has locations in Montpelier and the Burlington airport. Sweet and savory crêpes ranging $5–13 as well as burgers and salads. Fondue in winter.

In Winooski

♿ **Sneakers Bistro & Café** (802-655-9081; sneakersbistro.com), 28 Main St. Open daily 7–3. Big, heavy breakfasts such as a range of Benedicts and Kahlúa-dipped French toast have attracted lines down the block for decades.

Misery Loves Co. (802-497-3989; miseryloves covt.com.com), 46 Main St. Open Tues.–Sat. for lunch and dinner; Sun. brunch. This former food truck made its name with its nap-inducingly heavy sandwiches and burgers. They're still served at lunchtime, but dinner is seriously innovative, with groundbreaking platings of seafood and local veggies that earned the co-chefs James Beard Foundation award recognition. Their bakery, across the street at 25 Winooski Falls Way (802-497-1337), serves Stumptown Coffee Roasters brews and creative pastry daily. Try a loaf of levain, made from spent grain used in the beer at nearby Four Quarters Brewing.

♿ **Mule Bar** (802-399-2020; mulebarvt.com), 36 Main St. Open daily 3 PM–1 AM. This craft beer and comfort food establishment is almost always busy, but worth braving the crowds. Sit at a high table or outside for charcuterie and cheese, homemade pasta, or a burger. The funky 16-tap list changes constantly, but is always packed with surprises from Vermont and farther afield.

♂ ♿ **Our House Bistro** (802-497-1884; our housebistro.com), 28 Main St. Open daily for dinner. Weekday lunch is replaced by a popular brunch on the weekend. The stuffed Dutch pancakes here give Sneakers' brunch a run for its money. At dinner, signature "twisted comfort food" includes an eclectic mac-and-cheese menu. (Surf-and-turf mac! Peanut-butter-and-jelly mac!) Meatloaf and fries are served in miniature fryer baskets.

❂ ❀ **Dharshan Namaste Asian Deli** (802-654-8000), 212 Main St. Open daily for lunch and dinner. A Nepalese and Vietnamese couple fuse their native cuisines at this homey little restaurant. Dumplings and uncommonly flavored versions of Vietnamese bun and Nepalese chow mein fill the menu, but come for the sweet-and-hot, cilantro-laden fried chicken wings.

Along Williston Road (Route 2)

♂ ♿ **Al's French Frys** (802-862-9203; als frenchfrys.com), 1251 Williston Rd., South Burlington. Open daily for lunch, dinner, and late night. This 1944-vintage house of grease boasts an America's Classics award from the James Beard Foundation. In-season, try the black raspberry or mint creemees. Cash only.

❂ ♂ **The Bagel Place** (802-497-2050; the bagelplacevt.com), 1166 Williston Rd., South Burlington. The bagel sandwiches here are served in a café surrounded by reclaimed wood from vintage Vermont barns. Try the perfectly balanced Italian sandwich, or a Caprese, filled with fresh mozzarella, tomato, basil, and prosciutto. For dessert, try the marzipan bagel.

♂ ♿ **Wooden Spoon Bistro** (802-399-2074; woodenspoonbistro.com), 1210 Williston Rd., South Burlington. Chef Adam Raftery trained in the Virgin Islands, and his flavors hark back to the tropics as well as his Vermont upbringing. Casual tacos and wings share menu space with upscale steak and seafood. It's a great way to choose your own culinary adventure before a show steps away at Higher Ground (see *Entertainment*).

❂ ♂ **Parkway Diner** (802-652-1155), 1696 Williston Rd., South Burlington. Open daily breakfast and lunch. The Worcester Lunch Car might be of a 1950s vintage, but the food here isn't. Barbecue seitan and quirky specials such as fried pork on a cheddar biscuit with chipotle Hollandaise share menu space with a Platonically ideal hot turkey sandwich, made from a freshly roasted bird each day.

In Essex

❂ ❀ ♂ ♿ **Café Mediterano** (802-878-9333; cafemediterano.com), 17 Park St. Open Tues.–Sat for lunch and dinner. Gyros, falafel, and baklava join Bosnian owner Barney Crnalic's Old Country street food at this modern café. Sip a European coffee or Stella Artois with garlicky cevapi sausages or soft-and-flaky spinach pies called burek.

❀ ♂ ♿ **Firebird Café** (802-316-4265; the firebirdcafe.com), 163 Pearl St. Open daily for breakfast and lunch. California boy Jake Tran imports the burritos and breakfast he enjoyed as a kid to Vermont. Breakfast and lunch are both served all day, so you can order a smoked salmon eggs Benedict with poblano cream sauce alongside a kicking pork carnitas burrito in tangy salsa verde.

❂ ♂ ♿ **Sukho Thai Restaurant** (802-878-2788l; sukhothaiessex.com), 21 Essex Way. Open Wed.–Sun. for lunch and dinner. Vermont-born chef-owner Seth Giffin spent his Culinary Institute of America externship cooking for no less than the royal family of Thailand. His cuisine mixes dishes familiar to Americans

Alice Levitt
CROISSANT FRENCH TOAST AT FIREBIRD CAFÉ, ESSEX JUNCTION

such as pad Thai and fried rice with authentic stews, soups, and fish dishes.

In Richmond
Sonoma Station (802-434-5949; sonomastation .com), 13 Jolin Court (off Bridge St.). Open for dinner Wed.–Sat. Reservations suggested. Chef-owner Monica Lamay fuses Vermont, California, and France together in this casual, pine-floored country bistro housed in a vintage-1854 feed store. You might begin with the crab-and-avocado napoleon with cilantro vinaigrette, then dine on lavender black pepper crusted ahi tuna.

♪ ⚅ **Parkside Kitchen** (802-434-7787; onthe risebakery.net), 39 Esplanade St. (corner of Bridge St.). The owners of the Kitchen Table Bistro remade the former On the Rise Bakery as a more casual version of their from-scratch locavore kitchen. There's wood-roasted mac-and-cheese, southern fried chicken, and flatbread on the savory side. But don't leave without trying a chocolate-potato doughnut or apple fritter.

In Hinesburg
♪ ⚅ **Bristol Bakery** (802-482-6050; bristol bakery.com), 16 Main St. Open daily for breakfast and lunch. Dinner every day but Sun. Bagels, croissants, and other baked goods are this spot's raison d'être, but savory specialties include fresh, local salads; tacos; and huevos rancheros.

♪ ⚅ **Hinesburgh Public House** (802-482-5500; hinesburghpublichouse.com), 10516 Rt. 116. That's not a typo: The extra *h* in this restaurant's moniker is a reminder of a time in history when the town did indeed spell its name that way. But the only thing old-fashioned about

this community-supported eatery is its menu of foods sourced from the town's own farms. Chicken-corn chowder uses Vermont Smoke & Cure bacon produced out back, while burgers are served from buns produced by a tiny local bakery.

On Shelburne Road (Route 7)
✪ ♪ ⚅ **Tilt Classic Arcade & Ale House** (802-489-5350; tiltvt.com), 7 Fayette Dr., South Burlington. Open daily for dinner and late night. This grown-up arcade sports vintage pinball and video games, but even if you aren't a player, the organically driven, GMO-free menu makes this one of Vermont's most accessible gastropubs. The 24-tap line includes hip beer and cider from around the country. The basic burger is made with local beef, Shelburne Farms cheddar, a beer-battered onion ring, and garlic confit aioli.

In Shelburne
✪ ♪ **Rustic Roots** (802-985-9511; rusticrootsvt .com), 195 Falls Rd. Breakfast and lunch Wed.–Sat., dinner Friday and Saturday. Named *Seven Days* newspaper's best new restaurant in Vermont in 2013. Everything is made from scratch here, including breads, condiments, and cured meats. The French-inflected menu changes with the seasons, but the Rustic Breakfast—two eggs, coffee-maple sausage, fennel-rubbed Canadian bacon, and a buttery popover—is a staple worth many a return visit.

In Williston
⚅ **Chef's Corner Café Bakery** (802-878-5524; chefscornervt.com), Rt. 2A just north of Rt. 2 intersection. Gourmet chef-inspired salads and sandwiches as well as breakfast seven days a week. The South African chef-owner knows his way around European-style pastries. There's also a location in Burlington's South End (802-660-7111, 208 Flynn Ave.).

TILT CLASSIC ARCADE & ALE HOUSE, SOUTH BURLINGTON
Alice Levitt

✪ 🍴 ✎ ♿ **Sushido** (802-288-8052), 19 Taft Corners. Open daily for lunch and dinner; Sunday is dinner only. This homestyle Japanese hole-in-the-wall replaces fancy atmosphere with Japanese game shows on TV. Service is super fast, so you'll get your pork katsu curry, udon beef soup, or sushi dinner in mere minutes. There are Japanese groceries, too, should you need to scratch your Pocky itch.

TEAROOM Dobra Tea (802-951-2424; dobratea.com), 80 Church St. (entrance on Bank St.), Burlington. Open 11–11 daily. The first North American branch of what started as a Czech teahouse chain, this temple to tea connoisseurs offers more than 100 varieties from around the globe, all served as they would be in their homeland. Each pot is freshly brewed at the precise temperature and time required. In the back you can shed your shoes and lounge on pillows, the way a tea drinker would in Uzbekistan.

COFFEEHOUSES Muddy Waters (802-658-0466), 184 Main St., just up from Church St., Burlington, open every day, all day. Excellent coffee, homemade desserts, vegan specials, smoothies, beer, and wine by the glass in a dimly lit, brick-walled den with sofas, lots of reading material, and earnest conversation. Bring a book or project—this is the spot for the artistic crowd. Sometimes there is live jazz.

Uncommon Grounds (802-865-6227; ug vermont.com), 42 Church St., Burlington. They roast their own here, offering a large selection, along with teas and Italian-syrup-based drinks. Down a piece of chocolate cake while perusing the day's papers, which are laid out on wooden holders. Outdoor seating in summer.

Maglianero Café (802-861-3155; blog .maglianero.com), 47 Maple St., Burlington. The direct-sourced coffees and teas attract professionals and hipsters alike. So do the excellent pastries and ice creams available at the counter. In summer, food trucks park out front, making Maglianero a one-stop shop for lunch, dessert, and a dose of caffeine.

Speeder and Earl's (speederandearls.com). A slim counter and coffee bar downstairs at 104 Church St. (802-860-6630), and a zany shop at 412 Pine St. (802-658-6016), both in Burlington. Both are open daily. The roastery's fun, flavored beans include Black Forest chocolate and maple French roast varieties.

Radio Bean (802-660-9346; radiobean.com), 8 N. Winooski Ave., Burlington. This Bohemian coffeehouse doubles as the best place for unplugged music acts, including frequent stops by Burlington's better-known musicians. Multiple shows each day mean cocktails replace coffee well into the night. Head two stores over to Light Club Lamp Shop for dessert and yet more tunes.

✴ Entertainment

Note: For current arts and entertainment in Burlington, check the websites of **Burlington City Arts** (burlingtoncityarts.org) and *Seven Days* (sevendaysvt.com), the latter of which is the alternative newsweekly that's available free at most area businesses. Also see *Special Events* at the end of this chapter.

MUSIC ♪ **Vermont Symphony Orchestra** (802-864-5741; 800-VSO-9293; vso.org), based in Burlington. One of the country's first statewide philharmonics presents a concert series at venues including the Flynn Center (see *Theater*) and Shelburne Farms (see *Must Do*), as well as children's music series, outreach programs, residencies, and choral and chamber concerts throughout the year.

Burlington Choral Society (802-878-5919; bcsvermont.org). This volunteer, 100-voice choir presents several concerts a year.

The Discover Jazz Festival (802-863-7992; discoverjazz.com), Burlington, 10 days in early June, a jazz extravaganza that fills city parks, clubs, restaurants, ferries. Ticketed shows and free open-air events.

THEATER Flynn Center for the Performing Arts (802-86-FLYNN; flynncenter.org), 153 Main St., Burlington. The city's prime stage for music and live performance is a refurbished art deco movie house, now home to regional, national, and international plays, musical comedies, concerts, dance troupes, and lectures. Constantly evolving, it houses the Amy Tarrant Art Gallery and is the home of Burlington's **Lyric Theatre Company** (lyrictheatrevt.org). Next door and down the stairs, the FlynnSpace black box hosts professional **Vermont Stage Company** (vtstage.org)—known for contemporary and original works—as well as the excellent **Flynn Arts Summer Youth Theater**, which performs two shows each summer.

Royall Tyler Theatre (802-656-2094; uvm theatre.org), 116 University Place, on the University of Vermont campus, Burlington, stages a seasonal repertory of classic and contemporary plays.

Main Street Landing Performing Arts Center (802-864-7999; mainstreetlanding.com), 60 Lake St., Burlington. A nonprofit, independently run complex that acts as a forum for local production groups. The neo-Victorian brick complex facing the waterfront houses a 130-seat theater and a film presentation room; a crêperie, The Skinny Pancake (see *Eating Out*), operates downstairs.

Saint Michael's Playhouse (802-654-2281; saintmichaelsplayhouse.org), at St. Michael's College, Colchester, presents four Equity theater performances each summer. The college theater department also puts on a show each spring and fall (smcvt.edu).

Lane Series (802-656-4455; uvm.edu/lane series) sponsors major musical and theatrical performances around Burlington fall through spring.

DRIVE-IN ❧ **Sunset Drive-In** (802-862-1800; sunsetdrivein.com), 155 Porter's Point Rd., Colchester. In summer, the four screens show nightly double features, after the "Let's All Go to the Lobby" short, of course. There's also a snack bar and a playground.

LIVE MUSIC VENUES For jazz, blues, rock, and dance clubs, check out these nightspots, in Burlington: **Nectar's** (802-658-4771; liveat nectars.com), 188 Main St., where Phish got their start, and above it **Club Metronome** (802-865-4563; clubmetronome.com) for live bands and DJs. **Red Square** (802-859-8909; redsquarevt.com) and **RiRa Irish Pub** (802-860-9401; rira.com) both have live music most nights. **Drink** (802-860-9463; come2drink.com) specializes in comedy and jazz, while **Radio Bean** (see *Coffeehouses*) and **Skinny Pancake** (see *Eating Out*) are also sure bets for live music. **Higher Ground** (802-652-0777; higher groundmusic.com), 1214 Williston Rd., South Burlington, is the state's best place for live music and events such as the Winter Is a Drag Ball, with a ballroom and smaller Showcase Lounge. Bands and music publications alike report it as New England's best live music venue. **The Old Lantern** (802-425-2120, oldlantern.com) in Charlotte boasts the largest maple dance floor in the state in a restored 1800s barn.

✳ Selective Shopping

Downtown Burlington boasts the Church Street Marketplace (see the sidebar and churchstreet marketplace.com) as well as the Burlington Town Center (burlingtontowncenter.com), an indoor two-level mall. Burlington's South End (seaba.com), clustered around the Pine St. area, brings to light some of the area's artsy and industrial-inspired shops.

If you head outside Burlington on Williston Rd. /Rt. 2 you'll reach the Dorset Street area with the University Mall (umallvt.com). Farther down Rt. 2 is the Taft Corners shopping area of Williston, which includes Maple Tree Place and the Majestic 10 movie theater (shopmtp.com). Rt. 15 from Burlington to Essex via Rt. 289 leads to the Essex Shoppes & Cinema (essex shoppes.com).

ANTIQUES Architectural Salvage Warehouse (802-879-4221; greatsalvage.com), 11 Maple St., Essex Junction. The place to explore vintage artifacts salvaged from old houses, such as crystal doorknobs, clawfoot tubs, marble sinks, and stained-glass windows.

Champlain Valley Antiques Center (802-985-8116; vermontantiquecenter.com), 4067 Shelburne Rd., Shelburne. Tom Cross has an ever-changing collection of Vermont furniture, folk art, crocks and jugs, and historical items.

🐾 ❧ **Upstairs Antiques** (802-859-8966), 207 Flynn Ave., Burlington. Open daily 10–6. Dave Robbins offers a hodgepodge of collectibles, from furniture to books to housewares.

Barge Canal Market (802-859-8966; barge canalmarket.com), 377 Pine St., Burlington. A small group of local retailers bring their finds to this consignment-style showcase of antiques and local goods.

ART GALLERIES & CRAFTS STUDIOS *Note:* See also *Cultural Attractions* and vermontcrafts .com for a full list of studios and info on Open

---

CHURCH STREET MARKETPLACE

The city's shopping and dining hub, the Church Street Marketplace (churchstmarket place.com) extends four car-free blocks, from the graceful Unitarian Church, designed in 1815 by Peter Banner, to City Hall at the corner of Main St. Outdoor concerts often take place at its head, and the bricked promenade is spotted with benches and boulders from different parts of the state. The marketplace buildings themselves, a mix of 19th-century and art deco styles, house more than 100 shops and an ever-growing roster of restaurants. Stop at a café to watch the colorful parade of Burlingtonian people and pups as they walk by. Chances are, at least one street musician will serenade you. Unlike Boston's Quincy Market, Church Street is a public thoroughfare, open daily and geared as much to residents as to tourists.

House Weekend, held every Memorial Day weekend.

Montstream Studio & Art Gallery (802-862-8752; kmmstudio.com), in 129 St. Paul St., Burlington. Open daily except Sun. Native-born watercolorist and oil painter Katharine Montstream depicts the lake and mountain landscapes of the Burlington waterfront and downtown area in greeting cards, prints, and paintings.

Lawrence Ribbecke (802-658-3425; ribbecke glass.com), 377 Pine St., Burlington, features over 500 types of glass including stained-glass masterpieces depicting the local landscape.

Dug Nap (802-860-1386; dugnap.com), whose animals and locals evoke a dark humor reminiscent of Gary Larsen's *The Far Side*. Nap shows his work by appointment at his studio, which is only a block south of City Hall at 184 Church St., Burlington.

Frog Hollow on the Marketplace (802-863-6458; froghollow.org), 86 Church St., Burlington. The Vermont State Craft Center showcases everything from furniture and art glass to hand-woven scarves and jewelry of every sort.

Bennington Potters North (800-205-8033; benningtonpotters.com), 127 College St., Burlington, sells kitchenware, home furnishings, glass, woodenware, and the ever-enduring Bennington Pottery. A good selection of seconds in the basement.

Furchgott Sourdiffe Gallery (802-985-3848; fsgallery.com), 86 Falls Rd., Shelburne, has rotating shows and does restoration and framing.

The Vermont Gift Barn (802-658-7684; vermontgiftbarn.com), 1087 Williston Rd., South Burlington. An overview of Vermont-made products, from specialty foods and weavings to jewelry, pottery, furniture, fine art prints, and glass.

BOOKSTORES The Crow Bookshop (802-862-0848; crowbooks.com), 14 Church St., Burlington. Well-stocked shelves of new, used, and remainder books in two rooms with creaky floors and great prices.

♂ **Flying Pig Children's Books** (802-985-3999; flyingpigbooks.com), 5247 Shelburne Rd., Shelburne. Former teachers Josie Leavitt and Elizabeth Bluemle have created an award-winning bookstore with close to 40,000 titles for kids and adults.

✿ ♂ Phoenix Books (802-448-3350; 802-872-7111; phoenixbooks.biz), 191 Bank St., Burlington; 21 Essex Way, #407, Essex. This independent chain of two has a fine selection of

local books and popular (and kids') titles. The Essex location boasts a café that serves coffee and wine along with its snacks.

FARMS Vermont Wildflower Farm (802-425-3641; vermontwildflowerfarm.com), 3488 Ethan Allen Hwy., Charlotte. Open May–Oct., daily 10–5. Paths lead through 6 acres of wildflowers in fields and woodland settings with flowers and trees labeled. There's a large gift shop and "the largest wildflower seed center in the East."

Charlotte Village Winery (802-425-4599; charlottevillagewinery.com), 3968 Greenbush Rd., Charlotte. A winemaking operation with a viewing deck overlooking acres of pick-your-own blueberry fields. Free wine tastings daily Memorial Day–Dec.

♂ Shelburne Vineyard (802-985-8222; shelburnevineyard.com), 6308 Shelburne Rd., Shelburne. Open daily year-round. Taste nine wine varieties for a $7 fee that includes the glass. Tours explain the winemaking process; tables and chairs overlook undulating vines with the lake in the distance. The on-site shop includes Vermont edibles and such novelties as wine racks made from antlers.

♂ Lang Farm (802-316-1210; langbarn.com), 51 Upper Main St. (Rt. 15), Essex Junction. Antiques center, nursery, and garden shop open daily, year-round. Links at Lang Farm operates here (see *Golf*), and the barn is most notably known as a wedding and event venue. In fall, there's a corn maze.

✿ ♂ Sam Mazza's Farm (802-655-3440; sam mazzafarms.com), 277 Lavigne Rd., Colchester. Open daily, year-round. The farm's market clearly labels what was grown on-site and uses those ingredients in its outstanding country-style baked goods. A petting zoo, pick-your-own berries, and an autumn corn maze attract families.

♂ Shelburne Orchards (802-985-2753; shelburneorchards.com), 216 Orchard Rd., Shelburne. Over 80 acres of apple trees dot this delightful local treasure for apple picking and some of the area's best local food-related events. Open daily with a farm store; picnickers always welcome. Special deals for seniors.

♂ Adams Apple Orchard & Farm Market (802-879-5226; upickvermont.com), 986 Old Stage Rd., Williston. Pick-your-own apples and large farm market selling Vermont products and tasty doughnuts; open daily mid-Apr.–Dec.

FARMERS MARKETS ♂ The Burlington Farmers Market held Sat. in City Hall Park (winter in Memorial Auditorium) is a fun place to stroll with the kiddies past artful pies, plants, fruits, cheeses, breads, and veggies, along with African samosas, honey meads, and Tibetan take-out. At the back are crafts, jewelry, clothes, and art. It can get crowded.

The area has the most concentrated location of farmers markets in the state. Essex Junction, Hinesburg, Jericho, Milton, Richmond, Shelburne, South Burlington, Underhill, Westford, Williston, and Winooski all have weekly markets in-season, some monthly in winter. For all locations, times, and details, see vermontagriculture.com.

FOOD AND DRINK Lake Champlain Chocolates (802-864-1807; lakechamplainchocolates.com), 750 Pine St., Burlington. Vermont's premier chocolate company offers free tours (and samples) at its Burlington factory, plus a delectable souvenir selection, including seconds. A café serves flavored coffees, hot chocolate drinks, chocolate ice creams, and more. A store and scoop shop is also located at 65 Church St. For a meal including more than chocolate and more chocolate, head to South End Kitchen (see sidebar).

Snowflake Chocolates (802-899-3373; snowflakechocolate.com), 81 Rt. 15A, Jericho

Corners. Bob and Martha Pollak have handcrafted chocolates at this store since 1986. Try the sea-salted caramels.

The Great Harvest Bread Company (802-660-2733; greatharvestburlington.com), 382 Pine St., Burlington, also provides a sandwich-ordering and eating area for its varied loaves and fruit-filled pastries. The cinnamon swirl and apple-cheddar breads are our favorites.

Magic Hat Brewing Company (802-658-BREW; magichat.net), 5 Bartlett Bay Rd., South Burlington (turn off Rt. 7 at the Jiffy Lube). A continuously expanding microbrewery offering tours, samples, and retail shop; navigate the complex and interactive website for hours, events, and giveaways.

See other breweries in the sidebar.

✪ **Chef Contos Kitchen & Store** (802-497-3942; chefcontos.com), 65 Falls Rd. The Charlie Trotter protégée, whose family owned the famous Chez Paul in Chicago, sells hard-to-find, cult gourmet goods and cookware at her elegant store. Check the website for the not-to-be-missed classes.

SPECIAL SHOPS Peace and Justice Store (802-863-8326; pjcvt.org), 60 Lake St., Burlington, run by the city's active Peace and Justice

BURLINGTON'S ARTISTIC SOUTH END
Though Church Street may be Burlington's sunny heart, bohemian Pine Street is its artistic soul. Businesses located between Main Street and Flynn Avenue are a highly concentrated mix of galleries, studios, and eclectic restaurants. For lunch, there's old standard **Myer's Bagel Bakery** (802-863-5013), *the* place for Montreal-style bagels, smoked sandwiches, and excellent baked goods. Just across the street, **Four Corners of the Earth** (802-657-3869) serves up the world between two slices of bread in the form of sandwiches with flavors including Jamaican Avocado and Iraqi Turkey. **Feldman's Bagels** (802-540-0474) handles the New York side of things with local cream cheese shmears and matzoh ball soup. **South End Kitchen at Lake Champlain Chocolates** (802-864-0505) serves up salads, a signature pork mole, and a parade of sweets for three meals a day.

On the artistic side, the **S.P.A.C.E. Gallery** (802-578-2512) hosts monthly group shows of the artists whose studios are located in the building, known as the Soda Plant for its previous factory tenant. **ArtsRiot** (802-540-0406) is not just a gallery, but a multipurpose event space, hosting concerts, movie screenings, and even yoga. Its restaurant features locally inspired, chef-driven takes on fast food, but the kitchen also opens up to pop-up meals including a popular Ethiopian night. **SEABA Center** (802-859-9222) hosts regular shows featuring members of the South End Arts and Business Association and offers frequent classes. It also puts on one of Burlington's biggest events of the year, the South End Art Hop (see *Special Events*). **South Gallery** (225-614-8037) shows the work of 30 contemporary Vermont artists who push the boundaries far beyond barnscapes. Don't miss the world's tallest filing cabinet on your right as you head toward 208 Flynn Avenue and its **Flynndog Gallery**. The space is actually just a long hallway filled with revolving local works, but there's lots to see and **Chef's Corner South End** (802-660-7111) serves its European pastries and exquisite soups right in the building.

Center, a source of alternative publications and fair-trade crafted items—jewelry, cards, clothing—all purchased from wholesalers committed to nonexploitation and social justice. Check the events bulletin board.

Gardener's Supply (802-660-3505; gardeners.com), 128 Intervale Rd., Burlington. One of the largest catalog seed and garden suppliers in New England, with a retail store and nursery adjacent to demonstration gardens along the Winooski River in Burlington's Intervale.

Apple Mountain (802-658-6452; apple mountain.net), 30 Church St., Burlington, is a Vermont-products gift and food shop; socks, ceramics, jewelry, scents, books, and more.

✪ **Old Gold** (802-864-7786; oldgoldvt.com), 180 Main St., Burlington. A well-cultivated collection of vintage clothing is the main draw here, but colorful new clothes and accessories meet the aesthetic, too. Looking for a costume? This is the place.

Horsford's Nursery (802-425-2811; horsford nursery.com), 2111 Greenbush Rd., Charlotte. It's worth visiting this 100-year-old farm just to roam the bounty of blooming flowers, perennials, and the two antique glass greenhouses.

Harrington's (802-985-2000; harringtonham .com), 5597 Shelburne Rd., Shelburne, sells the corncob-smoked meats and other goodies prepared at HQ on Rt. 2 in Richmond. Across the street from the Shelburne Museum, buy a variety of prepared foods or get a sandwich made to

order. Check out **Arabesque** (802-985-8732; arabesquevt.com) next door for fine gifts, baby accessories, and home decor. **The Shelburne Country Store** (802-985-3657; shelburne countrystore.com), 29 Falls Rd. (Rt. 7), Shelburne, encloses several gift galleries under the same roof—a sweets shop, cards, foods, housewares, lamp shades, and more.

✳ Special Events

⅃ *Early January:* **Vermont Cat Show** (catshows.us/vermontff.com). Vermont Fancy Felines pose for ribbons and rest between rounds in lavish travel homes on display at the Sheraton Burlington. The people-watching is even more interesting than the cats.

⅃ *Late January:* **Vermont Farm Show** (vtfarmshow.com). This long-running show is interesting even to non-agrarian types. Held at the Champlain Valley Exposition, highlights include a statewide farmers market and a cook-off among state legislators.

♪ *Early February:* **Burlington Winter Festival/Penguin Plunge**, Waterfront Park—snow and ice sculptures, vending (enjoy burlington.com),and the annual icy dip into Lake Champlain to benefit Special Olympics Vermont (penguinplunge.org).

Saturday before Lent: **Magic Hat Mardi Gras** (magichat.net)—Burlington hums with a packed crowd for this parade and block party on the Church Street Marketplace.

BEER, HERE!

Vermont boasts more cheesemakers and brewers per capita than any other state. But while the curds require lots of rural space to keep cows, beer makers seem to mushroom daily in the old warehouse spaces of the Burlington area. The late Greg Noonan, founder of **Vermont Pub & Brewery** (see *Eating Out*), is widely considered to be the father of Vermont's craft brewing scene. Just down St. Paul St. from his old stomping grounds, American Flatbread Burlington Hearth (see *Eating Out*) is home to **Zero Gravity Craft Brewery**, whose constant rotation ranges from IPAs to a harvest gruit ale containing carrots, chervil, and blackberries. On Pine St., **Citizen Cider** (802-448-3278) provides a pubby alternative to beer drinking with its range of local apple libations served alongside corn dogs and poutine. **Magic Hat Brewing Company** (802-658-2739) and **Switchback Brewing Co.** (802-651-4114) are the biggest producers on the scene, and both offer regular tours at their factories in South Burlington and Burlington, respectively. Down Shelburne Rd., **Fiddlehead Brewing Company** (802-399-2994) fills growlers perfect for enjoying over woodfired pies from **Folino's Pizza** (802-881-8822) just across the hall in the same Shelburne building. **Four Quarters Brewing** (fourquartersbrewing.com) in Winooski invites guests to its tasting room on weekends and hosts frequent events. Many other breweries are too small as of this writing to host regular visitors, but check the **Vermont Brewers Association** website (vermontbrewers.com) to see them all. And don't forget to get your tickets early for the **July Vermont Brewers' Festival** (vtbrewfest.com). Tickets to the bacchanal are known to sell out in hours.

Alice Levitt
FOUR QUARTERS BREWING, WINOOSKI

& *March:* In odd years the **Vermont Flower Show** (greenworksvt.org) is held at the Champlain Valley Exposition—three days of color and fragrance to mark the end of winter. **Maple Open House Weekend** (vermontmaple.org) is the last weekend in March—sugarhouses everywhere open their doors.

& *Late April to early May:* **Vermont Restaurant Week** (vermontrestaurantweek.com). Restaurants statewide offer prix fixe menus for $15, $25, or $35. Organizer *Seven Days* newspaper also hosts foodie events to keep the gustatory pot flowing over.

Memorial Day weekend: **Key Bank Vermont City Marathon & Relay** (runvcm.org)—hundreds participate, thousands spectate; activities all over Burlington. **Vermont Open Studio Weekend** (vermontcrafts.com)—art galleries and crafts studios across the state open their doors for demos and sales.

Early June: **Festival of Fine Art** (artsalivevt .org)—local Burlington shops and restaurants fill up with Vermont art. **Discover Jazz Festival** (discoverjazz.com)—for 10 days the entire city of Burlington becomes a stage for more than 200 musicians. **Lake Champlain International Father's Day Fishing Derby** (my champlain.net)—held annually on Father's Day.

Late June: **Burlington Food & Wine Festival** at Waterfront Park, Burlington—tastings and pairings from Burlington's best chefs and their favorite wines. **Vermont Quilt Festival** (vqf .org), New England's oldest and largest quilting event, at the Champlain Valley Exposition.

♂ *July 3:* **Burlington Independence Day Celebration** (enjoyburlington.com) on the Burlington waterfront and in the harbor—the state's most intense fireworks display over the lake

with live bands, children's entertainment, parade of boats, and lots of vending.

Mid-July: **Vermont Brewer's Festival** (vtbrewfest.com)—local microbreweries ply their stuff under tents at Waterfront Park.

August: **Lake Champlain Maritime Festival** (lcmfestival.com), Burlington waterfront—a historic boat festival held in conjunction with the lake Champlain Maritime Museum by day and well-staged rock concerts at night. ♂ & **Champlain Valley Fair** at the Champlain Valley Exposition in Essex Junction (cvexpo.org), late August—a traditional county fair with livestock and produce exhibits, pig races, rides, and an embarrassment of rich food.

September: **Burlington Book Festival** (burlingtonbookfestival.com), three days of readings, lectures, workshops, book signings, and events. ♂ **Shelburne Farms Harvest Festival** (shelburnefarms.org)—an annual festival held at this working and educational farm on the shores of Lake Champlain. ♂ At the **Small Farms Food Festival** at Shelburne Orchards (shelburneorchards.com), local farms offer tasting menus, live bluegrass, apple picking, sweet cider, and doughnuts. **South End Art Hop** (seaba.com)—a tour of some 400 art studios in Burlington's South End with a fashion show, music, food, workshops, and demonstrations.

October: **Vermont International Film Festival** (vtiff.org), a week's worth of independent, documentary, and outsider films, at area cinemas. 🎃 ♂ & **East Charlotte Tractor Parade** (tractorparade.com), held in front of Spear's Corner Store in East Charlotte—tractors of all sizes with drivers of all ages parade through the tiny center of one of the Burlington area's most thriving agricultural communities. & **Essex Fall Craft & Fine Art Show**, Champlain Valley

EAST CHARLOTTE TRACTOR PARADE

Rachel Carter

Exposition, Essex Junction, could be the state's largest crafts fair (vtcrafts.com). **Vermont Tech Jam** (techjamvt.com) is an annual expo of tech companies producing cutting-edge technology in the Green Mountains. **Haunted Forest** (thehauntedforest.org) is a family-friendly theatrical Halloween celebration with hundreds of jack-o'-lanterns lining the trails at Catamount Outdoor Center in Williston. **Nightmare Vermont** is an adult-geared haunted event held in rotating indoor venues (nightmarevermont.org).

✍ ♿ *Early December:* **Vermont International Festival** (vermontinternationalfestival.com)— food, crafts, dance, and music from around the world, at the Champlain Valley Exposition on Rt. 15 in Essex Junction.

✍ *December 31:* **First Night Burlington** (firstnightburlington.com), the end-of-the-year gala—parades, fireworks, and myriad performances that transform downtown Burlington into an alcohol-free "happening."

THE NORTHWEST CORNER
INCLUDING THE ISLANDS, ST. ALBANS, AND SWANTON

Interstate 89 is the quickest but not the most rewarding route from Burlington to the Canadian border. At the very least, motorists should detour for a meal in St. Albans and a sense of the farm country around Swanton. We strongly recommend allowing a few extra hours—or days—for the route up the Lake Champlain Byway and through the Champlain Islands: Vermont's unspoiled Martha's Vineyard.

THE ISLANDS The cows, silos, and mountain views couldn't be more Vermont. But what about those beaches and sailboats? They're part of the picture, too, in this land chain composed of the Alburgh peninsula and three islands—Isle La Motte, North Hero, and South Hero.

The Champlain Islands begin their straggle 30 miles south from the Canadian border. Thin and flat, they offer some of the most spectacular views in New England: east to the highest of the Green Mountains and west to the Adirondacks. They also divide the northern reach of the largest lake in the East into two long, skinny arms, freckled with smaller outer islands. It's a waterscape well known to fishermen and sailors.

This is Grand Isle County, Vermont's smallest. It was homesteaded by Ebenezer Allen in 1783 and has been a quiet summer retreat since the 1870s.

In the 19th century, visitors arrived by lake steamer to stay at farms. Around the turn of the 20th century a railway spawned several hotels, and with the advent of automobiles and Prohibition, Rt. 2—the high road down the spine of the islands—became one of the most popular routes to Montreal, a status it maintained until I-89 opened in the 1960s.

Happily the decades since, like the interstate, seem to have passed these islands by. Isle La Motte is the smallest and quietest of the islands. It's crossed and circled by narrow roads and linked to the mainland by trails beloved by bicyclists. St. Anne's Shrine near the northern tip marks the shore on which Samuel de Champlain first set foot in what would be Vermont in 1609. Near the southern tip of the island, Fisk Farm, formerly a major source of the island's distinctive black marble, is now an arts center and a "quarry preserve" with intriguing fossils. It's a clue to what's on view a short bike ride away at the Goodsell Ridge Preserve, part of the world's oldest reef. A short and fascinating video explains it all, and you begin to notice fossils embedded in the island's distinctive stone houses.

A summer destination first, this is also a great place to visit in September and October when its many apple orchards are being harvested and bicycling is at its best. Ice fishing fills inns in midwinter, as this area of Lake Champlain offers some of the state's finest angling opportunities—and a growing subculture as well. Just leave driving a truck onto the ice for the occasion to the locals.

ST. ALBANS AND SWANTON Once an important railroad center, the city of St. Albans (population 6,918; surrounded by the town of St. Albans, population 6,392) is still the Franklin County seat. The community's place in the history books was assured on October 19, 1864, when 22 armed Confederate soldiers, who had infiltrated the town in mufti, held up the three banks, stole horses, and escaped back to Canada with $208,000, making this the northernmost engagement of the Civil War.

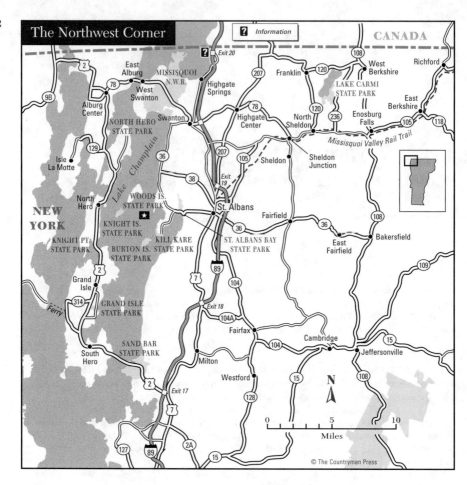

One of the raiders was wounded and eventually died, as did Elinus J. Morrison, a visiting builder. The surviving Confederates were arrested in Montreal, tried, but never extradited; their leader, Lieutenant Bennett H. Young, rose to the rank of general. When he visited Montreal again in 1911, a group of St. Albans dignitaries paid him a courtesy call at the Ritz-Carlton.

It was after the Civil War that St. Albans boomed as headquarters for the Central Vermont Railroad. At one time this was the largest railway in New England, employing more than 1,700 people just in St. Albans. This and the story of the St. Albans Raid are dramatized in the St. Albans Historical Museum.

Swanton (population 6,427) occupies a flat area circled by farmland and intersected by the Missisquoi River. Archaeological digs have unearthed evidence that Algonquin tribes lived here as far back as 8000 BC. The French settled the area about 1748, naming it 15 years later for Thomas Swanton, a British officer in the French and Indian Wars. Due to its proximity to the Canadian border (only 6 miles north), Swanton witnessed a fair bit of smuggling in the 19th century and during Prohibition.

During World War I the long-abandoned Robin Hood–Remington Arms plant produced millions of rounds of ammunition for the Allied armies. Today a sizable chunk of the population is of Abenaki origin, and the Abenaki Tribal Council and museum are based here.

The idyllic village green park is home to a pair of swans, a tradition since 1963, when Queen Elizabeth II sent the town a pair for its bicentenary, thinking its name had something to do with swans.

GUIDANCE Lake Champlain Islands Chamber of Commerce (802-372-8400; 800-262-5226; champlainislands.com), 3501 Rt. 2, North Hero. Next door to the Hero's Welcome General Store, this office is open year-round and publishes a list of accommodations, restaurants, and marinas.

Franklin County Regional Chamber of Commerce (802-524-2444; stalbanschamber.com), 2 N. Main St., St. Albans. Open weekdays. Facing Taylor Park, with plenty of easy parking, this is a friendly office stocked with brochures.

The Swanton Chamber of Commerce (802-868-7200; swantonchamber.com), 34 Merchants Row, Swanton. A seasonal information booth at the north end of the village green.

Lake Champlain Byway (Lake Champlain from Grand Isle to Addison Counties) operates a useful website: lakechamplainbyway.com.

GETTING THERE *By car:* From New York State and Montreal, Rt. 2 from Rouses Point, and from Vermont, Rt. 78 from Swanton (an exit off I-89). From Vermont on the south, I-89, Exit 17, to Rt. 2, which runs the length of the islands. St. Albans is Exit 19 off I-89.

By ferry: **Lake Champlain Transportation Company** (802-864-9804; ferries.com) offers year-round, 15-minute ferry crossings between Gordon's Landing, Grand Isle, and Cumberland Head, New York.

By train: **Amtrak** (800-USA-RAIL; amtrak.com) runs the Vermonter from St. Albans to Washington, DC. There's a ticket office near the corner of Lake and Federal Sts.; local taxi service is available.

MEDICAL EMERGENCY Call **911**. **Northwestern Medical Center** (802-524-5911; 800-696-0321), St. Albans.

Marine emergencies: Call 802-372-5590.

✳ Must See

St. Anne's Shrine (802-928-3362; saintannesshrine.org), 92 St. Anne's Rd., Isle La Motte. Open late-May–mid-Oct., free admission. An open-sided Victorian chapel and 13 shoreside acres mark the site of Vermont's first settlement, a French fort built in 1666. There are daily outdoor Masses in summer and Sunday services as long as weather permits. A gold statue devoted to Our Lady of Lourdes that once stood in the Burlington Cathedral dominates the property, a gift in 1991 from the Burlington Diocese. The shrine has a public beach and picnic area in a large pine grove, presumably descended from what Samuel de Champlain described as "the most beautiful pines I have ever seen" when he stepped ashore in 1609 on this spot. Champlain himself is honored here with a massive granite statue, which was carved in Vermont's Pavilion at Montreal's 1967 Expo. The History Room—upgraded for the 400th anniversary of his arrival—displays artifacts that have washed ashore over the years. Camping is offered seasonally for those making a pilgrimage.

✐ ⅃ **St. Albans Historical Museum** (802-527-7933; stamuseum.com), 9 Church St. (top of Taylor Park), St. Albans, open May–Oct., Tues.–Sat. This artifact-rich museum fills a three-story, 1861 brick schoolhouse. Exhibits include an old-time country doctor's office, complete with vintage medical instruments; Civil War artifacts; and period fashion. The century-old waiting room with a ticket office and telegraphic equipment is the setting for models of both a 1923 roundhouse and a steam locomotive, as well as plenty of Central Vermont Railroad memorabilia. A diorama of the town uses lights and narration to demonstrate the action of the St. Albans Raid. Samples of the stolen currency are on display. The Western Abenaki Exhibit includes a birch-bark canoe, tools, and arrowheads. There's also a children's room and a French heritage exhibit.

Hyde Log Cabin (802-828-3051; historicvermont.org), Rt. 2, Grand Isle. Open July 4–mid-Oct, Sat.–Sun. 11–5. Built by Jedediah Hyde in 1783 when the area was a wilderness accessible only by water, the cedar log cabin was restored in 1956. The Grand Isle Historical Society has furnished it with 18th-century artifacts—furniture, kitchenware, toys, tools, clothing, and atmosphere. At age 14, Hyde enlisted in the Revolutionary War. From the spoils, he received a surveyor's compass and theodolite, which he later used to survey Grand Isle and other parts of the state. This cabin housed 150 years' worth of Hydes at a spot about 2 miles southwest of where it stands today.

President Chester A. Arthur Historic Site (802-828-3051; historicvermont.org), 455 Chester Arthur Rd., Fairfield. A 1950s replica of the little parsonage in which the 21st (and usually under-rated) president lived as an infant can be found 10 miles east of Fairfield on Rt. 36 (open July 4–mid-Oct., Sat.–Sun. 11–5). In the visitors center exhibits examine the controversy over the actual site of Arthur's birth, which had an impact on the question of his eligibility to serve as president. Arthur's conduct as president in light of his reputation as a leading New York State political boss is also examined.

THE WORLD'S OLDEST REEF AND ISLE LA MOTTE'S BLACK MARBLE

Four hundred eighty million years ago, the plot of land now known as Goodsell Ridge Preserve on Reef Road in Isle La Motte was home to squiggly-mouthed cephalopods, snail-like gastropods, and moss animals known as bryozoa. **Chazy Reef**, which underlies the southern third of the island, was once a biologically diverse community of some of the earth's earliest invertebrates. Thanks to the efforts of Linda Fitch, owner of the **Fisk Farm**, visitors can tread over fossils as they learn more about the roughly half-billion-year-old reef, the planet's oldest.

In 2014 Fitch and her team at the Isle La Motte Preservation Trust debuted a new program at Goodsell Ridge in order to better illustrate the deep prehistory on display. *A Walk Through Time* takes visitors on a constitutional of just less than a mile. Each foot of the exhibit represents approximately a million years of the earth's natural history, with 71 illustrated signs explaining the changes that took place.

The exhibit was created by Sid Liebes, a scientist at Hewlett-Packard, and was displayed in California, Michigan, and Switzerland before Fitch transported it to the preserve. Touring the reef and its 81 acres of trails is free. There's a staffed interpretive center (open seasonally, Wed.– Sun. 11–4), which has a small collection of its own and a video dramatizing the history of the reef playing on a loop.

Goodsell Ridge isn't the only place to catch a striking view of the earth's early days. The **Fisk Marble Quarries** on West Shore Rd., the oldest in the state, were first used by the French in 1664 to make a kiln for Fort St. Anne, Vermont's first colonial settlement. The Fisk family acquired them in the 1780s, working them over four generations. In 1884 the quarries passed to Nelson W. Fisk, who recognized their potential as a high-end construction material. When polished, this black marble was magnificent, a coveted medium for facades such as New York's Radio City Music Hall, the U.S. Capitol building, and the Vermont State House. Nelson also shipped boatloads of apples, lumber, even ice to markets farther south. In 1897, as lieutenant governor, he hosted President William McKinley at the family mansion, now the site of **Fisk Farm**. It was while Vice President Teddy Roosevelt was visiting in 1901 that McKinley was fatally shot, and it fell upon Fisk to break the news to the next president.

In the nearby **Isle La Motte Historical Society** (Rt. 129, 4 miles south of the bridge; open July–Aug., Sat. 1–4), an 1840s stone school building and blacksmith shop, displays include a piece of local stone that's been partially polished, graphically illustrating that the stone used in many local buildings is marble. It also displays the cane chair used by President McKinley and Vice President Theodore Roosevelt during their stays at the Fisk mansion, and the industrial looms of weaving entrepreneur Elizabeth Fisk, who, with her prominent husband, acted as their hosts.

FISK QUARRY PRESERVE, ISLE LA MOTTE

Alice Levitt

ICE FISHING gets hot when lakes and ponds form a solid 6 inches of ice. By mid-January the season is in high gear, lasting until March, depending on "ice-out." The Lake Champlain Islands are especially popular because the season can gear up in December; there are numerous smaller bays and access points spread throughout the island region and Missisquoi Bay. Ice fishing lends itself to a jolly environment where family, friends, and children can all participate together, creating the on-ice shanty culture that is so Vermont—plus there is a good chance fish can be caught for dinner. Trout, pike, bass, walleye, perch, and smelt are all popular catches from the Alburgh Passage west to Broad Lake or east to the Inland Sea. Captain Gilly Gagner of Bronzeback Guide Service (see *Fishing*) offers fully equipped charters and is a true Lake Champlain specialist. Holiday Harbor Lodge (see *Fishing* and *Lodging*) specializes in ice fishing as a destination with housekeeping accommodations, shanty rentals, tackle shop, and enthusiastic ice fishing advice and community. Vermont Outdoor Guide Association (voga.org) operates an informational website, while license, fees, maps, and safety protocol is at vtfishandwildlife.com.

✪ **Missisquoi National Wildlife Refuge** covers 6,729 acres on Lake Champlain's eastern shore in Swanton north to Alburgh. Containing most of the Missisquoi River Delta and where it flows into Missisquoi Bay, the refuge began in 1943 under the authority of the Migratory Bird Conservation Act. Predominantly wetlands, the refuge consists of still waters, riverine floodplain forests, and emergent wetlands as well as open fields and hardwood forests in the upland landscape. Open from dawn to dusk year-round, the visitors center is open mid-May–mid-Oct. See *Birding, Boating, Fishing,* and *Green Space.*

✳ To Do

BICYCLING With its flat roads (little trafficked once you are off Rt. 2) and splendid views, the islands are popular biking country. From the chamber of commerce (see *Guidance*) be sure to secure the free Champlain Islands Bikeways map/guide, detailing five interpretive theme loops that thread gently rolling terrain. Isle La Motte is especially well suited to bicycling. One of the most dramatic bike trails in Vermont is the 12.5-mile "Island Line" thrusting out across Lake Champlain from Colchester along a former bed of the old Rutland Railroad. Lake views don't get any better than this, and it's flat to boot This is also the location of Vermont's sole bike ferry, which operates May–Oct. Adult day passes are $8; season passes retail for $40. Look for info at localmotion.org. The Missisquoi Valley Rail Trail is a 26.5-mile converted Central Vermont Railroad trail; see the sidebar.

Rental bikes: **Hero's Welcome General Store** (802-372-4161; heroswelcome.com) in North Hero Village; **Allenholm Farm Bicycle Rent Shop** (802-372-5566; allenholm.com) in South Hero; **Ken's Island Peddler** (802-372-4809) in Grand Isle also offers repairs; and **Porter's Bike Shop** (802-868-7417) in Swanton for rentals and vintage sales.

BIRDING Located on one of the major flyways, the islands are particularly rich in bird life: Herons, eagles, ospreys, and cormorants, among others, migrate through the area. Prime birding sites include the South Hero Swamp and Mud Creek in Alburgh and the Sand Bar Wildlife Refuge across from

---

Missisquoi Valley Rail Trail (802-524-5958; mvrailtrail.com), St. Albans to Richford. This 26.4-mile-long trail has been converted from an abandoned Central Vermont Railroad bed into a path for cross-country skiing, biking, walking, snowmobiling, and just plain strolling—but not for ATVs or dirt bikes. Be sure to secure the excellent free Bicycling & Walking Guide to the trail, available by request or online from the Northwest Regional Planning Commission (802-524-5958; mvrailtrail.com) and the Franklin County Regional Chamber (see *Guidance*). The trail runs cross-country from St. Albans to Sheldon Junction, then winds along the Missisquoi River (and Rt. 105) to Enosburg Falls and on up to Richford, at the Canadian border. The map/guide details access, rental sources, and parking along with handy info including where to find phones and ice cream. Most people do the trail in segments, given the round-trip factor. Porter's Bike Shop (802-868-7417), 116 Grand Ave., Swanton, is a find for out-of-luck bicyclists. Pauline Porter carries an impressive array of bike parts and can salvage a doomed trek when something on your bike gets broken. Rentals available.

The Missisquoi National Wildlife Refuge (802-868-4781; fws.gov/northeast/missisquoi), 29 Tabor Rd., 6 miles northwest of Swanton, off Rt. 78. The visitors center is open May–Oct., weekdays 8–4:30, Sat. 10–2, for this extraordinary 6,729-acre wildlife and waterfowl refuge. The center is worth a stop even if you can't hike or boat. The grounds are open dawn–dusk, year-round. Exhibits showcase detailed local geology and the history of human habitation as well as bird and animal life. The Black Creek and Maquam Creek Trails wind through brushland, timberland, and marsh, adding up to about 1.5 miles (a two-hour ramble); both are appropriately marked for the flora and fauna represented. The refuge provides habitat for over 200 species of birds. Hawks, marsh birds, songbirds, and great blue herons are frequent visitors, and migratory birds stop over on their voyage from northern breeding areas to wintering areas farther south. Most of the refuge is accessible only by boat (see *Boating*). There are two public boat landings, fishing from the Missisquoi River, and blueberry picking in the bog off Tabor Rd. in July and Aug. The walking trails convert to cross-country ski use in winter; for details, get a copy of the free brochure published by the U.S. Fish and Wildlife Service. Open most of the time, but call ahead to confirm. Dress in light colors and bring insect repellent if you're visiting in the hotter months, then do a thorough tick check after you depart. We mean it. The incidence of Lyme disease has increased notably in Vermont in recent years.

Sand Bar State Park. See also Knight's Island and Alburgh Dunes State Parks under *Green Space*. Just east of Alburgh, the Missisquoi National Wildlife Refuge (see the sidebar) is the region's prime birding area and protects Shad Island, the largest blue heron rookery in Vermont. An interpretive center features exhibits on local birds, including birdcalls. Wildlife viewing also at North Hero (protected turtle nesting beach), Alburgh Dunes (Vermont's only sand dunes), and Lake Carmi (140-acre peat bog) State Parks (vtstateparks.com).

BOAT EXCURSIONS **Driftwood Tours** (802-373-0022), North Hero, offers several daytime, sunset, and moonlight cruises in a boat that seats a maximum of six passengers. Captain Holly Poulin offers nature and fishing tours and also does dinner cruises in conjunction with the North Hero House. The trips take two hours and leave from the North Hero House Marina.

Ferry Cruise (802-864-9804; ferries.com), Rt. 314, Grand Isle. If you don't get out on the water any other way, be sure to take the 15-minute ferry to Plattsburgh, New York, and back; or visit **Kill Kare State Park** in St. Albans and take the ferry to **Burton Island State Park** (802-524-6021; vtstateparks.com).

BOATING Rental boats are available in North Hero from **New England Power Boat** (802-372-5131; nepbvt.com) and **North Hero Marina** (802-372-5953; northheromarina.com). **Hero's Welcome** (802-372-4161; heroswelcome.com) and the **North Hero House Marina** (802-372-4732; northherohouse.com) rent kayaks and canoes only. In South Hero, **Apple Island Resort Marina** (802-372-3922; appleislandresort.com) offers powerboats, kayaks, canoes, rowboats, and pontoon boats. **Ladd's Landing Marina** (802-372-5320; laddslandingmarina.com), at the bridge in Grand Isle, also offers sailboats, powerboats, canoes, kayaks, and boat slips. Canoe, kayak, row- and pedalboat rentals also at Vermont State Parks (vtstateparks.com) on water including **Grand Isle**, **Knight Point**, **Alburgh Dunes**, **Kill Kare**, **Burton Island**, **Lake Carmi**.

FISHING Lake Champlain is considered one of the finest freshwater fisheries in America. With the right bait and a little luck, you can catch trout, salmon, smelt, walleye, bass, pike, muskellunge, and perch. **The Missisquoi National Wildlife Refuge** (see *Must Do* and *Birding*) is a source of walleye, northern pike, largemouth bass, bullhead, white perch, and yellow perch.

Holiday Harbor Lodge (802-372-4077; holidayharborlodge.com) in North Hero is a year-round fishing resource with live bait, tackle shop, dock rentals, and ice fishing shanty rentals (see *Must Do*).

Bronzeback Guide Service (802-868-4459; bronzebackguideservice.com) in Highgate Springs is a fully equipped charter offering guided fishing tours, bait and tackle, ice fishing trips, and shanty rentals (see *Must Do*).

Fishing is popular at many of the state parks—see vtstateparks.com. Fishing licenses are required in Vermont—info at vtfishandwildlife.com.

GOLF ♂ **Alburg Golf Links** (802-796-3586; alburggolflinks.com), Rt. 129, 3 miles west of South Alburgh; 18 lakeside holes, gentle, shady terrain. **Links on the Lake Restaurant** serves lunch Tues.–Sun. during golf season and dinner Sat.–Sun. in summer (see *Eating Out*).

Apple Island Resort (802-372-9600; appleislandresort.com), Rt. 2, South Hero. A nine-hole, par-3 executive golf course. Pro shop, rental carts and clubs.

Champlain Country Club (802-527-1187; champlaincountryclub.com), Rt. 7, 3 miles north of St. Albans in Swanton. An 18-hole course built in 1915, some holes terraced. Pro shop and Clubhouse restaurant.

Enosburg Falls Country Club (802-933-2296; efccvt.com), Rts. 105 and 108, N. Main St., Enosburg Falls. A hilly, reasonably priced 18-hole course with friendly staff and good views from the restaurant.

Richford Country Club (802-848-3527), Golf Course Rd., Richford. A hilly, scenic nine holes, just half a mile from the Canadian border. Established 1929.

Wilcox Golf Course (802-372-8343; wilcoxcove.com), Rt. 314, Grand Isle, offers nine lakeside holes, golf carts, pro shop, rentals, and cottage rentals (see *Lodging*).

HISTORICAL ATTRACTIONS Abenaki Tribal Museum and Cultural Center (802-868-2559), 100 Grand Ave., Swanton. Usually open Mon.–Fri. 9–4 (call ahead to confirm). A former filling station houses headquarters for the Abenaki Tribal Council and this small museum, with clothing, tools, and crafts. The stars of this exhibit are the ceremonial headdresses, canoes, and the intricate handwoven baskets. A mile north of Swanton on Monument Rd. is the former site of an Abenaki Christian mission marked by a historical market and totem pole.

& **The Swanton Historical Society Railroad Depot Museum** (802-868-3892; swantonhistorical society.org), 58 S. River St., Swanton. Open Wed. and Sat. 11–3 in summer; by appointment the rest of the year. The first passenger train arrived here in 1863, and by the time this depot was built in 1875, the town was a transportation hub. Note the separate ladies' and men's waiting rooms and the scores of historical photos and artifacts. Now it houses the local historical society and tells the story of the railroad's impact on the area.

♂ **Vermont State Parks** (802-241-3655; vtstateparks.com) and the history of the Civilian Conservation Corps (CCC) are worth exploring as many of the park structures and components still remain from when they were built during the Great Depression when the CCC was created to offer work for young men. There are nine state parks in Vermont's Northwest Corner. See St. Anne's Shrine, St. Albans Historical Museum, Hyde Log Cabin, and the President Chester A. Arthur Historic Site under *Must See*.

SWIMMING ♂ **Alburgh Dunes State Park** (802-796-4170; vtstateparks.com), Alburgh. This little-trammeled area features the longest sandy beach on Lake Champlain, and its shallowness makes it excellent for swimming with young ones; rare flora and fauna. Call for directions or ask locally.

♂ **Knight Point State Park** (802-372-8389; vtstateparks.com), located on the southern tip of North Hero, is the best place to swim, especially for children. A former farm facing The Gut, a quiet, almost landlocked bay, its grounds include a fine brick house and a nature trail that loops around the point. From the sandy beach you can watch boats pass through the drawbridge between the islands. Canoes and rowboats are available for rent, and there are picnic tables with grills.

♂ **Sand Bar State Park** (802-893-2825; vtstate parks.com) fills to capacity on sunny weekends in summer, but this oasis with its shallow, sandy beach and adjacent 1,000-acre wildlife refuge is a fine place to relax on weekdays. Picnic tables, boat rentals, great for young children.

ST. ANNE'S SHRINE, ISLE LA MOTTE
Alice Levitt

✔ **Lake Carmi State Park** (802-933-8393; vtstateparks.com) in Enosburg Falls is the state's largest campground with two beaches for campers (see *Green Space*), but also has a day use swimming beach with nature center and boat rentals.

Grand Isle, Kill Kare, and Burton Island State Parks also have swimming areas, leaving the region no shortage of swimming spots.

✳ Winter Sports

CROSS-COUNTRY SKIING/SNOWSHOEING ✔ **Hard'ack Rec Area** (802-370-2380; hardack.org)
on Congress St. in St. Albans offers a free and local outdoor space for kids with groomed cross-country ski trails, snowshoe trails, ice skating, sledding, and even downhill skiing and snowboarding with a 700-foot rope tow; bring your own equipment.

Hero's Welcome General Store (802-372-4161; heroswelcome.com) in North Hero rents cross-country skis and snowshoes for the land and thick ice surrounding Lake Champlain. Many of the bike and walking trails make for excellent cross-country skiing and snowshoeing in winter.

ICE SKATING ✔ **Collins Perley Sports & Fitness Center** (802-527-1202; collinsperley.com),
890 Fairfax Rd., St. Albans, has a public skating rink with rentals.

✔ **Hard'ack Rec Area** (see *Cross-Country Skiing*) operates a rink free to the public; equipment rentals are *not* available.

✔ Ice skating on **Lake Champlain** when North Hero Bay is frozen is quintessential Vermont winter fun. A variety of skate rentals can be found across the street at **Hero's Welcome General Store** (802-372-4191; heroswelcome.com).

✳ Green Space

Ed Weed Fish Culture Station (802-372-3171; vtfishandwildlife.com), Bell Hill Rd., Grand Isle. Just beyond the Plattsburgh, New York, ferry on Rt. 314, look for the large hatchery (it's precisely 2 miles up Rt. 314 from Rt. 2), open 8–4 daily. Fish are brought to the facility as freshly spawned eggs (up to 2.2 million eggs at any one time), incubated, then transferred to a series of tanks; well worth checking out.

Mud Creek Wildlife Area (vtfishandwildlife.com), off Rt. 78, Alburgh, offers nature trails, a good spot for viewing waterfowl.

Also see the **Missisquoi National Wildlife Refuge** under *Must Do*. Practically in Alburgh, this is the area's largest nature preserve and includes a major interpretive center, worth a stop even if you lack time to walk, fish, or boat there.

The **Fisk Quarry Preserve** and **Goodsell Ridge** on Isle La Motte are described in our box *The World's Oldest Coral Reef.*

St. Albans Bay Park (stalbanstown.com), 4 miles west on Rt. 36, is a good place for picnics, with several tables and grills stretched out along the waterfront, but the water is too shallow and weedy for decent swimming.

KAYAKERS ON NORTH HERO HOUSE BEACH
North Hero House

Kill Kare State Park (802-524-6021; vtstateparks.com), once a fashionable summer hotel site and then, for years, a famous boys' summer camp; on Point Rd. off Rt. 36, St. Albans Bay. Surrounded on three sides by the lake, it affords beautiful views and can therefore be crowded on weekends, but it's usually blissfully quiet other days; swim beach, playgrounds, boat launch, rowboat rentals, and shuttle (fee) to Burton Island.

Burton Island State Park (802-524-6353; vtstateparks.com), a lovely, 250-acre island, is reached from Kill Kare by park boat or by your own. Facilities include 17 tent sites, 26 lean-tos, and a 100-slip marina with electrical hookups and 15 moorings. Campers' gear is transported to campsites by park vehicle. Fishing off this beautiful haven is usually excellent. Also accessible for day use; nature center, swim beach, food concession, hiking trails, boat rentals.

♦ **Lake Carmi State Park** (802-933-8383; vtstateparks.com), at 460 Marsh Farm Rd., Enosburg Falls. Take Exit 19 off I-89 and drive 2 miles on Rt. 104; 1.5 miles north on Rt. 105; 3 miles north on Rt. 108. Set in rolling farmlands, the 482-acre park has 140 tent/trailer sites, the largest camping area in the state. Facilities include two cabins and 35 lean-tos, some on the beach of this sizable lake; nature trails; boat ramp and rentals. Lake Carmi is the state's fourth largest.

Also see and *Swimming* and *Campgrounds.*

✴ Islands Lodging

Note: See *Guidance.* The chamber of commerce lists numerous rentals and lakeside cottage clusters. Vermont Lake Sales & Rentals (vermont lakerentals.com) and Porch Light Property (porchlightpm.com) are prime sources.

RESORTS ◑ ⚲ ♦ ⌖ North Hero House (802-372-4732; 888-525-3644; northherohouse .com), 3643 Rt. 2, North Hero 05474. Open Apr.–Oct. This century-old summer hotel offers a lakeside-resort feel and stunning views. It has become a popular spot for boaters, bikers, and Lake Champlain enthusiasts, a happening place. Owner Walter Blasberg has made substantial improvements over the years. Amenities include a glass-enclosed greenhouse sitting area, Oscar's Oasis pub, the Main Dining Room (see *Dining Out*), and the waterside Steamship Pier Bar & Grill (open seasonally). The North Hero House Marina features a long, grassy dock at which Champlain steamers once docked; boat and slip rentals are available. Try paddle surfing or a sunset cruise. The shorefront is also good for fishing, swimming, and dips in the hot tub. Rooms are air-conditioned and have private bath. There are 9 in the Main Inn and 17 more in lakeside buildings. Many rooms have private porch. In summer, $125–350 per couple B&B, off-season $110–225; children under 5 free; $35 per additional person. The inn also hosts small business meetings, weddings, and other events. Check the website for special events and packages.

⚲ ☀ ⚲ **Shore Acres Inn & Restaurant** (802-372-8722; shoreacres.com), 237 Shore Acres Dr., North Hero 05474. Open Apr.–Dec. This pleasant motel resort commands one of the most spectacular views of any lodging place in Vermont. Set in sweeping, peaceful, beautifully groomed grounds, 23 comfortable rooms face the lake and the Green Mountains. Four of the guest rooms are in the garden house and still offer views of the lake, but are a longer walk. The rooms are each decorated with locally handcrafted furniture. Breakfast is included, and dinner can be enjoyed in the Lake Champlain Room (see *Dining Out*). Amenities include lawn chairs, two clay tennis courts, a driving range, lawn games, game room, waterfront dockings and moorings, and a 1.5-mile private shore for swimming. Dogs are $20 the first night, $5 per night thereafter. High seasons run $168.50–252.50, low seasons $119–172.

INNS AND BED & BREAKFASTS Thomas Mott B&B (802-796-4402; thomas-mott-bb .com), 63 Blue Rock Rd., Alburgh 05440. Open May–Oct. This 1830s lakeside farmhouse is splendidly sited on a quiet back road along Alburgh's eastern shore, handy to the Missisquoi Nature Reserve and located on the Lake Champlain Bikeways route, and within a 20-minute car ride of the Missisquoi Rail Trail. Hosts Susan and Bob Cogley are longtime residents delighted to help plan your stay in the area. Bring your own alcohol (the stores close at 6 PM) to enjoy over a chat with your amiable hosts. The four Victorian-style guest rooms all have private bath and lake views—three have queen beds and one has twins. There is also plenty of common space inside and out as well as bike storage. Guests are welcome to swim, fish, and play horseshoes or croquet. $140–160 includes a homemade breakfast that might include homemade yogurt along with treats made from local produce. Dinner available upon request. Children over 12 welcome.

THE BEACH AT SHORE ACRES

Rachel Carter

Ruthcliffe Lodge & Restaurant (802-928-3200; 800-769-8162; ruthcliffe.com), 1002 Quarry Rd., Isle La Motte 05463, open Mother's Day–Columbus Day. Way out at the end of Old Quarry Rd., this lakeside compound includes a small motel and lodge with a total of six rooms, all with private bath and many featuring lakeside panoramas. Mark and Kathy Infante include a full country breakfast with the stay. Multicourse Italian American dinners are served nightly in-season. There's a 40-foot water's-edge patio for dining, as well as the cozy knotty-pine dining room in the lodge. Swimming and fishing are out the front door; rental boats and bikes are available. Rates range from $142.50 per couple for a room with a full bath to $152.50 for a two-room adjoining unit with a bath and a half; $15 per extra person, children over 6 welcome. Inquire about the Meadow House cottage rental and different packages.

♂ **The Ransom Bay Inn** (802-796-3399; 800-729-3393; ransombayinn.com), 4 Center Bay Rd., Alburgh 05440. Open May–Dec. A stone house built beautifully in the 1790s, originally a stagecoach stop, set back from Rt. 2 within walking distance of a small beach. Innkeepers Richard and Loraine Walker speak English and French and have maintained the inn to be worthy of its Vermont Register of Historic Places designation. Seasonal dining is available seven days a week in summer (see *Dining Out*). Guests are accommodated in two large and airy rooms plus two smaller ones, all nicely furnished with period antiques and private bath. $120 gets you a full breakfast with their specialty: homemade croissant French toast.

♂ **Allenholm Orchards Bed & Breakfast** (802-372-5566; allenholm.com), 150 South St., South Hero 05486. Open year-round. Pam and Ray Allen offer the Island Orchard Suite—a bedroom furnished in family antiques, including a queen-sized canopy bed, and a large living room with additional bed, a TV, and a full-sized pool table, plus a full private bath, patio, rose garden, and private airport. A country breakfast featuring homegrown apples is served upstairs in the dining room or, if you prefer, on your patio. The suite is on the lower level of the Allens' modern home; it opens onto Vermont's oldest commercial orchard, with more than 100 acres of apples. Established in the 1870s, it's now owned and operated by the sixth generation of Allens. $115 per couple for the bedroom, $175 for the entire suite.

♂ ♂ **Ferry Watch Inn** (802-372-3935; ferrywatchinn.com), 121 West Shore Rd., Grand Isle 05458. Open May–Nov. This wonderfully restored home, originally built in 1800,

overlooks the broad lake with spectacular views of the Adirondacks. Janet and Troy Wert offer three guest rooms (two with shared bath, one with private bath) with antique double beds renowned for their comfort. The property is within walking distance of a nine-hole golf course. A barn is available for weddings and events. $110 per room with shared bath or $130 with private bath includes full country breakfast. Weekly rate values available.

♂ **Adams Landing** (802-372-4830; adams landingvt.com), 1 Adams Landing Rd. Extension, Grand Isle. Open year-round. In this lovely big, rambling, secluded house on the west shore, Sally Coppersmith and Jack Sartore offer two rooms with shared bath ($130–155) and a suite with private bath, a fridge, and library ($220). Rates include breakfast and afternoon refreshments. Children 11 and older welcome. Inquire about Kelsey House, a fully equipped two-bedroom house with a lovely wraparound porch overlooking Lake Champlain.

○ **Crescent Bay Farm** (802-372-4807; crescentbaybb.com), 153 West Shore Rd., South Hero 05486. Open late spring to early fall. This restored 1820s farmhouse is a working farm on

TINY CASTLES DOT THE LANDSCAPE OF SOUTH HERO

Alice Levitt

CAMPING AT GRAND ISLE STATE PARK

the quiet, southern end of the island, near Snow Farm Winery, owned by the same family. Four guest rooms, three with private bath ($130 includes breakfast), are furnished in country antiques. Two generations of the Lane family operate this working homestead, raising llamas for wool and home-spun yarn; you'll also find pigs, a maple sugaring operation, cats and dogs, flower gardens, lake views, and one of many miniature stone castles scattered around the Champlain Islands.

MOTEL/HOUSEKEEPING COTTAGES

♂ ♂ & **Fisk Farm** (802-928-3364; fiskfarm .com), 3849 West Shore Rd., Isle La Motte 05463. Open May–Oct. Owner Linda Fitch offers two lovely guest cottages for weekly rentals (shorter periods are considered early and late in the season) on the former site of the Fisk family estate. The Stone House, built of wood and stone next to the main house, is a beauty, with only a fireplace for heating. It's said that the petite Shore Cottage was built as a playhouse in North Hero and brought across the ice. The three-bedroom Hemond House is also available in the village of Isle La Motte. The gray stone Fisk mansion now lies in ruins, a reminder of its history—it was in the house that Teddy Roosevelt first heard the news that William McKinley had been shot in 1901. The front garden is the setting for Sunday-afternoon teas. The horse barn has been renovated as an art gallery and live music venue as well as a wedding and event destination. Rates begin at $700 per week for the Shore Cottage and $900 for the Stone House (both of which have their own kitchens). Grills are available, and guests may help themselves to the herb garden.

🐾 ♂ & **Holiday Harbor Lodge** (802-372-4077; holidayharborlodge.com), 8369 Rt. 2,

North Hero 05474. Open year-round, specializing in fishing and outdoor recreation; this is the hot spot for ice fishing in winter. Bruce and Joanne Batchelder cater to outdoors enthusiasts and have created an environment with amenities to boot: fish cleaning stations, a live bait and tackle shop, ADA-accessible docks with charging facilities, boat rentals, fishing gear rentals including ice fishing shanties, swimming and fishing docks, a fishing guide service, lawn games, outdoor grills, a living room, a covered porch, and picnic tables. Six motel rooms and six fully equipped kitchen waterfront cabins are available ranging $95–175, depending on season. Pets can be accommodated for an additional fee.

🐾 **Wilcox Cove Cottages & Golf Course** (802-372-8343; wilcoxcove.com), 3 Camp Court, Grand Isle 05458. Open June–mid-Sept. This homey, lakeside cottage colony and nine-hole public golf course is less than a mile from the ferry. Each of the seven cottages has a living room, dining area, fully equipped kitchen, one bedroom with twin beds, bathroom with shower, and one or two screened porches. They are completely furnished except for sheets, pillowcases, and bath and kitchen towels, and can be rented for $625–775 a week including greens fees. Golf is $18 per day, and pets are welcome. Occupancy is limited to two adults; additional guests are $15 per day and must be arranged in advance; cots are not available.

CAMPGROUNDS See Kill Kare, Burton Island, and Lake Carmi State Park Camping under *Green Space*. The complete rundown on state parks is at **vtstateparks.com** (888-409-7579). For a list of private campgrounds and RV parks, visit campvermont.com. Also see Apple Island Resort below.

♂ **Grand Isle State Park** (802-372-4300), 36 E. Shore Rd. south, Grand Isle 05458. Open mid-May–mid-Oct. Vermont's second largest (and most visited) state campground has 117 tent/trailer campsites, 36 lean-tos (no hookups), and four cabins on 226 acres, with a beach, playground, nature trail, and recreation building. This family-friendly campground is perfect for smaller children and a family's first camping trip.

♂ **Homestead Campground** (802-524-2356; homesteadcampground.net), 864 Ethan Allen Hwy., Exit 18 off I-89 in Georgia 05468, offers 160 shaded campsites with water and electric hookups, laundry facilities, hot showers, cabin and camper rentals, a playground, and two swimming pools. Seasonal RV rentals; May 1–Oct. 15.

🏕 ⚓ **Apple Island Resort** (802-372-3800; appleislandresort.com), 71 Rt. 2, South Hero 05486. Open May–Oct. Direct lakefront camping and an RV campground that includes RV site rentals with hookups, campsite rentals, and cottage and cabin rentals. A fully operational resort with a marina (see *Boating*), golf course (see *Golf*).

REMOTE CAMPING North Hero State Park (802-372-8727) has 11 wooded tent sites and nine lean-to sites; all are remote with limited services. The park has drastically reduced its camping services to improve the habitat. The effort has paid off: This is a now great park for wildlife viewing. The campsites cannot be reserved; unlike other state parks they are first come, first served.

Knight Island State Park by way of **Burton Island State Park** (802-524-6353). The *Island Runner* (802-524-6353), a ferry operated between Memorial Day and Labor Day by the state, crosses the water to Knight Island on weekends from Kill Kare and Burton Island every couple of hours, weekdays only from Burton Island. There's even an optional gear delivery service. The seven campsites at Knight Island are primitive (there are no facilities)—even clothing is optional! To maximize privacy, campsites are hidden from public view. Not to be missed is the brochure-guided "Walk of Change" that explores island ecology.

Woods Island State Park (802-524-6353), 2 miles north of Burton Island. Primitive camping is available on this mile-long, quarter-mile-wide island of 125 acres. Five widely spaced campsites with no facilities are linked by a trail. The island is unstaffed, although there are daily ranger patrols; reservations for campsites must be made through Burton Island State Park (see above). There is no public transportation to the island; the best boat access is from Kill Kare.

✳ St. Albans and Swanton Lodging

RESORT ⚓ ♿ **The Tyler Place Family Resort** (802-868-4000; tylerplace.com), 175 Tyler Place, Highgate Springs 05460. Open late May–mid-Sept. One of the country's oldest family resorts (since 1933) continues to thrive on 165 acres of woods, meadows, and a mile of undeveloped lakeshore. Faithful partisans have been returning year after year for five generations of the Tyler family's management (more than 25 members of the family are currently involved). They provide just about every conceivable form of recreation for adults and children (infants–16 years of age), with separate

programs and dining for each group (special arrangements for infants). There are heated indoor and outdoor swimming and wading pools, six tennis courts, and equipment for kayaking, fishing, sailboarding, and more. For adults there is yoga, massage, a variety of workshops, and well-planned time away for romance; Montreal is less than an hour's drive. Accommodations vary: You'll find the contemporary inn plus 27 cottages, a farm, and a guesthouse, for a total of 70 cottages and family suites, over 40 with a fireplace. Each unit has two or more bedrooms, air-conditioning, and a pantry or kitchen. The inn has a spacious dining room with good food, and a big lounge with bar. Stays are usually Sat.–Sat. All-inclusive rates begin at $120 per adult and $91 per child. Reduced-rate packages are available at both ends of the summer season.

BED & BREAKFASTS ⚓ 🏕 **Tabor House Inn** (802-868-7575; taborhouseinn.com), 58 Homestead St., West Swanton 05488. Location, location, location! This 1890s mansion is the shores of Maquam Bay, an arm of Lake Champlain, and borders the 6,700-acre Missisquoi Wildlife Refuge. Innkeeper Jennifer Bright came to an auction held by the previous owners, never meaning to buy the place, but here she is on Tabor Point with four guest rooms including the vast (600 square feet) Lake Shore Suite with a private balcony and Jacuzzi, upstairs above the well-named "Great Room." There is also a 60-foot screened-in porch overlooking the lawn and lake. A full breakfast is included in the rates ($100–220 depending on season; open year-round). Dinner can be arranged, not a bad idea as you probably won't want to stir once you are here. Pets can be accommodated.

⚓ 🏕 ⚓ **Back Inn Time** (802-527-5116; backinntime.us), 68 Fairfield St., St. Albans 05478. Built by Victor Atwood, a railroad magnate during the Civil War, this house is an easy walk from the center of town. The handsome Victorian is home to sloping lawns, gardens, and four outdoor porches. The living room, chandeliered dining room, and library look much as they would have in the 1860s, but rooms are all modern luxury. Six guest rooms, all with private bath, include two master bedrooms with fireplace. Bedding and toiletries are of optimal quality, a hint of the relaxation to come with an on-site massage, concert, or cooking class. The food is organic and local at a dinner that's available with reservations. $119–169 includes a full breakfast.

🐾 🏕 ⚓ **Sampler House Bed & Breakfast** (802-893-2724; 888-501-8775; samplerhouse .com), 22 Main St., Milton 05468, handy to I-89 exits about halfway between Burlington and St. Albans. This 1830s cape, on a quiet street off Rt. 7, offers two comfortable, tastefully furnished air-conditioned rooms (one upstairs and one ground level), each with private bath. A bright, dual-level suite to the rear of the house, with a full kitchen, sofa, and satellite TV in its sitting room, also has an upstairs bedroom whose bath includes a jetted tub and overhead rain shower. $95–145 includes breakfast. $20 per day per pet. In each room the detailing, especially in the baths, reveals Peter's woodworking skill. Breakfast is Deborah's domain and includes something freshly baked as well a hot dish and cheese plate. Dinner can be prearranged. Inquire about the Elderberry Lodge as a rental option.

♂ ♨ ✍ **Grey Gables Mansion** (802-848-3625; 800-299-2117; greygablesmansion.com), 122 River St., Richford 05476. A turreted mansion built around 1890 by local lumber baron Sheldon Boright, this is a Queen Anne Victorian with hardwood floors, period wallpapers, stained glass, a wraparound porch, and a widow's walk. Guests enter past the carved walnut-and-mahogany staircase, and can linger in the fireplaced living room or in the library. The five antiques-filled guest rooms all include a full bath and cable TV. Dinners are available by prearrangement and served in the colorful downstairs pub. Bikers will be interested in the Missisquoi Valley Rail Trail connecting to St. Albans. The VAST snowmobile trail passes right outside, and there are numerous packages. It's also just a 20-minute drive to skiing at Jay Peak. $99–139 includes a full breakfast. Inquire about murder mystery weekends and resident ghosts.

♨ ☼ ✍ ⅙ **Buck Hollow Farm** (802-849-2400; 800-849-7985; buckhollow.com), 2150 Buck Hollow Rd., Fairfax 05454. Way off in rolling farm county some 10 miles southwest of St. Albans, this is a beautifully renovated 1790s carriage house set on 400 acres. Each of the four rooms includes antiques, a queen-sized four-poster bed, and TV. Guests are encouraged to use the outdoor hot tub and the heated pool or browse the antiques shop. In winter there's cross-country skiing on the property. $125 per room, including full country breakfast. $20 extra each night per pet.

♨ ✍ **Country Essence B&B** (802-868-4247; countryessence.com), 641 Rt. 7, Swanton 05488. Cheryl Messier provides two pretty rooms with private bath. Rooms are reached by a private staircase entrance in an 1850s homestead on 12 groomed acres with a playground and swimming pool. $100 per room with country breakfast. English and French spoken.

Parent Farmhouse B&B (802-524-4201; parentfarmhouse.com), 854 Pattee Hill Rd., Georgia 05468. Lucy and Roger Parent offer three rooms with shared bath. The handsome 19th-century brick farmhouse with distinctive oval windows is near Lake Champlain, with plenty of walking and biking opportunities and on-site antiques shop. $65–120 includes homemade continental breakfast. No credit cards or pets; call to inquire about children.

OTHER LODGING La Quinta Inn & Suites (802-524-3300; lq.com), 813 Fairfax Rd., Rt. 104, at Exit 19 off I-89, St. Albans. Several of the 81 guest rooms are suites; complimentary continental breakfast, indoor pool, and fitness room, rates for families, seniors, and business groups. Rates start at $85.

✳ Where to Eat

The Islands

DINING OUT ⅙ **Blue Paddle Bistro** (802-372-4814; bluepaddlebistro.com) 316 Rt. 2, South Hero. Open year-round for dinner Tues.–Sat. This large, colorful gathering place showcases local art in the upstairs dining room. To get it off the ground, owners Mandy Hotchkiss and Phoebe Bright gave paddles to investors. Now the paddles cover the walls, and the unpretentious café hums with activity year-round. Outdoor deck in summer.

Lake Champlain Room at Shore Acres Inn & Restaurant (802-372-8722), 237 Shore Acres Dr., North Hero. Reservations for dinner are a must much of the time. Also open for breakfast June–Aug. The dining room's large windows command a sweeping view of the lake, with Mount Mansfield and its flanking peaks in the distance. The fare caters to the needs of both picky eaters and more adventurous palates, as evidenced by the presence of the islands' only Korean ssam dish. The chocolate pie is famous.

❂ **North Hero House Main Dining Room** (802-372-4732; 888-525-3644; northherohouse .com), 3643 Rt. 2, North Hero. Open year-round, weekends only in the off-season, daily in busier seasons; call ahead. Reservations recommended. Dine on the glassed-in, lake-view veranda of the historic old inn, at one of the umbrella-covered tables on the lawn and outdoor patio, or in the glass-covered greenhouse (also used for private parties). Produce is grown in on-premise gardens. $18–27. **The Steamship Pier Bar & Grill** is open July and Aug. on the waterfront at the North Hero House Marina—a sought-after spot in summer.

Ransom Bay Inn (802-796-3399; 800-729-3393), 4 Center Bay Rd., Alburgh. Open for dinner daily in summer, some weekends in other seasons; call ahead. Longtime innkeepers Richard and Loraine, both culinary school graduates, have created an attractive dining space in the downstairs of their historic stone inn. In summer tables are all set out on a deck overlooking the garden. In fall there's fireside dining. The meats are all organic. Entrées range $12–24 and also feature treats from their on-site bakery.

✪ **Zach's Café at the Gallery** (802-378-4591, grandisleartworks.com), 259 Rt. 2, Grand Isle. Wed.–Sat. 10–3;. Sun. brunch 9–2. Dinner Thurs. 6–8. Reservations necessary for dinner. This multi-room gallery features the work of 75 artists, but the real virtuosity is in the kitchen of chef Zach Labelle. Throughout the week, Labelle whips up soups, sandwiches, and breakfast from ultra-local ingredients. On Theme Night Thursday, he uses island-grown meats and produce in $25, three-course dinners hinging on a different cuisine each week, from Korean to Greek.

EATING OUT ♦ (ᐧᑊᐧ) **Hero's Welcome General Store** (802-372-4161; heroswelcome.com), Rt. 2, North Hero Village. Open daily year-round. An upscale general store that serves deli sandwiches, baked goods, and coffee with waterside seating.

HERO'S WELCOME

Rachel Carter

No Name Tiki Bar & Grill at North Hero Marina (802-372-5953; northheromarina.com), 2253 Pelot's Point Rd., North Hero. Open seasonally in summer. You eat on the porch, no more than 10 people at a time, and the pool next door invites you in to pass the time between courses. It's not gourmet, but there's a full bar with six beers on tap.

🍴 **Links on the Lake at Alburg Golf Links** (802-796-3586; alburggolflinks.com), 230 Rt. 129, Alburgh. Lunch daily except Mon., dinner Fri.–Sun., seasonally. Country club food (read, simple sandwiches) is served in a setting that's a cut above: the Alburg Country Club.

🍴 **South End Café at Hall's Orchard** (802-928-3091), 4445 Main St., Isle La Motte. Located in an 1828 Scottish stone house adjacent to Hall's Orchard, the café is open May–Oct. (days vary, call ahead) for breakfast and lunch, mostly in the form of homemade pastries and sandwiches. But the real draw is the stock of sweet-but-potent ice ciders pressed on premises.

✪ **Broken Arrow** (802-777-6357), 59 Rt. 2, South Hero. Eben Hill got his start concocting flavor combinations as a bartender. His résumé includes the restaurants of six James Beard Foundation award-winning chefs, including Mario Batali at Lupa Osteria Romana and Tom Colicchio at Craft. His own eatery is somewhat less prepossessing, but the green trailer known as Broken Arrow is still a foodie destination. Tacos are filled with wild mushrooms or ancho-braised pork, mangoes, and crunchy cabbage slaw. Local, grassfed burgers are topped with Cabot cheddar.

✪ **Papa Pete's Snack Bar** (no phone), 35 Bridge Rd., North Hero. Days spent lolling in nature call for barbecue, and this is the only place on the islands to get it. Pulled pork and ribs emerge from a pig-shaped smoker at this seasonal stand located at the junction of North Hero and Alburgh. Take a dip in the lake while you wait.

St. Albans & Swanton

DINING OUT ✪ 🍴 **One Federal Restaurant & Lounge** (802-524-0330; onefederalrestaurant.com), 1 Federal St., St. Albans. Open seven days a week for lunch and dinner. Former New England Culinary Institute instructor Marcus Hamblett uses produce from his family farm to supply this classic American restaurant. There are no big surprises on the menu, but food is prepared with exceptional flavor and polish. Start with poutine or crunchy chicken fingers. Entrées range from a juicy, $29 rack of lamb to a $9 veggie wrap. For a true taste of terroir, try the Vermonter burger, a local beef patty stacked with Cabot cheddar, crispy bacon, and a grilled apple, then drizzled with maple syrup. Outdoor seating in summer.

♿ **Thai House** (802-524-0999; thaihousevt .com), 333 Swanton Rd., St. Albans. Open for lunch and dinner except Sun. There's a wide selection of well-prepared Thai favorites here, but also some showstoppers, including whole fried fish and soufflé-like Thai custard with sticky rice.

EATING OUT ♪ ♿ **Bayside Pavilion** (802-524-0909), 15 Georgia Shore Rd., St. Albans. Open daily for lunch and dinner. Drive from Taylor Park down Lake St. 4 miles until it dead-ends at Lake Champlain; this 1920s roadhouse is on the corner. Full bar, moderate prices, kids' menu, live music on weekends. Dinner entrées $14.95–21.95. In summer, dock seating overlooks St. Albans Bay.

♥ ♪ ♿ **Maple City Diner** (802-528-8400), 17 Swanton Rd., St. Albans. Maple is indeed the theme at this diner owned by the couple behind One Federal. Sap buckets decorate the walls and plates are filled with bacon waffles drenched in maple butter. Don't have time for a meal? Grab a giant cupcake or Black Forest cake.

Mimmo's Pizzeria Restaurant (802-524-2244; mimmositalian.com) 22 S. Main St., St. Albans. Domenico (Mimmo) Spano grew up in Italy and continues to emphasize Euro hospitality at his casual pizzeria. Pizza, pasta, and sandwiches take up most of the menu, but leave room for a big plate of fried-to-order zeppoli.

✳ Entertainment

❁ ♂ ♥ **Music at Snow Farm Vineyard** (802-372-9463; snowfarm.com), 190 West Shore Rd., South Hero. If you fancy meeting the locals, a popular event is the Thurs.-evening summer music series beginning at 6:30 on the vineyard's lawn. The music ranges, over the course of the season, from classical to rock. It's free, and all you need to bring is a picnic and a chair (bug spray wouldn't be a bad idea, either). You can buy wine and dinner, including woodfired pizza, on-site. Picnicking begins at 5 PM.

♂ ♥ **The Arts at Fisk Farm** (802-928-3364; fiskfarm.com), 3849 West Shore Rd., Isle La Motte. A music series in the Fisk Farm Tea Gardens runs Sun., June–Sept., with art and crafts shows in the Horse & Carriage Barn. Free except for refreshments. There is a charge for the Concerts in the Barn—Pro Series: music by professional chamber groups on select Saturdays in June, July, and Aug. Both are sponsored

by the Isle La Motte Preservation Trust. See also *Lodging*.

♥ ♪ **Knight Point State Park** in North Hero hosts **Music in the Park** in July and **Shakespeare in the Park** in Aug. Bring a picnic. Info at vtstateparks.com or champlainislands.com event calendars.

♥ ♪ ♿ **Enosburg Falls Opera House** (802-933-6171; enosburgoperahouse.org), 123 Depot St., Enosburg Falls. An 1892 structure that fell into decades of disuse until the community mustered the funds to restore it. The intimate stage is the site for year-round events, including Vermont Symphony Orchestra concerts, plays, musicals, and a variety of live-music events. Tickets and schedules online.

♂ **Grand Isle Lake House** (802-372-5024; grandislelakehouse.com), 34 East Shore Rd., Grand Isle. Built on Robinson's Point as the Island Villa Hotel in 1903, this is a classic mansard-roofed 25-room summer hotel with a wraparound porch, set in 55 acres of lawn that sweep to the lake. From 1957 until 1993 it was a summer girls' camp run by the Sisters of Mercy. Since 1997 it has been owned by the Preservation Trust of Vermont, which has restored the upstairs rooms beautifully, as it has the lobby, kitchen, and dining rooms. It plays host to a variety of public concerts, including ones featuring the Vermont Symphony Orchestra, and is available for large weddings and retreats.

✳ Selective Shopping

ANTIQUES The usual count is half a dozen shops, but they are all seasonal and tend to close as one thing, open as another. Standbys include **Junk and Disorderly**, 304 Rt. 2, South Hero; the **Back Chamber Antiques Store**, North

BROKEN ARROW FOOD TRUCK ON THE ISLANDS IN SOUTH HERO

Alice Levitt

Hero Village; and **Tinker's Barn**, gifts and antiques at 479 Rt. 2, South Hero. Also check with **Alburgh Auction House**, Lake St., Alburgh (802-796-3572).

ART GALLERIES AND CRAFTS STUDIOS

McGuire Family Furniture Makers & Vermont Clock Company (802-928-4190; mcguire familyfurnituremakers.com; vermontclock.com), Isle La Motte. Open year-round, but call first. Two generations of this talented family are involved in the day-to-day production of antique reproduction furniture in spare, heirloom, Shaker, and 18th-century designs: four-poster beds, pegleg tables, grandfather clocks, dressers—anything you want designed, some of it surprisingly affordable. The McGuires also handcraft replica Shaker and early American clocks.

Grand Isle Art Works (802-378-4591; grand isleartworks.com), Rt. 2 in Grand Isle, operates almost year-round; times/dates depend on the season, with updates on the website. Housed in a quirky 1797 farmhouse, this gallery displays and sells art from a wide selection of Vermont artists, both well known and obscure. Zach's Café at the Gallery serves edible art of its own and breakfast, lunch, and weekly dinners.

Island Craft Shop (802-372-4152), a cooperative located behind Hero's Welcome in North Hero Village, is open daily mid-May–mid-Oct. Works of local and area artisans.

FARMERS MARKETS

One of Vermont's strongest agricultural regions, the Northwest Corner abounds in farmers markets with farm-fresh and local food, products, and gifts in Grand Isle, Isle La Motte, South Hero, Enosburg, Richford, and St. Albans. See vermont agriculture.com for dates and times.

🐾 ♫ **Carman Brook Maple & Dairy Farm** (802-868-2347; 888-84-MAPLE; cbmaplefarm .com), 1275 Fortin Rd., Swanton. Daniel and Karen Fortin run a modern dairy operation that welcomes curious vacationers. Depending on the season, you can tour the cutting-edge barn, watch maple syrup being made, choose a variety of maple products, or take the five-minute hike past the barn to the Abenaki Medicine Caves, known among the locals as the mystical spot where generations of Abenaki gathered medicinal herbs and sought cures. Gift shop, daily tours (call ahead).

ORCHARDS ♫ Allenholm Farm

(802-372-5566; allenholm.com), 111 South St., South Hero. Open mid-May–Dec., 9–5. A sixth-generation, 100-acre apple orchard, Vermont's oldest, with a farmstead selling Vermont cheese,

honey and maple syrup, jams and jellies, and Papa Ray's famous homemade pies. There's also a petting paddock filled with friendly farm dwellers seeking a snack. See also *Biking* and *Lodging*.

♫ ((ψ)) **Hall's Orchard** (802-928-3226; hall homeplace.com), 4461 Main St., Isle La Motte. This apple and pear orchard produces a range of ice ciders. The 1820s brick house sits across from the orchard, which has been in the same family since the house was built and now houses the South End Café (see *Eating Out*).

♫ **Hackett's Orchard** (802-372-4848; hacketts orchard.com), 86 South St., South Hero. Perennials, maple syrup, fruits, berries, and fresh-picked vegetables in summer; apples, cider, and pumpkins in fall. The farm stand has a family picnic play area and wagon rides. Fresh cider doughnuts are a specialty, as are the homemade fruit pies. Open May–Dec.

♫ **West Swanton Orchards and Cider Mill** (802-868-9100), Rt. 78, West Swanton. Open June–Nov. A family-owned orchard with 11 varieties of apples, a cider mill, and a gift shop featuring Vermont products and homemade baked goods. Take a walk on the nature trail that winds through the 62 acres of trees.

WINERY Snow Farm Vineyard

(802-372-WINE; snowfarm.com), 190 West Shore Rd., South Hero. Open May–Dec. Vineyard tours are offered daily in summer and early fall. Visitors enter a barnlike building that is the winery showroom with a tasting counter. There, over wine and local cheese and meats, they learn that this is still a relatively new operation (opened in 1997). Initially it processed and bottled wine from grapes grown in New York's Finger Lakes, gradually replacing them with grapes grown on the farm's 14 acres. (Also see *Entertainment*.)

SPECIAL STORES ((ψ)) Hero's Welcome

General Store (802-372-4161; 800-372-HERO; heroswelcome.com), 3643 Rt. 2, North Hero. Former Pier 1 CEO Bob Camp and his wife, Bev, have transformed this 19th-century landmark into a Vermontiana equivalent of the chain store: There's a bit of everything, including a café and bakery, gift shop, art gallery, as well as Vermont gourmet food products, toys and sporting goods, wine, and books, all adding up to a unique community gathering spot. They offer canoe, kayak, bike, ice-skate, cross-country ski, and snowshoe rentals as well as a boat launch.

Vermont Nut Free Chocolates (802-372-4654; 888-468-8373; vermontnutfree.com), 10 Island Circle, Grand Isle, just off Rt. 2. This venture—exactly what it sounds like—has been so successful, it's moved to the Island Industrial Park—but it's still worth finding. The retail store is open weekdays, year-round, 9–5.

✐ **Heroes Kingdom** (802-524-3446), 74 N. Main St., St. Albans, is a great place to nourish your inner geek. Manga, classic comics, graphic novels, and games all find a home here.

✐ **The Eloquent Page** (802-527-7243; the eloquentpage.com), 70 N. Main St., downtown St. Albans. Donna Howard stocks over 35,000 used and collectible books, with a big section on Vermont and a wide variety of doll, dollhouse, and children's titles.

✐ **Maple City Candy** (802-524-6755; maple candyvt.com), 22 N. Main St., St. Albans. Anything you could imagine made from sap including maple fudge, maple sugar candy, maple popcorn, maple cotton candy—even a maple Champ! The shop also operates as an old-fashioned candy store.

✷ Special Events

Also see *Entertainment*.

🎿 ✐ *Mid-February:* **Great Ice in Grand Isle** (802-372-8400; champlainislands.com). Two weeks of frozen fun on Lake Champlain's North Hero Bay that kick off with a Christmas tree fire on the lake with a bagpipe entrance. Events include ice hockey, ice fishing derby, state park lake trek, ice golf, dogsledding, ice skating, sledding, and indoor pursuits such as a pancake breakfast and movie night. Check the website for a complete schedule.

✐ *Late April:* **Vermont Maple Festival** (802-524-5800; vtmaplefestival.org), St. Albans. For three days the town turns into a nearly nonstop "sugarin' off" party, courtesy of the local maple producers, augmented by a parade, crafts and antiques shows, a pancake breakfast, specialty food show and sale, rides, and other events.

Late May: **Abenaki Heritage Celebration** (802-868-2559; abenakination.org), on the green, Swanton—a powwow with costumed dancing, Native music, foods, books, and crafts.

✐ *First weekend in June:* **Vermont Dairy Festival** (802-933-8891; vermontdairyfestival.com), Enosburg Falls. Milking contest, baking contest, midway rides, cow plop contest, crafts fair, pageant, and more.

July 4: **Parades** and **barbecues** in South Hero and Alburgh.

✐ *Early July:* **Great Race Triathlon** (802-524-2444; stalbanschamber.com). Run, bike, and paddle race in St. Albans Bay. **Bay Day** is held the same weekend as a beach day for families, followed by fireworks.

Second weekend in July: **Champlain Islands Open Farm & Studio Tour** (802-372-8400; openfarmandstudio.com). Tour the Champlain Island vineyards, farms, and markets and meet the artists, growers, and animals living and working on the Lake Champlain border. **Taste of the Island** is held in conjunction with the event at Grand Isle Art Works and offers tastes of local restaurants and a gathering place for the weekend's events.

✐ *Early August:* **Franklin County Field Days** (802-868-2514; franklincountyfielddays.org), Airport Rd., Highgate. Classic old-time country fair with cattle exhibits, crafts fair, games, rides, musical entertainment, tractor, horse, and oxen pulls, cattle judging, draft horse show.

🎣 ✐ *August:* **Lake Champlain Bluegrass Festival** (802-482-7766; lakechamplainmusic .com) Palmers Field, Alburgh. Bluegrass and camping festival with national, regional, and local bluegrass bands, banjo and fiddle contest, crafts. Day or festival rates, free camping, pets in camping area only, children under 12 free.

Columbus Day weekend: **Island Harvest Days** (802-372-8400; champlainislands.com), South Hero—orchards open for picking, berry pies, cider doughnuts, crafts show, farmers market.

✐ *Early December:* **Running of the Bells** (802-524-2444; stalbanschamber.com), St. Albans. Enjoy local holiday flair at this dress-up holiday stroll through town where families dress as their favorite Christmas characters. The event kicks off the **St. Albans Festival of the Trees**.

ICE FISHING DERBY IN GRAND ISLE
Raven Schwann

Stowe Area and North of the Notch

5

Smugglers' Notch Resort

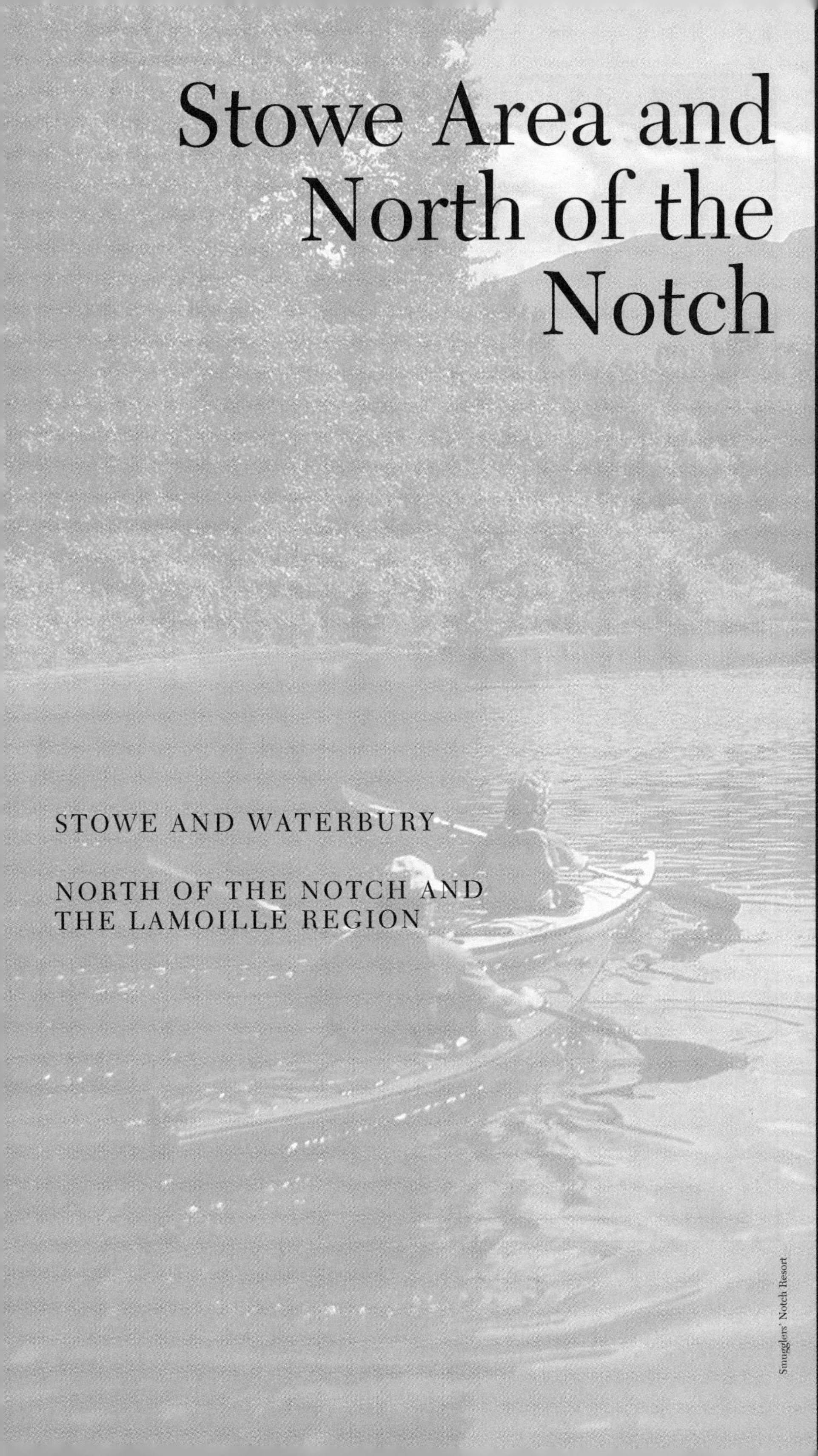

STOWE AND WATERBURY

NORTH OF THE NOTCH AND THE LAMOILLE REGION

Stowe Area and North of the Notch

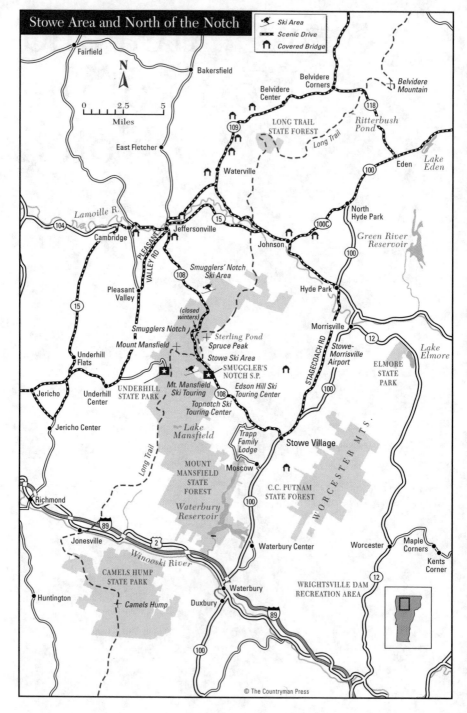

Ski Area
Scenic Drive
Covered Bridge

Fairfield

Bakersfield

N

0   2.5   5
Miles

East Fletcher

Belvidere
Corners

Belvidere
Center

Belvidere
Mountain

118

LONG TRAIL
STATE FOREST

109

Ritterbush
Pond

Long Trail

Waterville

100

Eden

Lake
Eden

Lamoille R.

104

Cambridge

15

Jeffersonville

North
Hyde Park

100C

Johnson

Green River
Reservoir

PLEASANT VALLEY RD

108

Smugglers' Notch
Ski Area

100

Pleasant
Valley

15

Hyde Park

(closed
winters)

Smugglers Notch

Mount Mansfield

Sterling Pond

Spruce Peak

Stowe Ski Area

SMUGGLER'S
NOTCH S.P.

Morrisville

12

Underhill
Flats

UNDERHILL
STATE PARK

Mt. Mansfield
Ski Touring

108

Edson Hill Ski
Touring Center

Stowe-
Morrisville
Airport

STAGECOACH RD

100

ELMORE
STATE
PARK

Lake
Elmore

Jericho

Underhill
Center

Topnotch Ski
Touring Center

Jericho Center

Long Trail

Lake
Mansfield

Trapp
Family
Lodge

Stowe Village

WORCESTER MTS.

MOUNT
MANSFIELD
STATE
FOREST

Moscow

C.C. PUTNAM
STATE FOREST

Richmond

Waterbury
Reservoir

100

89

Jonesville

2

Winooski River

Waterbury Center

Worcester

Maple
Corners

Kents
Corner

CAMELS HUMP
STATE PARK

12

Huntington

Camels Hump

Duxbury

Waterbury

89

WRIGHTSVILLE DAM
RECREATION AREA

100

© The Countryman Press

STOWE AND WATERBURY

Stowe is best known for scoring Vermont a spot on the map as the "ski capital of the East." But the mountain town is also a year-round vacation destination and the state's premier spa locale. Stowe's 200-year-old village looks like a classic Vermont village should look, set against the massive backdrop of Mount Mansfield, which looks just like Vermont's highest mountain should look. Waterbury is one of Vermont's most centrally located and accessible towns (Rt. 100 south from Stowe off I-89's Exit 10). It's home to the nerve centers of both Ben & Jerry's and Keurig Green Mountain, but small businesses thrive downtown.

Stowe Mountain Resort established its ski area in 1938, and the same outfit continues to maintain its reputation for world-class skiing and riding. The alpine skiing and snowboarding at Stowe continue to be outstanding. The cross-country ski network totals more than 150 km, with many trails meandering off the high walls of the cul-de-sac in which the resort nestles.

But truth be told, Stowe attracts more visitors in summer and fall than it does in winter. From June through mid-October it offers golf, tennis, theater, as well as hiking, biking, fishing, and special events every week. Mountain biking has become especially popular thanks in part to the Trapp Family Lodge's extensive backcountry trail system, which offers 50 miles from beginner to expert. Between Stowe Mountain Resort and the mountains it connects, there are ample discovery options, from gondola riding to extensive hiking.

STOWE RECREATION PATH

Stowe Area Association

Low-key natural beauty can be found along the 5.5-mile Stowe Recreation Path that parallels the Mountain Road, and at many of the smaller mountain lodging establishments. Both Stowe and Waterbury's roads meander through cornfields, wildflowers, and raspberry patches, branching very quickly away from the commercial center to reveal a more unspoiled Vermont.

Waterbury and Stowe are excellent pivots from which to explore northern Vermont: 30 miles from Burlington, just over the Notch to the unspoiled Lamoille Valley, and a short drive from both Montpelier and Barre on one hand and the Northeast Kingdom on the other, with the Mad River Valley just past Waterbury on Rt. 100.

Stick and mud season rates are lowest. Lodging options range from funky to fabulous, including a number of self-contained resorts as well as inns, lodges, motels, and condominiums.

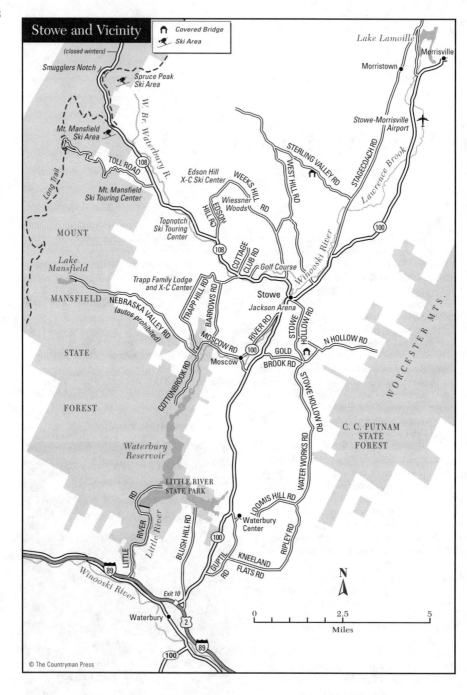

Stowe and Vicinity

Covered Bridge
Ski Area

(closed winters)

Smugglers Notch

Spruce Peak Ski Area

W. Br. Waterbury R.

Mt. Mansfield Ski Area

Long Trail

TOLL ROAD

108

Mt. Mansfield Ski Touring Center

Edson Hill X-C Ski Center

WEEKS HILL

Wiessner Woods

WEST HILL RD

STERLING VALLEY RD

STAGECOACH RD

Lake Lamoille

Morrisville

Morristown

Stowe-Morrisville Airport

Laurence Brook

100

Topnotch Ski Touring Center

EDSON HILL RD

MOUNT

Lake Mansfield

MANSFIELD

108

COTTAGE CLUB RD

Golf Course

Winooski River

Trapp Family Lodge and X-C Center

NEBRASKA VALLEY RD (autos prohibited)

TRAPP HILL RD

BARROWS RD

RIVER RD

Stowe

Jackson Arena

STOWE HOLLOW RD

N HOLLOW RD

STATE

MOSCOW RD

100

Moscow

GOLD BROOK RD

COTTONBROOK RD

FOREST

Waterbury Reservoir

STOWE HOLLOW RD

WATER WORKS RD

C. C. PUTNAM STATE FOREST

WORCESTER MTS.

LITTLE RIVER STATE PARK

RD

LITTLE RIVER

Little River

BLUSH HILL RD

LOOMIS HILL RD

RIPLEY RD

Waterbury Center

100

GUPTIL RD

KNEELAND FLATS RD

89

Winooski River

Exit 10

Waterbury

2

100

89

N

0   2.5   5

Miles

© The Countryman Press

Rachel Carter

WATERBURY RESERVOIR

The Stowe Area Association has been in business since 1936, matching visitors with lodgings they can afford and enjoy.

Until recently, most Stowe-bound visitors knew Waterbury, 10 miles down Rt. 100, simply as an I-89 exit. But a food and drink renaissance has changed that. In the brief downtown between the traffic light and the railroad station, there's an embarrassment of excellent places to grab an artisan pizza, a plate of smoked meat, or a hard-to-find beer. Waterbury Reservoir, accessible from Waterbury Center, is the obvious place in this area to swim and paddle a canoe or kayak.

GUIDANCE The Stowe Area Association (802-253-7321; 877-247-8693; gostowe.com), 51 Main St., Stowe 05672. The SAA publishes seasonal guides, makes lodging reservations, and maintains an expansive, professionally staffed welcome center, open daily 9–5, Sun. 11–5.

The Waterbury Tourism Council maintains an excellent website, waterbury.org, and stocks a self-serve kiosk in the Shell station on Rt. 100 by the I-89 exit.

GETTING THERE By bus: Vermont Transit/Greyhound (800-552-8737) stops in Montpelier with connections from Boston, New York, and points south.

By train: Amtrak from Washington, DC; New York City; and Springfield, Massachusetts, stops in Waterbury.

By plane: The Stowe-Morrisville Airport, 7 miles north, provides private plane services and charters. Burlington International Airport, 34 miles away, is served by major carriers (see "Burlington Region").

By taxi: Peg's Pickup/Stowe Taxi (800-370-9490). Nolan's Taxi Service (802-888-2255). More at gostowe.com.

By car: From most points, I-89, Exit 10, and 15 minutes north on Rt. 100.

GETTING AROUND During winter season and select peak weekends in summer and fall, Stowe Mountain Road Shuttle (802-223-7BUS; gmtaride.org) circles the 7 miles between the village and the mountain for free. Pick up a schedule at the SAA welcome center (see Guidance).

MEDICAL EMERGENCY Call 911. Copley Hospital (802-888-4231), 528 Washington Hwy., Morrisville.

✳ Must See

Mount Mansfield (802-253-3500; stowe.com), the highest point in Vermont—4,395 feet at the Chin—yields a truly spectacular view, accessible primarily in summer, unless you can clamber up to the summit from the Cliff House restaurant at the top of the gondola over ice and snow. In summer there are two easy ways up: the Toll Road and an eight-passenger gondola. **The Mount Mansfield Auto Toll Road** (802-253-3000) begins 7 miles up Rt. 108 from the village of Stowe; look for the sign on your left just before the Inn at the Mountain. Open late May–mid-Oct., 9–4, weather permitting. Motorcycles and bikes not permitted. First laid in the mid-19th century, this steep, winding road led to a now demolished hotel that served the public until 1957. The road also serves as a ski trail in winter. It climbs to the Mount Mansfield Summit Station, just below the Nose (4,062 feet). A half-mile Tundra Trail follows the Long Trail (red-and-white blazes on the rocks) north to Drift Rock (the trek should take 20 minutes); another mile along the trail brings you to the summit of Mount Mansfield (4,395 feet). The round-trip takes two hours. A naturalist is on hand May–Nov. The **Gondola Skyride** (802-253-3000; stowe.com) at Stowe operates mid-June–mid-Oct. at Mount Mansfield, weather permitting, 10–4:30 PM. The eight-passenger gondola runs from Midway Lodge to the Cliff House; half an hour's trek brings you up to the Chin. However you get there, the view from the summit (the Chin) is spectacular on a clear day: west across 20 miles of farmland to Lake Champlain; east to the Worcester Range across the Stowe Valley; north to Jay Peak (35 miles distant) across the Lamoille Valley; and south, back along the Green Mountains, to Camels Hump. Mount Washington is visible to the east, Whiteface to the west.

Smugglers Notch is the high (elevation: 2,162 feet), extremely winding and narrow stretch of Rt. 108 just north of Mount Mansfield, with 1,000-foot cliffs towering on either side. The first carriage road through this pass wasn't opened until 1894, but the name reflects its heavy use as a route to smuggle cattle down from Canada during the War of 1812, not to mention hooch during Prohibition. One of two formally designated State Scenic Roads in Vermont, Smugglers Notch is known for its colorfully named rock formations: Smugglers Head, Elephant Head, the Hunter and His Dog, the Big Spring, Smugglers Cave, and the Natural Refrigerator. The Long Trail North, clearly marked, provides an easy, mile-plus hike to Sterling Pond, a beautiful spot at 3,000 feet, and fish-stocked, too. Elephant Head can be reached from the state picnic area on Rt. 108; a 2-mile trail leads to this landmark—from which you can also continue on to Sterling Pond and thence out to Rt. 108 only a couple of miles above the picnic area. No one should drive through Smugglers Notch without stopping to see the Smugglers Cave and to clamber around on the rocks. The Notch is closed in winter, inviting cross-country skiing and snowshoeing.

Stowe Recreation Path is a 5.3-mile paved path that begins in Stowe Village behind the Community Church, winds up through cornfields, wildflowers, and raspberry patches, and parallels Mountain Rd. (but at a more forgiving pitch). It's open year-round to walkers, joggers, bicyclists, in-line skaters, and cross-country skiers. The path features spots for swimming and fishing as well as landmark bridges and access to local shops and restaurants. Note the **Quiet Path** along the West Branch River, a mile loop off the main path (it begins across from the Golden Eagle) reserved for walkers (no mountain bikers or in-line skaters).

THE VERMONT SKI & SNOWBOARD MUSEUM
Rachel Carter

Vermont Ski & Snowboard Museum (802-253-9911; vtssm.com), Old Town Hall, 1 S. Main St., Stowe. Open Wed.–Mon. See the actual lifts that carried the first skiers up the Vermont mountains and the ski equipment they used to come down. Discover how dozens of tiny ski areas grew into the handful of mega resorts that dominate the industry today. Watch old ski movies and vintage ski footage on a giant plasma screen. More than 10,000 items chronicling winter sports in Vermont. The museum shop sells ski-related gifts.

Note: For Ben & Jerry's Ice Cream Factory Tours see *To Do—For Families.*

AIR RIDES For **hot-air ballooning**, inquire at Stoweflake Mountain Resort and Spa (802-253-7355; stoweflake.com). Whitcomb Aviation's **Stowe Soaring**, based at the Stowe-Morrisville State Airport (802-888-7845; 800-898-7845; stowesoaring.com), offers **glider rides**, instruction, and rentals. Also see the Gondola Skyride on Mount Mansfield in *Must See*.

BIKING Mountain biking is to spring, summer, and fall in Stowe what skiing is to winter. Diverse trail system development at signature destinations like the Trapp Family Lodge has beefed up Stowe's appeal to mountain bikers. **Trapp Family Lodge** (802-253-5755, trappfamily.com) offers trail passes and rentals. Stowe rental sources are **AJ's Ski & Sports** (802-253-4593; 800-226-6257; ajssporting goods.com), **Pinnacle Ski & Sports** (800-458-9996; pinnacleskisports.com), the **Nordic Barn** (802-253-6433; nordicbarnvt.com), and **Skier Shop** (800-996-8398; skiershop.com) in Stowe. Neophytes usually head for the 5.5-mile **Stowe Recreation Path** (see *Must See*); next there's a 10-mile loop through part of the Mount Mansfield State Forest and into the Cottonbrook Basin.

BOATING Canoes and kayaks can be rented from **Umiak Outfitters** (802-253-2317; umiak.com), Stowe. Umiak also offers river trips, lessons, and guided trips on the Winooski and Lamoille Rivers, on Lake Champlain, and throughout the state. **Bert's Boats** (802-644-8189; bertsboats.com) also offers a variety of group tours.

⊘ **CARRIAGE RIDES** Gentle Giants Sleigh & Carriage Rides (802-253-2216; gentlegiantsrides .com) in Stowe offers sleigh and carriage rides. **Trapp Family Lodge** (802-353-5813) offers wagon and carriage rides, while draft horses pull guests in sleighs at **Stowehof Inn & Resort**.

COVERED BRIDGES The **Gold Brook Bridge** in Stowe Hollow, also known as Emily's Bridge because Emily is said to have hanged herself from it (due, so the story goes, to unrequited love), is the most famous "haunted structure" in the state (take School St. about 8 miles to Covered Bridge Rd.). There is another picturesque bridge spanning Sterling Brook off Stagecoach Rd., north of the village.

DISC GOLF The Center Chains Disc Golf Course and Harwood Union Disc Golf Course are both in Waterbury. More info at gmdgc.org.

FISHING The Little River in Stowe is a favorite for brook trout, along with Sterling Pond on top of Spruce Peak and Sterling Brook. **Catamount Fishing Adventures** (802-253-8500; catamountfishing .com), run by Willy Dietrich, is located in Stowe. It offers year-round guide service, including ice fishing. The **Fly Rod Shop** (802-253-7346; flyrodshop.com) in Stowe carries a full line of gear and offers full- and half-day guided tours.

FITNESS The Swimming Hole (802-253-9229; theswimmingholestowe.com) has an Olympic-sized pool, toddler swimming area, waterslide, fitness center with group-sized rooms, aqua aerobics, personal training, and swimming instruction. **West Branch Yoga** (802-253-4330; westbranchyoga .com) is open year-round, seven days a week, and evenings.

MOUNTAIN BIKING NEAR TRAPP FAMILY LODGE

Trapp Family Lodge

FOR FAMILIES ⊘ ♿ **Ben & Jerry's Ice Cream Factory Tours** (802-882-1240; 866-BJ-TOURS; benjerry.com), located on Rt. 100 in Waterbury, 1 mile north of Exit 10. No American ice cream has a story, let alone a taste, to match that of the Vermont-made sweet and creamy stuff concocted by high school buddies Ben Cohen and Jerry Greenfield, whose personalities linger though they have sold the company to Unilever. More than two decades ago they began churning out Dastardly Mash and Heath Bar Crunch in a Burlington garage; they have now outgrown this seemingly mammoth plant, Vermont's number one attraction. Ice cream is made Mon.–Thurs., but a half-hour tour of the plant is offered daily 10–6 (9–8 in

THE SPA CAPITOL OF THE NORTHEAST

Names such as Canyon Ranch and Golden Door get all the national attention, but tucked in the peaks of Stowe, a battle rages for spa supremacy. The competition is fierce, but the benefits belong to guests looking for a place to relax to the max. And each of the resorts welcomes eager customers even if they're not bedding down at the hotel.

The **Spa at Topnotch** (802-253-8585; topnotchresort.com) and the **Spa at Stoweflake** (802-253-7355; stoweflake.com) both offer over-the-top service. At Stoweflake, facilities include 30 treatment rooms, a Hungarian mineral soaking pool, an aqua solarium, and a 102-degree massaging waterfall. The 120 treatments include a maple sugar body polish, for a local touch.

But they're not the only ones willing to scrub you down with maple or seasonal Vermont botanicals. In 2013 Topnotch underwent a $15 million face-lift. That includes an improved program at the already sought-after 35,000-square-foot Topnotch Spa. The crown jewel is the "Pathways to Wellness" program, which tailors the experience to each guest.

Each "pathway" ($294–492) includes a set of treatments, plus choices made by the individual. Guests willing to shell out the big bucks for the "Restorative Pathway" package take an active role in their wellness with a private yoga session, access to all fitness classes on-site (they include pool exercises and Pilates), and a custom energy healing session to go with their massage and facial.

The **Spa at Stowe Mountain Lodge** (802-760-4782; stowemountainlodge.com) is no less indulgent. Perhaps it could be seen as the thinking man's (or woman's) R&R destination, what with offerings including craniosacral massage and chakra balancing along with the usual rubs and scrubs.

Located in the village of Stowe, the **Green Mountain Inn** (802-253-7301; greenmountaininn .com) offers an updated health club including an outdoor pool and a partnership with Stowe Village Massage, also a yoga practitioner. The **Golden Eagle Resort** (802-253-4811; golden eagleresort.com) offers massage, aromatherapy, and Reiki with fewer bells and whistles.

But when staying in the spa capitol of the Northeast, why choose only one?

GREEN MOUNTAIN INN POOL

Green Mountain Inn

Stowe Area Association

FLY FISHING

The gift store, selling an amazing number of things relating to cows and Vermont, is open 10–7, as is the Scoop Shop. The tour includes a multimedia show, a look (from an observation platform) at the production room, and a free sample of one of the many "euphoric flavors." The grounds include picnic facilities and some sample black-and-white cows. The fee of $3 adults, $2 seniors (ages 12 and under free), has remained steady for years.

✍ *More ice cream:* Ice cream is popular in Stowe and can be enjoyed in a quaint setting at **Depot Street Malt Shop** (802-253-4269); dripping with eclectic flavors at **I. C. Scoops** (802-253-0995); and at **Lake Champlain Chocolates** at "A Special Place" (802-241-4150) on Rt. 100 in Waterbury—also a one-stop shopping place for Vermont products.

✍ **Apple Tree Learning Centers** (802-253-4321; appletreelc.com) offers a year-round series of "discovery camps" for kids visiting the Stowe area ranging from bouldering and climbing to biking and nature exploration.

✍ **Kid's Summer Mountain Adventure Camps** (802-253-3685), based at Stowe Mountain Resort, offer age-appropriate activities for kids ages 4–12, ranging from outdoor excursions to ropes courses and sports. The camps also "take the kids to mountain attractions so you don't have to" (see *Alpine Slide*).

✍ **Stowe Golfpark** (802-253-9951) at the Sun & Ski Inn, Mountain Rd., offers 18 holes of miniature golf (May–Oct., 10–9:30).

GOLF Stowe Country Club & Vermont Golf Academy (802-253-4893; stowe.com) is an 18-hole course with a 40-acre driving range, putting green, restaurant, bar, pro shop, and school. The Stowe Mountain Club offers up an additional 18-hole course for members and resort guests named among the *Golf Magazine* "top 10 new places to play." **Stoweflake Mountain Resort & Spa** (802-253-7355; stoweflake.com) has a nine-hole, executive course and is adjacent to the Stowe Country Club, offering golf packages. **Ryder Brook Golf Club** (802-888-3525; 866-888-5810; ryderbrookgc.com), Rt. 100, 6 miles north of Stowe in Morrisville, offers nine holes, a driving range, putting green, rentals, and snack bar. **Blush Hill Country Club** (802-244-8974; bhccvt.com) is a picturesque nine-hole course in Waterbury, with restaurant and pro shop.

HIKING AND WALKING See Stowe Recreation Path, Mount Mansfield, and Smugglers Notch in *Must See.*

Green Mountain Club (GMC) (802-244-7037; greenmountainclub.org), a few miles south of Stowe Village on Rt. 100 in Waterbury Center, maintains a Hiker's Center stocked with hiking maps, guides (like the popular *Long Trail Guide* and *Day Hiker's Guide to Vermont*), and gear. Inquire about workshops and special events. Information is also available at the Stowe Area Association (802-253-7321; gostowe.com).

Popular local hikes include **Stowe Pinnacle**, a 2.8-mile climb; and **Mount Hunger** (4 miles), the highest peak in the Worcester Range. **Taft Lodge** (3.4 miles) is steep but takes you to the oldest lodge on the Long Trail. **Belvidere Mountain** in Eden is a 3½-hour trek yielding good views in all directions. **Ritterbush Pond** and **Devil's Gulch**, also in Eden, are about 2½ hours round-trip, and **Elmore Mountain** in Elmore State Park is a 2- to 3-hour hike with spectacular views.

Camels Hump, from Waterbury. See "Burlington Region" for details. This trail is also detailed in *50 Hikes in Vermont* (Backcountry Publications). One trail starts from Crouching Lion Farm in Duxbury; it's a 6½-hour round-trip hike to the unspoiled summit of Vermont's third highest mountain. Pick up a map at the GMC Hiker's Center (see above) and sign in at trailheads.

Little River Trail System, Mount Mansfield State Forest, Waterbury. There are seven beautiful trails through the Ricker Basin and Cotton Brook area, once a settlement for 50 families who left behind cellar holes, stone fences, cemeteries, lilacs, and apple trees. Accessible from both Stowe and Waterbury. See also "Barre/Montpelier Area" for hiking in the Worcester Range.

Note: Northern Vermont—Hiking Trails, published by Map Adventures of Portland, Maine (207-879-4777; mapadventures.com), is worth picking up. Again, sign in at trailheads if you can.

HORSEBACK RIDING **Edson Hill Manor Stables** (802-253-7371; edsonhillmanor.com), Stowe, offers guided trail rides (also pony rides) through its upland wilds and fields, geared to various levels, also lessons. **Topnotch Stables at the Nordic Barn** (802-253-6433; topnotchresort.com), Mountain Rd., also offers trail rides and lessons.

ROCK CLIMBING Check with **Umiak Outfitters** (802-253-2317; umiak.com) in Stowe for instruction and ropes course. Warm up on the **Climbing Wall** at Stowe Mountain Resort (802-253-3500; stowe.com).

✷ **SWIMMING** **Waterbury Reservoir**, the best local beach, is accessible from Little River State Park and from Waterbury Center State Park (see *Green Space* and *Campgrounds*). **Sterling Falls Gorge, Moss Glen Falls**, and the swimming holes in **Ranch Valley** are all worth checking; ask locally for directions. The nonprofit community pool is **The Swimming Hole** (802-253-9229; theswimmingholestowe.com), featuring a competition-sized pool in a barn with a toddler and child swimming area and waterslide. Many lodging places also have their own pools that nonguests may use for a fee.

TENNIS The Topnotch Tennis Center (802-253-9649; topnotchresort.com), Stowe. Highly acclaimed with four indoor and six outdoor courts, pro shop, instruction, ball machines, round-robins, and over 30 programs; open daily (hours vary).

Inn at the Mountain Tennis Club (802-253-3656; stowe.com), six well-maintained clay courts adjacent to the Inn at the Mountain, open daily (hours vary).

Free public courts can be found at the town recreation area off School St. A number of inns have courts available to the public; inquire at the Stowe Area Association (802-253-7321; gostowe.com).

✳ Winter Sports

CROSS-COUNTRY SKIING A 150 km network of trails that connects ski centers in this area adds up to some of the best ski touring in New England. Given the high elevation of much of this terrain, the trails tend to have snow when few other areas do, and on windy, icy days, cross-country can be better in Stowe than downhill. All four touring centers (in Stowe) honor the others' trail tickets (if you ski, not drive, from one to the next).

○ **Trapp Family Lodge Cross-Country Ski Center** (802-253-5755; trappfamily.com). Located on Trapp Hill Rd., off by itself in the upper reaches of the valley, this is one of the oldest and most beautiful commercial trail systems—40 km of set trails and a total of 85 km of trails at elevations of 1,100–3,000 feet. The basic route here is up and up to a cabin in the woods, a source of homemade soups and chili. Start early enough in the day and you can continue along ridge trails or connect with the Mount Mansfield system. Lessons, equipment rental and sales, and a refreshment lounge are all available, as well as guided and backcountry tours.

HORSEBACK RIDING NEAR STOWE
Stowe Area Association

Stowe Mountain Resort Cross-Country Ski Center (802-253-3688; stowe.com), Mountain Rd. Located near the Inn at the Mountain, this center offers 35 km of set trails, plus 45 km of backcountry trails, at elevations of 1,200–2,800 feet. It's possible to take the Toll House lift partway up the Toll Road and ski down (a good place to practice telemarking). You can also take the quad close enough to the summit to enable you to climb to the very top (via the Toll Road)

Trapp Family Lodge

**CROSS-COUNTRY SKIING AT THE TRAPP
FAMILY LODGE**

for a spectacular view out across Lake Champlain; the descent via the Toll Road is relatively easy. Another beautiful trail circles Sterling Pond high in the saddle between Spruce and Madonna mountains (accessible via chairlift). Connecting trails link this system with the Trapp Family Lodge trails (see above) along some of Stowe's oldest ski trails, such as Ranch Camp and Steeple, dating to the 1920s, as well as new backcountry trails (and tours) winding along the curved inner face of the mountain.

Edson Hill Manor Ski Touring Center (802-253-7371; edsonhillmanor.com), Edson Hill Rd. Relatively uncrowded on the uplands north of the Mountain Rd., the area offers 30 miles of set trails, 25 more on outlying trails at elevations between 1,200 and 2,150 feet; instruction, rental, sales, full lunches, and guided tours available.

Topnotch Ski Touring at the Nordic Barn (802-253-6433; topnotchresort.com), Mountain Rd., Stowe. Novice to expert, a total of 20 km of groomed trails on 120 private acres; instruction, equipment rental at the Nordic Barn; trails through Topnotch Resort.

Remember: Backcountry skiing is best done with a guide if you don't know the area. **Umiak Outfitters** (802-253-2317; umiak.com) offers backcountry tours as well as a moonlit dinner tour special.

DOWNHILL SKIING & SNOWBOARDING ✷ **Stowe Mountain Resort** (800-253-4SKI; stowe.com for information, snow reports, and slope-side lodging). In 2012 Stowe unveiled a new high-speed quad, one of many improvements included in a 15-year mountain expansion plan upgrading facilities and operations, and linking Stowe's two neighboring mountains, Mount Mansfield and Spruce Peak.

Stowe regulars ski Mount Mansfield in the morning, switching after lunch to south-facing Spruce Peak across Rt. 108, now connected by the skis-on "Over Easy" transfer gondola. The new Spruce Camp Base Lodge is now the resort's central base, with restaurants, shops, rentals, indoor and outdoor

STOWE

Stowe Mountain Resort

fireplaces. It adjoins a pedestrian plaza with more shops and restaurants and the dramatic new six-story Spruce Mountain Lodge and Spa, plus "mountain cabins" (posh condos) and private homes. High-speed quads now number three, and New England's first fully automated snowmaking system keeps the slopes dusted top-to-bottom. Backcountry stretches and main trail navigation continue to develop, and the 90-second "Over Easy" Gondola from Mansfield to Spruce eliminates the need for constant shuttles. Mount Mansfield, whose famous Front Four trails plunge almost vertically down its legendary face, has a quad and double to get you to the top (wear a neck warmer, goggles, and sunscreen). Under the Octagon Café, these expert slopes feature tree-shaded glades and some of the longest trails in the East, though you also have the option of half a dozen intermediate trails that snake down at more forgiving angles. It's an easy traverse from this side of the mountain to the trails served by the eight-person, high-speed gondola to the elevated Cliff House, from which long, ego-building runs like Perry Merrill sweep to the valley floor. Freestyle terrain parks (small, medium, and large) and half-pipe can be accessed from anywhere on Mount Mansfield.

Lifts: 8-passenger gondola, intermountain transfer gondola, 3 high-speed quad chairlifts, 4 double and 2 triple chairlifts, 2 surface.

Trails: 116, also glade skiing; 25% expert, 59% intermediate, 16% beginner.

Vertical drop: 2,360 feet on Mount Mansfield, 1,550 feet on Spruce Peak.

Snowmaking: Covers 80% of the terrain trails served by all of the 12 lifts.

Facilities: 3 base lodges each offer food and services with rentals and ski shops at Mansfield and Spruce; restaurants include Cliff House (see *Eating Out*) atop the busiest lift, Octagon Café, The Great Room, The Cottage, and the award-winning Solstice (see *Dining Out*).

Ski school: 200 instructors; a lift especially designed for beginners at Spruce Peak, where novices learn to make the transition from easy to intermediate trails; advanced ski school program at Mount Mansfield.

Night skiing: More than 20 acres on Mount Mansfield are lighted Thurs.–Sat. nights 5–9.

For children: Day care from 6 weeks to 6 years in Cubs Infant Daycare. The Children's Learning Center offers day care or a combo of care and lessons at Spruce Peak.

Rates: See stowe.com for current ticket prices.

ICE SKATING Ice skating is available at the Olympic-sized **Jackson Arena** (802-253-6148) in the village. Call for public skating times. The town of Waterbury has a large skating arena with rentals called the **Ice Center of Washington West** (802-244-4040; icecenter.org).

SLEIGH RIDES See *Carriage Rides*.

SNOWMOBILING Stowe Snowmobile Tours (802-253-6221; stowesnowmobiletours.com) offers rentals and tours of the Mount Mansfield State Forest, and is also a source of information about local trails.

SPRUCE PEAK AT STOWE

Stowe Mountain Resort

SNOWSHOEING Umiak Outdoor Outfitters (802-253-2317; umiak.com) offers guided moonlit snowshoe tours, fondue and gourmet dinner tours, even a package tour at the Ben & Jerry's Factory in Waterbury so you can snowshoe before you eat the ice cream. **Trapp Family Lodge Cross-Country Ski Center** has designated more than 15 km of its trails as snowshoe-only. The **Stowe Mountain Resort Cross-Country Center** has cut 5 km of dedicated trails and permits snowshoers on all 80 km of its cross-country trails. **Topnotch Resort** has also designated some snowshoe-recommended routes, and permits snowshoes on all 20 km of its trails.

The obvious place to go is, of course, up the unplowed stretch of Rt. 108 into Smugglers Notch, and the more adventurous can also access more than 40 miles of hiking terrain on

and around Mount Mansfield, but it's best to check with the **Green Mountain Club** (see *Hiking and*
Walking), which also sponsors a February Snowshoe Festival. Local rental sources are plentiful, and
many inns offer snowshoes for guests to use. Pick up a copy of Northern Vermont Adventure Skiing, a
weatherproofed map/guide detailing trails throughout the region. It's available at Umiak and other
local stores in Stowe.

✴ Green Space

For fees and reservation rules, see *Campgrounds* in "What's Where." Note that state parks are staffed
seasonally, but can be accessed year-round. All state parks on lakes have boat rentals during the open
season.

Mount Mansfield State Forest is the largest state forest in Vermont—27,436 acres—much of which
lies on the other (western) flank of the mountain. The 10-mile Cottonbrook Trail starts at Cottonbrook Rd. off Nebraska Valley Rd. in Stowe. Follow the blazes.

Smugglers Notch State Park (802-253-4014; vtstateparks.com), Stowe 05672; 10 miles up Mountain Rd. (Rt. 108) from Stowe Village, a small and quaint park with camping available.

❂ Elmore State Park (802-888-2982; vtstateparks.com), Lake Elmore 05657. Drive 14 miles north
of Stowe on Rt. 100, then east to Morrisville, south 5 miles on Rt. 12; 709 acres with a beach, bathhouse, concession stand, rental boats, camping, CCC community center, hiking trail up Elmore
Mountain with fire tower.

Waterbury Center State Park (802-244-1226; vtstateparks.com), Waterbury Center 05677. A very
popular swimming beach with spectacular views and fun boating activities.

Little River State Park (802-244-7103; vtstateparks.com), Waterbury 05676, on Waterbury Reservoir with miles of historic hiking trails. See *Hiking and Walking*.

Wiessner Woods (802-253-7221; stowelandtrust.org). An 80-acre preserve with nature trails maintained by the Stowe Land Trust. The entrance is on Edson Hill Rd., the next right after the entrance
to Stowehof Inn.

✴ Stowe Lodging

Most accommodations are found either in
Stowe Village or along—or just off—the 7.2-
mile Mountain Rd. (Rt. 108), which connects
the village with the ski slopes.

RESORTS

In Stowe 05672

♂ ♨ ♿ **The Trapp Family Lodge** (802-253-
8511; 800-826-7000; trappfamily.com), 700
Trapp Hill Rd., is a mountain resort in the
European tradition modeled on the Austrian
schloss once owned by the family of *Sound of
Music* fame. Johannes von Trapp and son Sam
von Trapp live nearby and remain involved in
the property's day-to-day operations, including
their own Austrian-inspired lagers at the new
Trapp Family Brewery. The 96-room lodge
includes a 12-suite luxury wing and offers ample
common space: a charming greenhouse sitting
room, three common rooms with fireplaces, and
a library, cocktail lounge, large dining room, and
conference facilities. Over 100 time-share guest-
houses and 21 "fractionally owned" villas
(inquire about vacancies) are arranged in tiers on
the slope below, commanding sweeping views of
the Worcester Range. The inn's 2,500 acres are
webbed with cross-country ski and mountain
biking trails, also good for splendid walks. There

are tennis courts and a spring-fed pool as well as
an indoor pool, a sauna, and a workout room in
the Fitness Center. Beer brewed with mountain
springwater, mountainside-reared Scotch Highland cattle, and produce grown year-round in
the greenhouse keep the Trapp Family Lodge
forging ahead with growing involvement from
younger-generation Trapps. A sugarhouse operates in early spring, live music plays in summer,
and a two- or three-day minimum is mandatory
in peak periods like foliage and Christmas.

THE TRAPP FAMILY LODGE

Rachel Carter

Inquire about packages, and about nature walks, snowshoeing, sleigh rides, fly-fishing, birding, yoga, and children's, exercise, cross-country, and backcountry ski and bike programs. Rates range $225–550 depending on seasons and holidays; children under 12 are free.

♂ ❀ ✿ ♿ **Edson Hill Manor** (802-253-7371; 800-621-0284; edsonhill.com), 1500 Edson Hill Rd. A former Colorado mining prospector's country estate set on 38 acres on a high slope, the Manor was built in the 1940s with brick from the old Sherwood Hotel of Burlington. Most of the living room beams were hewn for Ira and Ethan Allen's barn, which stood in North Burlington for more than a century. Each of the nine Manor guest rooms and 15 Carriage House units has a unique personality, most with wood-burning fireplaces. With clean and bright spaces throughout, the furnishings and fixtures combine a classic Vermont look and feel with chic one-of-a-kind components. That aesthetic reaches to the dining room, too, where chef Chad Hanley prepares dishes with a taste of the Green Mountains such as pork belly with arugula salad and a maple-poached egg. Facilities include stables, outdoor pool, multiple ponds, and 4.4 km of cross-country trails. $209–399 per couple.

♂ ✿ ♿ **Green Mountain Inn** (802-253-7301; 800-253-7302; greenmountaininn.com), 18 S. Main St. Lowell Thomas, President Chester Arthur, and President Gerald Ford were guests in this brick-and-clapboard landmark, which dates back to 1833, when it was built as a private home. According to legend, a deceased horseman by the name of Boots Berry has tap-danced above Room 302 since his untimely end

GREEN MOUNTAIN INN

Green Mountain Inn

Rachel Carter

THE TRAPP FAMILY LODGE CONCERT MEADOW

in 1902. Other rooms don't include friendly ghosts, but do include perks such as fireside double Jacuzzi, DVD player with surround sound, marble bath, and original artwork. The reasonably priced downstairs Whip Bar & Grill serves comfort food to make the stay feel like home. Afternoon tea and cookies are served in the living room. $139–389 for rooms (two-night minimum stay on weekends); more for suites, apartments, and two- to three-bedroom town houses. Guests enjoy complimentary use of Athletic Club facilities, located just on the other side of the year-round outdoor heated pool. Kids can enjoy a substantial game room while parents mingle at wine and cheese parties.

❍ ♂ ❦ ✿ ♿ **Stowehof Inn** (802-253-9722; 800-932-7136; stowehofinn.com), half a mile off Rt. 108 on the road to Edson Hill. This Swiss-chalet-style structure was built in 1949 and remains a retro fantasy world—part hobbit hole, part Swiss chalet. From the moment you step through the sod-roofed, porte-cochere entrance on two tree trunks, you are transported. No two of the 46 guest rooms are alike (some are suites; a few are fireplaced demi-suites with optional kitchenette), but all come with private bath and balcony with superlative views. The main floor is furnished like the inside of a castle, with meandering hallways, fireplaced nooks and libraries, a conference room shaped like a covered bridge, and mementos like the divining rod that located the water source for the building. Windows everywhere let in the view. *Four Seasons* was filmed here and the ambience remains solid while the amenities and comforts stay with the trends. Facilities include the lower-level **Coslin's Pub** and game room, **Emily's Fine**

Dining (see *Dining Out*), tennis courts, a triangular pool with mountain views, indoor pool, sauna, fitness room, Jacuzzi, tennis courts, and cross-country ski trails connecting with the larger network. Rates start at $84 midweek and climb to $299 for the best rooms on a holiday weekend, with minimum stays required. All lodging packages include breakfast.

○ ♂ ♥ ♂ ♿ **Topnotch Resort and Spa** (802-253-8585; 800-451-8686; topnotchresort.com), 4000 Mountain Rd. A $15 million renovation in 2013 means fully renovated rooms; a grand, modern lobby; and vast outdoor spaces fun for man, child, and beast. For meals, there's the hip-but-relaxed **Roost** or the stately, glass-sided **Flannel** (see *Dining Out*). Everything from standard hotel accommodations to sumptuous resort homes place guests in the lap of luxury. The spa (see *Fitness*) provides spacious showers, whirlpools, steam rooms, saunas, and leather-chaired fireplace lounges in superb new facilities, including a 60-foot-long indoor pool with skylights and a throbbing waterfall. The Ledges, recently added family units, come with two or three bedrooms and all the bells and whistles. The red Nordic Barn down and across Mountain Rd. serves as a cross-country ski center in winter (50 km of groomed trails connect with other trail systems in Stowe) and a riding stable. $187.50–410 for a regular room; $545–2,000 for homes.

♂ ♥ ♂ ♿ **Stoweflake Mountain Resort & Spa** (802-253-7355; 800-253-2232; stoweflake .com), 1746 Mountain Rd. The small ski lodge that the Baraw family opened more than 30 years ago has mushroomed into a spa and 120-room resort (including 9 luxury suites and 60 town houses of various sizes). There are bright, comfortable, inn-style rooms in the original lodge and many nicely furnished motel rooms in the garden wing (besides its own motel wing, the resort includes the former Nordic Motor Inn). The Stoweflake Spa (see *Fitness*) includes a Cybex circuit, racquetball/squash court, indoor pool, Jacuzzis, saunas, 30 treatment rooms, and a glass-roofed Aqua Solarium containing a Hungarian mineral pool and a heated jet-filled "pond" with a 15-foot waterfall made to replicate Stowe's moss-covered Bingham Falls. There are also tennis courts, badminton, volleyball, croquet, horseshoes, a putting green, and a brand-new nine-hole executive par-3 golf course, not to mention the Stowe Country Club right next door. The hotel's long-standing fine-dining restaurant is no more, but Charlie B's Pub serves three meals a day. $189–542 per room or suite; $239–1,161.50 for townhouse units; dining, spa, and getaway packages.

♂ ♥ ♂ ♿ **Stowe Mountain Lodge** (802-253-3560; stowemountainlodge.com), 7412 Mountain Rd. This resort indeed has a lodge theme, but it's a Disney version, all soaring ceilings, marble floors, and stone walls lined with birch trees. Guests of this centerpiece of the $400 million Spruce Peak alpine village enjoy 312 guest rooms, a spa and wellness center, ski-in/ski-out access, privileges at Stowe Mountain Club (the resort's private 18-hole golf course), and a heated outdoor pool. Solstice restaurant (see *Dining Out*) features farm-to-table cuisine; **Hourglass Bar** serves more relaxed versions of the same.

♨ ♥ ♂ ♿ **Golden Eagle Resort** (802-253-4811; 800-626-1010; goldeneagleresort.com), 511 Mountain Rd. Under new ownership since 2014, the 12-unit motel that Herb and Ann Hillman bought in 1963 evolved through two generations into an 80-acre complex with 94 units. Accommodations range from standard hotel rooms to mini suites and one-bedroom suites. Two-bedroom apartments and a full house are available for larger families. Family geared as well as owned, it offers a lot for children. Amenities include a playground as well as an attractive health spa with indoor pool, large whirlpool, sauna, exercise equipment, and massage services. There are also outdoor heated pools (swimming lessons are offered); a clay tennis court; fish-stocked ponds; shuffleboard, badminton, lawn games, and game rooms; and **The Colonial Café** serves breakfast. $99–579 depending on season and room type or suite (children 12 and under are free) plus a 5 percent resort fee; fully handicapped-accessible rooms available.

♨ ♥ ♂ ♿ **Commodores Inn** (802-253-7131; 800-447-8693; commodoresinn.com), 823 S. Main St., Rt. 100 south. All 72 large rooms have

TOPNOTCH

RachelCarter

a private bath, but request one in the back for a view of the lake. There's a living room with a fireplace, sports lounge, quiet rooms, and a game room; also three Jacuzzis and saunas and an indoor and outdoor pool. The Stowe Yacht Club Dining Room overlooks a 3-acre lake on which model sailboat races are regularly held, not to mention canoeing, kayaking, and fishing— all part of a stay. $98–178. Children 5 and under stay free, 6–12 pay $5 for breakfast; pets are welcome for $10 per night.

INNS AND BED & BREAKFASTS

In Stowe 05672

♂ ☼ ✔ **The Stowe Inn** (802-253-4030; 800-546-4030; stoweinn.com), 123 Mountain Rd. Listed on the National Register of Historic Places, this rambling old inn is set just above Stowe Village at the base of the Mountain Rd. There are 16 rooms with private baths in the inn itself and 20 "country lodge rooms" in the Carriage House (more of a motel/lodge style), most of which allow pets. Guests share spacious common areas with fireplaces, a game room with billiards, a Jacuzzi in the main building, outdoor pool, and the River House Restaurant. Children under 12 stay free, and continental breakfast is included. Rates range $99–179 in low season; $169–359 high season and holidays.

Rachel Carter

STOWEFLAKE SPA

STOWE MOUNTAIN LODGE

Stowe Mountain Resort

♂ & **Stone Hill Inn** (802-253-6282; stone hillinn.com), 89 Houston Farm Rd., 3 miles from the village, off Mountain Rd. With only nine rooms, owners Linda and George Fulton cater to couples. This is a romantic hideaway with a newly refurbished great room. Guest rooms feature two-sided gas fireplaces facing a king bed and a Jacuzzi. There's also a private entrance to 9-acre grounds with woodland gardens and walking trails. Rates of $245 per night off-season, up to $425 for holidays and peak foliage, include afternoon cocktail hour and a full breakfast.

♂ ✿ ✔ **Fiddler's Green Inn** (802-253-8124; 800-882-5346; fiddlersgreeninn.com), 4859 Mountain Rd., 5 miles from the village toward the mountain. Less than a mile from the lifts, this yellow 1820s farmhouse can sleep no more than 18 guests (making it great for small groups) in seven small but comfortable guest rooms. Our favorite is tucked under the eaves within earshot of the stream. Guests gather around the fieldstone hearth in the living room and at the long table off the sunny kitchen. Hammocking is out back by the stream, and hiking or skiing are close by. A cabin retreat is also available to rent. $99–135 B&B; dinner possible on request (BYOB). Families welcome.

✿ ✔ **The Inn at Turner Mill** (802-253-2062; 800-992-0016; turnermill.com), 56 Turner Mill Lane. Sequestered in the pines by Notch Brook, off Mountain Rd. just a mile from the lifts, this complex was splendidly built in the 1930s by an eccentric woman doctor. Its 10 wooded acres include a mountain stream swimming hole, and outdoor pool. The two guest rooms and two apartments are decorated with handcrafted log furniture and have cable TV, private bath, fridge, and coffeemaker. Owners Greg and Mitzi Speer offer a guide service to the best mountain biking, rock and ice climbing, and other adventure sports as well as snowshoe rentals and a trail to ski from the quad to the back of the inn. The old Civilian Conservation Corps ski trails (now cross-country ski trails) are within easy striking distance. $75–85 per room. No meals.

♂ **Brass Lantern Inn** (802-253-2229; 800-729-2980; brasslanterninn.com), 717 Maple St. (Rt. 100), is a welcoming B&B at the northern edge of the village. Since 2009, George and Mary Anne Lewis have made constant upgrades to this renovated 1800s building with planked floors and comfortable common rooms. The nine guest rooms are furnished with antiques and country quilts; all have private bath, and six have whirlpool tub and gas-burning fireplace. Seven have HD TVs with digital cable, too. There's also an outdoor hot tub and classic game room. A three-course farm breakfast using local ingredients and showcasing Chef George's talents and afternoon tea and cookies are included in the rates: $135–255, depending on room and season. Children over 8 are welcome.

♨ ♂ **Auberge de Stowe** (802-253-7787; 800-387-8789; aubergedestowe.com), 692 S. Main St. This 18th-century brick farmhouse and converted carriage house is a find. Shawn and Chantal Kerivan offer six rooms, including a pair of two-bedroom suites, all with private bath. The house is right on Rt. 100 along the river, but there is a view and a sense of space in the back. Amenities include a welcoming dog and cat, a comfortable living room, a large lawn, and a hot tub. Fondue dinners are offered during ski season. $79–199 (before tax) includes a substantial continental breakfast with homemade pastries. The owners speak both German and French.

Inn at the Mountain (802-253-3656; 800-253-4754; stowe.com), 5781 Mountain Rd. The Stowe Mountain Resort's Mountain Rd. inn with easy access to the Toll House lifts on Mount Mansfield. Facilities include **Fireside Tavern** restaurant, clay tennis courts, swimming pools, and wellness center. Off-season begins at $85 and extends to $360 during holidays. Children under 12 stay free. A grouping of condominiums located high up with great views (see *Condos*).

Mountain Road Resort (802-253-4566; 800-367-6873; mountainroadresort.com), 1007 Mountain Rd. A one-of-a-kind art collection separates this ultramodern ski lodge from the pack. The inn comprises two buildings with 31 guest rooms, several smaller buildings, and 16

acres of woods. Owner Eben Burr believes the inn houses the largest non-museum collection of emerging and midcareer artists in the United States and all of the art is for sale, with all proceeds going directly to the artists. Rooms include private patios and porches and 32-inch flat-screen TVs. There's locked storage for skis and snowboards. Once off the slopes, guests are welcome to enjoy pools, hot tub, and sauna or a massage. Fresh-baked goods are served with apple cider, lemonade, and tea each afternoon, along with drinks at the bar. Rooms $99–359, depending on season.

Elsewhere

☃ **Inky Dinky Oink, Ink** (802-253-3046; oinkink.com), 117 Adams Mill Rd., Moscow 05672. The playful name reflects the artwork of innkeeper Liz LeServiget, who houses guests in two air-conditioned rooms in this renovated 1840s farmhouse. One room has two single beds that can be joined together, the other a double bed with a two-tiered outdoor deck, private entrance, and private bath with Jacuzzi. Art and books are everywhere. $135–155. Pets okay (with restrictions). Check out Liz's art gallery, classes, and the organic farm stand out front. Her produce and other regional foods figure in breakfast and afternoon tea served in the tea garden when weather permits.

MOTELS ♂ **Arbor Inn** (802-253-4772; 800-543-1293; arborinnstowe.com), 3214 Mountain Rd. This is the former home of Olympian Billy Kidd. All 12 rooms and suites have a private bath and are furnished with antiques, equipped with TV and a small fridge. Two rooms have fully equipped kitchens; four have a fireplace, and two come with two-person whirlpool tubs. Common space includes a game room, pool table, and outdoor pool and Jacuzzi. Amenities include two fieldstone fireplaces, spectacular views of Mount Mansfield, and English gardens in summer. $100–240 per room with full breakfast.

♨ ♂ **Alpenrose** (802-253-7277; 800-962-7002), 2619 Mountain Rd. This tiny motel has just seven rooms, three of which are efficiencies with kitchenettes; one family with an efficiency (sleeps five) and one standard room. There's direct access to a cross-country network and the Stowe Recreation Path. $80–140; inquire about weekly and holiday rates.

CONDOS/RENTALS ♨ **Butler House** (802-253-7422; butlerhousestowe.com), 128 Main St. Laura and Paul Biron maintain six modern apartments in this 1830 home in the center of downtown. Each room includes a kitchen or kitchenette that includes a Keurig brewer. Some rooms have gas fireplaces and all retain their original pine floors. $99–369; inquire about weekly rates.

Stowe Country Homes (800-639-1990; stowe countryrentals.com) handles condos and houses. **Rentals at Stowe** (802-253-9786; rentalsat stowe.com) also rent homes and condos. **Stowe Mountain Resort** operates magnificent mountainside condo and rental villages—one of the leading features of the multiyear expansions. Among them are the **Townhouse and Lodge Condominiums at Inn at the Mountain** and the **Stowe Mountain Lodge Condominiums and Townhouses** at Spruce Peak. All info at stowe.com. If you're hoping more for a village feeling than a slope-side, **the Green Mountain Inn** offers a lovely selection of apartments and town houses in Stowe Village—green mountaininn.com.

♂ ✿ **The Village Green at Stowe** (802-253-9705; 800-451-3297; vgasstowe.com), 1003 Cape Cod Rd., Stowe 05672. Seven nicely designed buildings set on 40 acres (surrounded by the Stowe Country Club links) contain 73 two- and three-bedroom town houses, all brightly furnished. A recreation building has a heated indoor pool, Jacuzzi, sauna, and a swell game room; also an outdoor pool and two tennis courts. $200–535, low to high season.

🐾 ✿ ♿ **Mountainside Resort at Stowe** (802-253-8610; 800-458-4893; mountainsideresort .com), 171 Cottage Club Rd. Halfway between the mountain and town, these one- to four-bedroom condos offer a resort feel with complete indoor fitness and pool center, nice yard space with grills, tennis and basketball courts, game room; all services. $160–375 depending on season and rooms.

MI CASA KITCHEN & BAR, STOWE

Alice Levitt

CAMPGROUNDS ✿ ✿ **Nichols Lodge** (802-253-2929) **& Gold Brook Campground** (802-253-7683), 1900 Waterbury Rd. Just under 2 miles south of the village of Stowe off Rt. 100. Large campground with camping-resort-style Nichols Lodge; tent and RV camping, rentals on-site. Call for rates, including off-season.

See also *Green Space* and vtstateparks.com for state parks.

✳ Waterbury Lodging

INNS AND BED & BREAKFASTS ✿ ✿ **The Old Stagecoach Inn** (802-244-5056; 800-262-2206; oldstagecoach.com), 18 N. Main St., downtown Waterbury. A classic stagecoach inn built in 1826 with a triple-tiered porch but substantially altered in the 1880s, when a millionaire from Ohio added oak woodwork, ornate fireplaces, and stained glass. There are eight guest rooms and three efficiency suites, all tastefully furnished but widely varied—from a queen-bedded room with a sitting area, fireplace, and private bath to small rooms with a shared bath. Two efficiency suites are studios; the other has two bedrooms and a sitting area. Many of the rooms are large enough to accommodate families. Sophie, the African gray parrot, sits by the fireplace in the living room adjoining the library, with its fully licensed bar. Rates range $90–200 per room, depending on season. A full breakfast, including a selection of hot dishes, is included. Pets allowed in suites.

✪ ♂ ✿ ✿ **Grünberg Haus** (802-244-7726; 800-800-7760; grunberghaus.com), 94 Pine St., Rt. 100 south of Waterbury. This secluded, Tyrolean-style chalet with carved balconies has 11 guest rooms, 8 with private bath, and three cottages where pets are allowed for $5 per night. Included is a full breakfast of homemade breads and baked goods, a fresh fruit creation, and a main dish such as ricotta-stuffed French toast in a dining area with huge picture windows overlooking dozens of feeders, making for exceptional bird-watching. Facilities include a garden deck and self-serve pub and game room. Hiking and snowshoe trails behind the inn feed into a 20 km cross-country trail system. The dark-wood-beamed common rooms include a large fieldstone fireplace. In winter the inn offers discounts at Stowe, Sugarbush, Bolton, and Mad River Glen (all within easy striking distance). Dog in residence. Rooms start at $135; cabins go up to $195 during foliage.

♂ ✿ **Moose Meadow Lodge** (802-244-5378; moosemeadowlodge.com), 607 Crossett Hill, Waterbury. Greg Trulson and Willie Docto have created an enchanting mountain sanctuary

Rachel Carter

BIRD-WATCHING BREAKFAST AT GRÜNBERG HAUS

with Adirondack touches in this cedar log inn. The spirit is Ernest Hemingway with panache: mounted trophies, exposed wood walls, a wrap-around deck with mountain views, a large stone fireplace, and exotica (trophies include a water buffalo from Uganda and a 155-pound black bear). The four guest rooms are rustically luxurious with private bath; two have a two-person steam bath, and the basement hot tub seats five. The tree house next door is a two-story "glamping" spot on stilts, overlooking a pristine pond. The 86 acres are blissfully secluded, with a trout-stocked swimming pond, a tree-surrounded bonfire area, and countless trails. Snowshoes are available at no charge. You may choose to tackle the 25-minute uphill hike to the Sky Loft, a glass-enclosed mountaintop gazebo with 360-degree views. Rates of $199–475 include an imaginative gourmet breakfast.

MOTELS ✋ ♿ **Best Western Waterbury Stowe** (802-244-7822; 800-621-7822; bestwesternwaterburystowe.com), 45 Blush Hill Rd., Exit 10 north, I-89. This typical motel boasts an atypical dining option: chef Robert Barral's second outpost of **Café Provence**. When not supping on southern French fare, splash in the large indoor pool with a glass roof, or burn it off at the full-sized fitness center with high-end weight and aerobic equipment, hot tub, and sauna. A few luxury suites have whirlpool bath and fireplace. $125–250 per couple in regular seasons, from $114 in low.

CONDOS/RENTALS 🐾 ✋ **Stowe Cabins** (802-244-8533; stowecabins.com), Rt. 100, Waterbury Center 05677. Tucked into a pine forest whose logging roads become cross-country ski and snowshoeing trails in winter. Completely furnished one- and two-bedroom units with kitchen, WiFi, and TV. Standard and

deluxe rooms (gas fireplaces); $119–269 per room/season, double occupancy.

CAMPGROUNDS Little River Camping Areas (802-244-7103; 800-658-6934 off-season reservations), 3444 Little River Rd., Waterbury 05676. Six miles north of Waterbury on the 830-acre Waterbury Reservoir: 81 tent and trailer campsites, including 20 lean-tos, plus swimming beaches, playgrounds, boat launch, boat rentals, ball field, nature museum, hiking, and snowmobile trails in Little River State Park.

See also *Green Space* and vtstateparks.com for state parks.

✳ **Where to Eat**

In Stowe

DINING OUT ♿ **Blue Moon Cafe** (802-253-7006; bluemoonstowe.com), 35 School St., Stowe Village. Open for dinner Tues.–Sun, closed in mud and stick seasons. Reservations necessary. Owner Jim Barton serves "contemporary American" dishes with Mediterranean and East Asian influences. Appetizers under $15, followed by entrées $16–36 such as foraged mushroom risotto or seared mahimahi with grapefruit, fennel, and avocado puree.

Emily's Fine Dining at Stowehof Inn (802-253-9722; stowehoffinn.com), 434 Edson Hill Rd., secluded on a hillside. Open for dinner nightly May–Oct., Dec.–March. The Alpine-inflected fine dining here includes four kind of fondue. Schnitzel is always on the menu as well. **Coslin's Pub** downstairs offers less formal fare, including bratwurst with sauerkraut. Inquire about sleigh rides around the 29-acre property before your meal.

Solstice at Stowe Mountain Lodge (802-253-3560; stowemountainlodge.com), 7412 Mountain Rd. Open for breakfast, lunch, and dinner during ski, summer, and fall seasons; limited hours in off-seasons. A soaring space with an open kitchen and unsurpassed views of Spruce Peak Mountain any time of day. With furniture hand carved by Vermont-based artistic woodworkers Parker Nicholls and Charles Shackleton, and custom pottery pieces designed by Miranda Thomas, Solstice offers a feast for all the senses. The menu, at once refined and casual, changes with the seasons, but always includes the signature truffled pot roast. Dinner reservations requested. Entrées range $26–34. **Hourglass Lounge** has more casual dining, including flatbreads and build-your-own burgers and grilled cheese.

✋ **Crop Bistro & Brewery** (802-253-4765; cropvt.com), 1859 Mountain Rd. Open daily for lunch and dinner. Naked trees line the central bar at this expansive restaurant. If that's too nouveau for your taste, there's a traditional, dark wood bar in another of the many rooms. Order a sampler board of six 4-ounce samples of the ever-rotating beers brewed in-house. Snack on mussels in blood-orange curry or fried avocado, then crunch on a hulking platter of fish-and-chips. Entrées $13–27.

○ ♂ ♿ **Flannel at Topnotch Resort & Spa** (802-253-8585), 4000 Mountain Rd. Open daily for breakfast, lunch, and dinner. A daytime gem, with a curving wall of windows that maximize the superb view of Mount Mansfield and, weather permitting, its attractive patio dining. Chef Cortney Quinn knows diners eat with their eyes first, and that informs the bright colors of dishes such as beet pappardelle and dayboat scallops with sweet pea risotto. Sunday Funday brunch includes a waffle sandwiches and a Bloody Mary bar. A special menu of flatbreads and sandwiches is served poolside. **The Roost**, with its central shuffleboard table/dining bar, serves up small plates, simple suppers, plus cheese and charcuterie plates until late.

♂ **Harrison's Restaurant & Bar** (802-253-7773; harrisonsstowe.com), 25 Main St. Open nightly for dinner beginning at 4:30. When a fire burns in this basement restaurant's hearth come winter, diners may feel like they've descended into a modern hobbit hole. Seafood and steaks are a specialty. Nothing groundbreaking, but basics such as crabcakes, or chicken with caramelized apples and cheddar cream sauce, are prepared with flair.

♂ **Plate** (802-253-2691; platestowe.com), 91 Main St. Dinner Wed.–Sun. The winner of *Seven Days* newspaper's best new Vermont restaurant outside Chittenden County. Paneled with dark wood and artfully hung with nests of bare lightbulbs, this petite restaurant has style to spare. California-style salads pack a walloping punch of flavor, but save room for a mason jar of banana pudding. Entrées $16–25.

Trapp Family Dining Room (800-826-7000, ext. 5733; trappfamily.com), 700 Trapp Hill Rd. Open daily for breakfast and dinner; reservations required. A dress code is in effect, and cell phone use is prohibited. Produce originates in the gardens and greenhouse, maple syrup from the on-premise sugarhouse, and beer from the Trapp Family Brewery. The menu always boasts Austrian-inspired dishes such as schnitzel and sauerbraten along with creative, seasonally inspired grub. Desserts include a cheese plate with tastings from Waitsfield's Trapp Farmstead.

Alice Levitt

THE DOGGIE BAG, GRACIE'S, STOWE

EATING OUT Whip Bar & Grill (802-253-4400; thewhip.com), 18 Main St. at the Green Mountain Inn. Open daily; lunch begins at 11:30, dinner 5:30; Sunday brunch is a specialty. This old tavern, decorated with antique buggy whips, a brass dumbwaiter, and vintage photos, boasts Stowe's first liquor license, from 1833. In summer there's patio dining and a view of lawns and the pool; in winter the focus is on a roaring hearth. The food includes light fare such as burgers and lobster rolls as well as stir-fries and turkey dinner.

○ **Phoenix Table and Bar** (802-253-2838; phoenixtableandbar.com), 1652 Mountain Rd. Lunch and dinner daily, weekend brunch. This sleek, masculine restaurant uses co-owner Jack Pickett's BSA 441 Victor Shooting Star motorcycle as a centerpiece of a culinary road trip. The regional American cuisine hops from chicken-and-waffles to banh mi to the Technicolor flavor of harissa-marinated steak in chimichurri. Whatever you order, don't miss the jiggly perfection of the chocolate-hazelnut panna cotta.

♂ ♿ **Gracie's Restaurant** (802-253-8741; gracies.com), 18 Edson Hill Rd. Dinner daily from 5:30. Sue and Paul Archdeacon's dog-themed pub has fireplaces burning at both ends and an open kitchen cooking dinner. There are more than 85 items on the menu, including burgers, steaks, and seafood. But the real reason to sit between the walls covered in dog portraits is the Doggie Bag, a white chocolate bag filled with mint-chocolate mousse, served over thick hot fudge.

Piecasso Pizzeria & Lounge (802-253-4411; piecasso.com), 1899 Mountain Rd. Lunch and dinner daily. There's a growing nightlife scene at this modern take on the New York–style pizzeria, but families are just as welcome as the cool kids. Besides the locally focused pizzas, you may be treated to an organic green salad topped with lobster or fettuccine with wild mushrooms. Don't forget to pair it with a Vermont beer or cider.

Depot Street Malt Shoppe (802-253-4269), 57 Depot St. Open daily for lunch and dinner. A fun, 1950s decor with a reasonably priced diner-style menu to match, including 1950s-style fountain treats like malted frappes, egg creams, and banana splits.

Sushi Yoshi (802-253-4135, sushistowe.com), 1128 Mountain Rd. Open daily for lunch and dinner. Birch trees line the dining room of this chic eatery specializing in well-prepared, Americanized Japanese cuisine. Seating areas include hibachi tables, a sushi bar, and a martini bar, as well as traditional tables. Bento boxes are a great way to try a little bit of everything.

The Bench (802-253-5101; benchvt.com) 492 Mountain Rd. Daily dinner. Nearly every dish at this wood-covered restaurant and pub touches fire before hitting the plate. Start with wood-roasted mussels, then tear into a wood-fired pizza topped with duck confit, local Brie, and pears.

BREAKFAST ❂ **Dutch Pancake Cafe at the Grey Fox Inn** (802-253-5330), 990 Mountain Rd. Open daily for breakfast only. There are flat, American-style pancakes available here, but ignore those. Instead, go for the puffy, buttery Dutch ones, served in 80-some different varieties. We recommend the apple-and-bacon version, soaked to your liking in sweet stroop.

BREAKFAST AND LUNCH ❧ & **McCarthy's Restaurant** (802-253-8626), 454 Mountain Rd. next to the Stowe Cinema. A local gathering place with quick, cheerful service and deep, wooden booths. Daily specials for breakfast and lunch, plus a big breakfast menu and a wide selection of soups and sandwiches on homemade breads. Boxed lunches to go.

❂ ❧ **Trapp Family Lodge DeliBakery** (802-253-5705; trappfamily.com), 700 Trapp Hill Rd. Watch Trapp Lager being brewed while you wait for your Austrian-style pastry or a bratwurst with sauerkraut. There's afternoon tea across the parking lot in the **Lounge**.

APRÈS-SKI There are reputedly 50 bars in Stowe. Along Mountain Rd., the landmarks for après-ski are **The Rusty Nail Bar & Grille** (802-253-6245; 1190 Mountain Rd.) and the **Matterhorn Restaurant** (802-253-8198; 4969 Mountain Rd.); both serve up regular live music. **The Pub at Grey Fox** (802-253-5330; 990 Mountain Rd.) has a groovy selection of concert DVDs and big screens on which to show them. **Burt's Irish Pub** (802-253-6071; 135 Luce Hill Rd.) is a friendly townie bar with excellent Colombian food. **Sunset Grille & Tap Room** (802-253-9281; 140 Cottage Club Rd.) serves barbecue and pub grub until midnight.

In Waterbury

DINING OUT Hen of the Wood (802-244-7300; henofthewood.com), 92 Stowe St. Open for dinner Tues.–Sat. Reservations a definite must—at least a week in advance or even more. In 2008 *Food & Wine* magazine named chef and co-owner Eric Warnstedt one of "the best new chefs in America." Now he's one of the godfathers of the Vermont locavore movement, with numerous James Beard Foundation nominations under his locally crafted belt. Just a

CHEF ERIC WARNSTEDT SPIT-ROASTS A LAMB AT HEN OF THE WOOD, WATERBURY
Alice Levitt

quarter mile from the I-89 exit, the restaurant is housed in a vintage-1835 gristmill overlooking a waterfall. The menu is divided into snacks, small plates, and entrées such as rabbit leg with buttered celery root, parsnips, and cranberries. Co-owner William McNeil's award-winning wine list extensive, with many available by the glass, including the in-house imprint. Inquire about special wine-tasting events.

✪ **Michael's on the Hill** (802-244-7476; michaelsonthehill.com), 4182 Waterbury–Stowe Rd. (Rt. 100), Waterbury Center. Dinner Wed.–Mon. Swiss chef-owner Michael Kloeti describes his cuisine as "locally driven innovative European." The ambience is elegant yet relaxed and the food, reliably delicious. The menu changes to make use of what's best that season, but there's always a stellar gnocchi dish and chocolate fondue.

EATING OUT Juniper's Fare Café (802-244-5504; junipersfare.com), 23 Commercial Dr. Open for breakfast and lunch Mon.–Sat. Buffet brunch Sun. The Church of the Crucified One runs this café, using produce from the church's greenhouse. But don't be put off by this casual but comfy spot's religious background; the marinated chicken club is worth more than the sum of its parts. A creemee window cools down travelers in summer.

The Reservoir Restaurant & Tap Room (802-244-7827; waterburyreservoir.com), 1 S. Main St. Daily dinner, weekend lunch. A leg lamp à la *A Christmas Story* greets diners to this pub known for its assiduously researched 38-tap list, the largest in the state. Comfort food made from Vermont ingredients includes fried

RABBIT STEW EN COCOTTE AT MICHAEL'S ON THE HILL, WATERBURY

Alice Levitt

chicken, a wide variety of burgers, and fish tacos.

✪ **Prohibition Pig** (802-244-4120; prohibition pig.com), 23 S. Main St. Daily dinner, lunch Fri.–Mon. Beers here include suds brewed in-house. Still, old-fashioned, "medicinal" cocktails inspire this restaurant's name and its exceptional bar. Never had a smoked ice cube? You may well find it here. A smoker also turns out the restaurant's eponymous "pig" and other barbecue, but the burgers are local favorites, too. Don't miss the panko-fried pimiento cheese, a classic on the southern-fried menu.

✳ Entertainment

Spruce Peak Performing Arts Center (802-760-4634; sprucepeakarts.org) is a technically advanced 420-seat theater created to be the cultural soul of Stowe Mountain Resort's Spruce Peak community. Professional musicians from a variety of genres, dance, theater, and other staged artistic expressions dominate the schedule.

Stowe Theatre Guild (802-253-3961; stowe theatre.com), staged upstairs at the Akeley Memorial Building in Stowe Village, offers a series of four or more musicals, including classics and newer works, each summer.

Stowe Performing Arts (802-253-7792; stowe performingarts.com) presents a series of spring and summer concerts in village locations, as well as concerts by distinguished orchestras and performers staged in summer in the natural amphitheater of Trapp Meadow. Patrons are invited to bring a preconcert picnic. The setting is spectacular, with the sun sinking over Nebraska Notch.

Waterbury Festival Players (waterbury festivalplayers.com), at the Waterbury Festival Playhouse. Staging spring–fall productions, this "semi-professional" theater company utilizes local talent from across central Vermont.

Stowe Cinema 3 Plex & Lounge (802-253-4678), at the Stowe Center, Rt. 108. Standard seats as well as a bar viewing area for first-run films.

✳ Selective Shopping

ART GALLERIES AND CRAFTS STUDIOS
Helen Day Art Center (802-253-8358; helen day.com), the former wooden high school in Stowe Village, open in summer daily noon–5 except Mon., closed Sun. too in winter. The changing art exhibits are frequently well worth checking out. The Stowe Historical Society operates the mid-19th-century Bloody Brook

Schoolhouse museum located next door and is open on request in summer months.

Stowe Craft Gallery & Design Center (877-456-8388; stowecraft.com), 55 Mountain Rd., Stowe. Open 10–6 daily. Outstanding crafts from throughout the country including contemporary glass, furniture, jewelry, and ceramics. The interior design showroom on Main St. features lighting, rugs, hardware, and furniture.

Little River Hotglass Studio & Gallery (802-253-0889; littleriverhotglass.com), 593 Moscow Rd., Moscow. Wed.–Mon., check out these varied art glass creations.

Ziemke Glass Blowing Studio (802-244-6126; zglassblowing.com), 3033 Rt. 100, Waterbury Center. Open every day but Thanksgiving and Christmas. Artist Glenn Ziemke crafts his classically inspired glassware and art on-site and sells it exclusively here.

Stowe Gems (802-253-7000; stowegems.com), in the village near the Helen Day Art Center at 70 Pond St. Closed Sunday and most Tuesdays. Barry Tricker polishes and sets exquisite stones, including tanzanite, tourmaline, Tahitian pearls, and freshwater pearls.

West Branch Gallery & Sculpture Park (802-253-8943; westbranchgallery.com), 17 Towne Farm Lane, Stowe, 1 mile up Mountain Rd., behind the Rusty Nail. Open Tues.–Sun. 11–5. Indoor/outdoor space promoting emerging and midcareer artists of contemporary sculpture and exhibitions in glass, oil, steel, stone, and mixed media.

FARMERS MARKETS The Waterbury, Stowe, and Stowe Mountain Resort Farmers Markets are held seasonally. Details at vermontagriculture.org.

FLEA MARKETS The Waterbury Flea Market (802-244-5916), the biggest in northern Vermont, rolls out its tables every weekend May–Oct., 7–7 (weather permitting), on a grassy, 10-acre roadside spot on Rt. 2 just north of the village (Exit 10W off I-89).

FOOD AND DRINK A Special Place (802-244-6334), 2653 Waterbury–Stowe Rd. (Rt. 100), Waterbury, 1.4 miles north of Ben & Jerry's, open year-round. A one-stop place for Vermont products: Cabot Annex Store, Snow Farm Vineyard Tasting Room, Lake Champlain Chocolates, The Kitchen Store at J. K. Adams, Danforth Pewter, Rocking R Vermont T-Shirts & Gifts, Green Mountain Camera, Ziemke Glass Blowing Studio. **Cold Hollow Cider Mill** (800-3-APPLES; coldhollow.com), 3600 Waterbury–Stowe Rd. (Rt. 100), Waterbury, is

one of New England's largest producers of fresh apple cider; visitors can watch it being pressed and sample the varieties. The cider doughnuts emerge hot from the fryer, ready to melt in your mouth. The retail store in this big red barn complex stocks every conceivable apple product plus plenty of Vermont swag and gifts. There's lunch, including hearty locavore sandwiches at the **Apple Core Luncheonette**. Open year-round, daily 8–6.

(ʜ) **Green Mountain Coffee Visitor Center and Café** (877-TRY-BEAN; waterburystation .com), housed in the renovated 1867 working Amtrak station, Park Row, Waterbury. Open daily 7–6. Displays tell the story of Green Mountain Coffees from around the world, available for a nominal donation along with pastry, light lunches, and WiFi.

Harvest Market (802-253-3800; harvestat stowe.com), 1031 Mountain Rd., Stowe. A high-end take-out spot featuring fresh-baked country breads and other baked goods as well as house-made granola, an espresso bar, Vermont cheeses, gourmet items, and prepared foods.

Trapp Family Brewery (802-826-7000; trapp family.com), Trapp Hill Rd., Stowe. This micro-brewery is located on the lower level of the Deli-Bakery (see *Eating Out*) at the Trapp Family Lodge, drawing its springwater on location. Three lagers—Golden Helles, Vienna Amber, and Dunkel Lager—are on tap at the Trapp Brewery in addition to a rotating seasonal brew.

The Alchemist (802-244-7744; alchemistbeer .com), 35 Crossroad Rd., Waterbury. As of press time, this Waterbury-based maker of beloved Heady Topper beer was closed to the public, but hoping to move to Stowe to expand—and once again allow guests to its cannery.

SPECIAL STORES Bear Pond Books (802-253-8236), 38 Main St., Stowe Village. Open daily. A family-owned, independent bookstore with an entire section devoted to Vermont books.

Shaw's General Store (802-253-4040, heshaw .com), 54 Main St., Stowe Village. Established in 1895 and still a family business, a source of shoelaces and cheap socks as well as expensive ski togs and Vermont souvenirs.

Stowe Mercantile (802-253-4554; stowe mercantile.com), 38 Main St., Stowe. A diverse country store with a large, eclectic selection of clothing and gifts.

Stowe Mountain Lodge Shops, 7412 Mountain Rd. In contrast with most hotel boutiques, the shops in Stowe's newest, most dramatic and upscale hotel fill a free-flowing space inviting shoppers to wander. Top retailers represented include Simon Pearce, Shackleton Thomas, and Polo Ralph Lauren.

Nebraska Knoll Sugar Farm (802-253-4655; nebraskaknoll.com), 256 Falls Brook Lane, Stowe. Lewis and Audrey Coty's sugarhouse is open Mar.–Oct., selling maple products at "sugar house prices." Sited up beyond Trapp Meadow, it's a lovely little drive.

Stowe Street Emporium (802-244-5321; stowestreetemporium.com), 23 Stowe St., Waterbury. A 19th-century storefront in downtown Waterbury with treasures from near and far, open year-round.

✴ Special Events

Mid-January: **Stowe Winter Carnival** (stowe wintercarnival.com) is one of the oldest in the country, showcasing nationally sanctioned ice sculptures.

Last weekend of February: **Stowe Derby** (stowederby.com), the country's oldest downhill/cross-country race—a 10-mile race

STOWE ANTIQUE AND CLASSIC CAR SHOW
Stowe Area Association

from the summit of Mount Mansfield to Stowe Village—usually attracts about 300 entrants.

Late June: **Stowe Wine & Food Classic** (802-253-0399; stowewine.com). Three days of wine tastings, pairings, live auction, gala dinner, seminars, and the Grand Tasting Event, offering small bites from an impressive roster of Vermont's best chefs.

Summerlong: **Exposed! Outdoor Sculpture Exhibition** (802-253-8358, helenday.com), Helen Day Art Center, tours with the sculptors. Maps available.

July 4: **Stowe Independence Day Celebration** (802-253-7321) starting at 11 AM midtown—parade, food, games, performers, fireworks. Separate festivities in the village of Moscow, too small for its own band, so they parade to the music of radios.

Mid-July: **Stoweflake Hot-Air Balloon Festival** (800-253-2232; stoweflake.com)—annual balloon launch and tethers with live music, food, a beer garden, and kids' activity corner.

Mid-August: **Antique & Classic Car Show** (802-253-7321). Over 800 models on display, three days, 8–5. Parade, car auction, corral, fashion-judging contest, auto-related flea market, plus a Saturday-night Oldies Street Dance and Block Party.

Mid-September: **Annual British Invasion** (802-253-5320; britishinvasion.com). North America's largest all-British sports car show—contests, food, displays at Mayo Farm Events Field, Weeks Hill Rd., Stowe. **Oktoberfest** (802-253-7321; stoweoktoberfest.com), Jackson Arena—a three-day fest with oompah bands, parade, Bavarian food, microbrews, and children's tent.

Pre-Halloween: **Lantern Tours** (802-244-1173; stowelanterntours.com), mid-Sept.–Oct. 31. Carry an antique lantern on a "ghost walk" through Stowe, hearing tales of the village's resident ghosts. It's really an excuse to learn the town's history, including putting stories to many of the names at the downtown cemetery. Walks begin at the visitors center on Main St.

Second weekend of October: **Stowe Foliage Art & Craft Festival** (802-253-7321), Stowe Events Field. Three days of juried art and fine crafts from 160 exhibitors, wine tasting, music, magicians, and a special "off the grid" section.

NORTH OF THE NOTCH AND THE LAMOILLE REGION

Vermont's most dramatic road winds up and up from Stowe through narrow, 2,162-foot-high Smugglers Notch, then down and around cliffs and boulders. The route is at its best in autumn, just before falling leaves give way to the snow that will close the road for the winter. Just as the road's twists seem like they'll never end, motorists are startled by the apparition of a condominium town rising out of nowhere (Smugglers' Notch Resort, a self-contained, family-geared village that accommodates some 3,200 people). However, as Rt. 108 continues to descend and finally levels into Jeffersonville on the valley floor, it's clear that this is a totally different place from the tourist-trod turf south of the Notch. This is the Lamoille Region, what people who live there call "a Vermonter's Vermont," with real downtowns and true working landscapes.

Smugglers Notch leads north to Cambridge, one of several towns worth exploring along the Lamoille River. Jeffersonville has been a gathering place for artists since the 1930s, and Johnson, 9 miles west along Rt. 15, is also now an art center. It's easy to see why artists like this luminous landscape: open, gently rolling farm country. The Lamoille River itself is beloved by fishermen and canoeists, and bicyclists enthuse about the little-trafficked roads.

While Smugglers Notch is a memorable way to approach, the prime access to the Lamoille Region is Rt. 100, the main road north from Stowe, which joins Rt. 15 (the major east–west road) at Morrisville, the commercial center for north-central Vermont. Just west on Rt. 15 is Hyde Park, the picturesque county seat, famed for its summer theater.

North of the Lamoille Region is the even less-trafficked Missisquoi River Valley, and between the two lies some highly unspoiled country.

GUIDANCE Lamoille Region Chamber of Commerce (802-888-7607; 800-849-9985; lamoillechamber.com), 34 Pleasant St., Morrisville 05661, covers the area with an office that's open year-round. An information booth at the junction of Rts. 15 and 100 at the Morrisville Mobil station is open May–Oct. **Smugglers' Notch Chamber of Commerce** (smugnotch.com) operates a useful website and information booth at the Mobil station in Jeffersonville at the junction of Rts. 100 and 15.

GETTING THERE *By air:* See "Burlington Region." Given 48 hours' notice, Smugglers' Notch Resort arranges transfers for guests.

By train: **Amtrak** stops at Essex Junction (800-872-7245; amtrak.com).

By car: When the Notch is closed in winter, the route from Stowe via Morrisville is 26 miles, but in summer via Rt. 108 it's 18 miles from Stowe Village. From Burlington, it's 30 miles east on Rt. 15 to the intersection with Rt. 108 in Jeffersonville. If you're coming from the Northeast Kingdom, access is on Rts. 15, 109, and 108.

MEDICAL EMERGENCY Call **911. Copley Hospital** (802-888-4231), Morrisville.

✳ Must See

✿ **Smugglers Notch**. During the War of 1812, Vermonters hid cattle and other supplies in the Notch prior to smuggling them into Canada to feed the enemy—the British army. A path through the high pass existed centuries before European settlement, but it wasn't until 1910 that the present road was built, which, with its 18 percent grade, is as steep as many ski trails and more winding than most. Realizing that drivers are too engrossed with the challenge of the road to admire the wild and wonderful scenery, the state's Department of Forests and Parks has thoughtfully provided a turnoff just beyond the height-of-land. An information booth here is staffed in warm-weather months; this is a restful spot by a mountain brook where you can picnic, even grill hot dogs. The Big Spring is here and prior to your climb, you can ask about hiking distances to the other colorfully named landmarks: the Elephant Head, King Rock, the Hunter and His Dog (an outstanding rock formation), Singing Bird, the Smugglers Cave, Smugglers Face, and the natural reservoir. See the "Stowe and Waterbury" chapter for details about the trails to Sterling Pond and Elephant Head.

✳ Must Do

○ **ArborTrek Canopy Adventures** (802-644-9300; arbortrek.com). Thrill seekers and nature lovers alike will be inspired soaring through the backcountry forest of Smugglers' Notch Resort suspended in the air on 4,500 feet of ziplines. Following an extensive review and practice session, guides lead you on a nature walk and then up into your first tree. From there—safely hooked into a complete harness—you soar through the tree canopy and over mountain brooks, with views of the mountains in special clearings. The tour lasts 2½ to 3 hours, and reservations are a must. Minimum age is 8; participants 16 and under must be accompanied by an adult. There are also weight, health, and basic mobility requirements.

✳ To Do

BICYCLING *Rentals:* ✿ Mountain bikes for adults and children can be rented from **Three Mountain Outfitters** (802-644-8563; smuggs.com) at Smugglers' Notch Resort in full- or half-day increments. Child carriers are also available to rent.

The broad spectrum of back roads in this region make for excellent mountain biking. Our best advice is to pick up the Lamoille County Road Map, published by a partnership of the Smugglers' Notch and Lamoille Regions Chambers and the Stowe Area Association. There are several sections of rail-trails along the Lamoille River that make for great biking. Some are developed recreation paths such as the **Cambridge Greenway**, running 1.5 miles from Cambridge to the **Poland Covered Bridge** in Jeffersonville. Other parts of the former railroad trail are less developed . . . for now. Exciting news: The **Lamoille Valley Rail Trail** is currently in development to pick up the end of the **Missisquoi Valley Rail Trail** (see "Northwest Corner") and extend a continuous rec path to St. Johnsbury. Be sure to check with the chambers for updates.

CANOEING AND KAYAKING The **Lamoille River** from Jeffersonville to Cambridge is considered good for novices in spring and early summer; two small sets of rapids. More challenging rapids can be found in sections from **Lake Lamoille** to Johnson.

Bert's Boats (802-644-8189; bertsboats.com), at 73 Smugglers View Rd. in Jeffersonville, rents canoes and kayaks and offers shuttle service, tours, and instruction. Customized paddles can include a tour to Peterson Gorge or Boyden Winery (with camping).

ARBORTREK CANOPY ADVENTURES TOUR
Rachel Carter

Green River Canoe & Kayaks (802-644-8336) operates from 155 Junction Hill Rd. in Jeffersonville. Guided canoe and kayaking trips, especially ecotours led by trained naturalists; also instruction and rentals.

Umiak Outfitters (802-253-2317; umiak.com) operates rentals and rapids instruction at the junctions of Rts. 15 and 108 in Jeffersonville from Memorial Day to Labor Day.

COVERED BRIDGES *In and around Jeffersonville:* Look for the **Scott Bridge** on Canyon Rd. across the Brewster River near the old mill; the 84-foot-long bridge is 0.8 mile south on Rt. 108 from Rt. 15. To find the **Poland Bridge**

FISHING AT CADY'S FALLS

Rachel Carter

(1887—walking only) from the junction of 108 and 15, drive east on 15 and take first left on Cambridge Junction Rd. Heading west on Rt. 15 toward Cambridge Village, look for Lower Valley Rd.; the **Gates Farm Bridge** (1897) is a few hundred feet from where the present road crosses the river.

In Waterville and Belvidere: Back on Rt. 109, continue north to Waterville and, at Waterville Town Hall (on your right), turn left; the **Church Street Bridge** (1877) is in 0.1 mile. Back on Rt. 109, continue north; the **Montgomery Bridge** (1887) is east of the highway, 1.2 miles north of town hall. Go another 0.5 mile north on Rt. 109 and turn right; the **Kissin' Bridge** (1877) is in 0.1 mile. Continue north on Rt. 109, and 1.5 miles from the Waterville Elementary School (just after the bridge over the North Branch), turn left and go 0.5 mile to the **Mill Bridge** (1895) in Belvidere. Back on Rt. 109, continue north 0.9 mile, then turn left to find the **Morgan Bridge** (1887). See the Jay Peak chapter for a description of six more covered bridges another dozen miles north in Montgomery.

In Johnson: Take Rt. 100C north from its junction with Rt. 15 for 2.6 miles and turn right; the **Scribner Bridge** (around 1919) is 0.3 mile on your right.

Note: For detailed descriptions of all these sites, see *Covered Bridges of Vermont* by Ed Barna (The Countryman Press).

DISC GOLF Two courses can be found: The Woods at Smugglers' Notch and the Johnson State Disc Golf Course—info at gmdgc.org.

FISHING The stretch of the Lamoille River between Cambridge and Morrisville reputedly offers great fly- and spin fishing for brown trout. Lake Eden and Lake Elmore offer diverse shorelines for good bass fishing. Fishing licenses at vtfishandwildlife.com.

Green Mountain Troutfitters (802-644-2214; gmtrout.com), 233 Mill St. (Rt. 108S), Jeffersonville. Fishing gear, clinics, and guided tours.

Smugglers' Notch Resort (802-644-8851; smuggs.com) offers frequent fly-casting clinics, fly-fishing stream tours, and seasonal fishing outings.

GOLF Copley Country Club (802-888-3013; copleycountryclub.com), Country Club Rd., Morrisville, is a nine-hole course open Apr.,–Oct.

Bakersfield Country Club (802-933-5100), 201 Old Boston Post Rd., Bakersfield, is a nice drive north on Rt. 108 for an 18-hole course open from when it's warm enough to when it's too cold.

HIKING Prospect Rock, Johnson. An easy hike yields an exceptional view of the Lamoille River Valley and the high mountains to the south. Look for a steel bridge to the Ithiel Falls Camp Meeting Ground. Hike north on the white-blazed Long Trail 0.7 mile to the summit.

Belvidere Mountain–Ritterbush Pond and **Devil's Gulch**. These are basically two stretches of the Long Trail; one heads north (3½ hours round-trip) to the summit of Belvidere Mountain, the other south (2¾ hours round-trip) to a gulch filled with rocks and ferns. Both are described in the Green Mountain Club's *Long Trail Guide.*

Sterling Pond, Jeffersonville. This is one our favorite hikes, accessible from the top of the Notch parking area, beginning across the road from the information booth. Look for the LONG TRAIL sign and register. Follow the white blazes to a T-intersection (about 35 to 45 minutes up). Turn left at the sign for Sterling Pond Shelter. It's a short walk to the "the highest trout pond in the state." For views, follow the trail around the end of the pond, through the woods, and turn left off the Long Trail, up a short rise to a clearing at the top of Sterling Lift. Return by the same route.

Elmore Mountain, Elmore. A surprisingly steep hike for 2,600 feet, Elmore Mountain showcases particularly beautiful hardwood forests once you reach the summit, with a fire tower on top and sweeping views of the agricultural and rugged landscape below (vtstateparks.com).

HISTORIC ATTRACTIONS The Noyes House Museum (802-888-7617), 122 Main St. (Rt. 100), Morrisville. Open Fri.–Sat. 10–4, June–Aug., Sat. only Sept.–Oct.; guided tours. Admission by donation. Carlos Noyes was a 19th-century banker who spent much of his fortune expanding this 1820 Federal-style homestead. Its 18 rooms and carriage barn contain one of the state's best collections of Vermont memorabilia, including an 1,800-piece Cheney pitcher and Toby jug collection, and Indian Joe's canoe. The staff regularly curates new exhibits showcasing specific aspects of history's day-to-day life, including Victorian etiquette, and funerary practices during the Civil War.

HORSEBACK RIDING ✔ **LaJoie Stables** (802-644-5347; lajoiestables.com), 992 Pollander Rd., Jeffersonville. Horseback riding offered all year, including trail rides, pony rides, and overnight treks. Also sleigh and wagon rides.

LLAMA TREKS ✔ **Northern Vermont Llama Co.** (802-644-2257; northernvermontllamaco.com), 766 Lapland Rd., Waterville. Treks depart from the Smugglers' Notch Resort and head into the backcountry. Geoff and Lindsay Chandler offer half-day treks in summer and by appointment in fall. Snacks are provided, and llamas will carry additional snacks you bring. Call for rates and to reserve. Back at the farm, purchase stuffed animals made from the wool shorn from your new friends. The farm is also home to mini donkeys and Christmas trees.

✔ **Applecheek Farm** (802-888-4482; applecheekfarm.com), 567 McFarlane Rd., Hyde Park. Trek on "wilderness trails." While you're there, take a tour, pick up meats, produce, and bread at the farm store, and inquire about special events.

PICNICKING There are several outstanding roadside picnic areas: on Rt. 108, 0.2 mile north of the junction with Rt. 15 at Jeffersonville, four picnic tables (one covered) on the bank of the Lamoille; on Rt. 108 south of Jeffersonville Village on the east side of the highway; on Rt. 108 in Smugglers Notch itself (see *To See*); on Rt. 15, just 1.5 miles east of the Cambridge–Johnson line.

SCENIC DRIVES Four loop routes are especially appealing from Jeffersonville:

Stowe/Hyde Park (44-mile loop). Take Rt. 108 south through Smugglers Notch to Stowe Village, drive up the old Stagecoach Rd. to Hyde Park (be sure to see the old Opera House), and head back through Johnson.

Belvidere/Eden (40-mile loop). From Jeffersonville, Rt. 109 follows the North Branch of the Lamoille River north to Belvidere Corners; here take Rt. 118, which soon crosses the Long Trail and continues to the village of Eden. Lake Eden, 1 mile north on Rt. 100, is good for swimming and boating; return on Rts. 100, 100C, and 15 via Johnson.

Jericho/Cambridge (38-mile loop). From Jeffersonville, drive southwest on Pleasant Valley Rd., a magnificent drive with the Green Mountains rising abruptly on your left. Go through Underhill Center to the junction with Rt. 15. At Rt. 15, either turn right to head back to Cambridge or continue south on Jericho Center Rd.; return via Jericho and Rt. 15 to Cambridge Village, then drive back along Rt. 15 to Jeffersonville.

Jeffersonville/Johnson (18-mile loop). From the junction of Rts. 15 and 108, head north on Rt. 108, but turn onto Rt. 109 (note the Poland Covered Bridge on your right). Take your first right, Hogback Rd., which shadows the north bank of the Lamoille River most of the way into Johnson. Stop at the Rt. 15 and 100C junction for water from the Johnson Spring; return via Rt. 15.

SWIMMING Brewster River Gorge, accessible from Rt. 108 south of Jeffersonville (turn off at the covered bridge).

✔ **Smugglers' Notch Resort** (802-644-8851; 800-451-8752; smuggs.com) features multiple elaborate water parks with eight heated pools and four waterslides in summer, plus a winter pool.

✔ **Lake Eden** (802-635-7725) on Rt. 100 north from Morrisville is a large lake with a popular swimming recreation area open Memorial Day–Labor Day.

✔ **Cady's Falls** in Morristown is a waterfall swimming area located above Lake Lamoille. Parking area on Stagecoach Rd.

Smugglers' Notch Resort
TENNIS AT SMUGGLERS' NOTCH

TENNIS Courts and programming at **Smugglers' Notch Resort** (800-419-4615; smuggs .com), a summer program of clinics and camps for adults and children, and daily instruction at the TenPro Tennis School.

WALKING The **Cambridge Greenway** (see *Bicycling*) recreation path runs 1.5 miles along the Lamoille River from Jeffersonville east.

Lamoille County Nature Center (802-888-9218; lcnrcd.com), Cole Hill Rd., Morrisville. Two nature trails offer easy walking and the chance to see deer, bear, a variety of birds, and lady's slippers in early summer. Inquire about programs offered in the outdoor amphitheater.

✳ Winter Sports

CROSS-COUNTRY SKIING Nordic Ski and Snowshoe Adventure Center (802-523-2754; smuggs.com), Smugglers' Notch Resort. Narrow trails wind up and down through the trees, then climb meadows away from the resort complex, for a total of 30 km of cross-country trails and 24 km of snowshoe trails. Rentals are available, including telemark, skate skiing, and snowshoe rentals. Lessons and tours are given, and there's a warming hut with cocoa and a woodstove.

Smugglers Notch. The steep, rocky stretch of Rt. 108 that is closed to traffic for snow season is open to cross-country skiers. Guided tours are offered by the Nordic Adventure Center (see above).

DOGSLEDDING By the Dozen Dogsledding (802-858-4836; bythedozendogsledding.com) offers one- to two-hour, 6-mile dogsledding tours at **Boyden Valley Farm** (see *Farms*) in Cambridge. Also inquire about dog carting and dog-powered scooters.

DOWNHILL SKIING AND SNOWBOARDING ⚲ Smugglers' Notch Resort (800-451-8752; smuggs.com), Jeffersonville. In 1956 a group of local residents organized Smugglers' Notch Ski Ways on Sterling Mountain, a western shoulder of 3,640-foot-high Madonna. In 1963, development began to transform the area known as Madonna Mountain into a self-contained, Aspen-style resort. Six hundred fifty condominiums later, "Smuggs" is a major ski destination poised over a natural snow bowl. A satisfying variety of terrain is spread over three interconnected mountains: beginner trails on Morse Mountain (2,250 feet), intermediate runs on midsized Sterling Mountain (3,010 feet), and expert and glade skiing on Madonna, the highest of the three, with its spectacular long-distance views. (A shuttle links the base areas.) A warm-up hut serves hot meals atop Sterling Peak, and a full range of restaurants lies at the base (see *Where to Eat*).

It soon becomes clear why many Vermont skiers bypass Stowe for "Smuggs": The crowds are thinner, the prices lower, and the trails as challenging. After all, this is the site of the only triple-black-diamond run in the East, a sheer drop halfway down Madonna known as The Black Hole. One trail goes 3.5 miles, making it northern Vermont's largest vertical descent, a whopping 2,610 feet. But you also find the opposite extreme: Sir Henry's Learning and Fun Park at the base of Morse Mountain is a mini slope with two conveyor belts, a great place for toddlers (and older beginners) to cut their teeth.

Lifts: 6 double chairlifts, 2 surface.

DOGSLEDDING

Rachel Carter

Trails: 78, including two 3.5-mile trails; 25 percent expert, 56 percent intermediate, 19 percent beginner.

Vertical drop: 2,610 feet.

Snowmaking: 61%.

Facilities: Mountain Lodge, base lodge with ski shop, rentals, cafeteria, pub. The reception center/ski shop at Morse Mountain has a Village Center, source of rentals and tickets; the complex also includes a ski shop, deli, country store, and restaurant/snack bar. Top of the Notch warming hut is at the Sterling chair terminal. Snowboarding.

Ski school: Children's ski and snowboard camp, group and private lessons for all ages and abilities. Beginners enjoy Morse Mountain while intermediate and advanced skiers and riders take on Madonna and Sterling Mountains.

For children: Day care for kids 6 weeks–3 years. Discovery Dynamos Ski Camp for 3- to 5-year-olds—all day with hot lunch and two lessons, games, and races. Adventure Rangers Ski and Snowboard Camps for 6- to 10-year-olds: all day with hot lunch and two lessons; games and races. The Notch Squad is for kids 11–15. Mountain Explorers Ski Program for 16- to 17-year-olds begins at noon daily; lesson and evening activities; 2 teen centers.

Rates: $70 for a 1-day, 3-mountain adult lift ticket; $52 ages 6–18 and seniors 65 and older. Kids 5 and under ski free.

Note: See the *Lodging* sidebar for packages that greatly reduce ski-week rates. A 5-day ski week, which automatically includes lessons for all children and beginners, is usually the best option.

March (bargain season) is a great time to come. This far north snow lingers long past midseason, augmenting the manmade base.

SKIING AT SMUGGLERS' NOTCH

Smugglers' Notch Resort

BOARDING AT SMUGGLERS' NOTCH

Smugglers' Notch Resort

SLEIGH RIDES ✧ **Applecheek Farm** (802-888-4482; applecheekfarm.com), 567 McFarlane Rd., Hyde Park. John and Judy Clark's gentle Belgians, Sparky and Sam, take you through the woods by day or night. Hot beverage and farm tour included. Bring your voices and instruments! Wagon rides offered in the warmer months.

✧ **LaJoie Stables** (802-644-5347; lajoiestables .com), 992 Pollander Rd., Jeffersonville. Hour-long sleigh rides are offered all winter. In summer, they're replaced by pony rides.

SNOWMOBILING Green Mountain Snowmobile Adventures (802-644-1438), 300 Stoney Meadow Ln., Jeffersonville. Day and evening tours leave from Sterling Ridge Resort (see *Lodging*); inquire about packages.

Smugglers' Notch Resort (802-644-8851; smuggs.com) offers snowmobile tours daily in winter from the snowmobile trailer next to Morse Mountain Grille.

✳ Lodging

RESORTS ⚐ 🍂 ♫ **Sterling Ridge Resort** (802-644-8265; 800-347-8266; sterlingridge resort.com), 155 Sterling Ridge Dr., Jeffersonville 05464. Sterling Ridge is a secluded log cabin village with a variety of attractively furnished accommodations scattered among fields, ponds, and flower beds. Scott and Sue Peterson have built 18 one- and two-bedroom log cabins ($140–195, two-night minimum stay), each nicely designed with a fireplace, cathedral ceiling, fully equipped kitchen, and outdoor grill. For more spacious accommodations, try the two- to three-bedroom "Field & Stream," built exclusively for the magazine; the three-bedroom Wilderness Cabin; the four-bedroom Pond House; or the seven-bedroom Mansfield House. The inn's 360 acres are webbed with 20 km of trails; facilities include a hot tub and outdoor pool. Mountain bikes, boats, and snowshoes are available. Pets in some cabins.

INNS AND BED & BREAKFASTS 🍂 ♫ **Nye's Green Valley Farm Bed & Breakfast** (802-644-1984; nyesgreenvalleyfarm.com), 8976 Rt. 15 W., Jeffersonville 05464. Marsha Nye Lane and her husband, David, preside over this 1810 brick Colonial, a former stagecoach tavern. It's a homecoming for her—though there were several owners before she scooped it up and restored it, her great-grandfather purchased the property in 1867. Today it accommodates guests in four air-conditioned rooms, two with private bath. Common rooms are furnished with rare antiques, including a collection of handblown inkwells. In addition to the farm and gardens—which provide a memorable breakfast—there is a pond, a year-round campfire pit, and the Lanes' antiques shop. $75–95 for a farmhouse room; the guest cottage across the road is $125; the new barn apartment is $140.

🍂 ♫ **Smugglers Notch Inn** (802-644-6607, smuggsinn.com), 55 Church St., Jeffersonville 05464. Originally built in 1790, the inn remains historic and full of character. Each of the 11 rooms has a private bath. A restaurant, tavern, and bakery keep guests fed, while a hot tub and in-room massage help with sore après-ski muscles. Rates are $89–129 and include a $5 coupon per person to any of the inn's restaurants. $10 for extra cots.

Fitch Hill Inn (802-888-3834; 800-639-2903; fitchhillinn.com), 258 Fitch Hill Rd., Hyde Park 05655. Handy to many parts of the North Country, this 18th-century hilltop house is filled with six air-conditioned guest rooms, each with private bath. Most are named for a state (our

favorite is Vermont), all tastefully furnished and equipped with ceiling fans; two are able to accommodate more than two people. Two rooms, New Hampshire and Green Mountain, come with a small kitchen, two-person whirlpool tub, and fireplace. $139–189 in high season, $99–149 in low, includes a full breakfast and afternoon snack. Children over 8 are welcome in Green Mountain Suite.

⚐ ♿ **The Governor's House in Hyde Park** (802-888-6888; 866-800-6888; onehundredmain .com), 100 Main St., Hyde Park 05655. This is the place for a taste of *Downton Abbey*. Suzanne Boden has completely restored this sumptuous mansion to reflect the styles of 1893—when the house was erected—and of 1759 when the Longfellow House, after which it was designed, was built in Cambridge, Massachusetts. There are eight guest rooms, six with private bath. Boden serves an elegant afternoon tea in the library on Thurs. and Sun. and alfresco suppers when there is a production at Hyde Park Opera House across the street. Guests are invited to arrive early for lemonade and croquet on the expansive lawns, or simply to sit on the back portico and enjoy hors d'oeuvres (BYOB) as the sunsets behind the mountains. $125–265 includes three-course breakfast, and tea. Inquire about the "Elope to Vermont" package or the renowned Jane Austen Weekends.

🍂 ♫ **Village Victorian** (802-888-8850; 866-266-4672; villagevictorian.com), 107 Union St., Morrisville 05661. All five guest rooms in this 1890s Victorian have queen bed and private bath, with an air conditioner in each; there are two rooms in the annex across the street. There's also a fully furnished, winterized lake cottage on Shadow Lake, about 30 miles northeast. $90–150 includes full breakfast. Discounts for longer stays and "no use" service option. Inquire about afternoon tea parties.

Thistledown Inn (802-279-6120; thistledown inn.com), 201 Park St., Morrisville 05661. High school teacher, beekeeper, energy healer, and now innkeeper Sheila Tymon operates this Victorian-era bed & breakfast with a deep commitment to eco-friendly practices and products. Her organic breakfast showcases Vermont's working landscape—and her own honey. Five guest rooms, two with private bath, are furnished with Vermont-crafted furniture. Inquire about holistic workshops and retreats. Rates are $119–159 (breakfast included), less for singles; children 12 and older welcome. Get a 5 percent discount for taking the simple "eco challenge."

✪ ♂ ✦ ♿ **Smugglers' Notch Resort** (802-644-8851; U.S. and Canada 800-451-8752; UK 0800-169-8219; smuggs.com), 4323 Rt. 108 south, Smugglers' Notch 05464. While "Smuggs" remains a serious ski resort throughout the winter season, year-round it's geared to families and other groups. The result is an atmosphere akin to a family summer camp with endless activities. But there's no need for youthful energy to take part—free shuttle vans and canopied golf carts taxi guests wherever they want to go within the 100-acre core grounds of the 1,000-acre property.

Throughout the summer vacation season Smuggs maintains an exceptionally well-organized (and reasonably priced) family program. Upward of 400 kids weekly ages 3–17 participate in four age-appropriate camps, orchestrated by counselors who return year after year. The fun never stops with the children's camp programs: fishing, movies, nature hikes, tennis, music and dance, arts and crafts, disc golf, and more. Facilities include six different playgrounds, a nature center, a Ping-Pong/arcade room for rainy days, the FunZone indoor play area with climbing inflatables, and two teen centers with music, movies, video games, and organized activities. Despite the absence of a natural lake, there is water everywhere: eight pools, four with waterslides, plus elaborate creations like Little Smugglers Lagoon—a faux cave with a waterfall, fountains, spouts, and a shallow "river" that

RUM RUNNER'S HIDEAWAY

Smugglers' Notch Resort

♂ ♞ ♿ **Maple House Inn** (802-888-6565; maplehouseinnofvt.com), 103 Maple St., Morrisville 05661. This former religious retreat is now a four-suite bed & breakfast, all with private bath and kitchenette. An indoor flamingo-inspired pool with Milky Way ceiling, wet bar, hot tub, and waterfall rock wall is great fun for guests (children of all ages are welcome, and there are toys and snacks just for the kids). The Galaxy of Stars 45-seat home theater boasts an old-fashioned popcorn machine and plays films per guests' requests; also available for retreats and weddings. Rates include breakfast and run $119–199.

MOTEL ♂ ♞ ♥ ♿ **Sunset Motor Inn** (802-888-4956; 800-544-2347; sunsetmotorinn.com), 160 Rt. 15 W., Morrisville 05661. There are 55 comfortable units here, some with whirlpool bath and refrigerator, as well as three fully equipped three-bedroom houses with easy access to Smugglers' Notch and an outdoor pool. The family-friendly **Stonegrill Restaurant & Pub**, whose specialty is grilling meat on a heated volcanic rock, is right next door. Rates $89–185, houses $179–330. Kids 12 and under stay free. Pets allowed in some rooms.

propels youngsters around one end of the pool in inner tubes. There's also Rum Runner's Hideaway, a pristine, 8-acre lake high up the mountain with canoes, paddleboats, and a water trampoline.

With the extensive children's programs, parents can go off and do their own thing without worrying, be it tennis lessons, golf, guided mountain

Smugglers' Notch Resort

SMUGGLERS' NOTCH OFFERS CHILDREN'S ACTIVITIES.

hikes, day trips to Montreal, art or yoga classes, cooking demonstrations, wine or chocolate tastings. There are also family-geared facilities and activities including mini golf, evening bonfires, and fireworks; Thursday is "Country Fair Day," with games, face painting, and pony rides. A variety of summer vacation packages allows families to choose one matching their interests. Basic inclusions in all packages are lodging, use of the pools and waterslides, guided hiking, use of facilities such as the FunZone, and family and adult entertainment.

Altogether there are more than 650 condominium units in a variety of shapes accommodating a total of 3,200 people. Condos are grouped into four "neighborhoods," each with its own central facilities. All offer full kitchen facilities, TV, phones, Internet access, and in-building access to laundry facilities. Units are all privately owned and vary widely from studios, to five-bedroom suites, to luxury units with Jacuzzis. Some are wheelchair accessible. Most are roadside but some are slope-side or up in the woods. Package prices are based on the season as well as the number of people and services rather than on specific accommodations.

In winter a Club Smugglers' vacation package includes lodging, lift tickets for both alpine and Nordic trails, use of the FunZone, pool, tubing, and family entertainment. The resort's website (smuggs.com) has information on seasonal packages, activities, and an online vacation planner.

CAMPGROUNDS ✍ **Brewster River Campground** (802-644-6582; brewsterriver campground.com), 110 Campground Dr., Jeffersonville 05464. Open mid-May–mid-Oct. Twenty tent sites, group camping pavilion, three small trailer sites (not suitable for vehicles with indoor plumbing), and a tepee, lean-to, cabin, and apartment on 20 secluded acres with a 40-foot waterfall and a river where you can pan for gold. There's a fire pit, picnic tables, and a modern bathhouse (free hot showers); no pets (but there's a local kennel). Tent sites are $25 per night; hookups $30; $43 for the lean-to or tepee; cabin is $55, and apartment is $80.

🐾 ✍ **Common Acres Campground** (802-888-5151; commonacres.com), 1781 Rt. 100 N., Hyde Park 05655. Open mid-May–mid-Oct. RV and tent sites at the edge of the Northeast Kingdom. Lots of fun for children with go-carts, mini golf, paintball, pool, arcade, picnic areas, and hiking and biking trails.

🐾 ✍ **Mountain View Campground** (802-888-2178; mountainviewcamping.com), 3154 Rt. 15 E., Morrisville 05661. RV, tent sites, and cabins on the Lamoille River. Swimming pools, playground, multiple outdoor game areas.

Both **Elmore State Park** and **Smugglers' Notch State Park** offer camping; remote camping accessible only by canoe is at **Green River State Park**. Info at vtstateparks.com.

✴ Where to Eat

DINING OUT 🖋 ᕹ **158 Main** (802-644-8100; 158main.com), 158 Main St., Jeffersonville. Serving breakfast, lunch, and dinner daily except Mon. and closing Sun. at 2. This menu, chock-full of "innovative traditionalism," features organic vegetables from local farms; big, fresh salads; and the usual steaks, sandwiches, and flatbreads. The high-ceilinged, hardwood-floored dining room, formerly a dry goods store, shares space with a bakery selling fudge-covered brownies, cookies, Italian- and French-style baguettes, and whole wheat loaves fresh from the oven. Dinner entrées range $9–24. The **Jeffersonville Pizza Depot** is located upstairs. Fully licensed bar with good wine and a few local beers on tap.

✪ 🖋 **Hearth & Candle** (802-644-1260; smuggs .com), 4323 Rt. 108, Smugglers' Notch Resort, Jeffersonville. Open daily. Reservations recommended. If you have kids, there's a room for you. Hate them? Another area will keep you from the madding crowd. Or if you're just in it to wash away your sorrows, there's room at the bar. All this segregation means you're in for precisely the experience that you want from the Notch's only fine-dining establishment. Conservative diners will find classics such as potpie, but wild boar with ricotta gnocchi and salads filled with housemade bacon keep foodies satisfied. Entrées $24–35.

EATING OUT

In Jeffersonville

🖋 At **Smugglers' Notch Resort** (802-644-8851; smuggs.com). **Green Mountain Deli** serves breakfast and lunch daily; **Riga-Bello's** is a pizza joint with lunch, dinner, and take-out; and **Morse Mountain Grille** is a reasonable, casual restaurant serving breakfast, lunch, and dinner daily.

🖋 **Stella Notte** (802-644-8884; stellanotte .com), Rt. 108 across from Smuggs. Family-friendly Italian; traditional pastas and seafood. A lounge downstairs for après-ski and nightlife has a killer burger made from Boyden beef.

Cupboard Deli (802-644-2069), at the junction of Rts. 15 and 108. Located at the Citgo gas station, the deli has a giant selection of homemade and ready-made sandwiches. It's nearly impossible to leave without a few selections from the exhaustive collection of home-baked goods. The s'mores bar is not to be missed.

✪ 🖋 ᕹ **The Family Table** (802-644-8920; familytablevt.com), junction of Rts. 15 and 108.

Open for all three meals, Thurs.–Mon. Home cookin', if your dad happened to have two degrees from Johnson & Wales. The family-friendly, large menu has all the staples, prepared better than you're used to.

🖋 ᕹ **Brewster River Pub & Brewery** (802-644-6366; brewsterriverpubnbrewery.com), 4087 Rt. 108. Open daily. This chef-owned pub isn't your average fryolator-focused nightspot. Order duck wings and wild mushroom risotto to go with your house-brewed Saison, Porter, or IPA.

✪ 🖋 ᕹ **Burger Barn** (802-730-3441), 4968 Rt. 15. Open daily in-season. You may see a Burger Barn food truck elsewhere in the region, but this green-and-cow-spotted trailer spawned the mobile business. Using beef from Boyden Farm just down the road as a canvas, chefs make glorious burger art in this unexpected setting. Try the Ethan Allen burger, with Cabot sharp cheddar, grilled apples, and homemade cranberry-garlic mayo.

MTN Seasons Woodfired (802-644-5446), 4008 Rt. 108. The "Vermont-style" bagels here are boiled in maple syrup before baking for a shiny, subtly sweet crust. Try the Probiotic sandwich before or after hitting the slopes: It's filled with housemade gingery kimchi and local Does' Leap chèvre.

In Johnson

🖋 ᕹ **Edelweiss Bakery & Café** (802-635-7946), 325 Lower Main St. west. Breakfast and lunch, Tues.–Sat. The European-style bakery is downstairs, with a dining space upstairs in this converted Victorian on the edge of town. It's also the home of House Wolf K-9 Dog Biscuits. Grab yourself a sandwich to go and a little something for your furry friend.

(ᵢᵢᵢ) **Loving Cup Café** (802-635-7423; lovincup cafe.com), 38 Lower Main St. Breakfast, lunch, and afternoon snacks seven days a week. Laid-back student hangout with art on the walls and

AT EDELWEISS BAKERY

Rachel Carter

fresh-brewed java, teas, and smoothies; also panini and sandwiches. You order in the kitchen of this 19th-century house and sit down in the mango-colored living room or in the former dining room.

(ᵗⁱᵖ) **Downtown Pizzeria & Pub** (802-635-7626; thehubvt.com), 21 Lower Main St. Open Tues.–Sun. for dinner and late night; frequent live music and karaoke. It's often difficult to find real, New York-style pizza in the Green Mountains. Here, it's the real deal, served with Vermont beers.

In Morrisville

✍ ♿ **10 Railroad Street** (802-888-2277; 10railroadstreet.com), 82 Lower Main St. Open Wed.–Sun.; lunch, brunch, and dinner. The railroad setting inside this historical train station includes human-sized tracks to chug from table to bathroom. The upscale comfort food consists of classics such as a BLT and mac-and-cheese, both stuffed with lobster.

❂ ♿ **Lost Nation Brewing** (802-851-8041; lostnationbrewing.com), 254 Wilkins St. Taproom open 11:30 AM–9 PM, Wed.–Sun. This house belongs to some of Vermont's favorite craft brews (see *Wine and Beer*), including salted, coriander-flavored Gose. But the guests of honor are meals handcrafted as carefully as the suds. The dry-rubbed, smoked pork shoulder is served on focaccia from nearby Elmore Mountain Bread. It can all be enjoyed inside or in the outdoor biergarten.

APRÈS-SKI The best après-ski after a day at Smuggs (smuggs.com) is found right there for outdoor mountain events, or by heading into the **Bootlegger's Lounge** at the base of Smuggs's Madonna Mountain. Across the street is the downstairs lounge at **Stella Notte** (stellanotte.com—see *Eating Out*), which has live music most weekends. For a bit more local flair, head to **Brewster River Pub & Grill** (802-644-6366), formerly the raucous Brewski. As you head back to Jeffersonville, you can still stop at **The Family Table** (familytablevt.com—see *Eating Out*), which will tempt you into a full dinner, or head into the historic **Village Tavern** (smuggsinn.com) at the Smugglers Notch Inn (see *Lodging*).

✳ **Entertainment**

Lamoille County Players (802-888-4507; lcplayers.com) at the Hyde Park Opera House, 85 Main St., Hyde Park. A community theater that stages four productions a year, including at least two musicals. The opera house is the proud owner of one of Vermont's legendary

painted curtains, completed in 1911 by Charles Hardin Andrus.

Cambridge Arts Council (artsfestvt.com) stages concerts, coffeehouses, and contra dances in Jeffersonville and Cambridge; check the website. It also puts on Festival of the Arts—see *Special Events*.

Dibden Center for the Arts (802-635-1476; jsc.edu), Johnson State College, Johnson. A 500-seat theater plays host to music, theater, dance, and comedy performed by students and local residents as well as regional and national professional acts.

Bijoux Cineplex 4 (802-888-3293; bijou4.com), 4 Portland St. (Rt. 100), Morrisville. Traditional downtown movie house; all shows $5 on Thurs.

✳ **Selective Shopping**

ANTIQUES *Note:* Rt. 15 from Cambridge to Morrisville is a great drive for antiquing. Shops and outlets may vary, and include:

Smugglers' Notch Antiques (802-644-2100; smugglersnotchantiques.com), 906 Rt. 108 S., Jeffersonville. This dairy-barn-turned-antiques-center contains 10,000 square feet of antiques, specializing in custom-made and antique furniture.

The Buggyman Antiques Shop (802-635-2110), 853 Rt. 15 W., Johnson. Open Fri.–Sun. 10–5, more in summer. A big old barn and 18th-century farmhouse filled with antiques and estate sale items. Impressive collection of wagons, buggies, and sleighs.

Nye's Green Valley Farm Antiques (802-644-1984), 8976 Rt. 15, Jeffersonville. Weekends in winter, daily in warmer months. Old Vermont farmhouse furnishings and a wide selection of American pressed glass. See also *Lodging*.

ART GALLERIES AND CRAFTS STUDIOS *Note:* For full artisan listings, visit vermontcrafts.com and make note of Vermont Open Studio Weekend every Memorial Day weekend (see *Special Events*).

Visions of Vermont Gallery (802-644-8183; visionsofvermont.com), 94 Main St., Jeffersonville. Open Tues.–Sun. After getting its start showcasing the landscape paintings of Eric Tobin, Visions of Vermont has expanded to include three galleries and dozens of Vermont artists.

♿ **River Arts** (802-888-1261; riverartsvt.org), 74 Pleasant St., Morrisville. Offers classes, exhibitions, and events throughout the year. Check website for schedule.

& **Bryan Memorial Art Gallery** (802-644-5100; bryangallery.org), 180 Main St., Jeffersonville. Open 11–4, daily in summer, Thurs.–Sun. in spring and fall; by appointment in winter. Built by Alden Bryan in memory of his wife and fellow artist, Mary, this mini museum features a dynamic collection representing more than 200 New England landscape painters in revolving exhibits.

Vermont Studio Center (802-635-2727; vermontstudiocenter.org), 80 Pearl St., Johnson. Since 1984, this nonprofit center has absorbed more than two dozen buildings in the village of Johnson. The lecture hall is a former meetinghouse, and the gallery, exhibiting the work of artists in residence, is in a former grain mill one street back from Main, down by the river. As host to 600 international writers and artists annually, this unique program stages frequent gallery shows, readings, and lectures open to the public.

FARMERS MARKETS Johnson and Morrisville both hold seasonal farmers markets. A year-round Farmers Artisan Market is held at the River Arts Center in Morrisville the second Saturday of the month. More info at vermont agriculture.com.

FARMS ♂ ♪ **Applecheek Farm** (802-888-4482; applecheekfarm.com), 567 McFarlane Rd., Hyde Park. A real Vermont farm success story, this multigenerational family farm grew from a dairy and maple sugaring operation to one of the most revered grassfed poultry and meat producers in the Northeast. Eggs, raw milk, emu oil, and maple syrup are all available at the farm store. Animals include cows, chickens, pigs, guinea fowl, emus, ducks, and turkeys. Tours, special events, wagon rides; catering for weddings and events is offered at the farm's banquet hall. See also *Llama Treks* and *Sleigh Rides*.

♂ ♪ **Boyden Valley Farm** (802-598-5509; boydenfarm.com), 64 Rt. 104, Cambridge. This splendid former dairy farm bordering the Lamoille River—in the family for four generations—is now known for its beef and wine. Boyden beef can be found in restaurants throughout this book. Over 100 acres of maple trees also supply the farm's maple syrup operation; farther pastures are covered with grapes (see *Wine and Beer*). See *Canoeing* for a guided paddle to the farm with camping. Seasonal attractions include a summer concert series that includes the Cambridge Music Festival (see *Special Events*), hayrides, a corn maze, and

dogsled rides (see *Dogsledding*). The Barn is also host to some of Vermont's most elaborate farm weddings.

WINE AND BEER Boyden Valley Winery (802-644-8151; boydenvalley.com), 70 Rt. 104, Cambridge. An impressive collection of Vermont wines is crafted on this farm. More than 8,000 grapevines and local Lamoille Valley fruit make up Boyden Valley red, white, fruit, and dessert wines as well as the innovative Vermont Ice Cider brand. Stop in for a tasting in the restored 1875 carriage barn. Check the website for info on tours, tastings, and special events.

& **Rock Art Brewery** (802-888-9400; rockart brewery.com), 632 Laporte Rd., Morrisville. Open Mon.–Sat. 9–6. Stop in for a tasting and tour at this established brewery, known for a growing collection of 20-some varieties. Grab some growlers on-site to take home.

& **Lost Nation Brewing** (802-851-8041; lostnationbrewing.com), 254 Wilkins St. This 7,000-barrel brewery takes its cures from rare European beer styles. Kegs and growlers are available to take, or choose a seat in the taproom (see *Eating Out*) to try several varieties.

SPECIAL STORES Johnson Woolen Mills (802-635-2271; 877-635-WOOL; johnson woolenmills.com), 51 Lower Main St., Johnson. Open year-round, Mon.–Sat. 9–5, Sun. 10–4. Although wool is no longer loomed in this picturesque mill, Johnson Woolen Mills clothing is still made on the premises, as it has been since 1842. This mill's label can still be found in shops throughout the country, and its famous, heavy green wool work pants and checked jackets are a uniform for Vermont farmers young and old. Although there are few discounts at the factory store, the selection of wool jackets and pants—for men, women, and children—is exceptional.

Three Mountain Outfitters (802-644-8563; smuggs.com). Located at Smugglers' Notch Resort; seasonal sports clothes, skis, snowboards, boots, helmets, as well as toys, shoes and boots, T-shirts, and accessories.

Marvin's Butternut Mountain Country Store (802-635-7483; butternutmountainfarm .com), 31 Main St., Johnson. Open Mon.–Sat. 9–5:30, Sun. 11–4. This is the retail outlet for the Marvin family's Butternut Mountain Farm maple products, plus a variety of Vermont specialty foods and gifts.

Ebenezer Books (802-635-7472), 2 Lower Main St. W., Johnson. Open Mon.–Sat. 10–6. An inviting independent bookstore specializing in new and used children's books, fiction, and local authors as well as toys, CDs, and art.

Brick House Book Shop (802-888-4300), 632 Morristown Corners Rd., Morrisville. Open Tues.–Sat. 2–5 or by appointment, best to call ahead. Proprietor Alexandra Heller has amassed 70,000 old books, fiction and nonfiction, hardcover and paperback, in this Vermont treasure connected to her home.

& **Vermont Maple Outlet** (802-644-5482; vermontmapleoutlet.com), 3929 Rt. 15, Jeffersonville. A nice selection of cheese, syrup, handmade jams, gift boxes, and numerous maple products. Open daily 9–5.

✳ Special Events

Also see *Entertainment*.

✍ *Last weekend of January:* **Smugglers' Notch Heritage Winterfest** (smugnotch.com)—the main event is a primitive biathlon with muzzle loaders and snowshoes; also skiing, snowshoeing, theater, fireworks, sleigh rides, lasagna dinner, and contra dance.

✍ *Mid-February:* **Northern Vermont Snowshoe Race & Family Snowshoe Festival** (smuggs.com)—a day of snowshoe treks, walks, and races for all ages held at Smugglers' Notch Resort.

Memorial Day weekend: **Open Studio Weekend** throughout Vermont (vermontcrafts.com), where artisans open their studios for tours and shopping.

✍ *July 4:* **Fourth of July Celebration**, Jeffersonville and Smugglers' Notch Resort (802-644-1118; smuggs.com)—an outstanding small-town parade and celebration with carnival fun, games, crafts, cow-flop bingo, and a frog-jumping contest on the green behind the elementary school. Evening brings food live music and fireworks at Smugglers' Notch Resort.

✍ *Late July:* **Lamoille County Field Days** (802-635-7113; lamoillefielddays.com), Rt. 100C, Johnson—a classic small-town agricultural fair with family-friendly entertainment.

✍ *Labor Day:* **Cambridge Area Rotary Fun Run & Walk** (rotarycambridge.org)—a 5K footrace (or walk) for all ages and ability levels on some fine Vermont back roads; town celebration with race awards, barbecue on the green, and flea market to follow.

Early September: **Cambridge Music Festival** (cambridgemusicfestival.com)—a daylong showcase of Vermont musical acts at Boyden Valley Farm.

✍ *First Saturday of December:* **Festival of Lights** (802-888-7607; lamoillechamber.com)—a winter holiday jubilee in downtown Morrisville with sleigh rides, home tours, and Santa.

The Northeast Kingdom

Christina Tree

THE NORTHEAST KINGDOM

You know, this is such beautiful country up here it should to be called the Northeast Kingdom of Vermont.

It was in 1949 that Senator George Aiken made this remark to a group in Lyndonville. The name he coined has since stuck to Vermont's three northeastern counties: Orleans, Caledonia, and Essex.

This is the state's most rural and lake-spotted corner, encompassing more than 2,000 square miles, including 37,575 acres of public lakes and ponds and 3,540 miles of rivers. Aside from a few dramatic elevations, such as Jay Peak on its northwestern fringe and Burke Mountain at its heart, this is a predominantly high, open, glacially carved plateau of humped hills and rolling farmland, with some lonely timber country along the northern reaches of the Connecticut River.

For many decades neither Burke Mountain nor Jay Peak had much impact on surrounding communities in summer and fall. That has changed. Patrons from both sides of the border are drawn to Jay Peak's 18-hole golf course, to the spectacular new water park and ice arena, and to Kingdom Trails—more than 100 miles of biking, hiking, and skiing trails that web the high country surrounding the village of East Burke as well as on the ski mountain itself, now under the same ownership as Jay Peak and renamed Q Burke, with plans to transform into a more multifaceted resort.

In the era of trains and steamboats large hotels clustered on in Newport on Lake Memphremagog, and around dramatic and fjordlike Lake Willoughby; both Newport and Island Pond were busy rail junctions. Currently the focal points have shifted from the lakes to the ski areas, given their year-round appeal and lodging base, but the quieter corners of this magnificent region continue to attract creative spirits, and family farms survive in this locavore era.

Within the Kingdom lodging options range from working farms to ski resorts and include an unusual old lake resort (Quimby Country), several inns and lakeside cabin clusters, a limited number of B&Bs, and plenty of summer rentals. All the amenities are here: golf, tennis, and horseback riding as well as hiking, biking, boating, and fishing. Winter sports include ice fishing, tracking, snowshoeing, some of New England's best snowmobiling, and superb skiing, cross-country at Craftsbury Outdoor Center and at Haven's Notch as well as downhill skiing at Jay and Q Burke.

The key to this Kingdom is following farm roads and—in the process of finding an isolated craftsperson, a maple producer, or a swimming hole—stumbling on breathtaking views and memorable people. Frequently you come across traces of the Kingdom's oldest thoroughfare, the 48-mile Bayley-Hazen Military Road, which runs diagonally across the region. It was begun at Wells River on the Connecticut River in 1776 by General Jacob Bayley, and continued in 1778–79 by General Moses Hazen as far as Hazen's Notch (a plaque on Rt. 58 tells the story). It was a flop as an invasion route but served settlers well after the Revolution when it came time to establish towns in this area.

The Northeast Kingdom has a story to tell. Listen at a lunch counter, in a general store, at a church supper, at a county fair, or during the peerless Northeast Kingdom Foliage Festival. Tune in with Howard Frank Mosher's beautifully written books—*Northern Borders*, *Where the Rivers Flow North*, *A Stranger in the Kingdom*, *Disappearances*, and *On Kingdom Mountain*. Kingdom-based filmmaker Jay Craven has turned three of these into films.

Like many of the world's most beautiful places, the Northeast Kingdom's preservation is fragile. National Geographic Center for Sustainable Destinations has chosen it as one of the few areas in this country to partner with through its "geotourism" plan, working with the Northeast Kingdom Travel & Tourism Association (see *Guidance*).

While this is the single most distinctive corner of the entire state, 2,000 square miles is too large an area to describe without recognizing the ways in which it divides into regions. The first, at least for those of us approaching from the southeast, is the **St. Johnsbury Area**, including nearby Q Burke Mountain. The second is what is generally called the **Heart of the Kingdom**, the high, magnificent farm country surrounding Craftsbury/Greensboro and, closely linked to it, the Barton/Lake Willoughby area just north. The Canadian border country around **Jay Peak**, **Newport**, and the **Lake Memphremagog** area has its own look and feel, as does the wilder, former lumber company country around **Island Pond** and beyond to the east.

FISHING This entire area is a fly-fishing mecca, drawing serious anglers to wilderness brooks and ponds as well as rivers and lakes. Most general stores sell three-day fishing licenses (see *Fishing* in "What's Where" for fishing regulations). Check in the *Vermont Atlas and Gazetteer* for local access points to ponds. Rental boats, bait, and tackle are available at the sites listed under *Boating*. Check the Vermont Fish and Wildlife Department's site, **regulations.com/vermont/northeast-kingdom,** for details about what's available locally. Guides can also be found through the **Vermont Outdoor Guide Association** (800-425-8747; voga.org) and through local fishing-geared lodging. In early May head for the **Willoughby Falls Wildlife Management Area** east of Orleans to see wild rainbow trout climb the falls, jumping high to clear the whitewater to reach their spawning ground. **Willoughby** is known as the prime fishing lake; check out the **Clyde River** for brook trout and landlocked salmon, the **Barton River** for trout and perch. **Lake Memphremagog** is good for smelt, smallmouth bass, and walleye, in addition to salmon and trout, but also has plenty of milfoil. **Seymour Lake** is (at this writing) milfoil-free and known for bass and lake trout. **Holland Pond** and **Echo Lake** are known for rainbow trout, and **Norton Pond** is known for fighting pike. Ice fishing is particularly popular on Memphremagog and Seymour Lake. There is a state fish hatchery in Newark; **Newark Pond** has an access and is good for yellow perch along with trout. The **Willoughby River** is known, especially in early spring, for rainbow trout, as are the **Barton** and **Black Rivers**. The **Clyde River**, acclaimed as the first river in the country to have a dam removed for environmental reasons, is known for landlocked Atlantic salmon. Lodging geared to fishermen includes **Quimby Country**, a self-contained resort that includes 70-acre Forest Lake, half a mile from 1,200-acre Great Averill Pond, both lonely and remote but good for trout and salmon; rowboats can be rented here by the day, also handy to a stretch of the Upper Connecticut River that's known for trout. In the Jay Peak area the **Trout River** deserves its name.

The Kingdom also offer exceptional **canoeing, cross-country skiing and snowboarding, hiking,** and **mountain biking.** Check *To Do* throughout this section.

GUIDANCE The Northeast Kingdom Travel and Tourism Association (802-626-8511; 800-884-8001; travelthekingdom.com), a nonprofit umbrella organization promoting the area, has an exceptional website with themed maps showing lodging hiking, biking, and paddling, and more. Also check each section for local chambers of commerce and welcome centers.

BORDER CROSSINGS AND REQUIREMENTS Derby Line, Vermont, and Stanstead, Quebec, represent a major border crossing (I-91 continues north as Hwy. 55), linking up with the major east–west highway between Montreal and Quebec City. Less busy crossings include: **North Troy** (Rt. 243), **Norton** (Rt. 114 to Canadian Rt. 147), and **Beecher Falls** (Rt. 3 to Rt. 253). Passports or equivalent documents such as a NEXUS or U.S. Passport Card are required for U.S. citizens reentering by car. At this writing U.S. citizens are permitted to bring in Quebec cheese (except goat and soft cheeses such as Brie), apples, tinned meats (with the exception of goat and lamb), and a 1-liter bottle of wine duty-free.

The Northeast Kingdom

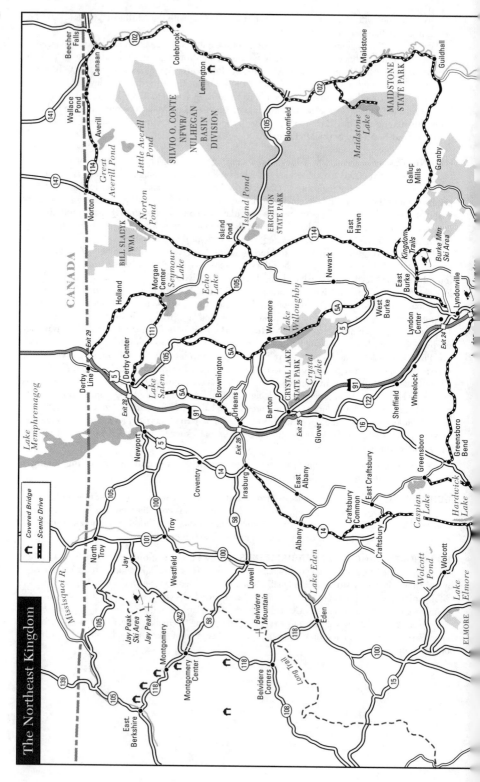

Covered Bridge **C**

Scenic Drive

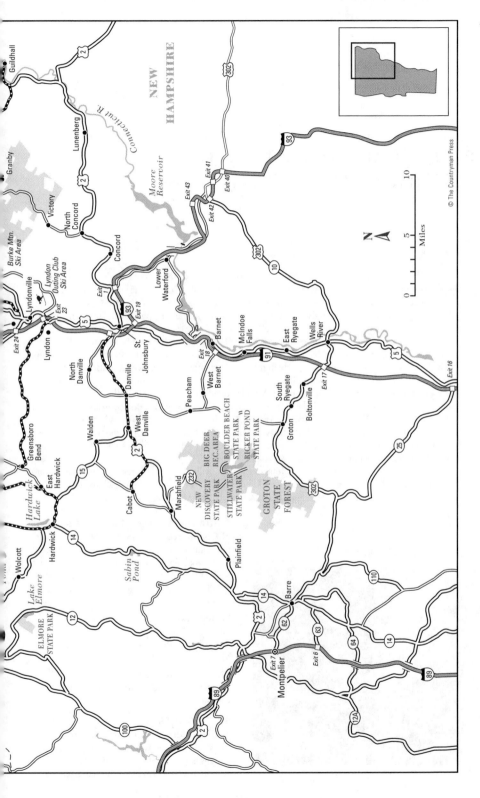

© The Countryman Press

ST. JOHNSBURY AND
BURKE MOUNTAIN

With a population of about 7,600, St. Johnsbury is the shire town of Caledonia County and largest community in the Northeast Kingdom. Thanks to members of the Fairbanks family, who began manufacturing their world-famous scale here in the 1830s, it is graced with a superb museum of natural and local history, a handsome athenaeum, and an outstanding public academy. The general late-19th-century affluence that St. J (as it is affectionately known) enjoyed as an active rail junction and industrial center has been commemorated in ornate brick along Railroad Street and in the fine mansions along Main Street, set high above the commercial downtown. In the 1960s, when Fairbanks became a division of a conglomerate—which threatened to move the scaleworks south—townspeople themselves raised the money to subsidize a new plant. This is a spirited community boasting one of the country's oldest town bands (performing Monday nights all summer in Courthouse Park), a busy calendar of concerts, lectures, and plays, and all the shops and services needed by residents of the picturesque villages along the Connecticut River to the south, the rolling hills to the southwest and northwest, and the lonely woodlands to the east. Less than a dozen miles north, the wide main street of Lyndonville is also lined with useful shops. Nearby Q Burke Mountain draws skiers from throughout the Northeast in winter.

As Rt. 2 climbs steeply west from St. Johnsbury to Danville, a spectacular panorama of the White Mountains unfolds to the east. The village of Danville itself is a beauty, and the back roads running south to Peacham and north to Walden follow ridges with long views.

DOWNTOWN ST. JOHNSBURY

Christina Tree

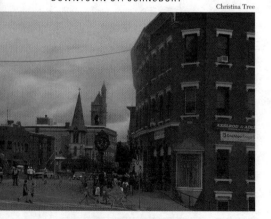

GUIDANCE Northeast Kingdom Chamber of Commerce (802-748-3678; 800-639-6379; nekchamber.com), 2000 Memorial Dr., Suite 11, St. Johnsbury 05819. Open daily 8:30–9 with walk-in info. A source for brochures and for lodging, dining, and general information on the region.

St. Johnsbury Welcome Center, in its vintage railroad station, is open year-round: in summer and fall Mon.–Sat. 9–6, Sun. 10–4; in winter Mon.–Fri. 9–5, Sat.–Sun. 10–2.

Also see the **Northeast Kingdom Travel and Tourism Association** (travelthekingdom.com) website.

GETTING THERE *By car:* I-93 makes the Northeast Kingdom far more accessible from the southeast than is still generally realized: Bostonians can be in St. Johnsbury in three hours. Note that I-91 works like a fireman's pole, a

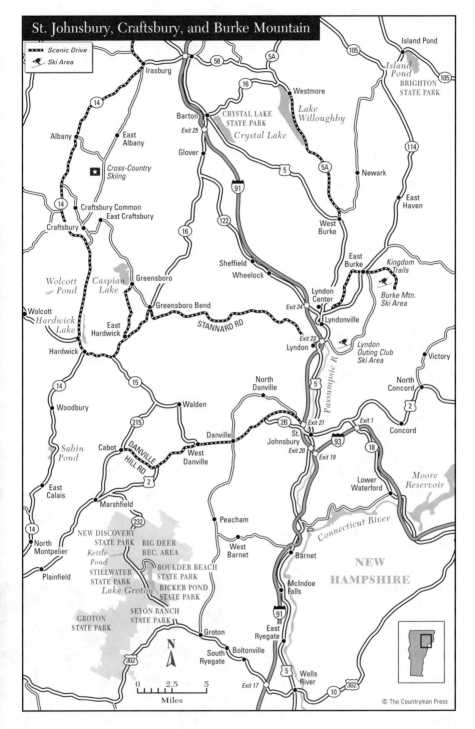

St. Johnsbury, Craftsbury, and Burke Mountain

🚗🚗🚗 Scenic Drive
⛷ Ski Area

Island Pond

105

Island Pond

BRIGHTON
STATE PARK

105

Irasburg

58

5A

16

Westmore

14

Barton

CRYSTAL LAKE
STATE PARK

Lake Willoughby

Albany

East Albany

Exit 25

Crystal Lake

Glover

5

5A

114

Newark

Cross-Country Skiing

91

East Haven

14

Craftsbury Common

East Craftsbury

122

West Burke

Craftsbury

16

East Burke

Kingdom Trails

Sheffield

Wheelock

Wolcott Pond

Caspian Lake

Greensboro

Lyndon Center

Burke Mtn. Ski Area

Wolcott

Hardwick Lake

East Hardwick

Greensboro Bend

STANNARD RD

Exit 24

Lyndonville

Hardwick

14

15

North Danville

5

Exit 23

Lyndon

Passumpsic R.

Lyndon Outing Club Ski Area

Victory

Woodbury

Walden

North Concord

2

215

Danville

2B

Exit 21

Concord

Sabin Pond

Cabot

DANVILLE HILL RD

West Danville

St. Johnsbury

93

18

Exit 20

Exit 19

Moore Reservoir

East Calais

Marshfield

2

Lower Waterford

Peacham

232

Connecticut River

NEW DISCOVERY STATE PARK

BIG DEER REC. AREA

West Barnet

Barnet

**NEW
HAMPSHIRE**

14

North Montpelier

Kettle Pond

STILLWATER STATE PARK

BOULDER BEACH STATE PARK

Plainfield

Lake Groton

RICKER POND STATE PARK

McIndoe Falls

SEYON RANCH STATE PARK

91

GROTON STATE PARK

Groton

East Ryegate

N ↑

South Ryegate

Boltonville

302

5

302

0   2.5   5

Miles

Exit 17

Wells River

10

© The Countryman Press

quick way to move north–south through the Kingdom. In snow, beware the high, open, 16-mile stretch of highway between Lyndon Center and Barton known as Sheffield Heights.

By bus: **Rural Community Transportation** (802-748-8170; riderct.org) offers service from **Montpelier** (linked by bus and train to New York City and Boston) to St. J.

✳ Towns and Villages

Barnet (population 1,700). An old Scots settlement encompassing the villages of McIndoe Falls as well as East and West Barnet and Barnet Center. The village of Barnet itself is on a curve of the Connecticut River, almost lost today in a curious intertwining of I-91 and Rt. 5. **Goodwillie House** (802-633-2891) in Barnet Center, built in 1790 by a Scottish pastor, served as a stop on the Underground Railroad and now houses the collections of the Barnet Historical Society; unfortunately it's only open by request and on Fall Foliage Day. Drive to West Barnet to find **Harvey's Lake** (good for both fishing and swimming); along the way stop by the 1870s **Ben Thresher's Mill** (open Sat. 10–2 July–Sept., and daily during foliage season). The beautiful round red **Moore Barn** sits above the Passumpsic River in East Barnet (north on Rt. 5 from Barnet). Also see the **Karmê Chöling Shambhala Meditation Center** (karmecholing.org) under *Lodging*.

Burke (population 1,750; chamber of commerce 802-626-4124; burkevermont.com). The town includes Burke Hollow and West Burke, but it's the village of East Burke that's home to **Q Burke Mountain** (see *Downhill Skiing*) and **Burke Mountain Academy**. In summer and fall the big draw is **Kingdom Trails** (see *Biking*). The village is a busy cluster of lodging places, restaurants, and shops around the Kingdom Trails base area, a general store, and a gas station. **The Burke Mountain Clubhouse** (802-626-9823), 368 Rt. 114, is a library with paintings and a historical collection; it's open Sat. with coffee and doughnuts, also for frequent events.

Concord (population 1,200). Six miles east of St. Johnsbury on Rt. 2, Concord is a proudly built village with an unusual number of columned houses. The **Concord Museum** is upstairs in the tower-topped town hall; there's a picture of St. Johnsbury's Railroad St., painted in the 1940s, on its stage curtain. A plaque declares this to be the site of the country's first "Normal School" to train teachers in 1823, founded by the Reverend Samuel R. Hall, who is also credited with inventing the blackboard. **Miles Pond** offers boat access, as does **Shadow Lake** in Concord Center.

Danville (population 2,334; danvillevt.com) is set high on a plateau, with a bandstand and Civil War monument in the center of its large green. The town hall was built as the county courthouse, and the small, square Passumpsic Savings Bank is one of the safest strongholds around, thanks to devices installed after it was last held up, in 1935. Danville is headquarters for the **American Society of Dowsers**. **Dowser's Hall** (802-684-3417) is open weekdays 9–5; note the summer concerts on the green (see *Entertainment*) and the Danville Community Fair in August. **West Danville** is a crossroads (Rts. 15 and 2) cluster of two general stores and a major crafts shop (see *Selective Shopping*). One of the world's smallest libraries sits across the road at **Joe's Pond** (named for a Native American beloved by early settlers), beside a public beach with picnic facilities. The water from Joe's Pond is said to empty, eventually, into Long Island Sound, while that from Molly's Pond (a mile south, named for Joe's wife) presumably winds up in the Gulf of St. Lawrence.

DOWNTOWN EAST BURKE

Christina Tree

Lyndon (population 6,000). An up-and-down roll of land encompasses the villages of Lyndonville, Lyndon Center, Lyndon Corner, Red Village, and East Lyndon, and the neighborhoods of Vail Hill, Pudding Hill, Darling Hill, and Squabble Hollow. Lyndon isn't a tourist town, but it offers real, down-home hospitality and **five covered bridges**. The village of Lyndonville was developed by the Passumpsic River Railroad Co. in the 1860s. Besides a handsome (long gone) station and a number of brick rail shops, the company laid out broad streets, planted elm trees, and landscaped Bandstand Park. **Lyndon State College** is on Vail Hill (T. N. Vail was the first president of AT&T; he came here to buy a horse and ended up buying a farm, which eventually turned into 20 farms, much of which is now occupied by the campus). Lyndonville's famous product is **Bag Balm**, manufactured since 1899 in the middle of town. Band concerts are held Wed. evenings during summer months in Bandstand Park, also Lyndonville. The **Lyndon Area Chamber of Commerce** (lyndonvermont .com) maintains an information center in the **Lyndon Freight House** (see *Eating Out*), which also showcases the town's railroading history. The Caledonia County Fairgrounds are the site of frequent events; the **Caledonia County Fair** itself runs for five days in early August.

Peacham (population 730). High on a ridge overlooking the White Mountains, this is a tiny but aristocratic village settled just after the Revolution, with a fine new library at the four-corners. Peacham's handsome homes and setting have attracted retired professors, literati, artistic luminaries, and ambassadors. All three Peachams (South, East, and Center) are worth exploring, as are the roads between. **Peacham Library** (802-592-3216) at the center of the village offers restrooms and a gallery; across the way is the new, community-owned **Peacham Café** (peachamcafe.org). During Foliage Festival the village stages "Ghost Walks," with current residents impersonating long-deceased counterparts, in hilltop **Peacham Cemetery**—which tells its own story and offers one of the best views in the Kingdom any day.

✳ Must See

St. Johnsbury Athenaeum (802-748-8291; www.stjathenaeum.org), 1171 Main St., St. Johnsbury. Open Mon.–Fri. 10–5:30, Sat. 9:30–3; closed Sun. The cost for the art gallery is $8 for adults; 12 and under are free. Completed in 1871, the athenaeum was conceived and created by Horace Fairbanks, who personally selected the paintings for the art gallery and the original 9,000 leather-bound books for the library. In 1873 the art gallery was added with paintings by Hudson River School artists, including Asher B. Durand, Sanford Gifford, and Albert Bierstadt, whose large painting *Domes of the Yosemite* is the centerpiece. Natural light through an arched skylight enhances the effect of looking into the Yosemite Valley. The art gallery is at the rear of this fascinating public library, a National Historic Landmark, which has seen extensive renovations that include extending the second-floor ceiling an additional 18 feet to reinstate the original Athenaeum Hall lecture space (now open stacks), uncovering arched windows, subtly inserting an elevator, and restoring and replacing the original skylights in the art gallery.

LOCAL ATTRACTIONS Maple Grove Farms of Vermont (800-525-2540; maplegrove.com), 1052 Portland St. (Rt. 2 east), St. Johnsbury. Apr.–May open weekdays 8–5; June–Dec. also weekends 9–5; Jan.–Mar., call for hours. Billed as "the world's oldest and largest maple candy factory"—in business since 1915—this is an old-fashioned factory in which maple candy is made from molds. A film in the adjacent museum depicts maple production and displays tools of the trade. The gift store stocks many things besides maple.

The American Society of Dowsers (802-684-2565; dowsers.org) is headquartered in Dowser's Hall (open weekdays 9–5), 184 Brainerd St., just off the common in Danville; the bookstore sells books, tapes, and dowsing equipment. Check out the labyrinth in the rear of the building. The ancient art of dowsing is the knack of finding water through the use of a forked stick, a pair of angle rods, or a pendulum. The society has thousands of members throughout the world.

🐾 🦴 Stephen Huneck's Dog Mountain, Gallery, and Dog Chapel (800-449-2580; dogmt.com), 143 Parks Rd., marked from Rt. 2 east of St. Johnsbury. Gift shop open May–Oct. Mon.–Sat. 10–5, Sun. 11–4; closing at 4 every day in winter. Chapel and grounds are open at all time. The full-scale wooden chapel "welcomes all creeds and breeds. No dogma allowed." Seven surrounding acres are planted in wildflowers, and visitors are welcome to bring

THE ATHENAEUM INTERIOR AFTER A RECENT RESTORATION
John Sherman courtesy of St. Johnsbury Athenaeum

Fairbanks Museum and Planetarium (802-748-2372; fairbanksmuseum.org), 1302 Main, St. Johnsbury. Open year-round, Mon.–Sat. 9–5, Sun. 1–5 (closed Mon., Nov.–Mar.). $8 adults, $6 seniors and ages 5–17; $5 for planetarium shows, which are Sat. and Sun. at 1:30 year-round, 11 and 1:30 daily in July and Aug. A wonderfully Victorian-style "Cabinet of Curiosities," said to be the oldest science education museum in the nation and the state's only public planetarium, the Fairbanks is much more as well. "I wish the museum to be the people's school . . . to teach the village the meaning of nature and religion," explained Franklin Fairbanks at the museum's 1891 dedication.

The main hall is capped by a 30-foot-high, barrel-vaulted ceiling, its floor lined with Victorian-style cabinets displaying thousands of stuffed animals: from mice to a vintage 1898 moose, from bats to bears (including a superb polar bear), birds galore (from hummingbirds to passenger pigeons), reptiles and fish, insect nests. Founder Franklin Fairbanks was passionate about nature, and the collection represents most native species of mammals and birds as well as many gathered from around the world, a total of 3,000 specimens. An extensive and varied geologic collection, started by Franklin Fairbanks, is also displayed, along with a living exhibit of local wildflowers in bloom. The balcony, which circles the entire hall level, is lined with historical displays depicting local 19th-century life (including the Civil War) and exhibits drawn from a 5,000-piece collection representing most of the world's far corners—Malaysia, the Orient, the Middle East, and Africa—by the Fairbanks family and their friends. Altogether the museum displays 160,000 objects. Note the new computer-operated Omniglobe.

In the **planetarium**, which seats just 50 people, you learn about the night sky as it appears in the Northeast Kingdom. The museum is also a U.S. weather observation station, and its daily *Eye on the Sky* forecasts are a fixture of Vermont Public Radio (VPR). The weather station is in the basement, worth a visit to see exhibits telling the story of the Fairbanks family and their scales and an interactive kids-geared exhibit. There is a fine little gift shop. The museum archives include a resource library for studies and information about the Northeast Kingdom. Ambitious exhibits in the main gallery change seasonally. The annual Feast with the Beasts (late June) celebrates local foods in the main gallery. Check the website for special events.

(or email) photos of their beloved animals to grace the chapel walls. The gallery showcases the late artist's stylish, carved wooden animals and bold, fanciful furniture, panels, and jewelry, and his children's books, featuring his black Lab Sally. A total of 150 acres are webbed with snowshoeing and hiking trails. Dogs are welcome everywhere on Dog Mountain, inside and out.

Bag Balm (802-626-3610; bagbalm.com). Developed in 1899 as an antiseptic ointment for cattle, Bag Balm proved particularly effective for chapped udders and is still used by Vermont farmers. Its campy, old-fashioned green tins now appear in Madison Avenue pharmacies and ski resort boutiques, at far higher prices than they fetch locally. Inquire about weekday-morning tours of the small factory on Lyndonville's Main St. (Rt. 5). The company, which has been owned by the same family since it opened its doors, still employs just four workers "on the floor." Bag Balm is sold here, also at Lyndonville Hardware and nearby Freighthouse Restaurant.

COVERED BRIDGES Five are in within the town of **Lyndon**—one 120-foot, 1865 bridge across the Passumpsic, 3 miles north of town off Rt. 114; one as you enter town, a genuine 1869 bridge moved from its original site; two in Lyndon Corner (one dating from 1879, the other from 1881, both west off Rt. 5); the fifth in Lyndon Center on Rt. 122. Pick up a map at the **Freight House** in Lyndonville. See *Scenic Drives* for directions to the recently restored **Greenbank's Hollow Bridge** in South Danville.

The Great Vermont Corn Maze (802-748-1399; vermontcornmaze.com), Patterson Farm, 1404 Wheelock Rd., North Danville. Open Aug. and Sept., 10–5; Oct., 10–4 (until the second to last Sunday). It takes from 40 minutes to two hours to thread the miles of pathways between walls of corn. "Cheater Poles" along the way permit a quick exit. A barnyard nature center, gardens, and "Miney's Korny Kid Korn Maze" are geared to younger children. Call first if the weather is questionable. Everyone we've talked to who has found this place has been enthusiastic, but we've also spoken to people who never did find it. Begin at the blinking light on Rt. 2 in Danville and head north; it's best to download the map on the website.

White Mountains rise like a white wall in the distance. This actually works better if you are driving east from Danville. Either way, be sure to pull off (there's an eastbound pullout) to appreciate the panorama.

Danville Hill Road. Continue west on Rt. 2 from West Danville to East Cabot; after Molly's Pond, take the right-hand turn—Danville Hill Rd., marked for Cabot. This is a high road with long mountain views; note the Cabot Creamery Visitor Center in Cabot.

Burke Mountain. A 2.5-mile auto road leads to the summit of Burke Mountain (3,267 feet). From the parking lot it's just a few steps through the trees to one of the most sweeping views of the White Mountains and points east. From the top of the lifts (on the other side of the parking lot), another superlative view encompasses Lake Willoughby and the Green Mountains to the west. Bring a picnic. This preserve was formerly the 10,000-acre Darling State Forest, donated to the state in 1933. The road was constructed by the Civilian Conservation Corps. The toll road and campground are open May–late Oct.

Darling Hill Road from Rt. 114 in East Burke, 5 miles south to Rt. 114 in Lyndonville, follows a ridge past a magnificent former estate that once encompassed many old homesteads and still offers great views. The bright yellow 38-room mansion, on a private drive, has been beautifully restored.

Danville to Peacham via Greenbanks Hollow. Near the Danville Green two roads head south for Peacham. Follow the road posted for Dowser's Hall, rather than Peacham Rd. This runs right through the covered bridge in Greenbanks Hollow, recently neatened up with picnic benches and a historic plaque describing this "forgotten village." In 1849 Benjamin Greenbank converted an existing mill into a five-story wooden textile factory, the centerpiece of a village that was completely destroyed by fire in 1885. Only the stone foundations of the mill, the rushing stream, and the bridge survive.

Lyndon to Greensboro Bend. An old ridge road with splendid views, 17-mile **Stannard Mountain Road** is unpaved but usually well graveled most of the way, best traveled in summer and fall. Check locally, though, because there are occasional washouts. The views are best driving west.

✳ To Do

FISHING is huge here. The Kingdom is pocked with glacial lakes and laced with streams. For regulations, check under Fish & Game at nekchamber.com. Check out **Harvey's Lake** in West Barnet, the **Moore Reservoir**, **Shadow Lake**, and **Miles Pond** in Concord, **Ricker** and **Levi Ponds** in Groton State Forest, as well as the **Lamoille**, **Passumpsic**, **Moose**, and **Connecticut Rivers**. Local lakes are also good for salmon, lake and rainbow trout, and perch. There are trout in the streams, too.

BIKING

Kingdom Trails Association (802-626-0737; kingdomtrails.org). The East Burke area is webbed with over 100 miles of trails, a composite of systems on Darling Hill, around the village, and on Burke Mountain itself. In winter there are separate trail systems for cross-country skiing, snowshoeing, and fat-tire biking. It's maintained by a nonprofit conservation organization that receives permission from over 50 landowners. Trails thread pastures and woods and vary from narrow singletrack and double-diamond downhill trails on Burke Mountain itself to wide old logging and fire roads. Also on Burke Mountain the **Q Burke Bike Park** offers five lift-accessed bike trails. Two are excavated jump trails; the other three are singletrack trails accessed via a ride up the Sherburne Express Chairlift (lift tickets required). Many trails within the system offer glorious views. Rave reviews have positioned the network as a strong magnet for bicycle clubs from throughout the East, with roughly half its patrons now coming from Quebec. The Kingdom Trails association's office in the middle of the village offer changing rooms, passes, and local information. Pick up a map and a pass (day passes are $15 adults, $7 ages 8–15; year passes are $75 per individual and $150 per family; under 7 and over 70 are free). Bike rentals are available across the road at **East Burke Sports** (802-626-3215; eastburkesports.com) or in Lyndonville at **Village Sports Shop** (802-626-8448; villagesportshop.com). Check the website for trail updates and conditions; note the trails designated for winter biking.

A handicapped-accessible fishing platform has been constructed in **Passumpsic Village** on the Passumpsic River.

At **Seyon Ranch** in Groton State Park (see *Lodging*) there is squaretail trout fishing, with flies only, from boats rented at the site.

GOLF St. Johnsbury Country Club (802-748-9894; 800-748-8899), off Rt. 5 north, open daily mid-May–Oct. This is an outstanding PGA-rated, 18-hole course, truly one of the Kingdom's gems. The original nine holes were designed in 1923; nine more were added by Geoffrey Cornish. Amenities include cart rentals and **Greenside Restaurant**.

Kirby Country Club (802-748-9200), 5 miles east of St. Johnsbury on Rt. 2 in Kirby. Open daily Apr.–Nov. Marc Poulin's evolving, challenging nine-hole course and clubhouse offer great views. Reasonably priced.

HIKING AND WALKING TRAILS See *Green Space*, as well as Kingdom Trails Association under *Biking*. Request a copy of *Hiking in the Northeast Kingdom* (800-884-8001; travelthekingdom.com).

HORSEBACK RIDING D-N-D Stables (802-626-8237) in East Burke. Guided rides for all abilities on trails that extend from the farm to local snowmobile and cross-country trails, as well as the Kingdom Trails system. Younger children are welcome to ride in the ring. Rides are tailored to the rider (maximum of four) and can be as long as desired.

PADDLING East of St. Johnsbury, the Moore and Comerford Reservoirs, created by dams, are good for canoeing (there are two boat launches in Lower Waterford)—as we found out one evening, listening to birdcalls and watching a baby beaver swim steadily toward a beaver lodge beneath the pines. Below the Comerford Dam, the stretch of the Connecticut River south to McIndoe Falls (now the McIndoe Dam) is excellent, and the portage around the dam isn't difficult. Other rivers that invite canoeing are the Passumpsic and Moose, which join the Sleeper at St. Johnsbury. A boat launch on the Moose River can be accessed from Concord Avenue in St. J, and look for a boat launch on the Passumpsic in Passumpsic Village, 5 miles south of St. Johnsbury. Canoe and kayak rentals are available from **East Burke Sports** (802-626-3215; eastburkesports.com) in East Burke and from **Village Sport Shop** (802-626-8448), 511 Broad St., Lyndonville. Boat rentals are available from **Injun Joe Court** (802-684-3430; injunjoecourt.net), Rt. 2, West Danville. This area is pocked with lakes, and launches are shown on the state map. Request a free copy of the map/guide Waterways of the Northeast Kingdom (800-884-8001; travelthekingdom.com).

SWIMMING There are public beaches on **Harvey's Lake** in West Barnet; **Joe's Pond** in West Danville; **Molly's Pond** in Marshfield; **Miles Pond** in Concord; and within **Groton State Forest**, notably at **Boulder Beach State Park** (802-584-3823; vtstateparks.com). If you can find it, also check out **Ticklenaked Pond** in Ryegate (off Rt. 302 west of Wells River). There are public pools in St. Johnsbury and in Lyndonville.

TREE CLIMBING New England Tree Climbing (802-684-9795; newenglandtreeclimbing.com), Penny Hill, Danville. No joke. This is a serious skill, pitched to climbers ages 7–70. Inquire about the three-hour, basic "Tree Climbing Experience" and more extensive courses.

✳ Winter Sports

CROSS-COUNTRY SKIING AND SNOWSHOEING Kingdom Trails Cross-Country Ski Area (802-626-6005; kingdomtrails.org). The nonprofit Kingdom Trails Association (see *Biking*) maintains a 20 km system with spectacular views on Darling Hill. It is best accessed from the trailhead at the Vermont Children's Theater on Darling Hill Rd. (the spot from which the photo on the cover of this book was taken). Rentals, lessons, and guided tours originate at the KT **Nordic Welcome Center** in the Granary Building across from the **Wildflower Inn**. Twelve km of trails are groomed for skate/classic skiing; additional trails are groomed for backcountry Nordic. No dogs please. *Note:* There are separate trails for snowshoeing and fat-tire winter biking.

&. **Seyon Ranch State Park** (802-584-3829; vtstateparks.com). This isolated 1890s hunting/fishing lodge deep in Groton State Forest has been winterized and caters to cross-country skiers with 5 miles of groomed trails.

Also see **Craftsbury Outdoor Center** under *Winter Sports* in "Heart of the Kingdom."

BURKE MOUNTAIN ACADEMY RACER   Christina Tree

DOGSLED TOURS Hardscrabble Mountain Dogsled Tours (802-626-9895), based in Sheffield. Keith Ballek offers runs through his woods of various lengths, from a 2-mile ride on the sled to a "Mushers Package" in which you are invited to drive the team. Keith is happy to meet patrons at the post office in Sheffield (not far from Burke Mountain) and drive them up to his base cabin.

DOWNHILL SKIING AND SNOWBOARDING Q Burke Mountain (888-BURKE-VT; skiburke.com), East Burke. "The Vermonter's Mountain" is a big peak with a respectable vertical, known for excellent terrain and reasonable prices. In 2014 it acquired new owners and a "Q" (for Ary Quiros, the new president and CEO). It's now a sister property to Jay Peak and major expansion is planned, utilizing funding from the federal EB-5 immigration program. A midmountain 116-suite (studio to three-bedroom) hotel and conference center is slated to open for the 2015–16 ski season. This is the home of Burke Mountain Academy, a prep school for aspiring racers, known for the number of graduates who become Olympic contenders (over 50 Olympians).

Lifts: 2 quad chairlifts (1 detachable), 2 surface lifts.

Trails and slopes: 50 trails, 110 acres of glades.

Elevation: 3,267 feet.

Vertical drop: 2,011 feet.

Snowmaking: 80%.

Snowboarding: 4 terrain parks, season-long freestyle program.

Tip: Best intermediate trail is East Bowl, a 2-mile old-style trail that winds with natural contours, offering breathtaking views of the Presidential Range.

Facilities: Sherburne Base Lodge includes glass-walled Tamarack Grill as well as a cafeteria; a mid-slope lodge with its Bear Den Lounge serves the upper mountain. Trailside lodging is offered in dozens of privately owned condos (Burke Vacation Rentals: 802-626-1161; Burke Mountain Rentals: 888-282-2188; Burke Slopeside Lodging: burkeslopesidelodging.com, 802-626-3066). Also check with the Burke Area Chamber of Commerce (burkevermont.com), the best way to compare local lifts and lodging packages, including local motels and B&Bs.

Programs: Kids' programs during weekends and holiday periods; ski school, rentals.

Rates: $64 adults, $49 juniors; half-day, multiday, student, and Vermonter discounts.

SLEIGH RIDES Wildflower Inn (see *Lodging*) arranges sleigh rides for guests and will accommodate nonguests when possible. **Haden Tanner** (802-467-3639), a farrier in Sutton, also offers sleigh rides.

SNOWMOBILING Given the extent of the trail system, accessibility to the trails from local lodging places, and dependable snow cover, this area is becoming as well known among snowmobilers as it is to cross-country skiers. The trail systems, however, seldom cross. Contact the **Northeast Kingdom Chamber of Commerce** (802-748-3678; 800-639-6379; nekchamber.com) for a list of the local clubs from which you must purchase a VAST membership in order to use the trails. Rentals are available from **All Around Rental Store** (802-748-7841), St. Johnsbury. Also see *Snowmobiling* in "Island Pond and Beyond."

✳ Green Space

Groton State Forest (802-584-3829; vtstateparks.com), off Rt. 232 (which runs north–south, connecting Rts. 2 and 302). This 25,600-plus-acre forest is the second largest contiguous landholding by the state of Vermont. It's a scenic and rugged place, best known for its five separate campgrounds (see *Campgrounds*) and fishing, but it also harbors Lake Groton and both Osmore and Ricker Ponds. There's an extensive year-round trail system. The area was intensively logged, beginning in 1873 with the opening of the Montpelier & Wells Railroad that ran through the forest, ending in the 1920s when most of the timber had been cut. Subsequent fires further altered the landscape from evergreens to mostly maple and birch. The naturalist-staffed **Groton Nature Center** (802-584-3823) in **Boulder Beach State Park** (a day-use area featuring a swim beach on Lake Groton), marked from Rt. 232, is open June–early Sept. and serves as the information source for the forest and the trailhead for the 2.5-mile trail to Peacham Bog. Seyon Ranch State Park (see *Lodging*) is on Noyes Pond in another part of the forest, catering to groups, fishermen, and cross-country skiers. Favorite hikes in the **Groton State Forest Trail System** include the **Peacham Bog Natural Area** and two trails to the summit of **Owls Head Mountain** (there's a summer road as well as a trail), where a handsome old CCC wood-and-stone watchtower commands spectacular views.

Victory Basin, alias Victory Bog. This 4,970-acre preserve administered by the Vermont Fish and Wildlife Department includes a 25-acre boreal bog with rare plant life, 1,800 acres of wetlands, 1,084 acres of hardwoods, and 71 acres of clearings and old fields. The dirt road access is via Victory; there are three parking areas: Mitchell's Landing, Lee Hill, and Damons Crossing.

Waterford Dam at Moore Reservoir. New England Power offers guided tours of the huge complex of turbines. There are also picnic sites and a boat launch here. The approach is from the New Hampshire side of the Connecticut River, just below Lower Waterford, Vermont, off Rt. 135.

In St. Johnsbury

Fred Mold Park, near the confluence of the Passumpsic and Moose Rivers, is a great picnic spot by a waterfall and old mill. **The Arlington Preserve**, accessible from Waterman Circle, is a 33-acre nature preserve with woods, meadows, and rock outcroppings.

See also *Biking, Hiking and Walking Trails*, and *Camping*.

✳ Lodging

& **Rabbit Hill Inn** (802-748-5168; 800-76-BUNNY; rabbithillinn.com), 48 Lower Waterford Rd. (off Rt. 18), Lower Waterford 05848. Brian and Leslie Mulcahy welcome you to this pillared landmark. All 19 rooms and suites are romantic confections, 15 with working fireplace, many with canopy bed (no twins), in-room Jacuzzi for two, and "indulging" bathrooms. They are divided between the main house and the neighboring 1795 Tavern House. All are themed so they vary widely in look and feel, from the luxurious North Woods cabin style of Cedar Glen, complete with a mounted bass above the hearth and a log canopy bed, to "Tiffany" with a pencil-post bed and classic country inn furnishings. Check out choices on the website. There's a capacious living room, a full-service bar in the Snooty Fox Pub, and a cozy game room/library. Children should be older than 14—really, this is all about couples stealing time together. Summer golf privileges, winter cross-country skiing and snowshoeing. The inn is set in a tiny, classic village with the delightful Davies Memorial Library across the road. $170–375 per couple most of the year, $210–415 in high season, breakfast, afternoon tea, and gratuities included. Dinner is available. While just 9 miles from downtown St. Johnsbury, the inn faces the White Mountains and is a 20-minute

drive down I-93 to attractions and skiing in New Hampshire's Franconia Notch.

✪ ♂ ☆ ✎ & **The Wildflower Inn** (802-626-8310; 800-627-8310; wildflowerinn.com), 2059 Darling Hill Rd., Lyndonville 05851. Depicted by coincidence on the cover of this book, this is one of Vermont's best family-geared resorts. It clusters around a 19th-century farmhouse set high on a ridge with a spectacular view across

RABBIT HILL INN, LOWER WATERFORD

Christina Tree

Christina Tree

THE WILDFLOWER INN SITS HIGH ON
DARLING HILL

surrounding hills and valleys. It's surrounded by
its own 530 acres, with extensive flower gardens
and trails maintained for hiking, mountain biking, and cross-country skiing. There's a full-
service bike shop with rentals and repairs on-
site. Jim and Mary O'Reilly have eight children
(five boys, three girls), and have fitted rooms
and condo-style suites with child-geared amenities, such as small rockers and diaper-changing
tables, but no TVs. The idea is to get children
out of their rooms and let them find one
another in the playroom, the outdoor play structures, the petting barn, the pool (there's one for
toddlers), or the Playbarn. For older children a
sports complex offers basketball, a batting cage,
tennis court, playing field, and (also a big appeal
for parents) the beckoning system of the Kingdom Trails (see *Biking*). For cross-country skiers, Kingdom Trails maintains a network right
at the inn; for alpine skiers and boarders Burke
Mountain's trails are minutes away. Adult
spaces include a sauna, an attractive parlor, and
a library—stocked with games and the kind of
books you really want to read. The landscaped
pool commands a spectacular view of rolling
hills, and there are also lawn games and walking
trails. Dinner is in Juniper's (see *Dining Out*),
and for children there's the occasional option of
parent-free dining at Daisy's Diner, a 5:30–9:30
dinner and activity program (summer only).
Breakfast is a three-course production, and
afternoon snacks are also served. Upstairs in the
main house, two family suites have great views.
Twelve rooms and 11 suites, some with and
some without views, include a romantic hideaway with whirlpool bath in the old schoolhouse
(with view). There's also Grand Meadow, a two-
bedroom retreat sleeping eight with two baths
(a Jacuzzi in one), full kitchen, dining and

lounging area, and view. Rates are $235–500
per couple in high season B&B, $150–320 in
low plus $25 per child over age 3; $10 for ages 3
and under. Singles pay $35 less. Dogs are $35
per stay. Special packages.

INNS AND BED & BREAKFASTS

In the St. Johnsbury area

✪ ☕ ✿ ♿ **Emergo Farm B&B** (802-684-2215;
888-383-1185; emergofarm.com), 261 Webster
Hill, Danville 05828. Just north of the village,
this strikingly handsome, prizewinning working
dairy farm has been in the same family for six
generations. Our stay in the upstairs front room,
tastefully furnished with family antiques, and
with private bath and view of the White Mountains, was one of the most pleasant of the summer. There is also a two-bedroom apartment
with full kitchen and sitting room. Older children only, please. The farm's 230 acres include
a hilltop with panoramic views of much of the
Kingdom. Historical and present-day farm tours
are offered (there are 140 head of cattle, 90
milking cows). Lori Webster is a hospitable
host. Rooms from $120.

Estabrook House B&B (802-751-8261;
estabrookhouse.com), 1596 Main St., St. Johnsbury 05891. Maurine Hennings has painstak-
ingly restored this handsome, vintage-1856
painted lady on the quiet, residential end of
Main St. and within walking distance on the
Fairbanks Museum and Athenaeum. The house
is spacious, comfortable, and uncluttered. Most
of the second-floor, antiques-furnished guest
rooms share a bath ($125); one is private ($150);
$95 for a small room with twin beds. The feel is
that of staying in a friend's house. There is

HEAVEN'S BENCH AT THE WILDFLOWER INN
IS A WEDDING VENUE

Christina Tree

ample common space, including a "media room/ library." In her former life Maurine was constantly on the road for her company, so she's especially sensitive to the needs of solo travelers. Rates include a full breakfast.

The Old Homestead (802-633-4016; 877-OLD-HOME; theoldhomestead.com), 157305 Rt. 5, Barnet 05821. Gail Warnaar plays the oboe and bassoon, sells music for double-reed instruments, and offers five rooms in her 1850s village home, which faces Rt. 5 and backs on gardens and meadow. Two second-floor rooms (private baths) feature porches overlooking the grounds, while a small first-floor single room with a spool bed (shared bath) is appealing. Common space is comfortable, and musical groups will find rehearsal space. From $98 includes a breakfast of fruit and fresh-baked bread.

Christina Tree

THE VILLAGE INN OF EAST BURKE

In the Burke Mountain area

♂ 🐾 ♿ **The Inn at Mountain View Farm** (802-626-9924; innmtnview.com), 3383 Darling Hill Rd., East Burke 05832. Like the Wildflower Inn, this is part of a onetime 9,000-acre hilltop estate owned by Elmer Darling, a Burke native who built the brick creamery in 1890 to supply dairy products to his Fifth Avenue Hotel (it used to churn out 600 pounds of butter a month and 70 pounds of cheese per day). The inn also includes the neighboring "Farm House" and the magnificent red barns and other outbuildings. Its 440 acres spread across a high ridge and are laced with paths, part of the Kingdom Trails network (see *Biking*) maintained for walking, mountain biking, and cross-country skiing. Marilyn Pastore has tastefully decorated the 14 guest rooms (private baths), which are divided between the Creamery and the Farm House with its three "luxury suites," each with gas fireplace and Jacuzzi. A sauna is accessible to all guests. The centrally air-conditioned Creamery houses the inn's sitting room and a dining room serving breakfast to guests. The inn is a favorite for weddings and reunions, given its renovated Morgan horse barn. $175–354 includes a full breakfast and tea. Inquire about special packages.

○ 🐾 ♥ ✿ **The Village Inn of East Burke** (802-626-3161; villageinnofeastburke.com), 606 Rt. 114, East Burke. The Willy family's comfortable, affordable B&B offers genuine hospitality and many rarely found amenities, like a fully equipped guest kitchen; an inviting living room with a fireplace, books, games, and satellite TV; a weatherproofed Jacuzzi near the extensive gardens (guests are invited to pick what's in-season); and a streamside picnic/lounging area. All five rooms have private bath and are

comfortably, tastefully decorated, each different and varying in size—one with a sleeping loft and large enough to accommodate families— but all are the same price, $99.95 ($89.95 midweek) per night per couple ($150 for the three-bedroom apartment) plus $25 per extra person. Rates include a full-choice breakfast next door in the dining room of (former) Will's Restaurant, now the base for Chris Willy's catering business. Locked storage, air, and tools for bicyclists, who are also welcome to shower after rides even if they've checked out.

Willoburke Inn and Lodge (802-427-3333; willoburke.com), 638 Rt. 114, East Burke 05832. This welcome addition to village lodging combines a 19th-century Greek Revival home and a neighboring lodge on 5 brookside acres on the edge of the village. A totally renovated barn, the lodge has a contemporary feel with spacious open raftered "lobby" sitting areas and a fireplace. The eight guest rooms (with private bath) are nicely, simply fitted with locally crafted furniture; try for one of the four back rooms (two up/two down) overlooking the Dishmill Brook. $150–170 for rooms in the lodge with continental breakfast and afternoon snack, $255 for a two-bedroom apartment (sleeping six) with a full kitchen and living room overlooking the brook. Locked area for bicycles and skis.

Note: See the **Kingdom Trails** website (kingdomtrails.org) for more about mountain-bike-geared area lodging.

Branch Brook Bed & Breakfast (802-626-8316), 36 Branch Brook Lane, Lyndon 0849. Ann Tolman's 1850 house is only minutes but seems many miles from the I-91 exit. It has long, graceful parlor windows and a front room with a pencil-post canopy bed, locally crafted from cherrywood and worthy of brides. Other inviting rooms are tucked under exposed beams along an el, furnished with antiques. All but two of the five have private bath. Prices are $90–120 per couple with a hearty breakfast prepared on Ann's English Aga cooker. Two of Lyndon's five covered bridges are within walking distance.

🍁 **Moonlight Inn Vermont** (802-626-0780), 801 Center St., Lyndonville 05851. Shirley Banks welcomes visitors with genuine western friendliness, while Dick Banks is the quiet, capable Vermonter. Their spacious Victorian house on a quiet side street offers comfortable common space and three second-floor guest rooms, one with twins, all with private bath. A serious quilter, Shirley offers lessons and quilting weekends. $95 includes tax as well as a full breakfast.

Elsewhere

MOTOR LODGES 🐾 🎣 **Fairbanks Inn** (802-748-5666; stjay.com), 401 Western Ave. (Rt. 2 east), St. Johnsbury 05819. This three-story, 45-unit, surprisingly luxurious motel on the outskirts of town has central air-conditioning, cable, dataports, outdoor heated pool, and fitness center privileges.

🎣 **Comfort Inn & Suites** (802-748-1500; comfortinn.com), off I-91, Exit 20, Rt. 5 south, St. Johnsbury 05819. A 107-unit high-rise motel with an indoor heated pool, a fitness center, a video arcade, cable, dataports, direct VAST trail access.

🎣 **Colonnade Inn** (802-626-9316; 877-435-5688), 28 Back Center Rd., Lyndonville 05851. A two-story, 40-unit motel just off I-91, Exit 23. Standard motel rooms, cable TV and phone, continental breakfast.

RENEWAL CENTERS FOR BODY AND SPIRIT Karmê Chöling Shambhala Meditation Center (802-633-2384; karmecholing.org), 369 Patneaude Lane, Barnet 05821. Receptionist: 9–5 weekdays, 1:30–5 weekends. The oldest (founded in 1970) and probably still the best of New England's Buddhist meditation centers, Karmê Chöling follows the Tibetan Buddhist path of understanding one's own mind through meditation. What began as a small center in an old farmhouse now includes 540 wooded, path-webbed acres, six meditation halls, a practice pavilion, an azuchi (Zen archery range), a large organic garden, private guest rooms, and dining facilities. The centerpiece remains the original, now expanded farmhouse with its beautiful Main Shrine Room. Visitors are welcome (call beforehand), but this is all about one- to seven-day retreats (many are geared to weekends) on a variety of themes but with the practice of "mindfulness meditation" at their heart. The daily routine begins with a 6:30 wake-up call and continues until 10:30 lights-out. Space to sleep in the Main Shrine Room is included in the cost of a program.

Stepping Stone Spa and B&B (802-626-3104; steppingstonespa.com), 1545 Darling Hill Rd., Lyndonville 05851. Sited in 570 acres along a high ridge with panoramic views and access to the Kingdom Trails system, this four-room inn was designed and built from scratch as a spa inn by Joan and Richard (Dick) Downing. Check the website for descriptions of the professional spa staff and spa menu. The inn is a short walk from a ridgetop, medieval-style Catholic chapel with superlative views, also built by the Downings. $159–199 per couple includes breakfast. This is also a day spa with massages and a menu of other spa options available to the public.

OTHER LODGING ♿ **Seyon Lodge State Park** (802-584-3829; vtstateparks.com). This 1890s hunting/fishing lodge on Noyes Pond—Vermont's only public fly-fishing pond—is deep in Groton State Forest, staffed and open year-round except for stick and mud seasons. It caters to fishermen, cross-country skiers, snowshoers, and snowmobilers in-season, offering double and queen beds, and there are bunk rooms with shared baths, accommodating a total of 16, serving up to 30 for meals. It's also popular with small groups, which take advantage of the conference space with a hearth. $75–85 per room, meals extra.

CAMPGROUNDS Groton State Forest (802-584-3829; vtstateparks.com) in Marshfield and Groton. This 25,623-acre preserve offers five separate campgrounds, each an individual state park, all accessed from Rt. 232. **New Discovery Campground** (802-584-3042) has a total of 47 campsites, 14 of them lean-tos; beach privileges and hiking trails; primitive camping. **Stillwater Campground** (802-584-3822), on the west side of Lake Groton, has a total of 63 tent sites, 16 lean-tos; campers' beach and boat launch; rental boats, dump station. **Ricker Pond Campground** (802-584-3821) has a total of 33 campsites, 22 of them lean-tos, on the south side of Ricker Pond; campers' beach, rental boats, nature trail, dump station. **Big Deer State Park** (802-584-3822) has 28 tent/trailer sites (no hookups) near Boulder Beach and Groton Nature Center with many miles of trails. **Kettle Pond** (802-426-3042), on the south side of the pond, has walk-in fishing, group camping, hiking, and snowmobiling. For an overview of Groton State Forest, see *Green Space*.

Burke Mountain Campground 802-626-7300; skiburke.com), a small campground on Burke Mountain with five lean-tos and room for 26 tents, is geared to hikers and bikers.

Note: Reasonably priced rentals abound in this area; check listings on the websites listed under *Guidance* and Google "vacation rentals" plus "Vermont."

✳ Where to Eat

DINING OUT

In the St. Johnsbury area

Bailiwicks on Mill (802-424-1215; bailiwicks finerestaurant.com), 98 Mill St., St. Johnsbury. Open daily for dinner from 5, Fri.–Sat. for lunch, Sun. brunch. A pleasant ambience in a 19th-century mill with an appealing diner menu, from eggplant napoleon ($19) and Korean BBQ chicken finished with cilantro-mint pesto ($23) to Green Mountain Ribeye ($32). There's also an attractive wine and martini bar.

Rabbit Hill Inn (802-748-5168; rabbithillinn .com), 48 Lower Waterford Rd. (Rt. 18), Lower Waterford. Open to outside guests by reservation, space permitting. The elegant dining room holds just 15 tables, and both food and atmosphere are carefully orchestrated. There's candlelight, and music many nights, to complement an à la carte menu that might include Vermont-raised pork loin, roast saddle of lamb, and chicken dumplings. Gorgeous desserts. $17–37.

Creamery Restaurant (802-684-3616), Danville. Open Tues.–Sat. from 3 PM. A former creamery with a blackboard menu featuring homemade soups, curries, and pad Thais, along with salads, pies, and a choice of meat and seafood dishes. Breads and soups are homemade, and salad comes with all dinners. Entrées $14–24; there's a less expensive pub menu.

❧ **Juniper's at The Wildflower Inn** (802-626-8310; wildflowerinn.com), between Lyndonville and East Burke on Darling Hill Rd. Open (except Nov. and Apr.) Mon.–Sat. 5:30–9. Reservations advised if you want a table on the sunporch, overlooking a spread of hills and valleys. You can dine on filet mignon ($25), but entrées on an extensive menu average $15 and tend toward comfort foods like "slow cooked shepherd's pie," roast all-natural pork, and Vermont-raised lemon-herb chicken. There are "Junior Juniper" plates for kids. Entrées come with warm rolls and salad. Sandwiches and burgers are also available. Much of the beef served is from all-natural belted Galloway cattle raised here on Darling Hill. Salads and sandwiches are also served. Vermont beer featured.

EATING OUT

In and around St. Johnsbury

✪ **Dylan's Café** (802-748-6748), 139 Eastern Ave., St. Johnsbury. Open Mon.–Tues. 11–4, Wed.–Sat. 11–9, this outstanding café owned by rock star Neko Case is housed in a former post office next to Catamount Arts (see *Entertainment*), cheery and spacious with art and fresh flowers, booths and tables, seasonal outdoor seating. Generous lunch salads and tasty sandwiches—even the BLT is Vermont-smoked bacon with locally grown spinach and tomatoes. Dinner specials.

The Wine Gate (802-748-3288), Railroad St., St. Johnsbury. Open Mon.–Fri. 11–2, Thurs.–Sat. 5–closing. Housed in a former rail warehouse beside the handsome station that's now the region's major welcome center, this is an attractive space with a lunch menu featuring a wide choice of cold and hot panini and salads. There are also reasonably priced entrées and a tapas menu.

Cantina di Gerardo (802-748-0598), 378 Railroad St., St. Johnsbury. Open for lunch Mon.–Sat.; dinner nightly except Tues. A family-run restaurant with authentically southern Italian fare: pizzas, hot and cold sandwiches, classic red-sauce dishes, daily specials, wine and beer.

♿ **Anthony's Restaurant** (802-748-3613), 321 Railroad St., St. Johnsbury. Open 6:30 AM–8 PM Tues.–Sat.; closing at 4 Sun.–Mon. Anthony and Judy Proia have run this cheerful family-geared diner since 1979, remodeling it several times to make it handicapped accessible and give it a homier feel. Regulars still gather around the counter, and there are booths as well. Breakfast is big: corned beef hash, specialty omelets, and about everything else you can think of. "Specials" at all three meals. The fries (try sweet potato) and onion rings are made fresh, along with the soups; pies are a point of pride. Prices are getting up there.

❧ **Good Fellas Tavern & Restaurant** (802-748-4249), 59 Parker Rd., just off Rt. 2, east of Danville Village. Open Wed.–Sat. 4–9, Sun. 11:30–8. Known for homemade soups, seafood, steaks, and pasta, this is a reliable country restaurant with a sports bar, a separate dining area, and a seasonal deck that's great for families.

Mooselook Restaurant (802-695-2950), Rt. 2, east of Concord. Open from 6 AM daily for all three meals. Basic comfort food. For visitors the bonus is what's on the walls: dozens of vintage photos of what this area was all about more than a century ago.

Upper Valley Grill (802-584-3101), junction of Rts. 302 and 232, Groton. Open 6 AM–8 PM; till

9 Fri.–Sat. Handy to Groton State Forest, this is a welcoming oasis at the junction of two lonely roads. Bill Kane's general store has a friendly, U-shaped counter in back, good for hearty breakfasts, homemade soups, apple pie, and daily specials.

Kham Thai Cuisine (802-751-8424), 1112 Memorial Dr. (Rt. 5 north), St. Johnsbury. Open daily 11–9, Sun. noon–8. A great addition to local dining options, known for fresh ingredients and spices, reasonably priced, reliable.

Bentley's Bakery & Café (802-864-3385), 20 Hill St. (just off Rt. 2), Danville. Open Apr.– Dec., Wed.–Fri. 6:30–4:30, weekends 8–1. A pleasant stop for coffees, soup, quiche or panini, and desserts.

In Lyndonville

Café Sweet Basil (626-9713; cafesweetbasil .com), 32 Depot St. Open for lunch Wed.–Fri. 11:30–2, for dinner Wed.–Sat. 5:30–8:30. An appealing ambience with an interesting menu. We lunched on a grilled tomato soup and quesadilla.

Miss Lyndonville Diner (802-626-9890), Rt. 5 south. Open from 6 AM until supper, famed for breakfast, including strawberry pancakes with whipped cream, also pies, homemade French toast, and jumbo eggs. This is one of the best of Vermont's surviving vintage railroad car diners.

🍴 **Valley View Family Restaurant and Tavern** (802-626-8685), 774 Main St. Open for all three meals. A popular spot for everything from breakfast omelets to steaks, pleasant atmosphere, reasonable prices, good service.

🍴 🍴 **Farmers Table at the Freight House** (802-626-1174), 1000 Broad St. Open daily 6:30 AM–9:30 PM. Local dairy farmers Eric and Cathy Paris have salvaged and restored this middle-of-town former freight station (1868), transforming it into a combination restaurant/railroad museum, information center, and ice cream parlor. The menu features local meats, fresh greens and veggies, fresh-baked breads, and the fluffiest of omelets plus Carmen's popular ice cream (64 flavors). There's more: Starbucks coffee and a crafts gallery upstairs. This is one of 2 buildings left from the 22 built here by the Boston & Maine. This village sprang into existence with the 1860s arrival of the railroad and remained an important rail yard for the B&M until the 20th century. Most local families have railroad ties, and memorabilia has come pouring in. Walls are hung with early-1900s photos, and a model train circles a diorama of a 1940s Lyndonville. Frequently, too, a real freight train still comes rumbling by.

Stage Food and Music (802-427-3344; stage foodandmusic.com). Open daily 11–9; until 11 Fri.–Sat. The idea here is local food, brew, and music—and it works. Check the website for live nightly entertainment.

Trout River Brewery (802-616-9396; trout riverbrewing.com), 645 Broad St. (Rt. 5.). Open Fri. and Sat. 4–9 in winter, Thurs. too in summer. Hand-tossed pizzas as well as a selection of ales and other draft brews, made on the premises. The three signature beers here are Rainbow Red (medium bodied), Scottish Ale, and Hoppin' Mad Trout; also seasonal specials. Inquire about tours and tastings.

In East Burke

🍴 **The Pub Outback** (802-626-1188; thepub outback.com), out back of the Northeast Kingdom Country Store. Open daily 5–9, later Fri. and Sat. This former cow barn is now a cheerful pub with a full menu, from soups to pitas, veggies, burgers, sandwiches, steaks, pastas, great onion rings, the works. Children's menu. Full bar.

Tamarack Pub & Grill (802-626-7390), Sherburne Base Lodge, Q Burke, East Burke. Open Thurs.–Sun. from 4 most of the year. A genuine neighborhood pub feel because it is and hopefully stays that way, comfortably worn and welcoming. Pub food.

Mikes Tiki Bar (mikestikibar.com) and **The Vermont Food Truck** (802-626-177), open daily 11–9 during biking season at the base area for Kingdom Trails singletrack mountain bike network, East Burke. In the middle of the village but tucked back beside the Kingdom Trails

THE VERMONT FOOD TRUCK SERVES MOUNTAIN BIKERS IN EAST BURKE. Christina Tree

parking lot and its shower house, the thatched bar and truck together supply reasonably priced food and drink (30 mostly local beers on tap).

Northeast Kingdom Country Store (802-626-4611), 466 Rt. 114, East Burke. Order from the large deli menu and get paper-wrapped sandwiches on homemade bread to eat at bright oilcloth-draped tables in the center of the store.

East Burke Market (802-626-5010), 461 Rt. 114, the village's genuine general store with a solid deli as well as burgers and homemade baked goods. We picked up a freshly made chicken salad on whole wheat and munched it on a nearby ridge.

Peacham Café (peachamcafe.org), housed in the former fire station beside the general store in the middle of Peacham Village. Generally open 9–2, but closed some days so check. This new community-owned café is getting rave reviews for fresh, local, and imaginative fare, seasonal soups and salads, house-roasted local meats, quiche, and fresh-baked goods to eat in or to go.

BREWS Hill Farmstead Brewery (802-533-7450; hillfarmstead.com), 403 Hill Rd., Greensboro. Open Wed.–Sat. noon–5. This back-road farm is now a mecca for beer lovers who come to sample growlers and tote home as many bottles as they can manage, given that this is the only place you can buy the bottles and the selection of ales—all brewed in Shaun Hill's family barn. Available on draft mostly in local places.

✳ Entertainment

Catamount Arts (802-748-2600; 888-757-5559; catamountarts.org), 115 Eastern Ave., St. Johnsbury. The former Masonic Temple is a venue for this long-established, nonprofit arts center features nightly screenings in two theaters: the larger Cinema 1, screening popular films, and the smaller Cinema 2 with regional premieres, mini series, and programs devoted to Vermont filmmakers. There's an extensive video library, and a gallery showcasing local artists; also live performances, periodic coffeehouses, and special events.

Star Theater 802-748-9511), 18 Eastern Ave., St. Johnsbury. Cinemas 1-2-3; first-run movies.

♪ Vermont Children's Theater (summer only: 802-626-5358), Darling Hill Rd., Lyndonville. Sited next to the Wildflower Inn, this is a genuine theater in a former hay barn. Local youngsters (some 120 are usually involved) perform amazingly well. Performances in July are by thespians ages 7–18. Tickets $8 adults, $4–6 for youngsters.

Band concerts: **St. Johnsbury Town Band concerts**, weekly all summer at the bandstand in Town Hall Park, Mon. 8 PM. **Lyndonville Town Band concerts**, every Wed. in summer at 8 PM; **Danville** concerts on the green, Sun. at 7 in July and Aug.

✳ Selective Shopping

ANTIQUES SHOPS Route 5 Antiques & Collectibles (802-626-5430), Rt. 5, Lyndonville. Open daily, except Tues., 10–5. A multidealer and consignment shop.

Antiques & Emporium (802-626-3500), 182 S. Wheelock Rd., Lyndonville. Open daily 10–5, except Tues. Housed in a former grade school, a multigroup shop with everything from rugs and clocks to furniture, pottery, and prints.

BOOKSTORES Boxcar & Caboose Bookshop (802-748-3551; 800-754-9830; boxcarandcaboosee.com), 394 Railroad St., St. Johnsbury. St. Johnsbury Academy history teacher Scott Beck and wife, Joelle, own this bright, well-stocked downtown store, with a large children's section and café.

CRAFTS SHOPS AND ART GALLERIES

In the St. Johnsbury area

Note: St. Johnsbury's most famous art gallery is the St. Johnsbury Athenaeum (see *To See*).

❂ Northeast Kingdom Artisans Guild (802-748-0158; nekartisansguild.com), 430 Railroad St., St. Johnsbury. Open Mon.–Sat.; closed Mon. off-season. This magnificent cooperative shop showcases work by more than 100 Vermont artists in many media.

Joe's Pond Craft Shop (802-684-2192; joespondcrafts.com), 2748 Rt. 2 west, West Danville, adjoining Hastings Store at the junction with Rt. 15. Open May–Dec., Tues.–Sun. Deborah Stresing can usually be found at her loom behind the counter in the barn she has filled with well-chosen quilts, baskets, block prints, woodworking, floorcloths and rag rugs (her own), cards, felted bags—the work of close to 40 craftspeople in all.

Sanderson's Wooden Bowls (802-626-9622; vtbowls.com), 2902 Rt. 114, East Burke. Call ahead. The showroom displays work by this husband-and-wife team who fashion their signature wooden bowls from burls and tapped sugar maples. They also fashion smaller items like key chains and pens from deer and moose antlers.

FARMS AND FARM STANDS Brigid's Farm (802-592-3062), 123 Slack St., Peacham. Call ahead. A small farm with sheep, angora goats, and dairy goats with a weaving studio and mittens, hand-spun yarns, spinning wheels, natural dye extracts, and supplies sold.

Snowshoe Farm (802-592-3153; snowshoe farm.com), 520 The Great Rd., Peacham. Open year-round, but call. Ron and Terry Miller breed alpacas and process their fiber, selling it along with hand-knit or woven alpaca products.

At **Emergo Farm** (see *Lodging*) guests are invited to join in farm chores, and visitors are welcome to tour the dairy barns.

Chandler Pond Farm (802-626-9460), 528 Burroughs Rd., South Wheelock. Visitors welcome May–Oct. for the farm stand and walking trails. A 600-acre farm with a commitment to sustainable technique and diverse products: dairy, meat, syrup, vegetables, fruit, and flowers. Check the website for current offerings and directions.

COUNTRY STORES Hastings Store (802-684-3398), West Danville. Jane Hastings is the third generation of her family to manage the store and post office serving "64 people in the village and the 300 cottages on the lake." Garey Larrabee, Jane's husband, is known locally for his homemade sausage and the doughnuts and blueberry cake he makes fresh each morning. Built as a 19th-century stagecoach stop, the rambling, double-porched store is positioned picturesquely across Rt. 2 from Joe's Pond. Jane Larrabee happens to be a justice of the peace and frequently performs waterside weddings; four couples have been married right at the counter. Hastings doesn't sell gas, beer, or wine, and there's no lunch counter, but you'll find all that next door at **Joe's Pond Country Store**. According to Deborah Stresing, owner of Joe's Pond Craft Store, housed in between the two, it's a symbiotic relationship.

Marty's First Stop (802-684-2574), Rt. 2, east of Danville. Open 5:30 AM–9 PM. Dedicated as we are to promoting classic old-time general stores, this is an exception we have to acknowledge: a Mobil station with an extensive grocery and deli, filling a real need for locals and for visitors headed for vacation rentals. It's also good for homemade soups, generous grinders, and more.

Kerrigan's Market & Deli (802-467-8800), 4080 Rt. 5, West Burke. A general store with a full-service deli and pizzas.

Also see **Peacham Café** and **East Burke Market** under *Eating Out*.

SPECIAL SHOPS Caplan's Army Store Work & Sportswear (802-748-3236), 457 Railroad St., St. Johnsbury. It's getting harder and

harder to find a genuine army-navy store, and this is the genuine article. Established in 1922 and still in the same family, a serious source of quilted jackets, skiwear, Woolrich sweaters, hunting boots, and such; good value and friendly service.

Moose River Lake and Lodge Store (802-748-2423), 370 Railroad St., St. Johnsbury. Open except Sun. 10–5; in summer Sun., too (11–4). Antiques, rustic furniture, and accessories for the home, camp, or cabin: taxidermy specialties, deer antlers and skulls, prints, pack baskets, fishing creels and snowshoes, folk art, an extensive wine collection, and more.

✪ **Artesano Mead** (802-584-9000; artesano mead.com), 1334 Scott Hwy., Groton. Check the website for varieties (including sparkling and spiced meads), tours, and special events. Housed in Groton's former general store, this family-owned enterprise produces mead—a rich golden wine made from honey—using their own and other Vermont bees. Artesano was founded by Mark Simakaski and Nichole Wolfgang after they returned from the Peace Corps in South America. The couple work together to capture the flavor of the Green Mountains in their mead.

Samadhi Store and Workshop (802-633-4440), 30 Church St., Barnet. Open Mon.–Fri. 9–4:30, Sat. 11–3:30. An offshoot of nearby Karmê Chöling, selling singing bowls and gongs, robes, teas, Vermont-made raku incense bowls, lacquerware from Japan and Korea, locally made meditation benches and tables, and meditation cushions and yoga mats made on-site.

Diamond Hill Store (802-684-9797), 11 E. Rt. 2, Danville. This former general store is now a sleek emporium specializing in handmade chocolates, wine, and gifts, also antiques.

SUGARHOUSES Rowell Sugarhouse (802-563-2756), 4962 Rt. 15, Walden. Visitors are welcome year-round, 9–5. Maple cream and candy as well as sugar; also Vermont honey and sheepskins, crafts, paintings.

Goodrich's Sugarhouse (802-563-9917; goodrichmaplefarm.com), just off Rt. 2 by Molly's Pond in East Cabot. A family tradition for seven generations, open to visitors Mar.–Dec. with a full line of award-winning maple products.

Goss's Sugar House (802-633-4743), 101 Maple Lane, Barnet. Gordon and Pat Goss have won a blue ribbon for their syrup at the Caledonia County Fair. They welcome visitors, sell year-round, and will ship.

High Meadow Farm (802-467-3621), East Burke. The sugarhouse is open in-season. Call for directions.

✳ Special Events

February: **Snowflake Festival Winter Carnival**, Lyndonville–Burke. Events include a crafts show, snow sculpture, ski races for all ages and abilities, sleigh rides, music, and art.

Last weekend of March: **Open sugarhouses** (vtmaple.org). **WinterBike** at Kingdom Trails (kingdomtrails.org), East Burke.

Late April: **World Maple Festival** (world maplefestival.org), St. Johnsbury.

Memorial Day weekend: **Annual Vermont Open Studio Weekend** (vermontcrafts.com).

June: **Tour de Kingdom** (tourdekingdom .com), first weekend, a competitive and recreational century ride from Burke through the Lake Region, 15, 25, 50, and 75 miles for all ages. Midmonth: **Vermont Invitational Lumberjack Competition** at Q Burke. **Cultural Heritage Festival**, third week, at Lyndon State College. Late June, **New England Mountain Bike Festival**.

June–October: **Farmers markets**, in downtown St. Johnsbury Sat. 9–1; in Craftsbury Sat. 10–1; in Danville Wed. 9–1; in Hardwick Fri. 3–6.

July: **Peacham Independence Day festivities** include a Ghost Walk in the cemetery, with past residents impersonated by present ones. **Burklyn Arts Council Summer Craft Fair**, Sat. closest to July 4, in Bandstand Park, Lyndonville. **Stars and Stripes Festival**, last weekend, Lyndonville—big auction, parade featuring Bread and Puppet Uncle Sam, barbecue.

August: **Danville Fair**, first weekend, on the green features a parade with floats, more than 75 years of tradition. **Annual Kingdom Triathlon** (kingdomtriathlon.org), held midmonth

at Lake Salem, comprises a 500-yard swim, 13-mile bike ride, and 5-mile run. **Caledonia County Fair**, third week, Mountain View Park, Lyndonville—horse, pony, and ox pulling; cattle, sheep, alpaca, rabbit, and swine shows; midway, rides, demolition derby, music. **Q Burke Bike-n-Brew Fest**.

September: **Burke Mountain Bike Race**, first weekend after Labor Day, up the Toll Road. **Burke Fall Foliage Festival**, last Saturday.

September–October: **Colors of the Kingdom**, held in mid-September, pairs St. Johnsbury autumn festival with Fairbanks Museum fall event: crafts fair, farmers market, planetarium show, parade, trains rides, and more. **Northeast Kingdom Fall Foliage Festival**, the last week in September or first one in October. Seven towns take turns hosting visitors, feeding them breakfast, lunch, and dinner, and guiding them to beauty spots and points of interest within their borders. In Walden the specialty is Christmas wreath making; in Cabot there's a tour of the cheese factory; in Plainfield, farm tours; in Peacham, a Ghost Walk and crafts fair; in Barnet the exceptional historical society house is open, and guided tours of back roads are outstanding. The day in Groton includes a parade, lumberjack's breakfast, and chicken pie supper. For details, contact the Northeast Kingdom Chamber (see *Guidance*).

October: **Autumn on the Green** in Danville, first Sunday, includes the **Cabot Apple Pie and Cheese Festival**.

November: **Old Fashioned Game Supper** in Danville (since 1921).

First weekend of December: **Burklyn Christmas Crafts Market**—a major gathering of North Country craftspeople and artists in the Lyndon Town School. **North Pole Polar Express** (Lyndon).

HEART OF THE KINGDOM

In this high, open farm country, fields roll away to distant mountains and woods are spotted with small lakes and large ponds. Get lost along the well-maintained dirt farm roads that web this area. Find your way to Craftsbury Common, with its white homes, academy, and church; to the beach on Caspian Lake in Greensboro; to the Stone House Museum in Brownington and the Bread and Puppet Museum in Glover.

Barton boomed in the late 19th century, when six passenger trains a day stopped in summer, bringing guests to fill the town's big hotels (long gone) or the gingerbread "camps" (still there) on Crystal Lake. Lake Willoughby with its dramatic, fjordlike "Gap" was a far better known destination more than a century ago than now.

What this area now offers, besides beauty, is a sense of discovery. So much is here, but quietly. On the hottest of days there's plenty of space on its beach at the foot of Lake Willoughby. On the best snow day of the season you may ski alone on the Craftsbury Outdoor Center trails.

GUIDANCE The **Heart of Vermont Chamber of Commerce** (802-472-5906; heartofvt.com) serves surrounding towns, including Walden, Craftsbury, Greensboro, Cabot, and Woodbury.

Barton Area Chamber of Commerce (centerofthekingdom.com) serves the southern part of this region and has listings of summer lakeside cottages.

✳ Villages

Barton (population 2,780). The hotels are gone, but Crystal Lake remains beautiful, with a clifflike promontory on one side and public beaches at its northern rim. There is golf here, and the town of Barton itself packs a number of services into its small downtown. The **Crystal Lake Falls Historical Association** maintains the Pierce House Museum, 97 Water St. (open June–Aug., Sun. 1–5), next to the old-fashioned office of the *Barton Chronicle*, an excellent weekly covering much of Orleans and Essex Counties.

Brownington Village is a crossroads full of outstanding, early-19th-century buildings, the core of a once proud hill town long since eclipsed by such valley centers as Barton, Orleans, and Newport. There are 19th-century flower and heirloom herb gardens behind the Eaton House and a spectacular panorama from the wooden observatory up in a meadow behind the church. A descriptive walking tour booklet is available at the **Old Stone House Museum** (see *To See*).

Cabot (population 2,000). Known during the War of 1812 for its distilleries, this distinctly upcountry village is now famed for its cheese. The **Cabot Farmers Co-op Creamery** is Vermont's major cheese producer, and its visitors center is a popular attraction. Cabot is called the mother of the Winooski because the river rises in four of its ponds. Technically the town is in Washington County, but it's tightly bound into the network of Kingdom roads and farms.

Craftsbury (population 1,162; townofcraftsbury.com). Few places convey such a sense of tranquility and order as the village of **Craftsbury Common**. In summer, petunias bloom in window boxes, and the green of the grass contrasts crisply with the white fences. In winter, the general whitewash of this scene contrasts with the blue of the sky. Throughout the year there are nearby places to stay and books to check out at the desk in the new **Craftsbury Public Library** (802-586-9683) with its

SOUTH BEACH AT LAKE WILLOUGHBY

rockers on the porch, comfortable reading corners, WiFi, and imposing portraits of Ebenezer Crafts and his son Samuel. Due to debt, Ebenezer was forced to sell his tavern in Sturbridge, Massachusetts (the still-popular Publick House). He made his way here over the Bayley-Hazen Military Road, eventually bringing his family and 150 of his Sturbridge neighbors this way on sleds. Ebenezer was quick to establish a school. Samuel, a Harvard graduate who served three terms as governor, founded Craftsbury Academy, which still functions as high school for the town. **Babcock House Museum** (802-586-2825), beside the library, houses the Craftsbury Historical Society collection. The **Sterling College** campus adds to the mix. In East Craftsbury the **John Woodruff Memorial Library** (802-586-9692) preserves the look of the general store (vintage 1840s) while offering its stock of 20,000 books, including many children's titles, to visitors as well as residents. Many farmers welcome visitors to their sugarhouses during sugaring season in late March and early April and sell syrup from their farmhouses year-round. Inns and B&Bs offer year-round lodging, and the **Craftsbury Outdoor Center** offers one of the most extensive and dependable cross-country ski networks in New England; its summer sculling program is also nationally recognized. An extensive web of well-surfaced dirt farm roads meander in all directions, beloved by bicyclists and horseback riders. In 1930 Craftsbury had close to 100 farms, each with an average of 10 cows. In 2010 there were still 1,760 cows, and many farms had diversified. **Craftsbury Public House**, a former 19th-century inn that stands on 5 acres in the lower village (107 South Craftsbury Rd.), is under restoration as a nonprofit project. Due to open in autumn 2015, it will include a community gathering, exhibition, and performance space as well as a restaurant and upstairs accommodations. In winter it will also serve as a trailhead link between the Craftsbury Outdoor Center and Highland Lodge Nordic trail networks; the property, which borders the Black River, will be a public park.

Greensboro (population 770). Shaped like an hourglass, **Caspian Lake** has a century-old following. The unusual purity of its water is checked three times weekly in-season by its association of cottage owners—who include noted authors, educators, and socialites—all of whom mingle in **Willey's Store**, one of Vermont's most genuine and extensive village emporiums, in the center of Greensboro. You'll also find a public beach in the village and walking trails east of the village, which also maintains superb cross-country skiing trails in winter. Greensboro claims Vermont's oldest (nine-hole) golf course. The **Greensboro Historical Society** (802-533-2457), 29 Breezy Ave., is worth a visit, open most days in summer.

Hardwick (population 3,174). This hardscrabble little commercial center is making national news as a center for reinventing local agriculture. It's home to Vermont Soy (produced from local beans) and to the nonprofit Center for Agriculture Economy and a Vermont Food Venture, an incubator for businesses like the area's current success stories, Wolcott-based High Mowing Organic Seeds, Craftsbury-based Pete's Greens, and Greensboro-based Jasper Hill Cheese. At Claire's Restaurant and Bar, a community-funded cooperative (see *Dining Out*), the motto is "Local ingredients open to the world." This isn't the first time Hardwick has channeled local resources to a wider world. Its Victorian architecture is a reminder of the town's heyday as one of the world's major granite processors. The granite was actually in Woodbury, 5 miles south, whence it arrived by rail. Thousands of skilled European craftsmen moved to town beginning in the 1870s and continuing into the 1920s; a number of French Canadians remain. The Lamoille River runs through town, good for fly-fishing, beneath the swinging (pedestrian) bridge linking Main Street with parking. East Hardwick is also worth finding. **The Hardwick Historical Society** (802-472-8555) is housed in the former Hardwick Depot. The **Hardwick Town House** (see *Entertainment*) is noted for its hand-painted stage curtains and frequent concerts, live productions, and lectures.

✳ Must See

MUSEUMS & ATTRACTIONS ⌀ **The Old Stone House Museum** (802-754-2022; oldstone housemuseum.org), 109 Old Stone House Rd. off Rt. 58 east of Orleans in Brownington. Open May 15–Oct. 15, Wed.–Sun. 11–5 for guided tours; last tour at 4. $8 adults, $7 county residents, 2 students. **Athenian Hall**, a striking, four-story, 30-room granite building with a clerestory, completed in 1836 as a dormitory for the Orleans County Grammar School, houses the collections of the Orleans County Historical Society Museum. The building is all the more dramatic, set among the village's scattering of early-19th-century houses and the surrounding 55 acres of farmland. Its story is compelling. The school's headmaster and the building's architect was Alexander Twilight (1795–1875), the first African American to attend an American college (Middlebury, 1823) or serve in a state legislature (Vermont House of Representatives, 1836). A visitors center is housed in the circa-1830 Alexander Twilight House, from which guided tours depart to view the Old Stone House. Here, some rooms have been restored while others showcase special exhibits and historical collections from towns throughout Orleans County (including tools, paintings, furniture, and decorative arts). The Lawrence Barn features an exhibit titled *A Hard Row to Hoe: Two Centuries of Farming in Orleans County*. Inquire about special, year-round workshops. **Old Stone House Day**, second Sunday in August, represents one of the Kingdom's biggest annual events with a farmers market, picnic, kids' activities, live music, crafts demonstrations, and more. Any day, pick up the walking tour guide to the Brownington Historic District—and don't miss the view from the observatory tower on Prospect Hill. This is one of the most magical places in Vermont. Check the website for year-round special events and workshops. The federal-style Samuel Read Hall is a venue for wedding receptions and other special events and classes. There's also a working blacksmith shop and a perennial garden, maintained by the Four Seasons Garden Club.

Bread and Puppet Theater Museum (802-525-3031; breadandpuppet.org), 753 Heights Rd. (Rt. 122), Glover. Open mid-June–Oct., 10–6. The internationally known Bread and Puppet Theater tours in winter, but much of the year the weathered, vintage-1863 dairy barn is open to anyone who stops (free, but donations welcome). It houses one of the biggest collections and some of the biggest puppets in the world: huge and haunting puppet dwarfs, giants, devils, and other fantastic figures of good and evil, the artistic expressions of German-born Peter Schumann, who founded the Bread and Puppet Theater in 1962 and moved it to Glover in 1974. Inquire about tours, but usually visitors wander and wonder. Publications, postcards, and "Cheap Art" are sold in the shop. Sat. and Sun. in July and Aug., performances are staged in the outdoor arena in the neighboring field and in the timber-frame theater.

⌀ **Cabot Creamery Visitor Center** (802-563-3393; 800-837-4261; cabotcheese.com), 2878 Main St., Cabot Village (no way can you miss it). Open year-round: June–Oct., daily 9–5; the rest of the year, Mon.–Sat. 9–4, from 10 in Jan. Cabot—cooperatively owned by dairy farmers since 1919—has been judged "best cheddar in the world" at the industry's olympics. The center showcases its history with a video and offers tours, every half hour, of "Cheddar Hall" to view the cheesemaking (token fee per person over age 12 includes samples). The store features all of Cabot's many dairy products, along with other Vermont products. Call ahead to check when cheese is being made and inquire about the week's specials.

LAKES Lake Willoughby, Westmore. Vermont's most dramatic lake, nearly 5 miles long and more than 300 feet deep, shaped like a stocking with a foot toward the north and Mount Pisgah and Mount Hoar rising to more than 2,500 feet on opposite sides at the southern end. See *Boating, Fishing, Swimming*, and *Lodging*.

Crystal Lake, Barton. Roughly 3 miles long and about 1 mile wide, in places more than 100 feet deep, this glacial lake is beautifully sited between rough-hewn mountains. Crystal Lake State Park (see *Swimming*) is justly popular; summer rental cottages can be found through the Barton Area Chamber of Commerce. Also see *Fishing*.

The town of Glover also harbors three small, fish-stocked lakes: **Daniels Pond**, **Shadow Lake**, and **Lake Parker**.

✳ To Do

BIKING This pristine area offers hundreds of miles of dirt and logging roads. Request the excellent bike map for the Kingdom from the **Northeast Kingdom Travel and Tourism Association** (800-884-8001; travelthekingdom.com).

Craftsbury Outdoor Center (802-586-7767; craftsbury.com), Craftsbury Common, rents fat-tire bikes and offers a great jumping-off point for exploring over 200 miles of dirt roads through glorious farm country, also on 20 km of singletrack snowshoeing trails on its own 400 acres. Also see *Lodging*.

BIRDING The most famous birds in the Kingdom are the peregrine falcons that nest on Mount Pisgah on Lake Willoughby. Falcons return in spring, nest during summer, and leave by August. Early morning and late afternoon are the best times to see them from the north end of the west-facing cliff. Over 100 species of birds have been spotted around Lake Willoughby alone. **Siskin Ecological Adventures** (siskinea.org) offers tours to lesser-known spots like the bird sanctuary on the Barton River.

BOATING Craftsbury Outdoor Center (802-586-7767; craftsbury.com), Craftsbury Common, has offered nationally acclaimed summer sculling programs for 35 years. Three-, four-, six-, and seven-day sessions run late May–Sept. Open to all ages and skill levels. Sessions include tailored coaching, video analysis, demo equipment, and access to the swim beach, massage, nature trails, and mountain biking with lodging and three daily meals. Canoes and kayaks can also be rented for use on Great Hosmer Pond.

🐾 **Clyde River Recreation** (802-895-4333; clyderiverrecreation.com), 2355 Rt. 105, West Charleston. Kayak, canoe, and paddle-boat rentals, guided tours on the Clyde River, shuttle service, and fishing. Pets welcome.

NorthWoods Stewardship Center (802-723-6551; northwoodscenter.org), 10 Mile Square Rd., East Charleston (5 miles west of Island Pond), offers rental canoes on the Clyde River, also guided canoe expeditions on a variety of waters. **White Caps Campgrounds** (802-467-3345) at the southern end of Lake Willoughby rents canoes and kayaks. Boats are also available at **Brighton State Park** in Island Pond (see *Green Space*). **Anglin' Boat Rentals** (802-626-4523; anglinboatrentals.com) delivers rental aluminum fishing boats to local lakes.

Northern Forest Canoe Trail. For an overview of a 174-mile route through northern Vermont, see northernforestcanoetrail.org.

FISHING Also see the introduction to "The Northeast Kingdom."

Lake Eligo and **Caspian Lake** in Greensboro, and **Little** and **Great Hosmer Ponds** in Craftsbury. The **Lamoille River** in Hardwick is good for trout and perch. Also see **Clyde River Recreation** under *Boating*.

BIKING THE BACK ROADS AROUND
CRAFTSBURY OUTDOOR CENTER

Perry Heller

GOLF Mountain View Country Club (802-533-9294), Greensboro, nine holes. Established 1898; open to nonmembers midweek only. Use of carts permitted only for health reasons.

Orleans Country Club (802-754-2333), Rt. 58, near Lake Willoughby. Apr.–Nov.; 18 holes, rentals, instruction.

Lake Willoughby Golf (802-723-4783; lakewilloughbygolf.com), Westmore. This hilltop nine-hole family-friendly course is well worth finding. Check the website for directions.

Barton Golf Course (802-525-1126), Telfer Hill Rd., Barton. Apr.–Sept., 18 holes, cart rentals, low fees.

Grandad's Invitational, Newark. This nine-hole course is a local legend. Ask around for directions and leave your fee in the mailbox.

Kris Dobie
RUNNING AT CRAFTSBURY OUTDOOR CENTER

HIKING AND WALKING Mount Pisgah and **Mount Hoar**, Lake Willoughby. Named respectively for the place where the Lord sent Moses to view the Promised Land and for the place Moses' brother Aaron died after the Lord commanded him to go there, these twin mountains, separated by a narrow stretch of lake, form Willoughby Gap. Both are within the 7,000-acre Willoughby State Forest and offer well-maintained hiking trails. Mount Pisgah (2,751 feet) on the east side of the lake (access marked from Rt. 5A) has fairly short climbs yielding spectacular views of the White Mountains; trails up Mount Hor (2,648 feet) begin on the Civilian Conservation Corps road, 1.8 miles west of its junction with Rt. 5A, and also offer panoramic views of the Green Mountains to the west. For details, consult *50 Hikes in Vermont* (Backcountry Guides) and *Day Hiker's Guide to Vermont* (Green Mountain Club).

Wheeler Mountain. The trail begins on Wheeler Mountain Rd., which leaves the north side of Rt. 5, 8.3 miles north of West Burke and 5 miles south of Barton Village. From the highway, the unpaved road climbs 1.9 miles to the trailhead.

Bald Mountain. There are excellent views from the newly restored fire tower at the summit of this, the tallest peak in the Willoughby Lake area. Trails ascend to the summit from both the north (Lookout's Trail, 2.8 miles) and the south (Long Pond Trail, 2.1 miles). From the north side of Bald Mountain, you can hike on trails and wilderness roads all the way to the summit of Mount Hoar; Haystack Mountain (a side trip) has excellent views and two trails. Details can be found in *Day Hiker's Guide to Vermont* (see *Hiking and Walking* in "What's Where").

HORSEBACK RIDING Perry Farm (802-754-2396) in Brownington offers sleigh and carriage rides drawn by Morgan horses through the Brownington Historic District.

RUNNING Craftsbury Outdoor Center (802-586-7767; craftsbury.com), Craftsbury Common, offers five, six-, and seven-day camps late June–Aug., some fall weekends. Different sessions focus on training for triathlons, marathons, road racing, Masters running, and just plain fun and fitness. Camps are open to all ages and abilities; the reasonably priced all-inclusive price covers coaching, lodging, and three daily meals.

SCENIC DRIVES West Burke to Westmore. The stretch of Rt. 5A along Lake Willoughby is one of the most breathtaking anywhere.

Lake Willoughby to Island Pond shortcut. An easy route to navigate from Westmore on Lake Willoughby: Turn north in the middle of the village on Hinton Ridge Rd. and follow it through high, rolling farmland and forest (never mind name changes) until it reaches a T intersection. Turn right and right again onto Rt. 105 into Island Pond. The reverse direction is even more beautiful but too tricky.

Greensboro Village to East Hardwick. The road passes through Hardwick Street (that's the name of the hamlet) and a fine collection of Federal and Greek Revival houses; from Greensboro Village to Hardwick it makes a bee-line through high and open farm country; and from Craftsbury Common north to Rt. 14 through Albany and Irasburg, it follows the rich farmland of the Black River Valley.

SWIMMING There are state facilities at **Brighton State Park** (802-723-9702) in Island

NORTH BEACH AT LAKE WILLOUGHBY
Christina Tree

Pond, a large beach that is sandy and shallow for quite a way out, great for children. **Crystal Lake State Beach** (802-525-6205), 90 Bellwater Ave., Barton (just east of the village off Rt. 15), is open daily late May–Sept., with lifeguard, bathhouse (built of stones quarried on the lake and built in the late 1930s by the CCC), and picnic facilities; and **Pageant Park**, a mile farther east on Rt. 16, is a town-owned park open daily until 10 PM, with a bathhouse and camping (primarily tenting). **May Pond**, also along Rt. 16 in Barton, is a great spot for swimming, canoeing, and kayaking. **Lake Willoughby** has small public beaches at both its northern and southern tips.

✔ **Caspian Lake**, Beach Rd. in the middle of Greensboro Village. This is a great spot for small children, with gradually deepening, clear water. There's a large, free parking lot and space to spread blankets.

✔ **Shadow Lake Beach** in Glover is marked from Rt. 16. The most accessible of Glover's three lakes, with free parking; also good for small children.

✳ Winter Sports

✪ **Craftsbury Outdoor Center Nordic Ski Center** (802-586-7767; craftsbury.com), Craftsbury Common, grooms 85 km of well-marked trails for skating and for diagonal stride. Thanks to their elevation and Craftsbury's exceptional grooming, they also represent the most dependable cross-country skiing in the Northeast, opening in mid-November and usually skiable well into April. Geared to top athletes but also to skiers of every ability, the center offers a new Activity Center with rentals and instruction (also see *Lodging*).The only major New England cross-country system that's nowhere near an alpine ski hill, these trails web the kind of red-barn-spotted farmscape that's equated with, but increasingly rare in, Vermont. They traverse rolling fields, woods, and maple and evergreen groves, with stunning views of the distant Green Mountains. The center maintains the former Highland Lodge trail network, accessible via a connecting trail (our favorite part of the network); shuttle service to that trailhead is offered on weekends. Home to the late-January Bankworth Craftsbury Ski Marathon, one of Vermont's standout cross-country ski winter events. Daily trail passes available.

SNOWMOBILING Northeast Kingdom Snowmobile Map is free from the **Northeast Kingdom Chamber of Commerce** (800-639-6379). Island Pond is the snowmobiling capital of the Kingdom, from which groomed VAST (**Vermont Association of Snow Travelers**; vtvast.org) trails radiate in all directions. The local Brighton Snowmobile Club maintains a snow phone: 802-723-4316. **Kingdom Cat Corp.** (802-723-9702; kingdomcat.com) on Cross St. in Island Pond is the snowmobile rental operation in the area, and offers guided tours.

CROSS-COUNTRY SKIING AT CRAFTSBURY OUTDOOR CENTER

John Lazenby

SLEIGH RIDES Perry Farm (802-754-2396) in Brownington offers hay- and sleigh rides for groups of up to 10 people.

✳ Green Space

Barr Hill Nature Preserve, Greensboro. Turn right at the town hall and go about half a mile to Barr Hill Rd. (another left). The trails at Barr Hill, managed by The Vermont Nature Conservancy, overlook Caspian Lake. Don't miss the view from the top. In winter ski and snowshoe trails are maintained by the Craftsbury Outdoor Center.

Hardwick Trails, Hazen Union School, Hardwick. Six miles of nonmotorized nature and recreational trails wind through the woods behind the high school in the middle of the village.

✷ Lodging

♨ 🐾 **Craftsbury Outdoor Center** (802-586-7767; 800-729-7751; craftsbury.com), 535 Lost Nation Rd., Craftsbury Common 05827. Recreational programs are the big attractions here, with accommodations for 90 guests divided between two rustic lodges: 35 rooms sharing lavatory-style hall bathrooms, 7 with private bath, 2 efficiency apartments, and 4 housekeeping cottages sleeping four to eight. Three meals are served, buffet-style, in the dining hall. Guests come for the programs offered: running, sculling, mountain biking, and cross-country skiing, along with winter Road Scholar programs; or they stay and enjoy the outdoors at their own pace. Facilities include swimming and paddling at Lake Hosmer, mountain bike rentals, a fitness room and sauna all on around 400 acres, and in winter, simply the best network of cross-country ski trails in the East. $108–160 single/$190–280 double late May–mid-Oct. in rooms, $314–344 double occupancy in cabins, kids (7–12) $40, including three plentiful meals with vegetarian options. Winter prices are $104–270 single, $188–381 double, extra person $90; kids $41. Pets are allowed in two lakeside cottages ($80 cleaning fee). (See also *Biking, Boating, Running,* and *Cross-Country Skiing.*)

♿ **WilloughVale Inn and Cottages** (802-525-4123; 800-594-9102; willoughvale.com), 793 Rt. 5A, Westmore 05860. This contemporary, traditionally designed inn and cottages now represent the only lodging on Vermont's most dramatic lake. Guests can swim from the dock, or take advantage of canoes, kayaks, and paddle boats. Windows maximize the view. Guest rooms in the inn itself include three "luxury suites" with fireside Jacuzzi and private porch, one with a living/dining room and kitchen, and seven attractive rooms with private bath, phone, and TV (one handicapped accessible). Across the road there are three housekeeping cottages (one and two bedrooms) with fireplaces right on the lake, and 4 two-bedroom "lake view" cottages up behind and above the inn. A taproom and light dinners are available; continental breakfast is also available for guests. Standard rooms with queen beds in the main inn are $104–249 in summer and fall; cottages are $299–339. Substantially less in off-seasons. This is a luxurious but lonely spot. The restaurant (see *Dining Out*) is open for dinner, varying schedule (call ahead).

✪ ♨ ❀ **Rodgers Country Inn** (802-525-6677; 800-729-1704; rodgerscountryinn.com), 582 Rodgers Rd., West Glover 05875. Not far from Shadow Lake, this proud old farmhouse has been in Jim Rodgers's family since the 1800s. Far from any traffic, it's surrounded by its 350 acres, beckoning guests out for a walk down to the beaver pond or a bike along miles of hard-packed farm roads. Shadow Lake is good for swimming, boating, and fishing. There's plenty of common space—an enclosed porch, living rooms (flat-screen TV and VCR), and a game room with Ping-Pong table. We've stopped by over the years but it wasn't until we spent a night here this year that we realized what makes this place so special. A full breakfast, included in $65 single, $80 per couple, is served in the bright dining room off the open kitchen. The food is farm fresh and delicious, and there's good conversation between guests and hosts. Snowmobilers and cross-country skiers (Craftsbury Outdoor Center is nearby) are both welcome. Inquire about a winterized cabin sleeping six to eight with direct access to VAST trails near the beaver pond and an older, seasonal one, sleeping seven, by a small pond off by its own private pond. Weekend rentals are available.

✪ ♨ **The Kimball House** (802-472-6228; kimballhouse.com), 173 Glenside Ave., Hardwick 05843. This is a capacious, handsome 1890s painted lady set high above downtown Hardwick. Sue and Todd Holmes began hosting guests after their four children moved on. All three guest rooms are upstairs (one has twin iron beds) and share two full baths, one upstairs and one down. Sue is a hospitable host and delighted to help guests explore. There's plenty

RODGERS COUNTRY INN

Christina Tree

of common space, plus a big wraparound porch and backyard. $99–119 per couple includes a full breakfast. A light dinner is offered with advance notice.

Mill Village Road B&B (802-586-6937; mill villageroad.com), 468 Mill Village Rd., Craftsbury 05827. A small, pleasant B&B in a renovated 1860s house just down the road from the Craftsbury Outdoor Center. $125 for two, $95 single includes a full breakfast.

Mountain Lake Cottages (802-525-3072; vermontmountainlakecottages.com), 52 Old 5A Rd., Westmore 05860. Open Apr. 15–Oct. 15. A line of 10 exceptional log cottages all facing directly on Lake Willoughby above a sloping lawn, a total of more than 4 acres with an expanse of waterfront. This prime location was understandably the site of one of the lake's major 19th-century hotels. The two-room cottages have stone fireplace in the sitting/dining area along with full kitchen, heat, and front porch. Owner Renee Leveille is a hospitable host, inviting guests to swim off the dock and venture out onto the lake in a rowboat or kayak. Amenities include a rec hall, a tennis court, and a little take-a-book/leave-a-book library. Mid-June–Aug., $200 per night, $1,295 per week; less in spring and fall.

Also see **Mountain View Dairy Bed & Breakfast** in the Newport/Jay Peak chapter. It is betwixt and between.

✳ Where to Eat

DINING OUT Vermont Supper Club (802-472-7053; vermontsupperclub.com), 41 S. Main St., Hardwick. Open Tues.–Sat. 4–10, Sun. 10–2 for brunch then until 8. Past patrons of Claire's will recognize the venue of this new upscale restaurant. Chef Peter McLyman and wife Marie now fill the fine-dining niche in the middle of Hardwick. Dinner menu choices might include Wiener schnitzel with pan-fried roasted garlic spaetzle, and grilled ahi tuna served with sweet pepper coulis and basmati rice. Entrées $19–32. A full bistro menu featuring flatbreads is also offered.

Positive Pie (802-472-7126; positivepie.com), 87 S. Main St., Hardwick. Open daily 11:30–9:30, bar until 10:30 or 11. Despite the bar and big screen, this place appeals to families. There's a long list of specialty pizzas, some gluten-free and vegan, as well as salads, poutine, and serious entrées like honey-glazed pork loin.

Gills Bar & Grill at WilloughVale Inn and Cottages (802-525-2123; willoughvale.com), Rt. 5A, Westmore. Open Fri.–Sat. in winter; Wed.–Sun. in May–June and Sept.–Oct.; Tues.–Sun.

Christina Tree
VIEW FROM THE KIMBALL HOUSE, HARDWICK

in July–Aug., but call to check. Tables overlook Lake Willoughby. The atmosphere is casual. Entrées range from fish-and-chips ($11.95) to New York strip sirloin ($24.95).

EATING OUT 🍴 ((ͦ)) **The Parker Pie Co.** (802-525-3366; parkerpie.com), 161 County Rd. in the back of the Lake Parker Country Store, West Glover Village. Open except Mon., 11–9; until 10 Fri.–Sat. Bistro menus on Wed., music in the original space Thurs., music or live performances upstairs above the new dining room (check website) Sat. nights. A renowned foodie destination in the back of the village store featuring thin-crust New York–style pizza, cooked on stone, with locally sourced toppings that include veggies and cheeses as well as smoked sausage and bacon, a dazzling choice of specialty pies. A dozen revolving beers on tap and wine by the glass. Local greens, sandwiches, and nachos are also available.

🍴 ((ͦ)) **Parker Pie Wings** (802-334-9464; parkerpiewings.com), 2628 Airport Rd., Coventry. Overlooking the runway at the Orleans County Airport doesn't sound like a likely good food destination—until you get there. The small airport is 2.6 miles off Rt. 5 high on a plateau, and the restaurant windows face west. There was a beautiful sunset the evening we visited. The pizza bianca had plenty of garlic as well as fresh asparagus and caramelized onions. Dozens of very local farms are listed as producers, and the choice of local beers on tap is just what you'd expect from a Parker Pie offshoot. A country singer was tuning up as we left.

Christina Tree

CRAFTSBURY GENERAL STORE IS A SOURCE OF PIZZA

✒ **Parson's Corner** (802-525-4500; parsons corner.com), 14 Glover Rd. (Rt. 16 on the southern edge of Barton). Open except Tues. 5–2:30. This cheerful, family-owned eatery serves breakfast all day and daily specials (Monday it's meatloaf). Soups, slaw, ice cream, and a lot more made from scratch. Children's menu. The last time we tried to stop for lunch, there wasn't a space to be had.

Connie's Kitchen Bakery & Deli (802-472-6607; conskitchen.com), 4 S. Main St., Hardwick. Mon.–Fri. 6:30–5, Sat. 7–3. From-scratch buttermilk doughnuts, breads, cream pies, cookies, and brownies (gluten-free options). You'll also find daily soups—maybe butternut squash or black and white Mexican bean—lunch deli sandwiches on a choice of housemade breads, salads, daily specials.

(•)) **Buffalo Mountain Café** (802-472-8800), upstairs at the co-op, 39 Main St., Hardwick. Open Mon.–Fri. 8–3, Sun. 9–1. This little café above the food co-op is a favorite meeting spot despite the limited number of tables. Lunch on the day's quiche and soups or salad or build your own sandwich. Curried chicken salad and a wide choice of veggie options are on the menu. For breakfast, you can have a veggie scrambler.

The Village Restaurant (802-472-5701), 19 Main St., Hardwick. Open Wed.–Sun. 6–3. Sited at the junction of Rts. 14 and 15, this landmark little diner can fill the bill. Recently totally renovated, and under new ownership, it's cleaner, cozier, with better views of the Lamoille River than before. A good stop in Hardwick for families. Particularly good for breakfast, especially if you like hash browns, this is the spot that has locals raving.

Craftsbury General Store (802-586-2440; craftsburygeneralstore.com), 118 S. Craftsbury

Rd. A happening place since Emily McLure took over. A well-stocked store featuring local products, also a choice of pizzas, salads, build-your-own as well as signature sandwiches like chèvre caprese and Craftsbury cheese steak, kids' menu, everything as local as possible.

TEA Perennial Pleasures Nursery and Tea Garden (802-472-5104; perennialpleasures .net), East Hardwick (posted from Rt. 16). Tea-room open Memorial Day–Labor Day, noon–4; closed Mon. English-born Judith Kane and her daughter Rachel serve a traditional "Cream Tea" (cucumber sandwiches, daily-made scones, and fresh cream) and offer an assortment of teas, cold drinks, and cakes and savories. Judith makes her own strawberry jam. Many come just for the gift shop, known for its splendid summer hats as well as jewelry, clothing, books, gardening tools, and more. The 3 acres (open May–mid-Sept., 10–5) represent more than 800 varieties of flowers and herbs, featuring phlox and heirlooms such as lemon lilies, golden glow. Free garden tours Sun. at noon, mid-June–Aug. Teas are $10.95–25.95, depending on order.

✳ Entertainment

Bread and Puppet Theater Museum (802-525-3031; breadandpuppet.org), Rt. 122, Glover. The internationally known Bread and Puppet Theater with its huge and haunting puppet dwarfs, giants, and devils performs Sun. in July and Aug. at 3 PM in the outdoors area and Fri. and Sat. nights in the timber-frame theater. Also see *To See*.

PERENNIAL PLEASURES NURSERY AND TEA GARDEN IN EAST HARDWICK

Christina Tree

Craftsbury Chamber Players (800-639-3443; craftsburychamberplayers.org) has brought chamber music to northern Vermont for 40 years. The series runs mid-July–late Aug. Check the current schedule for performances at the Hardwick Town House, the Presbyterian Church in East Craftsbury, and Fellowship Hall in Greensboro. Most performers are faculty members at the Juilliard School of Music in New York City.

Hardwick Town House (802-472-8800; hardwicktownhouse.org), 127 Church St., Hardwick. Home to the Northeast Kingdom Arts Council and the Craftsbury Chamber Players, this 1860 schoolhouse also hosts a variety of programs: film, drama, music, lectures, and other live performances. The stage features a vintage hand-painted curtain.

Summer Music from Greensboro (summer musicfromgreensboro.net). Late July–Aug., a series of chamber and other music concerts.

Circus Smirkus (802-533-7443; smirkus.org), 1 Circus Rd., Greensboro. June–mid-Aug, this is a nationally recognized program cultivating acrobatic and other circus skills for children— ranging from a "smirking weekend" for 6- to 8-year-olds to advanced sessions and performances in more than a dozen towns all over New England.

The Music Box (802-586-7533; the musicbox vt.org), 147 Creek Rd., Craftsbury. Built as a piano-tuning studio and offering exceptional acoustics, this is a frequent venue for concerts and performances.

Craftsbury band concerts at the band shell on the common, Sun. at 7 in July and Aug. In **Greensboro**, concerts on the dock at Caspian Lake are sponsored by the Greensboro Association, summer Sun. at 7:30.

✴ Selective Shopping

ART AND CRAFT Mill Village Pottery (802-586-9971), 6 Mill Village Rd. (on the way to Craftsbury Outdoor Center), Craftsbury Common. Open summer and fall, usually off-season, too, but call ahead. Lynn Flory specializes in one-of-a-kind vessels and unusual functional ware such as the "Yunan steamer," a lidded ceramic pot with a conical chimney in its center, designed to retain vitamins and minerals.

✪ **Miller's Thumb Gallery** (802-533-2045; millersthumbgallery.com), 14 Breezy Ave., middle of Greensboro Village. Open May 15–Oct. 15, daily from 11. Art and quality craftsmanship in many media, including wearable art and furnishings, housed in an old gristmill with its raceway still visible through a window in the floor.

Greensboro Barn (802-533-9281), 491 Country Club Rd., Greensboro. You will find Jennifer Ranz here at her pottery wheel in this standout, vintage-1886 barn most days in summer and fall. The high-fired glazed stoneware is dishwasher safe. There are also limited-edition watercolor reproductions of Vermont landscapes.

SPECIAL SHOPS Red Sky Trading (802-525-4736; redskytrading.com), 2894 Glover St. (Rt. 16), Glover. Doug and Cheri Safford's red barn store is an irresistible mix of good things to nibble (including old-fashioned doughnuts), local produce and products, cheese and eggs, garden art, antiques, and kitsch.

Evansville Trading Post (802-754 6305), Rt. 58 between Orleans and Lake Willoughby. Open early May–Oct. A crafts cooperative for Clan of the Hawk, the local Abenaki Indian band. The 39-acre tribal grounds are the scene of a big powwow the first weekend in Aug. and a crafts show the last week in July.

BOOKS ❧ **Galaxy Bookshop** (802-472-5533; galaxybookshop.com), 41 S. Main St., Hardwick. Open from 10 except Sun., until 7 Wed.–Fri. This full-service bookstore is a delight to step into. A mural of Hardwick with a night sky rendition of the "galaxy" runs across one wall, above shelves full of books. Many Vermont writers and unusual titles are featured along with a strong children's section. An armchair invites lingering, and the frequent author readings and special events attract a far-flung community. Sandy Scott and Andrea Jones preside over this mid-village shop.

GENERAL STORES Willey's Store (802-533-2621), Greensboro Village. Open 6:30–6, Sun. 8–1. One of the biggest and best general stores

RED SKY TRADING IS A MUST-STOP IN GLOVER.

Christina Tree

Christina Tree
CURRIER'S QUALITY MARKET IN GLOVER

in the state, in business over 100 years; an extensive grocery, produce, and meat section, local dairy products (check out Constant Bliss cheese, made in Greensboro), hardware, toys, and just about everything else you should have brought for a vacation but forgot. Don't miss the upstairs with its selection of everything from flannel shirts and buttons through yard cloth and boots . . . and then there's the large hardware wing. Helpful staff will help you find what you are looking for and occasionally sell you something you never thought of wanting.

Currier's Quality Market (802-525-8822), Glover. Open year-round daily, Mon.–Sat. 6–9, Sun. 9–6. James and Gloria Currier's general store is a must-stop if just to see the 948-pound stuffed moose and a variety of formerly live animals lurking in the aisles and festooned from the rafters of this old-style emporium. In addition to staples and a good deli counter with hot specials, this is a major sporting goods store, selling fishing and hunting licenses and stocking extensive gear.

Craftsbury General Store (802-586-2440), 118 S. Craftsbury Rd. Currently a source of handmade specialty pizzas and picnic fare as well as toys, local eggs, wine, and staples. Grab a paper and coffee and sit by the woodstove. See *Eating Out.*

FARMS AND FARM STANDS Pete's

Greens (petesgreens.com), 266 S. Craftsbury Rd. Open late May–Oct. south of Craftsbury Village. Look for the colorful signs and roof planted in flowers and veggies. Pete Johnson's certified-organic vegetable farm supplies restaurants and stores through much of Vermont. Founder of Hardwick's Center for Agricultural Economy, he has pioneered year-round organic farming in this area. The farm stand carries local

meats and cheese along with as many as 100 varieties of vegetables in high season; also locally produced staples such as grains, honey, and syrup. Still, it's not a big place, and it's not staffed. Payment is on the honor system.

○ **Hazendale Farm** (802-533-7107; hazendale farm.com), 2853 Hardwick St., Greensboro. Open from mid-May, 10–5, for flowers and vegetable starts; from July 4 weekend, 8–6, for full stock; 10–5 mid-Sept.–late Oct. David Allen is a third-generation owner who switched from dairy to organic vegetables and fruit more than 35 years ago. This is a major source of local beef, veggies, and flowers, also PYO in July and Aug., corn maze in Aug., Sept.

Stillmeadow Farm (802-755-6713), 158 Urie Rd., South Albany. Open May–July. Call before coming. The dairy cows are gone but the greenhouses at this handsome farm, one that's been in the same family since the 1830s, are worth a visit. Elizabeth Urie sells a variety of vegetable plants and flowers; hanging baskets and planters are specialties.

Willoughby Gap Farmstand (802-467-9847; willoughbygap.com), Rt. 5A just south of Lake Willoughby. Open June–foliage, Tues.–Sun. 11–6. MORE THAN A FARMSTAND, the sign proclaims, and this is true. There are farm-grown veggies, pickles, maple popcorn, plus handmade quilts and other crafted items, picnic tables, goats, chickens, and a series of special events, like a sugar-on-snow party in July.

PETE'S GREENS IN CRAFTSBURY IS A FAMOUS KINGDOM FARM STAND.
Christina Tree

Agape Hill Farm (802-472-3711; agapehill farm.com), 618 Houston Hill Rd., Hardwick. Open May–Oct. Llama trail walks and farm tours that include feeding the farm animals (including sheep, chicken, pigs, ducks) and guiding llamas through an obstacle course, experimenting with fiber art.

MAPLE SYRUP Gebbie's Maplehurst Farm (800-258-7699), 2183 Gebbie Rd., Greensboro. Peter and Sandra Gebbie are major local maple producers, perpetuating a business that's been welcoming visitors for generations. **Sugarmill Farm** (802-525-3701), Rt. 16 south of Barton Village. Mid-Mar.–mid-Nov. The Auger family sell their own syrup; sugar-on-snow in-season.

Sugarwoods Farm (802-525-3718), 2287) Rt. 16, Glover. Open May–Sept., 8–4:30; Feb.–Apr., Sat. 8–1. A major outlet for maple syrup, candy, and sugaring equipment.

GARDENS Vermont Daylilies (802-533-2438), behind Lakeview Inn, Main St., Greensboro. Over 500 varieties of daylilies with display gardens; also potted daylilies, hostas, and garden perennials on sale. The gardens are always open, while the store is open May–Sept. 10–5. **Perennial Pleasures Nursery**. See *Tea*.

✳ Special Events

Last weekend of January: **Craftsbury X-C Ski Marathon** (craftsbury.com)—a great classic technique event open to skiers of all skills; 25 and 50 km races for the true competitors, 10 for ordinary skiers. All begin and end at Craftsbury Common, traversing the network of high, dependably snowy trails maintained by Craftsbury Outdoor Center and Highland Lodge. Food stops are a feature.

Last weekend of March: **Open sugarhouses** (vtmaple.org).

May: **Annual Vermont Open Studio Weekend** (vermontcrafts.com) on Memorial Day weekend. **Hardwick Spring Festival**, last

ANNUAL X-C SKI MARATHON AT CRAFTSBURY OUTDOOR CENTER

John Lazenby

weekend, includes a parade, crafts fair, and chicken BBQ.

June–October: **Farmers markets**, in Craftsbury Sat. 10–1; in Hardwick Fri. 3–6.

June: **Antique Gas/Steam Engine Show** at the Old Stone House Museum in Brownington (oldstonehousemuseum.org).

July: The **July 4 parade** in Cabot is the best around (802-563-2279). **Antiques and Uniques Fair** in Craftsbury Common. **Stars and Stripes Pageant**, last weekend.

August: **Circus Smirkus** (802-533-7443), Greensboro. A children's circus camp stages frequent performances. **Old Home Days** (802-586-7766), Craftsbury Common—parade, games, crafts. **Orleans County Fair**, last week, in Barton, an old-fashioned event at the extensive fairground—horse, pony, and ox pulling, harness racing, stage shows, demo derby, tractor pull, arts, crafts, and agricultural exhibits. **Kingdom Farm & Food Days** (kingdomfarmand food.org). **Clan of the Hawk Pow Wow** at the Evansville Trading Post (see *Selective Shopping*). **Old Stone House Day** (oldstonehouse museum.org) open house, picnic lunch, crafts demonstrations at the museum in Brownington Village.

M
emphremagog is Vermont's second largest lake, stretching from Newport, 32 miles north to Magog, Quebec. Once a busy rail junction and destination in its own right, Newport is reclaiming its lakefront. There's an attractive boathouse, a departure point for daily lake cruises and for a lakeside walkway/bike path that runs along the lake to the Canadian border at Derby Line.

At this writing there is also a grand plan for Newport's downtown revival. Whether or not it materializes, a significant change has been set in motion.

Jay Peak Resort, 18 miles west of Newport, is now the area's big destination and economic engine. For half a century this northernmost of the Green Mountains has been a ski area known for its natural snow cover, attracting a loyal following, primarily from Montreal. In the past few years it has developed quickly and dramatically into a major year-round destination with a championship 18-hole golf course, the Northeast's largest weatherproofed water park, a professional hockey arena, and a wide choice of lodging and dining options. It has done much of this with funding through EB-5, a federal immigration visa program through which foreigners can obtain a green card by investing a minimum of $500,000 in a "depressed area." Orleans County qualifies with one of the highest unemployment rates in the country. At this writing the plan is to invest further funding from this program in new industries and a new downtown block in Newport.

At present Newport is still far quieter than in the days when the 400-room Memphremagog House stood beside the railroad station, Newport House was across the street, and the New City Hotel was nearby. Guests came by train from Boston and Philadelphia. Lindbergh came with his *Spirit of Saint Louis*, and there was a racetrack and a paddle-wheeler. Today many Newport visitors are from Quebec and bring an appreciation for good food that's reflected in the area's newest and bilingual menus.

The waters of Quebec and Vermont mingle in Lake Memphremagog, and the international line runs right through the Haskell Opera House in Derby Line—the audience in America attends concerts performed in Canada. Even the major border crossing (passports or equivalent documents required) at Derby Line isn't especially busy. There are four more rural crossing along this border, which divides two very different cultures. As the French say, "Vive la difference!"

We encourage everyone to cross the border into the Eastern Townships region, which complements this northern edge of the Kingdom with its rolling agricultural landscape, resort amenities, vineyards, and distinctly French ambience. Since 1974, when French was declared the official language in the province of Quebec, there's a sense that you have flown across the Atlantic when in fact you've driven little more than half an hour north of the border. Still, Americans are welcomed and understood.

East of Newport you are quickly in little-trafficked lake country: Lakes Derby and Salem, Seymour and Echo all have good fishing, and dozens of smaller ponds have boat launches. West of Jay Peak, Rt. 242 plunges down in into sleepy Montgomery, where the prime attraction is still its six covered bridges.

GUIDANCE Vermont's North Country Chamber of Commerce (802-334-7782; vtnorthcountry .org) maintains a walk-in visitors center, 246 the Causeway in Newport, open daily year-round: Mon.– Sat. 10–4, Sun 1–4.

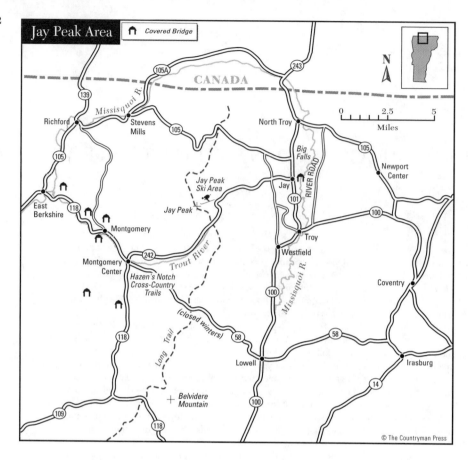

Jay Peak Area ⌂ *Covered Bridge*

© The Countryman Press

Jay Peak Area Chamber of Commerce (802-988-4120; jaypeakvermont.org) publishes a handy map/guide available from P.O. Box 426, Jay 05859.

Vermont Welcome Center (802-873-3311) on I-91 south in Derby Line, half a mile south of the border. Daily 7–7, with restrooms, Green Mountain coffee, live attendant, information.

For the Eastern Townships of Quebec, see **easterntownships.org**.

✳ Communities

Newport (population 4,520; discovernewport.com). The city has reclaimed its lakefront with a marina and 6-mile walking/running/biking path. Its past splendor is recalled in archival photos mounted by the **Memphremagog Historical Society** of Newport in the State Office Building. Step into the vintage 1868 **Goodrich Memorial Library** for a sense of the era. The beautifully built **Gateway Center** (84 Fyfe Dr.) with parking offers a public marina and restrooms and (theoretically at this writing) food; well worth checking. **Newport Parks & Recreation** (newportrecreation.org) also maintains **Gardner Memorial Park** with extensive playing fields and a picnic area by the Clyde River (across the footbridge from Vermont's **North Country Chamber Visitor Center**) and maintains a 35-acre park with camping at **Prouty Beach**. Check their website for seasonal information about rental kayaks, canoes, and skateboards.

Montgomery (population 1,201) is known for its six covered bridges (see *To See*). It began as a lumbering center and was for a long time one of the world's major producers of timothy grass seed. The Montgomery Historical Society's collection is housed in an 1835 wooden church, open June–Sept. at stated hours; the society also sponsors Saturday-evening concerts on the common in July and Aug.

Christina Tree

NEWPORT CITY DOCK & GATEWAY CENTER

Lunch and shopping can be found 2 miles east in **Montgomery Center**, crossroads of Rt. 242 (to Jay Peak) and Rt. 118 (north to Richford and south to Stowe). It's also the terminus for Rt. 58, which angles back through **Hazen's Notch** over a high woods pass and down through fields into Lowell. An inviting drive in summer, it's open only for the first 4 miles in winter, just far enough to access the magnificent and dependably snowy trails at **Hazen's Notch Cross-Country Ski and Snowshoeing Center**.

Derby Line/Sanstead, Quebec. Unfortunately the post-9/11 security at this border has created a wall between two communities that have been historically knit. The international line famously runs between the stage and audience of Derby Line's Haskell Opera House (see *Entertainment*). **La Vielle Douane**, the former customs station, remains a popular stop for all three meals, but Americans have to go through the new station to get to it.

North Hatley, Quebec (population 772). Some 20 miles north of Derby Line on Lake Massawippi, this village was founded in the 1770s by loyalists who moved north from New England during the Revolution. It became a fashionable resort for wealthy American southerners, who sold their summer homes in "Yankee land" after the Civil War. In 1900 there were 15 summer hotels here, one with 365 rooms. The village is charming, with its lakeside shops, cafés, and walkway—a magnet for tourists from Montreal.

Magog, Quebec (population 23,880; 800-267-2744; tourisme-memphremagog.com). A 19th-century textile town, Magog is now a resort center with a lively downtown and a lakeside walkway and bike path; it's a departure point for excursion boats.

✴ To See

LAKES Lake Memphremagog, Newport. Vermont's second largest lake stretches 32 miles north to Magog, Quebec. Only 5 miles are within the United States. The name is said to be Abenaki for "Beautiful Waters." On the western shore look for Owls Head, a distinctive monadnock that's also a ski area, and for the monastery of **St. Benoit du Lac** (see below). Also check listings under *Boating, Fishing,* and *Swimming*.

Seymour Lake. There is a public beach in the tiny village of Morgan Center, also the spot to rent boats for fishing for landlocked salmon. In winter this lake is peppered with fishing shanties, and there is a system of ungroomed cross-country trails.

Northeast Kingdom Tasting Center (802-334-1790; nektastingcenter.com), 150 Main St., Newport. This former hardware store is now a bright, open market with high ceilings and a contemporary, industrial feel, the venue for three dozen Vermont artists and a place to sample local syrup and spirits, meat and cheese. In a back corner **Jocelyn and Cinta's Bake Shop** is an open kitchen filled with busy bakers and the aroma of breads, cakes, and pies—made with all-natural local ingredients, no preservatives. The **Vermont Eden Ice Cider Company** (edenicecider.com), based in nearby West Charleston, has fermenting tanks in the basement (tours offered). It's featured at **The Tasting Bar**, a central attraction in the center that also offers samplings of Vermont-brewed spirits like Dunc's Mill elderflower rum from St. Johnsbury and Bar Hill Gin from Caledonia Spirits in Hardwick. A seasonal tasting plate with drink pairings; "4 bites and 4 sips" is $9. You'll also find a film on maple syrup production and a selection of products from **Butternut Mountain Farm**.

THE NORTHEAST KINGDOM TASTING CENTER IS NEWPORT'S NEWEST ATTRACTION.

Christina Tree

Echo Lake. Much smaller than Seymour Lake and adjoining it on the south, this lake is circled by a dirt road and gently rolling hills. There is also public boat access. Good fishing for trout and landlocked salmon.

Jay Peak summit. The spectacular view from the top is accessible via the 60-person tram at Jay Peak Resort. See the sidebar.

Montgomery and its covered bridges. Montgomery boasts a grand total of six Town lattice covered bridges: one right in Montgomery Village over Black Falls Creek; one south on Rt. 118; another nearby but 3 miles off Rt. 118 on West Hill on an abandoned side road over a waterfall; another northwest on Rt. 118 over the Trout River; and two in Montgomery Center, both a mile west of Rt. 118 over the Trout River (see our area map). Montgomery Village itself is picturesque.

Abbaye de St. Benoit du Lac (819-843-4080; st-benoit-du-lac.com), 1 Rue Prinicipale, Austin, Quebec. Open daily. This French Benedictine monastery, founded in 1912, is sited on the west shore of Lake Memphremagog. It's an imposing building with a landmark tower. The resident monks welcome visitors for daily Mass and daily Eucharist (11 AM) and vespers (5 PM), at which Gregorian chant is sung. The big, popular shop sells monastery products such as cheese and hard cider, as well as books and recordings of Gregorian chant, vestments, and religious articles. In autumn the orchards are open for PYO. The easiest route from Newport is via the North Troy border crossing, then through Mansonville, South Bolton, and Austin. The shop is open Mon.–Sat. 9–10:45 and 11:45–5; Sun. noon–5 in summer, closed in Sun. in winter. Retreats are offered for men in a guesthouse on the grounds and for women in a neighboring convent.

✳ To Do

BIKING **Newport–Derby Line Bike Path** takes you from downtown Newport up along the eastern shore of Lake Memphremagog on the old railbed to the Canadian border and beyond. You will need to stop and have your passport checked at the border.

See **vtnorthcountry.org** for a detailed list of area bike routes. Bike rentals from **The Great Outdoors** (59 Waterfront Plaza).

The **Missisquoi Valley Rail Trail** (see "Northwest Corner") begins in Richford and runs 26.4 miles west to St. Albans. A time-honored and -tested 22.6- or 33.7-mile ride in the Jay area begins at the Black Lantern Inn (see *Lodging*) in Montgomery Village, passes two covered bridges along Rt. 118 north, and takes you to East Berkshire; you can continue to Enosburg Falls, where **Lake Carmi** offers camping and swimming, or turn onto Richford Rd., looping back to Montgomery or up into Canada.

BOATING ✪ **Northern Star Lake Cruises** (802-487-0234; vermontlakecruises.com), City Dock & Gateway Center, Newport. Sailing May–mid-Oct., 11–4, weather permitting. The *Northern Star* is a spiffy replica of a 1920s luxury cruise boat and was sailing the inland waterway before Captain Chris Johansen had her shipped across the mountains to Lake Memphremagog. According to Johansen, it took five weeks to take her apart to ship and seven to put her back together again (the only other vessel to have made a similar transit is the M/S *Mount Washington* currently sailing Lake Winnipesaukee in New Hampshire). The enthusiastic crew offer live narration of what you see on this international cruise across the Canadian line. Check the website for catered and other special cruises. At this writing the company operates Sully's (see *Eating Out*), a source of sandwiches and light fare with tables on the deck overlooking the marina. Plans call for expanded service here, plus bike rentals for use on the adjoining waterfront recreation path.

Newport Marine (802-334-5911) at Farrants Point on Lake Memphremagog rents aluminum boats with small motors, also pontoons.

The 86-mile-long **Missisquoi River** makes a complete loop around Jay, passes briefly through Quebec, and continues across Vermont to empty into Lake Champlain. The upper half of the river near Jay offers fast water in spring; the lower reaches are gentle and broad, good spring and summer ground for beginners and those who enjoy traversing outstanding rural landscapes.

Montgomery Adventures (802-370-2103; montgomeryadventures.com), 262 Deep Gibou Rd., Montgomery Center. Canoe and kayak rentals, tours and shuttle service.

FISHING See the introduction to "The Northeast Kingdom."

GOLF The **Jay Peak Championship Golf Course** at Jay Peak Resort (jaypeakresort.com); see the sidebar.

Newport Country Club (802-334-2391), off Mount Vernon St., overlooking the lake. Eighteen holes, rentals, instruction, restaurant; Apr.–Nov.

Dufferin Heights Golf Club (819-876-2113), Stanstead, Quebec. May–Nov. Nine holes, cart rentals, restaurant.

HIKING The **Long Trail** terminates its 262-mile route at the Canadian border, 10 miles north of Jay Peak, but the trek up Jay itself is

THE 18-HOLE GOLF COURSE AT JAY PEAK
Jay Peak Resort

SKIING—AND SPLASHING—AT JAY PEAK

Jay Peak Resort (802-988-2611; 800-451-4449; snow conditions 802-988-9601; jaypeakresort .com), 4850 Rt. 242. Jay.

In winter, storms sweep down from Canada or roll in from Lake Champlain, showering Jay Peak with dependable quantities of snow. This phenomenon is better known in Montreal (one hour's drive) than in Boston (four hours) let alone New York City (six hours), and for three decades the resort's owners were Montreal based. However, over the past several years—since Jay's longtime president and CEO, Bill Stenger, acquired it in 2008—Jay Peak has been making waves felt throughout the northeastern United States and Canada.

Jay's glitziest attraction, the Pump House, is a 50,000-square foot glass-enclosed water park that literally makes waves year-round. Next door is a National Hockey League–sized ice arena and two major new condo-style hotels—The Tram Haus and the Hotel Jay. This new complex is sited at the base of the ski trails. Down the road a clubhouse with an attractive Clubhouse Grille serves the new 18-hole championship golf course and doubles as a Nordic ski center in winter.

Much of this transformation has been ingeniously financed by the EB5 federal program that encourages foreign investment by expediting the procurement of green cards by immigrants in exchange for a $500,000 investment in a project that provides jobs in high-unemployment areas. At this writing Jay Peak has attracted more than 500 investors from 74 countries. The results are worth a trip to see. The resort continues to evolve.

SKIING/BOARDING While there's an easy-intermediate trail (Northway) off the summit, Jay Peak regulars duck into glades right off the top. Jay's 20 glades and extreme chutes are what draw many of its regulars, who like to strike out into 150 acres of backcountry terrain. Unlike regular runs, wooded trails ("glades") cannot be covered by manmade snow and so require a lot of the natural stuff, which is what Jay Peak has in spades: an average of 350 inches annually. That's twice the snow many New England areas receive.

The original trails here are in an area called State Side, on a shoulder of Jay Peak. Still considered some of the toughest runs in Vermont, they were carved 50 years ago by local residents.

THE AERIAL TRAM DEPARTS FROM BESIDE TRAM HAUS LODGE   Jay Peak Resort

An enterprising Kiwanis group (it included the parish priest) convinced the Vermont Legislature to reroute existing roads up over the high ridge from which Jay's access road rises, thus linking it to northwestern Vermont as well as to the Northeast Kingdom. They imported an Austrian skimeister to create a true trail system and ski school. In the early 1960s Weyerhaeuser Corporation acquired the ski area and installed a Swiss-built tramway to Jay's Peak, which it topped with a Sky Haus tram station, a building that emphasizes the crest of the summit and gives it a distinctly Matterhorn-like cap.

Admittedly, given its exposed position, Jay can be windy and frigid in January and February (we try to visit in March), the reason—along with spectacular snowfall—that regulars are drawn by "off-piste" skiing through glades and into the backcountry beyond. In nearby Hazen's Notch, cross-country skiers also find some of the most dependably snowy and beautiful trails in New England.

Jay Peak Resort

POWDER SKIING AT JAY PEAK

Lifts: 60-passenger aerial tramway; 3 quad chairs, 1 triple, 1 double; 1 T-bar, 1 moving carpet.

Vertical drop: 2,153 feet.

Trails and slopes: 76 trails, glades, and chutes totaling more than 50 miles of skiing, spread over 2 peaks, connected by a ridgeline; 100-plus acres of gladed terrain.

Off-piste skiing: 100-plus acres.

Snowboarding: 3 terrain parks; board demo center, rentals, instruction.

Snowmaking: 80% of the total 385 acres.

Snowshoeing: Weekly snowshoeing walks led by a naturalist.

Facilities: Austria Haus, Tram Haus, and State Side base lodges with cafeteria, pub, and ski and rental shop. The Tower Bar. Alice's Table Restaurant. The Foundry Pub and Grille. Mountain Dick's Pizza. Taiga Spa. Aroma Café. Four-hundred-person conference center. The Drink pub. The Warming Shelter snack bar. Nursery and day care facilities. Rentals. Van service is offered from Burlington International Airport (80 miles away) and from the Amtrak station in St. Albans (a 45-minute drive).

Ski school: U.S.- and Canadian-certified instructors, adult and junior racing clinics, American Teaching Method (ATM). Telemarking instruction and rentals offered.

For children: Mountain Explorers for both skiing and snowboarding for 6- to 10-year-olds, Mountain Adventurers for ages 10–17, kinderski for ages 3–5. Day care for ages 2–7.

Rates: $72 adult, $57 junior, but far cheaper for multidays and with lodging packages, also student and zone rates.

Jay Peak Ski Touring Center
(800-451-4449), 4850 Rt. 242, Jay. The resort maintains 20 km of groomed cross-country trails emanating from the golf course; rentals and lessons.

Ice Haus (802-802-988-2710; open year-round). A professional-sized hockey rink designed primarily for tournaments but with time scheduled for public skating. Nominal admission, rental skates, also helmets, hockey sticks, skate sharpening.

Pump House Indoor Waterpark
(802-988-2710), open year-round. Glass walled with a retractable glass roof and 86 degrees every day, this roughly 50,000-square-foot phenomenon features "La Chute," described as a black-diamond waterslide with a 45 mph descent through twists, turns, and flips, part of "the only aqualoop on the continent." It also boasts the largest indoor activity river in the country and offers a kids' play area. $35 per day for ages 15 and older; $25 for younger kids.

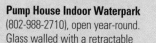
ICE HAUS HOCKEY RINK AT JAY PEAK
Jay Peak Reso

GOLF The **Jay Peak Championship Golf Course** (802-327-2184). Designed by Graham Cooke, this highly rated 18-hole course emphasizes natural features and offers some memorable views. Lessons and lodging at the clubhouse. From $37 for a nine-hole round with a cart. Ask about packages.

AERIAL TRAM to **Jay Peak summit**. The 60-person aerial tram hoists visitors to the 3,861-foot summit. The view sweeps from Mount Washington to Montreal, back across the lake, down the spine of the Green Mountains, and southwest across Lake Champlain to the Adirondacks. It operates daily during ski season and from the last weekend in June through Labor Day, then in foliage season mid-Sept.–Columbus Day.

what most hikers look for here. The most popular ascent is from Rt. 242, 1.2 miles west of the entrance to the ski area; the round-trip hike takes three hours. For details on this and the section of the trail between Hazen's Notch and Rt. 242, as well as the final, fairly flat leg to the border, see the *Long Trail Guide*, published by the Green Mountain Club, which maintains the trail and four shelters in this area.

✍ **Hazen's Notch Association** (802-326-4799; hazensnotch.org), 1421 Hazen's Notch Rd. (Rt. 58), Montgomery Center. Open May 15–Nov. 15. No trail fee, but contributions appreciated. Twenty miles of this network are maintained for hiking, winding through 2,500 acres of privately owned woods and meadows; it's 15 minutes to Bear Paw Pond. The 2-mile-long Burnt Mountain Trail ascends to the 2,700-foot summit of Burnt Mountain, an open summit with 360-degree views that include Hazen's Notch, the Jay Mountains, Mount Mansfield, and Lake Champlain. Stop by the welcome center on Rt. 58. Dogs must be leashed. Check the website for details about ecology day camps for children 6–9, Adventure Day and Overnight Camps for those 10–15, also about frequent nature walks and special events.

SCENIC DRIVES Big Falls of the Missisquoi. River Rd. hugs the river, paralleling Rt. 101 between Troy and North Troy. You can access the falls from either town or from Vielleux Rd. off Rt. 101 at its junction with Rt. 105. This last is the prettiest route, through farmland and through the

LODGING At this writing the resort can accommodate 4,000 in three condo-hotels and 500 condominiums clustered around the two base areas and the golf course. There is a 24-hour shuttle bus service.

Tram Haus: 57 attractive studio suites with cooking facilities, featuring locally made furniture and blankets, hung with artfully arranged photographs by employees. Facilities include restaurants (see *Dining Out*) and the Taiga Spa. From $110 per person. Many packages. **Hotel Jay:** 172 rooms, three restaurants, conference center, 38 fifth-floor penthouse suites, outdoor pool, the Foundry Pub & Grille, condo-style rooms, fitness facility restaurants and pubs. From $119 per person. Kids stay free.

DINING Tram Haus: Alice's Table (802-327-2323). Open for lunch and dinner, locally sourced menu, tables from an old barn. **Tower Bar** (802-327-2324), lunch and dinner (sports bar, music, pub menu). **Clubhouse Grille** (802-988-2770). Open for three meals. Many, many more options.

IT'S SWIM TIME YEAR-ROUND INSIDE THE PUMP HOUSE. Jay Peak Resort

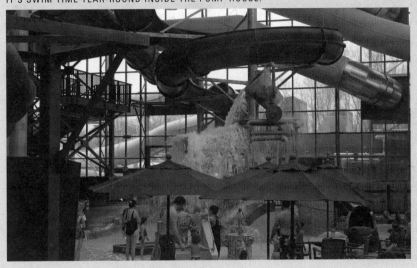

covered bridge south of the falls. Look for the unmarked pull-off in a grove of pine trees. The falls, thundering through a deep gorge, are awe inspiring.

Hazen's Notch. From Montgomery Center an unpromising narrow road, Rt. 58, climbs steeply east, quickly changing to dirt. In winter it's open only for the first 4 miles and is a popular ski-touring spot. In summer it's a beautiful road, dappled with sunlight through the thick foliage. Look for a picnic spot near the height-of-land, close to a clear roadside spring. A historic site plaque says the road through the high pass was built by General Moses Hazen in 1778–79, commissioned by George Washington himself. The road was begun in 1776, 48 miles to the southeast at the town of Wells River on the Connecticut River, and was intended to reach St. John, Quebec. It was abandoned on this spot in April 1779 when the news that British patrols might use it as an invasion route (it was meant to work the other way) reached the camp at Hazen's Notch.

SWIMMING In Newport try **Prouty Beach** (802-334-7951; newportrecreation.org/prouty-beach), 266 Prouty Beach Rd. This is a 35-acre lakeside park with a camping and disc-golf area as well as swim beach on Lake Memphremagog. On Seymour Lake there is a public beach in Morgan Center.

CROSS-COUNTRY SKIING ✪ **Hazen's Notch Association** (802-326-4799; hazensnotch.org), welcome center at 1423 Hazen's Notch Rd. (Rt. 58), Montgomery Center. Hazen's Notch is a road

CROSS-COUNTRY SKIING AT HAZEN'S NOTCH

Christina Tree

through a high pass that—like the more famous Smugglers Notch north of Stowe—is closed in winter. The original road dates from 1779, commissioned by George Washington. This is one of the first non-profit ski centers in Vermont, and still maintained by founder Rolf Anderson. It offers reliably snowy, well-marked trails for people of all abilities looping through woods and open meadows on 2,500 acres of private land, meticulously tracked for cross-country and snowshoeing (also see *Hiking*). You can ski up to 25 km without returning to the **Welcome Center**—but please check in and pay the trail fee. Trails offer fine views of Jay Peak and the Cold Hollow Mountains. Early and late in the season, this tends to be one of half a dozen cross-country networks in New England that have snow (elevation 900–2,800 feet). We last spent a beautiful morning skiing here on a March day that was too windy to ski at Jay Peak. Ten miles of dedicated snowshoe trails include the path up Burnt Mountain. Lessons and rentals, also full-moon snowshoe tours. No dogs or walking please.

NorthWoods Stewardship Center (802-723-6551; northwoodscenter.org), 10 Mile Square Rd., East Charleston (5 miles west of Island Pond off Rt. 105), is a 1,700-acre preserve with 35 km of groomed skiing and snowshoeing trails. Rentals and guided tours are offered.

DOGSLEDDING is offered by **Montgomery Adventures** (802-370-2103; montgomeryadventures .com), 262 Deep Gibou Rd., Montgomery Center.

✳ Lodging

RESORT See the sidebar for **Jay Peak Resort**.

INNS AND B&BS

In the Newport/Derby Line area
Little Gnesta B&B (802-334-3438; littlegnesta .com), 115 Prospect St., Newport 05855. On a quiet block a short walk from Main St. shops and restaurants, this house has been thoroughly restored as a B&B. Ruth Sproull was inspired by a trip to Sweden to create an uncluttered, restful atmosphere. White is the dominant color, and guests are asked to remove their shoes on entering. The four guest rooms are simply furnished, bright, and comfortable—two first floor and two second, all with private bath.

$85–135 includes a Swedish-style breakfast of crust breads, cheese, meat, and yogurt. Inquire about longer stays in Ruth's newly restored house across the street.

✪ ❀ 🐾 ❀ ⚓ & **Cliff Haven Farm Bed & Breakfast** (802-334-2401; cliffhavenfarmbedand breakfast.com), 5463 Lake Rd., Newport Center 05857. Mim LeBlanc's 19th-century post-and-beam farmhouse is a real gem. Set in their 300 acres, it overlooks Lake Memphremagog from a rise—which continues to rise through meadows to a swim pond near the height of their land. Our ground-floor guest room was really a spacious suite, tastefully and comfortably decorated. All four guest rooms have private bath with whirlpool tub; they're also fitted with gas fireplace, antiques, TV/VCR, microwave, and small fridge. $80–175 includes a full breakfast and afternoon tea, less if you stay three nights. Children under 12 are free. Well-behaved pets accepted but cannot be left alone.

Derby Village Inn (802-873-5071; derbyline villageinn.com), 440 Main St., Derby Line 05830. One of the town's proudest mansions (vintage 1909), this is now a hospitable inn, best known for its restaurant (see *Dining Out*)—but that's on a different side of the house than you access as a guest. There are five guest rooms, each with private bath, A/C, and a fireplace (electrified). $135–165 with a full breakfast, depending on room and season.

✪ ✿ Mountain View Dairy Bed & Breakfast (802-754-8494; mountainviewdairybedand breakfast.com), 725 Poutre Dr., Irasburg 05845. Off the beaten track, this is a third-generation 221-acre dairy farm with a truly spectacular view east across rolling hills. Denis and Carol Poutre are up at 4 every morning milking the cows, who spend most of the day decoratively distributed over the hill behind this tidy farmhouse. The three comfortable guest rooms are upstairs, sharing a large, immaculate bathroom. No one else was there the night we stayed. This is a great find for families as guests are invited into the barn to help with the milking and other chores, haying, and sugaring in-season; there are walking/snowshoeing trails. Denis has an easy laugh and Carol, a grandmother, looks ridiculously young and energetic; both enjoy their guests. Although this seems miles from anywhere, especially the first time you try to find it (don't use your GPS or you never will), it's not far from lunch and dining options. $100 per couple, $65 single, $30 per child includes a large country breakfast.

Lake Salem Inn (802-766-5560; lakesaleminn .com), 1273 Rt. 105, Derby 05829. This attractive inn with its columned porch is set on 7 acres overlooking Lake Salem. Joe and Mo Profera offer four guest rooms, all with private bath. The spacious first-floor library room ($125) has a queen-sized sleigh bed and a sitting area, the Zen Room ($125) is airy and tranquil, and both the Wyoming Room and the Hideaway have lake views and deck ($155). Common space includes a TV, books, and games; there's a back deck and boat dock. Rates include a full breakfast. Dinner is available to guests and the public on request (see *Dining Out*).

Water's Edge B&B (802-334-7726), 324 Wishing Well Ave., Newport 05855. Several miles north of downtown Newport, Pat Bryan's

contemporary house sits right on the edge of Lake Memphremagog. Common space is tasteful and includes a deck. The three guest rooms include a queen room with a lake view, a splendid corner queen with two windows on the lake ($120), and a suite with a sitting area and gas stove ($150). All rooms have private bath and TV. In summer guests have use of the canoe, rowboat, and dock; in winter there's snowmobile and ice-fishing access right out the front door. Bird-watching year-round. Rates include a full breakfast. Residents include two gentle Saint Bernards.

The Birchwood B&B (802-873-9104; birchwoodbedandbreakfast.com), 502 Main St., Derby Line 05830. Betty and Dick Fletcher's handsome 1920s village house has three spacious, antiques-furnished (the couple own an antiques store), immaculate bedrooms with private bath: the Double Bed Chamber (antique pineapple bed), the blue-and-white Queen Canopy Chamber, and the green-and-pink Twin Bed Room. The fireplace in the formally furnished living room is frequently lit, and guests gather around the long formal dining table for full, candlelit breakfasts. $120–125 includes breakfast. Children 12 years and older please.

A Place in Time (802-334-6950; aplaceintime bedandbreakfast.com), 235 Vance Hill Rd., Newport Center 05857. Vincent and Trish Buttice have nicely restored this 19th-century farmhouse and welcome guests to a first-floor suite with private bath. $109–129 includes a full breakfast.

THE BARN AT MOUNTAIN VIEW DAIRY B&B IN IRASBURG

Christina Tree

Newport City Inn & Suites (802-334-6558; 800-338-6558; newportcitymotel.net), 444 E. Main St., Newport 05855. This 82-room motel has units that vary widely, from $82 per couple weekdays in a standard room to $173 for a suite accommodating four. Facilities include an indoor pool.

In the Jay Peak area

Black Lantern Inn & Brew Pub (802-326-3269; blacklanterninn.com), 2057 N. Main St. (Rt. 118), Montgomery 05470. A white-pillared brick inn built in 1803 as the Montgomery Village stage stop, 10 miles west of Jay Peak, this is an appealing place to stay. With new ownership it has reclaimed its old name. The innkeeper is Greg Lucas. Fifteen rooms are divided between the main inn and neighboring Burdette House, all nicely decorated and varying from standard to a two-bedroom suite. Adirondack chairs are also positioned behind the inn with a view of Hazen's Notch. Some rooms have a fireplace or wood-burning stove and steam shower or whirl-pool bath. There is a low-beamed, charming dining room (see *Dining Out*) and a cozy brew-pub featuring Irish whiskey and the house handcrafted brew. Beyond the porch is the village with its six covered bridges, and from the back there is a hot tub under the gazebo with a view of Hazen's Notch, a venue for small weddings. Summer is low season: $120–210 per room in ski and foliage seasons, otherwise $85–190 ($120–345 for the three-bedroom) B&B.

♂ 🐾 **Phineas Swann Bed & Breakfast Inn** (802-326-4306; phineasswann.com), 195 Main St., Montgomery Center 05471. Darren and Lynn Drevik have brought the right touch to the village's premier B&B. Accommodations are divided among upstairs rooms in the main house, luxurious suites in the Carriage House, and fully equipped, dog-friendly apartments in River House. Common rooms are elegantly comfortable. In summer the deck and gardens invite you outside and down to the Trout River. Amenities include many bells and whistles plus long-distance toll-free phones and an outdoor hot tub. $139–179 for rooms, $159–599 for one- and two-bedroom suites (less off-season), includes a full breakfast and all-day snacks. Inquire about romance packages and periodic farm-to-table dinners.

❂ 🐾 **The Inn** (802-326-4391; theinn.us), 241 Main St., Montgomery Center. New York transplants Nick Barletta and Scott have thoroughly renovated and reopened this inn, formerly the Inn on Trout River. The feel now is that of a quirky boutique hotel, unfussily stylish, with accommodations ranging from a spacious honeymoon suite to economical family rooms and

Christina Tree
BLACK LANTERN INN & BREW PUB IN MONTGOMERY

bunkrooms. Pasfield, a renowned photographer, is the eye behind objets ranging from a wax bust of Elvis to a couch stenciled with images of automatic weapons that make the shared spaces feel like a secret museum. $139–209 (ski season is $179–249) includes a splendid full breakfast. Food is taken very seriously here, with a varied menu to match the decor. Also see *Dining Out*.

Jay Village Inn (802-988-2306; stayatjay.com), 1078 Rt. 242, Jay 05859. Three miles downhill from Jay Peak in Jay Four Corners, this classic log ski lodge is best known as a convivial restaurant and pub—but the rooms upstairs have been tastefully refurbished, all with private bath. There are seven double rooms, varying in size and shape, and four family suites (sleeping four to five). The quietest rooms are on the third floor and include our favorite, with a fireplace and sleigh bed. In summer there's a heated pool, and the outside hot tub gets year-round use. From $70 in summer and fall; during ski season from $75 weekdays; $95–229 weekends. The inn serves all three meals, 6:30 AM–9 PM (until 10 Fri.; see *Dining Out*).

Couture's Maple Shop and Bed & Breakfast (802-744-2733; 800-845-2733; maplesyrup vermont.com), 560 Rt. 100, Westfield 05874-9197. Pauline and Jacques Couture raised six children in this 1892 farmhouse while also maintaining a dairy farm and sizable maple syrup business. Three guest rooms with queen-sized bed and pullout couch share a bath; a family room (private bath) sleeps four. The cow barn is out the back door, and the sugarhouse is just up the hill. $95 per couple, $155 for the family room, includes a full breakfast served in the renovated farm kitchen.

Across the border

Hovey Manor (800-661-2412; hoveymanor .com), 575 Hovey Rd., North Hatley, Quebec, Canada J0B 2C0. A pillared southern-style lakeside mansion built in 1900 by the president of Georgia Power, set in 25 acres with lovely English gardens on the shore of Lake Massawipi. Owned by the Stafford family since 1979, the resort is a member of Relais & Châteaux. The 32 guest rooms and six suites are divided among the original mansion, icehouse, pump house, electric house, and caretaker's residence; several of the most luxurious are squirreled away in the trees, atop a bluff above the hotel, with decks overlooking the lake. They vary in size and decor, but most have lake views, many with fireplace, Jacuzzi, and balcony. Amenities include two beaches, a lakeside pool, exercise room, access to kayaks and sailboats, massage, yoga, and cross-country ski trails. Dining is central to the experience here. In addition to the formal dining room, a fireside pub is the venue for lunch, served in-season on the lakeside terrace. Check the website for rates and packages.

Auberge Ripplecove & Spa (800-668-4296; ripplecove.com), 700 Ripplecove, Ayer's Cliff, Quebec, Canada J0B 1C0. Founded by members of the Stafford family as a rough-hewn fishing lodge back in the 1940s, this is now another romantic resort, rivaling Hovey Manor in both food and facilities. You'll find 32 rooms, five suites, two cottages, 12 acres, and a recently added rustic-style spa with a lake view. Every room is different. Eighty percent have a fireplace and lake view, and many offer fireplace and whirlpool tub. There's also the original family-friendly log cabin (owned by the Staffords in 1945 when there was no electricity) and another three-bedroom cottage with a Jacuzzi, private pool, and water views. Here dining is also central to the experience, consciously a shade less "haute" than Hovey Manor. Owned by a different branch of the Stafford family, the two compete. It's literally in a cove near the southern end of Lake Massawipi. Heated pool, tennis court, bike path (bikes available). Check current rates; from $404 for two nights off-season.

✳ Where to Eat

DINING OUT

In the Newport and lakes area

○ ♿ **Derby Village Inn** (802-873-5071; derby linevillageinn.com), 440 Main St., Derby Line. Open Wed.–Sun. 4:30–close, also 2:30 for Sun.

brunch. A terrific addition to the area! Chef-owner Fritz Halbedl, a veteran of 14 years as an executive chef with Royal Caribbean Cruises, has created a bright, informally inviting dining room overlooking the garden in one of the town's grandest mansions. The Austrian-accented menu includes potato pancakes, bratwurst or knockwurst, and vegetarian strudel as well as schnitzels and (local) venison stew with mushrooms served over red cabbage and spaetzle. Entrées $19–25; patrons are welcome to dine on a mix of starters and entrées. With a sense of his place right on the border, Fritz also offers sauerbraten and chicken schnitzel poutines. There's a kids' menu and carefully chosen selection of draft beers.

○ **Newport Ciderhouse Bar & Grill** (802-334-1791) 150 Main St., Newport. Open Mon.–Sat. 11–9. Tucked into a bright, streetside corner of the Northeast Kingdom Tasting Center. There is a cheery, open feel to the space, which has quickly become the downtown place for lunch and dinner. Ingredients, including meats from the adjacent butcher shop, are locally sourced, with local brews and ciders on tap. Starters might include "Little Porks," crispy pork bites with a spicy soy glaze, and fried rabbit with sweet potato waffles. Dinner entrées $10–20.

♿ **Le Belvedere** (802-487-9147; lebelvedere \restaurant.com), 100 Main St. Open Wed.–Sun. 5–close. With windows and seasonal patio dining overlooking the lake, this place styles itself as "upscale dining" and has the prime in-town location, a large bar, and casually elegant atmosphere. Entrées from $14 for a chicken saltimbocca to $26 for New York sirloin and $32 for rack of lamb. Thursday sushi nights are the only way to fulfill a raw-fish craving for miles.

♂ ✿ **The Eastside Restaurant and Pub** (802-334-2340; eastsiderestaurant.net), 47 Landing St., Newport. Open for lunch and dinner weekdays, breakfast too on weekends; the Sun. breakfast buffet is big. A large old landmark with the best lake view of any restaurant in town, also a seasonal outdoor deck and dock. The reasonably priced lunch menu might include lamb stew and biscuits or grilled chicken salad. The salad bar can be a meal in itself. Many locals come just for dessert (try the pecan ribbon). Dinner entrées range from $12.95 for chicken 'n' biscuits to $27.95 for Alaskan king crab legs. Children's menu. Weddings are a specialty.

✿ **Derby Cow Palace** (802-766-4724), Main St. (Rt. 5), Derby. Open Tues.–Sun. 11–close, Mon. from 3 PM. Doug Nelson—owner of the largest local dairy operation and of Cow Town

Elk Ranch with 200 elk on 70 acres out back—owns this large, log restaurant, festooned with elk horns, specializing in meat, from burgers to prime rib and elk sirloin. We lunched on an elk burger. Dinner entrées $12.95–18.95. Fully licensed, with a bar menu.

Lago Trattoria (802-334-8222; lagotrattoria .com), 95 Main St., Newport. Open nightly from 5 PM. The decor is modern Italian, and chef-owner Frank Richardi claims not to fry anything except calamari. The menu includes pastas and staples like chicken Marsala and cacciatore. Pizzas from $13, otherwise entrées from $17 for Frank's homemade lasagna to $28 for lamb rack; fish and steak at market prices.

Vermont Pie and Pasta Company (802-334-7770; vtpiecompany.com), 4278 Rt. 5, Derby. Open Tues.–Sun. 11–9, until 10 Fri., Sat. Woodfired Neapolitan-style pizza with Vermont-sourced toppings is the specialty, but the large menu includes salads and burgers; dinner features seafood and steaks as well as pasta. Dinner entrées $14.99–25.99.

In the Jay Peak area

❦ **The Belfry** (802-326-4400), Rt. 242, between Montgomery Center and the Jay Peak access road. Open nightly 4–9, later on weekends. No reservations, and during ski season you'd better get here early (or late) if you want a booth. Built in 1902 as a schoolhouse, this is the area's most popular pub, and the food is fine. If you've been here a day or two, chances are you will recognize someone in the crowd around the mirrored oak-and-marble back bar. The soup is homemade, and the blackboard lists daily specials, like pan-blackened fish and grilled lamb chops. The set menu features "Belfry

THE DERBY COW PALACE IS THE PLACE FOR ELK SIRLOIN.

Christina Tree

Steak" ("price depends on the chef's mood"), salads, burgers, and deep-fried mushrooms. Wednesday is Italian night. Inquire about music.

Black Lantern Inn (802-326-3269; theblack lanterninn.com), 2057 N. Main St. (Rt. 118), Montgomery Village. Open 5–9. With its original name (for some years this was the Montgomery House) and new owner, this delightful low-beamed old dining room is once more a popular place to dine on seared duck breast or herbed steak (entrées $18–21). The inviting brewpub offers the area's largest selection of Irish whiskey and eight beers on tap, including the house handcrafted brew and the reasonably priced menu. We supped happily on jumbo lump crabcakes and butternut squash risotto.

The Inn (802-326-4391; theinn.us), 241 Main St., Montgomery Center. Open for dinner Thurs.–Sun. A big old upcountry inn dining room with a hearth and adjacent lounge are the setting for chef Jason Chartrand's inventive take on comfort foods, including pork chop with sautéed apples and apple brandy sauce, and lobster mac-and-cheese. Service on the outdoor deck in summer. Entrées $19–24 with a choice of "light plates."

Big Jay Tavern (802-326-6688; bigjaytavernvt .com), 3709 Mountain Rd., Montgomery Center. Open for dinner Thurs.–Mon from 4 (2 on Sun.). Five miles west on Rt. 242 from Jay Peak, this is a welcome addition to the local dining and après-ski scene. Chef-owner Nelson Cognac and his wife previously operated two popular neighborhood restaurants in the Boston area. The decor is rustic, and the hearty comfort foods are described as "Austrian meets Mediterranean." Signature dishes: baby back ribs with maple-ouzo glaze; polenta soup with garlic, tomato, and squash; and braised rabbit with apple, onions, and currants. Entrées $11–22. Check for music and other events.

Jay Village Inn (802-988-2306), 1078 Rt. 242, Jay. Open daily for three meals. A lively dining scene in a warm, informal lodge atmosphere with a big stone fireplace at the center of the dining room and the pub tucked into its own space. Pasta and $20 specials such as garlic sautéed shrimp and scallops or Delmonico steak.

❦ ♪ **Tastings Food & Spirits** (802-988-4063; tastingsinvt.com), 66 Main St., North Troy. Open Wed.–Sun. 4 PM–closing. Chef-owner Jeffrey Weiss has an impressive history as an executive chef at several Ritz properties and at Stoweflake in Stowe. The attractive restaurant in this 1890s border village hotel has become destination dining for the area. Appetizers

Christina Tree

TASTINGS FOOD & SPIRITS IN NORTH TROY GETS RAVES.

include hand-cut poutine with shaved Parmesan and truffle demiglaze as well as escargots with mushrooms, garlic, and brandy; the corn chowder is seasoned with thyme cloud and chili oil. A wide choice of entrées ranges from vegetarian pasta ($12) to herb-crusted rack of lamb ($31), with many choices below $20. A five-course tasting menu is $50, with wine pairings for an additional $20. Kids' menu also available. Inquire about the reasonably priced **lodging units** upstairs, with dining/lodging packages.

♪ **Hidden Country Restaurant** (802-744-6149; hiddencountryrestaurant.com), off Rt. 100, Lowell. Call ahead, but posted hours in summer are Tues.–Sat. 4:30–9 PM, Sun. 8:30–11 AM and noon–8. Open weekends in winter. Begun in 1988 by Joe St. Onge, this restaurant offers atmosphere that must be experienced to be appreciated. The specialty is prime rib. Big portions come with soup and salad bar. Rolls and desserts are housemade, and the specialty cocktails and Friday fish fry are famous. There's a trout pond for paid fishing and an eight-hole chip-and-putt golf course. No credit cards.

Note: **Hovey Manor** (hoveymanor.com) in North Hatley, Quebec, and **Auberge Ripplecove** (ripplecove.com) in Ayer's Cliff represent superb gastronomy, certainly this area's destination dining and in a class of their own. Check their websites for current menus. Admittedly, these inns are pricey, but Lake Massawippi offers a choice of lodging (see easterntownships.org). Serious foodies should dine at both of these inns at least once.

EATING OUT

In the Newport area
The Brown Cow (802-334-7887), 350 E. Main St., Newport, open daily 5 AM–1 PM, Sun. 6–1. This is a great spot to linger over breakfast.

Chef salads, steak dinners, homemade ice cream on homemade pie.

(ᵞ) **Newport Natural Market and Café** (802-334-2626; newportnatural.com), 194 Main St., Newport. Open Mon.–Sat. 8–8, Sun. 10–6. This attractive café offers a choice of a regular menu as well as vegan and vegetarian, a variety of espressos, fruit smoothies and herbal teas, panini, soups and wraps, smoked tempeh, a good salad bar, and wholesome baked goods.

Brenda's Homestyle Cookin' Restaurant (802-334-3050; brendashomestylecookin.com), 125 Main St., Newport. Open for breakfast and lunch daily, breakfast only Sunday. A down-home coffee shop that's surviving in the new Newport.

Roaster's Café & Deli (802-334-6556), 4267 Rt. 5, Newport, east of town. Open 6–2, great coffee, good food.

Also see **Brown Dog Bistro**, the **Derby Cow Palace**, and the **Vermont Pie and Pasta Company** under *Dining Out*.

In the Jay area
♪ **Bernie's Café** (802-326-4682), Main St., Montgomery Center. Open 6:30 AM–10 PM. Bigger than it looks from its greenhouse-style front, this is a genuine gathering spot for the area. Breakfast options include bagels and eggs any style, and the breads are baked daily, for sale separately as well as used in sandwiches. Soups are a luncheon specialty, and at dinner the menu ranges from sautéed scampi through pastas. Fully licensed with a pub in back. Chef-owner John Boucher frequently presides behind the counter.

NEWPORT NATURAL MARKET & CAFE
Christina Tree

Jay Village Store (802-988-4040), Rt. 242, Jay Village. Grill operates daily 6 AM–3 PM, sandwiches until closing (9 PM); Sun. from 7:30. We can vouch for breakfast. Panini are the house specialty. Request the "Lumberjack" (green onions, turkey, caramelized onions, maple mayo, and Vermont cheese). Seating at the counter and at tables in the solarium.

In the Seymour Lake area
Morgan Country Store (802-895-2726), Rt. 111, Morgan Center. Open 7–7, closed Sun. A genuine general store with a post office, live bait, and an extensive breakfast, lunch (burgers, sandwiches, salads), and pizza menu.

Along Route 5 south
Martha's Diner (802-754-6800), Rts. 5/14, Coventry. Open Mon.–Fri. 5 AM–2 PM, Sat. 5:30–1, Sun. 6–1. A classic 1950s chrome diner operated by the same family for 30 years, serving local diner fare with flair, excellent poutine and hash browns, fried chicken with buttermilk waffles, pea soup and much more.

✳ Entertainment

& **Haskell Opera House** (802-873-3022; in Canada 819-876-2471; haskellopera.org), Derby Line. This splendid vintage-1904 theater has perfect acoustics, three antique stage sets, a rare roll-up curtain depicting scenes of Venice, and a rococo interior. Its season runs May–mid-Oct. and includes performances by a resident theater company, opera, dance, and a variety of outstanding concerts. **QNEK Productions** (802-334-2216), the summer resident theater company at the Haskell, offers reasonably priced evening and matinee productions of musicals and other stock Broadway hits. Tickets for opera house performances are also available at the Woodknot Bookshop, Newport (802-334-6720).

The Piggery Theatre (819-842-2431; piggery .com), 25 Chemin Simard, North Hatley, Quebec. A long-established summer playhouse featuring plays, revues, and other performances, primarily in English.

Newport Gateway building (802-334-1005) on Lake Memphremagog is a frequent venue for summer–fall music.

Waterfront Cinemas (802-334-6572), 137 Waterfront Plaza, Newport. First-run films on three screens.

✳ Selective Shopping

In and around Newport
MAC Center for the Arts (802-334-1966; memphremagogartscollaborative.com), 158

Christina Tree
MAC CENTER FOR THE ARTS IN NEWPORT

Main St., Suite 2, Newport. Open (except Sun.) 10–5 in summer; closed Tues., too, in winter. This impressive new shop showcases the varied work of more than 50 local artisans. Check the website for workshops and special events.

◎ **The Pick & Shovel** (802-334-8370; pickand shovel.doitbest.com), 54 Coventry St. Don't miss Newport's mega general store, just off Main St., a vast complex selling everything from home improvement supplies and hardware to clothing for the whole family. If you can prove someone else is selling something cheaper, they will match the price. Don't pass up **Tim & Doug's Ice Cream**, another seasonal draw to this landmark spot.

The Great Outdoors (802-334-2831; great outdoorsvermont.com), 59 Waterfront Plaza, Newport. In summer the store features an extensive array of fishing gear and sells fishing licenses; four-season sporting goods. Rental bikes, kayaks, and canoes, also rental in-line skates, snowshoes, cross-country skis, and snowboards.

♪ **Wider than the Sky** (802-334-2322; wide rthanthesky.com), 158 Main St., Newport. This big, bright combination children's book and toy store is a winner.

Country Thyme (802-766-2852; 800-334-7905; countrythymevermont.com), 60 Rt. 111, Derby (near the junction of Rts. 111 and 5). Every inch of the ground floor in Kay Courson's house is crammed with gifts, toys, specialty foods, Christmas decorations, and more.

Kingdom Brewing (802-334-7096), 1876 Rt. 105, Newport Center. Tasting room open Thurs.–Sat. 3:30–6:30. Using a geothermal type of fermentation, American grains, and locally produced ingredients such as maple sap, spruce tips, and apples, Brian and Jenn Cook create a variety of light to robust beers. They dispose of the spent grains from the process by feeding them to the Black Angus beef herd on their farm.

Louis Garneau USA Factory Outlet (802-334-1036; louisgarneau.us), 3916 Rt. 5, Derby. Open daily 9–5, until 9 Thurs., Fri. Cyclists know this Canadian brand name well, and the outlet at their big new distribution center is a definite stop for those interested in gear.

In the Jay area

Jay Country Store (802-988-4040), Jay Village. Open daily. The center of Jay Village, selling papers, gas, food, and wine basics, also a deli (see *Eating Out*), plus an interesting assortment of gift items and cards.

Mountain Fiber Folk (802-326-2092; mtfiber folk.com), 188 Main St., Montgomery Center. Open Thurs.–Mon. 10–5. This is a cooperative selling hand-spun yarn as well as knitwear, art dolls, wall hangings, and knitting supplies.

Couture's Maple Shop (802-744-733; 800-845-2733), 560 Rt. 100, Westfield. Open year-round, Mon.–Sat. 8–6. A long-established maple producer: maple candy, cream, granulated sugar, pancake mix, and salad dressing, as well as syrup; will ship anywhere.

Jed's Maple Products (802-744-2095; jeds maple.com), 475 Carter Rd., Westfield. Syrup, candy, and frosted nuts. Inquire about the annual Mud Season Sugar on Snow Party.

Berry Creek Farm (802-744-2406; berry creekfarmvt.com), 1342 Rt. 100, Westfield. Farm stand sells local yogurts, cheese, bread, seeds, plants, and compost as well as their own produce.

In the Eastern Townships of Quebec

Vignoble Le Cep d'Argent (877-864-4441; cepdargent.com), 1257 Chemin de la Rivière, Magog. This is a long-established winery on the shore of Lake Memphremagog. The vintners are French, and tours are offered Apr.–Thanksgiving. A menu of fruit, local cheese, and crudités or a full meal is also available, as are samplings of its close to 20 products, from champagne to ice wines with a variety of table wines.

✿ **Verger le Gros Pierre** (819-835-5549; grospierre.com), 6335 Route Louis-St.-Laurent. This is a major orchard (8,000 apple trees, many varieties); also raspberries and strawberries in-season. About 20 minutes through farmland from the border at Norton. We visited on a September Sunday at the height of PYO season and feasted on crêpes stuffed with apples, ham, and cheese, served with sparkling cider. Plates of local cheese were also available, along with hard cider. A great place for families, with a playground and tractor rides.

✳ Special Events

February: **Newport Winter Carnival**. **Barton Snowmobile Races**. **Winter Festival**. **Mountain Mardi Gras** at Jay in late season.

March: **Sugaring** throughout the region.

May: **Open Studio Weekend** (vermontcrafts .com). **Dandelion Run** (dandelixnrun.org), late May—a half marathon largely on dirt roads through the dandelion fields of Morgan and Derby.

June: **Tour de Kingdom** (tourdekingdom.org), five days of riding.

July: ✪ **Kingdom Aquafest** (kingdomaquafest .com) is the premier event in the Newport area, with events throughout the first week of July. Check the website for schedule.

August: **Kingdom Triathlon** (kingdom triathlon.org). **Town of Jay Summer Fest** (augustwestfest.com), late August. **Kingdom Thunder** (kingdomthunder.org)—motorcycle ride for charity.

October: **Bean and Brew** festival at Jay Peak.

ISLAND POND AND BEYOND

T he crossroads of Vermont's lonely, northeasternmost corner, the village of Island Pond has the look and feel of an outpost. A historic marker in front of the city-sized depot reads: "Pioneer railroad planner John A. Poor's dream of an international railroad connecting Montreal, Canada, with the ice-free harbor of Portland, Maine, became a reality on July 18, 1854, when the first through trains met at this great halfway point on the Grand Trunk railway." During the late 19th century and into the 20th, Island Pond hummed with the business of servicing frequent passenger trains and freight trains trans-porting logs and wood pulp. No longer. Today Island Pond is a quiet village on a pond with an island in its center. Brighton State Park east of town offers calming and a sandy beach, and there's a pleasant pondside park in the village itself. The religious community Twelve Tribes (known locally as "The Tribe") has restored several Victorian houses and operates The Tannery, a destination clothing and shoe store. In winter Island Pond is the region's snowmobiling capital.

The lake-spotted woodland east and south of Island Pond is now largely publicly owned, much of it the Silvio O. Conte National Fish and Wildlife Refuge and teeming with moose, black bear, and other wildlife. There's great fishing in the waters in and around Quimby Country, the region's oldest and one of Vermont's most appealing resorts. Continuing east you hardly notice the short bridge across the Connecticut River (here a trout stream) as you cross from Canaan, Vermont, to Stewartstown, New Hampshire.

GUIDANCE Island Pond Welcome Center (802-723-9889; islandpondchamber.org), Rt. 105/114 at the south end of Main St. Open daily during summer, foliage, and snowmobiling seasons, but volunteer-dependent. A beautiful welcome center with restrooms as well as historical and crafts displays.

North Country Chamber of Commerce (northcountrychamber.org) covers this section of Vermont as well as the Colebrook and Connecticut Lakes regions of New Hampshire.

BORDER CROSSINGS are staffed 24 hours in Norton (Rt. 147), Canaan (Rt. 141), and Beecher Falls (Rt. 253). Passports required.

✳ To Do

Note: **NorthWoods Stewardship Center** (802-723-6551; northwoodscenter.org), 10 Mile Square Rd., East Charleston (5 miles west of Island Pond), is a 1,700-acre preserve with 40 km of walking/skiing and snowshoeing trails. Aside from its formal nature hikes, guided canoeing, and frequent out-reach programs, the center also serves as an informal clearinghouse for local canoe, fishing, tracking, and nature guides.

BOATING On the **Connecticut River**, Canaan is a good place to put in, but there are several rapids at the start. Canoeing is also good below Colebrook, New Hampshire, for 3 miles but then rather fast for an equal distance. (See also *Fishing.*)

Clyde River Recreation (802-895-4333; clyderiverrecreation.com), a quarter mile east of the junc-tion of Rts. 5A and 105 in West Charleston, rents kayaks, canoes, and small boats and offers drop-off and delivery.

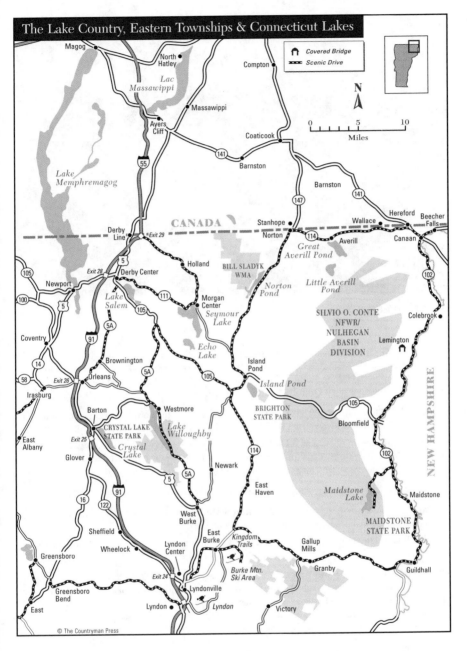

The Lake Country, Eastern Townships & Connecticut Lakes

Covered Bridge	
Scenic Drive	

N

0   5   10
Miles

Magog

North Hatley

Compton

Lac Massawippi

Massawippi

Ayers Cliff

Coaticook

55

141

Barnston

Lake Memphremagog

Barnston

147

141

Hereford

Beecher Falls

CANADA

Stanhope

Wallace

Derby Line

Exit 29

Norton

114

Averill

Canaan

Great Averill Pond

102

105

Derby Center

Holland

BILL SLADYK WMA

Norton Pond

Little Averill Pond

Exit 28

5

Newport

100

111

Morgan Center

SILVIO O. CONTE NFWR/ NULHEGAN BASIN DIVISION

Colebrook

Lake Salem

105

Seymour Lake

Lemington

5

5A

Echo Lake

Coventry

91

Island Pond

Brownington

Island Pond

14

5A

58

Exit 26

Orleans

105

BRIGHTON STATE PARK

105

Irasburg

Westmore

Bloomfield

Barton

Lake Willoughby

102

East Albany

Exit 25

CRYSTAL LAKE STATE PARK

Crystal Lake

Newark

114

Maidstone Lake

Maidstone

Glover

5

5A

East Haven

16

122

MAIDSTONE STATE PARK

91

West Burke

Sheffield

East Burke

Kingdom Trails

Gallup Mills

Granby

Guildhall

Greensboro

Wheelock

Lyndon Center

Burke Mtn. Ski Area

Exit 24

Greensboro Bend

Lyndonville

East

Lyndon

Lyndon

Victory

NEW HAMPSHIRE

© The Countryman Press

THERE REALLY IS AN ISLAND IN THE POND.

Christina Tree

FISHING See the introduction to "The Northeast Kingdom" for an overview. Biologist Ken Hastings of Colebrook, New Hampshire, with his **Osprey Fishing Adventures** (603-922-3800; ospreyfishing adventures.com), is the fishing guru for this stretch of the river, offering one- and three-day fly-fishing trips on his driftboat. Also see **Quimby Country** under *Lodging*.

HIKING Bluff Mountain (2,380 feet) looms over Island Pond to the north. It's a popular climb with spectacular views. The trail starts from Rt. 114, north of the village. Inquire locally for directions.

Monadnock Mountain (elevation: 3,140 feet), in Lemington, towers over the Connecticut River and Colebrook, New Hampshire. A trail runs west, beginning as a driveway off Rt. 102 near the bridge to Colebrook. An abandoned fire tower crowns the summit.

SNOWMOBILING The website **snowmobile.islandpond.com** has all you need to know.

SWIMMING There are state facilities at **Brighton State Park** (802-723-9702) in Island Pond, a large beach that is sandy and shallow for quite a way out, great for children.

Boulder Beach Day Use Area (802-584-3820) in Groton State Forest has a public beach, picnic area, snack bar, and bathhouse.

SCENIC DRIVES Island Pond Loop. This 66-mile loop circles the northeastern corner of Vermont, beginning in Island Pond and heading north on Rt. 114. The Canadian National Railway's Grand Trunk line from Montreal to Portland, Maine, hugs the highway the full 16 miles to Norton. This railway was once Montreal's winter lifeline to Europe, as goods could not be shipped into or out of the frozen port of Montreal during the coldest months. About halfway to Norton, near the south end of long and slender Norton Pond (there's a boat launch on Rt. 114), a gravel road to the left leads into the **Bill Sladyk Wildlife Management Area**, frequented by hunters, fishermen, and loggers. Just before you reach the tiny village of Norton (opposite slightly larger Stanhope, Quebec), the forest thins out and farmland reappears. Norton was the site of the notorious Earth People's Park, a 1960s-style, loosely governed hippie commune that once numbered hundreds of residents but is now state owned; no one is allowed to live there. The road passes several farms, a school, and the **Norton Country Store** (open daily), then swings abruptly eastward to avoid the imposing Canadian port-of-entry.

Eastern Townships detour (easterntownships.org). Some 15 minutes north on Rt. 147 brings you to Coaticook with "the world's largest pedestrian suspension bridge" (lit at night) spanning Coaticook

Christina Tree

ISLAND POND VILLAGE

Gorge. Compton is another 10 minutes' drive north. From Coaticook return on scenic Rt. 141 along Lake Wallace and into Canaan.

If you head eastward along the U.S. side of the border, Rt. 114 reenters the forest, passing a series of lakes, most of which are dotted with hunting and fishing camps. In Averill Gore (population 9) stop for bait and directions to the boat launch on Great Averill Pond at the **Lakeview Store** (open daily); owner Priscilla Roy sells locally handcrafted items. East of the store Forest Road leads to **Quimby Country**, one of Vermont's oldest and most appealing resorts (see the boxed description in *Lodging*). Shortly after passing Big Averill, you leave the St. Lawrence watershed and begin a rapid descent into the Connecticut River Valley. Halfway from Averill to Canaan, the road skirts the south shore of sizable Wallace Pond, almost entirely within the province of Quebec.

Canaan, 14 miles east of Norton. In the far corner of Fletcher Park (at the junction of Rts.114 and 141), the handsome 1846 Greek Revival building houses the Canaan Historical Society's changing exhibits upstairs. You barely notice the Connecticut River, here just a fledgling stream spanned by a brief bridge into West Stewartstown, New Hampshire.

These far corners of Vermont and New Hampshire form a North Country region of their own. Check out northcountrychamber.org for details. You may want to detour north up Rt. 3 to Pittsburg and the series of four lakes strung along the 22 semi-wilderness miles north of town. This stretch of Rt. 3 is known as "Moose Alley" for reasons scarily easy to grasp if you drive it on a summer evening. Diehard Connecticut River buffs may want to hike in to its source, a small pond accessible via a path beside the Rt. 3 border station (restrooms).

From Canaan our loop turns south on Rt. 102, through river-bottom farmland, through Lemington, and past the impressively long **Columbia covered bridge**, which demands a photo stop. This stretch of the river valley alternately narrows and widens, and the road tunnels through forest, broken occasionally by farms, fields, and glimpses of impressive mountains. In Bloomfield (the store may or may not be open) the Grand Trunk railroad line angles east across the road, heading for Portland. Here our route turns west on Rt. 105 (it's 16 miles back to Island Pond).

For another rewarding detour, however, continue at least the mile down Rt. 102 to the wooded path (on the left) into **Brunswick Springs**, once the site of a mineral springs resort. At this sacred Abenaki site, the resort's buildings repeatedly burned; only their foundations and an eerie cement stairway leading down to the riverbank remain. Please be respectful of the property, now owned by a local Abenaki group. Water from the sulfur springs still runs from spigots. Park next to the white wooden former town hall (on your left, heading south). The road in is usually chained off. It's roughly a 15-minute walk.

BIG AVERILL IS ONE OF THE AREA'S MANY LAKES KNOWN FOR GOOD FISHING.

Christina Tree

Another 4 miles south on Rt. 102 (and 5 miles in on a dirt road) brings you to **Maidstone State Park**, offering camping and swimming as well as fishing. The Connecticut River widens noticeably the farther south you drive on Rt. 102, and views of the White Mountains are increasingly dramatic. If you continue another 7 miles south to Guildhall, you are informed by a billboard-sized sign that the town was "discovered" in 1754, chartered in 1761, and settled in 1764, making it the oldest town in northeastern Vermont (by contrast, Norton was not settled until 1860). An attractive, square green is flanked by historically interesting buildings: a tiny courthouse, church, town hall (the Guild Hall, 1798), and an ornate 1909 Classical Revival library with stained-glass windows. An unassuming white-clapboard house serves as a county lockup.

Two miles downriver from Guildhall, a town road marked GRANBY runs west off Rt. 102, beginning as a paved road but becoming gravel well before reaching the tiny hamlets of Granby and Gallup Mills, about 8 miles from Rt. 102. This is wild, wooded, and boggy country, good for spotting moose and bear. Lumber camps and sawmills once peppered this area, and there was even a steam railway. The road finally descends about 8 miles west of Granby to reach Rt. 114, joining it a couple of miles north of East Burke. Take Rt. 114 some 12 miles north through rolling, mixed farm- and forestland to its junction with Rt. 105, 2 miles west of Island Pond.

✳ Green Space

Note: For more information on Vermont state parks, visit vtstateparks.com.

Brighton State Park (802-723-4360), Island Pond, 2 miles east on Rt. 105 to State Park Rd. Open mid-May–mid-Oct. Campsites are nestled in a stand of white birch trees on Spectacle Pond: 63 tent/trailer sites, 21 lean-tos, and a rental cabin. The park includes frontage on the south shore of Island Pond, where there's a day-use area that features a sandy beach (check to make sure it's open), a bathhouse with restrooms, and rental boats. Hiking trails include a leisurely trek to Indian Point and wildlife. Watch for moose and loons.

Maidstone State Park (802-676-3930), RR 1, Box 388, Brunswick 05905. Open Memorial Day–Labor Day. Five miles south of Bloomfield on Rt. 102, then 5 miles on dirt road, this is the most remote Vermont state park and retains much of its wilderness forest of maple, beech, and hemlock. The park's camping and day-use facilities are on Maidstone Lake, one of the most pristine in Vermont. It's home to lake, rainbow, and brook trout. Moose sightings and the call of the loon are common. There's a beach, picnic area, picnic shelter, hiking trails, 45 tent/trailer sites, and 37 lean-tos. Maidstone Lake is famed as a nesting area for loons, and the Nulhegan Basin is an important breeding habitat for migratory birds and nesting thrushes and warblers. Boreal forests in the basin support rare species such as spruce grouse, gray jay, Wilson's warbler, olive-sided flycatcher, rusty blackbird, black-backed woodpecker, and the three-toed woodpecker. A splendid, free Connecticut River Birding Trail/Northern Section map/guide is available locally; also see birdtrail.org.

Bill Sladyk Wildlife Management Area, off Rt. 114, south of Norton Pond: 9,500 forested acres, also accessible via a gravel road past Holland Pond from Holland Village, 11 miles east of Derby. A detailed map is available from the **Fish and Wildlife Department** in Waterbury (802-241-3700).

♿ **Silvio O. Conte National Fish and Wildlife Refuge, Nulhegan Basin Division** (802-962-5240; nulhegan.com), 5360 Rt. 105, Brunswick. Mailing address: P.O. Box 2127, Island Pond 05846. In 1999 when the Champion International Corporation announced plans to sell its holdings in Essex County, the U.S. Fish and Wildlife Service purchased this 26,000-acre tract (roughly 10 miles in diameter) that's home to rare animals and migratory birds. The Vermont Agency of Natural Resources acquired some 22,000 adjoining acres to form the West Mountain Wildlife Management Area; another 84,000 acres surrounding these preserves continue to be logged but with easements to protect their development. Over 100 species of birds nest in the Nulhegan Basin, which is home to moose, black bear, beaver, fisher, white-tailed deer, and coyote. The Nulhegan River and its tributaries harbor brook trout, bullhead, chain pickerel, chub, and more. The refuge is open to hunting, fishing, trapping, bird-watching, and hiking. It includes 40 miles of gravel roads, 17 miles of wooded pathways, and the Mollie Beattie Bog interpretive boardwalk (handicapped accessible). No biking. Request a map.

✳ Lodging

🐾 ♦ **Jackson's Lodge and Log Cabins**
(802-266-3360; jacksonslodgevt.net), P.O. Box
384, Canaan 05903. This is a find for families
looking for a reasonably priced lakeside vacation. Gloria Jackson is the second generation of
her family to maintain this appealing lineup of
15 log cabins along Lake Wallace. Open late
spring–fall. Two-bedroom cabins sleeping four
are $185 per night, $875 per week. Three-
bedroom cabins sleeping six are $200 per night,
$900 per week. Less in shoulder seasons. Ask
about Wayfarer's Rooms (with bath and private
deck), $85 double. Café open weekends to the
public for breakfast. The rustic central lodge is
also a venue for events and weddings. Lake
Wallace itself extends into Canada.

The Lakefront Inn & Motel (802-723-6507;
thelakefrontinnislandpond.com), 127 Cross St.,
Island Pond 05846. A two-story motel and a
main building houses the lobby and suites with
one or two bedrooms in the center of the village
overlooking the lake. Three of the 20 units have
built-in kitchenettes. A floating dock is reserved
for motel guests only during summer months,
and a heated multibay garage is available for

✪ 🐾 ♦ 🚹 **Quimby Country**
(802-822-5533; quimbycountry.com),
P.O. Box 20, Averill 05901. This is the
hidden gem of the Kingdom, one of
Vermont's most historic and family-
friendly resorts. Less than 3 miles from
Canada and 10 miles from New Hampshire, Quimby first opened as a fishing
lodge in 1894. It's set in literally thousands of acres of woodland, facing
Forest Lake and a short walk in the
woods from 1,200-acre Great Averill
Pond. Each of the well-spaced 20 cottages is different, but all have woodstoves or fireplaces in their living
rooms and are named for a fishing fly.
In the yellow-clapboard lodge a big
stone hearth is the focal point of the
book-lined common room. Many of the
Adirondack-style furnishings date back
to the 1890s, as do the polished
wooden tables in the spacious old-
fashioned dining room and the rockers
lining the porch, overlooking Forest
Lake.

Christina Tree

MAIN LODGE AT QUIMBY COUNTRY

Under the management of Hortense Quimby, daughter of the founder, this evolved into a
family-oriented resort, attracting an elite following so fiercely loyal that on Miss Quimby's death
in the 1960s, a group of regulars formed a corporation to buy it and to perpetuate the special
ambience. During July–mid Aug. all three meals are served; counselors take children on hikes
and swims, supervise rainy-day activities, and offer family-inclusive picnics on a remote beach as
well as a Friday sunset lobster feast at "The Rock" on Big Averill. Amenities include kayaks,
canoes, rowboats with trolling motors and sailboats, a tennis court, playground, and rec hall.
Rates are $200 per adult with all meals. If one of the 10 housekeeping cottages is available,
an EP rate without meals is available. May, June, and mid-Aug.–Oct., a cottage is $119 per
night, $35 for each extra occupant. Meals are available on an à la carte basis. Manager Ray
Wojckewch is an experienced fishing guide and offers a June fishing camp for teens. This is a
great place for birders and naturalists of all kinds (ask about the peat bog) as well as for fishermen, walkers, weddings, and reunions.

guests to work on servicing their snowmobiles in winter. Just across the way are public tennis courts, a beach, a picnic area, a boat launch, a lighted ice hockey rink, and a children's playground. Robert and Sharon Dexter are the innkeepers.

CAMPGROUNDS See Brighton State Park and Maidstone State Park in *Green Space.*

✳ Where to Eat

In Island Pond and beyond

❂ (𝔂)) **Common Sense Yellow Deli** (802-723-4453), 28 Cross St., Island Pond. Open weekdays 7–3, until 8 Thurs.; Sun. 10–6; closed Sat. A colorful, friendly eatery with a woodsy decor run by The Tribe, serving reliably tasty, healthy food: from-scratch soups, stews, chili, create-your-own-sandwiches, juice bar, carrot cake, maté drinks. Breakfast until 11. The bread and granola are homemade.

The Ponds Edge Pub & Eatery (802-723-4590), 69 Cross St., Island Pond. Open daily 11–9. This sports bar and reasonably priced restaurant makes a great addition to town. Nice atmosphere, generous portions.

Friendly Pizza (802-723-4616), 31 Derby St. (Rt. 105), Island Pond. Closed Mon., otherwise open from 11 until at least 9 PM. John Koxarakis offers a variety of pizzas.

Spa Restaurant & Outback Pub (603-246-3039), West Stewartstown, NH, just across the bridge from Rt. 114, Canaan, VT. Open daily for all three meals (from 4 most mornings). A cheerful diner that opens onto a more formal dining room for dinner as well as a pub on the lower level.

Quimby Country (802-822-5533), Forest Rd., Averill. During the summer season the resort's old-style dining room overlooking Forest Lake is open to the public for dinner. Call to check the set menu which varies in cost as well as content with the night. On Friday a full-blast lobster feast is held in a beautiful spot on Big Averill Pond.

Jackson's Cafe (802-266-3360) at Jackson Lodge (see *Lodging*) is a lovely dining room, open Memorial Day–Columbus Day, Fri. and Sat. 8–11 and Sun. 8–noon. Specials from $6.95, known for crêpes. The room is also available for wedding receptions and such.

Also see **April's Maple** (aprilsmaple.com) under *Selective Shopping.*

✳ Selective Shopping

Simon the Tanner (802-723-4452), Cross and Main Sts. Open daily except Sat., closing at 3 on Fri., otherwise 9–5, until 8 on Thurs. This is an unlikely spot for such a huge shoe store, but here it is selling a wide variety of name-brand shoes—Birkenstock and Clarks sandals, Dansko and Stegmann clogs, Doc Martens, work boots, winter boots, and a big selection of athletic shoes, all at below-usual prices. There is also a nice selection of men's, women's, and children's clothing, a bargain basement, and a line of natural soaps and body care products made by the Twelve Tribes. The store is owned and run by members of this international sect, which came to Island Pond several decades ago, restoring a number of houses and winning the respect of the community.

April's Maple (802-266-9624; aprilsmaple .com), 6507 Rt. 114, Canaan. Open Mon.–Sat. 10–5, Sun. 10–3. April Lemay is the energetic young entrepreneur who left for a corporate job, came home, and has established a major sugaring operation with nearly 15,000 taps on her grandparents' 800 acres. The gleaming Vermont-made evaporator is state-of-the-art, and shelves are filled with pure Vermont maple syrup plus other maple products, pancake mix, and other specialty foods. The sugarhouse has trails for hiking and snowshoeing, is handy to snowmobile trails, and has homemade chili and soup on tap. Inquire about complimentary tours—and be sure to try the irresistible Maple Cream Truffles when you stop in.

✳ Special Events

July 4 weekend: Parade, fireworks, boat parade, duck race, Island Pond.

Late June–August: **Friday Night Live**, vendors, and food, Island Pond.

Last week in August: **North Country Moose Festival** (northcountrychamber.org)—based in Colebrook, New Hampshire, a series of colorful events on both sides of the Connecticut River.

Friday of Labor Day weekend: Live music, BBQ, vendors, Island Pond.

INDEX